Aging in Contemporary Canada

Aging in Contemporary Canada

SECOND EDITION

Neena Chappell ✦ Lynn McDonald ✦ Michael Stones
University of Victoria   University of Toronto   Lakehead University

PEARSON

Prentice
Hall

Toronto

Library and Archives Canada Cataloguing in Publication

Chappell, Neena L.
  Aging in contemporary Canada / Neena Chappell, Lynn McDonald,
Michael Stones. —2nd ed.

Previous ed. written by Neena Chappell ... [et al.].
Includes bibliographical references and index.

ISBN-13: 978-0-13-201873-9
ISBN-10: 0-13-201873-X

1. Aging—Canada. 2. Gerontology—Canada. I. McDonald, L. 1947- II. Stones, M.J. (Michael J.) III. Title.

HQ1064.C2C423 2007   305.260971   C2006-906359-1

ISBN-10: 0-13-201873-X
ISBN-13: 978-0-13-201873-9

Editor-in-Chief, Vice-President of Sales: Kelly Shaw
Executive Acquisitions Editor: Ky Pruesse
Executive Marketing Manager: Judith Allen
Developmental Editor: Emily Jardeleza
Production Editors: Avivah Wargon, Katie Hearn
Copy Editor: Gilda Mekler
Proofreader: Anne Holloway
Production Coordinator: Sharlene Ross
Composition: Laserwords
Permissions Research: Emily Jardeleza
Art Director: Julia Hall
Cover Design: Kerrin Hands
Cover Image: Kerrin Hands

7 8 9 DPC 12 11 10

Printed and bound in Canada.

Chapter opener photo credits:

Chapter 1, Lisa Kyle Young/istockphoto.com/File Number 917830; Chapter 2, David Young-Wolff/Getty Images; Chapter 3, Steve Smith/Getty Images; Chapter 4, CP (Fred Chartrand); Chapter 5, Sharon Dominick/istockphoto.com/File Number 623624; Chapter 6, CP (Whitehorse Star–Chuck Tobin); Chapter 7, Michael Stones; Chapter 8, Kerri Picket/Getty Images; Chapter 9, Photodisc/Getty Images; Chapter 10, Lisa F. Young/istockphoto.com/File Number 1596065; Chapter 11, Anna Chelnokova/istockphoto.com/File Number 701993; Chapter 12, Piecework Productions/Getty Images; Chapter 13, Comstock Royalty Free Division; Chapter 14, Jupiter Images Unlimited/www.jiunlimited.com/Comstock.com Image #4843410; Chapter 15, Bruce Ayres/Getty Images; Chapter 16, Jupiter Images Unlimited/www.jiunlimited.com/Thinkstock.com Image #4855990.

Dedicated to Ellen Gee, one of Canada's
superb sociologists and gerontologists,
a colleague, and a friend, 1950-2002.

Contents

PREFACE   XI

ACKNOWLEDGMENTS   XIII

INTRODUCTION   XV

PART I   INTRODUCTION TO GERONTOLOGY   1

Chapter 1

Attitudes and Social Issues that Affect Older People   1

Introduction   2
Ageism as a Pervasive Social Attitude   3
Attributes of Attitudes   6
Attitudes and Elder Abuse   11
Attitudes and Later-Life Sexuality   16
Attitudes and Well-Being   20

Chapter 2

Population Aging   25

Introduction   26
Assessing Population Aging   26
Canada's Aging Population   29
What Causes Populations to Age?   32
Causes of Death   37
Differentials in Population Aging   40
Apocalyptic Demography   47

Chapter 3

Social Theory in Gerontology   55

Introduction   56
The Nature of Theory   57
Barriers to Theory Development in Social Gerontology   59
Theories within Social Gerontology   63

Chapter 4

Knowledge Building and Older People   85
Introduction   86
What Is the Nature of Research in Social Gerontology?   87

Why Do We Conduct Research?   88

Scientific Guidelines   90

Systems of Knowledge   92

The Challenges in Studying Aging   104

PART II COMMONALITIES AND DIVERSITY   114

Chapter 5

The Gendered Life Course   114

Introduction   115

Overview of the Changing Life Course   116

The Gendered Family Life Course   117

The Family Life Course of Older People   126

The Gender Wage Gap   128

The Intersection of the Family and Work Life Courses   131

Chapter 6

Aging and Ethnicity   136

Introduction   137

Ethnic Membership and Aging   137

Canada's Diverse Older Population   142

Theorizing about Ethnicity   152

The Wealth, Health, and Family Support of Ethnic Minorities   156

Implications for Policy and Practice   163

PART III HEALTH AND WELL-BEING   167

Chapter 7

Cognitive and Physical Performance   167

Introduction   168

Cognitive Performance   168

Aging and Physical Competence   180

Types of Physical Competence   183

Chapter 8

Mental Well-Being and Mental Disorder   191

Introduction   192

Mental Well-Being   194

Mental Disorder   206

Chapter 9

Health and the Determinants of Health   220

Introduction   221
Health during Old Age   221
Determinants of Health   229
Social Structure as a Determinant of Health   239

Chapter 10

Successful Aging   249

Introduction   250
Historical Overview   250
Inferences about Aging   251
Individual Differences on Age-Dependent Measures   255
Individual Differences Related to Later-Life Health and Well-Being   263

PART IV SOCIAL INSTITUTIONS   **270**

Chapter 11

Families and Aging   270

Introduction   271
The Structure of Aging Families   276
Structure of Extended Families   284
Mid-Life Families   284
Family Relationships in Later-Life Families   287

Chapter 12

Social Support and Caregiving   300

Introduction   301
Social Support: What Is It, and Why Is It Important?   301
Volunteering   311
A Special Type of Social Support—Caregiving   313

Chapter 13

Work and Retirement   328

Introduction   329
The History of Retirement in Canada   329
Retirement in the 21st Century   334
Explaining Retirement   339

The Link between Work and Retirement 343
Issues in Retirement: Who Retires, When, and Why? 345
Living in Retirement 353

Chapter 14

Pensions and Economic Security for Older Canadians 360

Introduction 361
The Retirement Wage: A History of Pensions in Canada 361
The Current Canadian Pension System 368
Employer and Individually Administered Programs 378
Why a B Grade for Canada? 382

PART V POLICY 392

Chapter 15

Health-Care System and Policy 392

Introduction 393
Historical Roots of Canadian Health-Care Policy 393
A New Vision 401
Reforming Canada's Health-Care System 402
Vested Interests 407
Pharmaceuticals 410
The Future? 412

Chapter 16

End-of-Life Issues 417

Introduction 418
Death and Dying in the 21st Century 418
Valuing Life 420
Care of the Dying 422
Family and Friends at the End of Life 430
Recognizing the Importance of the End of Life 434

REFERENCES 437
INDEX 481

Preface

Aging in Contemporary Canada is written from a social psychological perspective by authors who specialize in sociology and psychology. Instead of taking a biological or physiological perspective, it focuses on individuals and their social worlds. The book has been organized into five parts, outlined below.

Part I: Introduction to Gerontology

Chapters 1 to 4 provide students with an overview and explanation of what gerontology is, how we theorize about aging, and how we measure aging so that it can be studied. Chapter 1 begins with a discussion of ageist attitudes encountered in Canadian society, providing an individual perspective on aging. Attitudes toward violence, abuse, and sexuality are highlighted, revealing how many societal stereotypes are inconsistent with the realities of aging.

Chapter 2 describes the aging of the population in Canada and elsewhere, providing a broader social perspective beyond the individual. Various definitions of aging, including the construction of age 65 as the entry point for old age, are examined. Chapter 3 explains the theoretical foundations of gerontology and how thinking within the field has evolved over time. Research and the research process are the focus of Chapter 4. The key principles of the scientific method are reviewed, and a number of quantitative and qualitative methodologies are discussed in relation to the study of aging.

Part II: Commonalities and Diversity

In Part II, the focus of the text shifts to the commonalities and diversity found in later life, with an emphasis on gender and ethnocultural communities. Chapter 5 examines the gendered life course, looking at how many of gender differences begin early in life and continue throughout the life course. Cultural diversity within the context of aging and the importance of race and ethnicity to an understanding of aging are the central themes of Chapter 6. These are but two forms of diversity. Socio-economic diversity, for example, also permeates the aging experiences and is dealt with in all chapters.

Part III: Health and Well-Being

Physical, mental, and overall health aspects of aging are covered in Part III. The physical aspects of aging, including cognition, are discussed in Chapter 7, while Chapter 8 deals with mental well-being and mental disorder within the population aged 65 and over. The focus is on happiness, which seems to vary little over the life course. Chapter 9 turns to a general exploration of health, distinguishing between health and illness. Health beliefs and health practices are examined, as well as structural factors (such as socio-economic status and social support) that affect people's health even though many are unaware of the influence. Chapter 10 deals with successful aging, a topic of relevance to all of us. Overall well-being is intimately connected with aging well.

Part IV: Social Institutions

Part IV looks at some major social institutions—the family, social support, the workplace, and systems to provide economic security in old age —and the effects these have on the process of aging. Chapter 11 discusses families and aging, including changes that are evident in contemporary family structures, such as an increase in divorce and blended families. Chapter 12 examines social support, its importance for well-being and quality of life, and its critical role for seniors as their health declines. Caregiving is viewed as an aspect of social support, and its effects on both the giver and receiver of care are considered. Chapter 13 focuses on work and retirement, including a discussion of the flexible nature of retirement at the beginning of the 21st century. Chapter 14 examines the development of the pension system in Canada, what it looks like today, and what direction the future may hold. Because socio-economic status is a major correlate of health in old age, economic security takes on special importance.

Part V: Policy

The final section of this book examines two areas that have special relevance for policies that affect us as we age: health care and policy and end-of-life issues. Chapter 15 discusses the Canadian health-care system and health-care policy, including current attempts at health reform. Chapter 16 concludes the text with a focus on end-of-life issues, a tremendously important topic that has not received very much attention from researchers to date, especially those in the social sciences. During this period in our history, most Canadians can expect to live well past age 65, to have a prolonged dying process prior to death, and to leave behind loved ones who must cope with their absence.

Our hope is that *Aging in Contemporary Canada* conveys an accurate picture of the most current knowledge available about aging from a social psychological perspective, and that this will stimulate students' interest in aging. Every effort has been made to include the most current demographic and census data available at the time of writing. Each chapter also offers Learning Objectives, a Chapter Summary, a list of Key Terms, and Study Questions. These features are designed to help students develop a deeper and more critical understanding of the topics covered. We have also included numerous boxes throughout the text that feature articles, stories, or information that helps bring to life and more fully illustrate many of the most important issues related to aging. The relevance of aging, both personally and societally, will not wane, so it is important to understand its many facets in all of their complexity to ensure quality of life and care throughout the aging process.

Supplemental Materials

The new Text Enrichment Site for *Aging in Contemporary Canada*, found at www.pearsoned.ca/text/chappell, will benefit students and instructors alike. This website provides links to online sources for relevant statistical data.

Each chapter of the Instructor's Manual, provided free to adopters, includes a Chapter Outline, detailed Chapter Overview, and answers to the Study Questions posed in the text. This supplement is available online and can be accessed through the instructor link on the Text Enrichment Site or through the online catalogue text specific page which can be accessed at www.pearsoned.ca.

The Test Item File includes multiple-choice, true/false, short answer, and essay questions, as well as answers and is available online.

Acknowledgments

We would all like to thank the staff at Pearson Education Canada for their professional assistance. They have been helpful without being intrusive. They have kept us on appropriate timelines without being unrealistic. And they have been responsive to our needs and demands.

We would also like to thank the staff at the University of Victoria's Centre on Aging for assistance at every step of the long process of getting a book together. In particular, Lindsay Cassie and Tracy Hanton's skills and hard work ensured this book came to fruition.

In addition, we would like to thank the following reviewers for their helpful suggestions: Gura Bhargava, University of Calgary; Laurie Forbes, Lakehead University; Bonita Georgekish, Cambrian College of Applied Arts and Technology; Candace Kemp, The University of Western Ontario; Mary Ann Murphy, The University of British Columbia/UBC Okanagan; Jennifer Poudrier, University of Saskatchewan; and K. Victor Ujimoto, University of Guelph.

Neena Chappell: I would like to thank Michael and Kristen Barnes for their supportive acceptance of my many work commitments, including the undertaking of this book, and for their living proof of the social perspective. As well, many friends and colleagues challenge my thinking and support my endeavours.

Lynn McDonald: Thanks to Joanne Daciuk, Julie Dergal, Ron Jockheck, and Anthony Lombardo for research assistance and to the Faculties of Social Work at the University of Toronto and Calgary for their support. A special thank you to Laine Ruus of the Data Library Service at University of Toronto for her help with statistical data. I would also like to acknowledge my family for their continual encouragement.

Mike Stones: I would like to thank my wife, Lee, for supporting and putting up with me during the long hours spent writing this book, and my research collaborator, Al Kozma, recently retired from Memorial University. The three of us, made a great team and together learned a lot about aging. I also owe thanks to Sister Angela Fowler, Dr. Len Foley, Dick McNiven, Nettie Russell, and Dr. Gracie Sparkes, who showed me how to age well.

Introduction

Aging is an important issue in contemporary society in terms of both our own selves and the people who are significant in our lives. We all age. We age physiologically, socially, psychologically, and emotionally. We change over time. The experience of aging—how we age—varies over time and from society to society. At the turn of the 20th century in Canada, we could expect to die much younger than at the turn of the 21st century. Currently in Canada, virtually everyone, barring accidental death or death due to violence, can expect to live a long life—well into their seventies, eighties or beyond. This is historically unique—never before has this been true for society as a whole. Now, in industrialized societies, reaching at least age 65 has become the norm (see Chapter 2 for a detailed discussion of the demographics and definitions of old age). Some developing countries are rapidly approaching this position as well. Those who are currently elderly in Canadian society are the first cohort to have achieved this distinction, where the vast majority of their peers reach old age. This means that middle-aged adults, by and large, have parents who are still alive and children who know their grandparents. More and more young children know their *great*-grandparents. When children today look ahead, they can expect to live well into old age. What sort of meaning will this profound change have to society as a whole?

For Canadians, the aging of individuals and of the population is occurring within a culture that metaphorically searches for the fountain of youth, values youth, and associates vitality with youth. Despite the increase in the group of individuals who are now elderly, ageist stereotypes and attitudes prevail. The reasons for this are speculative. As an individualistic and capitalistic society, Canada places emphasis on individuals who are visibly contributing to the economy. Unlike more collectivist societies in which, historically, seniors were valued, respected, and considered wise, Canada's seniors are viewed as no longer productive because they are, by and large, retired. Within Canada, traditional Aboriginal societies tend to value elders more than mainstream society; similarly, immigrant groups originating in non-Western societies tend to place a higher value on older people than does the host society.

The outward or visible signs of biological aging are undeniable. Long before the age of 65, the body shows signs of aging: grey hair, baldness, wrinkles, decreasing agility. As Australian sociologist Turner (1995) points out, we age socially largely because of the body's visible aging. Phenomenologically, the inner self, or the subjective self (variously referred to as the *spirit*, the *internal*, the *soul*), remains useful, evolves, grows, and becomes wiser as we age. There is a disjuncture between the inner self and the external self. Modern Western society sees the physiological body, the external, and generalizes to the internal, producing what Turner refers to as the **paradox of aging**—a visibly deteriorated outer body coexisting in most cases with a vibrant, mature, and wise inner self. Biological aging is seen negatively as deterioration. The difficulty for seniors is that biological, visible change is then assumed to be associated with decline in the subjective sense of the inner self. Aging within Western society, then, is often a search to try to at least prevent, if not reverse, deterioration of the body, with much less attention paid to the nurturing of the subjective self. The huge growth in cosmetic surgery attests to our preoccupation with the visible signs of aging.

Aging has relevance for social institutions: the family, the educational system, retirement, health care, recreation, and so on. Families look different today than they did before: They are less likely to lose young people to death, and more generations are alive at the same time. Retirement, instituted just over 100 years ago in Germany, is now undergoing important changes, including much greater flexibility in its timing and form (part-time, full-time, contract work, etc.). As we hear in the news daily, our health care system is under attack as increasingly unaffordable. While this is popularly attributed to the aging of the population, there are good reasons to believe that the aging of the population itself will make only minor demands (1 to 2 percent per year) when the baby boom generation enters old age. Nevertheless, declining health is an important matter as we age, and all Canadians want a health care system that is appropriate to meet their needs. As the awareness grows that health includes more than sickness and treatment, interest in alternative forms of health care (including recreation and healthy lifestyles) is burgeoning. Overall, the relationships among social institutions, population, and individual aging is reciprocal. That is, the aging of the population affects society's institutions, and these institutions affect the individual experience of aging.

While academics often identify trends, and therefore focus on commonalities, it is important to understand that there is tremendous diversity in the aging experience. There are important differences by gender, for example. Not only do women live longer than men, but the aging experience is very different for women. For example, older women are far more likely to live alone, be poor, and be institutionalized in later life than is true for older men. Similarly, aging varies depending on whether you are a member of a minority ethnocultural group and, if so, of which group. Furthermore, aging differs depending on whether you are a member of that ethnocultural group within Canada or in your homeland. For example, aging as an elderly Chinese woman in Canada is different from aging as an elderly Chinese woman in Shanghai.

There are also differences depending on whether a person is rich or poor. Despite the existence of universal health care in Canada (covering physician services and hospital care), older people with money can afford to hire other types of assistance as well. They can afford better housing and they can afford luxuries such as spending time in warmer climates if they desire. Also, socio-economic status is a strong correlate of health: Those who are poor experience worse health in old age. There are also variations in terms of where a person lives within Canada. Aging in rural areas is distinct from aging in urban areas; aging in the harsh winters of Winnipeg is different from aging in the Niagara peninsula or Victoria.

The aging experience also varies depending on our social embeddedness. Some seniors are surrounded by family and friends, with strong social ties, whereas others live a more isolated (although not necessarily lonely) existence, interacting with a few close friends within a smaller social circle. While seniors share much with one another by virtue of their age, there is also tremendous diversity within this age group that spans over three decades (from the age of 65 to over 95).

Aging at both personal and societal levels is constantly evolving. In recent years, increased globalization has had a significant impact on Canadian society. Numerous technological advances, such as the Internet, and economic initiatives, such as the adoption of the North American Free Trade Agreement (NAFTA), have had a profound effect upon Canadian social policy. The long-term effect of these changes is still uncertain. For example, one viewpoint suggests that the "techno-logical imperative," rather than the needs of people, is increasingly what drives health care. A contrasting perspective believes that technology allows for improved health that would otherwise not be possible. The rapid changes taking place in so-cieties worldwide also often mean that seniors can be perceived as obsolete. However, there is great diversity among seniors in computer use, computer ownership, and use of the Internet. Since they are primarily not members of the paid labour force, sen-iors have fewer demands on them to learn this new technology. Some are interested in learning these new skills and can afford to, while others cannot.

Globalization also brings with it increased diversity, including ethnic diversity. Canada has become increasingly heterogeneous in its ethnic composition, especially over the last 20 years. In part, this is due to the increasing global mobility of labour. The movement of refugees—often displaced by globalization and related instabilities—plays a role as well. Increasing ethnic diversity has numerous consequences. It means that we have the opportunity to learn more directly about other cultural perspec-tives. It also means that social services should become more sensitive to cultural dif-ferences and more accessible to those who are not fluent in an official language. This has direct and immediate implications for health and social services for older adults.

A major issue for gerontology is that many policy changes (such as changes to the Canadian welfare state) are driven by global economic needs, but older adults by and large are not active members of the labour force. Consequently, their needs tend not to be taken into account. There has also been a politicization of aging at both the societal and individual levels. Individuals have become much more aware of the institutions that affect them within society and of the reasons why politicians make the policies and policy changes they do. Similarly, at the societal level, population aging has been used as a reason for social reform. We have heard that the pension system has to be reorganized or the baby boomers will bankrupt the system when they are old. Almost identical words are used in dis-cussions of the health-care system. As we will see, these issues are far more com-plicated than these simplistic charges suggest.

The issue of aging ultimately encompasses all of the diversity and variabil-ity of human society itself. The complex interaction of psychological, sociological, economic, and political factors is what makes the study of the aging individual in a social context so fascinating. As Canadian society evolves and changes to meet the many new challenges of the 21st century, so too does our understanding of and approach to aging. We hope that with every new question raised, we gain a greater appreciation of older people and of old age as an integral part of society.

Chapter 1

ATTITUDES AND SOCIAL ISSUES THAT AFFECT OLDER PEOPLE

Learning Objectives

In this chapter, you will learn about

- Ageist attitudes—what are their scope and implications?
- How education, health care, employment, legislation, and sexuality reveal ageism.
- The difference between attitudes and beliefs.

- The attributes of an attitude.
- Attitudes toward sexual abuse, later-life sexuality, and well-being.
- How attitudes toward such social issues as abuse, sexuality, health, and well-being differ from ageist stereotypes.

Introduction

"I think therefore I am." This famous quotation from Descartes defines one measure of what it means to be a human and alive. There is also a degree of truth in a reversal of that saying: I am what I think. What you think (e.g., about other people, your physical environment, your life) contributes to a sense of your own **self** as distinct from the selves of other people. Your thinking is part of your identity, affects your feelings (or vice versa), and helps to determine how you act. Although thoughts about social and other issues invoke processes rooted in the biology of our brains, our thoughts evolve with maturation and experience. For example, a comment attributed to many authors asserts that "A man who is not a liberal at 16 has no heart; a man who is not a conservative at 60 has no head." Our thoughts also reflect the period of history in which we live. This chapter examines attitudes and social issues that pertain to older people today.

Attitudes and beliefs refer to **cognitions**. Such cognitions are about something. The *something* might be discrete (e.g., a person), categorical (e.g., older people), temporal (e.g., an event), or hypothetical (e.g., the "big bang" theory of the origin of the universe). These cognitions are structured into what George Kelly (1955/1991) termed *personal construct systems*. These systems determine people's outlooks on their personal and professional life. A convergence of outlooks within a profession or among the public can influence the kinds of regulations, rules, and policies put in place to control behaviour. Consequently, the significance of attitudes extends beyond the individual, ultimately to the governance of society as a whole.

Attitudes to a category of people that are common within a society are called *stereotypes*. Common stereotypes include those based on racial, religious, and sexual characteristics. Such stereotyped attitudes and beliefs are always oversimplifications because the people within any category are heterogeneous except for the common characteristic that defines the category. This chapter begins with an overview of stereotypes of older people that find expression in public opinion, education, health care, employment, legislation, and lifestyle. Although stereotypes can and do affect the treatment of older people, stereotyped attitudes are not the only influence on such behaviour. Research since the 1920s that examined relationships between attitudes and **behaviour** arrived at some surprising conclusions. Consequently, the section following the overview examines the underpinnings of attitude research with respect to definition, measurement, and causal influences.

The remainder of this chapter looks at stereotypes of older people and evidence pertaining to that cohort. What are the attitudes of younger people; of older people? How does the evidence relate to these attitudes? The issues examined include personal and social concerns identified as important to all Canadians. What are these concerns? Read any newspaper or magazine nowadays to find that the concerns that occupy the minds and thoughts of Canadians include violence, sexuality, well-being, and the self.

Ageism as a Pervasive Social Attitude

Dowd (1980a) asserted that the status accorded to people in Western culture increases from youth to middle age but declines thereafter. This trajectory holds true regardless of the age, social class, or gender of respondents. The consequences include a stereotyping of older persons that is usually negative but sometimes positive (Palmore, 1990)—see Chapter 3 for more on the modernization theory of aging. The name for such stereotyping is **ageism.**

Some authors consider the roots of ageism to reside in fear and vulnerability toward aging and death (Martens, Greenberg, Schimel, & Landau, 2004; Martens, Goldenberg, & Greenberg, 2005). Put simply: old people forewarn young people of their own futures and it scares them. This fear may contribute to a marginalization of older people in industrialized countries and a reduction in their participation in social affairs (Blekesaune & Solem, 2005). Other factors suggested to contribute to ageism include the social separation of young and older cohorts in modern society (Hagestad & Uhlenberg, 2005). There is also evidence that negative information about the elderly contributes to ageist attitudes. Kojima (1996) examined population opinion surveys in Japan conducted between 1990 and 1995. During this period the proportion of respondents favourably disposed toward a large aging population fell and the proportion with unfavourable attitudes increased. Kojima (1996) explained that this trend coincided with extensive media coverage of record-low fertility rates in Japan and the introduction of government policies to slow the rate of population aging.

Regardless of the reasons for its appearance, the expression of ageism varies with history and culture. Comparative analysis of young people in the United States with those in countries like Germany and Turkey show differences in attitudes towards aging (McConatha, Schnell, Volkwein, Riley, & Leach, 2003; McConatha, Hayta, Rieser-Danner, & McConatha, 2004). German youth have more negative attitudes about aging than North Americans but consider "old age" to begin later. There are also gender differences, with females more negative about the aging of their bodies than males.

Researchers from Canada disagree about whether ageism is of social significance in this country. Over twenty years ago, Schonfield (1982) found that approximately 20 percent of respondents showed substantial ageist stereotyping, with evidence of some degree of stereotyping present in most respondents. He did not think that the former figure was especially high. Stones & Stones (1998) referred to ageism as a "quiet epidemic" that contributes to benign neglect or indifference toward older people as a social category, but not necessarily to interpersonal antagonism. They reminded their readers that ageism refers to stereotyping of older people as a social unit but may not lead to antagonistic behaviour in interactions with older people.

Research findings on ageism derive from many sources, including studies of undergraduate attitudes (Knox & Gekoski, 1989), health care (Butler, 1975), literary and dramatic productions (Berman & Sobkowska-Ashcroft, 1987; Donlon,

Ashman, & Levy, 2005), humour (Palmore, 1971), and legislative processes (Stones & Stones, 1998). One university library lists nearly 40 references on the attitudes of college students to the elderly(Montgomery, 2000). Some studies use composite scales to compare levels of ageism in different cohorts (Rupp, Vodanovich, & Crede, 2005). A Canadian composite scale developed by Knox, Gekoski, and Kelly (1995) provides a useful measure of stereotypes and attitudes. The Age Group Evaluation and Description (AGED) Inventory contains evaluative factors of Goodness and Positiveness, and descriptive factors of Vitality and Maturity. The following paragraphs describe the manifestations of ageism on topics that have received considerable attention from researchers.

Ageism and Education

Students' knowledge and attitudes about aging benefit from exposure to positive information. The prevailing educational philosophy in North America ignores aging as a topic during the high school years, thereby providing students with little information to counter ageist attitudes found throughout society (Couper, 1994). Several studies show that college students' attitudes about older people improve when they are given factual information, especially information highlighting the benefits of aging. Knowledge about aging increases with education (Palmore, 1988), and, not surprisingly, specifically with education in gerontology (Matthews, Tindale, & Norris (1985). Canadian studies by Knox, Gekoski, and Johnson (1984) and Gfellner (1982) found attitudes to be more positive among students who had positive interactions with older people.

However, a review of studies of medical students' knowledge and attitudes about aging surprisingly concluded that instructional modules in geriatrics have little impact (Beullens, Marcoen, Jaspaert, & Pelemans, 1997). The probable reason is that such modules deal only with sickness. The authors recommend including courses on gerontology and interaction with the healthy elderly. Similarly, Hawley, Garrity, and Cherry (2005) found that police officers have better knowledge about pathological than about normal memory in the elderly. Kane (2004) found that social work students perceived a lesser need for active intervention with old than with young clients because of differences in the problems frequently presented.

Ageism and Health Care

Many authors argue that ageism is pervasive in health care. Pulitzer-Prize-winning author Robert Butler (1974) told a Symposium on Geriatric Medicine: "Medicine and the behavioural sciences have mirrored social attitudes by presenting old age as a grim litany of physical and emotional ills." In nursing homes, he spoke of a policy of **pacification**—the overuse of medication as a substitute for humane attention through diagnosis and careful treatment (Butler, 1975). More than a decade later, van Maanen (1991) and Honeyman (1991) echoed Butler's sentiments to the Canadian Medical Association. Evidence from Canadian nursing homes also supports Butler's comments about pacification. Canadian homes use psychotropic medication no more than those in other countries; however, the physical restraint of residents is more frequent in this country (Canadian Institute for Health Information, 1998).

Ageist attitudes uphold fiscal assumptions of an "apocalyptic demography" (see Chapter 2) that influence health-care policy (Gee & Gutman, 2000). The assumptions are that (1) age brings about illness, (2) the treatment of illness incurs fiscal cost, and (3) population aging brings about an expectation of escalating cost. This reasoning seems to provide bureaucrats with compelling reasons to reconsider the wisdom of benevolent health-care policies. However, health economists have likened the apocalyptic demography hypothesis to a "zombie" that keeps walking despite its evident death (Evans, McGrail, Morgan, Barer, & Hertzman, 2001; Reinhardt, 2001). They argue that professional self-interest rather than demography contributes to projections of rising health-care expenditure. These projections justify increased income for health-care providers, distract attention from poor health-care practices, and provide a rationale for greater corporate involvement in health care (i.e., privatization—see Chapter 15). Evans and colleagues conclude that "we have nothing to fear from the aging of the population, only from those who continue to promulgate the fiction" (p. 188).

Ageism and Employment

The practice of mandatory retirement reviewed elsewhere in this book (see Chapter 13) invokes active discrimination based on age. Other negative stereotypes suggest that younger workforce members may lack requisite experience and that older workers may be unmotivated and inflexible. Such attitudes can have implications for recruitment, salary, and termination. Although some countries introduced legislation to promote workplace equity, findings suggest that ageist attitudes continue to affect mainly the youngest and oldest groups of workers despite the emergence of equal opportunities legislation (McVittie, McKinley, & Widdicombe, 2003; Duncan & Loretto, 2004).

Ageism and the Law

Lubomudrov (1987) examined misrepresentations by members of the United States Congress used to influence the legislative process. He found frequent instances of stereotypes, both negative (e.g., the elderly as poor, frail, ill-housed) and positive (e.g., the elderly as well off, politically potent) were frequent. The treatment of age as a prohibited ground for discrimination varies across provincial human rights codes in Canada. For example, under the terms of the *Newfoundland and Labrador Human Rights Code*, a senior can be denied access to public places or private dwellings, denied service, harassed, and even become the object of hate literature (Stones & Stones, 1998). Why is this? Because the Code makes age a prohibited ground for discrimination only between ages 18 and 65 years (the employment age span recognized at the time the Code was written). Although legislators did not intend to enshrine ageism within the Code, the omission of age as a prohibited ground for discrimination does precisely that.

Ageism and Sexuality

Starr (1985) writes that nowhere is ageism more obvious than in attitudes toward sexuality. The common belief is that older people have neither the interest in nor the capacity for a sexual relationship and that an older person who breaks this taboo must be deviant and immoral. Butler and Lewis (2002) and Stones and Stones (2004) support this conclusion with evidence from both historical and modern times. Although the development of the potency drug Viagra and the attendant publicity contributed to increased awareness of later-life sexuality (Stones & Stones, 2007), a taboo that lasted for over a millennium is unlikely to fade away abruptly.

The preceding examples of ageism illustrate its pervasiveness as a social attitude. However, ageism is just one attitude among many that social scientists have studied. In order to understand how attitudes (including ageism) relate to social issues of relevance to the elderly, we need to consider the concept of attitude more broadly. The following section examines how social scientists define and measure attitudes, differentiate attitudes from related concepts (e.g., beliefs), identify the attributes of attitudes, and take account of possible influences on attitudes.

Attributes of Attitudes

Definition and Measurement

Social scientists have studied attitudes since the 1920s. The true home of the concept, however, is in social psychology, where attitude remains "distinctive and indispensable" (Allport, 1935, p. 198). Definitions of attitude refer to (1) a tendency (2) to evaluate (3) an object with some degree of favour or disfavour (Eagly & Chaiken, 1993). In other words, an **attitude** represents a fleeting or enduring tendency to positively or negatively evaluate an **object**—which may be a person, a category of people (e.g., the elderly), or any other animate (e.g., dogs) or inanimate (e.g., global warming) instance, occurrence, or category. The **target** of an attitude is the person who experiences the object. To illustrate: In the sentence, "On waking up, I like a cup of coffee," the phrase "on waking up" delimits the tendency; the target is "I"; the evaluative term is "like'" "a cup of coffee" is the object.

Social psychologists were also among the first researchers to explore systematically different ways to measure attitudes. The main **measures** included

Thurstone's (1928) method of equal intervals, Guttman's (1941) cumulative method, and Likert's (1932) summative method.

1. Thurstone's (1928) method of equal intervals proceeds in three stages. Judges rate statements for the degree of favour or disfavour toward an attitude object. The items selected for inclusion are those that represent different levels on the evaluative dimension. Respondents rate their levels of agreement with each statement. This method fell into some disfavour because of its complexity.

2. Guttman's (1941) cumulative method uses statements ordinarily graded for degree of favour or disfavour toward the attitude object. If the measure is truly cumulative, respondents should disagree with all items below a threshold level but agree with all those above that level. The threshold level reflects the attitude.

3. Likert's (1932) summative method uses statements rated by respondents for level of agreement. The scores are summed across items (with negative items reverse-scored), and the attitude is represented by the summed score. This method is currently the most popular because of its simplicity.

Attitudes and Beliefs

An attitude is not the same as a belief. A **belief** is simply a statement that a respondent thinks is true. A statement like "Older drivers are at high risk of dying in road accidents" expresses a belief rather than an attitude. This belief may or may not be true but, by itself, it does not convey an evaluation. An *attitude* always conveys an evaluation. If somebody says, "Older drivers should be banned because they are a danger to themselves and others," "I hate driving because of all the slow and dangerous older drivers on the road," and "I won't be in a car with an older driver because they drive so badly I might be killed," it is reasonable to infer a negative evaluation. By the way, research on accidents does support a belief that seniors are at high risk of fatality in automobile crashes (Bédard, Guyatt, Stones, & Hirdes, 2001). However, one main reason is that older people are at increased risk of mortality if injured. Figure 1.1 provides an illustration with 1999 data from the Fatal Accident Reporting System (FARS) in the United States. The number of people killed in automobile accidents in which a fatality occurred exceeds the number of people uninjured or injured only for people aged over 60 years regardless of whether the occupant of the vehicle was the driver or a passenger. Younger people are more likely to be uninjured or injured than killed. Consequently, Figure 1.1 does not support the belief that older people *cause* more traffic fatalities than younger people. The odds of dying in a road accident do increase after age 60 years, but most people involved in fatal road accidents are young rather than old.

The distinction between attitudes and beliefs finds its counterpart in the types of measures used in research on ageism. Matthews, Tindale, and Norris (1985) described a Canadian "facts on aging" quiz that measured only beliefs about aging and the aged. In contrast, the Age Group Evaluation and Description (AGED) Inventory by Knox, Gekoski, and Kelly (1995) includes attitudinal content

Figure 1.1 DRIVER AND PASSENGER INJURIES IN FATAL MOTOR CRASHES
BY AGE

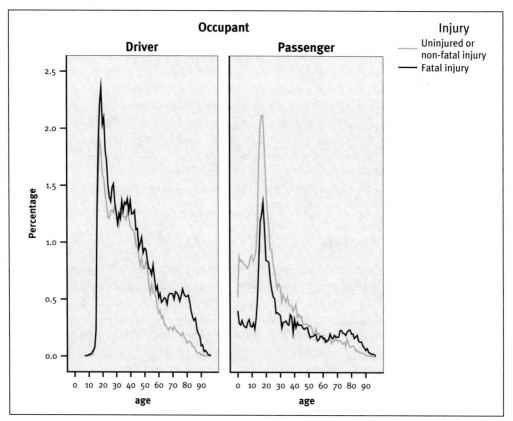

Source: Based on Fatal Accident Reporting System data, 1999.

(i.e., the respondents' evaluations of aspects of aging). The items on the AGED contrast bipolar pairs of adjectives (e.g., timid versus assertive) with the respondents asked to indicated the pole that best describes old people. Differences in research findings obtained with the respective types of measure likely relate to differences between beliefs and evaluative bias.

Attitudes and Response Consistency

Psychologists consider attitudes to belong to a category of concepts—variously termed latent variables, hypothetical constructs, or cognitive schemata—that also includes learning, memory, and personality (MacCorquodale & Meehl, 1948). These concepts (1) intervene between a stimulus and a response; (2) are inaccessible to direct observation; and (3) have properties that can be inferred from consistencies in the responses to related stimuli. The stimuli might be questions about something asked by an interviewer or items on a survey. The responses include the answers or other reactions (e.g., time to respond) to the stimuli.

We need the concept of attitude to account for consistencies and dissimilarities between different modes of responding to related stimuli. Although most attitude measures rely on self-report, the items may address cognitive, affective, and behavioural modes of responding. Most research shows that evaluative responses correlate across these domains (Breckler, 1984; Eagly & Chaiken, 1993; Zanna & Rempel, 1988). Campbell and Fiske (1959) refer to such consistency as *convergent validity*. The complement to convergent validity is discriminant validity, which means that items within one domain should correlate more strongly with each other than with items in other domains. Table 1.1 illustrates these distinctions by showing the expected levels of correlation between Likert-scale agreement with cognitive, affective, and behavioural attitude statements about old people. We expect high correlations between items that measure the same mode of responding and moderate correlations between items that measure different modes of responding, regardless of whether the statement is positively or negatively keyed.

Measures of ageism tend to conform to these expectations. Knox, Gekoski, and Kelly's (1995) Age Group Evaluation and Description (AGED) Inventory distinguishes between descriptive factors and evaluative factors. The former are cognitive and the latter affective. Rupp, Vodanovich, and Crede (2005) also find cognitive and affective distinctions in their analysis of responses to the Fraboni Scale of Ageism, and corresponding correlations with other measures of age-related attitudes.

Table 1.1 HYPOTHETICAL CORRELATIONS BETWEEN COGNITIVE, AFFECTIVE, AND BEHAVIOURAL RESPONSES ON ATTITUDE STATEMENTS ABOUT OLD PEOPLE

Item Type	Cognitive		Affective		Behavioural	
Items	*Old people are wise*	*Old people are mentally slow*	*I enjoy talking with old people*	*Old people bore me*	*I intend to volunteer in a seniors' centre*	*I want to work in the gerontology field*
Wisdom	*	High –	Moderate +	Moderate –	Moderate +	Moderate +
Slowness		*	Moderate –	Moderate +	Moderate –	Moderate –
Enjoyment			*	High –	Moderate +	Moderate+
Boredom				*	Moderate –	Moderate –
Volunteer Work					*	High+
						*

* Values of the hypothetical correlations include strength (moderate, high) and direction (+, −).

Attitudes and Behaviour

Social scientists traditionally assumed that attitudes have a predictive or even a causal relationship to behaviour. However, there was much debate about this issue during the 1970s. Wicker (1969) reviewed 42 mainly laboratory studies that included correlations between attitudes and behaviour. He found the correlations to be weak or non-significant in most of the studies. There were strong reactions to Wicker's paper. Hovland (1959), in an earlier account, had posited that attitude–behaviour correlations might be weaker in laboratory research than in survey research because the attitudes studied tend to be less important to the respondents. Furthermore, laboratory studies constrain the choice of actions to those chosen by the researcher, whereas people in natural settings express their attitudes by behaviours of their own choosing.

Probably the most compelling evidence was research showing a weak correlation of attitudes with discrete behaviours but stronger correlations with summed indexes of behaviour. Weigel and Newman (1976) provided an example in which they obtained correlations between attitudes toward environmental preservation with unobtrusive measures of behaviours taken six months later. The findings showed the correlations of attitude with discrete behaviours to average about r=.32, but the correlation with a summed index to be r=.62. The stronger correlation with the summed index was not a surprise. Somebody with a given attitude toward an object may express it unevenly for any number of reasons (e.g., fear of a social penalty if the attitude is unpopular), with attitude being only one among many influences on behaviour (Ajzen & Fishbein, 1977). Current theories tend to agree that attitudes have implications for behavioural inclinations rather than strong effects on specific behaviours (Eagly & Chaiken, 1993).

Influences on Attitudes

Many social theorists incorrectly assume that attitudes depend exclusively on learned experience. Campbell (1963) even defined attitude as an acquired condition. An implication of this hypothesis is that differences in attitudes arise from differences in experience. However, other researchers suggest a strong influence of personality or genetic predisposition (Costa & McCrae, 1980b; Olsen, Vernon, Harris & Jang, 2001). Attitudinal differences may depend less on nurture than on nature, and attitudes may be harder to change than many social theorists had contemplated.

Studies that purport to show genetic influences on attitudes use a twin research paradigm. This paradigm contrasts identical twins with fraternal twins. Because identical twins share fully common genes whereas fraternal twins have only 50 percent of genes in common, it follows that if attitudes have a genetic influence, the attitudes of identical twins should be more similar than between fraternal twins. Examples of studies that show greater similarity of attitudes between identical than fraternal twins include Waller and colleagues (1990), who studied religious attitudes, and Eaves, Eysenck, and Martin (1989) who showed a genetic influence on other attitudes. Recent Canadian research on twins provides consistent evidence of a genetic contribution to 26 of 30 attitudes.

The evaluative concept of attitude that emerges from the discussion in this section of the chapter has implications for consistency across different kinds of response and for behavioural inclinations across a range of situations. Although attitudes may relate to life experiences, predisposition may also affect resistance to change. The final sections of this chapter examine attitudes to social issues that affect older people. The attitudes of younger people are likely to affect their behaviour toward older people and the attitudes of older people are likely to affect their own behaviour.

Attitudes and Elder Abuse

Hudson (1991) clarified our understanding of elder **abuse** and neglect by providing a standard definition agreed upon by an international panel of experts. This definition refers to abuse as a special case of harmful behaviour that occurs in the context of a trust relationship. Abuse refers to destructive behaviour, while neglect refers to a failure to provide required help. The people that seniors should be able to trust include unpaid caregivers (e.g., relatives, friends) and professional helpers (e.g., doctors, nurses, lawyers). By this definition, confidence tricksters who prey on older people are committing crimes, but not abuse, because they are strangers and are not in a position of trust.

Similar definitions are in use throughout Canada (e.g., British Columbia Inter-Ministry Committee on Elder Abuse, 1992). Although such definitions capture the global meaning, they do not distinguish between types of abuse. One way to classify cases pertains to the kind of harm done (e.g., damage to the physical, mental, or financial well-being of seniors). Another way pertains to the type of social expectation the behaviour violates (e.g., legal, ethical, professional, or social standards of acceptability) (Stones, 1995). The latter has the advantage of consistency with the rule-based system that dominates legal logic.

The federal government and every Canadian province has attempted in various ways to combat elder abuse, beginning in the 1980s (Health and Welfare Canada, 1987, 1990). Ontario leapt ahead of the other provinces in 2002 with funding provided by its government for a Provincial Strategy to Combat Elder Abuse. This strategy complements the efforts of agencies, facilities, and community organizations by coordinating community services, training frontline staff, and raising awareness through public education (Stones, 2005a).

Ageism and Elder Abuse

Several Canadian authors implicate ageism as a category of or influence on elder abuse. Namiash (2000) refers to social or collective abuse, which includes ageism and its effects. McDonald and Collins (2000) remark on the inherent ageism in some theories about elder abuse (e.g., the social exchange **model**) that equate aging with increased powerlessness. Other authors suggest that ageism may reduce sensitivity to the expressed concerns of older people or a failure to take those concerns seriously (Wolf, 1997b).

Examples of ageism cited by these authors include a failure to treat complaints of abuse by old people as seriously as similar complaints by young people (Wolf, 1997b). The treatment of pain by physicians provides a related example from health care, with older people frequently receiving less aggressive treatment than younger people. Stones (2005b) reports that some physicians tend to treat agitation in old continuing-care residents by chemical or physical means rather than carefully investigating situational causes. Beaulieu (1995) cited similar prevalent practices in long-term care as examples of systemic abuse that would not be tolerated outside an institutional context.

Strength of Attitudes toward Abuse and Violence

There is a principle concerning group membership and attitudes pertaining to that group. Linville (1982) carried out early studies in what was to become a classical series by distinguishing between "in groups," to which the respondent belongs, and "out groups," to which the respondent does not belong. Linville found that attitudes toward out groups tend to be more extreme than toward in groups. In one study, she found the attitudes of college students toward (positive or negative) vignettes of an older person to be more extreme than toward comparable vignettes of someone their own age. She developed the complexity-extremity hypothesis to explain these findings: people have a complex understanding of their own group and thus moderate attitudes toward the object in question; people have a simpler, less differentiated understanding of out groups, and thus more extreme attitudes.

Research on attitudes toward violent behaviour shows a trend consistent with this hypothesis. More young than old people are the victims of violent crime. Statistics Canada regularly reports homicide rates more than 60 percent higher for people aged 15 to 44 years than for those aged 65 years and older. Consequently, one might think that younger people should have more fearful attitudes toward violent crime than older people have. Paradoxically, however, older Canadians have more fearful attitudes than younger Canadians (Statistics Canada, 2000b), with similar findings found among older and younger Americans (Dowd, Sisson, & Kern, 1981). Although such differences are open to multiple influences, the interpretation derived from the complexity-extremity hypothesis is that young people have a more complex understanding of violence in modern society than have older people, and this makes them less fearful.

The complexity-extremity hypothesis also applies to elder abuse. However, in their attitudes toward elder abuse, young people are an out group, whereas older people are an in group. Stones and Bédard (2002) found that young people disapproved more strongly of elder abuse and neglect than did older people. Stones and Pittman (1995) were able to relate the strength of negative attitudes of younger people toward elder abuse to other measures of attitude extremity.

Stones (2004) reports other evidence that group membership affects attitudes. Matched groups of older respondents living independently or in long-term care homes rated two sets of elder abuse items. The first set consisted of examples of abuse that could happen to any senior regardless of residence. The second set referred to abuse that could happen only in institutional settings. The findings show no differences between the groups on the generic items but more moderate ratings by long-term care than by community residents on the institutional abuse items (see Figure 1.2). Consequently, the findings with the institutional abuse items affirm the paradox that members of the in group have less negative attitudes towards examples of abuse than do members of the out group. Qualitative findings from the study indicated that the differences between groups did relate to a more complex understanding by the institution residents. For example, whereas most community residents considered the overuse of physical restraint to be unacceptable, the long-term care residents were more likely to mention safety issues and understaffing as relevant to their attitudes.

Other Findings on Attitudes toward Elder Abuse

Researchers began to study elder abuse by asking questions mainly of relevance to those professions involved in detection, treatment, and prevention. A major issue concerns the under-reporting of abuse—failure to report suspected abuse to the

Figure 1.2 **PERCENT OF GENERIC AND INSTITUTIONAL ABUSE ITEMS RATED "SEVERELY ABUSIVE" BY COMMUNITY AND CONTINUING-CARE RESIDENTS**

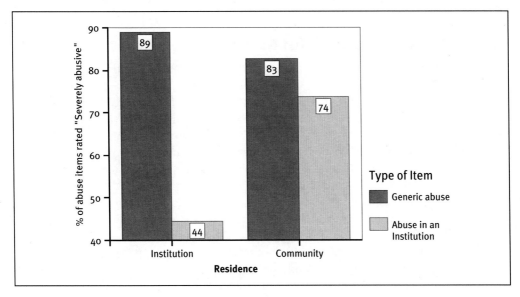

Source: Based on M.J. Stones & L. Stones. (2004). The language of elder abuse. Proceedings of Ontario Network for the Prevention of Elder Abuse Conference. Retrieved from http://onpea.org/Strategy/Communication/Conference04Eng.htm.

relevant authorities. Many social theorists liken elder abuse to an iceberg, with only a small proportion of cases coming to the attention of the legal and helping professions (Administration on Aging, 1998). The reasons usually given for under-reporting include the shame of seniors reluctant to disclose their experiences of abuse, or their fear of the family disruption that might result from such disclosure. Another reason, discussed in the preceding section, is that the more moderate attitudes toward elder abuse held by older people might mitigate inclinations toward disclosure to authorities.

Several studies examined attitudes toward elder abuse among non-professionals or compared attitudes across professions, between professionals and the public (Hudson & Carlson, 1998), younger and middle-aged people (Childs, Hayslip, Radika, & Reinberg, 2000), different occupations (Payne & Berg, 1999), and members of ethnic minorities (Hudson, Armachain, Beasley, & Carlson, 1998). The studies found overall similarity between the attitudes of professionals and the public but also some differences. Payne and Berg (1999) found the attitudes of nursing home professionals to differ from those of the police and college students. Older Korean-American women were less likely to perceive abuse than African-Americans or Caucasians (Moon & Williams, 1993).

Stones and Bédard (2002) attempt to explain these differences within a threshold model of attitudes. They reason that when different target groups rate behaviours for level of abuse, the groups are consistent about those behaviours evaluated as more or less abusive (e.g., "hitting a senior" is more abusive than "opening a senior's mail without permission"). (See also Stones & Pittman, 1995.) However, the target groups may differ in judging whether a certain behaviour exceeds a threshold for abuse. Stones and Pittman (1995) selected items that were close to the thresholds for inclusion in their Elder Abuse Attitude Test (EAAT).

Attitude Change and Elder Abuse

Educators such as Podnieks and Baille (1995) suggest that attitude change is among the key aims in the prevention of elder abuse: "Education is not only about acquiring information, it is also about changing attitudes, behaviours, and values" (p. 81). The targets of elder abuse education they identify include not only professionals, but also caregivers, the public, children, and seniors. Although seniors may actively avoid exposure to information about elder abuse (Vernon-Scott, 2003), Kipper (2001) found that such exposure may change their attitudes.

Little evidence is available about the outcomes of public education on elder abuse. Although Podnieks and Baille's (1995) review of elder abuse education cites no research on outcome evaluation, a subsequent study finds higher levels of reporting in communities that have higher levels of training for professionals (Wolf, 1999). In one Quebec study (Lithwick, Stones, & Reis, 1998), the first phase comprised four sessions of elder abuse education for members of 11 Community Senior Mistreatment Committees. The second phase involved a community awareness initiative organized and run by each committee. The committees had an average of 16 members, both men and women, drawn from the same ethnic community, with a mean age of 58 years. Committee members completed a battery of measures, including the Senior Behaviour Inventory (SBI), before and after the intervention. The SBI includes the Elder Abuse Attitude Test (EAAT; Stones & Pittman, 1995) and, as a validity check, "beneficence" items that a panel of 25 judges rated as not examples of "poor treatment" of seniors (Lithwick et al., 1997) (see Table 1.2).

Table 1.2 ABBREVIATED SENIOR BEHAVIOUR INVENTORY (SBI)

The following items refer to how people sometimes behave toward seniors. They only refer to behaviour by someone a senior has reason to trust. That person could be a relative or someone who takes care of the senior. That person could also be someone paid to help or look after the senior's affairs (e.g., doctor, nurse, homemaker, lawyer.) The questions do not refer to how strangers treat seniors. Do you understand the kinds of people the questions refer to? Please indicate whether the behaviours below are (1) not abusive, (2) possibly abusive, (3) abusive, (4) severely abusive, or (5) very severely abusive toward a senior if done by someone a senior has reason to trust. Remember that the questions do not apply to acts by a stranger.

Item	Not Abusive	Possibly Abusive	Abusive	Severely Abusive	Very Severely Abusive
EAAT items					
Steals something a senior values					
Pushes or shoves a senior					
Lies to a senior in a harmful way					
Opens a senior's mail without permission					
Withholds information that may be important to a senior					
Unreasonably orders a senior around					
Tells a senior that person is "too much trouble"					
Fails to provide proper nutrition					
Disbelieves a senior claiming to be abused, without checking					
Nonabusive (beneficence) items					
Asking a senior to contribute toward his/her own expenses					
Asking a senior to help with household chores					
Not buying an expensive watch a senior asked for as a birthday gift					

After the intervention, the largest gains in knowledge concerned resources to help mistreated seniors, Responses to the Senior Behaviour Inventory also showed that respondents had been sensitized to elder abuse. Attitudes toward elder abuse and neglect were more negative after the intervention, while responses to the beneficence items were unchanged.

Attitudes and Later-Life Sexuality

Butler and Lewis (2002) and Stones and Stones (2004) describe ageist depictions of later-life sexuality in folklore, the arts, Western religion, history, and the sciences. The features of these depictions include lack of sexual interest, incapacity, and moral prohibition. Box 1.1 illustrates sexual ageism from a senior's perspective.

Butler and Lewis (2002) describe folklore depictions of old people as likeable but asexual beings. However, the stereotypes are decidedly negative for older people who behave in sexually explicit ways. Whereas words that depict the behaviour of a sexually active young man have positive connotations (e.g., lusty, virile, stud), similar behaviour by an old man elicits pejorative expressions (e.g., lecherous, old goat, dirty old man). Folklore similarly depicts behaviour considered "provocative" or "seductive" in a young woman to show mental disorder, moral weakness, and a loss of dignity if present in later life.

In traditional literature and visual arts, the depiction of later-life sexual proclivity emphasized depravity and incapacity (Starr, 1985). A frequent character was the cuckold—a "sugar daddy" whose wealth attracts a young woman, who soon becomes unfaithful because of her partner's impotence. Such depictions in the arts and modern media affect the attitudes even of older people. Donlon, Ashman, and Levy (2005) find a correlation among people aged 60 or over between negative images of aging and the amount of television watched.

The preceding examples of sexual ageism are consistent with beliefs that originated from teachings by the early Christian church that sex is sinful outside the context of marriage and procreation (Stones & Stones, 2004). Consequently, sexuality in old people was seen as sinful because of limited procreative potential. These ideas originated with writings by St. Augustine (A.D. 354–430) who held that lust and passion are evils we must endure only to procreate the species. Although Protestant reformers attacked St. Augustine's doctrines in later centuries, the linkage of sex with sin continues to persist in our culture. Other major religions in the world (e.g., Taoism, Confucianism, Hinduism, Buddhism, and Islam) make no such connection. These religions traditionally embrace sexuality as a source of pleasure and solace; some consider it a means to enlightenment, and none stereotype sexuality in later life so negatively.

The quintessential religious condemnation of sexuality in older women occurred in the witch-hunting era in Europe during the 15th to 17th centuries. The official manual on witch hunting was the *Malleus Maleficarum* ("Hammer of

Box 1.1 Examples of Attitudes about Romance in Later Life

Marjorie Charles remembers that woman from St. John's telling five hundred seniors in Corner Brook they were sexy. It had been 18 years earlier—at the yearly convention of the Newfoundland Pensioners and Senior Citizens Federation. "And the funny thing was—she was right on the money," Marjorie recollects. "Even though she was young, from the university, and probably hadn't ever set a foot inside a fish plant, which usually means she knew naught worth telling. But I was wrong about that, b'y, was I wrong! That woman knew people, really knew people. No matter the wrinkles on my face and fingers a bit knurled with arthritis, that woman saw the person inside was the same as when I was 20."

Lee Stones has memories of that day, too. First terror, then amazement, finally joy mixed with humility. Strong emotions often accompany attitude change. The Federation's President wanted her to talk on "Putting the Zing Back into Your Relationships." He asked Lee to suggest ways to improve the romantic lives of older people. At first, Lee thought he was kidding. Did older people even have romantic lives? Sure, she sometimes saw some sweet old couple—probably married forever—holding hands in the park. But holding hands is far from passion, and isn't passion the key to romance? Also, most of her grandmother's friends were widows. Surely, they weren't lusting after romance, if only because of a shortage of men their age.

Just the thought of talking about romance to people like her grandmother gave Lee the shakes. The working families of her adolescent upbringing didn't talk much about sexuality. The edict was "Don't you fool around and you won't get pregnant!" That was about all she remembered of her at-home sexual education. The idea of sex

between her parents, even her grandparents (God forbid), was not only unspeakable but unthinkable. Such were the times a decade or more before the potency drug Viagra changed forever society's attitudes toward later-life sexuality.

But Mike Pickett, the federation's president, was insistent. A few months later, after much reading, thought, and discussion about the topic, Lee arrived at the convention floor.

"That's she, that's the one." Marjorie Charles remembers pointing Lee out to a friend. "I even went up to her and said, 'We really, really, look forward to your talk,' thinking only of smut. Wasn't I the catty one?"

Soon Lee found herself on stage before the microphone, hundreds of eager old faces looking up at her excitedly. "I controlled my nerves but at a price," she recalls. "My heart thumped to the rhythm of a fast Newfoundland jig. I asked myself for the umpteenth time, 'What madness made me agree to this? Will they think me presumptuous, even a hussy?'" And so, with much misgiving, she gulped in air and began.

"What was memorable," Marjorie recalls years later, "wasn't so much her advice, but her assumption that we needed advice. She could have been talking to somebody of her own age. She didn't treat us like people sexually dead—and I must admit, I acted dead in that way—but just in need of awakening. I did wake up right there and then, and so did many other people. We knew what we wanted, longed for even, widows like us. But we couldn't talk of it. To speak about sex and we'd face the youngsters' ridicule—even our children—specially our children. When she'd finished, we didn't just clap. Oh no! We cheered, drummed the floor with our feet, on and on, must've been for a good three minutes. What a racket, b'y! The reason was

(continued)

Box 1.1 *(continued)*

she saw us like we are and wasn't afraid to say so." "I learned so much from those people," Lee says now. "I told them what I knew, as though to friends. Of course I was unsure about whether I would shock them. But they shocked me. They shocked the sexual stereotyping right out of my head. I have no doubts now that people remain sexual to the end of their days. It was joyful to experience, but humbling because I'd been so wrong before. They changed my beliefs, my attitudes, and I think I changed theirs. What happened that day was that the formerly

unthinkable (to me) or unspeakable (to them) became open to discussion."
Lee Stones continued to give talks on later-life sexuality to avid audiences across Canada. She co-authored two editions of a book on the topic (Stones & Stones, 1996, 2004), and often acts as consultant for long-term care facilities to help staff, who are still reluctant to accommodate the sexual needs of residents. Two years after the Corner Brook convention, Marjorie Charles had a romance with a tourist from Nova Scotia. They married and settled near Halifax.

Witches," 1486), which equates the origins of witchcraft with carnal lust. This manual indicated that deviant sexuality could provide evidence for witchcraft. Records indicate that approximately 90 percent of witches were women, mostly aged in their 50s or 60s, and many had served as midwives. Women during this epoch had good reason to be modest in their sexual display.

Attitudes of Older People toward Sexuality

A major study by the American Association of Retired Persons (Jacoby, 1999) measured attitudes and beliefs in the context of later-life sexuality. The survey included items on sexual satisfaction, the relevance of sexuality to quality of life, and attitudes toward sex outside marriage. Figure 1.3 shows similar levels of sexual satisfaction between the sexes (although more females than males reported being very satisfied) and a decrease in satisfaction with age. The finding of somewhat higher sexual satisfaction in females than in males is consistent with findings from other studies (Matthias, Lubben, Atchison, & Schweitzer, 1997). Men in the AARP survey who were sexually satisfied were usually married to a partner perceived as romantic and sensitive to their needs. Sexually dissatisfied men had either no partner or a partner perceived as non-romantic. Sexually satisfied women usually had married partners perceived as sexually imaginative and exciting lovers. Sexually dissatisfied women were mainly without a partner. Consequently, much of the decrease in sexual satisfaction with age appears to relate to the absence of a partner in late life.

Figure 1.3 shows that the belief that sex is important to quality of life was more frequent among men than women but its prevalence decreases with age in both sexes. More women than men believe that sex outside marriage is wrong, and the belief is more prevalent with age in both sexes.

Figure 1.3 **ATTITUDES TOWARD SEXUALITY BY SEX AND AGE**

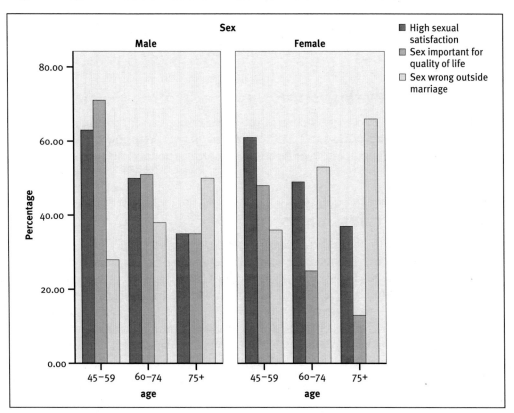

Attitudes toward Sexuality in Long-Term Care Homes

Long-term care brings special challenges because a significant proportion of residents have some form of dementia. Sexual expression in residents with and without dementia may bring different ethical challenges (Lichtenberg, 1997). For the cognitively intact, the issue of privacy is primary. For people with dementia, the question of competency may be paramount. Although there is no good reason to prevent people with dementia from enjoying a sexual relationship, it is important to respect their desires and ensure that they are not coerced or persuaded against their wishes.

One study found that long-term care staff were more likely than older people themselves to consider sexuality an important issue to be managed (Walker, Osgood, Richardson, & Ephross, 1998). Older people are more tolerant about homosexuals residing in nursing homes, and more likely to think that staff should facilitate access to erotica. On the other hand, more older people than staff think family members should be told if residents form a romantic attachment.

Although many long-term care institutions now provide privacy rooms to facilitate the sexual enjoyment of cognitively intact residents, there is little evidence on the outcome of such initiatives. The barriers to overcome include not only the attitudes of staff but also those of the residents, who may feel a mixture of benevolence, envy, or concern for those having romantic liaisons.

Attitudes and Well-Being

Well-being can be viewed as a continuum comprising mental and physical health at one pole and disease and disability at the other (also see the discussion in Chapter 10). Let's look at the attitudes first of professionals and then of the public at large.

Attitudes of Professionals

Professionals tend to be concerned with the disease and disability pole of the well-being continuum. The medical vernacular refers to old people as "a problem," senior activist Madeline Honeyman told the Canadian Medical Association in 1991 (Stones & Stones, 1996). They can be a problem to the physician because they are more likely to have chronic illnesses that typically necessitate longer consultations. Furthermore, because chronic diseases are not usually cured, as acute diseases can be, physicians may find treating older patients less rewarding. Older people are a problem to administrators of acute-care hospitals because they typically stay longer after admission. They may become known as "bed-blockers" if their discharge is delayed because of lingering illness and a failure to locate suitable alternative accommodation. Older people may even be a problem in continuing care homes, which are designed to house them, if they fail to fit in or comply with a home's routine. Treating the elderly as problems rather than people (i.e., dismissing their needs) is just one charge of ageism laid against health-care professionals.

Another charge is that health-care professionals give lower priority to older patients. Some research on this issue measures attitudes within the health-care professions whereas other research infers attitudes through analysis of health-care practices. Recent research on treatment priorities (Kane, 2004), pain (Brown, 2004), screening (Jerant, Franks, Jackson, & Doescher, 2004), and recruitment into clinical trials (Townsley, Selby, & Siu, 2005) all are consistent with ageist inferences. Other charges include the overuse of physical and chemical restraint to pacify residents in long-term care settings (Brink, Stewart, & Stones, 2004) and the use of ageist language that strips residents of autonomy and dignity (Nussbaum, Pitts, Huber, Krieger, & Ohs, 2005).

As a qualification to the preceding charges, no author argues that most or even a small minority of health professionals are overtly ageist—just the opposite, in fact—but rather that the health-care system makes some kinds of ageism invisible (e.g., pacification disguised as treatment) and that it ought not to tolerate ageism in any form. Health-care professionals work within strictures dictated by their professional organizations and by government policies. If ageism is inherent in those policies and practices, the blame extends to levels much higher than the direct interaction between the health-care professional and the older patient.

Attitudes of the Public

Despite the charges of ageism in acute health-care settings and continuing-care homes, the majority of consumers report satisfaction with their experiences in health care. Approximately 85 percent of patients report overall satisfaction with acute-care hospital experiences (CIHI, 2005). Similarly, about 85 percent of residents of Ontario continuing-care facilities report overall satisfaction, as do their families (HRCC, 2005). The residents' satisfaction is highest for medical care and lowest for the autonomy allowed them. Their families are least satisfied with the living environment and provisions for activities and entertainment.

Other research on public attitudes examines the positive pole of the well-being continuum. Most respondents of any age have a positive attitude about their health. Health Canada (2000) reports that 78 percent of seniors described their health as good, very good, or excellent. The AARP (1999) survey similarly shows that just over 80 percent of people aged 45+ years evaluate their health as good, very good, or excellent, with few differences due to cohort or sex. Ratings of perceived health are high among older Canadians (Kozma, Stones, & McNeil, 1991). In a 1999 telephone survey of 1000 representative Canadians sponsored by Manulife Financial, the majority of respondents perceived themselves as having good health; few said they worried about their health or felt depressed. There were no significant cohort differences on any measure, suggesting that attitudes toward personal health do not change with age (see also Chapter 10).

However, some caution is necessary in interpreting satisfaction ratings and other measures of well-being. As we said earlier, personality and enduring dispositions are important influences on attitude. This may help to explain why even older people with multiple chronic disorders continue to evaluate their personal health positively. We will discuss the role of life experience and personality further in Chapter 8.

Attitudes and the Self

Findings on attitudes toward the self by older people show two main influences. The first is a negative appraisal of a diminishing future. The second is a positive appraisal of themselves against other people.

In the AARP (1999) survey, respondents from all cohorts and both sexes thought they stood higher on a **life satisfaction** ladder five years ago than now, and expected to stand lower on the ladder five years into the future. These findings are consistent with Dowd's (1980a) claim of devaluation as people progress from mid-life to old age.

Another AARP survey examined attitudes toward physical attractiveness in a national telephone survey of over 2000 Americans (AARP, 2001). This survey asked respondents to rate their personal attractiveness on a 10-point scale and to estimate the age when physical attractiveness attained its peak. The findings show both negative and positive evaluations. Because the age of peak attractiveness is in the mid-life span, older respondents think their peak attractiveness is past. However, the mean rating of personal attractiveness by both older men and women is close to 6.5 on the 10-point scale. Consequently, the respondents continue to consider themselves as attractive even though the age of peak attractiveness is behind them.

Subjective age refers to ratings of looks and feelings relative to those of age peers (i.e., whether the respondent looks or feels younger or older than a reference group of other people the respondent's age). Findings by Montepare and Lachman (1989) showed a compressed range for subjective age. Teenagers had a subjective age older than their years; middle-aged and older respondents had a subjective age younger than their chronological age. Sato and colleagues (1997) replicated these findings in Japan with over 1800 respondents aged 8 to 92 years. Findings from the Canadian 1999 Manulife Financial survey also provide replication.

The research findings on attitudes toward the self include evidence for evaluations by older people based on both realistic and unrealistic considerations. Negative evaluations of personal status are realistic to the extent that they accord with ageism entrenched in Western culture. Positive evaluations of subjective age are unrealistic because the mean subjective age within any cohort should mathematically correspond with chronological age. Consistent findings that older respondents rate themselves subjectively younger than they would rate their age peers suggest that seniors devalue the latter because of their age. Consequently, the findings on subjective age may reflect the respondents' own ageist attitudes.

CHAPTER SUMMARY

The term used to describe stereotyped attitudes toward older people is ageism. Although some researchers argue that ageism is not a pervasive phenomenon, the evidence suggests otherwise. There is evidence for ageist attitudes in such diverse fields as literature and the arts, the sciences, health care, the law, and sexuality.

Key ideas to remember from this chapter:

- The definition of an attitude is a tendency to evaluate an object with favour or disfavour. Attitudes differ from beliefs in that the latter lack an evaluative component.

- Measures used in gerontological research may include attitudes, beliefs, or both; they may assess cognitive, affective, and behavioural modes of responding.
- Attitudes are predictive of general trends in behaviour rather than of behaviour in any specific situation.
- Influences on attitudes include enduring dispositions as well as life experiences.
- Elder abuse and neglect refer to behaviour toward older people by those in positions of trust. Ageist attitudes may exacerbate the frequency of elder abuse and present barriers toward the reporting of abuse.
- Attitudes toward elder abuse show reasonable consistency throughout society, but differ somewhat among different professions and across minority groups. Older people have less negative attitudes toward elder abuse and neglect than young people. This finding is consistent with other research that shows less extreme attitudes when rating an in group rather than an out group. There is limited but positive evidence that community education can change attitudes toward elder abuse and neglect.
- The Western world has a long history of ageist attitudes toward later-life sexuality. Although satisfaction with sexuality shows little change with age, satisfaction is lower among those without a partner.
- Charges of ageism against health-care professionals are legion. However, patients in acute and continuing-care settings report being satisfied. Ratings of health care by the public are mainly positive at any age.
- Attitudes toward the self have negative and positive trends. The trend is negative when evaluating the past with the present and future. The trend is positive when respondents compare themselves to other people their age. Both trends may reflect cultural devaluation of the elderly as internalized by the respondents.

KEY TERMS

self **(p. 2)**

cognition **(p. 2)**

behaviour **(p. 2)**

ageism **(p. 3)**

pacification **(p. 4)**

attitude **(p. 6)**

object **(p. 6)**

target **(p. 6)**

measures **(p. 6)**

belief **(p. 7)**

abuse **(p. 11)**

model **(p. 12)**

life satisfaction **(p. 22)**

subjective age **(p. 22)**

Study Questions

1. Define the term *attitude*. Discuss the relationship between attitudes and behaviour.

2. Is ageism a pervasive problem in Canada?

3. Are older people's attitudes toward elder abuse similar to those of younger people? Critically evaluate the evidence.

4. Discuss the common belief that older people have little interest in sexuality.

5. Provide evidence on whether older people have negative attitudes toward their health and their lives.

6. Explain the relevance of ageism to attitudes toward the self.

Suggested Readings

Special Issue on Ageism (2005). *Journal of Social Issues, 61*(2).

Olson, J.M., Vernon, P.E., Aitken Harris, J, & Jang, K.L. (2001). The heritability of attitudes. *Journal of Personality and Social Psychology, 80*: 845–860.

Matthias, R.E., Lubben, J.E., Atchison, K.A., & Schweitzer, S.O. (1997). Sexual activity and satisfaction among very old adults: Results from a community-dwelling medicare population survey. *Gerontologist, 37*: 6–14.

Stones, L., & Stones, M.J. (2004). *Sex may be wasted on the young.* 2nd edition. Toronto: Captus Press.

Chapter 2

POPULATION AGING

Learning Objectives

In this chapter, you will learn about

- A number of different ways population aging can be measured.
- Statistics on the aging of the Canadian population since the end of the 19th century, and its variation over time.
- The major cause of population aging.
- Epidemiological transition theory and its concern with changes in the causes of death as mortality declines.
- The major causes of death among elderly Canadians.

- "Compression of morbidity," a debated concept that posits that more and more people will live in a healthy state until just before their death.
- Gender, ethno-cultural and migration differences in old-age differentials.
- Apocalyptic demography, which refers to the view that demographic change—in this case, population aging—can be severely detrimental to a society.

Introduction

We are interested in aging from both an individual and a population perspective. The first chapter discussed the field from an individual perspective: how individuals perceive aging, their attitudes towards it, and others' attitudes toward old people. This chapter looks at aging from a macro point of view, taking the population as the focal point. We thus turn to demography, a sub-field within sociology and economics that studies the characteristics of a population and the dynamics of population change. One important aspect of a population is its **age structure** (also sometimes called *age composition*). The Canadian age structure is getting older; indeed, if this were not so, it is unlikely that books such as this would be written or that you would be taking a course in **gerontology**, which is the study of aging and the aged. While the demographic fact of population aging is central to gerontology, very few gerontologists are demographers. Typically, gerontologists take the demographics of aging for granted—or, at best, treat it as a backdrop to or justification for the phenomena that they study—and leave others to do the research on demographic change per se. While this division of labour works quite well, it is nevertheless important for beginning students of gerontology to have a basic understanding of the demography of aging.

In this chapter, we first look at the extent to which aging has occurred and is expected to occur in the Canadian population, and how Canada compares with other countries. We then turn our attention to the demographic processes that lead to population aging. This is followed by a discussion of the characteristics of the aged population in Canada. Next, we examine causes of death in relation to lowering mortality. The chapter ends with a discussion of apocalyptic demography—the exaggeration of the consequences of population change in general, and population aging in particular.

Assessing Population Aging

Assessing the degree to which a population is aged or aging depends upon the measurement that is used. Three common measures of population aging are discussed here. (*Note:* The data in this section, unless otherwise specified, are from Statistics Canada (2001b).)

Percentage Aged 65+

The most common measure of population aging is the percentage of the population that is aged 65 and over. (See Box 2.1 for a discussion of age 65 as the entry point for old age.) By rule of thumb, a population in which at least 10 percent of the population is aged 65 and over is deemed to be old. Canada is, therefore, considered to have an old population because 13.0 percent of our population was aged 65 and over in 2001 (United Nations, 2001).

Box 2.1 *Why Is Age 65 Years the Entry Point for Old Age?*

There is no logical reason why age 65 years is now considered to mark the commencement of old age. This age marker has been socially constructed, and it could just as easily be any other age. In order to understand this social construction, a little history is helpful. In the late 1800s, Otto von Bismarck, on the basis of advice from actuarial consultants, chose 65 years as the age at which his military personnel would be eligible to receive pension benefits. This decision was based on two factors. First, Bismarck believed that the promise of a pension would increase the loyalty and productivity of his employees. Second, making the age of pension eligibility 65 years would not be costly to Bismarck's coffers since the mortality levels of the time meant that most of his employees would likely die before that age or shortly after!

After this initial demarcation of the entry point for old age, the age of 65 years gradually became the norm, institutionalized first in a number of private pension plans and later in government pensions and other policies. It is noteworthy that the social construction of age 65 years as the starting point of old age had nothing to do with the characteristics of people and everything to do with meeting the needs of employers, both as a benefit to retain employees and as a way to be rid of older and more highly paid workers. Given increases in life expectancy and improvements in health, there is no reason why age 65 years will continue to be the socially defined entry point to old age. Canadian demographers Denton and Spencer (2002) foresee that age 70 years will gradually come to replace age 65 years.

The percentage of the population that is aged 65 and over is a simple and easily understood indicator of population aging—as the percentage increases, the population is aging. However, this measure does have limitations. It implies that populations with the same percentage aged 65 and over have identical age structures, but that is not necessarily the case; populations may have very different proportions of children, youth, and working-age adults. This measure also homogenizes the aged, implying that all persons aged 65 are the same; however, there are tremendous differences, on average, between people aged 65 or so and those aged 90 and over, for example. In recognition of this, Neugarten (1974) categorized the elderly population into: the young-old (aged 65 to 74), the middle-old (aged 75 to 84), the old-old (aged 85 to 89) and the frail-old (aged 90 and over). These distinctions are commonly used by gerontologists to help de-homogenize seniors, but it must be remembered that considerable variation exists even within these more age-delimited categories. For example, people aged 75 range from the very rich to the very poor, from the hale and hearty to the frail, from those living alone to those living in multi-generational households, from the fluent in English or French to recent immigrants with no facility with an official language, and so on.

Median Age

Another single measure of population aging is the **median age of the population**. By definition, one-half of the population is older than the median age and one-half is younger. As the median age increases, the population is aging. In Canada, the median age was 37.6 years in 2001 (United Nations, 2001). Usually, demographers consider a population with a median age of 30 to be "old"—therefore, by this measure as well, the Canadian population falls into the "old" category. However, the correlation between the two measures—median age and the percentage of the population aged 65 and over—is far from perfect. A population that ranks the oldest by one of these measures will not necessarily rank the oldest by the other measure.

Dependency Ratios

A number of types of age **dependency ratios** can be used to assess population age structure. These ratios attempt to measure the relative proportion of persons of "dependent" ages within a population. The assumption is that people of a certain age are necessarily dependent on others, and constitute a social burden. Thus, a dependency ratio is sometimes called "the dependency burden." Although this term is used less commonly now, its abandonment does not reflect a fundamental perceptual change but merely increased sensitivity to the ramifications of using pejorative terminology for groups of people.

The most frequently used dependency ratios take the total population of "working ages" of 15 (or 18) to 64—that is, the age range in which most people are in paid employment—as the non-dependent ages. Using the total population aged 15 (or 18) to 64 as the denominator, three dependency ratios are calculated: an **aged dependency ratio**, a **youth dependency ratio**, and a **total dependency ratio**. The aged dependency ratio is the number of persons aged 65 and over as a ratio of the number of persons aged 15 to 64 (or 18 to 64). In 2000, the aged dependency ratio in Canada was 183; that is, there were 183 elders for every 1000 persons aged 15 to 64. The youth dependency ratio is the number of persons aged 0 to 15 (or 0 to 18) relative to the population aged 15 to 64 (or 18 to 64). In 2000, the youth dependency ratio in Canada was 279; that is, there were 279 children aged 0 to 14 for every 1000 persons aged 15 to 64. Note that the youth dependency ratio is larger than the aged dependency ratio (279 vs. 183), indicating that despite the increasing number of seniors, there are still more children than seniors in Canada. The aged dependency ratio and the youth dependency ratio, when combined, form the total dependency ratio—the total dependent population (the old and the young) relative to the population considered to be non-dependent. In 2000, the total dependency ratio in Canada was 462 (183 + 279) persons for every 1000 persons in the non-dependent ages.

A second type of dependency ratio uses only the population aged 15 (or 18) to 64 who are in the paid labour force as the denominator in order to calculate the aged, youth, and total dependency ratios. Since the denominator is smaller because not everyone aged 15 to 64 is in the paid labour force, each of the three dependency ratios (aged, youth and total) is larger.

Another type of dependency ratio is the ratio of the number of persons aged 65 and over to those aged less than 15 years. In 2000 in Canada, this ratio was

656 (i.e., there were 656 elders for every 1000 children aged below 15). As an over-all measure of population aging, this ratio is superior to the others mentioned above. As we will see later in this chapter, fertility (the number of children born) and mortality (deaths in a population) are key demographic processes in population aging. This ratio captures the persons closest to fertility (the young) and mortality (the old), and thus is a better measure of population age than the previous dependency ratios.

Yet another type of dependency ratio is the **familial old-age dependency ratio** (Kart & Kinney, 2001). It is the ratio of the number of elderly parents (population aged 65 to 84) to the children who would support them (population aged 45 to 54). This ratio is taken as a proxy for the dependency burden of middle-aged children, although it is recognized that not all persons aged 65 to 84 need support from their children or have children, and that not all children are able or willing to provide support to elderly parents. The familial old-age dependency ratio in Canada in 2000 was 787; that is, there were 787 older parents for every 1000 persons in the ages likely to be their children.

All dependency ratios contain a problematic assumption regarding older people: that is, that they are all economically dependent. This assumption ignores a number of realities: some older people are members of the paid labour force; many older people pay taxes and contribute to the general economy in that way; and many older people are engaged in unpaid labour (as volunteers, as caregivers to spouses and/or grandchildren, for example) which contributes much to the Canadian economy. Dependency ratios also carry difficult-to-justify assumptions regarding other age groups. For example, not all people of working age are economically independent; the work of homemakers is not considered when the dependency ratio is calculated on the basis of the paid labour force; children can contribute in a variety of ways to the family economy. The fundamental problem, then, is the simplistic assumption of equivalence between age and economic productivity and the narrow conceptualization of economic usefulness as tied only to paid labour.

Canada's Aging Population

We now look at how the Canadian population has aged over the last 150 years, and how it is expected to age in the coming decades. Projections about the future age structure depend on assumptions about future levels of fertility, mortality, and migration. In particular, if our fertility rates were to undergo another boom, our future age structure would be younger than projected. Figure 2.1 presents data on the percentage of the population aged 65 and over from 1881 to 1993, with projections to 2036. It can be observed that our population has been aging continuously over the entire period; in other words, population aging is not new. However, certain time periods have experienced more rapid aging than others. Clearly, the decades to come will experience a large increase in the proportion of the population

Figure 2.1 **PROPORTION OF PEOPLE AGED 65 YEARS AND OVER IN THE TOTAL POPULATION, CANADA, 1881-2036**

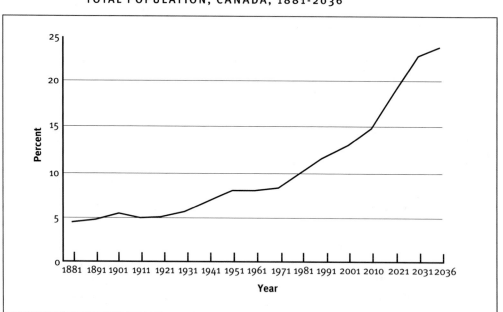

Source: Statistics Canada, *Population ageing and the elderly*, Catalogue No. 91-533 (April 7, 1993): 13.

aged 65 and over. This increase is a direct result of the aging of the baby boomers—the large cohort of persons born between 1946 and 1962—who will begin entering traditionally defined old age (i.e., age 65) in 2011. Between then and 2027, when the youngest baby boomers turn age 65, the ranks of the older population will grow substantially. The effect of the baby boom on the percentage of the population aged 65 and over will gradually dissipate; by 2050, most of the youngest boomers will be dead.

It is also important to note that the elderly population is itself aging, that is, among those aged 65 and over, there is an increasing number and percentage of persons who are aged 80 and over. In 2000, there were approximately 910 000 Canadians aged 80 and over, making up 3 percent of the total population. In 1981, the comparable percentage was 2.4 percent, and in 1961 it was 1.4 percent. In fact, the population aged 80 and over is proportionately the fastest growing age segment in Canada.

Canadian Population Aging in Comparative Perspective

Approximately 7 percent of the world's population is aged 65 and over, with a sharp division between more developed and less developed nations (see Table 2.1).

Table 2.1   **PERCENTAGE OF POPULATION AGED 65 AND OVER, BY REGION: CIRCA 2001**

REGION	PERCENTAGE
World	7
More developed countries	14
Less developed countries	5
Africa	3
Asia	6
Europe	14
Latin America (and Caribbean)	5
North America	13

Source: Population Reference Bureau (2001). *2001 World population data sheet*. Washington, DC: Population Reference Bureau, Inc.

The youngest populations occur in Africa; the oldest populations are in Europe. With 13 percent of our population aged 65 and over, the Canadian population is, comparatively speaking, quite old. However, many European nations are substantially older than Canada. For example, Sweden, Belgium, Italy, and Greece all have 17 percent of their populations aged 65 and over; and the figure is 16 percent in France, Germany, Spain, and the United Kingdom (Population Reference Bureau, 2001). In contrast, the percentage aged 65 and over is as low as 2 percent in Niger and Uganda in Africa and Bhutan in South Central Asia.

So far, we have been considering relative proportions only; absolute numbers are also important to take into account. The number of older persons in the continent with the greatest proportion of old people, Europe (including Russia), totals approximately 102 million; in Asia, the 6 percent figure translates into approximately 221 million elderly persons. India alone, with only 4 percent of its population aged 65 and over, contains about 44.1 million elders—almost 10 million more people than the total population of Canada (Population Reference Bureau, 2001). Thus, the developed and developing worlds face different age structure issues. In the North, we are dealing with a relatively high proportion of elderly, compared with other age groups; in the South (or the Third World), the issue is one of a large and growing *number* of elderly people, although they do not constitute a large fraction of the overall population. To the degree that elderly people require special resources (and only some do), the North faces a relatively smaller proportion of working-age people to support them. Southern countries, in contrast, are concerned about the sheer numbers of older adults who do or might need support.

What Causes Populations to Age?

The Important Role of Fertility

Why is it that developed countries such as Canada have an age structure that is so much older than that in developing countries? The answer may surprise you: the main factor accounting for population aging is declining fertility, as established by noted U.S. demographer Ansley Coale (1956) 50 years ago. As fertility declines, the number and proportion of children in a population decline, and the proportion of older people correspondingly increases. In youthful Africa, the total fertility rate (the average number of children born to a woman by the end of her childbearing years) is 5.3; in old Europe, the comparable figure is 1.4 (and the Canadian total fertility rate is 1.5) (Population Reference Bureau, 2001).

The reason that Canada (and the United States) has a younger population than most European countries is because we had a large and long baby boom after World War II, as noted above. The immediate effect of this boom was to increase the proportion of children and then young adults in our population, that is, to "young" our population. However, because the baby boom was followed by declining—and now low—fertility rates, its ultimate consequence has been only to delay population aging.

Although declining fertility is key to population aging, gerontologists have not devoted much attention to it as a research topic (although family size and number of children are studied by gerontologists in relation to aging families and social support, as shown in Chapters 11 and 12). Fertility levels and trends have been, and remain, the purview of demographers, who have identified a number of factors that acted as important causes of fertility decline in the West : urbanization and the declining value and increased costs of children in cities; the decline of the family wage and the consequent increase in women's labour force participation; increasing levels of education, particularly for women; the women's movement; and increasingly available and effective means to control reproduction (e.g., Balakrishnan, Lapierre-Adamcyk and Krotki, 1993; Ford and Nault 1996; Matthews, 1999). Apart from academic specialization, one reason why gerontologists have not studied fertility is that fertility has become less predictive of population aging as mortality rates have been lowered. After a population reaches a life expectancy at birth of 70 years, almost all young people survive past their risky first year; thus, any further declines in mortality are concentrated at older ages. These declines translate into relatively more growth in the older age groups, and therefore population aging.

Population Pyramids

It is common to graphically represent age structures by what are termed **population pyramids**; these illustrate the proportion of males and females in each age group (usually five-year age groups up to the older ages, where there is aggregation due to small numbers) in a population. There are three ideal types of pyramids: (1) expansive pyramids, which have a broad base (and look most like pyramids), reflecting a high proportion of children in the population, the result of high past and present fertility levels; (2) constrictive pyramids, in which the base is somewhat narrower than the middle, and which occur when fertility has been rapidly declining: and (3) stationary pyramids, which have a narrow base and approximately equal percentages of people in each age group, tapering off at older ages, and which are the result of a lengthy period of low fertility. Figure 2.2 presents Canadian population pyramids for selected years from 1881 to 2036. We can see that: in 1881, the Canadian age structure was expansive, reflecting high fertility which had not yet begun to decline; decreases in fertility are evident in the 1921 pyramid, as the base of the pyramid is narrowing; continuing constriction is interrupted by the baby boom, the beginnings of which can be observed in the 1951 pyramid; in 1991, the pyramid has taken on the classic characteristics of the constrictive type as a result of the significant decline in fertility that commenced in the mid-1960s; and the future pyramids in 2011 and 2036 increasingly take on the stationary shape.

Mortality Decline

While declines in fertility are the major cause of population aging, decreases in mortality (deaths) are important as well. This is more intuitive. Because we associate population aging with more older people, we automatically equate population aging with higher life expectancy (the flip side of lower mortality).

　　Life expectancy refers to the number of years that a person in a given country/population can expect to live. Conceptually, life expectancy is virtually identical to *longevity*; the difference between them lies in measurement issues. Life expectancy is calculated in a very strict way, using what is termed life table analysis (see Box 2.2); longevity is not associated with any particular statistical technique. Both life expectancy and longevity are distinct from **lifespan**, which, in demography, refers to the number of years that humans could live under ideal conditions. In other disciplines the concept of lifespan is sometimes used differently. In psychology, for example, it refers to developmental changes over the course of a human life.

　　Table 2.2 shows trends in life expectancy at birth and at age 65 for the period from 1921 (when Canada began a national system of death registration) to 2001. We can see that life expectancy increased steadily over the course of the 20th century. The major gains in life expectancy at birth were made in the earlier part of the period. For example, from 1921 to 1961, life expectancy at birth increased almost 10 years for males and nearly 14 years for females. Over this same period, life expectancy at age 65 increased a mere 0.6 years for men and 2.5 years for women. However, after 1961, life expectancy at age 65 increased more sharply. These trends indicate that young Canadians were the first to benefit from mortality

Figure 2.2 AGE PYRAMIDS, CANADA, 1881–2036

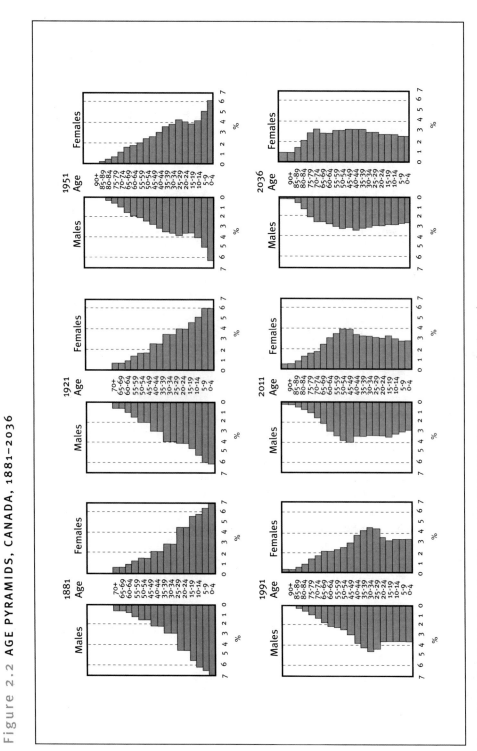

Source: Adapted from Statistics Canada, *Population ageing and the elderly,* Catalogue No. 91-533 (April 7, 1993): 18.

Box 2.2   *Measuring Life Expectancy*

Life expectancy is a summary measure of mortality in a population. Statistics on life expectancy are derived from a mathematical model known as a life table. Life tables create a hypothetical cohort (or group) of 100,000 persons (usually of males and females separately) and subject it to the age-gender-specific mortality rates (the number of deaths per 1,000 or 10,000 or 100,000 persons of a given age and gender) observed in a given population. In doing this, we can trace how, say, the 100,000 hypothetical persons (called a synthetic cohort) would shrink in numbers due to deaths as they age. The average age at which these persons are likely to have died is the life expectancy at birth. Life tables also provide data on life expectancy at other ages; the most commonly used statistic other than life expectancy at birth is life expectancy at age 65 years, that is, the number of remaining years of life that persons aged 65 years can expect to live.

Life expectancy statistics are very useful as summary measures of mortality, and they have an intuitive appeal that other measures of mortality, such as rates, lack. However, it is important to interpret data on life expectancy correctly. If it is reported that life expectancy at birth in a given population is 75 years in 2000, this does not mean that all members of the population can expect to live to the age of 75 years. Rather, it means that babies born in that population in 2000 would have a life expectancy at birth of 75 years, if they live their lives subject to the age-specific mortality rates of the entire population in 2000. This is not likely; as they age, age-specific mortality rates will almost certainly change in some ways. Also, older people in that population will have lived their lives up to the year 2000 under a different set of age-specific mortality rates. Thus, it is important to be aware of the hypothetical nature of life expectancy statistics.

---

reductions; it was only later that longevity in later life increased appreciably. This is the typical experience of developed countries.

It is not known whether life expectancy will continue to increase as we move through the 21st century, and indeed this is a subject of a fair amount of debate. Part of the debate concerns the length of the human lifespan. Some (e.g., Fries, 1983; National Institute on Aging, 1996) argue that Western populations are approaching a biologically fixed maximum or finite lifespan—probably in the range of 85 to 100 years. Others suggest that the human lifespan can be extended by many more years, due to advances in molecular medicine (Schwartz, 1998) or dietary improvements (Walford, 1983), for example. A third, intermediate position is that there is no rigid limit to the human lifespan and unforeseen biomedical technological breakthroughs could gradually increase our lifespan.

A considerable amount of research, based on the foundational assumption of a finite human lifespan, has focused on the concept of **dependency-free life expectancy** (also called *dependence-free life expectancy, healthy life expectancy, active life expectancy, disability-free life expectancy,* and *functional life expectancy*). These varying terms refer to the number of years that people in a given population can

Table 2.2 LIFE EXPECTANCY AT BIRTH AND AT AGE 65 YEARS, MALES AND FEMALES: CANADA, 1921–2001

	MALES		FEMALES	
	At Birth	*At Age 65*	*At Birth*	*At Age 65*
1921	58.8	13.0	60.6	13.6
1931	60.0	13.0	62.1	13.7
1941	63.0	12.8	64.6	13.4
1951	66.4	13.3	70.9	15.0
1961	68.4	13.6	74.3	16.1
1971	69.4	13.8	76.5	17.6
1981	71.9	14.6	79.1	18.9
1991	74.3	15.6	80.8	19.8
2001	77.0	17.0	82.1	20.5

Source: E.G. Moore & M.W. Rosenberg, with D. McGuinness (1997). *Growing old in Canada: Demographic and geographic perspectives.* Toronto, ON: Statistics Canada and ITP Nelson (p. 12); A. Bélanger, Y. Carrière, & S. Gilbert (2000). *Report on the demographic situation in Canada, 2000.* (Catalogue No. 91-209-XPE). Ottawa, ON: Statistics Canada, Table A9; Population Reference Bureau. (2005). *2005 World population data sheet.* Washington, DC: Population Reference Bureau, Inc.

expect to live in (reasonably) good health, with no or only minor disabling health conditions. Much of the research on dependency-free life expectancy tests, in varying ways, the validity of the **compression of morbidity** hypothesis, originally formulated by Fries (1983). This hypothesis states that, at least among Western populations, more and more people are able to postpone the age of onset of chronic disability; hence, the period of time between onset of becoming seriously ill or disabled and dying is shortening or compressing. The general idea is that we are moving to a situation in which we will all live hale and hearty lives until a very old age and then die quickly.

While some research finds support for the compression of morbidity hypothesis (Hayward, Crimmins, & Saito, 1998), until recently, more did not (e.g., Crimmins, 1990; Ford, Haug, Roy, Jones, & Folmar, 1992; Verbrugge, 1984), including Canadian research by Roos, Havens, and Black (1993) in Manitoba. However, it would appear that we are now experiencing more years that are dependency-free (Manuel & Schultz, 2001). This is good news; it suggests that more of the additional years we are living are years without disability.

As discussed in Chapter 15, one of the challenges for an aging society is that the biomedical model dominant in the Canadian health-care system is largely geared toward acute illness and often does not provide the most appropriate care for the chronic conditions seniors suffer. Even though recent research suggests that the onset of chronic conditions is later than it used to be, seniors still have many years living with these types of problems.

Research on dependency-free life expectancy in Canada reveals an important gender difference (Martel & Bélanger, 2000). While, at age 65, women can expect to live about four years longer than men, their expectation of dependency-free years of life is not quite a year more than that of men. In other words, older women will spend proportionately more of the remaining years of their lives (32.4 percent) in poor health than will men (21.1 percent). Gender differences in health in later life are discussed more extensively in Chapter 10.

The Role of Migration

It is commonly thought that one way to cope with population aging is to try to avoid it by "younging" the population through increased immigration. The reasoning is that because migrants tend to be young, their numbers will counteract population aging. However, migration plays a relatively small role in population aging, especially at the national level. Canada's Chief Statistician, Ivan Fellegi (1988) has estimated that Canada would have to allow in more than 600 000 immigrants per year in order for immigration to have a measurable impact on our age structure. The Canadian government sets its annual immigration targets in the neighbourhood of 200 000 to 225 000 (and has failed to meet these targets in recent years). An approximate tripling of the number of immigrants who enter Canada annually has not occurred and does not seem likely despite current plans from Ottawa at the present time. There are also additional costs for immigrant services, such as teaching English or French as a second language, and public opinion is less than enthusiastic about current levels of immigration, let alone increased levels. Following the terrorist attacks on September 11, 2001 on the World Trade Center in New York and the Pentagon in Washington, D.C., immigration has become even more difficult.

In summary, Canada's aging population is due to the combined effect of declining fertility and declining mortality, with international migration playing a fairly minor role. Historically, fertility has been the major determinant of our age structure. In the absence of another baby boom—which no one is predicting—and in the face of low fertility, mortality will take on increasing importance in determining our age structure.

Causes of Death

As mortality rates fall and a population becomes older, the causes of death—and relatedly, the ages of death—change. The **epidemiological transition** refers to changes in the causes of death that accompany declines in mortality (and consequent increases in life expectancy) (Omran, 1971). Gerontologists are particularly interested in causes of death since, in modern societies such as Canada, deaths are concentrated at old ages.

Epidemiological Transition Theory

Epidemiological transition theory has its roots in demography, not gerontology. It is less a theory than a description of the relationship between mortality decline and changes in the relative importance of different causes of death in the West. It posits that a society or a population goes through three mortality stages in its transition to a modern pattern. The first stage—the Age of Pestilence and Famine—is characterized by high death rates that vacillate in response to epidemics, famines, and war. It should be noted that epidemics and famines tend to go hand in hand, since malnourished people are particularly susceptible to infectious diseases. In the second stage, The Age of Receding Pandemics, death rates start to steadily decline and the proportion of deaths due to infectious diseases decreases as a result of the improved nutrition and sanitation and medical advances that accompany socio-economic development. Eventually, the third stage is reached—the Age of Degenerative and Human-Made Diseases—in which death rates are low (life expectancy at birth is over 70 years) and the chief takers-of-life are chronic diseases associated with aging, such as cardiovascular disease and cancer. It is implicitly assumed that infectious and parasitic diseases become less and less important, and that mortality levels and causes of death in the less developed countries will eventually come to mirror those in the West.

Omran's (1971) epidemiological transition model generally reflects the situation for countries in the West, at least for the period from the Agricultural Revolution until the late 20th century. Prior to the Agricultural Revolution, it is highly likely that malnutrition (starving to death) was a more important killer than infectious diseases (Barrett, Kazawa, McDade & Armelagos, 1998; McKeown, 1988). Once agriculture predominated, the denser settlement pattern of humans as well as closer proximity to animals and animal waste contributed to the spread of infectious diseases. One of the most spectacular examples of epidemic-caused loss of life in the West was the Black Death (the Plague), which hit hardest in the middle of the 14th century but which continued to reoccur for more than three centuries. By the eve of the Industrial Revolution, the Plague had virtually disappeared in Europe, as a result of changes in shipping, housing, sanitary practices, etc. that affected the way that rats, fleas and humans interacted (McNeill, 1973). Other types of infectious diseases (such as cholera, influenza, smallpox, pneumonia) remained important killers and were eventually conquered by improved nutrition, hygiene, and public health measures. Medical advances played a small role, although the smallpox vaccine was important (McKeown, 1976).

For the data that we have available for Canada, the epidemiological transition model is appropriate. The large increases in life expectancy at birth for 1921 to 1961, seen in Table 2.2, are the result of our control over infectious diseases that are important takers-of-life of infants, young children, and young women in childbearing. As Canadian society came to control these infectious diseases, mortality at young ages declined and life expectancy at birth increased. Over the latter part of the 20th century, deaths became concentrated at older ages, and the causes of death shifted to chronic, degenerative diseases.

The epidemiological transition model applies less well to the developing world. Western mortality decline, and the changing configuration of causes of death associated with it, was fuelled by socio-economic development. In contrast, in Third World countries, there is a much smaller relationship between mortality and economic development. In the post-World War II decade of the 1950's, mortality declines in many Third World countries were substantial. In those Cold War years, public health measures and death-reducing technologies were exported by the West (largely the United States) to many less developed countries, at least in part as an attempt to woo non-aligned countries towards the West and away from the Soviet Union. As a result, deaths due to infectious diseases fell dramatically, often in the absence of any significant economic development or modernization.

However, probably the biggest challenge to epidemiological transition theory comes from the emergence of new, and the re-emergence of old, infectious diseases in the latter part of the 20th century. This has led to debate about epidemiological transition theory's end stage. Is the third stage the final one? A number of fourth stages have been proposed, the most popular being the Age of Delayed Degenerative Diseases (Olshansky & Ault, 1986), corresponding to declines in death rates due to cardiovascular disease experienced in Western countries through the 1970s and 1980s. This stage conforms with the expectations of the compression of morbidity hypothesis discussed above. But now a radically different fifth stage is being proposed in light of increasing death rates due to viruses and bacteria (Olshansky, Carnes, Rodgers & Smith, 1997). Indeed, Barrett and colleagues (1998) view the trend of increasing mortality due to infectious disease as characterizing a new epidemiological transition altogether. However, Murray and Lopez (1996), taking both death and disability into account, argue that non-communicable diseases will take on increasing importance in the global burden of disease.

The emergence of new infectious and parasitic diseases (e.g., AIDS/HIV, Legionnaire's Disease, Lyme Disease, SARS), the re-emergence of diseases (e.g., smallpox, malaria) that we thought had been conquered, and the evolution of antibiotic-resistant strains of bacteria have led to a reappraisal of the possible future role of microbes in mortality. While it does not seem likely that infectious and parasitic diseases will overtake chronic, degenerative diseases as killers, it is difficult to predict the relative importance of the two major categories of death causation in the future. Much appears to depend on how successful we will be in controlling HIV/AIDS, which is estimated to have taken 3.1 million lives worldwide in 2004 alone. Another 39.4 million people are living with HIV (World Health Organization, 2004). Given the depression of the immune system that comes with AIDS, it is possible that this estimate is low; some persons with AIDS might be counted as dying from another infectious disease to which they were vulnerable.

Major Causes of Death among Elderly Canadians

As predicted by epidemiological transition theory, most deaths in Canada occur in old age and are the result of chronic, degenerative diseases. Circulatory diseases (which include heart disease and strokes as major categories) are the most important killer, and increasingly so with advancing age (see Table 2.3). Malignant neoplasms (cancers) are the second most important cause of death among elderly Canadian men overall, and are the leading cause among men and women aged 65 to 69. Respiratory diseases are the next most important cause of death. This category includes both chronic, degenerative diseases such as emphysema and chronic bronchitis as well as infectious diseases such as influenza and pneumonia. The latter may afflict the frail elderly who are suffering with chronic illness(es) as well. In such cases, the seemingly tidy distinction between infectious and degenerative disease becomes quite blurry.

Elderly women have lower mortality rates for all causes of death than elderly men, reflecting their higher life expectancy. However, women's mortality advantage decreases with age; at ages 65 to 69, women's overall mortality rate is about 60 percent that of men's but at ages 90 and over, the difference is only approximately 20 percent. There are some exceptions to this general pattern, however. The death rate for cerebrovascular disease (strokes) is higher for women than for men in the oldest age category. Also, the gender ratio in mortality due to respiratory diseases tends to stay high, and not narrow with increasing age. In addition, death rates due to suicide—although not a common cause of death—are much higher for elderly men, generally about five times as high as for elderly women.

Differentials in Population Aging

So far, we have been referring to the elderly/aged population as if it were homogeneous. However, this is not the case; the elderly Canadian population is very diverse. In this section, we examine some dimensions of this diversity, with a focus on gender, ethnocultural variables, and place of residence.

Gender

It is sometimes said that aging is a woman's issue. This is because elderly women outnumber elderly men by a substantial margin, and one that increases with advancing age. In 2001, there were 2.2 million Canadian women aged 65 and over compared with 1.7 million men; therefore, women make up about 57 percent of the total elderly population. However, among the Canadian population aged 85 and over, women make up nearly 70 percent of the total. The numerical dominance of

Table 2.3 CAUSES OF DEATH (PER 100 000) BY AGE AND GENDER—
POPULATION AGED 65 YEARS AND OVER: CANADA, 2001

MEN	65–69	70–74	75–79	80–84	85+
All Causes	1 952	3 194	5 229	8 736	17 124
Diseases of the Circulatory System	613	1 070	1 902	3 451	7 172
Ischemic heart disease	413	687	1 156	1 995	3 852
Cerebrovascular disease	85	167	347	721	1 493
Malignant Neoplasms	831	1 254	1 744	2 310	3 170
Bronchi and lungs	290	416	522	580	583
Prostate	60	125	250	429	781
Respiratory Diseases	120	253	522	1 011	2 226
Accidents and Adverse Affects (External causes of morbidity and mortality)	61	83	117	198	524
Accidental falls	11	17	29	71	213
Suicide (intentional self-harm)	13	21	21	14	27
WOMEN	**65–69**	**70–74**	**75–79**	**80–84**	**85+**
All Causes	1 160	1 861	3 088	5 503	13 703
Diseases of the Circulatory System	276	536	1 066	2 218	6 327
Ischemic heart disease	153	291	565	1 114	3 043
Cerebrovascular disease	53	113	243	567	1 564
Malignant Neoplasms	557	754	983	1265	1 682
Bronchi and lung	166	206	235	233	201
Breast	84	105	121	174	263
Respiratory Diseases	82	154	264	495	1 221
Accidents and Adverse Affects	24	37	68	120	407
Accidental falls	3	10	22	43	162
Suicide (intentional self-harm)	5	5	4	3	2

Source: Adapted from Statistics Canada Cat. No. 84-208 (October 16, 2003), 97F0003XCB2001001 (July 16, 2002), and CANSIM Database Tables 102-0522, 102-0529, 102-0530, and 102-0540.

women in old age results from gender differences in mortality and life expectancy. As we saw in Table 2.2, at age 65 women can expect to live about three and a half more years than men, and Table 2.3 indicates that women have lower death rates for most causes of death.

The general longevity advantage of women has important social and individual implications. For example, as will be seen in later chapters, it means that women are more likely to become widowed; to live alone; to be institutionalized; to be grandparents for a longer time; to be poor in old age since, in part, any savings have to be spread over more (possibly inflationary) years; and to deal with the physical difficulties of extreme old age without age peers able to provide support or assistance. Yet elderly women have shown their resilience, in part nurtured through the more intense and long-lasting personal relationships that women maintain over the course of their lives (Connidis, 2001). It should be kept in mind that the men who do live very long lives, especially the few who do not remarry, may face social isolation because there are very few other older men for companionship and because women are more likely to be the kin-keepers (Rosenthal, 1983) who keep family ties activated.

Why is female life expectancy so much higher than that of males? At least some part of the gender difference in mortality is biologically based. It is universally found that more male than female babies are born. While the magnitude of the gender ratio at birth (the number of male births per 100 female births) varies somewhat, it is almost always in the range of 103 to 107. There is some debate about why male births exceed female births, in part centred on the issue of gender differences in the number of conceptions. Overall, the research evidence suggests that more males are conceived, but that the male fetus is biologically weaker. However, that conclusion must be tempered with the fact that it is extremely difficult to obtain accurate data about fetal mortality in the first few months of pregnancy.

While there is uncertainty about gender mortality differentials in the early gestational period, data for the first year of life are very clear. In virtually all places and times, infant mortality rates are higher for males than for females. Quite a bit of evidence points to biological factors playing a role in the higher mortality of infant males. Despite their higher birth weights (a factor associated with infant survival) male babies are more likely to suffer from congenital abnormalities that lead to death and to have immune deficiencies associated with X-chromosome-linked genetic defects and with exposure to testosterone prenatally and in early infancy. This latter factor may also contribute to greater activity levels among boy babies, associated with higher accidental mortality (Waldron, 1998).

Similar biologically based factors contribute to gender differences in mortality across the life course, including the protective effect of women's XX chromosome structure against heart disease, especially at ages under 55 (Waldron, 1985) and a propensity to violence among men that can have lethal consequences (Boyd, 2000). The degree to which men are more violence-prone than women, and the reasons for it, are, however, hotly debated and it cannot be stated whether and how biology may be implicated.

While biological factors can explain part of the gender differences in mortality, these differences vary too much by time and place to be accounted for by biology to any great extent. What other factors are involved? One way to approach an answer to this question is to look at trends in the size of the gender differential in life expectancy over the course of the 20th century. Trends in mortality declines favoured women in the more developed countries from at least the beginning of the 20th century to the early 1980s. At the beginning of the 20th century, the difference is estimated to have been two to three years (United Nations Secretariat, 1988). In the middle of the 20th century, the average gender difference in life expectancy at birth (favouring females) in the more developed countries was approximately five years (United Nations, 2000); in Canada, it was 4.5 years (see Table 2.2). Mortality trends in different age groups contributed differentially to this overall trend of the widening of the gender gap in mortality. Nearly two-thirds of the widening can be attributed to mortality differentials among persons aged 65 and over; death rates for older women declined more quickly than death rates for older men. An additional one-quarter of the increase resulted from mortality trends among persons aged 55 to 64, for whom, as well, female death rates declined more than male death rates. Very little of the increase, less than 3 percent, was due to mortality among children aged 1 to 14. In contrast, trends in infant mortality operated to narrow the gender difference in mortality. High male infant mortality was overcome to a considerable degree so that eventually, for the most part, only the genetically caused higher susceptibility to death of male infants remained (United Nations Secretariat, 1988).

Differential trends in various causes of death contributed to the widening of the gender mortality difference. By far the most important reason for the widening in cause of death is diseases of the circulatory system. While there is variation from country to country; overall, of the different kinds of circulatory diseases, trends in ischemic heart disease played the biggest role in the three-year widening of the gap, with men's death rate due to circulatory diseases increasing over most of the 20th century while women's death rates were stable or declined. Rheumatic heart disease and strokes (for which women and men have more equal risks of death) have decreased in importance as takers-of-life. Thus, the composition of the circulatory disease category, with an increasing prevalence of ischemic heart disease, played a role in widening the gender mortality differential.

The increase in respiratory cancer among men and the slower decreases in circulatory system mortality among men have been attributed to smoking differences, in large part. Over the earlier years of the 20th century, men—much more so than women—took up cigarette smoking, the effects of which show up in mortality statistics among older age groups, given that cigarettes are slow killers (Retherford, 1975).

The second most important cause of death in explaining the widening gender differential in mortality is malignant neoplasms (cancer). At the turn of the 20th century, female mortality from cancer (especially breast cancer and cancers of the female genital organs) tended to be higher than male cancer mortality. However, over the course of the century, increasing rates of male mortality due to respiratory (e.g., lung) cancers served to widen the male-female mortality difference. In the United States for the period from 1900 to the early 1980s, shifts in the trends and pattern of cancer mortality accounted for more than one-third of the widening gender mortality differential; in other Western countries such as England/Wales and Australia, the contribution made by malignant neoplasms to widening the gender mortality ratio was even greater (United Nations Secretariat, 1988).

Other causes of death are much less important contributors to the widening gender mortality differential over the 20th century. For example, declines in maternal mortality, although very substantial, have had only a small effect; as well, trends in accident mortality and suicide have not played a big role. In contrast, declines in infectious and parasitic diseases—for which males in the West tended to have higher mortality than females—had an opposite effect, that is, to narrow the gender gap in mortality.

In the last 20 or so years, the gap between male and female mortality has narrowed somewhat. As we can see in Table 2.2, the biggest difference between male and female life expectancies at birth occurred in 1981, when it was 7.2 years; by 2001, it was only 5.1 years. The female advantage in life expectancy at age 65 has similarly decreased, from 4.3 years in 1981 to 3.5 years in 2001. It is still the case, though, that male mortality is higher than female mortality for virtually every major cause of death. The major factor accounting for the narrowing of the gender gap in mortality is that men have been experiencing greater declines in deaths due to circulatory diseases than women (Gilbert & Bélanger, 2001). Trends in cancer, particularly respiratory cancer, account for some of the decrease in the gender mortality ratio; women's lung cancer rates have increased substantially, reflecting, in large part, the later adoption of smoking by women (Wright, 1997).

If the gender differential in mortality is to be reduced, the preferable route is to decrease male mortality, not to increase female mortality! Smoking cessation is clearly required in order to achieve this. Also, research has shown that the gender gap in mortality is much smaller among the educated and economically advantaged segments of the population (Rogers, Hummer & Nam, 2000). This suggests that mortality level is, to a large extent, determined by social and economic factors and that improvements in male mortality are attainable.

Ethnocultural Variations

Canada's older adult population has the highest percentage of foreign-born or immigrant persons compared with other age groups; whereas 18.4 percent of the total Canadian population is foreign-born, 28.4 percent of Canadians aged 65 and over in 2001 were born outside Canada. Most foreign-born seniors have lived in Canada for a long time; for example, approximately 61 percent immigrated to Canada before 1961. During that period of time, Canadian immigration policy discriminated on the basis of ethnicity/race; hence, the majority immigrated from Europe (71 percent) and other Western countries. Thus, the majority of today's foreign-born seniors are of a Western European cultural background and have home languages that are relatively similar to Canada's official languages; in 2001, only 6.52 percent were members of visible minority groups. Many of the younger foreign-born population in Canada (those aged under 65) come from Asia. This reflects the fact that the current leading sender countries to Canada are the People's Republic of China, India, the Philippines, Hong Kong, and Pakistan (Citizenship and Immigration Canada, 1999). In other words, the older adults of the future will be much more ethnically diverse than today's seniors.

However, it is important not to discount minority elderly immigrants because their numbers are small. Every year, approximately 6000 elders immigrate to Canada; most are of non-European origins and most are family-class immigrants. As sponsored immigrants, they do not have economic resources, and are not eligible for any Canadian public pension until after 10 years of residence. Also, many lack the ability to communicate in either English or French. They represent a particularly vulnerable segment of the Canadian aged population, as do Aboriginal seniors, who make up a small percentage (4.1 percent) of the total First Nations population. Their small representation among First Nations is due to higher fertility and higher mortality levels among Aboriginals. However, a rapid aging of the Aboriginal population is expected; a doubling of the percentage aged 65 and over is expected by 2016. Since registered Aboriginal seniors are more likely than younger adults to live on reserves, their proportionate growth will affect locations that are not equipped to serve the aged and are, for the most part, impoverished.

Place of Residence and Migration

Age structures also vary by geographic region within Canada. Saskatchewan and Manitoba are our oldest provinces, with 15.1 percent and 14.0 percent respectively of their populations aged 65 and over. At the other end of the spectrum is Alberta, which has only 10.4 percent of its population in the 65 and over age group. The northern territories have even less; Yukon has 6.5 percent, the Northwest Territories 4.4 percent, and Nunavut 2.2 percent. Fertility differences across provinces are very small; therefore, the usually strong effect of fertility is not responsible for provincial variation in population age structure. Neither are provincial mortality differentials particularly large. Rather, migration plays the most important role. However, it is not migration of seniors that accounts for this pattern but migration of younger people. The have-not provinces of Manitoba and Saskatchewan are old because of high levels of out-migration of younger people; the have province of Alberta has received large numbers of young migrants in recent years. This illustrates that, while the current level of migration does not play an important role in affecting our national age structure, it can and does affect the age structure of smaller areas. However, in absolute numbers, the majority of elderly people live in the most populous provinces of Ontario, Quebec, and British Columbia.

Elderly Canadians are about as likely (76 percent) as non-seniors (79 percent) to live in an urban area. Canadian elders who live in rural areas face unique problems. While they are as well integrated into family and non-family support systems as urban elders, these supports are not as reliable because, for example, children live farther away, they have fewer personal visits, and they have fewer younger neighbours who can provide practical assistance. Transportation is a major concern of rural elders; they have less access to adequate transportation but more need for it, given the geographic dispersion of people, facilities, and services. Also, while rural Canada has sufficient spaces in institutional facilities for frail elders, services for those who need only limited formal help to live independently in the community have been lacking (Joseph & Martin-Matthews, 1994).

The foreign-born and Canadian-born elderly differ substantially in the size of the places in which they live. Among the Canadian-born, approximately one-quarter live in one of Canada's three largest cities (Toronto, Montreal, and Vancouver). However, about 40 percent of elders born in Europe and approximately 70 percent of seniors born in Asia live in one of the big three cities; and among the Chinese-born, the figure is 75 percent. Conversely, very small percentages of Asian-born elders live in smaller places (Gee, 1996). Other things being equal, then, the foreign-born, and especially those born in Asia, are in an advantageous position with regard to accessing services if they become frail. However, things are never equal, and we must remember that many Asian-born elders face language barriers in service access and delivery. For example, in a seven-city (Victoria, Vancouver, Edmonton, Calgary, Winnipeg, Toronto, and Montreal) study of more than 2000 Chinese Canadians aged 50 and over, Chappell (2005) found that only 23.1 percent reported they understood English well and fully 78.3 percent spoke Cantonese at home.

Canadian cities vary quite widely in age structure. Victoria, long known as Canada's retirement city, records 17.8 percent of its population as age 65 and over; however, several other places now equal or surpass that—Camrose, Alberta has 20.2 percent; Cobourg, Ontario has 21.1 percent; Penticton, B.C. has 24.2 percent; Elliot Lake, Ontario has 25.1 percent; and Parksville, B.C. has 31.0 percent. In contrast, Calgary has 9.0 percent, Oshawa has 10.4 percent, and Labrador City in Newfoundland has 2.6 percent of its population in the elderly age group. As with provincial variations in age structure, migration accounts for these differences. A combination of the migration of both non-seniors and seniors is at work.

Litwak and Longino (1987) provide a three-fold typology of senior migration. The first type shows up in the high percentages of the elderly in Victoria and the Niagara area and communities seeking to benefit from attracting seniors. **Amenity-oriented migration**, often associated with retirement, is mostly undertaken by young elderly married couples with higher than average income. The second type occurs at older ages and is precipitated by increased difficulty in performing daily tasks such as shopping, housework, and preparing meals. The senior moves to be closer to family members who are able to provide assistance. Since difficulty in performing daily tasks is exacerbated by the death of a spouse, widows are most likely to be involved in this type of move. The third type occurs at still older ages, and involves a move to an institutional setting. More than one-third of the population aged 85 and over reside in institutions, with a high pro-portion being widows. While we do not know a lot about the transition process to institutionalized living, it appears that a sizable proportion of seniors who live in institutions are there mostly because of the lack of adequate supports in the community (Moore & Rosenberg, 1994; Shapiro & Tate, 1988).

Older Canadians are less likely to move than are younger individuals; in a five-year period, about one-half of persons 20 to 59 changed their place of residence at least once, but fewer than one-quarter of those aged 60 and over did (Che-Alford & Stevenson, 1998). When elderly individuals do move, it tends not to be far; in 2001 only 1.2 percent of seniors moved out of their province or territory. Canadian data support the age-related model of senior migration proposed by Litwak and Longino. That is, the older the mover, the more likely it is that the move is motivated by declining health and a need to be closer to family. Canadian data also indicate that moves to smaller homes with special features (e.g., bathroom adaptations, street-level entrance, extra handrails, lifts) are common, posing challenges for the housing industry as the population continues to age (Che-Alford & Stevenson, 1998).

One unique aspect of Canadian migration in later life is the "snowbird phe-nomenon." **Snowbirds** are elderly Canadians who move, on a seasonal basis, to southern U.S. states such as Florida and Arizona. It has been estimated that as many as 250 000 elderly Canadians were annual snowbirds to Florida alone in the 1980s (Mullins & Tucker, 1988). The duration of stays varies, but rarely exceeds six months, probably since this would result in a loss of Canadian health-care benefits. Snowbirds rarely make a permanent move to the United States. Furthermore, snowbird migration is selective; the type of elderly persons who are most likely to engage in this seasonal migration are relatively young, mar-ried, of higher levels of income and education, and in relatively good health (Martin, Hoppe, Marshall & Daciuk, 1992).

We have been discussing many of the facts of the aging population in Canada, the reasons for this aging, how Canada compares with other countries of the world, and some of the diversity among Canada's seniors. We have not made a value judgement as to whether the aging phenomenon is primarily good or bad, either for the individuals involved or for the country as a whole. There are those who view the aging of the Canadian population as problematic. We turn now to discuss and assess apocalyptic demography, the view that the aging of the pop-ulation will cause disastrous consequences for the country.

Apocalyptic Demography

The term **apocalyptic demography** (sometimes also called voodoo demography) characterizes the oversimplified notion that a demographic trend—in our case population aging—has catastrophic consequences for a society (Gee, 2000). The complexity of aging is reduced to a one-sided negative view that our society cannot afford increasing numbers and percentages of older people. Apocalyptic demography is prominently seen in the media today, especially in discussions of medicare and the health-care system. According to Gee and Gutman (2000), apocalyptic demography consists of five interrelated themes:

(1) Aging as a social problem. Rather than celebrating the control over unwanted births and early deaths that population aging represents, it is viewed as negative, as a problem that needs fixing.

(2) The homogenization of older people. All older people are seen as the same. In particular, they are stereotyped as well off, e.g., as rich golfers and cruise-ship travellers, as "greedy geezers."

(3) Age-blaming. The elderly are blamed for overusing social programs and consequently for government debt/deficits.

(4) Intergenerational injustice. Older people are seen as getting more than their fair share of societal resources, and this inequity is predicted to lead to severe intergenerational conflict/clashes.

(5) The intertwining of population aging and social policy. Aging has become the guiding paradigm of the Canadian welfare state (McDaniel & Chappell, 1999). So, for example, social policy reform is guided by the idea that deep cuts have to be made to accommodate the increasing numbers and percentages of elderly in our population.

General Criticisms of Apocalyptic Demography

Is aging a social problem—the most basic postulate of apocalyptic demography? Much of the conclusion that aging is a social problem is based on looking at aged dependency ratios, and the extrapolation that the number/percentage of older people (considered to be dependants) is increasing too much. However, it is important to look at youth and total dependency ratios as well and not fixate on the aged dependency ratio alone; the youth and aged dependency ratios have counterbalancing effects on the total dependency ratio. Canada provides a particularly good example of these counterbalancing effects. In 1951, the total dependency ratio in Canada was 0.83 (that is, there were 83 dependants—old and young people—for every 100 persons in the working ages). In 2041, it is expected to be 0.82. This basically unchanged situation is caused by a large increase in the aged dependency ratio (from 0.14 to 0.46) accompanied by a large decrease in the youth dependency ratio (from 0.69 to 0.36). It is also interesting to note that in 2001, the overall dependency ratio was at a historical low point (.62) (Denton, Feaver, & Spencer, 1998).

This knowledge makes it difficult to accept the view that many of the social problems of the day are due to changes in the Canadian age structure and population aging in particular. Also, research shows that economic productivity is an important part of the equation; Canada will be able to afford an aging population with little difficulty as long as we experience at least moderate levels of economic growth (Denton & Spencer, 1999; Fellegi, 1988). Canada would be better off looking at ways to improve our economic productivity than worrying about increases in the proportion of the population that is aged and consequently cutting social programs.

Are the aged "greedy geezers" using more than their fair share of government monies? It is true that the largest portion of the social envelope goes to seniors, in the form of public pensions and medicare. However, the majority of elderly Canadians are far from wealthy and nearly one-half of old women without a spouse (mostly widows) live in poverty. As McDonald (1997) points out, poor seniors are invisible, unlike the seniors we see on cruises and golf courses. Also, research in both the United States and Canada reveals that age makes virtually no difference in public support for old-age social programs (Hamil-Luker, 2001; Northcott, 1994). A related question: Are the aged to blame for increasing costs in government spending, and, consequently, government debt/deficit? A considerable amount of research, much of it conducted by Robert Evans and his colleagues at the University of British Columbia, shows that population aging itself will account for only a small part of future health-care costs and will require little, if any, increase in public expenditures for health care (Barer, Evans & Hertzman, 1995; Evans, McGrail, Morgan, Barer & Hertzman, 2001).

Using administrative data from the province of British Columbia for the period from the mid-1970s to the late 1990s, Evans and colleagues (2001) report that acute-care hospitalization use rates fell dramatically, the result of declines in age-specific use rates (i.e., declines at all ages); the use of physician services increased substantially, resulting from rises in age-specific use rates that are associated with increases in the number of physicians per capita and in billings per physician (especially among specialists); and per capita expenditures on prescription drugs rose far faster (over the period since 1985, the only data available) than would be projected on the basis of changes in the age structure, even if one focuses on the elderly population alone.

What then has led to the increased health costs that are so often assumed to be the result of an aging population? An important component is rapidly rising costs for pharmaceuticals, the result of a combination of inflation and shifts in prescribing more expensive medications without scientific evidence of therapeutic benefit. The pharmaceutical industry is an important cost driver; one book dedicated to this issue is cleverly titled *Tales from the Other Drug Wars* (Barer, McGrail, Cardiff, Wood, & Green, 2000). Other factors include cost increases in the pricing and rate of uptake of new technologies and an oversupply of physicians (Evans et al., 2001). Thus, while it seems to make sense that an aging population leads to increased health-care costs, the evidence—at least in terms of hospital use, physician use, and pharmaceuticals—strongly negates the importance of age structure in affecting health-care costs. (More is said about this issue in Chapter 15.)

When Canada, and other Western countries, ran into trouble with government debt/deficit, it was widely attributed to increased spending on social programs, and the target of this supposed overspending was seniors. A number of Canadian economists have shown that the debt and deficit are not due to overspending on social programs (e.g., Fortin, 1996; Osberg, & Fortin, 1996; Rosenbluth, 1996), pointing the finger instead at Canadian monetary policy and especially the Bank of Canada. In particular, the Bank's decision in the late 1980s to reduce inflation led to increased interest rates, which in turn contributed significantly to Canada's growing debt. Fortin (1996) shows that anti-inflationary measures were the most important cause of our increased government debt.

The fourth theme—intergenerational injustice—is manifest in what is termed the **intergenerational equity debate**. On the one side are those who argue that the aged are getting more than they deserve from the public purse; that is, our society is organized such that there is generational inequity that favours the old. This theme has been promulgated by academic research and writing such as Samuel Preston's 1984 presidential address to the Population Association of America; by the work of economists such as Kotlikoff (1993) on generational accounting; and by the media. Although the intergenerational inequity perspective originated in the United States, it has found its way to Canada. We hear the argument that today's younger people are paying more to finance the pensions of the elderly than they will ever receive when they themselves retire. A stronger version of this side of the debate is that the Canada Pension Plan will no longer exist when today's young people are old; that it will have been completely depleted by earlier generations of older adults.

On the other side of the debate is the intergenerational interdependence perspective (Williamson & Watts-Roy, 1999). The proponents of this side emphasize that the generations are, and should continue to be, interdependent. Transfers across generations are both public and private; it is partial and biasing to focus only on public transfers, as do those who view intergenerational relations as unfair to the young. Older adults help younger ones in many ways—within the family setting, they assist with child care and provide cash gifts and loans to grown-up children to help with a down payment on a home, for example. Indeed, it has been estimated by Kronebusch and Schlesinger (1994) that, when taking all things into account over the course of their lives, parents give 50 percent more to their children than they receive. Outside the family, elders engage in volunteer activities and give to charities that benefit younger people. However, these private transfers (see Chapter 14) are not counted by those who only look at the costs of older adults with regard to pensions and health care. Proponents of intergenerational interdependence also point out that cuts to pensions and health care to seniors will adversely affect their children, who will have to provide care for their parents out of their own wallets. It is also important to note that our society is stratified in many ways other than age (e.g., gender, social class, ethnicity/race), and any attempts to dismantle old-age benefits—to promote generational equity—would negatively affect some groups of older people more than others, thus generating further inequities.

In terms of the fifth theme, if we believe that the elderly will bankrupt our society through their demands on the public health-care and pension systems, it is a simple step to move toward a dismantling of the old age welfare state—and the whole welfare state, for that matter—to counteract the societal burden of an aging population. Evidence of this can be seen in attempts to privatize pensions as much as possible and in the reductions in health-care spending (and associated privatization) that have been posed as inevitable due to population aging (also see Chapter 15).

It should be evident by now that the hard, dry facts on population aging are deceiving. Population aging is an intensely political issue; apocalyptic demography is playing an important role in shaping the future of a Canadian welfare state that will be "leaner and meaner." It is being used by those who favour a neo-liberal (that is, pro-free market and anti-welfare state) social agenda. For a debunking of apocalyptic demography, see three books published around the millennium: *Demography Is Not Destiny* (National Academy on an Aging Society, 1999) in the United States; *The Imaginary Time Bomb: Why an Ageing Population Is Not a Social Problem* (Mullan, 2000) in the United Kingdom; and *The Overselling of Population Aging: Apocalyptic Demography, Intergenerational Challenges, and Social Policy* (Gee & Gutman, 2000) in Canada. All present convincing arguments that population aging does not necessarily have dire social and economic consequences.

CHAPTER SUMMARY

This chapter, discussed the demography of aging, from a presentation of statistics to a discussion of the intertwining of population aging and politics.

Key ideas to remember from this chapter:

- The Canadian population has been aging since the beginning of the 20th century, and will continue to age for many decades to come, with a rapid aging expected when the baby boom generation arrives at age 65.

- The main driving force behind population aging is decreases in fertility; because fertility in Canada did not fall as quickly as in Europe and because we had a large baby boom after World War II, the Canadian population is somewhat younger than in many other parts of the Western world.

- There are many ways to measure population aging, and none is perfect. However, relying on aged dependency ratios to measure population aging contains a number of problems, including assumptions about dependency. It is important to examine changes in total dependency ratios and youth dependency ratios along with aged dependency ratios. When we do, we see the counterbalancing effects of a decreasing youth population and an increasing aged population. At the present time in Canada, we are at an historical low point in overall dependency, and our future total dependency in the years when the baby boomers are old will not be higher than it was in the middle of the 20th century.

- Life expectancy increased substantially over the course of the last century, with the major gains in life expectancy at birth made in the earlier part of the period. Young Canadians were the first to benefit from mortality reductions; it was only later that longevity in later life increased appreciably, a trend that is typical of developed countries.

- The compression of morbidity hypothesis states that more and more people are able to postpone the age of onset of chronic disability; hence, the period of time between the onset of becoming seriously ill or disabled and dying is shortening or compressing. The general idea is that, at least in Western countries, we are moving to a situation in which we will live in a healthy state until a very old age and then die quickly.

- Epidemiological transition theory deals with the relationship between mortality decline, on the one hand, and changes in the relative importance of different causes of death, on the other. As mortality declines, the changes in causes of death shift from infectious diseases to chronic diseases; this occurs in three stages. The theory holds quite well for Western countries like Canada, but is not as applicable to countries of the Third World. However, the theory is now being challenged by the emergence of new and the re-emergence of old, infectious diseases, beginning in the latter part of the 20th century.

- As predicted by epidemiological transition theory, most deaths in Canada occur in old age and are the result of chronic, degenerative diseases. In order of importance, the major causes of death are circulatory diseases (which include heart disease and strokes as major categories); cancer; and respiratory diseases (including both chronic degenerative diseases such as emphysema and chronic bronchitis as well as infectious diseases such as influenza and pneumonia).

- Elderly women have lower mortality rates for virtually all causes of death than elderly men, reflecting their higher life expectancy.

- Women's life expectancy at birth improved more than men's throughout most of the last century in Canada. At the turn of the 20th century, women could expect to live two more years than men. By approximately 1980, that difference had grown to 7.2 years. Although biological differences account for some of the greater longevity of females, social factors are responsible for this large increase in the gender gap in mortality over the 80-year period. In Canada, the mortality of older women (aged 55 and over) decreased much more rapidly than that of older men. Since the early 1980s, the gender gap in mortality has narrowed. This is due to more rapid declines in deaths due to circulatory diseases among men, along with increases in cancer deaths, especially lung cancer, among women. The overall trend is attributed to smoking, which women have taken up more than men in the last few decades.

- Canada's elderly population is diverse in age (from 65 to 100+) and gender. As well, more than one-quarter of Canada's senior population is foreign-born (which is much higher than for the non-aged population). Most foreign-born seniors are of European origins and have lived in Canada for a long time, with 61 percent immigrating before 1961. However, Canada is now receiving approximately 6000 elderly immigrants annually; most are of non-European origins and most are family-class immigrants with few economic resources and no eligibility for any public pension.

- Manitoba and Saskatchewan are Canada's oldest provinces. At the other end of the spectrum is Alberta, which has only 10 percent of its population in the 65 and over age group. These differences are largely due to migration, particularly of non-seniors. The territories have considerably fewer seniors than the provinces.

- Canadian elders tend to move less often, and less far, than younger people. However, some young-old, married and reasonably well-off seniors are part of the snowbird phenomenon, spending up to six months per year in a southern U.S. state like Florida or Arizona.

- Apocalyptic demography represents an exaggeration of the negative effects of population aging. The research evidence does not support an apocalyptic view of population aging.

KEY TERMS

age structure **(p. 26)**

gerontology **(p. 26)**

median age of the population **(p. 27)**

dependency ratios **(p. 28)**

aged dependency ratio **(p. 28)**

youth dependency ratio **(p. 28)**

total dependency ratio **(p. 28)**

familial old-age dependency ratio **(p. 29)**

population pyramids **(p. 32)**

life expectancy **(p. 33)**

lifespan **(p. 33)**

dependency-free life expectancy **(p. 35)**

compression of morbidity **(p. 36)**

epidemiological transition **(p. 37)**

epidemiological transition theory **(p. 38)**

amenity-oriented migration **(p. 46)**

snowbirds **(p. 47)**

apocalyptic demography **(p. 47)**

intergenerational equity debate **(p. 50)**

STUDY QUESTIONS

1. Find out how "old" your province is compared to the Canadian average. What accounts for its relative age?

2. Provide a critique of dependency ratios. What are their strengths, their weaknesses?

3. Why do Canadian women live longer than Canadian men? What are some of the social consequences of this longevity differential?

4. Evaluate epidemiological transition theory. Does it hold equally well for the West and the rest of the world? Do you think it will continue to be valid in Canada?

5. Do you think population aging is a crisis for Canadian society? Why or why not?

SUGGESTED READINGS

Gee, E.M., & Gutman, G.M. (Eds.) (2000). *The overselling of population aging: Apocalyptic demography, intergenerational challenges, and social policy.* Toronto: Oxford University Press.

Moore, E.G., & Rosenberg, M.W., with McGuinness, D. (1997). *Growing old in Canada: Demographic and geographic perspectives.* Toronto: Statistics Canada and ITP Nelson.

Murray, C.J.L., & Lopez, A.D. (1996). *The global burden of disease: A comprehensive assessment of mortality and disability from diseases, injuries, and risk factors in 1990 and projected to 2020.* Boston: Harvard School of Public Health on behalf of the World Health Organization and the World Bank.

Williamson, J.B, Watts-Roy, D.M., & Kingson, E.R. (Eds.) (1999). *The generational equity debate.* New York: Columbia University Press.

Chapter 3

SOCIAL THEORY IN GERONTOLOGY

Learning Objectives

In this chapter, you will learn about

- What theory is and how it is different from some related concepts.
- Barriers to theoretical development within social gerontology.
- Why theory is important.
- The challenges of level of analysis and assumptions about the relationship between the individual and society.

- Some details about the major theories within social gerontology.
- Life course theory.
- Some very recent theoretical perspectives that are challenging some core assumptions of gerontology.

Introduction

This chapter provides an introduction to the major theories of social gerontology, the majority of which have their origins in the United States over the last 50 years. While gerontological theory is not in crisis per se, two camps on the status of theory can be identified. One group is highly dissatisfied with the state of theory; a representative feeling is expressed in the following well-known quotation: "Gerontology is rich in data but poor in theory." (Birren & Bengtson, 1988: ix). This statement is made in the face of a large number of theoretical perspectives within social gerontology, many of which will be outlined in this chapter.

A second, and much larger, group consists of gerontologists who seem not to be concerned about theory and theoretical issues and, thus, are not worried about the general state of social gerontology theory. As Bengtson, Rice, and Johnson (1999: 3) state: "Many researchers in gerontology seem to have abandoned any attempt at building theory." In general terms, we can say that social gerontology is not without theory but that much of that theory has not developed over the years, in part because a substantial number of researchers have not made the theory or the theoretical underpinnings of their studies explicit. For example, a study by Bengtson, Burgess, and Parrott (1997) reports that an examination of eight leading gerontology journals found that 72 percent of articles did not mention any type of theory in relation to the findings. Similarly, Chappell and Penning (2001) characterize sociological gerontology in Canada as empirical, often without explicit theoretical content or direction.

This characterization of theory is very much married to research, as we will see in the next chapter. As pointed out by prominent American sociologist Robert Merton (1968), theory and research are two sides of the same coin—or at least should be. Scientific knowledge progresses when theory informs and directs research; in turn, research findings play an important role in theory development. Therefore, the separate study of theory (in Chapter 3) and research methods (in Chapter 4) in this text is somewhat artificial and does not reflect the real way that scientists proceed in their work—moving back and forth between theoretical and methodological issues and concerns. Keep in mind when reading Chapters 3 and 4 that the subject matter of both chapters intersect in the actual practice of knowledge building.

The chapter begins with an examination of what theory is. In the process, theory is distinguished from a number of related concepts, such as paradigm and fact. Given the dissatisfaction about gerontological theory—at least among a small but vocal group of gerontologists—we then turn to some factors that account for lack of theoretical development. Next we discuss why theory is important. Then, we look at two issues that gerontological theory building faces: (1) the level of analysis; and (2) the tension between differing assumptions about the relationship between individuals and society. These two issues form the basis for a classification of social gerontological theories. The last part of the chapter examines in more detail some key social gerontological theories. You will see that gerontology is not short on theories; rather, it is the application of theory in real-life research that is problematic.

The Nature of Theory

What Is a Theory?

In everyday life, we use the term theory quite loosely, often to refer to a guess or a hunch we have about something. For example, you will hear people say things like: "My theory is that old people vote more conservatively than young people do." Besides the fact that this statement is not true (older people's votes are distributed in much the same way as younger people's [Binstock, 1997]), it is not a theory in the way that scientists mean the term. Within science, theory has a specific meaning; Bengtson and colleagues (1999:5) define **theory** as "the construction of explicit explanations in accounting for empirical findings." The most important part of this definition is *explanation*—what theories do is explain something. They provide explanations by stating causal relationships that connect processes or events. Theories also do not explain just anything. They explain things that have been, or can be, empirically observed; that is, data-based findings (from any number of sources—interviews, administrative data, textual materials, laboratory trials, and so on). In the above statement about voting, there is no explanation. Neither is there empirical (data-based) confirmation that older people vote differently from younger people. Even if data did confirm a relationship between age and voting choice, there is still no explanation. At best, all we could do is predict voting behaviour without knowing why.

Some explanatory schemes are called theoretical perspectives, rather than theories. **Theoretical perspectives** are not as tightly organized as theories, offering more loosely linked explanations. Usually, theoretical perspectives are more descriptive and less explanatory than theories. However, in practice, the distinction between theory and theoretical perspective is quite blurry. While noting the distinction is useful to avoid confusion, for our purposes, the two terms mean basically the same thing.

Types of Theories

Theories are usually developed in two ways, either by deductive or inductive approaches. In a deductive approach, the theory is derived by a logical pattern of thought. Once the theory is thought through using rules of logic, the data gathering begins. The starting point for data collection is often a **hypothesis**, which is a testable statement about the relationship between two or more concepts derived from the theory. This approach has been associated with a more traditional type of science (hard science). In contrast, the inductive approach to theory begins with emphasis on gathering data and moves from specific observations (data) to the development of a theory. As we see in the next chapter, the deductive strategy accents the *testing* of theories and their subsequent revision resulting from new data, while the inductive approach accents the *creation* of a theory (Bryman, 2001).

Theories can also be classified by their level of abstraction. There are grand theories and middle-range theories (Bryman, 2001; Merton, 1967; Slife & Williams, 1995). In the earlier part of the 20th century, **grand theories** (that is, broad and general theories that focus on establishing universal principles) emerged in many disciplines, accompanied by optimism and confidence that science (both theory and methods) could understand and fix virtually all problems. Within gerontology, grand theories include, for example, *disengagement theory* and *modernization theory*.

Middle-range theories operate in a more limited domain, such as the buffer hypothesis (or theory) discussed in Chapter 6. The buffer theory argues that the social psychological processes of group identification help to buffer older adults from the challenges of aging. Middle-range theories represent attempts to understand and explain a limited aspect of the social life of older adults (Bryman, 2001).

Facts, Models, Theories and Paradigms

Facts are empirically established findings; they form the building blocks of theories. It is extremely important to note that facts are not cut and dried, with an essential meaning of their own; rather, *facts take on the meaning that theory gives them*. For example, let us take a fact from Chapter 2: women outlive men by a substantial margin, at least in Western societies. If we apply a biological theory to this fact, we might conclude that women have a physiologically and genetically superior constitution that enables them to live longer than men. This would provide an explanation based on physiology and genetics. If, on the other hand, we apply a sociological theory to this fact, we might provide an explanation based on social norms that both protect and constrain women (e.g., not engaging in physically hazardous work or leisure pursuits defined as masculine). Therefore a fact—here, that women outlive men—is not neutral. It takes on different meanings, depending upon the theory applied to it. The first theoretical interpretation *assumes* that the differences between men and women are physically based while the second *assumes* that the differences are socially constructed. In short, theories in social gerontology make assumptions about people that are not always explicit. We have to be on the lookout for these assumptions; if we accept the theory we also accept all the implications that come with the theory.

Facts that are confirmed, especially repeatedly, form **empirical generalizations**. Empirical generalizations can be linked together descriptively to form **models**. For example, the relationship between gender and longevity can be linked to levels of social and economic development. Models are not theories, although the terms *model* and *theory* are often used interchangeably. Models only offer descriptions (sometimes quite complex and sophisticated ones) but not explanations. In the above example, we still do not know *why* women outlive men to a greater degree in the more developed countries.

Families of theories can usually be grouped into **paradigms**. Paradigms are the world views that underlie different groups of theories. Thomas Kuhn (1962) first introduced the term paradigm in one of the most widely read books on the history of science. Kuhn argued that most of the time, researchers do normal science, in which a given *paradigm* is shared. However, every so often, there is a shift in paradigm; Kuhn calls this a scientific revolution. After a while, the new paradigm takes hold, and normal science takes place again (although a different kind of normal science, since the paradigm is different)—until another shift in paradigm (or revolution) occurs.

Following Kuhn, alternative theories have emerged from the interpretive critiques of traditional science to create new paradigms, with quite different world views. Some of these new paradigms that challenged traditional science are presented in the next chapter—the interpretive and critical paradigms. While the testing of a theory implies that we can understand people by using objective measures, inductive strategies usually focus on process and understanding and identify themes of meaning that emerge from the data (Glaser & Strauss, 1967). For example, theories like social exchange or age stratification theories, which fall under the umbrella of traditional science, were challenged by theories about understanding and meaning such as some feminist and political economy theories. According to Kuhn, this type of challenge creates a scientific revolution. These paradigmatic differences will be discussed further in the next chapter because they also influence the type of research method that is chosen to study older people.

Researchers are people, and just like everyone else, they carry deeply held and, often, unconscious assumptions about the world and how it operates—a paradigm. Their paradigms influence their choice of theory, and this is to be expected. However, their paradigms and all their assumptions may be hidden from them; then they go about their research not realizing (or caring, perhaps) that they are viewing facts through a lens that is consistent with the way they think things should be, rather than the way they actually are. When this happens, some facts (which do not fit with their paradigms) go unnoticed, and other facts may be given an interpretation or explanation that is comfortable, rather than useful or valid. These comments are not meant to be a criticism of any particular scholars. Uncovering deep-seated assumptions can be extremely difficult.

Barriers to Theory Development in Social Gerontology

Given the overlap between theory and research in the scientific enterprise, you may be wondering why research in gerontology has been criticized for its lack of theoretical attention and development. One reason is that a considerable amount of research in gerontology has been driven by attempts to solve immediate problems. While this is a laudable goal, it contains some dangers; perhaps most important is that the gerontologist's assumptions will not be unearthed or evaluated. Some of these assumptions may be just simply wrong, leading to wrong or partial findings and the implementation of solutions that are not likely to be successful. For example, if a researcher is charged with finding a way to reduce loneliness among a group of elderly people, he or she may assume that contact with pets will solve the problem—with no theoretical direction. He or she may then interview only those elders who seem enthusiastic about the idea of interacting with pets. When a pet visitation program is implemented, it should not surprise us that it is a failure. The researcher might have assumed that any pet would alleviate loneliness, without any guidance from a theory pointing to, for example, the importance of symbolic meanings of a pet. For example, the visiting pets may not have been the kind of pets they liked (dogs versus cats) or may have reminded the older adults that they could no longer keep their own pets.

Another stumbling block to gerontological theorizing, which applies to other scientific disciplines as well, is the general failure of earlier "grand theories" to meet expectations. (Bengtson, Rice & Johnson, 1999). Grand theories, in their generality, proved not to be adequate for solving all problems, especially specific applied problems. This resulted in a turning away from most aspects of these theories—perhaps a case of throwing out the baby with the bathwater. At the same time, gerontologists began to specialize in sub-areas, without attention to creating theories about aging or old age per se. The resulting scientific norms that developed (sustained by gatekeepers, such as journal editors, and the emergence of increasingly specialized journals) focused on the reporting of (often numerical or quantitative) findings and a lack of emphasis on theory.

Bengtson and colleagues (1999) identify a third factor: the relatively recent emergence in the social sciences of the **postmodern turn** (Foucault, 1972; Habermas, 1972; Rorty, 1991), a line of intellectual exposition emanating from Western European philosophy, art, and science. The postmodern intellectual discourse (which reached gerontology later than some other disciplines, such as sociology and anthropology) represents a significant challenge to theory, as well as to the whole scientific enterprise. The postmodern challenge rests on a number of interrelated propositions. One is that science itself and, therefore, the knowledge that it claims, is hierarchical: it belongs to the privileged classes only. The second, and related, idea is that scientific knowledge excludes the voices of the marginalized (the colonized and the minorities, including women, of the West): voices that are just as valid as those of so-called scientific authority. Third, reason itself—the basis of science, research, and theory—is attacked, as a holdover from the Western Enlightenment era. This translates into a rejection of scientific knowledge claims, since all knowledge is relative. Fourth, the relativity of all knowledge—scientific and non-scientific—lies in the fact that it is socially constructed, in both time and space.

In an ironic twist, this anti-imperialist movement in intellectual discourse has taken on its own imperial power. While postmodernism proposes that no universal truths exist, in practice, postmodernist discourse has taken on the quality of a universal truth. The overall dilemma for gerontological theory (and other social theory) is that on the one hand, postmodernism eschews theory and, on the other hand, more mainstream theories are viewed as inadequate. The end result is that theory development is in neutral.

The Importance of Theory

The above barriers to gerontological theory building matter only because theory matters. Bengtson, Rice and Johnson (1999) identify four ways in which theory is important.

1. *Theories integrate knowledge.* Theories summarize empirical findings and empirical relationships by incorporating them in a parsimonious way. In other words, theory synthesizes existing knowledge; without such synthesis, we would have a mass of seemingly unrelated and relatively meaningless findings.
2. *Theories offer explanations.* Theory goes beyond synthesis to provide an understanding of how and why phenomena are related. These explanations are provided in a way that can be tested. If subsequent research does not support the theory, or supports it only in part, the theory will be abandoned or modified.
3. *Theories provide predictions.* A good theory will provide predictions that will lead to future discoveries and the furthering of knowledge.
4. *Theories can offer interventions to improve our lives.* This is not a defining characteristic of theory in the way that explanation is, but sometimes the knowledge gained through the development of theory and its testing can be used to help alleviate social problems. In other words, theory has practical applications.

Most would agree that theory is an indispensable element in knowledge development. At the same time, it is important to remember that theories are, at best, partial explanations. Theories can provide a good explanation about that part of the social world upon which they cast their lenses.

Organizing Theories in Social Gerontology

The subject matter of gerontology is very large in scope. Bengtson, Rice and Johnson (1999) identify the three major foci of social gerontology as: (1) the aged; (2) aging as a process; and (3) age as a dimension of social structure. The aged and the aging process deal with individuals and their experiences, and hence are at the **micro-level of analysis**; theories attempting to explain individuals are **micro-level theories.** Age as an aspect of the social structure, in contrast, focuses on the **macro-level of analysis**; theories that deal with this dimension of aging are **macro-level theories**. While the micro–macro distinction is important, in reality, individuals and the societies in which they live are intimately and intricately interrelated. Can we really understand older and aging individuals without taking into account the broader social context in which they are embedded? Can we understand the social structure of age without, at the same time, looking at individuals and how they deal with that wider structure? Social gerontological theories often focus on either the micro- or the macro-level of analysis, reflecting what Marshall (1996: 14) characterizes as "a longstanding tension within social gerontology between the social psychological and the social structural levels of analysis." However, some theories, such as the life course perspective (discussed later in this chapter) attempt to bridge and link the micro- and macro-levels.

A recent article on the state of the art in social gerontological theory decries what is termed a trend toward "microfication" (Hagestad & Dannefer, 2001). Microfication involves an increasing tendency to focus on the characteristics of individuals and of micro (face-to-face) interaction, and to neglect macro-level phenomena, such as social institutions, social cohesion, social conflict, and norms and values. Hagestad and Dannefer (2001: 5) state that "few systematic attempts to develop a general approach for conceptualizing age beyond the individual level can be found." They attribute this state of affairs to three factors: (1) the general mood of social science theory at the present time, with its emphasis on individual agency; (2) a tendency to medicalize old age, viewing it as a problem that individuals face; and (3) research funding agencies, which tend to view aging as an individual problem.

Second, social gerontological theories differ in the assumptions made about the relationship between the individual and society—the distinction between normative and interpretive theorizing (Marshall, 1996). As we stated previously, the differing assumptions have methodological consequences. Normative theories assume that individual behaviour is determined by social norms (rules); people learn, through socialization, the norms of their society and generally abide by them. Methodologically, normative theories favour the traditional scientific method, and the use of deduction. In contrast, interpretive theories assume that people are creative in their use and construction of rules and do not automatically abide by them.

On the basis of these two axes—level of analysis and assumptions about the individual–society relationship—Marshall (1996) proposes a nine-cell classification of theories within social gerontology. In essence, his classification scheme is a refined description of the interpretive and scientific paradigms and how they might be linked. A simplified adaptation of Marshall's classification scheme is shown in Table 3.1, listing only the 12 theories that we will discuss in this chapter. Note that some of these theories have their origins in other disciplines: for example, social exchange is a theory from sociology; political economy perspectives existed in sociology, political science, and economics before being adopted by gerontologists. Others are offshoots of theories from outside gerontology: for example, age stratification theory and disengagement theory have roots in structural functionalism. The only theory that social gerontology can

Table 3.1 CLASSIFICATION SCHEME FOR SELECTED SOCIAL
GERONTOLOGICAL THEORIES

Level of Analysis	Individual/Society Relationship		
	NORMATIVE	**BRIDGING**	**INTERPRETIVE**
MACRO	Modernization		Political Economy
LINKING	Disengagement Age stratification	Life course Feminist	Critical
MICRO	Productive Aging Activity	Social Exchange	Continuity Postmodern

Source: Adapted from V.W. Marshall, 1996. The state of theory in aging and the social sciences. In R.H. Binstock & L.K. George, (Eds.). *Handbook of aging and the social sciences* (4th ed.), page 13.

(probably) claim as its own is the life course perspective, although one of its leading proponents, Glen Elder, argues that it has antecedents in structural functionalism and symbolic interactionism (Elder, 1992; Elder & Caspi, 1990).

Theories within Social Gerontology

We now examine each of the 12 theories that appear in Table 3.1. We start with the earliest social gerontological theories. After that, we will look at more recent theories, with an emphasis on life course theory. We conclude with an examination of emergent theories.

First-Generation Theories

All the early theories in social gerontology focused on individuals and particularly on how individuals can best adjust to aging, that is, increase their satisfaction with life.

Activity Theory Activity theory is a micro-level theory focusing on the individual's adjustment to old age. **Activity theory** holds that aging brings with it problems for individuals (i.e., decreases in life satisfaction) that can be alleviated by engaging in activities (Havighurst & Albrecht, 1953). Activity theory is sometimes characterized as the *implicit theory of aging*, meaning that it is implicitly held (and not actually stated) in a considerable amount of social gerontological research (Kart & Kinney, 2001). This theory is based on the proposition that older people—although they may face health declines—continue to have the psychological and social needs of earlier life. Activity theory posits that individuals who are able to meet their social and psychological needs through maintaining the activity level of middle life—through taking on new roles, friends, and activities—will be the best adjusted and most satisfied with life. Related to activity theory is the concept of **successful aging**. *Successful Aging* is the title of a book by Rowe and Kahn (1998) and was the theme of the 1998 Gerontological Society of America's Annual Meeting. The message of successful aging is primarily that older adults have significant abilities to prevent illness, to minimize losses in physical and mental function, and to enhance their engagement in life—prescriptions very similar to activity theory proposed over 40 years ago.

Some empirical research partially supports activity theory. In general, it has been found that older individuals who engage in a lot of informal social activities (e.g., visiting with friends) are more satisfied than those who do not, but that involvement in formal activities (e.g., participating in clubs, political parties, and so on) may (Aquino, Russell, Cutrona, & Altmaier, 1996; Caro & Bass, 1997) or may not (Lemon, Bengtson, & Peterson, 1972; Longino & Kart, 1982) enhance life satisfaction. Overall, empirical support for activity theory has been mixed, and a number of criticisms have led researchers to modify their thinking.

The first criticism is that activity theory assumes that taking on any kind of activity can substitute for the activities of the past. This view does not take into consideration the meanings that different people attribute to different activities. For example, one person may find volunteering at a local hospital very rewarding, whereas another person may find that same activity to be unpleasant. Second, activity theory assumes that psychological and social needs are stable over the adult years. However, it may be that a change in life circumstances (e.g., widowhood) can significantly alter an individual's psychological and social needs. Third, activity theory presumes that individuals have a high degree of control over their social situation. But do all older people have the means to reconstruct their lives, replacing old activities with new ones? Probably not; middle- and upper-class people are more likely to have the economic resources to facilitate such changes. Older people with very little money may find it difficult, even if they want to, to replace old friends or find activities that can compensate for lost ones. Fourth, activity theory has not been able to generate a generally agreed-upon conceptualization and measurement of activity (Achenbaum & Bengtson, 1994). With different researchers conceiving of, and measuring, activity in many different ways, it is difficult to gain a sense of an accumulated body of research that addresses whether and how activity is related to adjustment in old age.

Disengagement Theory Cumming and Henry's (1961) disengagement theory is, on one level, the direct opposite to activity theory. In contrast to activity theory, **disengagement theory** holds that individual adjustment in old age is accomplished through withdrawing (disengaging) from social life, letting go of social roles and activities. On the other hand, disengagement theory represented a new approach to theorizing on aging in that it shifted focus away from the individual and to the wider social structure. The fundamental proposition of disengagement theory is that aging is accompanied by a *mutual withdrawal* of individuals and society. That is, the society withdraws from the individual, which is viewed as functional for society; at the same time, the individual wishes to be less involved in social interaction. Thus, the process is normative and agreed on by all concerned (Cumming, 1963). Further, the disengagement process is inevitable and universal because it makes for social equilibrium: there are minimal disruptions to society when an old and socially withdrawn person dies. As you can see, this is a grand theory.

Disengagement theory created quite a reaction within gerontology, with gerontologists either for or against it, often quite vehemently. For the most part, however, subsequent research failed to find empirical support for disengagement. Also, some research suggests a social class dimension to disengagement; for example, Atchley (1971) found that retired university professors tended to be very much psychologically engaged in their profession, even if not socially engaged. Other occupations do not offer the same opportunity for involvement. Also, it is interesting that the research testing disengagement theory has tended to focus only on one side of the disengagement equation: individuals withdrawing from society. Very little research has taken disengagement theory to task on its proposition that society benefits from the withdrawal of its senior members.

The controversy around disengagement theory has continued, although not as vigorously as in the 1960s and 1970s. Hochschild (1975) argues that the theory contains three problems that have contributed to its continued controversy. First, the theory is hard to actually disconfirm (which is not a desirable quality for a theory). This is because Cumming and Henry (1961) created a number of categories for people who did not disengage (for example, they could be unsuccessful disengagers, exceptional people who re-engage, or disengagers who were "off-schedule" and would presumably eventually disengage). Second, the concept of disengagement is so broad that there may be many different types of disengagement, both psychological and social. For example, there can be disengagement from friends, from social activities, from material possessions, and so on. Third, disengagement theory does not pay attention to what the older individual is thinking or feeling. Behaviour that looks like disengagement to the researcher may not be viewed that way by the individuals involved.

Second-Generation Theories

Until the early 1980s, disengagement theory and activity theory were the dominant theories within social gerontology. Individual adjustment in later life was the focus of gerontological study. Even though disengagement theory introduced social structure to aging theory, research within both theoretical perspectives focused on aging individuals and satisfaction. Since then, a substantial number of different theories have been proposed and some more general social theories have been applied to the study of age and aging. We will now look at five of them—continuity theory, social exchange theory, age stratification theory, aging and modernization theory, and political economy of aging theory—going in general from the more micro to the more macro in focus. We will then give special attention to the life course perspective, given its recent popularity.

Continuity Theory   Like the activity and disengagement theories, continuity theory is a uniquely gerontological theory that focuses upon individual adjustment in later life. **Continuity theory** holds that as people age, they make choices in an effort to preserve ties with the past. Continuity can be both internal and external. Internal continuity refers to the coherence of a personal structure of ideas (based on memory). External continuity refers to the constancy of familiar environments and people. However, it is not the case that successful adjustment to old age means that people should remain in the past or should behave exactly as they did in mid-life (Kart & Kinney, 2001). Atchley (1989) reports that older people classify the degree of continuity in their lives as: too little, optimum, and too much. Too little continuity occurs when people perceive that their lives are unpredictable or discontinuous. This is associated with low levels of satisfaction, since individuals are not able to use their prior coping skills and strategies successfully. Too much continuity occurs when people feel that their lives are too predictable. New and/or enriching experiences do not occur. Optimum continuity exists when the pace of change in people's lives is in line with their personal preferences, personality, and societal expectations. "No change" is not the main implication of continuity theory; rather, it means that new experiences occur against a backdrop of familiarity. Also, continuity is not necessarily the same thing for all individuals. Some individuals, throughout their entire lives, particularly in later life, prefer quiet activities and a lot of "me" time; others want activity and a high level of social involvement. Therefore, a degree of correspondence between mid-life and later life is important for adjustment to old age, according to continuity theory.

While continuity theory is considered one of the main social gerontological theories, it has not been tested very much and has limitations. Perhaps the most obvious criticism is its lack of consideration of structural factors—if life is unpredictable because of a severe shortage of money (the result, for example, of low wages and seasonal work in the fishing industry, no private pension, and a work-related injury that led to early retirement), how is one to cope successfully in old age? Another query is: Is it ageist to assume, as continuity theory seems to, that mid-life is the standard for old age? Also, continuity theory does not take into account maladaptive behaviours in mid-life; presumably, they would not become adaptive if continued into old age (Kart & Kinney, 2001).

Social Exchange Theory   A variant of social exchange theory, originally set forth by George Homans (1961), has been applied to the subject of gerontology, especially by James Dowd (1975; 1980a, 1980b). **Social exchange theory** is concerned with person-to-person interaction, focusing on the calculations and negotiations that transpire between individuals as they seek to maximize rewards and minimize costs in their interactions. Rewards can be either material (e.g., money, property) or non-material (e.g., affection, approval). Costs refer to the loss of rewards. Social exchange theory rests on the propositions that people want to profit (i.e., receive more than they give) in their social interactions and that profit consists of a perception that rewards outweigh costs. The ability to profit from a social interaction depends upon the resources that persons bring to their exchange relationships. Exchanges work best and are most satisfying when the resources that individuals have are approximately equal; this makes for interdependency and not dependency. When one of the persons in a social relationship has substantially fewer resources, his or her ability to profit from the exchange is reduced.

Dowd (1975; 1980a, 1980b) argues that older people find themselves with fewer resources in exchange relationships. Since they cannot reciprocate, they are often forced to offer their compliance to others. And having to do what other people want you to do is not an enviable position to be in. Rather than be compliant, older people can choose to withdraw from relationships. For example, Sarah Matthews (1979), in a study of a centre for older women, observed a high rate of dropout, which, through interviews, she determined to be a calculated decision made by the older women to avoid the costs of interacting with the middle-aged staff at the centre who viewed them as old and, therefore, dependent. In other words, people with perceived disadvantages (few exchange resources) can protect themselves and their identity by avoiding people who define them in negative terms.

It is important to note that the resources that a person has may not be as important as the resources that he or she is *assumed* to have. In our society, it is assumed that older people lack resources—for example, that they have out-of-date skills and knowledge and inadequate physical strength. These assumptions underestimate the resources of older people, creating situations in which the seniors become powerless. For example, an older man is assumed by a prospective employer to be unable to work at a job requiring the use of a computer; an older woman is assumed by the police to have misplaced an item that she says has been stolen. The fact that the man is a computer wizard and that the woman has a wonderful memory may not figure into these social interactions. Thus, social exchange theory is a bridging theory (see Table 3.1) because it incorporates the ageism of the wider society into the person-to-person social interactions in which older people are engaged.

In an important empirical test of social exchange theory, Kart and Longino (1987) found only moderate support for the theory. In a study of 1346 retirement community residents in the United States, they report low inverse relationships between support (emotional, social, and instrumental) given, emotional and social support received, and life satisfaction. In other words, both seniors who gave more and those who received more had lower levels of life satisfaction. According to social exchange theory, we would expect only those who received more to be unhappy (due to lack of reciprocity). The finding that those who gave more were less satisfied is unexpected and is not consistent with social exchange theory's postulate that persons with more exchange resources will have more satisfying social relationships. A more recent study, however, finds higher levels of psychological well-being among elders with more exchange resources but also reports that social exchanges are not a very important determinant of well-being (Liang, Krause & Bennett, 2001). Nevertheless, this theory, especially given its "bridging" of individuals and society, has potential; reformulations based on empirical findings are needed.

Age Stratification Theory Age stratification theory was initially developed by Riley, Johnston, and Foner (1972). Unlike the other theories considered so far, age stratification theory is concerned with all age groups and not just the aged. It is more macro in focus, and views age not only as a characteristic of individuals but also as an important and dynamic element of the wider society.

The elements and processes involved in age stratification theory are presented in Figure 3.1. The age structure of a society consists of four primary elements (these are the boxes in Figure 3.1). The first element is *age strata*, which refers to groups that are based on age (e.g., youth, adults, the aged) and that have unequal status and opportunities in society. Riley (1971) argues that age strata share many commonalities with social classes, especially their hierarchical

Figure 3.1 **ELEMENTS AND PROCESSES IN AGE STRATIFICATION THEORY**

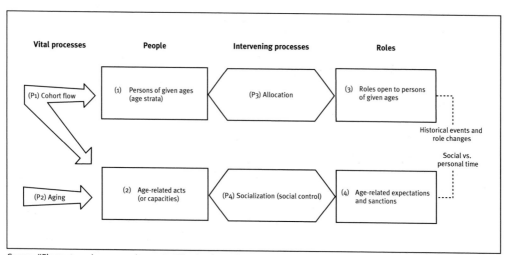

Source: "Elements and processes in age stratification theory." In *Aging and society: A sociology of age stratification*, edited by Matilda White Riley, Marilyn Johnson, and Anne Foner. © 1972 Russell Sage Foundation, 112 East 64th Street, New York, NY 10021. Reprinted with permission.

nature. As individuals age, they move from one stratum to another. The second element is *age-related capacities*. Each stratum differs from the others in the contributions that it makes to the wider society; that is, each stratum is characterized by age-related capabilities. These capacities depend on both biology and social/cultural definitions. The third element is the *social roles* based on age that are available to people. Some roles are directly linked to age (e.g., one must be 16 years old to drive; 65 years is considered the entry point for old age); other roles are only indirectly related to age. Regarding the latter, a society's normative system specifies the appropriate ages for persons to take on (or give up) given roles. We expect, for example, that undergraduate students will be approximately 18 to 23 years old; we expect that people will not be married at age 17 years. As this role linkage with age becomes looser, we can observe people in off-time roles (a 40-year-old first-year university student, a 16-year-old husband). However, the very fact that we notice they are off-time shows the workings of the age normative system. Fourth is *age-related expectations,* which refer to our expectations of how roles are performed by people of varying ages. For example, we do not expect a 20-year-old bride and a 40-year-old bride to act in the same way.

In addition, age stratification theory posits a set of processes that affects the degree of articulation between the above four structural elements and the patterning of individual lives. There are two basic processes and two intervening processes. The first basic process is *cohort flow* (the term **cohort** refers to a group of people who were born at about the same time and who experience a given event at the same time. For example, everyone born in 1980 is part of the same birth cohort). Cohort flow refers to all the factors that contribute to the shaping of the age strata—fertility, in particular, mortality, and migration (as we saw in Chapter 2). Age stratification theory views cohort flow as a process, since a cohort is continuously undergoing change: it loses members (due to death, emigration); it can gain members (through immigration). Also, any given cohort is mobile, as it moves from one age stratum to another. The second basic process is *individual aging*, referring to the physiological and maturational changes that occur over time. However, the differences between age strata cannot be accounted for by age alone; therefore, age stratification theory proposes two intervening processes.

One intervening process is *allocation*, referring to the process of assigning and reassigning people of various ages to suitable roles. (Of course, role assignment is based on more than age, but age is one important criterion that we use.) Role allocation by age, which is also known as age grading, is based on a number of factors, such as cultural values, economic conditions (e.g., when the economy is healthy, people tend to marry at younger ages), and the general shape of the age structure, or population pyramids, as discussed in Chapter 2 (e.g., the large cohort of the baby boom may result in delayed job opportunities for those younger than the baby boomers). When any of these factors change, the system of role allocation by age occurs. The other intervening process is *socialization*—the learning and internalization of the age stratification system that is necessary to ensure the smooth transition of people from one age stratum to the next. We are socialized about the age stratification system through direct observation and participation in small groups, such as the family, through books and other forms of media, and by formal organizations.

Age stratification theory has been influential in social gerontology; however, its importance has waned with the general decline of structural functionalist-based theories and their status quo orientation. In dealing with criticisms—such as the static nature of the concept of age strata and its focus on social equilibrium—its proponents are re-inventing this theoretical perspective under a new name—the *aging and society paradigm* (Riley, Foner & Riley, 1999). This theoretical perspective has introduced the notion of structural lag, referring to the disjuncture between the (limited) opportunities that our society affords older people and the growing numbers of competent elders. This represents a significant moving away from the concepts of age-related capacities and age-related expectations, so central to age stratification theory. Another new element is the idea of the emergence of an age-integrated society (Riley, 1997), in which age barriers are removed, and people of all ages interact together—which turns the concept of age stratification upside down. Riley, Foner, and Riley (1999) feel that age integration should demand the attention of the next generation of theory builders in social gerontology.

Aging and Modernization Theory   Aging and modernization theory is most closely associated with Donald Cowgill (Cowgill & Holmes, 1972). It is a grand theory of the macro variety, attempting to establish universal principles regarding the status of the aged. Its most general and important proposition is that the status of the aged declines with increasing modernization.

According to aging and modernization theory, four interrelated aspects of modernization are particularly salient in relation to aging. One aspect is the development of *health technology*, which includes improvements in sanitation and nutrition as well as curative and surgical medicine. Progress in health technology eventually operates to increase life expectancy, facilitating the aging of the population. With population aging, there is intergenerational conflict for jobs, which eventually results in the establishment of retirement. With retirement comes reduced prestige and reduced income for the aged. A second aspect is *economic modernization*, bringing with it many new specialized jobs, particularly in cities. The young will fill these jobs because they are more likely to have the training for them and they are more geographically mobile, that is, more likely to move to the urban centres where the jobs are. As a result, there is an inversion of status, with young people getting the better jobs and older people left in jobs that tend to become obsolete. The latter also creates a pressure toward retirement. Third, *urbanization* itself operates to lower the status of the aged. As young people migrate to urban areas, the role of the aged in the family changes. As elderly persons become geographically separated from their children and grandchildren, they become peripheral to the nuclear families of their children.

Also, the upward social mobility of the children creates a social distance between the generations. Fourth, increases in *education* lower the status of the aged. In premodern societies, elders are the repositories of knowledge, an important role that reinforces their status. With increases in education, older people lose this role as their children gain more knowledge and have more skills than the parents have.

While Cowgill wants his theory to apply to all societies, he does recognize that societies will have unique characteristics (termed extraneous factors) that affect the way that modernization relates to aging. For Western society, he identifies two unique factors. One is the work ethic, with its high value placed on industriousness, savings, time consciousness, efficiency, and individual achievement. These values serve to reinforce the decline in the status of the aged: people who no longer work. Second is the cult of youth, which is related to the work ethic and its emphasis on efficiency and so on. In a cult of youth, youth becomes a symbol of, and a means to, progress. By definition, then, older people are devalued: they are no longer young.

While offering important insights, aging and modernization theory has its limitations, and no longer enjoys the popularity it did in the 1970s. First, the concept of modernization in the theory is not well explicated and is used synonymously with a host of other terms, such as development, change, westernization, and progress. Indeed, it is often difficult to pinpoint when modernization actually begins, making tests of the theory very difficult. David Hackett Fischer (1977) argues that the decline of the status of the aged in the United States preceded any of the modernization changes that Cowgill's theory postulates as critical. Second, the theory, while aiming for universal applicability, appears to be ethnocentric, taking the West as the standard. Third, researchers have challenged the linear conception of modernization that is implicit in aging and modernization theory. Modernization tends to be a more dynamic process than it is seen to be in this theory. Fourth, aging and modernization theory homogenizes older adults of the past; they were not all affluent, powerful property owners.

Political Economy of Aging Theory While political economy theory has a long history in the social sciences, it has been applied to the subject of the aged and aging societies only fairly recently. In Canada, the leading gerontologists using this perspective are John Myles (1984; Myles & Quadagno, 1991) and Lynn McDonald (1996); Carroll Estes (1979) and Meredith Minkler are the gerontologists in the United States most closely associated with this perspective (Minkler & Estes, 1984); in the United Kingdom, relevant gerontologists include Alan Walker (1981, 1996) and Chris Phillipson (1982).

Canadian social gerontologists have tended to be more macro-focused than their American counterparts, and the political economy perspective has been more widely used in Canada than in the United States. The basic premise of **political economy of aging theory** is that the experience of old age and the treatment of seniors can only be understood within the context of the economy (both national and international), the state, the labour market, and the intersecting class, gender, age and racial/ethnic divisions in society (Estes, Gerard, Zones, & Swan, 1984). Inequality by age is an important element of the political economy of aging perspective; it seeks to uncover the structural conditions that create age inequality and the way that older people are defined and treated (Quadagno & Reid, 1999).

The political economy of aging perspective originated from Marxist and neo-Marxist critiques of age stratification theory (Quadagno & Reid, 1999). Specific criticisms include the facts that age stratification theory uses a static conceptualization of social structure; neglects political processes that create inequalities; ignores power relationships that play an important role in how roles and statuses are allocated; and does not consider the wide variation and diversity within age cohorts. The time had come for a social gerontological theory that focused on the dynamics of inequality and power relations, and the political economy of aging emerged to fill the bill.

According to Estes (1991: 31), the political economy of aging perspective is based on the following premises:

- The social structure shapes how older people are perceived and how they perceive themselves.

- The labels applied to both the elderly and social policy shape the experience of old age.

- Social policy and the politics of aging mirror wider social inequalities and the power struggles around them.

- Social policy reflects the dominant belief system that is crucial in enforcing, bolstering, and extending structured inequalities in the wider economic, political, and social order.

- We can see that social policy—and the state that is responsible for it—are crucial elements of this perspective. The state is especially important in the lives of older people, since they are more dependent on state policies than are younger adults. At the same time, however, the state's primary purpose is to ensure the well-being of the economy. This means that older people, who are largely outside productive labour, are in a precarious and tension-filled relationship with the state. Yet, state policy is also responsible for meeting social needs. Thus, a central concern of the political economy of aging perspective is the dynamic between the organization of work (capitalism) and social needs and how the contradiction between the two affects the aging process and the experience of aging (Estes, 1991).

According to this perspective, the problems faced by older people are socially constructed, not biologically determined. The political economy of aging perspective is critical of the structured dependency (Townsend, 1981) of the aged, viewing age-related dependency as a construction of economic, political, and social factors in 20th-century Western society. The state, through the institutionalization of retirement, for example, has played a key role in the dependency of the aged. This perspective is also highly critical of institutionalized medicine; by applying a medical model to aging, it has created an equivalency between aging and illness, has helped create the idea that aging is a problem, and has individualized aging, making it appear to be the private problem of individuals. At the same time, medicine and many helping professions have become an enterprise with a vested interest in the view that old people are dependent and in need of their help (Estes, 1979).

The political economy of aging perspective is sympathetic to the critique of apocalyptic demography, discussed in Chapter 2. This perspective takes note of the state's creation of crisis as a way to promote its own agenda. As Estes, Linkins and Binney (1996: 350) state, "(u)nderstanding the contemporary welfare state and its treatment of the aged requires ... attention to *crisis construction and crisis management* by the state and its political leaders." [italics added] The socially constructed "crisis" of population aging has much to do with the distribution and control of capital and much less to do with the demographics of the changing age structure. As noted by Myles and Quadagno (1991: 304–305), the fact that a greater proportion of people (i.e., the aged) exist on public pensions means that "an ever-growing and increasingly important portion of the national wage bill [is]... removed from the market... [and] workers, in their capacity as citizens, are able to claim a share of the social product independent of their capacity as wage earners." Such a shift is detrimental to the interests of capital; the state (aligned with capital) responds by constructing a crisis that allows it to reform pensions and health care, for example.

The Life Course Perspective   The life course theoretical perspective, with Glen Elder (e.g., 1985; 1994; 2000) as its major developer, is generally considered the dominant perspective within social gerontology at the present time, and for that reason receives more attention here. It has roots in age stratification theory and also draws heavily on prominent American sociologist C. Wright Mills's (1959) call for a theoretical orientation that encompasses individual biography and history and the intersections of biography and history within the social structure. This call is for a theory that links macro (history, social structure) elements and micro (or individual level) elements. Life course theory is considered the best attempt within social gerontology, to date, to make that linkage.

Before we look at the life course perspective, it is useful to distinguish among a number of concepts: life course, lifespan, life cycle, and life history. These terms are often used interchangeably; however, they do not refer to the same thing (Elder, 2000). *Life cycle* most precisely refers to the stages of parenthood, from the birth of the first child to the departure of all children (to set up homes of their own and, presumably, begin child-bearing). Normatively, this cycle is repeated from one generation to the next, although, in actuality, some people will not have children and will not be part of an intergenerational life cycle. The life cycle comprises a set of ordered stages, with the important transition points being marriage, the births of the first and the last children, and the departure of the last child (resulting in the empty nest stage). In other words, the life cycle concept focuses on the sequence of events and tells us little about age (e.g., marriage may be at 18 or at 30 years). A bigger limitation of the concept is its focus on ideal sequencing, which is increasingly being disrupted by common-law marriage preceding legal marriage and by divorce and remarriage, as seen in Chapter 5. In other words, the concept has become less and less applicable to more and more people.

Life history refers to a number of methods for collecting information about human lives over time. Information may be gained either from archival or administrative records or by interviews. Quite often, the former data source involves quantitative data, and statistical methods, such as life history event analysis (described in the next chapter). In contrast, interviews are more likely to yield qualitative data. Life history also refers to a self-reported narration of life; a narrative account by individuals in which the researcher takes a non-directive role, documenting the history only and not asking specific questions.

Within demography, the term *lifespan* refers to the maximum number of years that members of species can live, for example, approximately 120 years for human beings at the current time. In gerontology, *lifespan* refers to age-related biological and behavioural changes from birth to death (Elder, 2000). It is in this sense that we use the term in this chapter. This concept is closest to that of the life course. However, there is a difference between the span of a lifetime and the course of a life (Hagestad, 1990). The concept of life course is more macro; the life course reflects how society gives both personal and social meanings to the passage of time in a life. *Life course* can be defined as "trajectories that extend across the lifespan, such as family or work; and by short-term changes or transitions, such as entering or leaving school, acquiring a full-time job, and the first marriage. Each life course transition is embedded in a trajectory that gives it specific form and meaning." (Elder, 2000:1615) Thus, the focus of life course theory is on the transitions and trajectories that constitute an individual's life or the lives of similarly situated people.

The **life course theoretical perspective** is concerned with individuals as social personae, "tracing their pathways along an age-differentiated, socially marked sequence of transitions." (Hagestad, 1990: 151) These pathways occur over time. Time is an important concept within this theoretical perspective. There are three types of time: life time—or age; historical time—the historical era in which a life is embedded and the historical events that may affect it (e.g., Depression, war[s]); and social time—the ordering of life events/social roles by age-linked expectations and options like retirement (Elder, 1975; 1978). Research based on the life course perspective attempts to untangle the effects of age, history, and social structure on the pathways that make up the life course of individuals. The linking of age and historical time has benefited from the concept of cohort (persons born at the same time). If a historical event differentially affects people of different cohorts (or ages), then a **cohort effect** has occurred (Uhlenberg & Miner, 1996). For example, the Vietnam war era (and the protests that accompanied it and helped form a counterculture in the 1960s) had a different effect on the youth of the time than on middle-aged people. On the other hand, if a historical event has the same effect on people of all cohorts (ages), a **period effect** has occurred. The events of September 11, 2001 may be of this variety. Both period and cohort effects show the impact of historical influences on individual lives (Elder, 2000).

Age and social time are linked by the notion of normative timing. That is, societies have expectations about the "appropriate" age for individuals to take on or exit from social roles; these are sometimes called *social clocks*. Some of these expectations are formal (e.g., retirement at age 65 years); many more are informal, embedded in wider social and cultural norms. Settersten and Hagestad (1996) argue that age norms have three characteristics: (1) they are prescriptions for behaviour; (2) they are supported by widespread consensus in society; and (3) they are enforced through mechanisms of social control. Research indicates that individuals in Canada and the United States perceive age guidelines and express age preferences for role transitions (Gee, 1990; Settersten & Hagestad, 1996; Veevers, Gee & Wister, 1996); however, there is debate about whether these guidelines and preferences constitute age norms or not.

According to life course theory's main architect, Glen Elder (2000), it is organized around four major principles:

1. *The life course of individuals is embedded and shaped by their historical and geographical placement.* This principle refers to the cohort effect discussed earlier. That is, when societies are undergoing rapid social change, different cohorts are exposed to different structures of opportunities and constraints and to different cultural values. For example, people born in the earlier years of the baby boom (in Canada, those born between 1947 and 1952) faced much competition for jobs (due to the size of the cohort), but within an expanding economy in which jobs were quite plentiful. In contrast, their children (who are of a relatively small cohort, due to the low fertility of the boomers) faced less competition for jobs, but due to economic recession, there were very few jobs available when they reached young adulthood. Thus, the life courses of baby boomers and their children, at minimum, will vary due to economic differences. Also, within each cohort, variations will occur in terms of geography. For example, the "hippie" movement was more pronounced in large cities; the economic recession of the early 1980s hit certain parts of Canada harder than others.

2. *The impact of a transition or event depends on when it occurs in a person's life.* Social change or major events affect individuals differentially according to their age at the time of the change/event; this is sometimes called the "life stage principle." For example, if a country has compulsory military service, usually young people are conscripted and the military service tends not to have far-reaching consequences for the rest of their lives. However, during war time, older people are

engaged in military service. Late entry into the military in World War II had life-long consequences, such as increased risk of divorce, increased risk of work–life instability, and negative physical health effects in later life (Elder, 1987; Pavalko & Elder, 1990). Similarly, giving birth at age 15 years will likely negatively affect the educational attainment of the mother and consequently her work opportunities and earnings; we would not expect this if a mother has her first child at the age of 30 years.

3. *Lives are lived interdependently.* This principle is sometimes called "linked lives." Given that we all live in networks of shared relationships, the actions of one person can affect the lives of others. This is most easily seen in the family context. For example, if a young woman has a child at a very young age, she also makes her mother a grandmother at a young age. Research on African American women in Los Angeles shows that young motherhood can be associated with a rejection of responsibilities by grandmothers, with care being shifted up a generation to great-grandmothers (Burton & Bengtson, 1985). In contrast, women who become grandmothers at an "expected age" (i.e., their late 40s) are happy to take on the grandmother role. Canadian research (Mitchell & Gee, 1996a) on the home-leaving phenomenon also shows the effects of linked lives. Children who leave and return home (boomerangers) several times are viewed by parents as having a disruptive effect on their lives and their marriages; children who leave home and do not return, or return only once or twice, do not negatively influence the marital satisfaction of their parents.

4. *Individuals construct their own life course through their choices and actions, contingent upon the constraints and opportunities provided by history and social circumstance.* This principle gives centrality to the concept of human agency within life course theory. Individuals are not just passive recipients of whatever history and social structure present them with; they have agency, and can make good or bad choices or act wisely or unwisely. Life course theory does not reduce individual behaviour to a stimulus–response model, in which all individuals respond in a given way to a set of social factors. Thus, two people in the same historical and social situation may act differently; for instance, one may choose to drop out of school at 16, while the other goes to university; one may choose to remain in a bad marriage, and the other may leave it. The concept of *planful* competence has emerged to explain the different choices and actions of individuals; that is, individuals who in their youth are future-oriented and efficient are more likely to make "good" life-course decisions (Clausen, 1993). However, it seems that planful competence only holds when there are real opportunities open to individuals (Shanahan, Elder & Miech, 1997); when the economy is very bad, for example, no amount of planful competence helps individuals construct their life course in a favourable way. This suggests that different historical and social circumstances will affect the likelihood of certain choices or actions being taken. For example, obtaining a divorce before 1969 in Canada was very difficult; the chances of going to university are better now than they were 50 years ago.

The life course perspective is a dynamic one; it focuses on the complex interrelationships among biographical time, social time, and historical time. Hagestad and

Dannefer (2001) identify a number of critical issues for this theoretical perspective and the research emanating from it. They suggest that the theory has yet to artic-ulate a clear conception of social structure, with the effect that—despite the basic tenets of the theory—research has tended to be micro-oriented. Thus, we know more about lives at the micro-level than we do about lives at the macro-level. Similarly, the concept of "linked lives" has been studied in the context of indi-vidual relationships (e.g., mothers and daughters) but the role of macro-factors, such as social policy, in the linking of lives has not been considered. Also, some researchers have registered skepticism about the life-stage principle—that the effects of social change depend on the age of individuals. For example, Elder (1974) found that young people were more negatively affected by the Depression than were the older people. However, it may not necessarily be the case that the young are the hardest hit. If people have invested many years in something that becomes useless or redundant or loses its social value because of major social upheaval, they may be more negatively affected than young people who have invested little.

The concept of agency—which does explicitly focus on the individual—contains some problems as well. Settersten (1999) argues that life course theory to date has not paid attention to *how* individuals shape or change structures, and the reverse; he calls for an "agency within structure view." Also, life course the-ory may establish individual agency and social structure as an artificial dichotomy. In addition, agency is implicitly assumed to be a good thing in itself; life course theory neglects the dark side of agency, for example, risk, stress, and uncertainty (Settersten & Hagestad, 2001). In addition, we cannot necessarily assume that individual agency is effective in producing or shaping social structural change; we need to know the conditions conducive to efficacy of individual agency—conditions that are likely social in origin.

Third-Generation Theories

In recent years, some new theoretical perspectives have been applied to social gerontology from the structural perspective. Here we consider two of them—the feminist perspective and critical gerontology. While neither are "neat" the-oretical packages, both, in varying ways and in varying degrees (depending upon what is being focused on), share tenets with the political economy of aging perspective. We end with a discussion of productive aging, which is, at best, an emerging and popular theoretical perspective for understanding aging.

Feminist Theory In the past, non-feminist approaches to women and gen-der in the studies of aging represented two approaches: the simple addition of women into existing research studies or the control of the influence of gen-der relative to other factors such as levels of education or income. Scholars in these early studies confused research on women with feminist approaches and did little to advance theory. As Calasanti (2004:S306) has recently observed, " . . . feminist gerontologists theorize gender relations as forces that shape both social organizations and identities as men and women interact with one another." Gender relations are, at their core, constructed power relations that are embedded in social processes and institutionalized in ways that have consequences for life chances. What is more, according to this theory, because gender is relational, feminist gerontology encompasses men and women alike.

Be that as it may, there is no one feminist approach, either overall or with respect to aging. **Feminist theory** ranges from liberal feminism (which holds that men and women are equal and should have equal rights) to radical feminism (which focuses on women's subjugation due to patriarchal arrangements and argues that society must be fundamentally reorganized to address this problem). Within gerontology, a wide range of feminist approaches exists as well (Browne, 1998; Lopata, 1995). Given this diversity, providing the full scope of feminist gerontological theory is not possible here. Rather, our discussion is limited to general principles with which most feminist gerontologists would agree.

Feminist gerontology theory is based on the premise that gender is a fundamental organizing principle of society, operating over the life course of individuals. This does not mean that women and men are somehow different; rather, it implies something much more important: that gender is a structured aspect of our society. In other words, gender is socially constructed (not biologically determined) and the social construction of gender permeates all aspects of our society. With regard to biological determinism, leading feminist scholar Michele Fine (1992) states that feminist work must be intolerant of what is considered inevitable and natural. Since gender is an organizing principle of social organization, it is implicated in social stratification and inequality. Indeed, gender stratification—which occurs in work, family, leisure, and so on—is one of the ways in which patterns of (male) advantage and (female) disadvantage operate.

Gender and age operate together to lower the status of women as they age. As Garner (1999:4) writes: "Much of western society's view of women's worth is associated with a socially defined social attractiveness that clearly equates youth with beauty and the ability to attract men. Therefore, women lose their social value simply by growing old." However, while women lack social, economic, and political power, this does not mean that they must accept this. Resources permitting, women have individual agency to resist social definitions of powerlessness. Indeed, one of the goals of feminist gerontology is to empower women to resist societal definitions and rules. Gee and Kimball (1987), in one of the earliest feminist gerontological works in Canada, argue that older women do, in fact, resist their social and political marginality through the development of rich interpersonal ties.

Feminist theory has implications for the practice of research, that is, for methods. Feminist methods call for a dismantling of the power hierarchy between the researcher and the researched. Thus, older persons are transformed from subjects of research to real people engaged in a mutually beneficial (research) relationship. As well, feminist research and theory begin with the premise that the knowledge brought to the research venue by older persons is just as valid as the knowledge of the professional researcher; this is the concept of *multiple knowledges*. One task of the feminist researcher, then, is to give voice to the marginalized, often silenced members of our society, such as older women, validating their experiences and their worth as individuals. However, feminist theory goes beyond this, seeking to empower older women and to play an advocacy role for them. Thus, feminist scholars do not feel satisfied with pointing out, for example, the severe financial situation of many older Canadian women; they seek to alter pension policies to change this situation. Ideally, this is done collaboratively with older women and not just on their behalf, as participatory research is a hallmark of much feminist work. However, if some older women are physically or mentally limited in advocating for themselves, feminist scholars will operate alone.

The empowerment of older women is best seen in feminist practice, that is, for example, working with older women who require some type of social service. Feminist practitioners seek to empower older women by helping them establish new roles, identify their strengths, and use their knowledge (Garner, 1999). This is often done in small groups, in which older women share their experiences (and come to understand the social structural roots of problems shared), validate each other's sense of self-worth, and sustain each other through the development of meaningful relationships. While feminist practice aims to promote clients' independence and self-sufficiency, it, of course, also supports the client's rights to services and resources and seeks to educate others about older women's rights.

Critical Theory   Critical gerontology is also not a neat theoretical package. It could be viewed as a paradigm, subsuming a number of related theories. Here, we examine the main tenets of a critical approach to theory. In Chapter 4, we discuss it as a paradigm. It has roots in the Frankfurt School (neo-Marxism), postmodernism, the humanities, and feminism (Achenbaum, 1997). Also, it has sometimes been integrated with the political economy of aging approach (Estes, 1999). In this case, the concept of *moral* economy is added to that of political economy, with *moral economy* referring to the shared moral assumptions that underlie norms of reciprocity in a society. The moral economy approach makes explicit the cultural beliefs and values that underlie social policies and practices that affect older adults. For example, the Canadian moral economy has valued equity and access to health care for all, including older people, far more than that of the United States (Clark, 1999).

The essence of critical gerontology is *reflexivity*. That is, **critical theory** seeks a self-awareness and a deconstruction of the assumptions underlying mainstream social gerontological theories and research. At the same time, it focuses on a critique of the existing social order and its treatment of the aged, especially by exposing assumptions and myths that maintain the status quo. In addition, and in keeping with the principle of reflexivity, critical gerontology seeks to provide us with an understanding of the meaning of aging and old age.

In its extreme forms, critical gerontology represents a significant attack on mainstream gerontology because it questions the importance of causation—a central component of explanation, itself the defining characteristic of theories. In this way, some aspects of critical gerontology can be viewed as part of the postmodern turn in social theory, discussed earlier. Some forms of critical gerontology reject causation in the call for a rich understanding of life that is intrinsically situational—affected by history, culture, and geography. Critical gerontology assumes that the nature of aging is fluid (i.e., ever-changing), context based, and subject to individual agency. This non-static assumption represents a fresh approach to social gerontology related to the humanities as much as to the social sciences. Thus, the scientific search for knowledge that is generalizable is underemphasized, in favour of a more humanities-oriented understanding of fluidity and context in aging. However, critical gerontology retains some links to the social sciences. For example, like feminist gerontology, critical gerontology rejects hierarchical power relationships between the researcher and the researched, but, unlike postmodernism, it is still wedded to the idea of doing social research. In keeping with the centrality of reflexivity, critical gerontology seeks to provide us with an understanding of the meaning of aging and old age.

Postmodernism Postmodernism, as explained earlier, is actually anti-theoretical; however, the approach has been recently used in gerontology to "theorize aging" (Powell, 2006). It sometimes is linked to critical theory (Katz, 2005). Postmodern constructions of aging consider the cultural interaction between the aging body and the social context in shaping the way people experience their lifetimes. One strand of postmodernism in the study of aging is the Foucauldian analysis. Foucault, a sociologist, developed discursive tools to help us analyze the authoritative discourses embedded in public policies and professional practices in society, especially the power relationships between professionals and older people (Biggs & Powell, 2001). Stephen Katz in Canada has been a leader in this type of analysis, especially of the emergence of gerontology as a discipline (Katz, 1996).

Productive Aging The concept of productive aging was first introduced in 1982 by Robert Butler in Salzburg as a way of countering the prevailing ageism at the time. The Salzburg Conference resulted in an edited volume entitled *Productive Aging: Enhancing Vitality in Later Life* (Butler & Gleason, 1985). At present, "productive aging" appears to be a popular buzzword in gerontology, which is not surprising since the concept views aging in a positive light and suggests the potential of an aging population (Taylor & Bengston, 2001). According to Butler and Schechter, **productive aging** " . . . is the capacity of an individual or population to serve in the paid workforce; to serve in volunteer activities; to assist in the family; and to maintain, to varying degrees, autonomy and independence for as long as possible"(2001:824). Both society and the individual are responsible for ensuring older people meet their productive potential, making this a potential bridging theory. Unfortunately, as there are many definitions of productive aging, the conceptual and theoretical foundations have yet to be developed.

Research on productive aging has focused on the barriers that older adults face in aging productively, such as employment and retirement, caregiving, volunteering, and education and training (O'Reilly & Caro, 1994). One of the major pitfalls of this research, however, is the lack of a unified concept of productive aging. Taylor and Bengtson (2001) ask important questions about whether researchers are studying phenomena as they exist or simply attempting to alter reality by introducing the concept of productive aging.

Table 3.2 summarizes the theories discussed in this chapter.

Table 3.2 SUMMARY OF THEORIES

Theory	Author	Date of Emergence	Level of Analysis
Activity	Havighurst & Albrecht	1953	Micro
Successful Aging	Rowe and Kahn	1997	Micro
Disengagement	Cumming and Henry	1961	Linking
Continuity	Atchley	1971	Micro
Social Exchange	Dowd	1975	Micro
Age Stratification	Riley, Johnston & Foner	1972	Linking
Modernization	Cowgill	1972	Macro
Political Economy of Aging	Este	1979	Macro
Life Course Perspective	Elder	1985	Linking
Feminist	Browne	1980s	Linking
Critical	Phillipson	1990s	Linking
Postmodernism	Katz, Powell	1990s	Micro
Productive Aging	Butler	1982	Linking

Chapter Summary

This chapter has introduced you to a wide variety of theories within social gerontology and to some broad theoretical concerns of the discipline. It has been shown that social gerontology is not devoid of theories, despite the criticisms of a vocal minority about the state of theory. The issue seems to be less that there are no theories than that a considerable amount of research in social gerontology does not make its theoretical underpinnings explicit.

Key ideas to remember from this chapter:

- Theory and research are intimately related; one is useless without the other.
- The defining feature of theory is its provision of explanations. Theories can be distinguished from facts (the building blocks of theories), empirical generalizations (findings that are found repeatedly), models (descriptive linkages of empirical generalizations), and paradigms (world views that underlie theories).
- The barriers to theoretical development in gerontology include research driven by the need to solve immediate problems; the general difficulty with "grand theories"; and the postmodern turn.
- Theories are important because they: integrate knowledge; offer explanations; provide predictions; and can offer ways to solve problems.
- The three major foci in social gerontology are the aged, the aging process, and age as a dimension of social structure.
- Micro-level theories deal with the aged and the aging process; macro-level theories deal with age as a dimension of social structure.
- Social gerontological theories may also be categorized as interpretive or normative. These two axes—level of analysis and assumptions about the individual–society relationship—form the basis for a classification of theories in social gerontology, as seen in Table 3.1.
- The first-generation theories—activity theory and disengagement theory—focus on the adjustment of individuals to aging. In addition, disengagement theory is concerned with the wider society; its chief tenet is that aging is accompanied by a mutual withdrawal of individuals and society
- The second-generation theories, ranked from more micro-focused to more macro-focused, include continuity theory, social exchange theory, age stratification theory, aging and modernization theory, and political economy of aging theory. Life course theory—which links micro- and macro-levels—is currently the dominant theory.
- The life course perspective conceptualizes time in three ways: life time, social time, and historical time. Its four central principles are that the life course of individuals is embedded in and shaped by their historical and geographical position; the impact of a transition or event depends on when it occurs in a person's life (the "life stage" principle); lives are lived interdependently ("linked lives"); and individual agency is an important factor in the construction of a life course, contingent upon macro-level constraints and opportunities.

- Third-generation theories include feminist gerontology, critical gerontology, postmodernism, and productive aging. Feminist gerontology is based on the premise that the social construction of gender permeates all aspects of society and aging. Critical theory's main contribution is its focus on reflexivity of both researchers and the researched. Postmodernism "undresses" the darker side of aging in some instances and in others provides different interpretations of the aging body. Productive aging emphasizes the productive capacity of older people and their significant contributions to work, family, and community.

KEY TERMS

theory (p. 57)

theoretical perspectives (p. 57)

hypothesis (p. 57)

grand theories (p. 58)

middle-range theories (p. 58)

facts (p. 58)

empirical generalizations (p. 58)

models (p. 58)

paradigms (p. 59)

postmodern turn (p. 60)

micro-level of analysis (p. 61)

micro-level theories (p. 61)

macro-level of analysis (p. 61)

macro-level theories (p. 61)

activity theory (p. 63)

successful aging (p. 64)

disengagement theory (p. 64)

continuity theory (p. 66)

social exchange theory (p. 67)

age stratification theory (p. 68)

cohort (p. 69)

aging and modernization theory (p. 70)

political economy of aging theory (p. 71)

life course theoretical perspective (p. 74)

cohort effect (p. 75)

period effect (p. 75)

feminist theory (p. 78)

critical theory (p. 79)

productive aging (p. 81)

STUDY QUESTIONS

1. Why is theory important? What do you think is its most important function? What would happen if there were no theory?

2. Why is the distinction between micro- and macro-levels important in social gerontology? Do you think this distinction has caused any problems in our understanding of aging?

3. Choose a topic of interest to you. How would this topic be approached by political economy of aging theory? by life course theory? by feminist gerontology?

SUGGESTED READINGS

Bengtson, V.L., Burgess, E.O., & Parrott, T.M. (1997). Theory, explanation, and a third generation of theoretical development in social gerontology. *The Journal of Gerontology: Social Sciences, 52*, S72–S88.

Bengtson, V.L., & Shaie, K.W. (Eds.). (1999). *Handbook of theories of aging.* New York: Springer.

Biggs, S., Lowenstein, A., & Hendricks, J. (2003). *The need for theory.* Amityville, NY: Baywood.

Powell, J.L. (2006). *Social theory and aging.* New York: Rowman & Littlefield Publishers Inc.

Settersten Jr., R.A. (2003). *Invitation to the life course: Toward new understandings of later life.* Amityville, NY: Baywood.

Chapter 4

KNOWLEDGE BUILDING
AND OLDER PEOPLE

Learning Objectives

In this chapter, you will learn about

- Research in social gerontology.
- The focus of gerontological research on the explanation, description, and exploration of aging as a social process for both applied and policy purposes.
- How to avoid human errors in studying older people, by adhering to three main principles central to scientific inquiry: empiricism, objectivity, and control.

- Perspectives that challenge these principles, and contrasting beliefs about the nature of reality, the relationship between the researcher and older person, and how to build knowledge.
- Three overarching world views—postpositivism, interpretive/constructivist theory, and critical theory—that all employ different research methodologies.

- The postpositivist tendency to use cross-sectional and longitudinal surveys, secondary data analysis, experimental and quasi-experimental designs; constructivists' use of biographies, phenomenology, grounded theory, and ethnography; and critical theorists' use of the best methods suited to their research questions that help them challenge unjust social structures.

- The entanglement of age, period, and cohort effects unique to the study of aging and how these effects can best be separated.
- The flaws within all designs, including longitudinal designs.
- The critical importance of participation of the older person.
- The importance of ethical research in social gerontology.

Introduction

Are you aware that older people who are familiar with computer hardware and software report an increased sense of efficacy and life satisfaction (Karavidas, Lim, & Katsikas, 2005), or that 25 percent of women diagnosed with AIDS in 2000 were aged 45 years of age or older (Neundorfer, Harris, Britton, & Lynch, 2005)? Did you know that 20 percent of grandparent caregivers in skipped generation families (no parents, aunts, or uncles) are from First Nations in Canada (Fuller-Thomson, 2005), or that the physical abusers of older people are not always caregivers (McDonald, 2006a)? Contrary to what many people think, widows who live below the low-income cut-offs for Canada express satisfaction with their incomes (McDonald, Donahue, & Moore, 2000b). Much to everyone's surprise, during one of the worst floods in Canadian history, the cognitive functioning and self-assessed health for older flood victims with the greatest exposure to the crisis actually improved a year after the event (Havens, 2001).

All of the above knowledge about older people comes from research by social scientists who study aging. Many of the results are not obvious or challenge common stereotypes of older people and their social conditions. Social gerontologists are able to go beyond the obvious or commonly held beliefs by the use of the scientific method in their study of older persons. Two major features of the scientific method attempt to safeguard against human errors commonly made by researchers. The ideas that all knowledge—no matter how cherished a belief it represents—is provisional and that all knowledge is subject to refutation are at the heart of the scientific method. In this chapter, we review what social researchers study and why research in social gerontology is crucial. We describe the "many ways of knowing" about older people, the goals and methods of scientific inquiry, and the unique issues faced by social gerontologists.

What Is the Nature of Research in Social Gerontology?

The study of aging in a social context is different from the study of physical aging. While a researcher in geriatric medicine might be interested in the physical effects of the frailty of older people on the risk of death, a social gerontologist might focus more on the relationship between frailty and "aging in place" in the person's own home. The social study of aging is strongly rooted in the disciplinary research traditions of sociology, psychology, economics, anthropology, and the humanities. The central interest of the gerontologist is age—how it affects and is affected by such factors as the influence of ethnicity on aging, or vice versa, and the consequences of aging, including hospital use, widowhood, rural/urban mobility, and grandparenting. The first research on aging tended to focus on the aged as a special group in the Canadian population. These early researchers were inclined to see most of older persons' social circumstances as social problems and explored ways to solve these problems by intervening with individual older people and their families, or at the societal level by advocating for and altering social policies. The research methods social gerontologists employed tended to treat older people as a static group (all those Canadians over age 65 years), who were seen to be mostly homogeneous.

More recently, aging is viewed as a dynamic process seen through the lens of a life course perspective (see Chapter 3) where researchers pay attention to, ". . . the location and measurement of events and the processes of aging in time" (Alwin & Campbell, 2001). Social gerontologists attempt to study individuals as they move through both normative events (e.g., retirement) and non-normative events (e.g., war) across the life course on their way to later life, all within the context of an ever-changing society. For example, the horror of September 11, when the World Trade Center was struck by terrorists piloting commercial passenger planes, will follow many New Yorkers into old age. The life experiences of children who are destined to grow up without their natural fathers or mothers, or of men and women instantly thrust into widowhood, will be undeniably different. Recent studies of Holocaust survivors show that some of the survivors are particularly vulnerable to the changes associated with the normal aging process and are more at risk for committing suicide (Barak et al., 2005). Settersten (2006b) studied how wartime military service, especially during World War II, affected the short- and long range development of recruits. Thus, the focus of gerontological research has shifted to include the study of aging as a social process in addition to the aged as a static population category, taking what we call a long view of aging over the life course (Hagestad, 1990). Today, social researchers in gerontology are continually searching for more suitable ways to capture the flow of aging in a society that does not stand still.

Generally, researchers in social gerontology are interested in how aging processes affect people, how aging affects society in general, and how society affects the aging processes of individuals. Social gerontologists are also interested in the best ways to intervene to help older people improve their lives. For example, one researcher might want to know how leaving a job to care for an ill parent affects a woman's income in later life, while another researcher might want to know whether the Canadian pension system protects women against such contingencies. Another researcher with more applied interests might want to know what we could do to effectively help an individual woman faced with these circumstances. These researchers may all be from different disciplines that lead them to examine different aspects of the same issue and to study different relationships between the many factors involved. In the above example, the sociologist would be more concerned about the relationship between caregiving and income in later life, while the economist is more likely to focus on the capacity of the pension system. Furthermore, the two researchers might work together, in a partnership or in a multidisciplinary team, in an attempt to capture the multidimensional nature of aging processes.

The Canadian Association on Gerontology (CAG), founded in the 1970s, which publishes the *Canadian Journal on Aging,* represents the wide diversity of research activities across the country. The Association has six active divisions to represent the full research spectrum: biological sciences, health sciences, educational gerontology, psychology, social sciences, and social policy and practice (Martin-Matthews & Béland, 2001). Canadian research in gerontology ordinarily runs the gamut from curiosity-driven research about why things are the way they are to more applied research for policy and program development and for interventions, such as counselling for older persons (Chappell, 1995; Gee, 1997a)

Why Do We Conduct Research?

To Err Is Human

When we observe older people on our own, we often make errors that scientific enquiry can help us overcome. Often, our observations are inaccurate and selective; we sometimes overgeneralize; we might engage in *ex post facto hypothesizing*; we can be illogical, and sometimes, we prematurely stop the inquiry before we have all the information. Sometimes, we let our ego get in the way of our observations (Rubin & Babbie, 2005). As a visitor to a nursing home, you may conclude that the staff are rude to the residents, when, in reality, the offenders were the visitors to another resident. On the basis of a few cases, namely, your retired aunt and her two friends who complain about their new seniors' housing, you may wrongly conclude that seniors' housing is a poor living arrangement for all older persons.

Ex post facto hypothesizing means that you deduce something after the fact. For example, you were kind enough to take your older uncle and three of his friends to the hockey game, thinking that this would be a treat because they love hockey. When you arrive at the arena, they seem somewhat uncomfortable and a little agitated and want to go home before the end of the second period—something you never would have expected. Your new hypothesis is that the noise and the crowds were overpowering for them, a sensible line of reasoning, but one that may not be correct. This example of *ex post facto hypothesizing* is acceptable as long as you don't stop here without further testing your idea. You would not know if you were correct until you tested your hypothesis by collecting factual information from your uncle and his friends. Being illogical can also be problematic. Inferring that the neighbour next door neglects her old mother because she works all day is illogical because the link between the evidence and conclusion is weak.

The familiar saying "My mind is made up; don't confuse me with the facts" is a good example of **premature closure**. The problem of premature closure can be seen in earlier research claims that retirement was a chronological guillotine, since people often die shortly following retirement (McDonald & Wanner, 1990). If social gerontologists had stopped studying retirement, they would not have discovered that certain people self-select for retirement due to prior illness. *Ego involvement* is another way of saying that sometimes we have a vested interest in our views, a serious problem that can cloud our vision. An excellent example is the way some social gerontologists continue to claim that most elder abuse is the result of the unreasonable demands of caregiving. It is somewhat awkward for a social gerontologist to have to report that a family member purposely caused physical harm to an older relative, especially in light of the burgeoning research findings that families are supportive of their older members. It is also easier to blame the abuse on the demands of caregiving than to face the fact that the family member perpetrated a crime and could be reported to the police (McDonald, 2006a).

The Purpose of Social Science Research

Scientific inquiry helps prevent gerontologists from going astray in their attempts to understand the social processes of aging. Social scientists, like all scientists, are committed to explaining observed relationships or patterns of behaviour in the social world of older people. They want to reliably answer questions such as: Why do some older people and not others become depressed? Why do some people go back to work after they retire? Why does the erroneous belief persist that the aging of the Canadian population will bankrupt the health-care system? Why are some older people abused by their families?

Explanatory research helps to answer these why questions and leads to the development and testing of theories that help us understand social behaviour (see Chapter 3). In addition, by identifying and understanding patterns of behaviour like elder abuse, sometimes we can predict who will be abused and design preventive programs accordingly (Singleton & Straits, 2005). The ultimate aim of social gerontologists, then, is to produce valid and reliable knowledge that explains the social processes of aging, knowledge that is less subject to the errors of judgment noted above.

Although explanation is the ultimate goal of the social scientist, exploration and description are considered to be two additional **goals of science**. Social gerontologists may pursue the simple goal of exploration when they know very little about a topic, such as the aging of gay and lesbian adults. There is very little knowledge available about how gay people grow old and whether they face the same issues as everyone else (Donahue & McDonald, 2005; Herdt & de Vries, 2004). In this instance, the researcher would have to first explore whether there were any differences in the aging processes between homosexuals and heterosexuals before testing any theories about the differences. If the researcher wanted to describe gay individuals in Canada, the goal would be different again. The social gerontologist would want to provide a description of gay adults as to how many there are, where they live, how they age and so on, with the aim of obtaining facts, rather than opinions about them in old age. The goals of the social gerontologist, then, are to explore, describe, and ultimately explain the processes of aging. To achieve these aims, social gerontologists follow a number of standardized methods and procedures.

Scientific Guidelines

Social gerontologists adhere to the guidelines for the scientific method and follow a common process of justification (Singleton & Straits, 2005). These guidelines also provide assistance in evaluating the quality of existing research, as reported in the ensuing chapters. While these scientific rules or guidelines are often subject to dispute, they provide a blueprint for collecting data, which minimizes the chances of committing the errors examined above. The three key principles are *empiricism, objectivity,* and *control* (Singleton & Straits, 2005).

Empiricism relies on evidence gathered systematically through observation or experiment and means that research results can be reproduced and verified by other social scientists following the same rules. Empiricism is distinct from explanations involving the supernatural or the doctrine that all values are baseless and that nothing can be known. In short, the type of information based on intuition, unsupported opinions, or "New Age" psychics is not part of science because social scientists limit their questioning to those phenomena for which empirical data can be collected.

Reliability and validity relate to the adequacy of measurement. Reliability means that in repeated observations of the same event, the same data would be collected each time; **validity** refers to how well the measure represents the concept assessed.

Objectivity means that in conducting studies, researchers strive to avoid biases rooted in emotion, conjecture, or intellectual partiality—a goal rarely, if ever, achieved. At best, social scientists take objectivity to mean that a group of scientists can agree on the results of a given observation, until new observations appear to refute the earlier ones. Because of the requirement for objectivity, the logic, method, and analyses of research studies should be reported step by step so that they can be accurately reviewed by peers.

The need for **control**, the third guideline followed by social scientists, assumes that procedures have been used in the research study to eliminate, as much as possible, sources of bias and error that would discredit results. While a researcher may have a favourite explanation of why people 65 years of age and older watch more television than those aged 45 to 64 (Victorino & Gauthier, 2005; Chou, Chow, & Chi, 2004), the same researcher must also consider alternative explanations of the television-viewing patterns of older adults and use procedures to rule out these alternatives. The researcher's preferred hypothesis may be that older people watch more television because they have nothing else to do, but the researcher must first rule out competing reasons, such as the possibility that older people have less income so they avoid more expensive entertainment, such as going to the movies. Almost all procedures and techniques used by social gerontologists are designed to achieve control of alternative factors, which is not an easy task, since people cannot live out their lives in a controlled environment, such as in a laboratory.

The three principles informing scientific activity are generally used in the scientific process that is represented in Figure 4.1. Social scientists follow one of two systems of logic, depending on how theory is employed in the process. As depicted in Figure 4.1, there is a chain of events that social scientists can enter into at any point, depending upon their interest. Arbitrarily, starting at the top of the diagram, theories generate hypotheses or predictions; hypotheses are checked against observations in the world; the observations give rise to generalizations about the data collected; and the generalizations either support, contradict, or indicate the need to modify the theory. In this case, starting with theory, that is,

Figure 4.1 THE SCIENTIFIC PROCESS

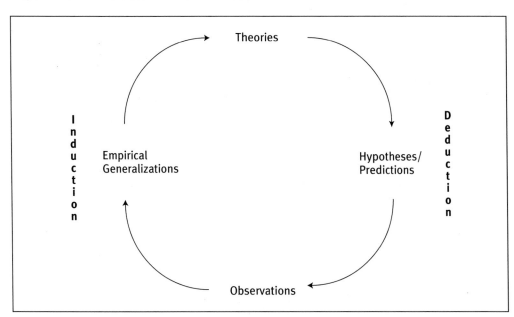

Source: Adapted from Walter Wallace (1975). *The logic of science in sociology.* Chicago: Aldine-Atherton. Used by permission.

going from the general to the particular, is an example of a **deductive approach** to research.

For example, if a social gerontologist employs a political economy perspective to examine the effect of ethnicity on income in old age, he or she might hypothesize that membership in a visible minority group is associated with lower income in old age, where ethnicity is treated as a structural variable that affects people's life chances and resources. The researcher would then interview visible minorities about their income in old age and determine whether the observations reflected the hypothesis. The researcher might find out that only visible minority women have lower incomes in old age and would then adjust the theory to reflect gender differences.

Conversely, the researcher could start with observations, using an inductive approach, which goes from the particular to the general. In the **inductive approach** to research, the gerontologist would first collect data from visible minorities about their aging experiences and, from the data, discover a number of patterns, one being that women from visible minorities have problems with their incomes in old age. This information, which is grounded in the data, could then be used to formulate a theory about aging within a visible minority group. At the outset, the researcher had no firm views on what would be found—the theory emerged from an examination of the data.

Systems of Knowledge

Some of the scientific rules or guidelines we presented above are currently contested in the social sciences, and the debate has spilled over into gerontology (Haldemann & Lévy, 1995). Two aspects of the scientific method that attract considerable debate are ideas about the nature of reality and the quest for objectivity—issues at the heart of the study of knowledge, or what philosophers call **epistemology**. Some scholars argue that there is no reality, and all we can do is examine each individual's subjective reality, while others counter that there is a "real" reality we can know, although not perfectly. Not surprisingly, those who favour a subjective reality usually believe that it is impossible to be objective, while those who believe there is an (imperfectly) knowable reality emphasize the pursuit of objectivity. Rather than enter into the debate, we present the different ways of knowing that are open to social gerontologists in their study of aging. While the epistemological differences might be insurmountable (Guba & Lincoln, 2005), gerontologists do not hesitate to take advantage of the complementary nature of the many methods available to them. Today, there are studies in gerontology that use several methods together, which results in a richer understanding of aging processes (McDonald, Dergal & Cleghorn, 2006; Laub & Sampson, 1998).

The various philosophical views that researchers hold about the nature of reality, objectivity, and how to collect information about social behaviour are sometimes called **paradigms** (Kuhn, 1970) or systems of knowledge. A paradigm or system of knowledge is (as noted in Chapter 3) an organizing tool that helps us understand the world view of a researcher and, thus, has important consequences for the practical conduct of research and our understanding of the research. Systems of knowledge are, of course, not mutually exclusive and frequently overlap. A system of knowledge usually has at least three components: (1) a view of reality (*ontology*); (2) an episte-mology of the nature of the relationship between the researcher and the subject; and (3) a methodology that specifies a way to gain knowledge about the world and how we know what we know is true (Guba & Lincoln, 2005). Research in gerontol-ogy commonly falls within three major paradigms: (1) positivism/postpositivism, (2) interpretive approaches, and (3) critical gerontology (Guba & Lincoln, 2005).

This is not to suggest that these are the only knowledge systems available to social gerontologists. Knowledge production is continually evolving, to the extent that there are almost always newer systems of thought hovering on the horizon. Arguments have been mounted for an ethnic or race paradigm that would look to a different epistemological framework to describe the experiences and knowl-edge systems of people outside the dominant paradigms mentioned in this chap-ter. Beginning work draws on oral history and critical race theory to unmask racism (Stanfield, 1994; Ladson-Billings & Donnor 2005). A feminist paradigm that starts with the standpoint of women's experiences and knowledge has also been examined by a number of scholars (Harding, 2004; Olesen, 2005) and has been used in gerontology by a number of researchers (Calasanti & Slevin, 2001; Ginn, Street, & Arber, 2001; Aronson, Denton & Zeytinoglu, 2004; McDaniel, 2004). Postmodernism (Katz, 1996; Powell, 2006) as Pauline Rosenau (1992) declares, haunts all systems of knowledge, calling into question the very foun-dation and core of the social sciences and posing challenges to every paradigm.

Positivist Approaches

Positivism in the social sciences represents an attempt to transfer the principles of the physical sciences directly to human behaviour, but over time and use, the principles have become more accommodating of human behaviour. Today, a num-ber of social scientists practise a more flexible form of positivism called **postp-ositivism**. This group of scientists tends to subscribe to the scientific principles noted above, although in a more flexible manner. They subscribe to the views that reality can be known, although not completely, that the aim of observation is to be objective but is never perfectly achieved, and that the methods used to study aging are mainly quantitative, as seen in Table 4.1. Quantitative methods rely more on the production of numerical data, which is presented in the form of gen-eralizable statistical findings. A simple measure of the health of older people—a rating scale ranging from excellent through very good, good, fair, to poor—has been found to be remarkably accurate (Menec & Chipperfield, 2001). When we state that 39.5 percent of Canadians 65 years of age and over rate their health as very good or excellent (Statistics Canada, 2006c), we are providing a reliable statistical snap-shot of the health of Canadians over age 65.

Table 4.1 COMPONENTS OF A PARADIGM

Components of a paradigm

Ontology	**Nature and form of reality**
• Postpositivism	• Real reality imperfectly known
• Interpretive/constructivist	• Reality socially constructed
• Critical theory	• Historical reality
Epistemology	**Relationship between the knower and known**
• Postpositivism	• Reality is independent of the knower
• Interpretive/constructivist	• Reality is dependent of the knower
• Critical theory	• Reality is transactional between knower and known
Methodology	**How do we gain knowledge?**
• Postpositivism	• Cross-sectional and longitudinal surveys, secondary analysis, experimental, quasi-experimental designs
• Interpretive/constructivist	• Biographies, phenomenology, grounded theory, ethnography
• Critical theory	• Social action research

While postpositivist gerontologists strive to be objective, they recognize that their studies are inevitably value laden. Their approach to theory is usually on the deductive side of the scientific coin (testing theory), although their research can also be inductive, especially if their goal is to explore a new topic. The studies within the postpositivist tradition favour three main types of research designs: (1) the social survey, (2) secondary data analysis, and (3) experimental and quasi-experimental designs.

Postpositivists also have a way of deciding if their research findings can be classified as knowledge. Social gerontologists working within this system of knowledge judge their information to be knowledge if the research results are valid and reliable, that is, the measurements are not open to error. Validity refers to how well our measure represents what we want to measure and not some other concept. There are a number of ways positivists think about validity, such as *content* or *face validity*, *criterion validity* and *construct validity*. In **content validity**, the researcher tries to ensure that the items making up the measure fully represent the measure. In **criterion validity**, the researcher will determine how similar the new measure is to one that is already known to measure the concept. One form of **construct validity** insures that the measure does not correlate with measures of opposing qualities. For example if anxiety is positively associated with life satisfaction, that might signal a problem to the researcher, because the two constructs are generally understood to be incompatible.

The Social Survey Surveys are probably the most widely used method within the postpositivist paradigm. A survey is best used when social gerontologists want to study a population that is too large to examine directly (Fowler, 2001).

This method basically uses a set of standardized questions contained in a questionnaire that can be administered by face-to-face conversations, telephone, mail, e-mail, or fax to older persons, agency personnel, policy makers, and so on. Surveys can be used for explanatory, descriptive, and exploratory purposes. **Cross-sectional surveys** can provide a freeze-frame of a population at one point in time; **longitudinal surveys** can interview people at several points in time. Surveys can be used in applied ways, such as determining whether older people's needs are being met in a specific community, or whether a meals-on-wheels program successfully provides meals for house-bound rural seniors. While surveys can be small and local, as in the cross-sectional survey of 1406 community-dwelling seniors in Manitoba (Chipperfield & Segall, 1996), they can also be large and national, such as the cross-sectional General Social Survey (GSS). Aging and Social Support, Cycle 16 of the GSS, carried out in 2002, collected data over an 11-month period from February to December 2002 from a list of individuals 45 years of age and older. The representative sample had approximately 25 000 respondents. The data from surveys can also be used over and over again for different research purposes by other gerontologists who did not participate in the original design of the study or the collection of data (**secondary data analysis**).

Most researchers who work within the postpositivist framework would agree that random samples are more useful than non-random samples. A random sample ensures that each person in the population of interest has an equal chance of being chosen for a study. As a procedure, random sampling is more likely to represent the heterogeneity of older people in the Canadian population, an important issue because research has shown repeatedly that there is increasing variability with advancing age (Dannefer, 1988).

Early research studies in Canada were sometimes not randomly selected and were, therefore, unrepresentative of the older people in the larger population. For example, the pioneer longitudinal study, the Ontario Longitudinal Study of Aging carried out between 1959 and 1978, was not a random sample and dealt only with the work and retirement of men. Although very important in the history of Canadian research because it was the first major longitudinal study, it completely overlooked the circumstances of women, as well as those of people from diverse ethnic groups. The social gerontologists using this study can only draw conclusions about the men in the sample because the sample was not randomly drawn, so there is no certainty that the findings apply to the Ontarian or Canadian population as a whole.

A related issue facing gerontological researchers has to do with statistically rare populations, which means certain small subgroups in the population. When social gerontologists attempt to locate people from rare groups, such as the oldest old (85+), physically abused seniors, or Chinese immigrant caregivers, these hard-to-reach populations require the use of special sampling techniques. Sometimes, researchers will oversample a certain group, such as First Nations older people, in order to have enough respondents to do a suitable statistical analysis.

While surveys are usually done relatively quickly and can be cost-effective, a few issues have to be considered (Hofer, Sliwinski, & Flaherty, 2002). Research has found that older people tend to have a higher non-response rate than younger people, especially in telephone interviews; the interviewer appears to have an influence on the older respondents' answers to questions; and older people seem to give more "don't know" responses (Herzog & Kulka, 1989). Specific effort must be made to try to counter each of these tendencies (through the training of interviewers, call backs, and so on).

Secondary Data Analysis Secondary data analysis, or secondary analysis, refers to the study of existing data initially collected for another purpose (Liang & Lawrence, 1989; Black, 1995; Lewis-Beck, Bryman & Liao, 2004; Bourque, Pushkar, Bonneville, & Beland, 2005). For example, a researcher interested in the relationship between the average number of hours women spend in caregiving and women's physical health might use a national data file, such as the General Social Survey, to analyze this relationship. The General Social Survey developed as a yearly survey to track social trends and provide immediate information on policy issues in Canada. Most university libraries in Canada house the public-use version of this data file, which means all identifying information has been removed from the file. That is, no individual who participated in the survey can be identified; everyone is anonymous.

Secondary data analysis uses data from many sources besides surveys, such as archival data (Vital Statistics), administrative files based on data from the records of organizations, such as social agencies or hospitals, and census data sets (Black, 1995). Secondary analysis can be used for any of the three purposes of research and is attractive because the analysis is inexpensive, requires few people, and takes less time. Secondary analysis is particularly useful for comparative studies that examine differences in aging processes across cultures or societies.

There is little doubt that secondary analysis has made an enormous contribution to gerontology in Canada. The Aging in Manitoba Study (AIM) is an excellent example. Over a 30-year period, the AIM data has been analyzed by at least 60 researchers. The contributions include more than 20 student theses and dissertations, 300 journal articles, book chapters, and conference presentations; and the study has been cited more than 2000 times in mainstream journal articles (Havens, 2001). The value of secondary analysis has been further emphasized by the Canadian government's recent Data Liberation Initiative, which, in partnership with Canadian universities, has made large national survey sample data files more easily accessible to Canadian researchers and their students. Most recently, Research Data Centres (RDCs) devoted to secondary analysis have been established at a number Canadian universities across Canada. The goal of the RDCs, managed by a partnership between Canadian universities and Statistics Canada, is to help strengthen the country's research capacity in social research and to support the policy research community by using existing data files.

Secondary data analysis, like all research methods, presents challenges to researchers. Although this methodology gives researchers access to large national, often longitudinal random samples, these surveys frequently leave out variables that the researcher might be interested in studying (Kasl, 1995). For example, a survey of interest may not measure mental health or stress levels, or it may not measure the concepts in a way that is consistent with the researcher's own theoretical perspective. If a social gerontologist is interested in a subjective measure of caregiver burden and the data file of interest offers only number of hours of caregiving per week, the researcher will have to abandon that particular data file or work around this shortcoming. A researcher may want to link separate data files such as tax files and the Survey of Labour and Income Dynamics, a Canadian longitudinal study of income. An example is a study by Trammer, Croxford and Coyte (2003), which links administrative data bases to determine the incremental use of health services by older adults with dementia. In brief, the challenge to the researcher using secondary data files is to work with the information available (Black, 1995).

Experimental and Quasi-experimental Designs   The classic experimental design is undoubtedly the gold standard for the postpositivist paradigm, mainly because it comes closest to meeting the three criteria required for causation: temporal ordering (in which the intervention clearly comes before the outcome), covariation (in which the intervention and outcome change together), and, the control of extraneous factors. In the classical experimental design, the aim is to determine whether an intervention (e.g., attendance at a senior centre) has an effect (e.g., reducing loneliness). Experiments require random assignment to the group that will receive the intervention, called the experimental group, and to the group that does not receive the intervention, called the control group. Random assignment means that each person is equally likely to be in either group; thus, the control group represents what the experimental group would have been like if it had not received the intervention. An intervention is introduced to the experimental group but not the control group, and if there is a difference between the two groups after the intervention, then the intervention is deemed to have had an effect (Singleton & Straits, 2005; Rubin & Babbie, 2005).

For example, researchers hypothesized that a family intervention program comprising caregiver education, stress management, and the development of coping skills, would reduce the burden of care in caregivers of Alzheimer's disease patients. Caregivers were randomly assigned to one of three groups: the family intervention or experimental group; a control group that was not given treatment but was simply interviewed in lieu of the intervention; and a control group that received no interview and no family intervention. The effectiveness of the family intervention was assessed by tests for measures of psychological distress and depression before and after the family intervention or interview, and at the same points of time for the second control group (Marriott, Donaldson, Tarrier, & Burns, 2000). At the end of the experiment, there were significant reductions in stress and depression in the family intervention group, compared with the two control groups. In contrast, a randomized control trial that evaluated an early psychiatric intervention for patients with psychological and behaviour problems living in residential care did not change 12-month health outcomes (Kotynia-English, McGowan, & Almeida, 2005).

Experimental designs with random assignment are often difficult to achieve. Sometimes, a design is not ethically feasible because it would mean delaying or denying service. Withholding help from a physically abused and confused older person is out of the question. There is also the problem of *intervention fidelity*, where the researcher is not sure that the intervention (e.g., counselling) was delivered to the experimental group exactly as intended. For example, if three therapists provide therapy to subjects in the experimental group, some therapists may have better skills or better judgment than others. Thus, each older person in the experimental group might receive a slightly different version of the counselling, and one would not be measuring the same intervention. Client recruitment and retention is also a serious problem, since the researcher often has to wait for referrals to a program and people sometimes drop out of a study if they find out they are in the control group. In addition, it is unlikely that we could ever control all the factors in the environment that would influence the aging process.

Given some of these problems, researchers often turn to quasi-experimental designs, which do not use random assignment and may not even have a control group. They do, however, have some of the characteristics of classical designs. For example, an experimental group receives an intervention but, instead of a control group, the study uses a comparison group that is not randomly assigned and, therefore, probably is not equivalent to the experimental group. To reduce such differences, researchers may use matching in selecting the control group. In a study of the effect of training professionals to train their colleagues to detect substance abuse by older clients, an experimental group was given a training program, and a comparison group of professionals who were matched with the experimental group on several factors (years of experience and level of education) was not trained (Peressini & McDonald, 1998). Although the program apparently improved the knowledge of the experimental group, the researchers could not rule out alternative explanations; even though the professionals were matched on important factors, the lack of random assignment means that the groups may still have differed.

As can be seen, postpositivists tend to use highly structured research methods that are informed by gerontological theories. Their goal is to understand social reality, which they believe can be known to some degree. Postpositivists usually treat their results as tentative and expect them to be tested in the future, according to set procedures. For these gerontologists, research is an unending and self-correcting process that strives to be as free as possible from political, ideological, and personal influences, against which the scientific method is a safeguard.

Interpretive Approaches

A research paradigm that contrasts with postpositivism is the **interpretive/ constructivism** approach to knowledge generation (Guba & Lincoln 2005). Social gerontologists who work within this paradigm or system of knowledge hold the view that you cannot adequately understand people by depending on objective measurements. They do not encourage research participants to be separate and apart from the researcher in an attempt to be objective. The researcher hopes to establish meaningful relationships with participants because the researcher wants to investigate the deeper meanings of the persons' experiences. While a post-positivist is interested, for example, in how, on average, older people rate their health on a standardized scale, an interpretive researcher is more interested in exploring the meaning of health to older people and the place of health within the context of their whole life.

Interpretive/constructivist researchers do not believe that objective reality—even if it exists—can be known (see Table 4.1). Rather, they believe that people interpret and construct their social world and that there are multiple realities that are equally viable. The relationship between the researcher and the older person as the subject is not objective but subjective and transactional. The older person is seen as an active participant in the research process, and an attempt is made to capture the person's life in a holistic manner. While theory is definitely important to interpretive researchers, they are less inclined to test theory than to generate theory from their data (the inductive approach; see Figure 4.1) at a mid-range level (see Chapter 3). The methodologies employed by interpretive researchers fall within the broader category of qualitative research, which explores the meanings of specific human experiences and generates "thick" descriptions of these experiences. Rather than statistics, the foundation of this approach is people's words, meanings, and conceptualizations.

Scholars within this research tradition have an embarrassment of riches when it comes to selecting a specific methodology—biographies, phenomenological approaches, grounded theory, case studies, and ethnographies, to name but a few (Denzin & Lincoln, 2005; Creswell, 1998). In addition, each of these broad traditions contains a multitude of data collection practices. The mainstays of the qualitative approach are in-depth interviews with subjects and/or with key informants (people in the know) and participant observation. In-depth interviews with older people may be spread over a number of interviews, depending on the purpose of the study and the amount of information to be collected. Participant observation requires the researcher to engage in prolonged participation as a member in a group, a community, an agency, and so on. The degree of membership varies from being a member of the group in the declared role of researcher to participating as a complete member of the group without revealing one's identity as a researcher. Content analysis is another technique sometimes used that covers a variety of ways to analyze any documents: formal records like medical files or agency files, newspaper editorials, advertisements, television shows, movies, and videotapes.

While qualitative methods vary somewhat, the underlying assumption is that a researcher can obtain a complex understanding of older persons and their worlds from ordinary observations and conversations (Gubrium & Holstein, 2000, 2003; Sankar & Gubrium, 1994). Standards for accepting or "warranting" knowledge are shifting in the direction of ethical considerations but were originally anchored in *credibility* (equivalent to validity) and *dependability* (equivalent to reliability) of the data. Credibility required such actions as prolonged engagement, triangulation (using more than one source of data), peer debriefing, and member checks, in which research participants evaluate the accuracy of the research (Erlandson et. al., 1993). Dependability meant creating an audit of the researchers' actions and maintaining a reflexive journal of the thoughts of the researcher. More recently, interpretive/constructivists have moved in the direction of postmodernism and tend to do away with research criteria. These scholars now depend more on moral issues that involve authenticity criteria (Guba & Lincoln, 2005:207).

Here, we look at the four most qualitative methods most commonly used to study older people.

Biographies　**Biography** covers a broad genre of approaches that provide methodological tools for studying aging and everyday life (Gubrium & Holstein, 2003; Wallace, 1994). Biographies include biographical studies, wherein the life story of a person is written by someone else; autobiographies, wherein people write their own life story; life histories, which report on an individual's life and how it reflects the cultural themes of society; and oral histories, which are used to collect people's experiences of significant historical events.

While they agree that biographies, in general, portray the meaning of being and growing old, scholars do not agree on the epistemological stance to be adopted by the biographer (Tierney, 2000). Some researchers use biographies to reveal the objective facts in a person's life; others seek subjective interpretations of a life narrative; and still others emphasize that the life course is a social construction made up in the interaction between the researcher and the subject (Gubrium & Holstein, 2003). Kemp (2005) carried out a life history study of relationships between grandparents and adult grandchildren. She asked both generations to recount the history of each relationship from their earliest possible recollections to their views of their present-day relationship. The study captured many of the positive dimensions of these relationships. One important finding was that the relationships grew more meaningful over time as both groups moved through the life course and experienced different life events.

The task of the biographer, then, is three-fold: (1) to have the time to collect information over a lifetime; (2) to learn about history; and (3) to focus on the ordinary, instead of the extraordinary, the marginal, or the deviant (Cresswell, 1998).

Phenomenology　As with everything else in the interpretive paradigm, there are a number of different schools of **phenomenology** to choose from: the descriptive school, which attempts to describe the essence of an experience; the interpretive school, which looks for the systematic interpretation of meanings of experiences, and the Dutch school, which combines the two preceding approaches (Moustakas, 1994; Creswell, 1998). Central to this approach, however, is the attempt to capture the fundamental, lived experience of an individual in reference to a specific concept or phenomenon.

An excellent example of phenomenological research is a three-year study by Porter, Ganong, Drew, and Lanes (2004) on the perspectives of women aged 80 to 94 about the characteristics of their homecare providers. Based on the women's views, they developed a new typology of providers that cut across the usual dichotomy of paid and unpaid caregiving to focus on type of care offered. In a study of widows, researchers explored how women interpreted their financial situation in widowhood and how they constructed their poverty to be normative (McDonald, Donahue, & Moore, 2000a). The phenomenological approach is challenging because it requires researchers to hold their own personal experiences in abeyance and set aside their own preconceptions of the phenomena under study. It is often difficult for us to set aside our own views and approach a study with a completely open mind (Moustakas, 1994).

Grounded Theory   While phenomenology emphasizes the meaning of experience, the intent of **grounded theory** is to discover theory or add to theory already developed. This methodology was first developed by sociologists Glaser and Stauss (1967), who argued that theories should be grounded in the data. Today, there are several strands of grounded theory, but overall, it is a very specific, highly developed set of procedures for generating a middle-range social theory. As the researcher collects data, insights and questions are generated and are pursued through further data collection. As concepts emerge from the data, the researcher engages in theoretical sampling of related events and activities, until no new information about the concepts emerges (Schwandt, 2001). In a Canadian study by Guruge and colleagues (2005), a grounded-theory approach was used to study staff-family relationships in continuing care from the perspective of staff. The data revealed three aspects of the unit manager's relationships with family members: establishing supportive entry for families into the management of the unit; building and preserving relationships, and dealing with the unmet needs of patients ("closing the loop."). In a study of dementia in African Americans, researchers used grounded theory techniques to uncover cultural and linguistic variations in the definition, recognition, explanation of, and response to, dementia and developed a preliminary model that described dementia in American African communities (Jett, 2006).

Even though grounded theory served at the front of the qualitative revolution, which helped make qualitative methods acceptable to gerontologists and other social scientists, it has been critiqued mainly by postmodernists as having an underlying positivist theme (Charmaz, 2000). Glaser's approach comes closest to traditional postpositivism with its assumptions of an objective external reality, a neutral observer who discovers data, and an unbiased reading of the data. Like other qualitative methods, though, it has made an important contribution to understanding the empirical worlds of aging persons by giving them voice and representing their reality as accurately as possible.

Ethnography **Ethnography** usually involves the description and interpretation of a social group or a culture and is both a process and an outcome. Ethnographers are ". . . outsiders wearing insider's clothes, while gradually acquiring the language and behaviours that go along with them" (Tedlock, 2000). The product of their efforts is usually an understanding of the intermingling perceptions of people and their patterns of behaviour, customs, and way of life. Ethnography, with its roots in anthropology, has been extended beyond sociology and is now used as a methodology in cultural studies, women's studies, folklore, literary theory, and performance art. At the heart of ethnography is the assumption that by entering into a close and prolonged relationship with people in their everyday lives, ethnographers can begin to understand better the behaviours of their subjects (Hammersley, 1992). Participant observation is one of the main ways that data are collected.

An eight-month study of the process of discharge decision making for older patients in a large acute-care hospital in Toronto uncovered a number of interesting processes (Wells, 1997). Over the eight months, the study collected data through participant observation, interviews, and content analysis of hospital charts. One of the more important findings was that the process of discharge related less to clinical outcomes than to factors such as the patient's social situation and pressure on the hospital to reduce prolonged stays. Health-care professionals in the hospital consistently held lower expectations for the patients than did the patients themselves. By the end of the study, the patients' perceptions turned out to be more accurate (Wells, 1997)! The results of this study had serious ramifications for the care of older people in hospitals. As this study illustrates, the challenge to the ethnographer is to have the time for prolonged observation.

Critical Approaches

The last paradigm we consider is the **critical paradigm**, which builds on an array of intellectual traditions, including those of Karl Marx and Max Weber, the writings of scholars from Frankfurt, Germany, in the 1930s, and, most recently, Jurgen Habermas (Estes, Linkins, & Binney, 2001). In Chapter 3, we noted that critical theory is not a neat theoretical package. Here, we view it as an overarching paradigm that includes a number of different strands of theory. Critical gerontology provides an approach to social gerontology ". . . that provokes and challenges assumptions, and that is grounded in a commitment, not just to understand the social construction of aging, but to change it" (Minkler, 1999). The distinguishing features of this perspective are a focus on the oppression of vulnerable people and a desire to effect change through a mutual process of research (Rubin & Babbie, 2005). Critical theory cuts a wide swath to cover feminism, empowerment practices, race and ethnic studies, and, at its outer boundaries, postmodernism (Katz, 2005; Biggs, Lowenstein, & Hendricks, 2003; Kincheloe & McLaren, 2005). When critical theorists make claims to be scientific, they attempt to offer rigorous explanations for the causes of oppression, such as economic dependence or ideological beliefs. These beliefs, in turn, are verified by empirical evidence and are framed by available economic and social theories in the process. Their explanations are also normative and critical, since they imply negative evaluations of current social structures.

The overall aim of the research process is to foster people's awareness of their oppression and to encourage social–political action. This paradigm generally subscribes to the view that reality is shaped by social, political, cultural, class, and gender divisions. Researchers in this tradition are not disinterested social scientists but, rather, share a transformative relationship with the research subjects in the research process. The type of research associated with this system of knowledge has been variously labelled social action research, participatory action research, critical ethnography, and participatory ethnography. In essence, the researcher discovers the meanings of situations to the participants (e.g., what it is like to be financially abused) and helps link these experiences to oppressive social, political, and economic structures (e.g., carelessness of banks) so that action can be taken by the participants (e.g., meeting with bank representatives to establish a monitoring system to protect older people's bank accounts).

Although there are a number of different versions of the method used, the differences are mainly about the degree to which the subjects participate in and control the research process and the extent of the social action. Many types of data collection techniques are used, including focus groups, surveys and in-depth interviews. The criteria for claiming that knowledge has been created is whether the research participants experience some form of emancipation; this is sometimes called "catalytic validity," meaning that the research is validated through meaningful action.

Improving the Quality of Life of Canadian Seniors is a national example of action research (Raphael, Brown, & Wheeler, 2000; www.utoronto.ca/seniors/). The goal of the project was to collect information about the factors affecting the quality of life of seniors in eight cities across Canada (Halifax, Quebec City, Montreal, Ottawa, Toronto, Regina, Whitehorse, and Vancouver). Seniors in each of the cities directed the activities of the projects and were supported by a local coordinator and a university researcher. For example, in Toronto, the research was directed by a Seniors Coordinating Committee, which used the knowledge and skills of seniors to explore and act upon government policy decisions that influenced the quality of their lives. The seniors wanted to know what government policies were affecting seniors, how these policies influenced their quality of life, what factors led governments to make the decisions they made, and what action could be taken to improve the quality of seniors' lives. In Toronto, 16 focus groups explored nine key policy areas from housing to belonging to a different ethnic community. The conclusion was that all three levels of government do not listen well to seniors' voices. With their results in hand, the seniors are designing action plans to address the issues that were raised in the research (Raphael, Brown, & Wheeler, 2000; www.utoronto.ca/seniors/).

Although we have not provided a review of all the research methodologies open to social gerontologists, it should be fairly obvious that there is a profusion of methods from which to choose. How one picks a method and/or combination of methods is guided by the research process. Normally, researchers are guided by the research questions they wish to answer (Chappell, 1995) and by their theoretical interests. A researcher interested in how older people feel about widowhood is more likely to choose a qualitative approach; one who wants to determine the average income of Canadian widows would use a quantitative approach. Another researcher wanting to know how older people feel about their incomes in old age might combine both approaches and use a theoretical framework that accommodates both methods, perhaps, the life course perspective. A feminist researcher may prefer a standpoint that sees the world from the point of view of a woman, while a political economist would prefer critical theory. We need as many methodological options as possible to address questions about aging processes. The complexity of the flow of cohorts through the age structure of society and through time demands nothing less (Riley, 1998).

The Challenges in Studying Aging

Although there are many different ways to approach the study of aging and a multitude of opportunities for methodological pluralism, several issues unique to aging challenge the social gerontologist. In this section, we consider the dilemma of age, period, and cohort effects, the main concerns in collecting data from older people, and special ethical considerations.

The Quandary of Age, Period, and Cohort Effects

An awareness of old age as a life-long journey embedded in a changing social context poses fundamental methodological issues for social gerontologists (Riley, 1998). If a researcher finds in a cross-sectional survey conducted in the 1990s that the frequency of computer use is lower in older age groups than in younger age groups, what would be the reason for the difference? The cross-sectional survey, a freeze-frame of behaviour at one point in time, tells us there are differences between age groups but cannot tell us why. Could the difference be a result of the aging process? Is it because this cohort did not have computers in their youth? Or is it because retired people do not have as much access to computers as people who go to school, work, or university? In our example, there is the possibility that three factors have influenced the changes between the age groups over time: aging, period, and cohort effects.

That older people do not use computer technology as much as younger persons do may be a result of growing old—an **age effect**. Perhaps, as people grow older, they find that they have less ability to manoeuvre a mouse and, therefore, do not use computers as much (Charness, Holly, Fedden, & Jastrezembski, 2004). There is also the possibility that the differences between the age groups might be due to a **cohort effect**. (Recall from Chapter 3 that a **cohort** is a group of individuals born around the same time, who often share a common history and social, economic, and cultural influences.) Older people today did not grow up in the company of computers and do not feel as comfortable around them as do younger cohorts. For example, the baby-boom echo, born between 1980 and 1995, have grown up with computer technology, whereas those born between 1940 and 1946 grew up with television. Those born between 1915 and 1919 grew up with radio.

Another explanation for the differences among the age groups could be the fact that the majority of older Canadians are not in the workforce and live on limited incomes. A major event that had a far-reaching effect on the Canadian economy during the study was the recession of the early 1990s. Older individuals with their restricted incomes saw the yields on their savings precipitously reduced (McDonald, Donahue, & Moore, 2000a). They may have wanted a computer, but the recession created so much economic uncertainty that they did not spend their money on what they probably saw as a luxury. The recession in the early 1990s in Canada had a significant effect on *all* Canadians and is called a **period effect**. Period effects are any historical or major event that occurs at the same time the researcher is measuring some aspect of the aging process. Common examples of period effects offered by researchers are world wars and depressions, because they have a profound influence on all age groups. However, more ordinary events, such as technological innovations (e-mail, for example), can also affect people in vital ways. Finally, there is the possibility that the differences in the use of computers may be a result of the combination of aging, period, and cohort effects.

The problem social gerontologists face is disentangling age, period, and cohort effects. In the early days of gerontological research, investigators made the mistake of interpreting cross-sectional age differences as if they referred to the process of aging. This type of mistake has been referred to as the **life course fallacy** (Riley, 1998). For example, in their examination of intelligence and aging, researchers found that younger age groups scored higher on intelligence tests than did older age groups. Many concluded that intelligence declined with age, but they were confusing age-related development and cohort effects (Schaie & Hofer, 2001). It was later found that older age groups had lower levels of education than younger age groups, which accounted for the difference, rather than age-related changes in intelligence (Albert et al., 1995). Fortunately, there are a number of designs researchers can use to circumvent this type of mistake.

Research Designs Specific to the Study of Aging

Longitudinal designs can help determine the ". . . impact of age versus cohort versus time or period. . . " in samples of aging people (Havens, 1995). This type of design allows researchers to directly observe changes in individuals and groups as they age and the consequences of these changes. Interviewing older people every year prior to retirement and every year after retirement has helped researchers understand the reasons for and the nature of the transition. Data collected from a cross-sectional survey could never truly capture what factors lead to changes in the work status of older people (see Chapter 13). These designs are typically very expensive and time consuming. However, in the last decade there has been increased recognition that longitudinal methods can be used over shorter time intervals and that existing data sets can be turned into longitudinal data by adding another round of data collection (Schaie & Hofer, 2001).

Panel Designs The most often used type of longitudinal study is the panel study, in which the same individuals in a sample are repeatedly surveyed about various aspects of their lives. In the United States, some studies span decades (such as the Baltimore Longitudinal Study of Aging, which started in 1958 and is still in progress). Depending on the study, people might be surveyed every year or every 10 years. The very first longitudinal study of aging in Canada mentioned above, the Ontario Longitudinal Study of Aging, started in 1959 and had annual follow-up for 20 years (Black, 1995; Havens, 1995). The National Population Health Survey, which started in 1994, interviews the same panel of Canadians every two years about their physical, mental, and social health. One of the explicit aims of the study is to examine the ". . . changes that people experience as they grow older." The federal government has made a commitment to fund this study for 12 years. Another longitudinal panel study in Canada is the Survey of Labour and Income Dynamics (SLID), which is the first national data file to collect data on the fluctuations in income that a typical family or individual experiences through time. The SLID, started in 1993, follows the same respondents for six years, and uses a split-interview format (people are interviewed twice a year, with different questions at each interview) so that each panel is interviewed 13 times over a spread of six years.

The Canadian Study of Health and Aging, started in 1991, followed 10 263 elderly people, using 18 study centres across Canada. The initial purpose of the study was to examine the prevalence of dementia and its subtypes by age and gender. This study was administered in two languages, and over 70 investigators were involved (Raina et al., 2004). Most recently, the Institute for Aging, one of the Canadian Institutes for Health Research, is deliberating on the establishment of the Canadian Longitudinal Study on Aging. The goal of this study of 50 000 Canadians followed for 20 years will be to examine the molecular, genetic, and cellular aspects of aging, together with the psychological and social aspects of aging—certainly an innovation in the history of Canadian gerontology (Havens, 2001).

Simple longitudinal designs, although more powerful than cross-sectional surveys, have their limitations. Sometimes, the duration of the study is too short to capture period effects, and unless there is more than one birth cohort sampled, the study can suffer from cohort-centrism. For example, the Survey of Labour and Income Dynamics is timely because it captures up-to-date changes made to the Canada/Quebec Pension Plan in the late 1990s and researchers can gauge the effects of this policy change (period effect) on retirement incomes. Riley (1987; 1998) warns against the fallacy of **cohort-centrism**, which erroneously assumes that members of all cohorts will grow older in the same way as members of one's own cohort. We should expect that research findings will change quite substantially as cohorts with differing experiences move in and out of the older population (due to death). The early baby-boomers (born between 1947 and 1959) are probably more likely to listen to the Led Zeppelin in their old age than current cohorts.

Cohort Designs An exceptionally useful longitudinal design, *cohort analysis*, allows researchers to study cross-sectional age-related differences, to observe age-related changes in a cohort over time, and to compare cohorts of the same age at different historical periods. Moreover, cohort analysis allows the researcher to study change across the life course. These designs, usually referred to as cohort sequential designs, follow more than one cohort longitudinally. The Aging in Manitoba study (AIM), started in 1971 (Havens 1997; 2001), conducted three independent cross-sectional studies of older Manitobans in 1971, 1976, and 1983. All three groups were then followed over time. The 1971 and 1976 groups were re-interviewed in 1983 to 1984, 1990, 1996, and 2001, and the 1983 group was re-interviewed in 1990, 1996, and 2001. Currently, AIM is the largest continuous population-based longitudinal study of aging in Canada. Figure 4.2 illustrates the design of this study.

Researchers using the AIM study can examine different age groups in any given year—they can compare the health of those aged 60 to 65 years with those 66 to 70 years of age from the cross-sectional survey in 1983–1984. They can also examine the same individuals aged 65 to 70 years at a minimum of three different time points, from 1971 to 1983 to 1990, to examine age changes within their cohort. Period effects can also be discerned by making comparisons of those who are the same age (e.g., 70 years) in 1971, in 1983–1984, and in 1990. Finally, researchers can assess patterns across the life course from one cohort to the other. While health may have deteriorated rapidly across the life course (three time points) for the 1971 panel, the 1976 panel did not show as rapid a decline over three time points. Figure 4.3 illustrates how a cohort sequential design can function. Figure 4.3 uses hypothetical data to show the various possible comparisons.

Figure 4.2 **DESIGN OF THE AGING IN MANITOBA STUDY (AIM)**

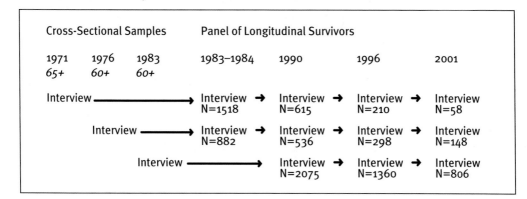

Source: Adapted from J.G. Chipperfield, B. Havens, & W. Doig (1997). Method and description of the Aging in Manitoba project: A 20-year longitudinal study. *Canadian Journal on Aging*, 16(1):612. Used with permission.

Figure 4.3 A HYPOTHETICAL COHORT SEQUENTIAL DESIGN

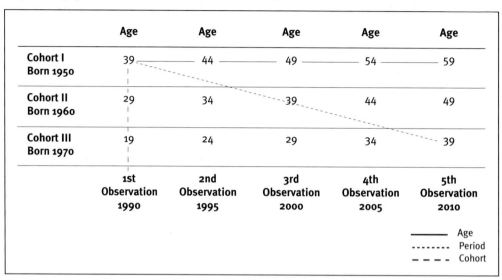

Source: Adapted from Morgan and Kunkel, *Aging: the social context*, P.18, copyright 2001 by Pine Forge Press. Reprinted by permission of Sage Publications.

Event History Analysis Another tool that is useful to social gerontologists is the **event history design** (Hirdes & Brown, 1994). Gerontologists often want to know when a particular life event will happen. For example, the bulk of the research on retirement has attempted to predict the age of retirement from paid employment, an issue that has serious ramifications for the costs of some government pensions. If people work longer they will spend less time in retirement, which can ultimately be cheaper for government. Event history analysis examines when and how particular events happen and their causes for individuals or groups (Alwin & Campbell, 2001). Using longitudinal data, the technique identifies how much time passes before an event occurs, the rates of occurrence of the event, and how the rates may change over time. In the last decade, in Canada, more and more workers who retire are actually returning to work. An event history analysis of a longitudinal data base, such as the SLID, would tell us how many years retirees spend in retirement before they go back to work, why they go back, what the national rates are for the reversal in any given year, and how the rates have increased or decreased over time. For example, event history analysis of data from the Longitudinal Study of Aging Danish Twins (764 identical and 1383 fraternal twins) showed that life is extended if there are strong social ties with a co-twin (Rasulo, Christensen & Tomassini, 2005).

Life Review Longitudinal designs may also include the use of diaries, letters, life stories, memoirs, biographies, and other kinds of data obtained by asking people to comment on the past (Alwin & Campbell, 2001). There are a number of interesting observations about life reviews found in the works of literary gerontologists about how culture invariably defines aging as a serious time of decline, even though other "positive stories" are available (Hepworth, 2005). These retrospective studies compare events and periods within the life of a single individual, focusing on time-marked events, relationships in the family, work, and community in a historical, cultural context. The *life* in the life review is the observant person moving through the changes encountered across the life course (Clausen, 1998). These studies help provide contextual realism, although they cannot be considered statistical designs (Alwin & Campbell, 2001). They are *retrospective*, since people are looking back over their lives, unlike panel studies, which are *prospective* because they measure attributes of individuals at regular intervals as they move forward in life. Sometimes these two features are combined when panel members are asked to fill in past history about jobs, family, and health, so there is often an interface between qualitative and quantitative approaches.

Related Methodological Issues

Although longitudinal designs are the strongest for studying age-related changes, they still have difficulties. Attrition from a longitudinal study can occur due to death, illness, and relocating, or because people no longer wish to participate in the study. For example, by the first follow-up in 1983–1984 of the AIM study, 58.6 percent of those respondents interviewed in 1971 or 1976 had died (Chipperfield, Havens, & Doig, 1997). There is also the problem of maintaining gender ratios representative of the population because of the difference in mortality rates between men and women in later life. For all designs, there are also measurement problems where a measure used at an earlier time is culturally unsuitable in later years or where it is difficult to determine the intervals between measurement.

A related issue is the need to construct culturally sensitive instruments when some of the respondents do not speak either of the two official Canadian languages. **Back translating** of questionnaires or linguistic equivalence means translating from English to the target language and back to English to see if they are similar. There is also the need for *measurement equivalence*, meaning that a measure developed in one culture will have the same value and meaning in another. A related idea is *metric equivalence*, which means that scores on a measure are comparable across cultures (Rubin & Babbie, 2005). Meeting these standards helps, as does using bilingual interviewers, but is not foolproof. Some concepts simply are not the same across cultures (Biribili, 2000).

The main problems with retrospective life reviews are fairly obvious because they are essentially cross-sectional. There is the problem of differential survival of the respondents. By definition, it is the life histories of survivors, who might have different histories than those who did not survive, that are studied. There is also the problem of the reliability of recall (Alwin & Campbell, 2001).

Data Collection

Besides design flaws, there are also issues related to collecting data from older people. Difficulties in obtaining data can be related to the diminishing capacity of the respondents over time. Some respondents may suffer sensory decrements, language erosion, cognitive deficits, chronic illnesses, or any combination of these. In life review studies, the rather demanding claims placed on a respondent that go well beyond a single interview can be onerous in terms of time and the "work" required to remember and locate archival materials.

Recent research by psychologists raises the question of how much age difference in circadian arousal contributes to performance differences on tests (Hasher, Goldstein, & May, 2005). **Circadian rhythm** refers to fluctuations in behaviour over a 24-hour period. These researchers found that younger adults' scores (on psychological tests) improve from morning testing times to afternoon times, while those of older adults decline. The 35 percent advantage for younger adults over older adults tested in the afternoon is reduced by 15 percent when both groups are tested at their peak times. It seems that the time of day we do our studies with older adults makes a difference in the results (Hasher, Goldstein, & May, 2005). A corollary is that younger adults probably do not do too well in early morning lectures!

Ethics

A number of potential ethical hazards occur in conducting research with any human subject. These risks are magnified for older individuals, especially the frail old, who are more vulnerable to unethical treatment. The most common problem areas are potential harm, lack of informed consent, and privacy. In the case of older people, harm can range from fatigue and stress caused by the simple process of collecting data to the withholding of a potentially beneficial experimental treatment from subjects in the control group. The older person might not live long enough to receive the treatment at a later date. A particularly poignant problem is the termination of a research project, especially a longitudinal project, where a meaningful social relationship has developed between the older person and the research team. The older person could be left feeling lonely and isolated.

Particularly relevant to the study of older people are the many issues surrounding informed consent (Gum, 2004). Frequently, it is difficult to determine who may give consent when the person is cognitively impaired. Among competent individuals, the unintentional threat of losing a service or a treatment may coerce an older person into participating. Even the promise of attention from the researcher may be enough to compel an older person to participate.

The right to privacy is the individual's right to decide when, where, to whom, and to what extent his or her behaviour will be revealed (Singleton & Straits, 2005). It is very easy to violate this right, especially with a captive audience, such as elderly persons in hospitals and nursing homes, where there is little privacy to begin with and no family member may be present to advocate on behalf of the older person.

The vast majority of social researchers do not plan to harm their subjects in any way. Nevertheless, to help ensure that a researcher does not engage in a potential violation of ethics, the Research Ethics Boards (REBs) at Canadian universities and ethics panels in most institutions and agencies approve the research before it can begin. All research conducted under the auspices of these organizations is subject to a thorough review by ethics committees, which ensure that researchers are ethically accountable. No research project can be implemented until the researcher is granted ethical approval.

CHAPTER SUMMARY

This chapter has reviewed the goals and methods of scientific enquiry in social gerontology. The focus of gerontological research has shifted from the study of the aged as a static category to the explanation, description, and exploration of aging as a dynamic social process. Generally, researchers in social gerontology are interested in how aging processes affect the individual and society and how society affects aging processes. They like to take a "long view" of people as they move through transitions in their lifespan.

Key ideas to remember from this chapter:

- To avoid human errors in studying older people, researchers adhere to three main principles central to scientific enquiry: empiricism, objectivity, and control.

- Researchers employ either deductive approaches (theory testing) or inductive approaches (theory development) in the scientific process.

- Although many gerontologists follow these principles, a number of new perspectives or paradigms have emerged over time that adopt contrasting beliefs about the nature of reality (ontology), the relationship between the researcher and the subject (epistemology), and how to gain knowledge about the world (methods). The various paradigms or systems of knowledge, therefore, employ a number of methodologies that match their world view.

- Postpositivists, who attempt to understand reality, use methodologies such as cross-sectional and longitudinal surveys, secondary data analysis, and experimental and quasi-experimental designs.

- In contrast, interpretive researchers, who believe in a subjective reality, attempt to capture the meaning of the human experience as it is expressed in the aging process and rely on a distinct set of methodologies such as biographies, phenomenology, grounded theory, and ethnography.

- Critical theorists, on the other hand, expose the injustices sometimes suffered by vulnerable people and try to change the social and cultural structures and policies that are the culprits. All types of methodologies are used in this paradigm; its distinguishing features are the involvement of subjects in the control and direction of the research process and the commitment to social change.

- Paradigms overlap; researchers who do not always agree on a world view select among the many methodologies open to them. Indeed, many employ several methods in a single study.
- An awareness of overarching paradigms in social gerontology not only helps situate research studies but also provides a guide to understanding the links between research questions, theory, and methods.
- There are a number of issues that are unique to the study of aging, particularly the need to disentangle age, period, and cohort effects—partially achieved by the use of longitudinal designs, such as panel and cohort designs, event history analysis, and life reviews.
- Longitudinal designs also have problems with follow-up, measurement, time intervals, and language, while all designs are subject to the capacity and willingness of older people to participate in the study. It is up to the researcher to ensure that no harm befalls the subjects, that they are fully informed about the study, and that their privacy is protected at all costs.

KEY TERMS

ex post facto hypothesizing (p. 88)

premature closure (p. 89)

goals of science (p. 89)

empiricism (p. 90)

reliability (p. 90)

validity (p. 90)

objectivity (p. 90)

control (p. 90)

deductive approach (p. 92)

inductive approach (p. 92)

epistemology (p. 92)

paradigms (p. 92)

positivism (p. 93)

postpositivism (p. 93)

content validity (p. 94)

criterion validity (p. 94)

construct validity (p. 94)

cross-sectional surveys (p. 95)

longitudinal surveys (p. 95)

secondary data analysis (p. 95)

interpretive/constructivism (p. 98)

biography (p. 100)

phenomenology (p. 100)

grounded theory (p. 101)

ethnography (p. 102)

critical paradigm (p. 102)

age effect (p. 104)

cohort effect (p. 104)

cohort (p. 104)

period effect (p. 105)

life course fallacy (p. 105)

cohort-centrism (p. 106)

event history design (p. 108)

back translating (p. 109)

circadian rhythm (p. 110)

STUDY QUESTIONS

1. Choose a research topic of personal interest to you in gerontology. Do you think you could be objective about the topic? How would you go about avoiding human error in your study?

2. What are the differences between the three major world views used to study the aging process? Do you prefer one over the other, and if so, why? Do you think you would feel comfortable using any of the three approaches?

3. Consider your own life and that of your grandparents. What differences would you expect between your aging and theirs? What are the sources of these differences?

4. What ethical obligations do researchers in social gerontology have to older people?

SUGGESTED READINGS

Giele, J.Z., & Elder Jr., G.H. (Eds.) (1998). *Methods of life course research: Qualitative and quantitative approaches.* Thousand Oaks, CA: Sage Publications.

Gubrium, J. F., & Holstein, J. A. (Eds.) (2003). *Ways of aging.* Oxford, UK: Blackwell.

Jamieson, A., & Victor, C.R. (2002). *Researching ageing and later life.* Philadelphia: Open University Press.

Martin-Matthews, A., & Béland, F. (2001). *Northern lights: Reflections on Canadian gerontological research.* Special supplement on the occasion of the 17th World Congress of the International Association of Gerontology. *Canadian Journal of Aging,* Vol 20 suppl. 1. (all articles).

Schaie, K.W., & Elder, G. (2005). *Historical influences on lives and aging.* New York: Springer.

Chapter 5

THE GENDERED LIFE COURSE

Learning Objectives

In this chapter, you will learn about

- How men's and women's family life courses differ.
- How gender affects the life course of paid work and retirement.
- The interrelationships between gendered family and work life courses.

- How life courses have changed over the last 100 years, more so for women.

Introduction

Gender is an important characteristic of individuals. Males and females differ biologically and genetically (XX versus XY chromosome composition). As a determinant of behaviour, however, most social scientists believe that learning is more important than biology, and one important component of our learning occurs through gender role socialization. That is, girls learn to be girls (and, later, women), and boys learn to be boys (and, later, men). What they learn, however, is dependent upon what the wider society deems gender-appropriate behaviour. Gender-appropriate behaviour varies tremendously cross-culturally, and it can also vary over time in societies undergoing change. Thus, while gender is a characteristic of individuals, it is one that is largely socially determined and socially constructed. However, gender is more than a characteristic of individuals; it is also an important—even a defining—aspect of social organization. In other words, our society is structured to advantage and privilege males (Gee & Gutman, 2000).

As noted in Chapter 4, age is both a characteristic of individuals and an aspect of social structure. Just as our society allocates roles and responsibilities to people on the basis of their ages, it also differentially places them on the basis of their gender. However, age and gender are not just two social markers; rather, age and gender intersect or interrelate. This means that one cannot be understood apart from the other. To understand aging, one has also to consider gender. For example, the "difference" between a young man and an old woman is greater than that between a young man and an old man. This chapter examines how aging and gender intersect by focusing on the different life pathways of men and women in Canadian society. However, it is important to remember that there are variations among women and among men. While gender is a very important dimension of people's lives, it does not eliminate the effects of other factors, such as social class, race/ethnicity, region, and so on.

Our discussion of the gendered life course is couched in the context of two revolutions that are transforming societies such as Canada. One revolution has already been discussed in Chapter 2—the longevity revolution, or increased life expectancy (and its effect on population aging). Second is a gender revolution, in which women's roles have substantially changed, with a majority of women now engaged in the paid labour force. As Moen (1996:172) writes: "Both [revolutions] are challenging old norms and ideologies about age and gender, as well as producing a **structural lag** in the roles and resources available to men and women." [emphasis added] Moreover, these revolutions are interrelated; as we saw in Chapter 2, women have benefited more from the increase in longevity.

Before we look at the substantive issues involved in the gendered life course, a methodological caveat is needed. By its very nature, the life course is a temporal phenomenon. This means that the best data to assess it are longitudinal, ideally panel data on the same individuals as they go through life, as described in Chapter 4. However, such longitudinal data are in short supply in Canada, and we almost always have to rely on cross-sectional data (see Chapter 4). By look-ing at cross-sectional data at different points in time, we can draw a general pic-ture of life course progression. However, as discussed in Chapter 3, we run the risk of confounding age, period, and cohort effects. Another difficulty in assess-ing the life course is that "it ain't over till it's over." So, for example, if we are looking at today's 20-year-olds, we do not know what their life course will be like 50 years from now, when they are 70 years old. If we have the data, we can com-pare today's 20-year-olds with people who are now, say, aged 70 years when they were 20 years old (i.e., 50 years ago). While such a comparison can tell us some things, it is not useful in assessing the life course of today's 20-year-olds—much of their lives have not happened yet. No data, not even the best panel data available, can help with this problem.

Overview of the Changing Life Course

First, let's look at two general dimensions of life course change. The first relates to the mortality reductions that were discussed in Chapter 2. The life course today is more predictable in that most deaths occur in later life. The unpre-dictabilities associated with loss of children, siblings, and spouses at a young age have lessened considerably. People can expect to enjoy many years in which parents and adult children jointly survive (Gee, 1990). While other unpredictable events in life (e.g., divorce) have increased, they do not take away from the great strides made in reducing deaths at young ages.

The other dimension relates to gender change. In the past, the life courses of people were highly gendered (although early deaths led to deviations, such as young widows working for pay to support their children). Men began working after their schooling was completed and continued working full time until retire-ment or until they could no longer work. Women's life courses were dominated by domestic tasks, and any work outside the home was secondary to that domes-tic work (although in farm settings, women did much work that directly con-tributed to the family income). Men's life courses were played out in the public sphere and women's in the private sphere, increasingly so as urbanization replaced farm life. As we progressed through the 20th century, this gendered public/private sphere distinction broke down. Women came to play a much big-ger role in paid labour; however, norms continued to stipulate that work in the home remain the responsibility of women. Women's lives became more fluid; they entered and re-entered the paid labour force over their life course. However, the workplace remained dominated by a male model of early and continued full-time employment (until retirement), and thus, women's involvement in the public sphere of paid work has been treated as marginal. At the same time, their unpaid work in the home has been taken for granted and undervalued.

The male life course was affected first by the institutionalization of retirement and then mandatory retirement (which continues to exist in five Canadian provinces) and later by an increasing trend of leaving and re-entering the paid labour force in later life, as discussed in Chapter 13. Retirement has less meaning in the female life course. When does a woman retire if she is a full-time homemaker? Even if she is a full-time paid worker, a woman's domestic work continues after she leaves the paid labour force. If her husband is ill, that domestic labour can increase to become a "full-time job" of caregiving but without pay. Given the different activities of men and women, the life courses of men and women continue to be gendered, but in different and more nuanced ways than in the past.

The Gendered Family Life Course

Women and men experience their families' lives in different ways. In this section, we examine some aspects of the difference between the genders in the taking on of family roles and the timing of family role transitions.

Marriage and Cohabitation

The vast majority of Canadian women and men marry at least once. Today's family life course varies from that of the past, however, with regard to common-law marriage/cohabitation. Cohabitation was virtually unheard of before the 1970s (although it may have been practised—invisibly—more than was thought); it was derogatorily referred to as "living in sin" and "shacking up." Now, it forms a part of the family life course for many Canadians, particularly in the province of Quebec (where it is called *union libre)*. Data from the 2001 Census reveal that approximately 10 percent of Canadians (or 2.32 million persons) over the age of 15 years live in common-law unions (Statistics Canada, 2004a), a 229 percent increase since 1981 (when the Canadian Census first began collecting data on cohabitation) (Statistics Canada, 1999a). Put in different terms, about 16 percent of all unions in Canada are common-law unions. However, there are strong provincial/regional variations. In Quebec, about 30 percent of all unions are cohabitating unions; the figures are even higher in the Northwest Territories (33.3 percent) and Nunavut (42.1 percent). In contrast, in Prince Edward Island and Ontario, about 11 percent of unions are common-law unions (Statistics Canada, 2002b).

Cohabitation varies by age and gender as well. In terms of age, as one might expect, younger people are more likely to be cohabiting. For example, nearly 21 percent of Canadians aged 25 to 29 years are currently cohabiting—more than double the percentage (9.8 percent) among those aged 45 to 49 years (Statistics Canada, 2004a). Men have higher rates of cohabitation than do women. However, these figures reflect current cohabitation only; from a life-course perspective, we want to know the numbers/proportions who have ever cohabitated and we want to understand the transition to cohabitation. In Quebec, 38.6 percent of women and 40.6 percent of men have ever lived in a common-law union; for the rest of Canada, the figures are 23.6 percent and 21.8 percent, respectively (Statistics Canada, 2004b). In other words, only in Quebec are men more likely than women to cohabit.

It is important to look at premarital and post-marital cohabitation separately. Looking first at premarital cohabitation (cohabitation that precedes a legal marriage), by age 35 years more than 70 percent of women and approximately 63 percent of men have ever lived in a common-law union. Therefore, women have higher rates of premarital cohabitation than do men, which is consistent with the fact that women marry (legally) at younger ages. A different picture emerges for post-marital cohabitation, however. Men are more likely to make the transition to post-marital cohabitation. For example, among divorced or separated persons aged 45 to 54 years, 25 percent of women and 36.9 percent of men are currently cohabitating (Statistics Canada, 2004b), and 30.9 percent of women and 42.8 percent of men have ever cohabited since their marital breakup (Wu, 2000). Overall, women are more likely to live in premarital common-law unions and men are more likely to live in post-marital common-law unions.

Whether it is a cohabiting relationship or a legal marriage, the ages of the men and women at the beginning of the union are different. Women tend to marry (or cohabit with) men who are older than they are. For example, in 2002, the median age at first marriage for men was about 29 years and for women 27 years (Statistics Canada, 2004c). While this age discrepancy was larger in the past (Veevers, 1984), it is still an important phenomenon. The fact that women marry (or cohabit) at younger ages than men do establishes what is called a **mating gradient**. The younger spouse (the wife in most cases) will have fewer resources, for example, less schooling, less job experience, less income. These small differences accumulate over time; the husband's job will be given priority, since it is more important to the economic well-being of the family. So, for example, the couple may move because of the husband's job; the wife will quit her job and have to start over again. Over time, then, the initially small economic difference between the husband and wife becomes a substantial gap. While other factors are also implicated in women's lower economic status, it is important to know that a relatively small age difference between a wife and her husband is involved as well. Gee (1995) argues that women face greater social pressures to marry and to marry early, helping establish a subtle process that increases women's economic dependency.

Fertility

The birth of children is an important transition in the life course of both men and women. However, we have data mostly for women (the General Social Surveys of 1990 and 1995 being an exception). In part, this represents administrative convenience for the government (which is responsible for most data collection on fertility in industrialized countries, such as Canada), but it also reflects a sexist bias in which women are assumed to be the primary parent due to biology alone. A dramatic change in the life course of Canadian women is a reduction in the number of children they bear. As we saw in Chapter 2, this decline in fertility is the primary cause of population aging.

Table 5.1 shows the average number of children ever born to women by the end of their reproductive lives (generally taken to be ages 45 to 49 years) from 1941 to 2001. (Data on children are collected only in census years ending in 1.) In 1941, these women (birth cohort of 1892 to 1896) had borne 4.2 children on average; in 1991 (birth cohort of 1942 to 1946), the comparable number was 2.2—a decline of approximately 50 percent. The women who produced the Canadian baby boom are represented in the data for 1971 and 1981; they bore on average 3.3 children. The baby boom, then, really did not encompass a large increase in children ever born to mothers, media coverage to the contrary. It is more accurate to say that the baby boom represented a stall in the overall trend of declining fertility in Canada in the 20th century. The baby boom was the result of a change in the timing of women's life course events, rather than a substantial increase in fertility. In the years of the baby boom, women married at younger ages and had their children at younger ages than did women both before and after them (Gee, 1980). Because of the pyramidal shape of the Canadian age structure in the mid-20th century, the proportionately large numbers of younger women led to greater numbers of babies being born (even though completed family size was only slightly elevated).

Table 5.1 also shows a convergence in the fertility behaviour of Canadian women. Not only are women having fewer children, they are also much more likely to have two children. Indeed, it is sometimes claimed that the two-child family has become the norm. At the same time, the percent of women having large families (six or more children) has plummeted. One reason for this convergence is a rapid fertility decline starting in the mid-20th century in Quebec, well known

Table 5.1   CHILDREN EVER BORN TO EVER-MARRIED WOMEN AGED 45–49 YEARS

YEAR	CHILDREN EVER BORN	2 CHILDREN	6+ CHILDREN
1941	4.2	15.5%	27.9%
1961	3.1	22.5%	14.9%
1971	3.3	22.0%	15.1%
1981	3.3	22.9%	12.2%
1991	2.2	38.1%	2.6%
2001	2.1	45.2%	0.2%

Source: Statistics Canda, *Family over the life course*, 1995 Catalogue No. 91-543 and from the General Social Survey, Cycle 15, 2001.

for its traditional pattern of very large family sizes. First Nations fertility levels, however, remain high (Suwal & Trovato, 1998).

However, these data—by their very nature—speak to the past. We have to wait until today's young women are in their late 40s to know how many children they will have had. Will more of them end up with no children, that is, never make the transition to parenthood? It is difficult to say, but it is important to keep in mind that levels of childlessness in the past were not particularly low. For example, among ever-married women born around the turn of the 20th century, approximately 13 percent never bore any children (Beaujot, 1995). Among ever-married women born in the middle of the 20th century, the comparable figure was approximately 10 percent. Whatever percent of today's young people may remain childless, the reasons may be somewhat different from those in the past. Childlessness may be either voluntary or involuntary. In the past, it is probably true that a higher proportion of women were childless for involuntary reasons, including infertility/sterility (of either the man or the woman) and the early death of husbands. However, it is possible that involuntary childlessness may increase, especially if women wait until later ages to try to become pregnant. We can already see evidence of this in the growth of fertility clinics and the use of reproductive technology to assist in impregnation (and the associated risks of multiple births and the psychological trauma of a high rate of failure). We do know, though, that young Canadian adults have not embraced the idea of childlessness. Data from the 2001 General Social Survey reveal that only 8.4 percent of men in their 20s and 10.7 percent of similarly aged women intend to have no children (Statistics Canada, 2004b).

While fertility has converged to a two-child average, some women go on to have a third child. What are their characteristics? Women who have a third child are more likely to have had their first child before the age of 25 years; have had a short interval between their first and second children; not be engaged in the paid labour force; not have a high school diploma; be born in a country other than Canada, the United States, and Europe; attend religious services frequently; and have two children of the same sex (Beaujot & Bélanger, 2001). Among Canadians with two children, the 15 percent who intend to have a third child are more likely to be regular attenders at religious services, Catholic, and in a remarriage (Wu & Wang, 1998). These sets of findings suggest that gender role orientations may lie at the heart of differences in fertility. Indeed, two Canadian studies find that gender role systems are an important determinant of family size, although in somewhat different ways. Jayachandran (2000) reports that couples who have an egalitarian gender role structure have fewer children; Matthews (1999) shows that women have fewer children than they desire because they have not been able to establish a satisfactory gendered division of labour in everyday life.

One of the recent changes in fertility behaviour in Canada is a postponement in the age at which couples have children. This is in sharp contrast to the baby boom mothers/parents, who married and bore children at the youngest ages in our history. The median age at first birth is now approximately 26 years for women and 30 years for men (Statistics Canada, 2004b). However, compared with other family life course events, the spread around the average age at first childbirth is large (Rajulton & Ravanera, 1995). In other words, while the overall trend in age at first childbirth is getting older, there is considerable variation, and some people continue to have children at young ages. It is important to keep this variation in mind; the media have tended to focus on late-age first-time mothers only, and it is easy to forget that young mothers exist as well. Early age at childbirth (and to a lesser degree, early age at marriage) is associated with becoming a lone parent in both Canada and the United States (Smith, 1998), which, in turn, is a major predictor of economic hardship. However, late age at childbirth does not guarantee economic advantage. As shown by Grindstaff (1996), even late age at the commencement of child-bearing does not protect Canadian women from economic disadvantage in terms of labour force partici-pation, the attainment of full-time work, and income.

The life course of Canadians has changed, as noted above, by the emer-gence of cohabitation as a common and accepted form of family living. When common-law marriages first gained popularity, children tended not to be born into them. However, children are increasingly being born into common-law marriage situations. For example, of all children born in Canada in 1983 and 1984, 9.8 per-cent were born into a common-law union; just 10 years later, the proportion had grown to 20.4 percent (Marcil-Gratton, 1998). (In Quebec, the figure for children born in 1993 and 1994 is 43.1 percent.). If one adds the figure of 20.4 percent to the percentage of children born to single mothers (about 9 percent), we can see that around 30 percent of children are now born outside (legal) marriage (Marcil-Gratton, 1998). Of course, these children may later live in a family with legally married parents, but the emerging trend is for parents in common-law unions not to marry, even when they have children. Thus, the link between (legal) marriage and child-bearing (and child rearing) appears to be weakening.

In keeping with the life course principle of "linked lives," the changing behaviour of parents has implications for their children. As we will see, com-mon-law unions tend to be more temporary than legal marriages; therefore, the children of such unions are more likely to eventually live in lone-parent fami-lies headed by their mother. For example, children born into a common-law union in which the parents do not subsequently marry are three times more likely to experience family breakdown than children born into a legal marriage not preceded by a common-law union (Marcil-Gratton, 1998). Also, they are more likely to experience family breakdown at a younger age, and as we will see later, families headed by mothers tend to be poor.

Divorce and Remarriage

Canada has seen a "revolution" in divorce in the last 35 years, in large part due to changes in divorce law. In 1969, there was a major liberalization in divorce; until then, adultery was the only legal grounds for divorce. A further liberaliza-tion in divorce law occurred in 1986, again making it easier for unhappy marriages to end by reducing the period of separation needed to be eligible for divorce. Consequently, divorce is now a relatively common event in the life course of men and women, although it is difficult to know what proportion of recent marriages will dissolve (as with fertility, we have to wait and see). However, among people born in the middle of the 20th century, 39 percent of men and 34 percent of women were no longer living with their (first) spouse after 25 years (Beaujot & Bélanger, 2001). With the recent increases in common-law unions, however, data on divorce prevalence become less meaningful. As argued by LeBourdais and Marcil-Gratton (1996), we need to have much better data on common-law marriages and their dissolutions in order to get a true picture of marital breakdown. This is especially true for Canada, which has much higher rates of common-law union formation than the United States.

However, there is a relationship between divorce and cohabitation. Numerous studies have shown that couples who cohabit and then legally marry are more likely to divorce (e.g., Hall & Zhao, 1995). Estimates by Beaujot (2000) suggest that the risk of divorce is double for marriages preceded by common-law unions. Thus, empirical research does not support the common belief that "trial marriage" operates as a testing ground to ensure marital success and longevity. On the other hand, it cannot necessarily be concluded that cohabiting itself makes a particular couple more likely to divorce. Rather, it appears that people who cohabit before marriage are a self-selected group who have more casual attitudes about relationships and are, thus, more prone to divorce if "the going gets rough" (Hall, 1996). Thus, the recent increase in cohabitation could lead to higher levels of union breakdown—both of the common-law unions themselves and of the legal marriages that may follow them. It will be recalled that men are more likely than women to engage in premarital cohabitation. Thus, women are more at risk of divorce after a premarital union that leads to marriage.

Rates of remarriage have declined, although about one-third of marriages involve at least one spouse who has been previously married. Recent data show that remarriage after divorce is more likely for men; 64 percent of divorced men but only 52 percent of divorced women remarry (Beaujot, 2000). As we have seen, men are more likely than women to be in post-marital cohabiting unions. Therefore, women are more likely to be living alone (if there are no young children) or heading a lone-parent family (if children are present) than are men. At least in part because of these differential post-divorce outcomes, women are more negatively affected economically by divorce than are men. Galarneau and Sturrock (1997) studied the financial effects of separation for Canadians who separated between 1987 and 1993. Among those with children under the age of 18 years living in the home, women experienced a 23 percent reduction in income in the first year and a 5 percent reduction after five years. For men, after five years, income had *increased* by 15 percent. Those who went on to form another union made gains after five years—18 percent for men and 14 percent for women. However, women were much less likely to form a post-divorce union.

Some argue that lower remarriage rates among women are the result of women's greater financial independence (e.g., Beaujot, 2000); the same argument has been made about divorce—that is, that increased divorce rates reflect women's financial independence as a result of their labour force participation. It has been found that in Canada, in marriages since 1969, women's labour force participation has not played a causal role in increased divorce (Hou & Omwanda, 1997). It has not yet been established whether women's participation in the labour force is a factor in their decreased likelihood of remarrying after divorce. However, given the negative financial implications of divorce for women, it seems likely that other factors are involved.

For example, McDonald and Robb (2004) found that separated and divorced women were the poorest among women aged 65 and over. Although income fluctuated over the 1993-to-1999 interval, the separated had the lowest before and after-tax incomes for all women in Canada in 1999. Living in Eastern Canada and having a lower level of education were also associated with lower incomes.

Lone Parenting

Women are far more likely to be lone parents than are men (McQuillan & Belle, 2001). This has always been the case; however, in the past, the major reason was the (early) death of husbands. In contrast, the main reasons today are births to never-married women and dissolution of both legal and common-law marriages. Of families with at least one child under the age of 18 years, nearly 19 percent are headed by a lone parent, with 15.6 percent headed by a lone mother (Statistics Canada, 2002a). Female-headed lone-parent families face a high likelihood of poverty. As shown in Figure 5.1, over half of lone female-headed families (with at least one child aged under 18 years) have incomes below Statistics Canada's Low Income Cut-offs (LICOs), sometimes referred to as the "poverty line." Part of the reason for the economic problems of female-headed lone parent families is the failure of fathers to provide (even court-ordered) child support (Richardson, 1992).

In the light of information showing paternal noninvolvement associated with divorce and non-marriage, Dumas and Péron (1992: 107) refer to an emerging "matriarchy" in the Canadian family. Gee (2000) argues against this interpretation, suggesting that rather than an end to **patriarchy**, what we are now witnessing is a shift in power (over women) from individual men to the state. Examples of the state becoming more involved in family life include legislation related to the best interests of the child and to parental fitness. Patriarchal control over the family continues, but in a different guise.

Same-Sex Unions

We have virtually no data on the numbers of persons in same-sex unions or their characteristics. However, we would be remiss in failing to mention this increasingly acknowledged and probably growing form of family living. It is likely that

Figure 5.1 PERCENTAGE OF FAMILIES BELOW LOW INCOME CUT-OFF BY
FAMILY STRUCTURE, FOR FAMILIES WITH AT LEAST ONE CHILD
UNDER 18, CANADA: 2000

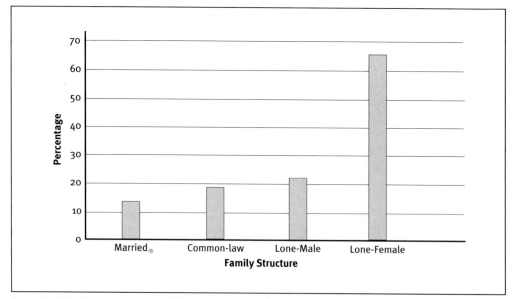

Source: Statistics Canada, *Income status (4) and Census family structure for Census families, sex, age groups and household living arrangements for non-family persons 15 years and over and sex and age groups for persons in private households (87), for
Canada, provinces, Census metropolitan areas and Census agglomerations, 1995 and 2000 – 20% Sample Data,* Catalogue No.
97F0020XCB01006 (May 13, 2003).

more men than women are engaged in same-sex unions (if we accept that more
men than women are homosexual), and it is also likely that at least some portion of the group of persons in same-sex unions has had previous heterosexual
marriages and/or has children.

Information about the family life course of gays and lesbians awaits the collection of data by federal bureaus, such as Statistics Canada. The collection of
official data on common-law unions was the subject of much debate in the 1970s
but came to pass in the 1981 census. Gay groups lobbied for official recognition
in the census prior to the 1996 and 2001 censuses. In the 2001 Census, 37 990
men and 30 415 women were with partners of the same sex (Statistics Canada,
2004a). The family life of these individuals is only now beginning to be researched
by gerontologists (Brotman, Ryan, & Cormier, 2003; Donahue & McDonald, 2005).

Widowhood

Women are much more likely to be widowed than are men. For example, among
Canadians aged 75 to 79 years, approximately one-half of women but fewer than

16 percent of men are widowed (Statistics Canada, 2002d). Overall, among the population aged 65 years and over, widows outnumber widowers by a factor of nearly five to one (Statistics Canada, 2002d). This differential is due, in large part, to the facts that women live longer than men, as we saw in Chapter 2, and that women tend to marry men who are older than they are, as discussed earlier in this chapter. Also, women are much less likely than men to remarry after the death of a spouse (Martin-Matthews, 1991; Wu, 1995). About 14 percent of widowers remarry, compared with only 5 percent of widows. Moreover, widowed men remarry much sooner than widows. As a result of these combined trends, elderly women are much more likely to live alone. Among the Canadian population aged 75 years and over, 49.8 percent of women and 21.1 percent of men live alone (Statistics Canada, 2002c).

Being Single

Being single refers to the never married in contrast to those who are unmarried, namely the widowed, separated and divorced (Connidis, 2001:79). The never married are often lumped together under the category "unattached" by Canadian researchers, a term used to cover the widowed, separated, divorced and never married. It is, of course, somewhat inaccurate to treat all unattached older adults the same, especially never-married individuals. The latter often do not have children, nor do they have ex-spouses, as do the separated or divorced. They have different levels of social involvement. The percentage of those 65 years of age and over that have never married (single) has never gone below 5 percent since the 1981 Census. In 1981 8.4 percent of older adults were single compared to 5.4 percent in 2001. Even though the proportion has fallen, the absolute numbers are growing because the older population is growing in Canada. In addition, younger cohorts in 2000 have higher rates of singlehood (10 percent of men and 7 percent of women aged 35 to 44 and 26 percent of men and 17 percent of women aged 25 to 34), rates which have the potential to continue to older ages (Statistics Canada, 2003h).

Whether gender is an important factor in understanding the lives of single persons is only beginning to be understood, since the research on single individuals is limited. The initial research suggests that older single women are more educated than married women and that single men tend to have fewer economic resources than married men (Seccombe & Ishii-Kuntz, 1994). Overall, never-married women have capitalized on a lifetime of work and make 96 cents for every dollar that is earned by their male counterparts, while married women earned 77 cents on the dollar in 1997 (Drolet, 1999). Single women tend to have larger social networks of family and friends and receive more familial support than single men (Barrett, 1999; Barrett & Lynch, 1999). Both single men and women undergo a change in a singlehood identity that occurs over time and is associated with a cultural timetable for marriage (Davies, 2003). In light of this finding, that singlehood is defined in terms of marriage, it is not surprising that Connidis calls for a " . . . reconceptualization of single life that does not implicitly accept marriage as the exclusive intimate relationship of adult life." (2001:92).

The Family Life Course of Older People

Present and Future

The family life course of the seniors of today is comparatively uncomplicated. They are the parents (for the most part) of the baby boomers, and were young at a time in Canadian history characterized by probably the highest degree of gendered behaviour. People tended to marry at relatively young ages, with husbands being older than their wives. They went on to have children, three on average. Divorce was not common, especially in the earlier part of their lives (although this does not mean that marriages were necessarily harmonious). Most marriages ended with the death of the husband. Women tended not to be major players in the labour force, certainly not when their children were young or when they were bringing up their children. A man's wage could support a family, and it was expected that men would "work" and women would look after the home and the people in it. This highly gendered division of labour was constraining, and it is no wonder that a women's movement developed in the 1960s. It also created economic vulnerability for women; they needed to stay married for financial reasons. When widowed (or abandoned in the pre-divorce liberalization days), women tended to fall into poverty (especially since husbands' benefits, if any, usually died with them).

In the 1970s—when today's seniors were middle-aged—things started to change. Large-scale increases in women's labour force participation began. On the family front, divorce became much easier, fertility started to decrease substantially, age at marriage began to increase, and cohabitation was beginning to become an acceptable living arrangement. All this suggests a decrease in the gendered division of labour and an increase in women's opportunities and life options. However, as noted by Moen (1996), structural lags still exist in the longevity and gender revolutions transforming our society. Women are still economically vulnerable, and often "one man away from poverty." The mating gradient still exists (for both marriages and common-law unions)—even if age at marriage is later for both men and women now—and continues to work to the financial advantage of men. Women, upon divorce or common-law union dissolution, are likely to head lone-parent families, which, as we have seen, are at high risk of poverty. To understand more about this structural lag, we turn our attention to the work life course.

Gender and the Work Life Course

We are all aware of the huge increases in women's labour force participation that have occurred in the last 30 years or so (see Table 5.2). In 1976, 42 percent of women were in the paid labour force; in 2004, the comparable figure approaches 58 percent. At the same time, male labour force participation has declined—from 72.7

Table 5.2   MALE AND FEMALE EMPLOYMENT, 1976–2004

	Women aged 15 Years and Over	Men aged 15 Years and Over	Women as a % of total employment
	% of all women employed	% of all men employed	
1976	41.9	72.7	37.12
1977	42.3	71.9	37.60
1978	43.4	72.0	38.20
1979	45.1	73.1	38.80
1980	46.4	72.8	39.59
1981	47.7	72.8	40.31
1982	46.5	68.4	41.24
1983	46.8	67.4	41.79
1984	47.7	68.0	42.02
1985	49.0	68.5	42.51
1986	50.2	69.5	42.77
1987	51.3	70.3	43.05
1988	52.7	70.9	43.51
1989	53.5	71.1	43.89
1990	53.7	69.9	44.38
1991	52.7	66.9	45.01
1992	51.9	65.0	45.30
1993	51.4	64.5	45.32
1994	51.8	65.1	45.29
1995	52.1	65.3	45.37
1996	52.0	64.9	45.46
1997	52.5	65.4	45.47
1998	53.6	65.9	45.75
1999	54.5	66.7	45.84
2000	55.4	67.3	46.00
2001	55.6	66.8	46.24
2002	56.6	67.1	46.55
2003	57.4	67.6	46.73
2004	57.8	67.8	46.84

Source: Statistics Canada, "Labour force historical review", 2004, Catalogue No. 71F0004XCB (February 18, 2005).

percent in 1976 to 67.8 percent in 2004 (Statistics Canada, 2006b, p. 103). Differential age patterns by gender are involved in these opposing trends. Among women, an increase in the labour force participation of the young (particularly young mothers) is implicated. In contrast, among men, as discussed in Chapter 13, declines in the labour force involvement of older men (voluntary and involuntary retirement) drive down male labour force participation rates. The overall increase of women in the paid labour force—so that now approximately 46 percent of workers are women—would lead us to conclude that gender equality is being approached in the workplace. However, an examination of the characteristics of women's labour suggests that much change will be needed before that conclusion can be made.

The Gender Wage Gap

Women in full-year, full-time employment earn approximately 71 percent of what men earn (Statistics Canada, 2006b, p. 139). Although this gender wage gap has narrowed since 1967, when the corresponding figure was 58.4 percent, it is still quite substantial (Shannon & Kidd, 2001). What causes it? Research in Canada has demonstrated that in any given year, less than one-half of the gap is due to differences between men and women in wage-determining characteristics, such as education, work experience, union status, and industry/occupation. The rest of the gender wage gap cannot be accounted for and is typically attributed to gender discrimination. This state of affairs exists despite the existence of "equal pay for equal work" and pay equity ("equal pay for work of equal value") legislation in most Canadian jurisdictions.

The gender wage gap is smaller for younger workers than for older workers (Gunderson, 1998; Statistics Canada, 1998a). The gap is also smaller for people with a university education but has actually fallen more since 1980 for those with less than a university education. Given women's increasing educational attainment, there would appear to be grounds for optimism about the future of the gender wage gap. However, Shannon and Kidd (2001) project that a substantial gap will still exist in 2031. One of the main reasons for this projection is the aging of the population. By 2031 the workforce will be more concentrated in the age groups where the pay gap is largest (Shannon & Kidd, 2001).

Part-Time Work

The above discussion of gendered wage differences relates to full-time workers only. However, men and women differ in their engagement in part-time work. In 2004, nearly 30 percent of women, but only 11 percent of men, worked part-time (Statistics Canada, 2005a). Men are more likely to work at part-time jobs in their later working years, whereas women are more likely to work part-time when they are younger and have very young children in the home. This employment pattern of women has long-term consequences for their income, since part-time work tends not to have pension benefits. This pattern is not necessarily women's choice. While some women choose to work part time, others can find only part-time work. For example, in 2004, 27 percent of women working part-time said they did not want to work full-time; however, 26 percent wanted full-time employment, but could find only part-time (Statistics Canada, 2006b, p. 110). Even when women do choose to work part time, their choice may not be an entirely free one, given the household workload that women continue to have (Baker & Lero, 1996).

Women's Wages in the Family

As a result of the gender wage gap and women's greater likelihood of working part-time (as well as the mating gradient), women's income contributes relatively little to total family income. As shown in Figure 5.2, women's share of the income in dual-income families (both married and common-law) is less than one-third. It is also notable that this share has not increased appreciably since the mid-1960s. Women remain the "junior partners" in their marriages and lack power as a result (Grindstaff & Trovato, 1990). However, women's incomes are important to families; it has been estimated that approximately 40 percent of Canadian families would be poor if both parents did not work outside the home (Duxbury & Higgins, 1994).

Figure 5.2 **EARNINGS OF WIVES AS A PERCENTAGE OF TOTAL INCOME IN DUAL-EARNER FAMILIES,* 1967–2003**

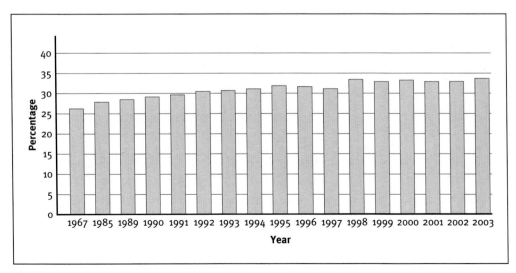

* Includes common-law unions

Source: Statistics Canada, *Women in Canada: A gender-based statistical report, 2005*, Catalogue No. 89-503 (March 13, 2006).

Labour Force Segregation

Women and men tend to work in very different occupations, as shown in Table 5.3. Women are concentrated in relatively few types of jobs—jobs in which other people are helped, for example, secretarial and clerical work, technical occupations like dental health care and librarians, health care and social assistance and educational services. Men are, on the other hand, concentrated in jobs in which people "do" things, rather than "help" people. This is not to suggest that all men have "good" jobs (for example, fishing is one of the main male occupations), but there is a greater likelihood that men will have jobs in which they are owners and/or managers. Table 5.3 also shows industrial segregation by gender. Men and women

Table 5.3   **THE GENDERED NATURE OF OCCUPATIONS**

Leading Women's Occupations*	Leading Men's Occupations*
Secretaries, recorders, and transcriptionists	Plumbers, pipefitters and gas fitters
Clerical occupations—general office skills	Heavy equipment operators
Cashiers	Supervisors—mining, oil and gas
Finance and insurance clerks	Central control and process operators in manufacturing and processing
Office equipment operators	Transportation officers and controllers
Technical occupations—libraries, archives, museums and art galleries	Machine operators—metal and mineral processing
Technical occupations—dental health care	Managers—protective services
Librarians, archivists, conservators and curators	Technical occupations—architecture, drafting, surveying and mapping
Industries in Which Women Predominate**	**Industries in Which Men Predominate****
Health care and social assistance	Construction
Educational services	Forestry, fishing, mining, oil and gas
Accommodation and food services	Transportation and warehousing
Finance, insurance, real estate, and leasing	Manufacturing

* Occupations in which more than 75 percent of workers are of one gender
** Industries in which more than 55 percent of workers are of one gender
Source: Statistics Canada, *Occupation–2001 national occupational classification for statistics (523), class of worker (6) and sex (3) for labour force 15 years and over, for Canada, provinces, territories, Census metropolitan areas and Census agglom-ereations, 2001 Census–20% sample data,* Catalogue No. *97F0012XCB01021* (February 11, 2003); and *Labour force historical review, 2004,* Catalogue No. *71F0004XCB* (February 18, 2005).

largely work in different industries. A good portion of the wage difference between men and women can be accounted for by their differential occupation and industry placement.

Why do men tend to concentrate in certain jobs and industries and women in others? Three different types of explanations have been put forth (Armstrong & Armstrong, 2001). One type of explanation focuses on the biological differences (such as in physical strength) between men and women, suggesting that these differences channel men into certain types of jobs and women into others. However, in today's workplace, brute strength is needed in very few jobs, and there does not seem to be any biological reason why men can be owners and managers and women cannot. Another set of explanations focuses on the ideas constructed by societies about what is appropriate work for women and for men, ideas that are transmitted from generation to generation by socialization and internationalization (by both females and males). Armstrong and Armstrong (2001) favour a third set of explanations, called **materialist explanations**. This set, based on political economy theory, focuses on the interacting material conditions of life in both the home and the workplace. The material conditions of family life mean that most women have to work for pay. At the same time, there has been a growing need for cheap and flexible labour. Women have been forced to take on marginal jobs for this reason, and also because of their household duties. The gendered segregation of work, in turn, leads men and women to develop different kinds of consciousness, which are passed on to children. As Armstrong and Armstrong (2001: 222) state: "Thus, the division of labour between the household and the formal economy perpetuates the segregation in the labour force, and the division of labour within each unit encourages the development of sex-specific attitudes and behaviour patterns."

The Intersection of the Family and Work Life Courses

The relationship between work and family over the life course differs dramatically for men and women. It is not an exaggeration to say that women's family and work life courses do not intersect easily. Despite the fact that most Canadian women work outside the home for a considerable period of time, both family and work life are structured on a one-earner (male) model. Women are still the primary homemakers and carers for others. Yet, the workplace is based on the assumption that workers do not have significant family/domestic responsibilities. Since work and family do not mesh for women, they end up making personal (private) accommodations. These accommodations may be made on the home front (e.g., having fewer children, lowering housecleaning standards); Bittman (1999) shows that the reliance on market substitutes (e.g., housecleaning services, fast food) is key in women's adaptations to domestic work overload.

Figure 5.3 TOTAL FERTILITY RATE AND LABOUR FORCE PARTICIPATION RATE OF WOMEN AGED 25–44, CANADA, 1950–2002

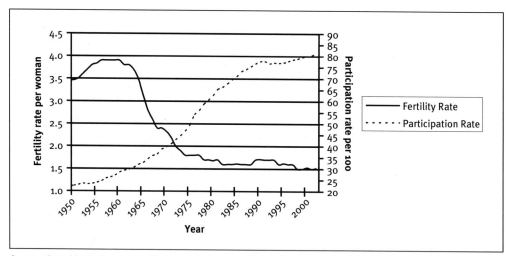

Source: Adapted from Statistics Canada, *Vital statistics, 1970,* Catalogue. No. 84-202; *Historical statistics of Canada, 1983,* Catalogue No. 11-516 (July 29, 1999); and *Labour force historical review, 2004,* Catalogue No. 71F0004XCB (February 18, 2005).

Workplace accommodations are also common (e.g., refusing promotions, working part-time). A vivid illustration of the conflict that women face in balancing work and family can be seen in Figure 5.3. As women have increased their labour force involvement, they have decreased the number of children they have. The direction of causation is not clear, however. Is it that women have fewer children because they work; or it is that women work outside the home because they have fewer children? Both, likely. It is interesting to note, though, that Canadian mothers have lower incomes than Canadian women who have never had children (Phipps, Burton, & Lethbridge, 2001).

The reason why women make accommodations is clear. Women continue to be the managers of the household, the cooks and the launderers, and the care-givers of others—husbands, children, parents. This unpaid work is not considered to be "real" work and is undervalued. At the same time, paid work is not "user-friendly" to women and families in many ways: (1) The care of children and elders cannot always be done around rigid workplace hours; hence women are absent from work for family reasons more than men—an average of 10 days per year for women versus about a day and half of work per year for men in 2004 (Statistics Canada, 2006b, p. 109). These absences also annoy employers, who tend to make conclusions about women's lack of work commitment; (2) Most workplaces do not provide childcare facilities, and the workplace hours of most day-care centres (8 a.m. to 6 p.m., Monday to Friday) may not correspond with women's work hours. A national childcare policy has been promised several times by different federal governments, but nothing has come to pass; (3) Most professional, "career-type" occupations contain age-related expectations about career progress. That is, one is supposed to make one's mark when young (in the 20s and 30s), when the demands of child-bearing and child rearing are most onerous.

As noted by Gee (2000), some employers are beginning to recognize the family–work conflicts of their female employees and are offering flexible hours (flex time), family-related leave, childcare, and the like. However, only large employers can afford these supportive options, leaving out a majority of women workers. Public policy changes would be of more benefit to more women. However, in the current environment of government cutbacks, such policy changes seem highly unlikely. At the same time, the reduction of social services reinforces and heightens women's obligations for the care of others.

The overall situation of women's employment and work–family conflict does not bode well for the future of Canadian women as they age. On the one hand, due to low fertility, older women will have few children to assist them should they become frail in later life. And, given the instabilities in marriages and common-law unions—and lower rates of remarriage than in the case of men—it is possible that more women in old age will be partnerless. Martin-Matthews (2000) projects that as many as one-half of women entering old age in 2025 will not be in any marriage. Being unattached is a major predictor of women's poverty in later life. It is sometimes assumed that older women in the future will be in much better financial shape than their mothers and grandmothers because of their participation in the paid labour force. However, the characteristics of female employment, as outlined above, suggest caution in making that assumption.

CHAPTER SUMMARY

In this chapter, we have looked at a number of facets of change and continuity in the gendered life course, focusing on family and work. We have seen that the intersection of history and biography has operated in different ways for men and for women.

Key ideas to remember from this chapter:

- The gendered aspect of the life course has changed over time. On the surface, gender differences are smaller; however, a more nuanced examination reveals that gender is a structured dimension of our society and that the life course continues to be gendered, although in more subtle and indirect ways than in the past.

- Men and women are both marrying at later ages. However, an age difference between husbands and wives continues, creating a mating gradient.

- Cohabitation is a new form/stage of the family life course for both men and women. Women are more likely to be premarital cohabiters and men are more likely to be post-marital cohabiters.

- One of the most dramatic changes in the family life course is declining fertility. Two children has become the norm. The average age of (first) child-bearing is older (especially compared with the baby boom period), but there is considerable variation in age at first motherhood. Children are now much more likely to be born into common-law unions.

- Divorce is a more commonly experienced life course event, although divorce data are becoming increasingly less meaningful with the growing incidence of common-law marriages. Divorce has negative economic consequences for women but not for men. Despite common-sense thinking and media portrayals, marriages preceded by cohabitation are more likely to end in divorce than marriages in which couples do not live together beforehand.

- Remarriage after divorce is decreasing, partially due to increases in cohabitation. Men are more like to remarry after divorce than are women.

- Women are more likely to be heads of lone-parent families, due to their lower remarriage rates and an increased tendency for children to be born to unmarried women. Lone-parent families are at very high risk of poverty and experience a shift from patriarchal control by men to patriarchal control by the state.

- Women are much more likely to be widowed. Among the population aged 65 years and over, widows outnumber widowers by a factor of five to one. Factors contributing to this gender differential include women's greater longevity, the fact that husbands are older than wives, and the higher rates of remarriage among widowers.

- *Single* refers to the never married; *unmarried* includes the separated, divorced and widowed. A reconceptualization of single life is needed that does not use marriage as the standard for comparison.

- The family life course of today's seniors is relatively uncomplicated, compared with that of younger Canadians. Today's seniors are less likely to have a history of cohabitation, divorce, and remarriage. The seniors of the future, on the other hand, will have had more complex family histories, and proportionately more of tomorrow's older women will have a life course involving paid labour.

- While family life course change has been substantial, there is a structural lag in the family–work interface for women. Women's labour force experience is marked by lower wages, part-time labour, and segregation by occupation and industry. Women's salaries make up only one-third of family income in dual-earner families.

- Both family and work life are based on a male, one-earner model. Accordingly, women make private accommodations to deal with work–family conflict.

- The characteristics of female paid labour, along with the accommodations women make, do not lead us to believe that the economic situation of younger women will be significantly better than that of today's elderly women. Their economic status may be further compromised by a greater likelihood of being unattached in later life—a major predictor of poverty in later life.

KEY TERMS

structural lag **(p. 115)**

mating gradient **(p. 118)**

patriarchy **(p. 123)**

materialist explanations **(p. 131)**

STUDY QUESTIONS

1. Interview some of your friends, and ask them how many children they expect to have. Consider what factors may lead to their having fewer children than they expect. Can you foresee any conditions under which your generation may decide to have more children?

2. What are the advantages and disadvantages of cohabitation? Do they differ for men and women?

3. Identify the major life course changes that have occurred, and are occurring, for men and for women. What are the major points of difference?

4. What public policy measures would help alleviate the work–family conflicts experienced by women?

5. Why do you think there has been such an increase in cohabitation?

6. If cohabitation is so common, why do we not have any social/cultural markers for the beginning or the end of this life transition?

SUGGESTED READINGS

Armstrong, P., & Armstrong, H. (2001). *The double ghetto: Canadian women and their segregated work* (3rd ed.). Toronto, Ontario: McClelland & Stewart.

Beaujot, R. (2000). *Earning and caring in Canadian families*. Peterborough, Ontario: Broadview.

Beaujot, R., Gee, E.M., Rajulton, F., & Ravanera, Z.R (1995). (Catalogue No. 91-643E). *Family over the life course*. Ottawa, Ontario: Statistics Canada.

Gunderson, M. (1998). *Women and the Canadian labour market*. Scarborough, Ontario: International Thompson Publishing for Statistics Canada.

Moen, P. (2000). The gendered life course. In R.H. Binstock & L.K. George (Eds.), *Handbook of aging and the social sciences* (5th ed.) (pp. 179–196). San Diego, CA: Academic Press.

Chapter 6

AGING AND ETHNICITY

Learning Objectives

In this chapter, you will learn about

- The importance of ethnicity and race in understanding aging.
- The ethnic origins of older Canadians.
- The immigration status of older Canadians.
- The visible minority status of older Canadians.

- Theorizing about ethnicity and aging.
- Health, wealth, and support of older ethnic minorities.
- Policy and practice with aging minorities.

Introduction

Virtually all countries in the world are ethnically diverse in that their populations are made up of groups of people with different ethnic ancestries. Canada has complex patterns of ethnic and linguistic diversity represented in various regions of the country. Indeed, in Canada, the census lists 200 ethnic groups in the population (Statistics Canada, 2003c). Canada is one of the most ethnically and racially diverse countries in the world, ranking after the United Kingdom, Singapore, and the United States (Pendakur & Henneby, 1998). In a multicultural society like Canada, the aged population clearly is not a homogeneous group. In 2001, about 30 percent of the population 65 years of age and over were members of ethnic or cultural groups, according to our analyses of the 2001 census data. To be an older member of an ethnic group, especially an older ethnic minority, is to experience environments substantially different from mainstream Canada.

Ethnogerontology is a new field in social gerontology that studies the influence of race, **ethnicity,** national origin, and culture on individual and population aging. Originally, ethnogerontology arose from a concern about the disadvantages experienced by ethnic minorities in the United States (Hooyman & Kiyak, 2005). The limited but growing research in ethnogerontology has shown that ethnicity and race have a profound influence on the aging experience, whether it be as a consequence of expectations for aging and preferred lifestyles, intergenerational differences, living arrangements, family supports, the use of ethnospecific health and social services, the problems of racism and discrimination, or any combination of these factors (Blakemore & Boneham, 1994; Hooyman & Kiyak, 2005). As an illustration, some Inuit do not subscribe to the view of healthy and active aging, the formula for successful aging that is promoted by mainstream Canadian culture. Rather, Inuit value the transmission of accumulated wisdom and knowledge to the young, an alternative view with implications for how Inuit will live their lives and how they will relate to younger generations (Collings, 2001).

In this chapter, we review how ethnicity and race influence the aging process, look at the ethnic makeup of Canada past and present, theorize about ethnicity, and explore the current circumstances of older Canadians with diverse ethnic backgrounds.

Ethnic Membership and Aging

Defining Ethnicity and Race

Ethnicity As would be anticipated, there are many ways of conceptualizing **ethnicity** and **race.** There has always been a question asked about one's origin on every Canadian census since confederation (Thomas, 2005). Since the inception of the census, people have been asked about their "origins," "race," "ethnic group" (first appeared in 1946), and, most recently, "ethnic-cultural ancestry" (Thomas, 2005:2). It is now argued that the census question about ethnic origin is interpreted as a question about individual identity (Thomas, 2005:3).

Some of the more common themes that appear in definitions of ethnicity include ancestral origin, a homeland or land of origin, a shared history of one's people and a shared identity, a language, sometimes a religion and, sometimes, a **culture** or subculture (Driedger & Chappell, 1987; Ujimoto, 1995; Vallee, 1998; Isajiw, 1999; Driedger, 2003). An **ethnic group** may be said to exist if group membership is defined by means of a characteristic normally inherited from one's parents, if the group has a distinct social structure, and if the shared ethnicity is recognized by individuals (ethnic identity) and by others (De Vries, 1995). The group's identity tends to be maintained over generations, not only because new members enter the society but also because members develop interest in their ancestry and identify with select aspects of the culture (James, 2003; Romanucci-Ross, De Vos, & Tsuda, 2006). What is important to remember, however, is that people have come to understand ethnic groupings as *fluid concepts* that change depending upon the social context. For example, it has been pointed out that the culture of ethnic groups is not necessarily a direct reflection of the original immigrant culture but rather a reconstructed ethnic culture in which traditions are developed on the basis of ongoing adaptations to the social environment in Canada (Fleras & Elliot, 1992:51).

Most gerontologists would agree that culture provides a world view for its members to the extent that the beliefs, values and agreed-upon behaviours provide some degree of personal and social meaning learned through tradition and transmitted through socialization. James (2003) makes it clear that all Canadians have a culture and that race, ethnicity and/or citizenship are not the only factors that influence their identity but "they are indeed characteristics by which individuals are identified in our society, around which selves are constructed, privileges are ascribed and mediated and consequences are experienced" (James, 2003:34). It is important to remember, therefore, that culture is only part of ethnicity and that culture and ethnicity are not interchangeable (Li, 1999). People of the same ethnicity do not necessarily share a common culture. Culture is not static and is subject to specific social conditions; it is not always uniform; it varies across historic times; and it is never safe to assume that there is a simple correlation between people, culture, and nation. An illustration of the complexity of culture is found in Box 6.1, a real story that happened in a large teaching hospital in a major Canadian city. The message is that familiarity with culture characteristics does always lead to clarity in a situation.

Ethnicity is important because it is one of the main factors that stratifies or contributes to the ranking of the social structure in a multicultural society like Canada. Within the social hierarchy, ethnic groups are perceived to have relatively different statuses, depending upon whether they belong to a majority ethnic group, such as the British groups in Canada (e.g., English, Scottish, Irish, and Welsh), or a minority group that comprises all other ethnic groups (Dreidger, 2003; Isajiw, 1999). Majority ethnic groups, because of their advantage of size, usually determine the nature of the societal institutions, and their culture becomes the overarching culture of the society within which minority groups coexist. The

Box 6.1 *The Complexity of Culture*

Mrs. J. was admitted to a large city hospital as a result of a serious heart attack. The treatment team believed that Mrs. J.'s children were translating their words accurately to the patient. However, a female Iranian cardiologist was able to decipher that at least one of Mrs. J.'s daughters was giving her inaccurate information about her condition. Mrs. J. was being told that she would completely recover as opposed to remaining chronically ill. When Mrs. J. asked the female cardiologist in Farsi what was wrong with her and whether she would recover, the cardiologist realized that she was in an untenable position

A family conference was held with the medical staff. During the meeting the eldest son spoke on behalf of the family and said that he would remove his mother from the hospital if she were told of the severity of her illness. He did not deny that false information had been given to his mother and said that the deception was in accordance with the values of their culture, which called on family to protect her. The Farsi-speaking doctor, who was from the same culture, disputed his claim of "culture of country" and suggested that he was really guided by his own family culture.

Source: Gerontology case studies, Faculty of Social Work, University of Toronto, 2005.

dominance of the majority group over the minority groups contributes to inequalities in a number of areas, especially when the minority groups are perceived to be a threat to the majority group's higher ranking in the social structure and, hence, resources (Johnson, 2006). However, an ethnicity other than British may not encompass minority status. Canadians belonging to Caucasian ethnic groups (e.g., Italians) may preserve their ethnic way of life and at earlier times were considered to be minorities, but are now generally considered to be part of the dominant group.

In the Canadian case, it is important to remember that Canada's French–English dualism has led to parallel institutions divided along linguistic lines so that Quebec is an exception to this observation. Although the French are a minority within the larger Canadian society, they are a charter group that has had a major impact in shaping the Canadian national character (Li, 1999). In contrast, the position of the Aboriginal peoples of Canada is quite different. In this "new world country," Aboriginal peoples have become a minority in the face of successive waves of immigrants who have subsequently been incorporated into the larger society (Laczko, 1997:112).

Within this complex plural structure is a larger web of interlocking hierarchies that allocate the resources of society according to power–dominance criteria associated not only with ethnicity, but also with age, gender, and class (Calasanti, 1996; Calasanti & Slevin, 2001). In essence, these statuses and their intersection influence a person's life chances, in terms of education, labour force participation, living arrangements, health status, and, ultimately, the quality of life in old age. To illustrate the effect of the combined forces of being a woman, an immigrant, and belonging to a visible minority, visible minority immigrant women in Canada have earnings 9 percent lower than those of white women (Pendakur & Pendakur, 1998; Basavarajappa & Jones, 1999; Li, 2000).

Although some scholars see ethnic membership in a group to be largely involuntary by virtue of recruitment at birth and socialization by parents and the community, others see ethnic identity to be partly a matter of subjective choice (Anderson, 1991; Blakemore & Boneham, 1994; Isajiw, 1999; James 2003). Both conceptions have important implications for aged ethnic group members. In the former case, changing ethnic identity can be a demanding psychological and social experience, as when moving to a different country. In the latter case, the self-identification with a specific ethnic group may act as a resource, providing a behavioural script and material resources to deal with new experiences, such as aging (Berry & Kalin, 1990). It is likely that both processes coexist, although more empirical support for these observations is required.

What is relevant is the implication that ethnic identity can wax and wane over the life course, consistent with the idea that ethnic membership can be fluid. One of the more important gerontological questions is whether ethnic identity is lost, retained, or strengthened in old age.

A number of scholars have warned that definitions of ethnicity warrant some caution in their usage. As is the case with aging in general, the variations within ethnic groups are often overlooked to the detriment of the aging individual (Dietz, John, & Roy, 1998; Whitfield & Baker-Thomas, 1999). As an example, in Canada, there are 11 Aboriginal language groups made up of more than 65 distinct languages and dialects represented among Aboriginal seniors (Health Canada, 1998a).

While earlier studies often compared ethnic groups without paying heed to what generations were being compared (Burr & Mutchler, 1993; Kamo & Zhou, 1994), today, researchers are more careful (Kobayashi, 2000; Hsu, Lew-Ting, & Wu, 2001). A generational approach to studying older ethnic group members takes into account the importance of socio-economic and political conditions encountered by each generation and, therefore, the different experiences of each generation and the nuances of the intergenerational relationships. The effect of the Holocaust, such as post-traumatic stress disorders suffered by many older Jewish Canadian survivors, has affected their relationships with the second generation (Safford, 1995).

Race Race and ethnicity are not synonymous. **Race** refers to physical appearance or, more specifically, the appearance of physical differences. Race is a category devised by others that places people with similar biological traits into a group. Essentially, race is a constructed social phenomenon (Isajiw, 1999; Li, 1999; James, 2003; Fluehr-Lobban, 2005). Physical traits, in themselves are not necessarily an identity-generating force because people tend to identify with their racial characteristics only as a response to being categorized and excluded by others in dominant positions. As a case in point, a participant in a study of Japanese Canadian families stated, "I don't think of myself as Japanese. I'm a

Canadian. The only reason I have to qualify my Canadian identity is because I look Japanese." (Kobayashi, 2000:193). What is more, this label can have real consequences for any Canadian. Despite the fact that black workers have education comparable with the population as a whole, they suffer higher levels of unemployment (Torczyner, 1997). This socially constructed category has a consequence that undoubtedly will stretch over a lifetime and be felt in old age. The concept of race also overlooks the ethnic diversity found in racial groups, such as the differences between African Canadians and those from the Caribbean (Foster, 1996). Without dwelling on the finer distinctions, race and ethnicity are different concepts that are not interchangeable, but both are important to the study of the aging process.

The Influence of Race and Ethnicity

The study of older people within their own ethnic group and in relation to other ethnic groups is important for a variety of reasons. First, different societies respond to the challenges of aging in different ways, and by understanding these processes, we can better understand what is culturally determined and what is age determined, and ultimately, the effect of ethnicity on age changes. Today, researchers are no closer to answers as to whether or not aging "levels" ethnic or racial differences (Rosenthal, 1983, 1986). The age-as-leveller concept posits that ethnic minorities do as well in the later years of their lives because aging challenges social, psychological, and physical abilities in unique ways that cut across ethnic boundaries (Williams & Wilson, 2001).

One of the main research controversies in the United States centres on the "crossover effect": African American mortality rates exceed those of Caucasian Americans until, at some age later in life, deaths among African Americans "cross over" and then decline relative to Caucasian Americans. This effect is attributed to selective survival and adaptation factors that cause those who survive to be more "hardy" (Markides et al., 1990). It is unclear, however, if the effect is a result of errors in collecting the date of birth of African Americans, or is a result of using cross-sectional surveys to study age effects (Williams & Wilson, 2001:168–169).

Second, ethnicity can act as a filter, influencing beliefs, behaviours, and interactions with society. By identifying culturally conditioned values in an older person's heritage, we can better understand the person's response to the aging process. In a study of younger and older Arab and Jewish people in Israel, ethnic background had a significant impact on the sources of the meaning of life, such as family, communal activity, and interpersonal relationships (Bar-Tur, Savaya, & Prager, 2001). Aging in an unfamiliar ethnic environment can cause distress for older people; conversely, membership in an ethnic community may act as an integrating force to buffer the stresses sometimes associated with aging (Strain & Chappell, 1984; Jacob, 1994). A study of elderly East Indian immigrants in Calgary found that when traditional living patterns were reversed (parents had to live with their children), the reported quality of life of the parents was poor (Murzello, 1991). In contrast, a longitudinal study of Korean immigrants to Canada found that increases in social support from family members and Korean friends lowered depression scores but support from the broader community had no effect on psychological distress (Noh & Avison, 1996).

Finally, incorporating the study of ethnicity into gerontology at the theory, research, and practice levels is necessary for understanding the aging of all old people. As the American gerontologist Calasanti has argued, using the knowledge from the standpoint theory (which refers to the perspective from where the person stands) exposes the racial/ethnic dynamics that shape aging experiences, including previously invisible aspects of the privileged group's experiences. Oppression is relational: "Oppression only exists to the extent privilege does, and vice versa" (Calasanti, 1996: 149). Framing the aging process to include both sides of unequal power relationships provides a more inclusive and complete picture of the aging process.

For example, during 2001 and 2002, there were 928 hate crime incidents reported by Canadian police forces. Fifty-seven percent of these crimes were motivated by race or ethnicity, 43 percent by religion, and about 10 percent by sexual orientation (Statistics Canada 2004e, 2005c). The 2002 Ethnic Diversity Study by Statistics Canada showed that 20 percent of visible minorities had experienced discrimination in the five years prior to the survey. The black respondents reported the highest levels of discrimination (32 percent) followed by the South Asians (21 percent) and then the Chinese (18 percent) (Statistics Canada, 2003d). It is difficult to imagine how a satisfactory old age is possible in a society where all Canadians do not have a right to dignity and respectful treatment, regardless of ethnic, racial, sexual, and religious differences.

Canada's Diverse Older Population

Ethnic Origin

Settlement and immigration have been the main constitutive factors in the history of Canadian society. Aboriginal peoples were the original settlers, followed by the English and the French, the two charter groups that formed the basis for all future interethnic relations in Canada (Laczko, 1997; Isajiw, 1999; Li, 1999). As Figure 6.1 shows, immigration over the century has fluctuated, with the largest waves of immigrants arriving in the 1910s, 1950s and 1990s (Boyd & Vickers, 2000). The composition of immigrant groups has been influenced by a host of shifting conditions: Canada's membership in the Commonwealth; alterations in immigration policies; the ups and downs of economic cycles in Canada and around the world; the displacement of people by wars and political strife; and economic globalization. For example, one of the largest waves of immigration was a result of labour market demands and immigration policy. From 1900 to 1915 Canada's economy grew so rapidly that the government instituted aggressive

Figure 6.1 IMMIGRATION TO CANADA, 1852–2004

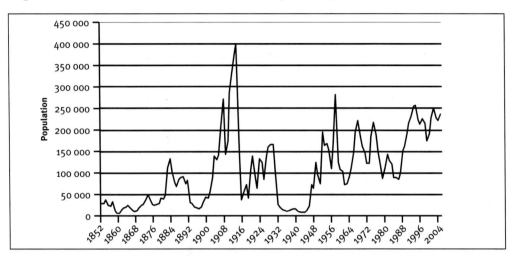

Source: Adapted from Citizenship and Immigration Canada, *Facts and figures, 2005: Immigration overview: permanent and temporary residents* (No. CI1-8/2004E). Ottawa ON: Research and Evaluation Branch. Reproduced with permission.

recruitment campaigns to boost immigration and attract more workers. Lured by the attraction of good jobs, the immigrant population grew from 13 percent to 22 percent between 1900 and 1911.

In the early 1800s, more than 15 000 men came from China as contract labourers to work on the Canadian Pacific Railway (CPR). Thousands of Jews fleeing Russia started to arrive at the same time, followed by Hungarians, who settled in Saskatchewan, and Ukrainians, who went to Manitoba. In 1899, the Doukhobors began arriving from Russia and settled in Saskatchewan and later in British Columbia. At the beginning of the 20th century, Indians, mostly Sikhs, came to British Columbia, as did over 8000 Japanese and Italians, who came to work on the CPR. As late as the 1950s, 80 to 90 percent of immigrants came from the United States and from European countries. This pattern began to change in the 1960s, when immigrants from Asia and other regions outside Europe began to arrive in greater numbers. By 1994, Europe accounted for only 17 percent of immigrants, while immigrants from Asia rose to 57 percent (Pendakur & Hennebry, 1998; Johnson, 2006).

According to the Canadian Census, **ethnic origin** refers to the ethnic or cultural group(s) to which the respondent's ancestors belonged. About 57 percent of the total Canadian population reported ethnic origins of British, French, or Canadian (mainly English or French Canadians) in 2001 (Statistics Canada, 2003i). Of the total Canadian population who report an ethnic origin other than British, French, or Canadian, German is the most frequently reported ethnic origin, followed by Italian, Chinese, Ukrainian, and North American Indian (Statistics

Canada 2005b). Aboriginal peoples made up about 3.4 percent of the total Canadian population in 2001 (Statistics Canada, 2005c).

The ethnic mix, however, varies by province because of the many different historical circumstances noted above. In Quebec, for example, Italian is the most frequently reported ethnic origin after British and French, followed by Aboriginal origin. In the territories, Aboriginal origin is the most frequently reported non-British or non-French ethnic origin.

As shown in Table 6.1, in 2001 there were 3 621 301 Canadians aged 65 years and over, representing 12.2 percent of the total population. British, French, and Canadian origins still dominate the 65 years and over age category. Of the people

Table 6.1 ETHNIC ORIGINS BY AGE CATEGORY, CENSUS CANADA 2001

Ethnic Origins	Percentage of Age Group		Percentage of Ethnic Group	
	0–64	65+	0–64	65+
Canadian	25.9	20.8	89.9	10.1
British	31.7	35.6	86.5	13.5
French	9.7	11.2	86.1	13.9
Other European	11.4	21.5	79.2	20.8
African	0.7	0.1	97.2	2.8
Arab	0.9	0.4	94.4	5.6
West Asian	0.6	0.3	93.2	6.8
South Asian	2.9	1.3	93.9	6.1
East and Southeast Asian	5.3	3.8	90.9	9.1
Latin, Central, and South American	0.5	0.1	96.6	3.4
Caribbean	1.2	0.6	93.6	6.4
Aboriginal*	2.0	0.7	95.5	4.5
Other	0.1	0.2	83.4	16.6
Multiple Other	7.1	3.3	93.9	6.1
	100.0%	100.0%	87.8%	12.2%
TOTAL N	26 012 362	3 621 301	26 012 362	3 621 301

* *Note:* There are many ways of defining the Aboriginal population, which can result in different estimates of the size. There is no single correct definition, and the choice depends on the type of analysis being conducted and the data used.
Source: Adapted from Statistics Canada, *Ethnocultural protrait of Canada, 2001 Census*, Catalogue No. 97F0010VCB2001001 (January 21, 2003).

65 years or older, 35.6 percent identify British ancestry, 11.2 percent French, and 20.8 percent Canadian roots. Older Canadians of single or multiple European backgrounds constitute the largest reported ethnic identity group after the British, French, or Canadian groups. With few exceptions, the ethnic mix of Canada's older people reflects the aging of the longer established immigrant populations that arrived in Canada at earlier times.

Thus, long-established ethnic groups will have higher proportions of older persons within their ranks than the "young" ethnic groups. While 12.2 percent of the Canadian population is 65 years of age or over, the proportions of old people among the British (13.5 percent) and the French (13.9 percent) are only slightly higher. European groups are the oldest, with 20.8 percent being over 65. In contrast, Aboriginal society is a very young society, with seniors accounting for only 4 percent of the total Aboriginal population (Figure 6.2).

Several significant shifts in the composition of the total Canadian population can be noted at a broad level. There has been a slow but gradual decline in the proportion of the French and the British in the total population. The French are currently down to about 15.8 percent from 19.6 percent in 1996, and the British are down from 23.9 percent to 20.2 percent. As well, in the last 40 years, there has been a dramatic increase in the Asian category. Before 1961, 3 percent of immigrants to Canada were born in Asia; between 1991 and 2001, this proportion increased to 58 percent (Statistics Canada, 2003d). In sum, from the 1960s onward, there has been a reversal of the proportion of Caucasian to non-Caucasian immigrants, particularly Asians, who constituted the largest groups of immigrants arriving annually in Canada in the 1990s. Obviously, it will take some time for population shifts to wend their way through the system to change the composition of the older Canadian population. Currently Canada's older ethnic population is not as diverse as are the younger cohorts. While 36 percent of those 65 to 74 years of age report at least one ethnic origin other than British, French, Canadian, or First Nations, 44 percent of Canadians aged 19 to 24 years report different origins (Mata & Valentine, 1999). What is significant is that the shifts indicate an increasingly greater role of the non-British and non-French ethnic groups among the elderly individuals of Canada. At the end of the 21st century, the older population will look very different from the current population.

We now turn to an examination of diversity among older Canadians.

Aboriginal Peoples

Of the total Aboriginal population in Canada, about 4 percent is 65 years of age or over; proportions are similar for First Nations and Métis (Statistics Canada, 2005c). Only 3.0 percent of the total Inuit population is age 65 years or older (see Figure 6.2). The number of Aboriginal seniors, while relatively small, soared 40 percent between 1996 and 2001, while the non-Aboriginal elderly population increased only 10 percent (Statistics Canada, 2003e). The projected growth in the

Figure 6.2 IDENTITY OF ABORIGINAL POPULATION 65 YEARS AND OVER

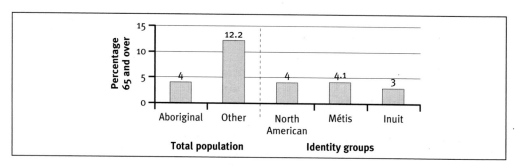

Source: Adapted from Statistics Canada, *Aboriginal peoples of Canada: highlight tables, 2001 Census*, Catalogue No. 97F0024XIE2001007 (January 21, 2003).

number of seniors varies by Aboriginal group and by place of residence. Future growth is projected to occur among registered Indians and Métis people living in urban areas. It is projected that by 2017, Aboriginals will constitute 4.1 of Canada's population. (Statistics Canada 2005c). In 2001, the life expectancy of First Nations women was just under 76 years, compared with 82 for the general population, and 70 years for First Nations men, compared with 77 for the general population (Government of Canada, 2005).

While beliefs, values, and customs vary widely among different nations, tribes, generations, and communities, some common beliefs underlie Aboriginal culture. Aboriginal values generally emphasize holism, pluralism, autonomy, community- or family-based decision making, and the maintenance of quality of life (Ellerby et al., 2000). Box 6.2 illustrates how these values can operate in a health-care setting. A major concern of Aboriginal peoples is the loss of their culture. The Cultural/Educational Centres Program was established by the federal government in 1971 to help First Nations and Inuit communities preserve, develop, and promote their culture and heritage.

Older Aboriginal peoples are a significant link with Aboriginal culture. In the oral tradition, culture is communicated through language. Transmission from one generation to the next is critical because Aboriginal languages cannot rely on immigration flows. As of 2001, about one-quarter (24 percent) of Aboriginal people reported that they had enough knowledge of an Aboriginal language to carry on a conversation—down from 29 percent in 1996 (Statistics Canada, 2003e). The Aboriginal languages reported as mother tongue have not changed over time, and the three largest groups remain Cree, Inuktitut, and Ojibway (Statistics Canada, 2002h). Seniors are twice as likely to speak an Aboriginal language as are younger people (Statistics Canada, 1999). About 95 percent of Inuit between 55 and 64 years, and all Inuit over age 65 years, reported using their mother tongue at home. The highest concentration of Aboriginal people is in the North (where

Box 6.2 *Caregiving and Aboriginal Values*

Mr. F, a 70-year-old Aboriginal elder male who speaks only Ojibway, is admitted to a tertiary care hospital for diagnostic investigation of possible prostate cancer.

Following the biopsy and other diagnostic tests, Mr. F, his son, the male interpreter, and the urologist meet. Addressing the son and the interpreter, the urologist explains that Mr. F has advanced cancer spreading to bone. When asked by the son about treatment, the urologist replies that any attempted curative treatment would probably cause more risk and discomfort than would pain relief and other palliative measures. The interpreter begins to translate the urologist's summary, but his explanation of the diagnosis is interrupted by the son, who says that he will communicate directly with his father. He states that the interpreter should not have used the Ojibway word *manitoc*, which denotes cancer through the cultural metaphor of "being eaten from within," and that direct reference to cancer

and his father's terminal prognosis will promote fear and pain. He adds that his father has given him responsibility to interpret and to act as his proxy decision-maker.

The son further opposes the physician's attempt to communicate the prognosis directly to Mr. F, stating that direct references to death and dying may "bring death closer." The urologist argues that Mr. F needs to understand his diagnosis to give informed consent for treatment. The son replies that he will not lie to his father but that he needs time to communicate with his father through a more gradual and indirect process. The physician and son finally agree that the son will involve other family members over the next 48 hours. The physician and family arrange to meet again in two days and, in the meantime, to hold a "sharing circle" in which patient, family members, and caregivers will discuss palliative care and answer Mr. F.'s questions.

Source: "Bioethics for clinicians: 18. Aboriginial cultures". Reprinted from *Canadian Medical Association Journal*, (October 3, 2000); 163(7), page(s) 845–850, by permission of the publisher. © 2000 CMA Media Inc.

they originally settled) and in the prairies, with approximately 31 percent of Aboriginals living on a reserve (Statistics Canada, 2003e). Aboriginal people represented 85 percent of the total population of Nunavut, 51 percent of the Northwest Territories, and almost one-quarter of Yukon. In Manitoba and Saskatchewan, about 14 percent of the population are Aboriginal compared to 5 percent in Alberta, 4.4 percent in British Columbia and 2 percent in Ontario (Statistics Canada, 2003e).

In Old Crow, Yukon Territory, the Vuntut Gwitchin use modern methods to honour their elders. Their website (http://www.oldcrow.ca/elders.htm) carries a column called "Here Are the News" from the *Whitehorse Star* that Edith Josee started writing in 1962 to keep a record of Old Crow and that she is still writing at age 77 years. She has captivated the hearts of Canadians, and several books have been written about her. She exemplifies an elder who has linked the past and the future to strengthen her culture and community.

A recent analysis of the 2001 Census data shows that Aboriginal people over age 65 are more likely to be widowed than other Canadians and twice as likely to reside with children over 14 years of age and to live in large households. Levels of postsecondary education are one-third those of the general Canadian population. Over one-third of older Aboriginal people work in unskilled labour, compared to 20 percent of non-Aboriginals. Employment rates are only slightly (1 percent) below those of older Canadians in general (McDonald, 2006). All of these factors affect their lifestyle and ultimately the quality of their old age.

Immigrants to Canada

A **landed immigrant** is a person born in another country granted the right to live in Canada permanently by immigration authorities. A relatively large proportion of older people in Canada are immigrants; 28.6 percent of the population aged 65 years and over in 2001 were immigrants, compared with only 17.7 percent of the population 64 or under in the same year (McDonald 2006). It is important to remember that the majority of older immigrants currently living in Canada have been here for a very long time. In fact, 61 percent arrived before 1961; 24 percent came in the 1960s and 1970s, while about 15 percent arrived between 1981 and 1996 (Health Canada, 1998b). The current older population "aged in place" in Canada; most were under 45 when they came.

It is less common for people to immigrate when they are already old. Only about 3 percent (fewer than 6,000) of those who immigrated to Canada in 2004 were 65 years of age or older (Citizenship and Immigration Canada, 2005:24).Approximately 80 percent of these people were **family-class immigrants**, 9 percent were **refugees**, and 2 percent were **economic-class immigrants** (Citizenship and Immigration Canada, 2005:24). The family class category in the *Immigration Act* stipulates that Canadian citizens and permanent residents have the right to sponsor the application of close relatives (spouses, dependent children, grandparents, brothers, and sisters). Family-class applicants are not assessed under the point system but are assessed for good health and character. Most importantly, the sponsor has to commit to support and house the applicant for up to 10 years, sometimes a problem for families (McDonald et al., 2001). Refugees are defined by the 1951 United Nations Convention on Refugees as people who may fear prosecution for reasons of race, religion, nationality, or political ideology and are outside the countries of their nationalities and who are unwilling to seek protection from those countries. Economic-class immigrants come to Canada for the purposes of business.

It is not always clear why older people immigrate to Canada. In a nonrandom study, 80 percent of newcomers indicated that they had come by their own choice; reasons included that they wanted to live with their children already settled here; they knew there were better health and social services for old people in Canada; and they liked the democratic political environment. The three most important reasons among those who felt they had no choice were that their children wanted them to help with family; their spouse had made the decision to come regardless of their wishes; or they could not continue to live alone in their home country (McDonald et al., 2001). A refugee will have different care needs from those of a family-class immigrant.

When we look at Table 6.2, we can see that Europeans represent half of all foreign-born seniors (50 percent of age group), with Southern Europeans holding a large share. Immigrants from the United Kingdom are the next largest group. About 32 percent of foreign-born people from the United Kingdom are elderly, compared with about 33 percent of Southern Europeans. On the other hand, of the people who came from East and Southeast Asia (China, Vietnam, Korea), 10.8 percent are age 65 years or older.

Senior immigrants are more likely to be married: 62 percent compared to 57 percent of non-immigrant Canadians of the same age. They are likely to have more children living at home: 26 percent of immigrants, but only 18 percent of those born in Canada, have three or more children over the age of 14 years living at home. Immigrants are more likely to have three people in their household than the rest of Canada, which averages only two persons per household. Even though immigrants are more likely to have substantially higher levels of education than the

Table 6.2 IMMIGRANTS BY PLACE OF BIRTH AND AGE

Place of Birth	PERCENTAGE OF AGE GROUP		PERCENTAGE OF ETHNIC GROUP	
	0–64	65+	0–64	65+
United Kingdom	8.9	19	67.6	32.4
Northern Europe	6.9	14.9	67.3	32.7
Southern Europe	9.7	17.7	71.1	28.9
Other European	9.4	17	71.3	28.7
Middle East	6.1	1.9	93.3	6.7
United States	4.2	4.3	81.3	18.7
India/South Asia	10.5	4.3	91.6	8.4
Southeast Asia	24.5	13.3	89.2	10.8
Africa	6.2	2.1	92.8	7.2
South/Central America/Caribbean	12.5	5.1	91.7	8.3
Australia	1	0.4	91.1	8.9
Column Total	100.0%	100.0%	81.7%	18.3%
Total N	4 525 098	1 013 957	4 525 098	1 013 957

Source: Adapted from Statistics Canada, *Immigration and citizenship, 2001 Census (immigrant status and place of birth of respondent, sex and age groups for population)*, Catalogue No. 95F0357XCB2001004 (April 23, 2003).

Canadian born (33 compared to 23 percent), and are more likely to be in professional/managerial professions (38 versus 31 percent), they have about the same unemployment rate as other older Canadians (McDonald, 2006b).

The Ethnic Diversity Survey carried out in 2002 in Canada of 42 500 people aged 15 years of age and over offers some interesting observations about ethnicity. Half of the respondents indicated that they had a strong sense of belonging to their ethnic or cultural group. Filipinos reported the strongest sense of belonging, followed by Indians, Portuguese, French Canadians, Chinese, and Italians. Not surprisingly, a larger proportion of the first generation (foreign born) reported a strong sense of belonging than subsequent generations born in Canada (57 versus 47 percent). Furthermore, the more recently they had arrived in Canada, the stronger their sense of belonging. In terms of ethnic customs and traditions, the first generation was more likely to rate them as important compared to second and third generations. The first generation was also more likely to stay in touch with family in the country of origin (Statistics Canada, 2003c). The information from this survey suggests that the attachment of people to their ethnic or cultural ancestry varies according to ethnic group, length of time in Canada, and the number of generations they have lived in Canada (Statistics Canada, 2003d).

Visible Minorities

Visible minority is defined by the *Employment Equity Act* (1995) as "persons, other than First Nations peoples, who are non-Caucasian in race or non-white in colour." Only a relatively small portion of Canadians 65 years of age and over are members of a visible minority group. According to the 2001 Census, 7.1 percent of the total population 65 years of age and older were part of a visible minority group. In comparison, 10.9 percent of those aged 45 to 64 years, 14.9 percent of those aged 25 to 44 years, and 15.8 percent of those aged 15 to 24 years were members of a visible minority group (McDonald, 2006b).

As seen in Table 6.3, of all the visible minorities over age 65 years, about 39 percent are Chinese, 21 percent are South Asian, and 13 percent are black. In the "Other" category, which accounts for 28 percent of visible minorities, 7 percent are Filipino and 6 percent are Arab. The Japanese (3.76 percent), Southeast Asians (3.85 percent), Latin Americans (2.77 percent), and Koreans (2.75 percent) are relatively smaller groups. The visible minorities are mainly "young" groups, with smaller proportions of older people than in the case of the total Canadian population, with the exception of the Japanese. In 2001, 16 percent of all those in the Japanese minority population were over the age of 65—higher than the figure for the Canadian population. As Table 6.3 indicates, about 10 percent of the Chinese are aged 65 years or over, coming closer to the percentage for the total Canadian population over age 65.

The majority of visible minorities, including aged members, live in cities. Seven of every 10 visible minority individuals in Canada lived in just three major

Table 6.3 ELDERLY AND NON-ELDERLY BY VISIBLE MINORITY STATUS

Visible Minority Status	As a Percentage of All Visible Minorities by Age Group		As a Percentage of the Total Population by Age Group	
	0–64	65+	0–64	65+
Chinese	26.34	38.98	90.00	10.00
South Asian	22.77	21.34	91.91	8.09
Black	15.63	12.48	93.02	6.98
Other	35.0	27.5	92.8	7.20
Filipino	7.97	7.00	92.37	7.63
Arab	7.75	6.18	94.31	5.69
West Asian	1.78	2.71	94.59	5.41
Latin American	5.80	2.77	95.70	4.30
Japanese	1.83	3.76	83.78	16.22
Southeast Asian	5.01	3.85	93.71	6.29
Korean	1.76	2.75	94.35	5.65
Other	2.56	2.31	92.17	7.83
Multiple	1.63	1.41	93.83	6.17
Total	100.00	100.00	87.8	12.2
Total N	2 780 495	261 155	2 780 495	261 155

Source: Adapted from Statistics Canada, *Ethnocultural portrait of Canada, 2001 Census (visible minority groups, sex and age groups for population)*, Catalogue No. 95F0363XIE2001004 (April 23, 2003).

metropolitan areas in 2001: Toronto (43 percent), Vancouver (18 percent), and Montreal (12 percent) (Statistics Canada, 2003a). Aging in an urban environment presents both challenges and benefits to older people from minority backgrounds. Large cities are more likely to have well-established ethnic communities with community institutions such as places of worship, recreational facilities, radio, newspapers, television, culturally sensitive health and social services, and traditional health care (McDonald et al., 2001). On the other hand, cities are very expensive, fast paced, and difficult to navigate, making services hard to access, not only to older persons but to their families as well. Jobs are hard to secure for older persons who do not speak the dominant language(s), and isolation is a genuine concern where informal support networks are at a premium, and where there are limited opportunities to create them.

The visible minorities have a slightly different demographic profile than non-visible minorities. Overall, visible minorities are more likely to be widowed; they are twice as likely to have young adults in the home; and their household size is almost twice the size of that of the non-visible minority population. Although they have a small advantage educationally (31 versus 26 percent have postsecondary education), they are no more likely to hold professional or managerial jobs than the non-visible minorities. If visible minorities are in the labour force at older ages they are slightly more likely to be unemployed (McDonald, 2006).

To summarize this section, Canada's population over age 65 is diverse but not as diverse as the upcoming younger cohorts, who will eventually age and change the ethnic composition of Canada's older people. In light of current immigration patterns, we can expect to see further declines in the numbers of those of British ancestry, an increase in the number of First Nations seniors in urban areas, and an increase in the numbers of visible minority elderly in urban areas as well. According to Statistics Canada's projections, the number of Canadians in visible minority categories is expected to increase to between 6.3 and 8.5 million by 2017, from approximately 4 million in 2001 (Bélanger and Malenfant, 2005). As a proportion of the overall population, visible minorities will constitute between 19 and 23 percent of the population in 2017. In 2001, the largest visible minority group was Chinese; but by 2017, the South Asian group may be the largest. The combined population of Chinese and South Asians is projected to reach between 3.2 and 4.4 million in 2017. Blacks will form the third largest visible minority group (between 948 thousand and 1.2 million). West Asians, Koreans, and Arabs are expected to increase at the fastest rate (Bélanger and Malenfant, 2005). The vast majority of visible minority adults live in urban areas so that they will be aging in a city as opposed to a rural environment. Although the impact of the projected demographic changes is uncertain, they do foretell a slightly different, older urban population that may have different needs. Whether we are prepared for these changes in Canada is highly questionable. We have little research on aging and ethnicity or, for that matter, on any minority groups and even less about new arrivals in Canada.

Theorizing about Ethnicity

Canadian gerontologists have not only conducted limited research on ethnicity and aging, they have also engaged in minimal theory development. It has been suggested that elderly members of ethnic groups have been too small to warrant much attention until recently, at least in the United States (Gelfand, 2003; Hooyman & Kiyak, 2005). While social gerontologists generally recognize that it is important to consider diversity, this factor has not been fully incorporated into research or theory (Hendricks, 1996).

In multicultural countries, such as the United Kingdom, the United States, and Australia, the focus of most of the research has been almost entirely on inequality, usually on the additive disadvantage of being old and belonging to a visible minority group (Dowd & Bengtson, 1978). In Canada, the limited research activity has been directed more at ethnic groups generally (e.g., French and English). One Canadian researcher has argued that research on diversity has been given short shrift because the sociological aging theories of inequality (e.g., age stratification, political economy) are not well suited to research on diversity and need to be rethought (McMullin, 2000). Whatever the cause, most theorizing has not overtaken the multiple jeopardy hypothesis, its competitor, the age levelling hypothesis, or the buffer hypothesis, which we will consider in this section.

Shared Perspectives

Assimilation and Modernization Theories   Conventional sociological theories have been the foundation of both gerontological theory and general theories of ethnicity (see Chapter 3). One broad perspective that has been applied is modernization theory, described in Chapter 3. Modernization theory links the lower status of older people to the increasing industrialization when simple societies are transformed into complex urban societies (Driedger & Chappell, 1987; Kim Hisata, Kai, & Lee, 2000). The theory has been used in a variety of ways, but mainly to explain differences among societies at different stages of industrialization, as in the case of developing countries (Olson, 2001). It can be used to study ethnic groups on a continuum of modernization and their attendant status. Modernization theory has been critiqued as being inconsistent with reality. Less modernized families do not necessarily support their ethnic elders any more than do modern families (Rosenthal, 1983).

Cut from the same structural functionalist cloth is the **essentialist approach** to understanding ethnicity, one of the oldest in sociology and anthropology. The argument is that "ethnicity is something given, ascribed at birth, deriving from the kin-and-clan structure of human society and something more or less fixed and permanent" (Isajiw, 1999: 30). It involves a set of "ready-made" attributes and an identity that an individual shares with others from birth. Offshoots of this approach treat ethnicity as a matter of identity, including what forces help maintain it or impel it to change. When scholars investigate assimilation and pluralism of ethnic groups, the core issue is ethnic identity (Li, 1999).

Assimilation theories go back to the Chicago School of sociology (e.g., Robert Park, W.I. Thomas, and F. Znaniecki) and suggest that minority groups will assimilate and lose their separate ethnic identities to a melting pot or through conformity or amalgamation with the dominant group (Driedger & Halli, 2000). Over time, the theories have been modified substantially to capture the many possible levels of assimilation or acculturation (Glazer & Moynihan, 1963; Driedger & Halli, 2000). Early studies of ethnic identity addressed how older people managed their ethnic identity in the face of aging and how identity changed from first generation to second and third generations, particularly among Japanese Canadians (Sugiman & Nishio, 1983; Ujimoto, 1995). A study of first- and second-generation Indo-Guyanese immigrants living in Ottawa found that first-generation immigrants had a greater identification with their Indo-Guyanese identity than the second generation, in private settings. In public settings, though, first-generation men were identified more with Canadians than were first-generation women (Clément, Singh, & Gaudet, 2006). A study of foreign-born Chinese who had immigrated to Vancouver and Victoria in old age showed that 49 percent felt more Canadian than Chinese; 37 percent felt more Chinese; and 14 percent felt equally Canadian and Chinese (Gee, 1999).

Assimilation theories lost some of their lustre over the years in the face of wide variations between and within ethnic groups and in response to multiculturalism policies in Canada that promoted **pluralism** (Fleras & Elliot, 1992). Spurred on by the complexity of ethnicity and its many levels and manifestations, researchers developed a multitude of continua that ran between assimilation and pluralism on a variety of levels, to include external and internal processes (Li, 1990; Dreidger & Halli, 2000). Pluralism suggested that ethnic groups retain a separate identity and do not always assimilate but still manage to live amicably in the Canadian community. Pluralism today usually refers to the Canadian multicultural mosaic that, at least in theory, values diversity (Fleras & Elliot, 1992).

Although assimilation may not be the norm, it is still studied in great detail in Canada. One of the main markers of ethnic assimilation is language, in particular the degree to which people use their language at home (De Vries, 1995). A study using 1981 census data concluded that there was enormous variation among older members of ethnic groups in the use of mother tongue and home language (Driedger & Chappell, 1987). Today, the majority of older Canadians speak at least one official language, but the proportion who do not is higher than among younger people. In 2001, 4.4 percent of Canadians over age 65 did not speak either English or French, compared with about 1.1 percent for younger age groups. Moreover, 13 percent of seniors, compared with 10 percent of younger people aged 15 to 64 years, spoke only a language other than English or French in their home (McDonald, 2006b). The proportion of older Canadians speaking a non-official language in their home has increased from 7 percent in 1981, likely reflecting changes in immigration patterns and the fact that older people maintain some aspects of their ethnic identity.

Age Stratification and Ethnic Stratification

Other approaches that cross-cut gerontology and ethnic studies are the structural frameworks used to explain aging and ethnicity. Like age stratification and political economy, **ethnic stratification** operates on the assumption of inequality in the social structure. Various ethnic groups are differentially incorporated into the larger society (aided and abetted by prejudice and discrimination) and membership in different groups confers different levels of resources, prestige, and power. The indicators of education, occupation, and income typically have been used to measure these positions. The **multiple jeopardy hypothesis** in gerontology represents the union of these two approaches (Markides, 1983; Gelfand, 1994). Early jeopardy theorists argued that if one were old and belonged to an ethnic group, especially a visible minority group, one was doubly disadvantaged. The jeopardy studies expanded to include multiple negative statuses, adding female gender and low social class. The alternative hypothesis, the **age levelling hypothesis,** as noted earlier, proposed that age effects cut across all racial and ethnic lines (Cool, 1981), levelling out inequalities found earlier in life.

Support for the jeopardy hypothesis has been lukewarm at best (Penning, 1983; Havens & Chappell, 1983; Wong & Reker, 1985), while some scholars have found little evidence to support the hypothesis (Chan, 1983; Havens & Chappell, 1983; Lubben & Becerra, 1987). The promulgators of the hypothesis found in their own cross-sectional study of African, Mexican, and Caucasian people some support with regard to income and self-rated health, but little support when it came to psychological well being (Markides, Liang, & Jackson, 1990). Many minority elders expressed high levels of psychological well being, a finding confirmed in a number of studies (Miner & Montoro-Rodriguez, 1999; Kobayashi, 2000). In other words, the external indicators of income, education, and occupation missed the mark; the social psychological processes of group identification and interaction were equally important.

Some have called the influence of psychosocial factors the **buffer hypothesis** (Miner & Montoro-Rodriguez, 1999). A direct test of the role of family psychological factors, compared with structural factors (acculturation, socio-economic status), in an American study of Hispanics, found that collectivistic family values held by older Hispanics were the most important factors correlated with high levels of well being (Miner & Montoro-Rodriguez, 1999:443). Conversely, a Canadian study of foreign-born Chinese elders found that ethnic identity did not compensate for low income. Gee (1999) found evidence that Chinese immigrants with lower incomes were less likely to identify themselves as Chinese. The author hypothesized that a Canadian identity may be more helpful to the descendants of poor older Chinese.

Although some scholars (Markides et al., 1990) suggest that the jeopardy hypotheses have come to the end of their run, much of the recent interest (McMullin, 2000) in diversity still addresses the same issues of multiple statuses, albeit from a broader base and within ethnic groups.

Constructing Ethnicity A recent trend in theorizing about ethnicity and aging is a constructivist perspective. Both age and ethnicity are negotiated and constructed in everyday life. As Nagel (1994: 162) observes ". . . culture is not a shopping cart that comes to us already loaded with a set of historical cultural goods. Rather, we construct culture by picking and choosing items from the shelves of the past and the present." At the outset, in social gerontology, political economists argued that age was a socially constructed category emanating from policies on aging, such as state pension plans. These gerontologists were joined later by feminists who added race and ethnicity to the mix, arguing that the experiences of ethnic minorities and older women were conditioned by the intersection of their social class, gender, and ethnic statuses. Their research investigated how these factors affected experiences (Calasanti, 1996; Estes, Mahakian, & Weitz, 2001). Exploration of the various ways in which ethnic minorities construct retirement or how older ethnic minority women in Canada foster and reshape their identities would be examples of this work. Dosa's study of aging Canadian Ismaili women who immigrated to Canada shows how a woman's life story is an "... embodiment of a homeland that can be (re)imagined only in her new country" (Dosa, 1999: 268). In Kobayashi's (2000) study of third-generation children (Sansei) and second-generation parents (Nisei), she found that while the majority of Japanese children believed in the longstanding values of filial piety, fewer adult children identified with being Japanese Canadian.

The theories addressed above provide several different lenses through which we can examine ethnicity and its effects on the social and psychological aspects of aging. Unfortunately, the net result is often fragmentary. Most of the theories do not have the capacity to capture the effects of ethnicity at the structural level and its link to the psychological and family levels. The theories are especially weak in reflecting the effects of multiple generations within ethnic groups. To apply any of the aforementioned theoretical perspectives with confidence at this time would be a risky business. The life course perspective, with its emphasis on the complex interrelationships among biographical time, social time, and historical time and its potential to link the individual and the structural, has been flagged as having promise (Rosenthal, 1987; Ferraro, 1997) but has rarely been used in the study of ethnicity and aging. Fry makes a strong argument that time is actually problematic in a life course perspective because of the cultural knowledge that is the foundation of the measurement of chronological time (2003: 272). According to this scholar, the life course is a cultural construct, based on cultural definitions of time and the uses of age. In short, we have only begun the theoretical work in this area.

The Wealth, Health, and Family Support of Ethnic Minorities

The Economic Resources of Older Minorities

A recent study of the economic resources of senior immigrants, visible minorities, and Aboriginals indicated that the ethnic stratification hypothesis operates at older ages. Using the Census 2001 data, the results showed that Aboriginal peoples, followed by visible minorities and lastly, immigrants, are the most likely to be below the low-income cut-offs (LICOs) of Statistics Canada. A person falls below the LICO if he or she spends a higher proportion of income on the necessities of life than does the average Canadian. Using Census 2001 data, 18 percent of the general senior population falls below the LICO. All minority groups were economically worse off than the majority: 23 percent of visible minorities, 19 percent of immigrants, and 31 percent of Aboriginal peoples 65 years of age and over were below the LICOs. The burden of poverty was carried by women in all instances, with an alarming 36 percent of older Aboriginal women, 25 percent of visible minority women and 24 percent of immigrant women below the low income cut-offs (McDonald, 2006b).

Sources of income were similar for immigrants and Canadian-born older adults. Immigrants received slightly lower government transfer payments, but the difference was less than $400 apart, no doubt because most older immigrants have been here long enough to collect a full Old Age Pension.

Visible minorities did not appear to benefit much from either the public or private pensions systems in this study. They received over $1000 less than other Canadians from government sources and $3500 less from work-related pensions (McDonald, 2006). The difference could reflect such factors as length of time in Canada, facility with the official languages, educational credentials, and barriers in the labour market.

While many new senior immigrants are pleased to be in Canada, the problem of financial dependence surfaces repeatedly (McDonald et al., 2001; Leung & McDonald, 2002). In interviews with 142 newcomer seniors to Canada, 35 percent reported financial difficulties to be a major problem (McDonald et al., 2001). Most are retired, with little opportunity for employment; they lack their own economic resources and are ineligible for full Canadian pensions or reciprocal pensions from their country of origin. Thus they have nowhere to turn, except to family. Many are forced to live in multigenerational households, and although they often participate in household chores and childcare to help out, they are still totally dependent on family for most of their needs. That only 11 percent of newcomer seniors were able to make a financial contribution to their own families is most telling (McDonald et al., 2001). Their lack of independence in a reduced social world where everything is foreign, including the spoken language, becomes even more challenging if illness strikes or if their adult children have their own problems.

The economic circumstances of Aboriginal seniors is strikingly different from Canadian seniors overall and represents a legacy of poor education, high unemployment, residential segregation, inadequate housing, lack of social services, malnutrition, and poor health (Driedger & Chappell, 1987; Wister & Moore, 1998). Given a lifetime of racial discrimination and inequality, it is not surprising that the mainstay of Aboriginal peoples' income in old age is the public pension system (McDonald, 2006b). Of all minority groups, they receive the largest total government transfer payments, ($13 000 versus $12 000) making them the most dependent on government (McDonald, 2006b).

The high poverty rates experienced by aging ethnic minorities and older Aboriginal women, in particular, is a serious problem in danger of being ignored. Most Canadians believe that the "poverty issue" associated with elderly persons has been solved, in light of the plummeting poverty rates for the older population as a whole (see Chapter 14). If there ever was a case for treating a private problem as a public issue, this would be an important example. As the dollars directed to health and social services for older people shrink, those with the fewest economic resources and with the weakest claim on the Canadian pension system are at risk of the greatest harm.

Health

Population-based information on immigrants' health status, disability, and life expectancy indicates that the **healthy immigrant thesis** applies to Canada (Chen, Ng, & Wilkins, 1996). Fundamentally, immigrants of all ages are healthy on arrival in Canada, but compared with native-born Canadians, they lose this advantage over time (Ng, Wilkins, Gendron & Berthelot, 2005; Newbold, 2005). Immigrants who come to Canada from Europe, the United States, or Australia and who have higher levels of education, occupational status, and higher incomes, report very good or excellent health, compared with those who come from Asia, Africa, and South America (Dunn & Dyck, 2000; Newbold & Danforth, 2003). A recent Canadian study found, however, that the hypothesis applies only to recently arrived middle-aged immigrants but not to recent immigrants 65 years of age and over; older adults have worse health than their Canadian counterparts on arrival to Canada. Older immigrants' health needs are different than the middle-aged and are likely to follow a different trajectory (Gee, Kobayashi, & Prus, 2004). What is more, poor financial circumstances early in life become more closely associated with poor health in later life: health risks accumulate over time for the poor (Prus, 2004).

Data from the National Population Health Survey (NPHS 1996–1997) show that ethnicity is related to health status. Fewer than 25 percent of seniors born in Canada, the United States, Europe, Australia, and Asia reported fair or poor health, while more than 33 percent of seniors born in Central and South America and Africa reported fair or poor health. Seniors who have lived in Canada for 10 years or more reported the same level of health as native-born older Canadians. In contrast, 40 percent of recent immigrants perceived their health to be fair to poor (Maurier & Northcott, 2000:48). The effect of race on the health of older Canadians suggests that there is a racial disadvantage, at least for seniors living in Ontario. Maurier and Northcott (2000), using the NPHS, found that approximately 40 percent of Caucasian seniors, compared with 33 percent of non-Caucasian seniors, in Ontario reported excellent to very good health. In light of the poor economic circumstances of Aboriginal peoples, it is not surprising the National Council on Aging asserts that they are the unhealthiest Canadians.

Several investigations indicate that the prevalence of chronic diseases among the immigrant population converge with that of the Canadian population over time (Chen, Ng, & Wilkins, 1996). In a study of Chinese elders in British Columbia, it was found that they suffered from as many chronic conditions as the older Canadian population (Chappell, Lai, & Gee, 1997; Chappell & Lai, 1998). At the same time, we know that the rate of diabetes is higher in specific ethnic minority groups, including South Asians and African Canadians (NACA, 2005). Even though the health of Aboriginals is improving (Government of Canada, 2005), Aboriginals are at least three times as likely to have diabetes as the general population (Health Canada, 2002). Older persons of Aboriginal ancestry have very high rates of disability, compared with the general older population. On the basis of the *First Nations Peoples Survey*, 1991, Wister and Moore (1998) reported that among those 55 years of age and older, the rate of disability was 66.5 for all First Nations peoples, compared with 37.4 percent for other Canadians of the same age (see Chapter 9).

Most scholars and clinicians agree that there is a strong interaction between culture and mental health (e.g., Pang, 1998; McCracken et al., 1997; Black, Kyriakos, & Miller, 1998; Meier, 2000; Bajek, Blare, Grewa, Karlso, & Nazroo, 2004, Peng & Lettner, 2004; Abramson, Trejo, & Lai, 2002; Almeida & Fenner, 2002; Chappell, Havens, Hollander, Miller, & McWilliam, 2004). In Canada, there is a steady increase in the suicide rate with age among immigrants: where suicide rates tend to level off after ages 35 to 44 among the Canadian-born, elderly immigrants have the highest rates of suicide (Malenfant, 2004). Several studies of immigrant elderly Chinese in Canada found rates for depression higher than those of the general elderly population, especially among women (Lai, 2000a; 2000b; 2004a). To underscore this finding, elderly Chinese women in the United States have a suicide rate 10 times that for older Caucasian women (Butler, Lewis, & Sutherland, 1998). A nationwide study found that greater identification with Chinese cultural values, along with encountering more cultural barriers, resulted in a higher probability of depression among elderly Chinese Canadians (Lai, 2004b).

Several researchers have found that culturally specific belief patterns about illness and health that influence views on illness and health-care utilization (Chung, 1994; Cook, 1994; Kopec, Williams, To, & Austin, 2001). Some of the identified belief patterns include more deference to authority/compliance, courtesy/desire not to offend, stoicism, and different types of social obligations (Morioka-Douglas, Sacks, & Yeo, 2004). For example, cultural factors may have a substantial effect on the reporting of pain. French Canadians and non-English Europeans have greater odds of reporting pain (Kopec et al., 2001). A study of Japanese, Korean, and Chinese Canadians 65 years of age and older, found that elderly Koreans expressed the most dissatisfaction with their health (Ujimoto, Nishio, Wong, & Lam, 1995), whereas an earlier study found that Koreans reported few mental health problems because they experience the symptoms of mental illness as physical symptoms (Kim, 1987). Anthropologist Peter Collings (2001), in his study of successful aging among Inuit, discovered that there was no such thing as good health in old age; what mattered was the ability to manage declining health successfully.

About half of the Chinese elderly people in a British Columbia study used traditional Chinese medicine (TCM) for minor and major illnesses, which the researchers found to be associated with religious beliefs and a preference for

Box 6.3 *Well-Being*

Among the Gitksan and Wet'suwet'en, there is no mother tongue word for health. However, they do have a word for strength, which is interchangeable[with] health. They also speak of well-being. This well-being is associated with high self-esteem, a feeling of being at peace and being happy... This includes education. It includes employment. It includes land claims. It includes resource management. All of these lead back to wellness and well-being.

Source: People to people, nation to nation: highlights from the report of the Royal Commission on Aboriginal peoples. Page 96. The Commission, 1996. Reproduced with the permission of the Minister of Public Works and Government services and courtesy of the Privy Council Office, 2006.

traditional Chinese medicine (Chappell & Lai, 1998:35). Another study found that older Chinese Canadians were more likely to use TCM and Western medicine together if they had pain or had been hospitalized. Users of TCM had strong to moderate beliefs about using TCM (Tjam & Hirdes, 2002).

In a B.C. study of Chinese elders, a multivariate analysis showed no relationship between the use of health services and the ability to speak English, immigration history, or country of origin (Chappell & Lai, 1998). However, more than 90 percent of the elders reported using physician services with some Chinese staff, probably because they had an opportunity to use their own language. Overall, service use of physicians and home-care services were the same for Chinese elders as for the rest of the senior population. Marriage, longer residence in Canada, and a strong ethnic identity increased the chance of an older Chinese person getting a physical examination (Lai & Kalyniak, 2005). A study of Chinese older adults across Canada found that even though the group reported poorer mental health and higher rates of depressive symptoms than the general older population, they used fewer mental heath services (Lai, 2004b). The same study found that only 5 percent of older Chinese used home-care services (Lai, 2004c) Immigrant older adults to Ontario from Asia, Central America, South America, and Africa used fewer home-care services than the Canadian-born and immigrants from Europe, America, and Australia (Maurier & Northcott, 2000).

In the senior newcomer study, lack of information about services and language barriers were the two most important reasons why services were not used, even if they were needed (McDonald et al., 2001). In the United States, an analysis of three national data files on service use found that living arrangements, health status, number of functional limitations, region, and health insurance affected utilization of service more than race or ethnicity (Markides & Black, 1996). At the same time, another study found that medical and psychosocial interventions that were ethnically sensitive increased ethnic minority utilization of services (Miller et al., 1996).

Aboriginal people in Canada are frequently dissatisfied with the contemporary health system, given its superficial acknowledgement of holism. As a result, many health services are being transferred to the control of First Nations and Inuit communities in a bid to provide culturally sensitive health services (Health Canada, 2002). This will likely benefit seniors, some of whom, according to one study, go out for less than an hour a day on the reserve (Frideres, 1994).

The need for research on ethnicity and health and service utilization at older ages is obvious. At this point, we cannot say what characteristics are shared across ethnic or minority groups or how each is unique. We do know that the health-care system is not organized to take their needs into account.

Family Support

The relationship between ethnicity and the provision of support to older persons from family has always been a focus of Canadian gerontologists, although the research has been a trickle, rather than a stream. Support from family is important because it is known to enhance health, especially mental health (Health Canada, 1999; Falcón & Tucker, 2000), it is known to relieve stress (Noh & Avison, 1996) and prevent loneliness (Williams & Wilson, 2001), and it is believed to contribute to a more culturally sensitive environment within the host society (Miner & Montoro-Rodriguez, 1999; see also Fiksenbaum, Greenglass, & Eaton [2006] and Karademas [2006] on the positive benefits of social support).

The underlying assumption driving the research is related to the earlier traditional–modern continuum for classifying ethnic groups. Presumably, more "traditional" ethnic groups have extended families available to them and, because of culturally conditioned norms of filial responsibility, are more supportive of older family members (Uijimoto, 1995; Keefe, Rosenthal, & Béland, 2000). Service providers and policymakers in health and immigrant settlement have indicated that social support has numerous advantages for immigrants and refugees to Canada, including developing a sense of empowerment, social and community integration, stress reduction, and improved physical and mental health; conversely, a lack of social support resulted in increased feelings of loneliness, loss of identity, and a knowledge deficit of available services and supports (Simich, Beiser, Stewart, & Mwakarimba, 2005; Simich, Beiser, & Mawani, 2003).

The evidence for ethnic differences in support, both instrumental (e.g., transportation, financial) and affective (emotional) has been mixed. The earlier Canadian research found few differences among ethnic groups (Chappell & Penning, 1984). Payne and Strain (1990) compared support patterns among four dominant ethnic groups in Canada. They did not find any conspicuous differences among British, French, German, and Ukrainian ethnic groups, possibly because of the assimilation of these groups into mainstream society. A study in Quebec examined caregiving in Haitian, Italian, and Chinese families and concluded that there were more similarities than differences among the groups (Guberman & Mahue, 2003/2004).

Research that examines more recent immigrants from a wider spectrum of ethnic and racial groups has found ethnic differences in support patterns. Using a non-random sub-sample from the CARNET Work and Family Survey, Keefe et al. (2000) discovered that respondents of southern European, Asian, and East Indian ethnic origin were twice as likely as those of British origin to provide three hours or more of help to senior members of their families. Filial obligation was an important value to all groups. **Co-residency** had the strongest influence on helping behaviour, followed by being female and older.

Other relevant Canadian studies have explored social support in single ethnic groups. Ho, Friedland, Rappolt, and Noh (2003) reported that social support helped Chinese Canadian women cope with the stresses of caring for relatives with Alzheimer's disease. Noh and Avison (1996) found that social support from Korean family members living in Toronto was more helpful than from the non-Korean community. Chappell and Lai (2001), who compared the level of life satisfaction of Chinese seniors living in Victoria (Canada) and Zuzhou (China), found that social support was more important to life satisfaction of the Chinese in Zuzhou. A closer look at social support indicated that living with others was important to the Zuzhou Chinese but not as important as geographical location (i.e., living in Victoria versus living in Zuzhou). The authors concluded that the differences in contributions to life satisfaction between the Canadian and Chinese seniors represented cultural differences. Kobayashi (2000), in her study of generational support between second-generation and third-generation Japanese Canadian families found that the value of filial obligation influenced the provision of emotional support and the quality of the support, but parents' health and socioeconomic status affected the provision of financial and service support.

Co-residency has typically been considered an indicator of a close-knit family with strong filial traditions that ensure support for elderly family members. The research is well established on co-residency of older persons with their adult children, but there is little data about the quality of support in these settings. The data clearly show that visible minorities, First Nations peoples, and immigrants live in larger households than do their counterparts, a finding replicated in most North American research (Thomas & Wister, 1984; Boyd, 1991; Kamo & Zhou, 1994; Gee, 1999; Kritz, Gurak, & Chen, 2000). In Canada, Chinese are one of the minorities most likely to live in complex households (Government of Canada, 1996a: 5-6; 1996b: 5-6). About 11 percent of Chinese immigrants aged 65 years and over live alone, compared with 25 percent for all immigrant seniors and 29 percent for Canadian-born seniors. Furthermore, a significantly higher percentage of Chinese seniors (65 percent) who do not live with their immediate family live with other relatives, compared with 29 percent of all immigrant seniors and 18 percent of Canadian-born seniors. In other words, Chinese Canadian families tend to be larger because of living patterns that can involve three generations (Li, 1998: 112). In Gee's study in Greater Vancouver and Victoria (1999), about half the Chinese elderly lived with at least one child in an intergenerational household setting.

Overall, most of the findings on co-residency suggest that later-life living arrangements among immigrants are influenced by the timing of immigration and ethnic and racial characteristics, which researchers treat as indirect measures of ethnic preferences. Basavarajappa (1998), using 1991 census data, discovered that the propensity for immigrant groups to live in three-or-more-generation households was influenced by lower incomes, the non-receipt of pension benefits, a shorter time in Canada, and widowhood. He also noted that 28 percent of immigrants living in three-generation households lived in crowded conditions. Gee (1999) underscores one of the main problems in the co-residency literature—the wide variation within ethnic groups. In her study, Chinese widows who lived alone reported lower levels of well-being, but they also indicated that they did not want to live with an adult child. Pacey (2002), using two data files, demonstrates substantial intra-group variations in Chinese living arrangements.

A number of researchers have attempted to untangle cultural preference from economic need as determinants of co-residency. Immigrants from poorer countries often cannot afford to support their parents in separate dwellings, nor can the senior immigrants support themselves because they are ineligible for government transfer payments. Living together and pooling resources becomes a very helpful economic strategy for both generations. A number of studies, however, have controlled for economic need and still find that some ethnic minorities choose to live in multi-generational families (Speare & Avery, 1993; Tennstedt & Chang, 1998; Wilmoth, 2001).

As the discussion has shown, there is growing evidence that membership in an ethnic group is related to different patterns of family support, especially for more recent immigrants to Canada. Co-residency appears to be one of the more important determinants for receiving help from family, although the reasons for co-residency are not entirely clear. As the ethnic composition of Canada continues to change, the research will have to explore these issues further.

Implications for Policy and Practice

It should be evident by now that policies and services need to be designed to take into account inter- and intra-ethnic differences among older people (Keefe et al., 2000; McDonald et al., 2001; Lai, 2004c). For example, a study comparing Chinese living in Victoria with those living in Vancouver found that the elderly Chinese in Victoria were healthier, probably because they faced fewer barriers to service delivery (Lai, 2003). How these services should be designed is another question. Some scholars argue that the needs of ethnic minority elders are best understood by members of their own groups and that these elders should be treated as distinct groups with their own sets of health and social services and policies. This view has led to calls for research and training programs that give special attention to ethnic minorities and for ethnic minority practitioners to be employed as service providers (Hooyman & Kiyak, 2005). Others have argued that social and economic inequalities across the life course should be alleviated and that services and policies should be culturally sensitive while being integrated into all services for the aged. Because we do not have enough research, the jury is still out on this matter, but in the meantime, the majority of social gerontologists recognize the many barriers ethnic elders might encounter when they require health and/or social services.

Language is a primary barrier to service, as is lack of knowledge of services, a reluctance to use formal Western health services stemming from different world views, the lack of transportation to services, the shortage of ethnically sensitive practitioners, and financial difficulties. In addition, given that most of the new senior immigrants to Canada have arrived through family reunification programs, there may be two generations of people who are new to Canada and who face the same issues (Keefe et al., 2000). Some studies have, therefore, recommended that the services for ethnic seniors include outreach to provide information about services, ethnically sensitive services for families, and services offered outside working hours and close to ethnic neighbourhoods, when possible (McDonald et al., 2001; Janevic & Connell, 2001).

A serious policy issue that requires immediate attention is the problem of poverty among First Nations peoples and visible minority seniors. Adjustments to pension policy and to immigration polices that do not penalize older ethnic citizens need to be examined.

CHAPTER SUMMARY

In this chapter, we have explored the diversity of older Canadians. One of the most important observations of the chapter is the fact that there is little research or theory development on older ethnic groups in Canada. What is more, the changing composition of the older population makes clear the need for new data to respond to the changing policy and practice demands of an aging ethnic and more urban population.

Key ideas to remember from this chapter:

- Ethnogerontology is a new field in social gerontology that studies the influence of race, ethnicity, national origin, and culture on individual and population aging.
- Definitions of ethnicity are fluid and can include a number of dimensions: ancestral origin, homeland or land of origin, a shared history of one's people, a shared identity, a language, sometimes a religion, and sometimes a culture or subculture.
- Race refers to physical appearance and is a category socially constructed by others that places people perceived as having similar biological traits into a group.
- There have been shifts in the composition of the Canadian population. The proportion of the British and French has gradually declined, while Asian immigrants have dramatically increased.
- Visible minorities make up 7 percent of the older population, and 4 percent of the First Nations population is 65 years of age or older.

- Most theorizing about aging and ethnicity has not developed past the multiple jeopardy hypothesis, its competitor, the age levelling hypothesis, or the buffer hypothesis.
- Immigrant visible minority seniors are more likely to live below the low income cut-offs of Statistics Canada than are the general population of seniors.
- Immigrants of all ages are healthy on arrival in Canada, but they lose this advantage over time. There is limited research indicating that non-Caucasian seniors may have poorer health than the general population of seniors. The research is inconsistent on the influence of ethnicity on service utilization.
- There is growing evidence for ethnic differences in family support. Co-residency appears to be one of the more important determinants for receiving help from family, although the reasons for co-residency are not clear.
- Whether ethnic seniors need ethnospecific services requires further research. Barriers to health and social services, especially language difficulties, strongly suggest that services, at minimum, should be ethnically sensitive, with staff who speak the language and understand ethnic differences.

KEY TERMS

ethnogerontology (p. 137)

ethnicity (p. 137)

culture (p. 138)

ethnic group (p. 138)

race (p. 140)

ethnic origin (p. 143)

landed immigrant (p. 148)

family-class immigrants (p. 148)

refugees (p. 148)

economic-class immigrants (p. 148)

visible minority (p. 150)

essentialist approach (p. 153)

assimilation (p. 153)

pluralism (p. 154)

ethnic stratification (p. 154)

multiple jeopardy hypothesis (p. 154)

age levelling hypothesis (p. 155)

buffer hypothesis (p. 155)

healthy immigrant thesis (p. 158)

co-residency (p. 162)

STUDY QUESTIONS

1. Do you think ethnicity has had any effect on how you live your life day to day? Do you think it will affect you when you are old?
2. What possible solutions do you see to the problem of poverty among older Aboriginals and visible minorities in Canada?
3. Do you think we should have an integrated or a separate service system for ethnic minority seniors? Why?

Suggested Readings

Gelfand, D. (2003). *Aging and ethnicity: Knowledge and services.* (2nd ed.). New York: Springer.

Chi, I., Chappell, N., & Lubben, J. (Eds.). 2001. *Elderly Chinese in Pacific Rim countries.* Hong Kong: Hong Kong University Press.

Olson, L. (Ed.) (2001). *Age through ethnic lenses: Caring for the elderly in a multicultural society.* Lanham, MD: Rowan & Littlefield.

Chapter 7

COGNITIVE AND PHYSICAL PERFORMANCE

Learning Objectives

In this chapter, you will learn about

- Cognition and its various aspects.
- The barriers with age to the processing of sensory information.
- Aging and different types of memory.
- Whether and how age impairs different aspects of intelligence.
- How people continue to retain cognitive expertise and creativity with age.
- How to measure physical competence and performance.
- Ways to distinguish levels of physical competence.
- How age and social trends affect physical competence.

Introduction

This chapter examines age effects on cognitive and physical performance. Cognition is a multi-faceted concept that includes sensory processing of information, memory, intelligence, creativity, and wisdom. Age does not affect these facets equally: some processes show decline, others remain stable, and yet others improve with age. Physical performance can also be measured in various ways. For applied purposes, a typological model may be used that groups people according to their level of physical capability. This chapter examines usual age trends in cognitive and physical performance, with ways to promote such performance in later life discussed more fully in Chapter 10.

Cognitive Performance

Cognition refers to sensation, perception, and thought as distinct from feeling and volition. Some authors consider cognition to be so important to the evolutionary genesis of our species that its retention contributed to the prolongation of the human lifespan (Allen, Bruss, & Damasio, 2005). Cognition starts from information. At the earliest stage of reception, information is nothing more than the activation of some cells rather than others in a sensory receptor. What happens then may include the following:

- In a seemingly miraculous way, the cognitive system detects patterns in this activation. The term for our awareness of detected patterns is **sensation**.

- Then the cognitive system holds some sensations in memory long enough for comparison with concurrent and subsequent sensations. We use the term **perception** to describe this process.

- Finally, the cognitive system operates on the perceptions by comparing them with perceptions experienced seconds, minutes, hours, weeks, years, and even decades before, the residues of which still endure within the brain. The quest for meaning among all these disparate perceptions is an aim of conscious thought.

The term for the residues of previous cognitive processing stored within the brain is **memory**. Memories fall into two main categories: memories of information processed at a particular time, known as *episodic* memories; and memories integrated into composite structures not specifically related to particular episodes, which fall under the rubric of *knowledge*.

An amazing feature of the human brain is that it is able to manipulate information stored in memory in similar ways to information received through the senses. The brain is able to detect differences, similarities, and incongruities between different bits of knowledge, and then create new knowledge or hypotheses about information not yet received. This kind of processing is analogous to intelligence and creativity, and its application to resolving important but uncertain issues in life goes by the term *wisdom*.

All the processes described thus far are susceptible to influences, both good and bad, associated with age. Processes can be enhanced by experiences that accumulate with age and knowledge that accumulates with experience. On the other hand, old age brings an increased risk of deterioration brought about by adverse age changes and disease. We shall confine discussion in this chapter to an examination of age trends in cognitive processes. Chapter 10 includes discussion of benefits to cognitive processing in later life; Chapter 8 discusses diseases that affect cognition.

Aging and the Sensory System

Information acquisition begins at the sensory systems. This section reviews changes with age in the important sensory systems that underlie the acquisition of visual and auditory information, as well as senses relevant to taste, smell, touch, temperature, pain, and the position of the body in space.

Vision   Recent reviews of vision suggest that two kinds of change occur at different ages (Fozard & Gordon-Salant, 2001; Kline & Schaie, 1996). Changes in the outer parts of the eye, such as the cornea and lens, begin to occur in many people between 35 and 45 years of age. The second kind of change affects the retina within the eye and occurs mainly in people aged 55 years and over.

Peripheral changes include a loss of flexibility in the lens, resulting in a decrease in the eye's ability to change shape to view objects at different distances—termed a difficulty in *accommodation*. This problem particularly affects vision for objects close to the eye, a condition termed *presbyopia*, which is why people with previously normal vision often require reading glasses in middle age.

There is also a yellowing of the lens with age. This change results in a reduction in the amount and quality of light passing through the lens to reach the retina. Because yellow absorbs the shorter wavelengths, the light at the retina of older people is deficient particularly at the blue-green end of the spectrum. However, the main problem caused by yellowing is that older people need more illumination to view objects than do younger people, with color constancy maintained by compensatory mechanisms.

Other peripheral changes include the development of cataracts and a decrease in pupil size with age. Both these conditions make more illumination a necessity for older people. Cataracts mainly affect people in their seventies and older. The condition results in opacity of the lens, blocking light from reaching the retina. Another consequence of opacity is glare, which results from scattering of the light as it passes through the lens. Susceptibility to glare presents particular problems for driving at night because the headlights of oncoming cars result in glare even in people with unimpaired vision. Although cataracts afflict up to 25 percent of people aged over 75 years, the condition is now treatable by simple surgical correction.

Because the consequences of peripheral changes extend to deficiencies with age in depth perception and field of vision, it is not surprising that the number of people requiring visual correction increases with age. The U.S. National Center for Health Statistics (1994) estimates that fewer than 50 percent of people in any cohort up to 44 years of age require corrective devices, compared to 80 percent or more in older cohorts.

The second category of change includes effects on the receptor cells in the retina. Two such effects are *age-related macular degeneration* (AMD) and *glaucoma*. The former affects the macula, which is a part of the retina particularly relevant for acute vision. A consequence of this condition is a loss in visual acuity, which if severe may necessitate the use of a strong magnifying glass for pursuits such as reading. Glaucoma involves high intraocular pressure that damages the optic nerve and affects the visual field. Although both AMD and glaucoma are diseases mainly affecting people over 55 years, the majority of older people show evidence of retinal damage (Fozard & Gordon-Salant, 2001), suggesting effects associated with normal living regardless of diagnosed disease.

Hearing   Losses in hearing, like vision, begin to be noticeable by mid-life (Wingfield, Tun, & McCoy, 2005). Fozard (1990) noted that one person in five had hearing difficulties between the ages 45 and54 years, compared with three-quarters of the population aged over 75 years, with the rates higher for males than females. Although external factors such as wax accumulation contribute to impaired hearing, the main cause is damage to the cochlea, which is the main neural receptor. This damage includes a loss of hair cells, which are the ear's equivalent to retinal cells in the eye, and problems of metabolism within the inner ear.

A prominent form of hearing loss is *presbycusis* (a loss of reception of high frequency sounds), which means that older people, especially men, often have difficulty hearing higher musical notes. Also common is *tinnitus*, the presence of high-pitched background noise that distracts and annoys those afflicted.

From a functional perspective, the main problem associated with hearing loss is the reduced ability to understand speech, which often leads to feelings of social isolation with its concomitant dilemmas. Bergman and colleagues (1976) found that various difficulties increased with age in the following order (i.e., from least to most):

- normal speech
- rapid speech
- listening to one speaker among many
- listening to speech in the presence of reverberation or echo
- listening to interrupted speech

These findings suggest that rapidity and distraction augment hearing difficulties in older people. They also point to ways to make speech more intelligible (e.g., slow-paced speech without interruption or external distraction). The conventional hearing aid provides only a partial solution because it amplifies the background noise as well as foreground speech. Advances in hearing aid technology and the acoustic ecology may rectify some of these problems (Fozard & Gordon-Salant, 2001).

Taste and Smell   Sensitivity to taste and smell show slight decline in late life, with some suggestion that sensitivity to sweet and salty tastes shows greater loss than sensitivity to bitter and sour tastes (Stevens, Cruz, Marks, & Lakatos, 1998). The implications are that older people may enjoy their food less than at a younger age and be less aware of smells indicating rotten food or toxins.

Touch, Temperature, and Pain   Gescheider (1997) reported that vibrotactile sensitivity (i.e., the ability to feel vibrations) declined substantially with age, especially with high-frequency stimulation. Losses in temperature sensitivity also occur with age (Stevens, et al., 1998), which may put older people at risk of hypothermia in cold Canadian winters.

The research is inconsistent about whether pain sensitivity decreases with age, although there is some evidence that older people under-report low-intensity pain but not high-intensity pain (Harkins, Price, & Martelli, 1986). It is difficult to study pain in natural settings, because perception of pain involves not just a painful stimulus but personality and emotion. Moreover, older people are more susceptible to disease and disability associated with pain. Research indicates that pain is a significant problem for many older people (Hadjistavropoulos, 2001). One study indicates that 50 percent of Canadian nursing home residents experience pain at least once a week, and 24 percent experience pain daily (Proctor & Hirdes, 2001).

Kinesthesis   Kinesthesis refers to awareness of the body's positioning as it moves through space. Some kinesthesis may be lost with age (e.g., reduced ability to touch one's nose with eyes closed) (Simoneau & Liebowitz, 1996). Low kinesthesis has implications for poor gait and balance, and a higher susceptibility to falls. A more extended discussion on balance and falls is provided later in this chapter.

Aging and Memory

Memory refers to the acquisition and retrieval of information. A model derived from James (1890) and elaborated by Atkinson and Shiffrin (1968) continues to provide a framework for structuring discussions about memory and aging. This model, illustrated in Figure 7.1, includes three stages of memory: sensory, short-term, and long-term. Memory starts with the inner circle (sensory) and moves outward. The area of the circles represents both the duration of storage and the amount of information retrievable.

Figure 7.1 **THE THREE STAGES OF MEMORY**

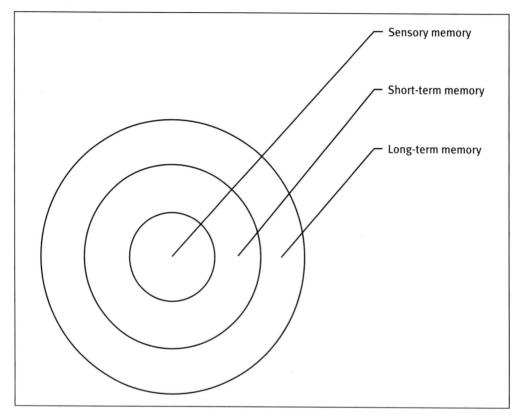

Sensory memory

Short-term memory

Long-term memory

Sensory Memory The **sensory memory** store holds information received from the environment for a very brief interval. Memory traces are called *icons* if the information is visual and *echoes* if auditory. The information persists in these stores only long enough to be processed and transferred to a store of longer duration (e.g., the sound of a word before the listener grasps its meaning). Studies on the masking of previous by subsequent visual information suggest a limited age effect on iconic memory; the minor age differences in sensory storage are unlikely to contribute greatly to any deficiencies in short-term memory (Craik & Jennings, 1992).

Short-Term Memory **Short-term memory** is an intermediate stage between sensory memory and long-term storage. It corresponds to the time information resides in consciousness while being processed for transfer to long-term memory. Short-term memory includes **primary memory** (passive storage) and **working memory** (active manipulation of information).

Tests of primary memory include the *Digits Forward* subtest of the Wechsler Adult Intelligence Scale (WAIS; Wechsler, 1958), in which respondents are asked to recall a sequence of digits after a single auditory presentation. Other tests of memory span use a non-meaningful sequence of words rather than digits. Most people are able to recall a string of six to eight digits, with no appreciable decline until very late in life except in cases of pathology affecting cognition (e.g., dementia) (Craik & Jennings, 1992).

Working memory involves mental manipulation of the information in consciousness into a form appropriate for long-term storage. An example is the *Digits Backward* subtest on the WAIS, in which the respondent recalls the presented sequence in reverse order. Recall on this test is typically lower than on the *Digits Forward* test by one to two digits, and unlike the latter, declines with age.

Evidence that working memory declines with age comes from both cross-sectional and longitudinal research (Hultsch, Hertzog, Small, McDonald-Miszlak, & Dixon, 1992). However, the reasons for this deterioration remain unclear. Salthouse and Babcock (1991) suggest that the deficiency may reside in processing rather than capacity or storage.

Long-Term Memory **Long-term memory** refers to a large-capacity storage system in which memories reside over prolonged durations. There are four main categories of long-term memory:

- **Episodic memory** refers to the remembering of discrete events;
- **Semantic memory** includes knowledge about concepts or events not necessarily associated with a single episode of acquisition (e.g., the provinces of Canada);
- **Procedural memory** involves the retention of skill (e.g., driving);
- **Prospective memory** is remembering to do something at a future time.

These four categories, although conceptually distinct, may show some correlation. There is ample evidence that people with higher general knowledge perform at higher levels on episodic memory tasks (Hultsch, Hamme, & Small, 1993). Because general knowledge involves retrieval from semantic memory, a relationship is evident. Similarly, disease may affect a range of cognitive performances, with the generalized memory loss in dementia being an extreme example. However, evidence also suggests that the memory systems operate independently. Tulving, Hayman, & MacDonald (1991) reported on the case of a brain-injured person with amnesia for past episodes in his life but retention of semantic and procedural memories (e.g., he remembered that his father taught him to play chess and the skills involved in playing chess, but failed to remember any game he ever played). Schonknecht, Pantel, Kruse, and Schroder (2005) find that among older people with mild cognitive impairment (i.e., impairment less severe than in dementia), only episodic memory declines significantly over a four-year period. In a recognition task, Parkin and Walter (1992) provided evidence that while younger people report that they *remember* items previously presented, older people more often report *knowing* that the items were present. This distinction between remembering and knowing appears to relate to retrieval from episodic and semantic memory, respectively.

Acquisition of Information into Long-Term Memory

The process of acquisition relates to activity performed in working memory. Older people can organize material for later retrieval as effectively as young people (Bäckman, 2001). Older people are, however, disadvantaged with unfamiliar information, material presented quickly, and tasks that require effortful rather than automatic processing (Hasher & Zacks, 1979). These deficits may indicate diminished resource capacity, low motivation, or the persistence of less effective processing strategies dating from their school years. However, when taught mnemonic (memorizing) techniques to aid retrieval, the recall of older people improves. These findings suggest that older people are indeed able to learn new ways of learning.

Retrieval from Long-Term Memory

Schonfield and Robertson (1966) were the first to show that the loss with age in the recognition of information is less than in recall. One reason for this discrepancy may be that **recall** invokes only episodic memory, whereas **recognition** brings semantic memory into play (e.g., the respondent may "know" an item through familiarity but not "remember" it from the learning trials). Because older people rely more on semantic memory than episodic memory (Parkin & Walter, 1992), their performance may benefit accordingly.

Another reason relates to organization. In order to recall information, a respondent has to retrieve not only the specific content but also the organization imposed on that content during acquisition. The necessity to retrieve organization is less pressing in recognition because the task itself provides cues to organization. An example is the recall of prose, which has a higher level of organization than the typical word list used in studies of memory, and which shows less loss associated with age. Older respondents show less loss with age in the recall of well-organized compared with poorly organized prose, and similarly benefit in word list learning after instruction on how to organize the material during acquisition (Hultsch, 1971). Craik and Jennings (1992) provide compatible evidence with findings that the presence of retrieval cues disproportionately benefits recall by older over younger persons.

A stereotype about old people is that they live in the past, remembering more about events decades past than current events. If this stereotype has any validity, do old people reminisce about the past because of a failure to acquire or retrieve recent memories or because earlier life events were more meaningful to them? (The lyrics of Bruce Springsteen's song *Glory Days* suggest the latter.) Our earliest memories usually date from about four and a half years of age and coincide with the development of the self-concept. Rubin (1999) reported that older adults have a higher frequency of autobiographical memories for the period from 10 to 30 years of age than for any other period. His interpretation is consistent with a *Glory Days* hypothesis: these memories capture events significant in the lives of the respondents. Similarly, Fitzgerald (1988) found that especially vivid memories by older people dated from a period of late adolescence to early adulthood.

Evidence on the retrieval of very old memories indicates considerable retention. Bahrick, Bahrick, and Wittlinger (1975) studied memory for high school classmates, the accuracy of which they checked against corresponding high school yearbooks. Their findings indicated that recall fell sharply during the three years since leaving school, but remained consistently above 60 percent until 25 years after graduation, after which time it continued to decline. Name and picture recognition showed minimal decline for 34 years after graduation, consistently remaining at about 90 percent, after which it declined steeply. These findings suggest that although distortion and inaccuracies may be present in long-term memory, memories from late adolescence persist with considerable accuracy for decades after the event.

Metamemory Metamemory refers to knowledge and beliefs about memory, including a person's own memory. The main age difference in metamemory concerns *self-efficacy*, which refers to beliefs about one's own memory (Hertzog, Dixon, & Hultsch, 1990). Older people are more likely than young adults to believe they have a bad memory; they report more memory failures and expect to perform worse in memory testing. However, the correlation between metamemory and actual memory performance is low; that is, what people think about their memory is not related to their actual memory.

Aging and Intelligence

Ideas about intelligence and its measurement underwent successive revisions during the past century. Galton (1883) in England measured **intelligence** by the ability to process sensory information, with more intelligent people presumed to make finer distinctions in modalities such as hearing, taste, and weight discrimination. Binet in France attempted to differentiate between children failing at school because of low intelligence and those failing for other reasons (e.g., low motivation). The Binet and Simon (1905) test measures ability to solve cognitive problems rather than to make sensory discriminations, and other countries adopted Binet's ideas about intelligence as well as his methods of measurement. Spearman (1927) in England supported Binet's assertion that intelligence includes a single ability to solve problems whatever the nature of the task presented. Wechsler (1958) in America developed the Wechsler Adult Intelligence Scale (WAIS) using different tasks to measure intelligence in different spheres of functioning. The WAIS differed from Binet and Simon's test with regard to the procedure used to compute levels of intelligence, better known as the *intelligence quotient (IQ)*. Whereas Binet and Simon used developmental age norms, Wechsler used norms associated with adult age ranges. Weschler's procedure provides for more meaningful estimations of intelligence within the adult age span.

Thurstone (1938) in America challenged Spearman's hypothesis that intelligence is a single ability that manifests itself to different degrees with different tasks. He proposed that intelligence comprises different and distinguishable mental abilities termed *primary mental abilities*. The multiple abilities model persists to the present day, although with variation in the ways of classifying these abilities. Schaie and Willis (1993) used Thurstone's model of primary mental abilities to evaluate age trends in intelligence. Their measures included

- verbal comprehension—evidenced by the ability to understand verbal information;
- word fluency—the ability to solve anagrams, to generate instances of a category;
- numerical manipulation—involved in arithmetic calculation;
- spatial orientation—concerned with spatial aspects of problem solving;
- associative memory—mainly relevant to rote learning;
- perceptual speed—speed of making distinctions in spatial problems;
- inductive reasoning—the extraction of rules linking the elements in a problem.

More recent models of intelligence have distinguished between the types of process that people use to solve problems. One such distinction is between *fluid* and *crystallized* intelligence (Horn, 1982). **Fluid intelligence** refers to mental abilities not acquired by learning from one's culture, but which may reflect individual differences in the integrity of the central nervous system. Horn assumed an increase in fluid intelligence with the maturation of the central nervous system, with a peak level achieved by the end of adolescence. Thereafter, he assumed fluid intelligence would decline because of age changes and other deleterious effects on the brain. **Crystallized intelligence** refers to problem-solving skills acquired from the culture. Such skills include the verbal abilities learned during school and from life experiences thereafter (e.g., vocabulary, practical, reasoning, concept formation). These abilities, more than fluid intelligence, contribute to the learning of new information in real-world (as opposed to laboratory) environments (Bier & Ackerman, 2005). Although Horn (1982) supposed crystallized intelligence to continue to increase with new learning throughout the lifespan, there is evidence for deterioration in advanced old age (Schaie, 1996).

Other models included Sternberg's (1984), which distinguishes between applications of intelligence to the inner world, the external environment, and their juxtaposition. Baltes (1993) differentiates the mechanical processes of intelligence from their pragmatic application, which can continue to improve to advanced age.

Age Trends in Intelligence Studies of age trends in intelligence use three types of research design. The early research mainly comprised cross-sectional studies that compared cohorts of different ages (e.g., young, middle-aged, and older people) at the same historical time. The usual interpretation of findings was that aging brought about losses. Subsequent studies were longitudinal (i.e., a single cohort measured at successive historical intervals) or combined cross-sectional and longitudinal components within the overall design (e.g., cross-sequential designs). Findings from these studies resulted in modification to the conclusion that aging inevitably causes decline in aspects of intelligence.

Cross-sectional findings on adult intelligence suggest overall declines with age that affect some tasks and abilities more than other skills. Wechsler (1972) noted steeper declines on spatial rather than verbal tasks that were due only partially to declining speed of performance. Recent findings replicate the steeper decline on spatial than on verbal tasks and implicate deterioration in a part of the brain called the cerebellum as a contributing factor (Lee et al., 2005). Schaie and Willis (1993) found verbal ability and numeric ability to show no substantial loss until age 60 to 70 years, compared with the other primary mental abilities, which began to deteriorate about three decades earlier. Horn (1982) reported that fluid intelligence begins to decline steadily after young adulthood, whereas crystallized intelligence continues to increase until advanced age.

Problems in the interpretation of cross-sectional data include a confounding of the effects of cohort and age in the research design. Schaie (1996) showed that successive cohorts over the 20th century had progressively higher scores on tests such as inductive reasoning, verbal meaning, and spatial orientation. These increases across successive cohorts probably relate to higher levels of education, improved nutrition, and better medical care. Because of this confounding, cross-sectional comparison between different cohorts likely resulted in an overestimation of the effects of aging on intelligence.

Because longitudinal research examines changes within cohorts over time, such studies avoid any confounding with cohort differences. Findings from these studies showed minimal decline over long time intervals. Canadian longitudinal research examined changes over intervals of 40 years or more (Arbuckle, Maag, Pushkar, & Chaikelson, 1998; Schwartzman, Gold, Andres, Arbuckle, & Chaikelson, 1987). The overall changes on tests of intelligence are low to age 65+ years. Performance gains are more likely on verbal tasks and losses more likely on spatial tasks. Those individuals with more years of education and who are more active are also more likely to show higher performance at all ages.

Other research studied different cohorts over intervals of three decades or more. Schaie (1996) reports little or no decline until age 60 years, slight decline until the mid-70s, followed by more pronounced deterioration. Although confounds in longitudinal research include higher rates of drop-out and death by those scoring lower on tests of intelligence, the preceding trends persist even after correction for such error. Consequently, it is fair to conclude that intelligence remains close to the levels in earlier life until long after the mandatory retirement age of 65 years.

Aging and Creativity

Creativity is a poorly understood concept, although one that differs from intelligence in the opinion of most theorists. A frequent distinction made by researchers is that intelligence implies convergent thinking, in which the respondent selects one correct response from several alternatives (e.g., the meaning of the word *antiquary*; the next number in a sequence beginning 1, 1, 2, 3, 5, 8 . . .). A precursor of creativity, on the other hand, is divergent thinking, in which the respondent generates multiple instances of a concept (e.g., possible uses of a sock). Convergent thinking may or may not require an extensive knowledge base to solve the problem, but creativity in the real world usually requires an extensive knowledge from which the creative act can emerge.

McCrae, Arenberg, and Costa (1987) conducted a comprehensive study of intelligence and creativity across the adult age span. They measured intelligence by a vocabulary test and creativity by four divergent thinking tests. The design included both cross-sectional and longitudinal methods of data collection. The findings indicated no relationship between vocabulary and divergent thinking, with the latter showing modest declines with age. These findings complement those by Ruth and Birren (1985), who found creativity to decline with age in cross-sectional research.

Findings on creativity outside of the constraints imposed by laboratory measures vary according to the criteria used to define a creative act or production. Early research suggested that the frequency of products judged as exceptionally creative peaked when the originators were in their 30s, thereafter showing gradual decline (Lehman, 1953). Dennis (1966) examined total productivity, rather than single masterpieces, of long-lived scholars in various disciplines, finding that their 60s was the most productive decade. Simonton (1990) concluded that the periods of high productivity coincided with the highest rate of producing masterpieces, with the ratio of the two unrelated to stage of career. What are we to make of these apparently discrepant findings?

Part of the answer is that creativity in the real world may take second place to other concerns as people age. Simonton (1990) suggested that for many creative people the need to be creative becomes secondary to a need to be wise. Successful people in our society often find themselves taking on positions with administrative responsibility in their later careers, which limits the time available for creative output. It is also true that the desire to foster creativity in others supplants for many people the desire to be creative themselves. Another reason is that once an innovator achieves success with a creative piece of work, social and commercial pressures may encourage that person to produce more of the same rather than chance something different. It is for reasons like these that some successful novelists and painters subsequently opt to reproduce variants on the pattern that brought them their early successes. Such considerations suggest that declines with age in the output of truly creative productions may have less to do with waning creative prowess with age than social influence that reward other than creative pursuits.

Aging and Wisdom

Baltes and Staudinger (1993) suggested that **wisdom** implies good judgment in important but uncertain matters of life. The basic dimensions of wisdom include the *mechanics of mind* and the *pragmatics of mind*. The former refers to the basic cognitive processing system, and the latter to factual and strategic knowledge and their relationship to problem solving in real life situations. Consequently, wisdom implies the application of expert knowledge that includes knowledge (both factual and strategic) about

- the basic pragmatics of life;
- the uncertainties in life;
- context;
- the relativism of values and goals in life.

These researchers suggest that three factors affect wisdom. First, wisdom is likely to increase with the knowledge gained through life experience. However, not everyone has the requisite life experiences, and aging brings about some decrement in the mechanics of mind. Second, personality traits such as openness to experience may foster one's knowledge about uncertainties and relativism. Third, specific experiences relevant to decision making may promote wisdom about those life domains. Consequently, the hypothesized relationship of wisdom with age may be secondary to its relationship with favourable life experiences.

The overall findings on age trends in cognition suggest that age changes are more manifest in the more basic cognitive processes (e.g., the sensory system, aspects of memory) than higher-level functions (e.g., intelligence, creativity). Wisdom may increase with age given favourable life experiences.

It is easy to find examples of people who retain superior cognitive skill in very old age. Box 7.1 provides examples of some notable people who were

Box 7.1   *Creativity in Old Age*

Consider the following people. What do they have in common?

Winston Churchill of Great Britain
Mao-Tse-Tung of China
Benjamin Franklin, the inventor
Michelangelo, the painter
Asa Gray, the botanist
Wilhelm Wundt, the father of modern psychology
Goethe, the author of *Faust* and other literary masterpieces
Cervantes, who wrote *Don Quixote*
Maggie Kuhn, founder of the *Gray Panthers* group of social activists
George Burns, the entertainer

None of them let age stand in their way of doing what they wanted. The world we know, is like it is today because of the likes of Churchill, Mao-Tse-Tung, and Charles de Gaulle of France, all of whom led the government of their countries when in their seventies. Asa Gray and Wilhelm Wundt both contributed seminal works to their respective sciences at ages beyond 75, and Franklin invented the bifocal lens when nearly 80. Goethe, Cervantes, and Michelangelo all produced their most famous literary or artistic creations at an age now termed the golden years. Maggie Kuhn pioneered a revolution for seniors when herself a senior. George Burns, who died at 100, was performing and acting well into his nineties. In the last interview we saw him give, he was still talking about how much he loved his late wife, Gracie, and he was still cracking jokes with sexual innuendoes.

All these famous people were at their cognitive best during old age.

Source: Adapted from Lee and Michael Stones (2004), *Sex may be wasted on the young.* Concord, ON: Captus Press.

at their cognitive best during their later years. They exemplify what Baltes and Baltes (1990) term the principle of **selective optimization** with **compensation**, whereby people select and practise those skills that are most important to them. The fact that the people listed in Box 7.1 were able to function at so high a level in late life is sufficient to dispel any myth that aging inevitably brings about irrevocable cognitive decline. Although few of us can hope to approach such levels of expertise at any age, a lesson we can learn from their lives is that through effort we can increase our chances of performing at our cognitive best in our old age.

Aging and Physical Competence

Physical changes with age occur at levels ranging from the cellular to whole body functions. Not all such changes occur because of the simple passage of time. Age changes may also reflect the effects of disease, disability, lifestyle, and the environment. Rowe and Kahn (1987) are among many who emphasize the significance of these distinctions, which are evident not just from comparison of individuals with different life histories and lifestyles, but also from differences between successive cohorts. The effects of age and cohort relate not only to physical functioning but also to physical structure, with height providing an instructive example.

Shephard (1978:20-22) acknowledged that people lose height with age mainly because of compression of the intervertebral disks and increasing kyphosis (curvature) of the spine. However, the reasons you are probably taller than your grandparents of the same sex include not only your youth. Anyone who has visited museums in Europe can tell you that people in medieval times were shorter than today; how else could they fit into those suits of armour, which look made for children not fighting men? Because of improved living conditions and diet, height increased by 1cm per decade in Britain during the last century (Shepard, 1978), which in terms of absolute magnitude approximates the loss of height per decade after 40 years of age.

What Is Physical Performance?

Gerontologists study physical competence to answer questions about what people of different ages usually do and are capable of doing. The term for what people do is **performance**. Developmental studies of physical performance include research on measurement, the elucidation of influences, and intervention to promote or sustain higher levels of functioning. The term for what people are capable of doing is **competence**, which relates to physical **fitness**. Research on competence examines issues similar to those on performance; it also includes studies of positive and negative influences on expert performance such as that displayed at elite levels of sport.

Measures of Physical Performance

A number of methods are available to measure habitual levels of physical performance in people of different ages. These measures include standardized retrospective interviews (van der Suiijs, 1972), retrospective activity questionnaires (Morris, Chave, Adam, Sirey, & Epstein, 1956), and current time budget diaries (Durin & Passmore, 1967). Indexes of habitual performance derived from such measures usually consist of the sum of the products of the time expended in different activities by their corresponding energy costs. Expressions of the latter include rates of energy expenditure (i.e., kilocalories, kilojoules), oxygen consumption, relative load (i.e., oxygen consumption compared with the maximal oxygen intake), multiples of basal metabolic rate (METs), and changes in heart rate (Andersen, Masironi, Rutenfranz, & Seliger, 1978). A Canadian measure of physical performance indexed the frequency of exercising enough to "get sweaty" (Godin, Jobin, & Bouillon, 1986).

Age Trends in Physical Performance

Levels of habitual physical performance by people of different ages differ depending on the period of history when the researchers collected the data. Andersen and colleagues (1978) reported that, before 1970, the time spent in demanding physical activity and the total energy cost of that activity declined with age for both men and women. This trend was evident in several countries (e.g., Czechoslovakia, Norway, Sweden, and the United States); it occurred because after young adulthood people replaced more strenuous physical pursuits (e.g., heavy physical labour, sport) with less strenuous activities (e.g., walking, gardening). Such declines in habitual performance with age have implications for physical competence. Shephard (1969) compared then-current findings on endurance fitness in the United States with 1938 findings by Robinson. The comparison showed lower levels of fitness in the more recent data, which the researcher attributed to lower levels of strenuous physical activity in the decades following World War II.

Findings after 1980 show higher levels of physical activity among older people than in earlier surveys. Stephens, Craig, and Ferris (1986) report on the frequencies of participants in the Canada Fitness Survey classified as "adequately active" (i.e., people whose activity was sufficiently frequent and strenuous to promote endurance fitness). Using data from the same survey, Kozma, Stones, and Hannah (1991) report on the frequencies of people classified as "active" (i.e., people who regularly engage in physical exercise for at least three hours per week). The findings indicate that although few older people fall within the "adequately active" category, more people aged over 60 years were "active" than people aged 40 to 59 years. Although a probable contributing factor is the *ParticipAction* campaign sponsored by the federal government to promote increased physical activity in Canada during the 1970s and 1980s, findings from other countries likewise show relatively high levels of exercising by older people. The examples include findings from Japan, where Harada (1994) reports higher rates of at least weekly participation in exercise or sport among people aged over 60 years than among middle-aged people.

Figure 7.2 shows more recent findings on the frequency of exercising. The data are from the 1999 Manulife Financial survey mentioned in Chapter 1 and show the mean number of 30-minute exercise sessions per week by men and women of different ages.

The findings for men show a roughly U-shaped curve, with the frequency of exercise lower in the 25-to-54 year age range than for men aged under 25 years, but with higher frequencies of exercise after age 55 years. The findings for women show an n-shaped curve, with the frequency of exercise after age 65 years lower than that for the peak exercise period of 35 to 44 years. Overall, 53 percent of men and 43 percent of all respondents are have three or more exercise sessions per week, with the lowest frequencies for men aged 45 to 54 years and women aged 65 years and over.

Figure 7.2   MEAN NUMBER OF 30-MINUTE EXERCISE SESSIONS PER WEEK, BY AGE AND SEX

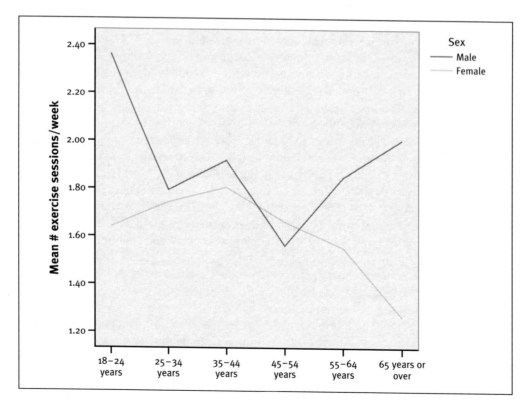

Types of Physical Competence

Physical competence is a broader concept than physical fitness but includes the latter. Although population studies of age trends in physical competence mainly use standardized measures of physical fitness, research undertaken for applied purposes considers physical competence within a typological framework that groups people according to level of competence.

Population Age Trends in Physical Fitness

The most extensive studies of age, gender, and physical activity effects on physical competence in this country use data from the Canada Fitness Survey (Stephens et al., 1986; Kozma & Stones, 1990; Kozma et al., 1991). The tests in this survey measured the number of push-ups and sit-ups within one minute, endurance fitness by a stepping test, handgrip strength, and trunk forward flexion. The ages of the more than 6000 participants ranged from the 20s to the 60s. The findings indicate most loss of competence with age for the push-up and sit-up tests, followed by the step test, followed by handgrip strength and flexibility, with generally greater losses by males than females.

These findings accord with a model proposed by Stones and Kozma (1986), which suggests that age loss is greater for activities with higher rates of expenditure of the available energy. The push-up and sit-up tests expend energy at a high rate because they engage a large muscle mass in near-maximal effort for a full minute. The stepping test also involves a large muscle mass but the effort is submaximal. Handgrip strength involves contraction of a small muscle mass for a very brief interval, and flexibility taxes energy only minimally. Although these findings are consistent with the proposed model, a limitation is that the model emphasizes power to the exclusion of other facets of activity (e.g., neuromuscular coordination) (Spirduso, 1995; Baker, Tang, & Turner, 2003).

A large study in the United States also provides support for Stones and Kozma's (1986) model. Kovar and LaCroix (1987) measured five work-related physical activities in a sample of nearly 10 000 participants aged 55 to 74 years:

- Mobility—walking a quarter-mile and walking up 10 stairs without resting
- Endurance—standing and sitting for two hours
- Freedom of movement—reaching up overhead and reaching out to shake hands
- Fine motor movement—grasping with fingers
- Strength—stooping, crouching, or kneeling, and lifting or carrying 10 pounds (4.5 kg) or 25 pounds (11.3 kg).

Over half (58 percent) of the sample completed all the tasks successfully. The proportion of participants who had trouble or were unable to complete the tasks increased with age and was higher for women than men. The tasks associated with the steepest loss of competence with age were lifting a 25-pound (11.3 kg) weight and standing on two feet for two hours. Of all the tasks, these two require the highest rates of energy expenditure over the short-term and long-term, respectively.

The Typological Perspective

Spirduso (1995:338–355) describes a hierarchical approach to understanding and measuring physical competence in old and very old people. This approach is useful for applied purposes because people of different abilities

- face different kinds of challenge;
- require different tools to provide sensitive measurement;
- need different kinds of intervention.

Spirduso identifies five groups based on differences in competence.

Physically dependent people are unable to perform some or all of the basic activities of daily living such as walking, bathing, dressing, and eating. People in this category need assistance with the basic tasks of life regardless of whether they live independently or in an institution. The reasons for physical dependency include debilitating physical illness and progressive neurological disorders such as Alzheimer's disease and related dementias.

The most discriminative measures of physical competence in physically dependent people are termed activities of daily living (ADL) measures. Probably the most widely used ADL measures in Canada derive from versions of the Resident Assessment Instrument (RAI) mandated for use by Ontario's complex continuing care facilities, psychiatric in-patient facilities, and community care access centres (Hirdes et al., 2000). These tools are also used in most of the other Canadian provinces and in countries around the globe. Embedded within the RAI tools are short and long ADL scales and the ADL hierarchy scale. As shown in Table 7.1, the latter includes four items—personal hygiene, toileting, locomotion, and eating—with the response scale measuring levels of competence from independence to total dependence on others (Morris, Fries, & Morris, 1999). Deterioration in activities of daily living relates to impending mortality in a study of non-demented elderly people (Schupf et al., 2005). The most frequent measures of physical competence include instrumental activities of daily living (IADL) and adaptive mobility (e.g., Kempen & Suurmeijer, 1990; Tinetti, 1986).

Physically frail people are able to perform the basic activities of daily living but lack the competence to undertake a full range of instrumental activities such as housekeeping, food preparation, and shopping. They are frequently homebound and require help from relatives or professional caregivers to remain independent. Their frailty may result from chronic or acute disease, accidents, and lifestyle. The predictors of physical disability most frequently reported in research include hypertension and arthritis, with cardiac disorders, cancer, bone injury, diabetes, obesity, smoking, and a high alcohol intake sometimes reported (Spirduso, 1995).

Table 7.1 **ITEMS ON THE RESIDENT ASSESSMENT INSTRUMENT ADL HIERARCHY SCALE AND THE IADL INVOLVEMENT SCALE**

ADL items	Response scale	IADL items	Response scale
Personal	Independent	Meal preparation	Did on own
hygiene	Supervision	Ordinary housework	Help sometimes
Toileting	required	Managing finances	needed
Locomotion	Limited assistance	Managing	Help always needed
Eating	Extensive assistance	medications	Performed by others
	Total dependence	Phone use	Activity didn't occur
		Shopping	
		Transportation	

Interventions with physically frail people aim to sustain existing levels of competence (i.e., to prevent deterioration) or to restore them to a higher level. The Resident Assessment Instrument Health Infomatics Project (RAIHIP) carried out in Ontario in 2000–2001 provides a profile of the kinds of intervention required. Of approximately 5500 assessments by Community Care Access Centres (CCAC) across the province to determine community care requirements, 53 percent were for home-care eligibility, 30 percent were post-hospitalization, and 11 percent were for chronic community care. Half of the people assessed were considered in need of home-care intervention, and one-third required assistance after hospitalization.

The prevention of falls receives much attention in Canada. As discussed in Box 7.2, falls are the leading accidental cause of death in later life. Every Canadian province has undertaken initiatives to prevent falls (Public Health Agency of Canada, 2005), with successful interventions usually combining physical exercise, home assessment, and education (Stones, Linkewich, Porter Brysch, Taylor, & Brink, 2004).

Physically independent people have competence in the basic and instrumental activities of daily living and are able to undertake light physical work and recreation (e.g., walking, gardening, golf). The majority of older people belong to this category. Most of them, however, neither participate in fitness activity nor concern themselves unduly with good health habits.

A Canadian tool to assess physically independent people is the *Standardized Test of Fitness* (1981), which is similar to the American Association for Health, Physical Education, Recreation, and Dance (AAHPERD) field test. Such tests

Box 7.2 *Falls and the Elderly*

A recent report on the prevention of injuries and falls in the elderly by the Provincial Health Officer of British Columbia included the following highlights:

- In British Columbia, more than 770 people aged 65 years and over died directly or indirectly from a fall in 2001. Falls generally account for over half the deaths due to injuries in elderly females and for over one-third the deaths due to injuries in elderly males.
- In British Columbia, there were over 26 000 hospital admissions of seniors because of falls and over 43 000 visits to emergency departments in 2001. The average hospital stay ranged from nine days in people aged 65 to 75 years to 14 days in those aged 85 years and over. The length of stay because of falls was more than twice that for all other causes of hospitalization in the elderly.
- Falls account for 90 percent of all hip fractures in the elderly, with a single hip fracture costing $24 400–$-28 000. The total direct health-care cost due to falls was $180 million in British Columbia in 1998.
- The human cost of falls is immense. Falls can cause enduring disability, chronic pain, depression, and a fear of falling that leads to restriction of activities. Nearly half the elderly who sustain a hip fracture never recover fully.

Source: Adapted from *Prevention of falls and injuries among the elderly: A special report of the Provincial Health Officer* (2004). Office of Provincial Health Officer, Ministry of Health Planning, Government of British Columbia.

---

measure competencies related to balance, endurance, flexibility, and strength. Intervention based on findings from such tests aims to improve physical fitness.

Another applicable measurement paradigm takes account of a broader range of functions. The concept of *biological* or *functional age* originated in Canada with the work of Murray (1951) at Dalhousie University. Researchers in other countries soon incorporated this concept into their own research (Heron & Chown, 1967; Borkan & Norris, 1980). The aim was to "find out how old a person *really* is" through assessment of physical and cognitive functions while statistically controlling for chronological age. Subsequent studies found functional age measures were able to predict fitness, health status, and mortality (Borkan & Norris, 1980; Botwinick, West, & Storandt, 1978; Stones & Kozma, 1988). Although the use of functional age measures diminished after Costa and McCrae (1980a) criticized the cross-sectional designs used in early research, Spirduso (1995) concluded that such batteries

- neither improve much on chronological age as a descriptor of the aging process nor predict rates of aging;
- are successful in discriminating groups differing in health and survival status.

Physically fit individuals generally exercise two or more times weekly for enjoyment, health, and well-being. They generally have good health habits, do not smoke, and refrain from excessive alcohol intake (Spirduso, 1995).

Measures of physical fitness for people within this category include field tests like the Canadian *Standardized Test of Fitness*. Although these tests are relatively inexpensive to administer, there are limitations to the accuracy of the information they provide. They may underestimate levels of fitness in older people because of their lower maximal heart rate (O'Hanley et al., 1987). Some researchers consider laboratory-based exercise stress tests as the *gold standard* measure of endurance fitness and prefer them for clinical assessment (Chodzko-Zajko, 1994).

The aims of intervention for people within the physically independent and physically fit categories are to sustain or improve their levels of fitness. Erik Larkin and Pamela Kipness were among the first in Canada to develop an exercise program for older people. This program, *Fitness with Fun and Fellowship (3F)*, started in St. John's, Newfoundland in 1977, and continues to this day with an enrolment of several hundred participants. As the name indicates, the aims of the program include making exercise an enjoyable experience within a socially supportive context. The participants exercise in groups graded according to fitness, with the context enriched by background music chosen to be lively and uplifting. The fitness instructors offer encouragement and support to all participants, with social support enhanced by many social events throughout the year.

Reasons for dropping out of exercise programs include illness, life changes, and personal factors. Stacey, Kozma, and Stones (1985) found participants who dropped out of the *3F* program to be relatively unhappy, with high levels of anxiety.

Physically elite people are those who score at the highest fitness levels for their age (Spirduso, 1995). They exercise most days and many compete in age-class or open-class athletic competitions. These older athletes enjoy sport, believe it to be beneficial, and relish the challenges of competition. For many of them, later life athleticism is a continuation of lifelong habits of competitive physical activity (Harada, 1994; Stones & Kozma, 1996). Older athletes in an Australian study (Dionigi, 2002) reported that competitive sport was enjoyable, helped them hold off aging problems, and gave them a sense of personal empowerment.

Canada has a good history of providing opportunities for older people to participate in sport. The First World Masters Track and Field Championship took place in Toronto in 1975, giving rise to the biennial World Veteran Games. These competitions regularly attract over 5000 athletes from around the globe. Canada also has a good track record for research on age effects in physical performance by elite athletes. Research on such performances (discussed further in Chapter 10) is useful for a number of reasons:

- The study of elite competence can clarify the processes of usual competence, including factors that promote and hinder competence as people age.
- Because elite physical performers are active, fit, and healthy, comparison of their physical performances at different ages may reflect intrinsic age trends—uncontaminated by disuse or disease.
- The study of trends in peak performance may facilitate prediction of the absolute limits of physical performance as people age.

CHAPTER SUMMARY

Cognitive and physical performance show trends that vary with age, experience, and the facet of performance studied.

Cognition refers to a set of processes that enable us to monitor information from the environment, filter that information, store some components in memory, integrate them with previous and subsequent information, make decisions, and behave in ways anticipated to change the environment. The processes of cognition include the sensory system, memory, intelligence, creativity, and wisdom.

Physical performance refers to what people do habitually; physical competence refers to what they are able to do. Models of the latter include a typological framework that classifies people according to their level of physical competence. Different measures are needed to provide accurate assessment of competence within each category.

Key ideas to remember from this chapter:

- The sensory system shows some deterioration with age in most modalities. However, many such changes are correctable to some degree (e.g., the use of glasses, hearing aids), and do not impair a person's capability to function effectively.
- Memory consists of several systems that appear to have some degree of independence. Sensory and primary memory show minimal effects of aging throughout most of the lifespan. Working memory, which involves a higher level of processing, does decline with age.
- Acquisition of information into long-term memory is less effective in older people, particularly if the information is presented rapidly or with few cues to organization. The provision of retrieval cues facilitates retrieval from long-term memory, with particular benefit to older people.
- Beliefs about memory held by older people include lower perceptions of efficacy.
- Studies of successive cohorts show that the apparent declines in intelligence found in earlier cross-sectional research on intelligence showed confounding by cohort differences. Studies that measure longitudinal change find minimal declines in intelligence until very late in life.
- Social context and life experiences appear to be stronger influences than age change on creative output and wisdom.
- Studies of habitual physical performance have mainly used measures of energy expenditure, with evidence that these levels decreased after World War II but increased in older people thereafter.
- Recent findings suggest that middle-aged Canadian men have lower expenditures than younger or older men, with an opposite trend in Canadian women.
- Population trends in physical fitness suggest that age decline is highest for activities that draw most heavily on the available energy.

- A typology of physical competence distinguished between five categories of people: physically dependent, frail, independent, fit, and elite.
- Physically dependent and frail people suffer from chronic disease and disability. Approximately 25 percent of the population aged 65 years and older are deficient in at least one instrumental activity of daily living and fall within these categories.
- Independent and (to a lesser extent) fit people may show losses in physical competence because of disuse of physical capabilities and other aspects of lifestyle. These categories subsume about 70 percent of the older population.
- Physically elite people comprise the top 5 percent of the population; their levels of physical decline provide the best data on intrinsic age effects.

KEY TERMS

cognition (**p. 168**)

sensation (**p. 168**)

perception (**p. 168**)

memory (**p. 168**)

sensory memory (**p. 172**)

short-term memory (**p. 172**)

primary memory (**p. 172**)

working memory (**p. 172**)

long-term memory (**p. 173**)

episodic memory (**p. 173**)

semantic memory (**p. 173**)

procedural memory (**p. 173**)

prospective memory (**p. 173**)

recall (**p. 174**)

recognition (**p. 174**)

metamemory (**p. 175**)

intelligence (**p. 175**)

fluid intelligence (**p. 176**)

crystallized intelligence (**p. 176**)

creativity (**p. 177**)

wisdom (**p. 178**)

selective optimization (**p. 180**)

compensation (**p. 180**)

performance (**p. 180**)

competence (**p. 180**)

fitness (**p. 180**)

physically dependent (**p. 184**)

physically frail (**p. 184**)

physically independent (**p. 185**)

physically fit (**p. 186**)

physically elite (**p. 187**)

STUDY QUESTIONS

1. Some sensory processes show deterioration with age. Which of these processes are the most likely to affect an older person's functioning and well-being? Give reasons.

2. Describe the various types of memory. Which types show the greatest challenges with age?

3. Does intelligence deteriorate with age?

4. How strong is the evidence that people retain creativity in very advanced age?

5. Explain why no single set of measures can provide for sensitive and useful evaluation at all levels of physical competence. What are the main types of measure?

6. Approaches to understanding physical competence include the typological model. What are the advantages and disadvantages of a typological model of physical competence?

Suggested Readings

Allen, J.S., Bruss, J., & Damasio, H. (2005). The aging brain: The cognitive reserve hypothesis and human evolution. *American Journal of Human Biology, 17,* 673–689.

Baltes, P.B., & Baltes, M.M. (Eds.) (1990). *Successful aging: Perspectives from the behavioural sciences.* Cambridge, UK: Cambridge University Press

Hultsch, D.F., Hertzog, C., Dixon, R., & Small, B.J. (1998). *Memory changes in the aged.* New York: Cambridge University Press

Schaie, K.W. (1996). *Intellectual development in adulthood: The Seattle Longitudinal Study.* New York: Cambridge University Press.

Spirduso, W.W. (1995). *Physical dimensions of aging.* Champaign, IL: Human Kinetics.

Chapter 8

MENTAL WELL-BEING
AND MENTAL DISORDER

Learning Objectives

In this chapter, you will learn about

- Measurement relevant to mental well-being.
- Personality as a resource for mental health.
- Whether most people are happy and satisfied with their lives.
- Influences on happiness and life satisfaction at different ages.

- How institutions caring for mentally ill and infirm older people evolved into their present forms.
- How mental disorders vary in frequency and expression in cohorts of different ages.

Introduction

Since the time of the classical Greek philosophers, a predominant theme in Western thought suggests that happiness is what most people want above all else. These philosophers used a question-and-answer game to illustrate this point (Stones & Kozma, 1980). They first asked respondents what they wanted most in life. Given an answer, their second question asked why that object or condition was so desirable. They continued to ask this latter question repeatedly until the respondent was unable to provide an answer different from the one that preceded it. For thousands of years, the last answer has always been the same. The respondents wanted to be happy, with happiness being the ultimate desire toward which all other desires led. Box 8.1 illustrates some responses obtained from undergraduates.

Box 8.1 *Mental Well-Being as the Most Desired Human Condition*

Mental well-being occupies a unique place in Western value systems. A thought game played since the time of the classical Greek philosophers involves a question-and-answer sequence. The questioner asks a respondent what that person desires most in life. Upon receiving an answer, the questioner asks a new question: "Why do you want that?" and repeats this same question until the respondent can provide no further reason for the last answer given. Typical question-and-answer sequences are as follows.

Questioner	Respondent 1	Respondent 2	Respondent 3
"What do you want most in life?"	"Right now? Money!"	"A responsible job after graduating."	"To meet someone and fall in love."
"Why do you want that?"	"So I can pay my tuition and buy a car."	"Because I think I have the ability to build a solid career."	"I'm a romantic. Eventually raising my own family is important to me."
"Why do you want that?"	"It'll make my life so much easier."	"Mainly because I want to make a *real* contribution to society."	"To feel excited about life, and fulfilled—doing the things I think are most important."
"Why do you want that?"	"I'll be happy, man!"	"So I can feel satisfied that I've done some good, made a difference to how things are."	"It'll make me content. If I never fall in love, I'd miss out on something very special."
"Why do you want that?"	"Just wanna be happy, man."	"That's it, really. I just want to be satisfied with my life."	"Being content. That is as good as it gets."

The conclusions the Greek philosophers drew from answers to this game were as follows:

- Happiness is valued for its own sake.
- Happiness is not valued for the sake of anything else.
- Happiness is the most valued of any human condition because only happiness is desirable for itself and for no other reason.

The concept known throughout most of history as **happiness** now falls under a rubric of mental (or psychological or subjective) well-being. A question that occupied the minds of philosophers throughout history, and scientists during the past half-century, concerns the nature of **mental well-being** and ways to attain that condition. Stones and Kozma (1980) concluded from a review of historical changes in theorizing about mental well-being that in thousands of years there were variants around three basic models:

1. Throughout most of history, philosophers considered mental well-being to be a consequence of virtuous activity—only the "good" could be happy.
2. During most of the past two centuries, philosophers represented happiness as the balance between pleasurable and unpleasant experiences.
3. During the past quarter-century, scientists found that mental well-being included a dispositional component that contributed to a differentiation between happy and unhappy people.

The theory that mental well-being relates to affective experience, rather than virtuous activity, represents a major departure from traditional Western thought. Early versions of this theory presumed that happiness is contingent on external influences that occasion pleasure or displeasure. This environmentalist perspective on happiness influenced political thought (e.g., the right to pursue happiness is part of the United States Constitution) and helped to justify the introduction of welfare systems in the 19th century. Although the environmentalist perspective on mental well-being probably remains predominant in popular discourse, scientific advances during the past quarter-century increasingly suggest that disposition (e.g., personality, genetic inheritance) makes a major contribution.

Nowadays, we consider mental well-being to fall within a broader concept of **mental health**. If we think of mental health as a continuum ranging from states of bliss to misery, mental well-being refers to the upper half-range of this continuum and mental disorder to the lower half-range. Although a substantial body of evidence related to mental well-being accumulated during the past decades, it is not surprising that most research on mental health focuses on the lower half-range. The reason is that ours is a problem-oriented culture. The presence of mental well-being is not a problem requiring a solution; mental disorder represents a range of problems that require differentiated solutions.

The major mental disorders that appear more frequently in later than earlier life include cognitive impairment because of dementia or delirium. The prevalence rates for most other mental disorders are less frequent in later than earlier life. However, an ongoing controversy with respect to mood disorder questions whether the lower prevalence in later life has more to do with diagnostic practices that fail to account for an altered expression of depressed mood as people age than a substantive reduction in prevalence (U.S. Department of Health and Social Services, 1999).

The organization of this chapter follows conventional practice by separating the discussion of mental well-being and mental disorder. The contents of the former include the measurement of mental well-being, the **distribution** of scores on such measures, and models of the concept. The latter section includes a historical overview of the treatment of mental disorder and discussion about cognitive impairment and other disorders in later life.

Mental Well-Being

Measurement of Mental Well-Being

Mental well-being refers to a subjective evaluation of overall quality of life. The various terms used to describe the concept include *happiness, life satisfaction, morale, and trait affect*. Researchers have used each of these terms to name measures of mental well-being that show acceptable reliability and validity (Kozma, Stones, & McNeil, 1991). (Recall from Chapter 4 that reliability refers to the confidence we can have in the scores provided by a measure; validity refers to the confidence we can have that the measure measures the concept it addresses.) A Canadian measure used in gerontological research across the world is the 24-item Memorial University of Newfoundland Scale of Happiness (MUNSH) (Kozma & Stones, 1980), later developed into a shorter 12-item scale known as the Short Happiness and Affect Research Protocol (SHARP) (Stones et al., 1995). These scales have high reliability as measured by inter-item consistency. Validity testing of the MUNSH showed high correlations with happiness ratings by the respondents, happiness ratings by informants knowledgeable about the respondents, and other measures of mental well-being. The scale also differentiated among groups of older people believed to differ in levels of happiness (e.g., community residents, residents of long-term care homes, psychiatric patients) (Kozma, Stones, & Kazarian, 1985; Kozma & Stones, 1987, 1988).

Potential problems with the validity of a scale include response set, extremity set, and impression management. **Response set** applies only to scales with categorical responses (e.g., the SHARP contains only "yes" and "no" response alternatives). It occurs if a respondent shows bias toward a particular choice regardless of the content of the item (e.g., yea saying refers to a bias toward the "yes" response). Studies found no evidence for response set on mental well-being measures in the vast majority of healthy and cognitively able older people, but some evidence of response set in respondents of very advanced age, low education, low socio-economic status, and impaired cognition (Kozma, Stones, & McNeil, 1991). Consequently, we should be cautious in interpreting mental well-being scores if there is any suspicion that respondents may fail to fully understand or respond appropriately to the item content.

Extremity set refers to a tendency to check extreme responses (e.g., the highest alternative on a 5-point scale). However, research provides convincing evidence that the distributions of scores have comparable meaning regardless of whether the extreme responses indicate high (Michalos, 1985) or low (Mann, 1991) mental well-being or level of affect (Larsen & Diener, 1987).

Impression management refers to positively biased responding because the respondents want to create a favourable impression (i.e., a socially desirable impression) or fear the consequences of negative responding. Hirdes, Zimmerman, Hallman, and Soucie (1998) illustrate the latter by suggesting that residents in institutions may fear repercussions if they express concerns about their care. Studies of impression management of mental well-being measures typically include two main features:

1. Respondents complete both the mental well-being measure and a measure relevant to impression management (e.g., a **social desirability** scale). If the two measures correlate highly, there is a suspicion that the former may be susceptible to impression management.

2. Proxy respondents estimate the level of mental well-being of each individual who provides self-report data. A proxy respondent is someone with good knowledge of the self-report respondent (e.g., a family member, a close friend, a primary care provider). The reasoning is that even if respondents bias their self-ratings to create a good impression, the proxy respondents should provide an unbiased estimate of mental well-being.

Findings with this type of design provide no good evidence for contamination of mental well-being measures by impression management regardless of age or type of residence (i.e., community versus institution). The MUNSH and other mental well-being measures show a high correlation between self-report and proxy respondents, with no comparable correlation between self-reported mental well-being and social desirability (Diener, Sandvik, Parvot, & Gallagher, 1991; Kozma & Stones, 1987, 1988; McCrae, 1986).

Other findings related to measurement show that differently named mental well-being measures correlate highly regardless of the label applied to the scale. Even though terms like happiness, life satisfaction, and morale have different nuances of meaning in everyday language, these nuances do not emerge in the scores from the scales—a person scoring high on a measure of morale is likely to have a similar score on a scale of happiness or life satisfaction. These high correlations led Stones and Kozma (1980) to conclude that all the indexes measure essentially the same construct, now termed mental well-being but known throughout most of Western history simply as happiness. The only consistent difference to emerge from this research on inter-scale correlation is that measures of mental well-being show a strong negative correlation with self-report measures of depression, suggesting that the latter lies at the opposite end of the mental well-being continuum (Kozma, Stones, & Kazarian, 1985).

Concepts related to mental well-being but with more restricted meanings include (1) life domain satisfactions, which refer to satisfactions with specific aspects of life (e.g., finances, health), (2) temporally specific mood states, and (3) affective style—also termed affectivity. Measures of these concepts tend to correlate positively with measures of mental well-being (McNeil, Stones, Kozma, & Andres, 1994; Stones & Kozma, 1986).

Distributions of Mental Well-Being Scores

One of the most frequently replicated findings on mental well-being during the past half-century is that most people score within the positive half-range on these indexes. If the index is on a 10-point scale (i.e., such that 10 is the most positive and 1 the most negative), the average score within the general population approximates 7 or 8 (Heady & Wearing, 1988). Figure 8.1 includes a recent distribution of mental well-being scores among Canadians from the 1999 Manulife Financial Healthstyles

Figure 8.1 DISTRIBUTION OF MENTAL WELL-BEING SCORES FOR CANADIANS

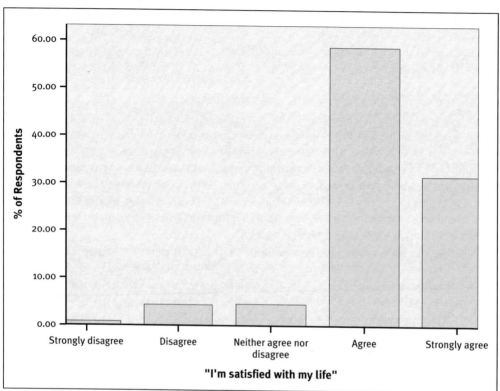

Source: Based on Manulife Financial (1999). *Manulife healthstyles study.* Toronto, ON: Market Facts of Canada Ltd.

Study. Approximately 90 percent of respondents rated themselves above the scale midpoint. Statisticians refer to such distributions as **negatively skewed**, meaning that most scores cluster near the positive pole with a tail at the negative end. Findings of negative skew on mental well-being measures transcend countries and demographic strata within countries (e.g., age, gender, social class) (Michalos, 1991; Near & Rechner, 1993). In other words, the findings are consistent from different countries, people of different ages, men and women, the rich and the poor. Such findings obtain from a range of measures that include

- mental well-being, life domain satisfaction, and affect indexes (Andrews, 1991; McNeil, Stones, Kozma & Andres, 1994);
- absolute and comparative estimates of well-being (e.g., personal well-being compared with age peers) (Heady & Wearing, 1998);
- self-ratings, multi-item scales, and ratings by other people (Kozma & Stones, 1988)
- unipolar measures and indexes of the balance between positive and negative affect (Kozma & Stones, 1980).

The few exceptions to the rule that population distributions of mental well-being score have negative skew include near-midrange levels of mental well-being for black South African youth during the Apartheid era (Moller, 1992), residents of long-term care homes (Kozma & Stones, 1987), and residents of psychiatric institutions (Kozma & Stones, 1987). The lowest mental well-being scores on record include findings from South Africa, where older Zulu return migrants in the 1980s provided scores below the midpoint on the scales. However, apart from the South African studies and studies of institution residents, the preponderance of findings show that the majority of community residents have positive scores on mental well-being measures.

Heady and Wearing (1988) wrote that some researchers appear defensive about such findings because traditional social science models convey an impression that unhappiness rather than happiness should be the prevailing condition (e.g., the "social pathology" and "relative deprivation" models in sociology; the "medical/clinical" model in psychology; the "rational actor" model in economics). Although some adherents to these theories have expressed skepticism about findings of overall happiness, the robustness of the latter with a diverse array of valid measures should cause such theorists to question their assumptions.

Demographic Influences on Mental Well-Being Distributions

Measures of happiness and life satisfaction generally show weak relationships with socio-economic indexes within and across countries (Diener, Sandvik, Seidlitz, & Diener, 1993; Myers, 2000; Myers & Diener, 1995). These measures also show similar distributions regardless of age and gender (Kozma, Stones, & McNeil, 1991). However, gender differences may appear in self-reports of depression. Figure 8.2 shows responses from a representative Canadian sample to the Manulife Healthstyles Study (Stones, 2001b) on self-rated depression. Although less than 20 percent of respondents agreed that they were "frequently depressed, down-hearted, or blue," more females than males agreed with this item. Findings reviewed later in this chapter show a similar gender difference in the prevalence of clinical depression.

A meta-analysis of nearly 300 studies of socio-economic influences on mental well-being showed the relevance of the quality, rather than the size, of an older person's social network (Pinquart & Sorenson, 2001b), with family contacts more important than those with friends. Although the absence of major life trauma was predictive of greater mental well-being (Lyubomirsky, 2001), longitudinal findings suggest that most people show recovery from the effects of such trauma. Other findings suggest that apart from life events related to health, most other life events have a minor influence on mental well-being (Ventegodt, Flensborg-Madsen, Andersen, & Merrick, 2006).

Figure 8.2 CANADIAN AGE AND GENDER TRENDS FOR SELF-REPORTED DEPRESSION

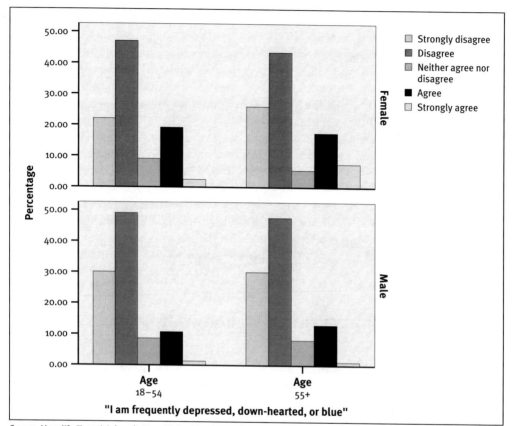

Source: Manulife Financial. (1999). *Manulife healthstyles study.* Toronto, ON: Market Facts of Canada Ltd.

Temporal Stability of Mental Well-Being

Longitudinal findings suggest that mental well-being retains stability as people age. Atkinson (1982) was probably the first to show minimal effects on stability because of major life changes. Studies by Kozma and Stones (1983) and Costa, McCrae, and Zonderman (1987) replicated this finding. Mussen, Honzig, and Eichorn (1982) analyzed mental well-being measures taken twice over 40 years. The findings showed that stability accounted for 15 to 30 percent of the total variability within measures. An analysis of earlier studies (cited by Veenhoven,1994) concluded that the stable component of mental well-being averages 40 percent or more over 10 years (Stones, Hadjistravopoulos, Tuokko, & Kozma,1995). Lykken and Tellegen (1996) reported comparable findings with a 10-year stability estimate of 50 percent in a study of aging twins. A study of nearly 1300 people showed—perhaps surprisingly—that less than 1 percent of the variability in changes in mental well-being resulted from a loss over the last three years in health, finances, or employment. In short, the evidence is abundant from longitudinal research that mental well-being measures retain considerable stability as people age.

Despite such evidence of longitudinal stability, a belief that mental well-being decreases with age continues to persist in our culture. Earlier textbooks on gerontology made frequent reference to losses associated with aging (e.g., in health, income, social networks) as contributing to an expectation of declining mental well-being. Shmotkin (1991:264) found evidence that older people also believe this myth. Most devalued their present and future expectations of life satisfaction in relation to the past: "Respondents of age 51 and over evaluated the past increasingly higher than the present, and respondents of age 66 and over evaluated the past even higher than the future." However, the actual distributions of well-being scores fail to support these expectations; no loss was found within the age range cited.

Models of Mental Well-Being

Current thinking generally follows one of three basic models of mental well-being: **bottom-up**, **top-down**, and **up-down** (Stones, Hadjistravopoulos, Tuokko, & Kozma, 1995). Figure 8.3 illustrates these models.

Figure 8.3 THREE MODELS OF MENTAL WELL-BEING

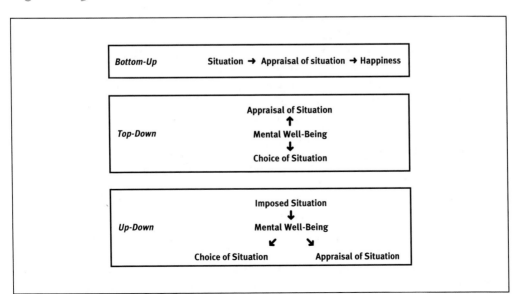

Bottom-Up Models Bottom-up models assume mental well-being to be a reactive state, with outside influences mediated through situational appraisal (e.g., life domain satisfactions, perceived burden, hassles). Consequently, the hypothesized causal sequence proceeds from an objective situation (e.g., a condition like socio-economic status or an event like a death or a marriage), which affects the cognitive appraisal of that situation, which in turn affects mental well-being.

The most comprehensive model of this type to originate from Canada is probably that described by Michalos (1991). Examples from gerontology include a study by Clyburn, Stones, Hadjistavropoulos, and Tuokko (2000) that compared several models of the impact of caring for Alzheimer's patients on the mental well-being of family caregivers. A bottom-up model received the most support in a Canada-wide study. This model assumes that objective features of caregiving (e.g., disturbing symptoms, kind of support received) affect the appraisal of caring (i.e., perceived burden), which in turn affects mental well-being as measured by a depression scale. Like most research that tested bottom-up hypotheses, the design of this study was cross-sectional. Other research within the purview of the model used experimental or therapeutic intervention designs.

1. *Cross-Sectional Research:* A substantial body of research used cross-sectional data to test support for bottom-up models. Some of these studies tested the overall correlation between objective situations and mental well-being rather than the correlations between the situation and appraisal, and appraisal and mental well-being, respectively. However, the support received from the overall correlations is limited. Michalos (1991) studied students from around the world, hypothesizing that demographic factors (e.g., income) correlate with situational appraisal (e.g., financial satisfaction), which correlate with mental well-being. Numerous studies of elderly populations similarly examined the relationships of mental well-being with demographic and situational appraisal indicators (Kozma, Stones, & McNeil, 1991). The findings show that although situational appraisals have moderate correlations with mental well-being at any age, knowledge about demographics or life situation has almost no predictive value. Myers and Diener (1995:17) commented: "Knowing a person's age, sex, race, and income (assuming the person has enough to afford life's necessities) hardly gives a clue." In other words, mental well-being has limited relationships with any demographic index or life situation measure.

   Kozma and Stones (1983) found that that perceived health and housing satisfaction showed the highest correlation with mental well-being in older people. Perceived health is predictive of mortality and recovery from illness. It correlates with both objective indexes of health and measures relevant to mental well-being (Benyamini, Idler, Leventhal, & Leventhal, 2000). The strongest support for the bottom-up model tends to derive from the moderate correlations between situational appraisal measures and mental well-being.

2. *Experimental Studies:* Bottom-up models also fare badly in experimental research. Kozma, Stone, Stones, Hannah, and McNeil (1990) used positive

and negative mood inductions to determine the effects on mood and mental well-being. These inductions required the participants to imagine or recollect experiences in their own lives that made them either happy or sad. The induction brought about substantial change in immediate mood but had no effect on mental well-being as measured by the MUNSH. These findings provide no evidence that mental well-being increases or decreases in response to experimental manipulations shown to change mood.

3. *Therapeutic Interventions*: Therapeutic interventions for older people include psychosocial programs intended to promote mental well-being. A well-known intervention is **reminiscence therapy**, in which participants reminisce about experiences and feelings in their past. Butler (1963) suggested this kind of intervention provides an opportunity to review past life and thereby provide a continuity of meaning with present experiences. He reasoned that for the majority of older people, participation in the intervention should promote mental well-being because it facilitates adaptation to their present life. Other forms of psychosocial intervention aim to increase personal **control** and daily responsibilities. Several studies tested the effectiveness of such intervention with residents of long-term care homes. The rationale is that the loss of personal control associated with institutional life causes a loss of mental well-being. Interventions that increase such control might bring the levels back to approach the pre-institutional level.

Findings from such studies provide some of the strongest support for bottom-up models. A factor contributing to this success is undoubtedly the low levels of mental well-being prevalent in long-term care homes. With a low baseline level of mental well-being, the chances of therapeutic success are higher than among people who start off with average levels of mental well-being. Consequently, adequate control groups are essential to ensure valid findings.

One study among long-term care residents divided participants into three groups: one reminisced about their past lives, one discussed current issues, and the third received no treatment. Both treatment groups showed major improvement in mental well-being, but there was no change in the control group (Rattenbury & Stones, 1989). The authors concluded that participation in group discussion, regardless of content, contributed to a gain in mental well-being.

A subsequent study examined the effects of reminiscence over 18 months in five institutions (Rattenbury, Kozma, & Stones, 1995). Compared with a control group that received no treatment, the participants in therapeutic reminiscence showed higher mental well-being over the study period, and lower rates of morbidity and mortality. The beneficial effects associated with the intervention were independent of pre-existing levels of illness and disability.

A recent meta-analysis of 20 controlled studies of reminiscence intervention showed statistically and clinically significant gains in mental well-being (Bohlmeijer, Smit, & Cuijpers, 2003) comparable to those commonly found for pharmacotherapy and psychological treatments.

Langer and Rodin (1977) conducted a classic study of the effects of increasing choice and responsibility in elderly long-term care home residents. One group of participants received information about choices in the institution and were encouraged to take on extra responsibilities. Many of them did. Another group received positive messages about life in the home but no encouragement to assume additional responsibilities. The group that took on extra responsibilities showed greater mental well-being and lower subsequent mortality.

Top-Down Models   Top-down models assume that mental well-being is more unchanging than changeable (Lykken & Tellegen, 1996). Mental well-being in this model is trait-like rather than state-like. The model envisions that happy people do things that make them happy, elicit pleasing behaviour from others, and get over troubles quickly. Unhappy people tend to avoid intimacy or new encounters, elicit unfavourable reactions from others, and brood over troubles. A happy person exposed to adversity tempers that appraisal with an optimistic outlook, whereas an unhappy person exposed to a fortunate occurrence still considers the cup to be half empty. Consequently, the top-down model suggests that mental well-being is a *cause* of individual differences in situational appraisals and situational choices rather than their effect (Lyubomirsky, 2001). An extreme example is bipolar disorder, in which afflicted individuals behave at different times like very unhappy or very happy people. Lykken and Tellegen (1996) cite this disorder as evidence that mood precedes behaviour in causal sequence rather than vice versa.

Because the model assumes that people appraise situations from optimistic or pessimistic perspectives (Peterson, 2000), it anticipates that life domain satisfactions correlate more strongly with mental well-being measures than do demographic indicators. An optimist sets goals and strives to attain them: a pessimist may give up. Peterson (2000) reviewed evidence that an optimistic outlook on life is predictive of lower mortality and morbidity, higher achievement, and success in life.

Support for top-down models is both indirect and direct. The former includes a failure to obtain convincing evidence that unfavourable or favourable life experiences affect the mental well-being in the long term (Atkinson, 1982; Costa, McCrae, & Zonderman, 1987). People adapt even to the gravest misfortune, such as acquired paraplegia, and winning a lottery does not ensure happiness. Chamberlain and Zika (1992) hypothesized that recent hassles might contribute more to an explanation of mental well-being than major life events. However, their findings showed prior level of mental well-being to be a stronger predictor of present happiness than recent hassles. Similarly, Kozma, Stone and colleagues (1990) found minimal changes in mental well-being due to emotion-evoking situations known to affect mood. These negative findings provide indirect support for the top-down model.

Research on **personality** provides direct support for the top-down model. Most theorists believe that personality remains constant across the full lifespan even though the ways in which people express their personalities vary with age and situation. Box 8.2 provides such an illustration. Personality theories include trait and stage theories, described in Box 8.3.

Box 8.2 *Stability and Change in Personality*

Mary McKeown is nothing if not a shrewd judge of character. In her 80s now, she recently participated in a research project on mental well-being in later life. Once the data collection was over, Mary insisted that the young researcher stay for a cup of tea before returning to the university. Then, she proceeded to tell him her opinions about life development, which was what she wanted to do the minute he told her the purpose of his research.

An immigrant to Canada, Mary brought with her, from Scotland, a toy mailbox designed to stimulate perceptual problem solving in infancy. The "letters" were plastic geometric shapes—like a star or a square—that the child "mailed" by pushing them through corresponding shapes cut in the lid of the box. When the infant succeeded in mailing all the letters, well, the idea was to pull off the lid, take out the shapes, and do it all over again! All Mary's three children loved that toy.

The pieces of wisdom Mary imparted to the young researcher came from her observations that each child used a different strategy to solve the mailbox problem and continued to deploy that basic strategy throughout life. She thought it showed that the basics of character were present in infancy and changed little—all her children now being in their 60s.

The oldest child, Rachel, would persist doggedly at the game—using whatever combination of insight and trial-and-error worked—never giving up until she mailed the last letter. Rachel's life course exemplified the potency of dogged determination. Intelligent and intuitive, though without the natural brilliance that made academic work easy, she consistently made the honour roll at school and university, usually while working at more than one job to help pay her way. She applied to the graduate program of a well-known business school, which offered her a place even without her finishing an undergraduate degree. It took her a year to complete a two-year MBA program and she never looked back. The rest is history—a job as troubleshooter in the automotive industry, sent to Europe to sort out problems in their Paris plant, back home with a promotion, marriage, off to the main plant in the United States, two children, promoted to the very top of her company in Canada, her children now at university, and Rachel soon to retire. Mary is very proud of her.

Matthew could never stick at anything for long. A brilliant, inquisitive, but impatient infant, he would play the mailbox game only until he made a mistake. Then he would stop playing, do something else, and come back to finish mailing only on some later whim. Matthew made the honour roll at school because of cleverness alone, certainly not because of the effort he made. A dropout from university, he became a hippie, travelling around Europe, Asia, and Australia, working at menial jobs in each country he visited just long enough to earn enough to finance a journey to some other exotic place. He returned to Canada in his late 20s for a journalism degree. Subsequently employed by a national newspaper in England, he became a foreign correspondent for most of his career. Only in his 50s did he return to Canada once more, this time as editor of a newspaper. Two years later, he took early retirement. He spends his retirement, not surprisingly, travelling abroad.

Sarah had a different way of playing the mailbox game. The first time she failed to mail a letter, she would lift up the lid, put all the shapes in the box, and with a radiant smile proclaim, "That was easy!" Mary remembers that Sarah never had much respect for conventions or rules. Often in trouble at school, but invariably able to overcome any difficulties by charm, she left without a high school diploma. A period of delinquency was followed by a spell in the armed forces, then she began to settle down. Sarah's attractiveness and charm earned her work in sales. She left sales to become a dancer, returned to sales, married, separated,

(continued)

Box 8.2 (continued)

worked again for a while, married for a second time, and became a mother. Always happy and charming, she continues to live life according to her own conventions.

The point made by Mary is that each of her children used strategies to overcome problems that changed very little from infancy on. The way her children played the mailbox game provided Mary with insight into their characters. Rachel was persistent, Matthew impatient and easily bored, and Sarah intuitive, charming, and unconventional. Mary believes that each person is born with a unique character and that upbringing and later experiences allow that character to develop but never change its basic form. Do you think she is right?

Box 8.3 Personality Theories

Trait models and stage models differ in presumptions about stability and change in personality. Costa and McCrae (1980a) proposed that the most important features of personality reduce to just five traits, known as the "Big Five": This is sometimes known as the **five-factor theory.**

1. neuroticism—anxiety, depression, emotional distress
2. extroversion—sociability, assertiveness, warmth
3. openness to experience—willingness to take risks, seek out new experiences
4. conscientiousness—organization, efficiency, dependability
5. agreeableness—empathy, sensitivity, cooperativeness.

Their research design included the administration of paper-and-pencil tests to huge numbers of people of different ages, with the traits identified by the use of a statistical procedure known as factor analysis. The findings provided evidence of stability of the mean levels across age groups, and evidence of interpersonal stability over time, suggesting that the big five traits retain stability over time. At least two of these traits—neuroticism and extroversion—correlate with mental well-being; people lower on neuroticism and higher on extroversion tend to be happier (Kozma, Stones, & McNeil, 1991; Ozer & Benet-Matinez, 2006). These two traits also show substantial contributions of heritability (Bouchard & McGue, 1990), meaning that genetics contributes substantially to their development.

Despite persuasive evidence that personality traits are stable, not everyone believes this to be true. Stage theorists like Cumming and Henri (1961) and McAdams and de St. Aubin (1992) suggest that middle-aged people emphasize generative concerns in their lives (e.g., contributing to their family and society), whereas the concerns of older people emphasize a review of the accomplishments and failures of their past life. Krueger and Heckhausen (1997) asked young, middle-aged, and older people to describe how their own personalities would change during subsequent decades of life. The respondents believed that age would bring about more undesirable than desirable changes on four of the big five traits (i.e., neuroticism, extroversion, conscientiousness, and agreeableness). However, there is little evidence to support this belief.

Personality traits and other stable resources that correlate with mental well-being include extroversion, neuroticism, meaning in life, perceived control, and optimism (Kozma, Stones, & McNeil, 1991; Diener, Suh, Lucas, & Smith, 1999).

Because these dispositions, like mental well-being, are stable over time, the findings suggest that mental well-being belongs with a constellation of other stable traits. However, probably the strongest evidence to support the top-down model derives from research on **heritability**.

A well-established research paradigm to estimate the effects of heritability compares identical and fraternal twins. Identical twins have exactly the same genetic inheritance, whereas fraternal twins are genetically no more similar than any brother or sister pairing. Refinements to the design include comparisons of each type of twin reared together or apart (e.g., because of adoption). Findings from the twin paradigm provide evidence for a substantial contribution by heredity to the mental well-being of both younger and older adults. Lykken and Tellegen (1996) estimate that approximately half the total variability between individuals at any given time, and 80 percent of the variability between individuals that is stable over time occurs because of heredity. These findings suggest that after accounting for temporary fluctuations (e.g., because of measurement error) only 20 percent of the differences between people in mental well-being arise because of environmental differences, with 80 percent attributable to genetic differences.

Although Lykken and Tellegen (1996) humorously interpreted their findings by suggesting that trying to be happier may be as futile as trying to be taller, this is an over-interpretation. Although 80 percent of the individual difference variability might be of genetic origin, previously cited findings of low scores on mental well-being measures by residents of long-term care homes and black South Africans during the Apartheid era suggest that situational effects are not trivial.

Up-Down Models   Up-down models incorporate both dispositional and situational influences on mental well-being. The top-down effects generally outweigh bottom-up effects because most people are able to choose their situations freely. (Even in circumstances beyond their control, people have choices on a day-to-day level.) Consequently, findings across a range of ages provide support for a model in which top-down effects are stronger than bottom-up effects (Kozma, Stone, & Stones, 2000; Mallard, Lance, & Michalos, 1997; Stones & Kozma, 1986). Stones, Hadjistavropoulos, Tuokko, and Kozma (1995) attempted to reconcile discrepancies in earlier research on external influences by suggesting that although mental well-being affects situational choices, situations externally imposed on people may affect mental well-being. Moller (1992) provided evidence consistent with this latter hypothesis.

Moller (1992) examined spare time use and mental well-being in 1200 black South Africans aged 16 to 25 years during the time of Apartheid. She found only 50 percent of the sample reported satisfaction with life, with the remainder either ambivalent or dissatisfied. Comparable proportions considered life rewarding or exciting versus frustrating or boring. Similarly, approximately 50 percent had a positive and 50 percent a negative outlook on the future. These distributions contrast dramatically with those of Canadians, whose ratings showed 90 percent endorsement of life satisfaction (Figure 8.1).

Although most theories suggest that mental well-being relates to the frequencies of positive and negative experiences (Diener, Sandvic, & Parvot, 1991), findings with time-use diaries suggest otherwise. More than 90 percent of Moller's sample pursued at least one "best liked" activity per day, with only 35 percent engaging in a disliked activity. Of the total activity units reported in the diaries, 94 percent were liked activities and 89 percent undertaken of free choice. Moller (1999:339) concluded as follows: "Superficially seen, black youth in South Africa lead very normal lives: they spend approximately one third of their time sleeping, working in jobs or learning at school, and on leisure activities including obligatory domestic duties." What was different about their lives was that crime, delinquency, riots, low opportunity for advancement, school boycotts, and pressures toward involvement in political conflict considerably limited their freedom of choice. They made the best of what they had but their environment restricted their range of options.

Likewise, residents in long-term care homes have a more limited range of options than people living in the community. Their activity preferences are limited not only by the regimens within the homes but also by cognitive and functional impairments. Figure 8.4 shows activity preferences (Morris, Murphy, & Nonemaker, 1995) for over 1500 residents of long-term care homes in Ontario in 2000–2001. The only activities enjoyed by more than half the residents were listening to music and engaging in conversation, and more than 60 percent of the sample enjoyed less than one-quarter of the activities listed.

In conclusion, up-down models are consistent with findings that

- mental well-being shows stability over time;
- personality and heredity are major influences;
- life domain indicators, burden, hassles, and mood measures are correlates;
- demographic indicators are generally poor predictors;
- an imposed negative environment negatively affects mental well-being;
- therapeutic intervention within such an environment may produce positive change.

Mental Disorder

At the opposite end of the mental heath continuum to mental well-being is mental distress. Mental distress encompasses many types of **mental disorders**. Psychiatry is the medical specialty concerned with the diagnosis and treatment of such disorders. Geriatrics is the medical specialty dealing with illness in older people. Their intersection is the subspecialty of psychogeriatrics, which focuses on the mental health problems of older people. Both psychiatry and geriatrics occupied lowly positions on the medical hierarchy for most of the past two centuries. A reason is that our society stigmatized both the insane and the impoverished elderly for much of this period. Nova Scotia geriatrician Roy Fox (1991) proffered this mocking depiction of geriatrics as viewed by colleagues in other branches of medicine: "A second-rate specialty looking after third-rate patients

Figure 8.4 ACTIVITY PREFERENCES IN MORE THAN 1500 LONG-TERM CARE HOME RESIDENTS

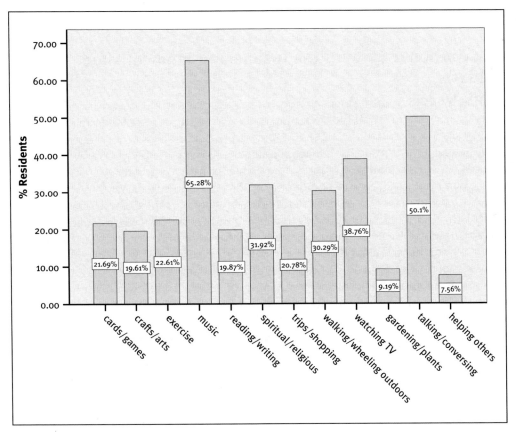

Source: Based on Resident Assessment Instrument Health Infomatics Project (2000–2001)

in fourth-rate facilities." Psychiatry's reputation fared no better in medical circles and public awareness.

For reasons that were more political (regarding the insane) or economic (for the impoverished elderly), institutional care became the accepted form of treatment for both populations. Depictions in Europe (Townsend, 1962) and North America (Butler, 1975) during the past half-century raised concerns about the quality of life in institutions for the aged. Psychiatric institutions elicited even harsher criticism. Researchers like Laing (1960), Goffman (1961), and Szasz (1961) provided powerful critiques, and movies such as *One Flew Over the Cuckoo's Nest* made the failings of psychiatry conspicuous to wide audiences. Such practices as frontal lobotomy and the overuse of electroconvulsive shock earned psychiatry much notoriety. Some former psychiatric patients, calling themselves psychiatric survivors, formed support networks, which continue to provide support and advocacy at local and provincial levels). This section of the chapter traces the history of institutional care in North America, before discussing common forms and treatment of mental disorder in later life.

Institutional Care for the Insane and Impoverished Elderly

Early Models North America imported models of institutional care based on experiences in Europe at the beginning of the 19th century. Large metropolitan insane asylums created during that century still exist in Canada, although with substantial reductions to the inmate populations since the 1980s, when advances in pharmacology made community care viable for many residents.

European psychiatric institutions before the 19th century were terrible places. The behaviour of mentally ill people scared the public and baffled physicians. The theology of a preceding era perceived many forms of social deviance as examples of sin. Although we now consider crime an act of volition and mental illness a loss of volition, the medieval theologian Thomas Aquinas interpreted insanity as possession by the devil. Residues of this thinking remained as the 18th century closed. Consequently, custodial institutions justified cruel treatment of the incarcerated insane as purging them of sin.

Such treatment horrified Philippe Pinel, who became administrator of an insane asylum in Paris. Incarcerated patients lived in gloom and squalor, tormented by brutal custodians, subjected to pitiless intervention (e.g., bleeding, blistering, emetics, purging), and some were kept in shackles for decades. Pinel's observations led him to introduce a more humane model of institutional care (e.g., replacing the more cruel attendants, providing adequate nutrition, making the environment more pleasing). Evidence of therapeutic success resulted in the wider adoption of this model. Comparable innovations at the York Retreat in England (established in 1796 by Quaker William Tuke) resulted in calmer patients despite the use of few restraints or medicaments. Another notable event of that era was clergyman Francis Willis's cure of the madness of King George III, after his physician's miserable failure became public knowledge. These successes heralded a change in institutional culture from punishment to the provision of care. The new world imported this model from Europe.

By the middle of the 19th century, a purely religious interpretation of insanity was on the wane in North America, with a rational (or medical) outlook gaining credence (Jimenez, 1987). This changing outlook raised questions about how to care for the insane, who in rural areas wandered freely about their communities, looked after by their families. Such a familial model of care was less viable in the industrialized cities, which became the home to increasing numbers of American families after the first half of the 19th century.

Rothman (1971) described the introduction of institutional care to the United States as coinciding with governmental anxieties about a disintegrating social structure. During the first half of the 19th century, with high rates of immigration and a large exodus from rural areas to the cities, the government of President Jackson faced a period of social upheaval. Its response to the perceived crisis included the creation of insane asylums, poor houses, and prisons as ways to prop up the crumbling social structure. Consequently, the early evolution of North American psychiatry accorded with a political agenda to restore social order. Although such analysis applies to change at a macro level of societal intervention, other researchers used similar concepts of social control to describe the micro-level treatment of patients within institutions. Goffman (1961) referred to "total institutions" in which the freedom of residents to act independently is made subservient to the smooth running of the organization.

Although institutional care for elderly persons also began for political reasons, these owed more to economics than social control. Forbes, Jackson, and Kraus (1987) describe the evolution of institutional care from its beginnings in Europe. After King Henry VIII dissolved the monasteries of England and Wales, the task of sheltering the old, poor, and vulnerable fell to the parishes. The parishes built poorhouses, also known as workhouses, in which residents did work in exchange for food and shelter. Poorhouses were unhappy places, without heart or dignity. The little care provided to the sick was by other inmates, known as pauper nurses, who were usually untrained older women. Discipline was strict and living conditions deliberately made harsh to discourage all but the most destitute from seeking poor relief. The parish wanted no parasites to feed. Unfortunately, the old and infirm, if they had no family able and willing to care for them, had few choices; the alternative to the poorhouse was death.

This was the culture transported across the North Atlantic. It had little tolerance of the old. Aboard ships arriving in New England or Nova Scotia, people who were maimed, lunatic, "vagrant" or too old to work were unwelcome. They were sent back home so as not to increase pauperism in the "Brave New World." However, the need for institutional care was pressing. Before long, poorhouses opened throughout Canada, patterned after those in Europe. These institutions mixed elderly people with the poor, sick, disabled, widowed, vagrant and drunkard, unless they were demented and sent to insane asylums. Seventy-six such institutions still existed in Ontario and 24 in Nova Scotia by the 1920s. Across Canada, more than 250 institutions for dependent and disabled people existed by the early 1940s, with two-thirds of the residents aged over 60.

Current Models   Psychiatric hospitals remained the main residence for severely ill patients throughout most of the 20th century. The treatments received by patients included physical intervention, such as prefrontal lobotomy, electroconvulsive shock, and pharmacological therapy, but with psychosocial interventions such as occupational therapy, group therapy, behaviour therapy, and therapeutic communities becoming part of standard practice. The effectiveness of psychiatric intervention came under increasing scientific scrutiny with standards and procedures for evaluation similar to those used in physical medicine.

Major changes in psychiatry occurred during the past quarter-century for two reasons. First, a consensus on diagnostic criteria and the publication by the American Psychiatric Association of successive editions of their *Diagnostic and Statistical Manual(DSM)* facilitated the reliable diagnosis of mental disorders, which in turn contributed to the more accurate evaluation of treatment effectiveness (APA, 1994). Second, success of long-acting tranquilizers in patients with psychosis, mood stabilizers in bipolar affective disorder, selective serotonin reuptake inhibitors in depression, and cognitive-behavioural intervention in neurosis meant that many patients who would previously have required prolonged institutional care were now treatable with short-stay institutional care or as outpatients. These developments contributed to the evolution of a community psychiatry model and the demise of the older psychiatric institutions in the 1990s, with short-stay inpatient care mainly provided in the psychiatric wards of acute-care hospitals.

Poorhouses failed to survive as a model of institutional care in Canada much beyond World War II. At this time, the introduction of new provincial and federal health funding plans changed the treatment of the old and infirm from a culture of despair to one of health care, with an emphasis on services to meet needs. The institutionalized elderly population increased more than tenfold from World War II to the early 1990s. However, the new nursing homes proved expensive, with the lack of acknowledged criteria for admission and good assessment tools resulting in inequitable admission practices. Many people in nursing homes had no real need for that level of care, and others in pressing need of such care remained without a bed for long periods. Starting at the end of the 1970s and into the 1980s, those at low levels of need were refused admission. Also, a home care model evolved that provided assistance to residents in their homes, thereby enabling them to retain independence for longer. Then during the 1990s the provinces normalized their criteria for admission to nursing homes, with standardized assessment tools introduced to measure need. Such functions are now the responsibility of multi-purpose agencies that function as gatekeepers with respect to the allocation of home care services and decisions about admission to nursing homes (e.g., the Community Care Access Centres in Ontario).

Advances in Evaluation

Although the quality of care in institutions for both psychiatric patients and elderly individuals continues to improve, complacency remains the enemy of progress. An influential school of thought suggests that comprehensive and regular assessment provides the key to enhancing quality of care. One such family of tools includes Resident Assessment Instruments (RAIs), increasingly used in Canada and many other countries throughout the world (Hirdes, Zimmerman, Hallman, & Soucie, 1998).

The RAI family includes Minimum Data Sets (MDS 2.0) for use in long-term care, home care (MDS-HC), and psychiatric institutions (RAI-MH). The version for long-term care became a mandated tool for all licensed nursing facilities in the United States early in the 1990s and in Ontario chronic-care hospitals in the mid-1990s. The development of the mental health tool (MDS-MH) took place in Canada under the direction of John Hirdes of the University of Waterloo, who was the leader of an international development team. This tool is now in regular use in psychiatric institutions throughout Ontario.

The primary aim of the RAI tools is to provide basic information for care planning purposes. However, the tools can also be used to compare quality of care across facilities and to estimate funding needs based on resource utilization within the resident population. The available evidence suggests that the RAI tools work fairly well for all three purposes, not least because international usage makes possible comparison not just within provinces or countries, but across countries.

Examples of the use of the MDS 2.0 include reports by the Canadian Institute on Health Information on the quality of care in Ontario chronic hospitals (CIHI, 1998). The findings include higher rates of physical restraint in Ontario facilities than in the United States and Europe (Ljunggren, Phillips, & Sgadari, 1997). Although institutions justify the use of physical restraint for reasons of safety—to prevent residents falling—other countries seem to prevent falls with less use of restraint. In contrast, the Ontario institutions have a lower prevalence of untreated cases of depression than most other countries. These comparisons provide guidance to improve care.

Diagnosis and Epidemiology of Mental Illness

Since the time of Hippocrates, physicians included conditions now considered mental illnesses in their classifications of disease (Kendall, 2001). They treated these conditions in much the same way as physical disorders, using potions, medicine, and other forms of physical intervention. However, the belief that insanity is similar to other diseases met with resistance during two periods in Western history. The first followed Thomas Aquinas's attribution of insanity to supernatural possession. The second occurred late in the 18th century, when physicians influenced by Cartesian mind-body dualism considered mental illness a disease of the mind rather the body. The psychoanalytic schools emerging of the end of the 19th century exemplify this philosophy, treating mental illnesses as psychogenic disorders amenable to psychotherapy. Medical opinion continues to be uneasy about this issue. Although modern physicians continue to treat mental illness with physical methods, the very title of the *Diagnostic and Statistical Manual of Mental Disorders* (*DSM-IV*, 1994) perpetuates a dualistic philosophy, albeit with some reluctance, as indicated in the introduction to the manual. The *DSM-IV* continues to be the bible of psychiatric diagnosis in North America.

Epidemiology is the study of the frequency of diseases. In the early 1980s, the National Institute of Mental Health in the United States. sponsored the

Table 8.1 BEST ESTIMATE OF ONE-YEAR PREVALENCE RATES FOR ADULTS AGED 18 TO 54 AND 55+ YEARS, ON THE BASIS OF EPIDEMIOLOGIC CATCHMENT AREAS, U.S. DEPARTMENT OF HEALTH AND SOCIAL SERVICES (1999)

DIAGNOSIS	PREVALENCE 18–54 YEARS	PREVALENCE 55+ YEARS
Any anxiety disorder	13.1%	11.4%
Any mood disorder (major depression)	7.1%	4.4%
Schizophrenia	1.3%	0.6%
Somatization	0.2%	0.3%
Antisocial personality disorder	2.1%	0%
Anorexia nervosa	0.1%	0%
Severe cognitive disorder	1.2%	6.6%
Any disorder	19.5%	19.8%

Source: U.S. Department of Health and Social Services (1999).

Epidemiological Catchment Area Survey (ECA) to provide the first comprehensive survey of mental disorders (Myers, 1984). This survey continues to influence thinking about the frequencies of different mental disorders at different ages (U.S. Department of Health and Social Services, 1999). The findings in Table 8.1 suggest that, with the exception of severe cognitive disorder and somatization, the prevalence rates are lower among people aged 55 years and older than in younger adults.

Other than severe cognitive impairment, the most frequent disorders in later life concern anxiety and mood. Phobias are the most frequent disorders at any age. **Agoraphobia** is probably the most devastating phobia because a person fearful of public places (elevators, planes, open spaces) suffers a restricted life, frequently becoming housebound. Agoraphobia is also distinctive because of panic attacks that occur for no apparent reason. Although major depression in later life (as diagnosed by *DSM-IV* criteria) is no more frequent that at younger ages, the following section shows that susceptibility to minor depression may be high in later life.

Depression in Later Life

Depression stands opposite to mental well-being on a mental health continuum. The symptoms of depression cited in *DSM-IV* (1994) include

- depressed mood (**dysphoria**)
- loss of pleasure (**anhedonia**)

- sleep disturbance
- appetite disturbance
- loss of energy
- difficulty in concentration
- low self-esteem
- psychomotor retardation or agitation
- suicidal thoughts

For a diagnosis of **major depression**, at least five symptoms, including dysphoria or anhedonia, must be present for most of nearly every day during a two-week period. The worldwide prevalence of depression indicates higher rates among women than in men, and for unmarried (e.g., divorced, separated) than married people (Weissman et al., 1996). Depression in older people increases the risk of mortality from physical illness (Schultz et al., 2000) and suicide (U.S. Department of Health and Social Services, 1999), contributes to cognitive decline in the non-demented elderly (Yaffe et al., 1999), and may be an early manifestation (rather than a predictor) of dementia (Chen, Ganguli, Mulsant, & DeKosky, 1999).

Although the prevalence of diagnosed major depression declines with age (with a one-year prevalence of 5 percent or lower in older people), the inference that older people have a lower susceptibility to depression is contentious. There is evidence that older people may present symptoms of depression differently than younger people. Such presentation includes a more frequent appearance of anhedonia than dysphoria (depression without sadness) and unexplained somatic complaints (Gallo, Rabins, & Hopkins, 1999). Consequently, it is possible that depression is underdiagnosed in later life, and that patients without dysphoria are at risk of undertreatment. Stones, Clyburn, Gibson, and Woodbury (in press) found a compatible trend, with a lower relationship of anhedonia than dysphoria to diagnosed depression in Canadian residents of long-term care facilities. The 1999 Surgeon General's report on mental health took note of such findings. That report includes discussion of a proposal for a new diagnostic entity of "minor" depression to encompass individuals with an otherwise atypical presentation of depression (U.S. Department of Health and Social Services, 1999).

A psychological model of depression—the *tripartite model*—also distinguishes between anhedonia and dysphoria, albeit with different terminology. This model includes as components low positive affect (anhedonia), negative affect (dysphoria), and somatic arousal (i.e., symptoms associated with bodily excitation) (Joiner, 1996; Watson, Clark, Weber, & Assenheimer, 1995). Anhedonia in this model is specific to depression, somatic arousal to anxiety disorders, with negative affect present in both conditions. Epidemiological research suggests dysphoria to be a more frequent condition than anhedonia. A study of lifetime histories of depression in people aged over 65 years revealed that 15 percent of men and 33 percent of women reported dysphoria of at least two weeks' duration, whereas 8 percent of men and 16 percent of women experienced anhedonia for a similar duration (Steffens et al., 2000). In elderly institutionalized populations, anhedonia rather than dysphoria may be the more frequent condition (Stones & Kirkpatrick, 2002). This finding suggests that depression in institutions mainly involves a loss of pleasurable experiences. Low positive affect is also related in several studies to the experience of meaning in life (King, Hicks, Krull, & del Gaiso, 2006).

Reports on the treatment of depression claim success in 60 to 80 percent of cases (U.S. Department of Health and Social Services, 1999), with the main forms of treatment including pharmacological intervention, electroconvulsive shock, and psychosocial intervention. A Canadian innovation in the treatment for depression in seniors was physical exercise (McNeil, LeBlanc, & Joyner, 1991). Subsequent research confirmed its effectiveness (Antunes, Stella, Santos, Bueno, & de Mello, 2005), with the size of effect comparable to antidepressant medication (Blumenthal et al., 1999). Because such findings show treatments for diagnosed depression to be successful in most cases, the resolution of issues about the accuracy of diagnosis in older people is of pressing concern.

Diseases That Impair Cognition

The two main conditions associated with impaired cognitive competence in later life are dementia and delirium. **Dementia** at this age most frequently takes the form of Alzheimer's disease and to a lesser extent vascular dementia. Both involve a progressive deterioration in cognitive competence because of changes within the brain, but they have different causes. **Alzheimer's disease** is associated with plaques and tangles in brain matter. **Vascular dementia** is caused by stroke or artery disease, which starves the brain of oxygen, and includes signs of focal neurological damage. **Delirium** is a disturbance of consciousness and cognition associated with a medical condition, the use or withdrawal of drugs, or other conditions. Box 8.4 shows the basic diagnostic criteria for the three conditions in the fourth edition of the *Diagnostic and Statistical Manual* of the American Psychiatric Association (*DSM-IV*).

A large study that estimated the prevalence of dementia in Canada was the Canadian Study of Health and Aging (Canadian Study of Health and Aging Working Group, 1994a). The study divided the country into five regions and sampled representatively from community and institutional settings, but excluded the territories, Indian reserves, and military units. The total sample included 9000 individuals aged 65 years or older. All participants received initial screening using a standard measure to identify cognitive impairment. All institution residents and those living in the community with impaired scores on the screening tool received a clinical examination to diagnose dementia. The definitions of dementia and Alzheimer's disease were those conventionally used.

The findings indicated that 8 percent of all Canadians aged 65 or over met the criteria for dementia. Half of these people resided in institutions and two-thirds

Box 8.4 *Diagnostic Criteria for Dementia and Delirium (DSM-IV)*

Dementia includes disorders with multiple cognitive deficits. The most common type in later life is Alzheimer's disease, with vascular dementia of lower prevalence.

Alzheimer's disease can be of early or late onset (>65 years), and occur with delirium, delusions, or depressed mood. Diagnostic criteria include the following:

A. Both (1) memory impairment and (2) at least one of language impairment, motor impairment, impaired recognition of objects, impaired executive functioning
B. The preceding result in impaired social or occupational functioning, and represent a decline from previous levels

C. Gradual onset and continuation of symptoms
D. The symptoms are not because of other forms of illness

Vascular dementia includes criteria A and B (above), and also

C. Focal neurological signs or symptoms
D. The deficits do not occur exclusively during a delirium

Delirium includes a disturbance of consciousness and cognition, associated with a medical condition, substance use or withdrawal, or multiple or unspecified etiology. The criteria include

A. Disturbance of consciousness
B. Disturbance of cognition
C. Development over a short period
D. Evidence of a contributing condition

Source: Adapted from American Psychiatric Association. (2004). "Delirium, dementia, amnestic, and other cognitive disorders." In *DSM-IV*.

were female, with the prevalence rate increasing with age. The specific rates for Alzheimer's disease and vascular dementia were 5.1 percent and 1.5 percent, respectively. The authors estimated that if the prevalence rate remained constant, the number of Canadians with dementia would double from 1994 to 2021 because of demographic changes in the population.

Risk factors for dementia included family history, low education, and head injury, with low risk associated with arthritis and the use of non-steroidal anti-inflammatory drugs. These risks are similar to those previously reported (Canadian Study of Health and Aging Working Group, 1994b). Recent findings on risk factors suggest that low physical activity in people aged over 65 years may be predictive of the onset of dementia within a six-year period (Larsen et al., 2006).

There is a predictable stage-by-stage progression of cognitive decline in Alzheimer's disease (Reisberg, Ferris, de Leon, & Crook, 1982). The symptoms in sequence include forgetfulness, then confusion, failure to recognize familiar people, loss of memory for recent events, disorientation, and finally the loss of all verbal ability. Other dysfunctions that accompany cognitive decline include lack of social involvement, behavioural disturbance, and limitations in everyday activity.

Delirium differs from dementia because its (1) onset is abrupt, (2) duration is usually brief, and (3) appearance coincides with that of another disorder. Martin, Stones, Young, and Bédard (2000) found that nearly 20 percent of consecutive admissions to an acute-care hospital related to an episode of delirium, usually beginning within the previous three days. Precipitating factors included

Figure 8.5 SCORES ON COGNITIVE PERFORMANCE SCALE AND SYMPTOMS
OF DELIRIUM MEASURE BY LONG-TERM CARE HOME
RESIDENTS WITH OR WITHOUT DIAGNOSED DEMENTIA

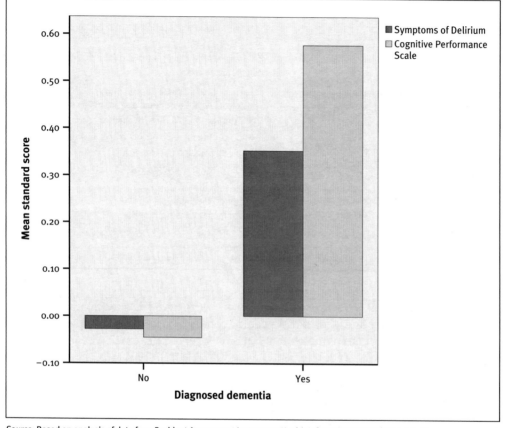

Source: Based on analysis of data from Resident Assessment Instrument Health Infomatics Project (2000–2001)

illness, medication, and the loss of control brought about by relocation to an unfamiliar (e.g., hospital) setting and associated medical procedures.

Delirium has adverse implications for early discharge and subsequent placement, especially if physicians in acute hospitals mistake the symptoms of delirium for dementia. Although such misdiagnosis tends to be less frequent now than a few years ago, patients with dementia do exhibit some of the symptoms associated with delirium. Figure 8.5 shows standardized scores on indexes of cognitive impairment and symptoms of delirium from over 1500 MDS 2.0 assessments of long-term care home residents. The mean scores on both cognitive impairment and the recent delirium index are higher in residents with than without diagnosed dementia.

CHAPTER SUMMARY

Key ideas to remember from this chapter:

- Mental health is a continuum ranging from well-being to distress.
- The distribution of mental well-being shows negative skew, with the bulk of people located at the high end and a tail at the low end.
- Approximately 80 percent of people at any age report that they are happy, and about 20 percent have a medical diagnosis indicating some form of mental distress. Although some theorists suggest that error in measurement contributes to the shape of negative skew, the evidence suggests otherwise.
- Mental well-being does not vary much with age in survey research, with no difference between gender groups in life satisfaction but more frequent reports of depressed mood in women than men. A diagnosis of clinical depression is also more frequent in women.
- Although mental well-being has low correlations with demographic indicators, remains stable despite changes in life conditions, and shows resistance to transient life changes that affect mood, the levels are low for residents of restrictive environments such as long-term care institutions. The probable reasons include a lack of choice.
- Psychosocial interventions in an institutional setting can improve mental well-being to some degree, and lower morbidity and mortality. However, mental well-being outside of institutions relates more to personality and genetic dispositions than life conditions. The relationship is so strong that some researchers conclude that trying to be happier is likely to be no more successful than trying to be taller.
- The treatment of mental disorder evolved from an institutional model to one emphasizing community care. Similarly, care of the infirm elderly evolved from the poorhouse to a combination of nursing home and home care. Although the current models continue to receive their share of criticism, it is important to acknowledge the immense progress in humanitarian care that has occurred during the past few decades. Ongoing advances include the development of comprehensive and regularized assessment protocols to detect problems, monitor change, and develop care plans.
- Although older people have rates lower than young people for most diagnosed mental disorders except cognitive impairment, the findings on depression may be misleading. Old people often express depression without sadness, but with a loss of pleasure. Depression in elderly people responds well to treatment.
- Dementia affects approximately 8 percent of Canadians aged 65 years and older. Its main forms include Alzheimer's disease and vascular dementia. The symptoms of dementia include a progressive impairment in cognition. Delirium also involves impaired cognition but onset is abrupt rather than gradual. Delirium arises in association with another medical condition.

KEY TERMS

happiness **(p. 192)**

mental well-being **(p. 193)**

mental health **(p. 193)**

distribution **(p. 193)**

response set **(p. 194)**

extremity set **(p. 194)**

impression management **(p. 194)**

social desirability **(p. 195)**

negatively skewed **(p. 196)**

bottom-up model **(p. 199)**

top-down model **(p. 199)**

up-down model **(p. 199)**

reminiscence therapy **(p. 201)**

control **(p. 201)**

personality **(p. 202)**

five-factor theory **(p. 204)**

heritability **(p. 205)**

mental disorders **(p. 206)**

epidemiology **(p. 211)**

agoraphobia **(p. 212)**

depression **(p. 212)**

dysphoria **(p. 212)**

anhedonia **(p. 212)**

major depression **(p. 213)**

dementia **(p. 214)**

Alzheimer's disease **(p. 214)**

vascular dementia **(p. 214)**

delirium **(p. 214)**

STUDY QUESTIONS

1. Older people tend to rate their present level of life satisfaction as lower than the level in earlier life. Does such a trend imply that mental well-being decreases with age? Discuss the evidence.

2. We assume that life conditions affect our mental well-being more than personality and genetics. Evaluate whether or not the evidence supports this assumption.

3. Most people in our society are happy. Is this statement borne out by the facts?

4. Evaluate levels of support for bottom-up, top-down, and up-down models of happiness.

5. Do older people differ from younger people in the frequency of psychiatric disorders?

6. Do the experience and expression of depression differ between old and young people?

SUGGESTED READINGS

Diener, E., Suh, E., Lucas, R.E., & Smith, H.L. (1999). Subjective well-being: Three decades of progress. *Psychological Bulletin 125*, 276–302.

Gallo, J.J., & Rabins, P.V. (1999). Depression without sadness: Alternative presentations of depression in later life. *American Family Physician, 60,* 820–826.

Kaszniak, A.W. (1996). The role of clinical neuropsychology in the assessment and care of persons with Alzheimer's disease. In R.J. Resnick & R.H. Rozensky (Eds.), *Health psychology through the life span* (pp. 239–264). Washington, DC: American Psychological Association.

Myers, D.G., & Diener, E. (1995). Who is happy? *Psychological Science, 6:* 10–19.

Ozer, D., & Bennet-Martinez V. (2006). Personality and the prediction of consequential outcomes. *Annual Review of Psychology, 57,* 401—421.

Stones, M.J., Rattenbury, C., & Kozma, A. (1995). Empirical findings on reminiscence. In B.K. Haight & J. Webster (Eds.), *The art and science of reminiscing: Theory, research, methods, and applications.* Washington, DC: Taylor & Francis.

Chapter 9

HEALTH AND THE DETERMINANTS OF HEALTH

Learning Objectives

In this chapter, you will learn about

- Which aspects of health decline as we age and which aspects improve.
- The difference between illness and disease.
- Wellness.
- The difference between defining health and being healthy.
- The concept of frailty.
- The lay explanations seniors use for their symptomatology and how, as we age, we begin to interpret many

symptoms and bodily changes as a normal part of aging even though not all are.
- Whether or not discrete personal health behaviours, such as nutritional intake, exercise, and sleep cluster with one another to constitute identifiable lifestyles.
- The effect that social structure, socio-economic status, gender, age, and culture have on our health.

Introduction

In this chapter, we turn to an examination of health and illness. The chapter begins with some statistics that provide us with a picture of the health and illness of Canada's seniors. We discuss the distinction between sickness (which includes both disease and illness) and health, as well as the more general concept of wellness. The chapter then turns to a discussion of the determinants of health, with a major focus on health beliefs, personal health practices, and social structure. Gender differences are highlighted throughout.

Health during Old Age

As we saw in Chapter 2, life expectancy is increasing and life expectancy of women continues to surpass that of men. The remaining life expectancy for people who have already reached age 65 is also increasing. Senior women have more years remaining than senior men (20.5 years after age 65 for women, almost four years more than for a 65-year-old man). But what about health? Is the common belief that our health declines as we age true?

It is chronic conditions that particularly afflict us in old age, and senior women suffer more from chronic health conditions than do senior men (71.5 percent versus 60.6 percent). As shown in Table 9.1, the most common chronic health problem is arthritis and rheumatism, followed by high blood pressure. Statistics Canada compared trends for major chronic illnesses between 1978/79 and 10 years later and reports, for older Canadians, no beneficial trends. Indeed, rates for diabetes, certain cancers, and asthmas have risen (Statistics Canada, 1999b). A Manitoba study found mixed results for seniors between 1985–87 and 1997–99 Rates fell for myocardial infarctions (heart attacks), strokes, cancer, and hip fractures but rose for diabetes, hypertension, and dementia (Menec, Lix, MacWilliam, & Soodeen, 2003).

The same picture of mixed results is evident for the baby boom generation. Wister (2005) notes that rates of cardiovascular disease, arthritis/rheumatism, hypertension, and bronchitis/emphysema have been declining from the 1970s to the late

Table 9.1   **PREVALENT CHRONIC CONDITIONS* AMONG CANADIAN SENIORS LIVING AT HOME**

Arthritis and rheumatism	47%
High blood pressure	43%
Moderate or severe pain or discomfort	17%
Diabetes	14%
Asthma	8%

*As diagnosed by a health professional.

Source: Adapted from the Statistics Canada CANSIM database http://cansim2.statcan.ca, tables 105-0202, 105-0210, 105-0201, 105-0211, and 105-0204

1990s. Simultaneously, rates have been increasing for diabetes, asthma, migraine headaches, respiratory diseases, and the total number of chronic conditions. How the changing face of chronic conditions among this generation will affect their illness experience in old age is as yet unknown. What we do know is that their experiences will be different from those of the current cohort of seniors. However, coronary heart disease and cancer will likely still be common in the years to come.

Often, how sick we consider ourselves to be relates not so much to the diagnosis per se but to the extent that it interferes with our lives. Older adults perceive their health not in terms of diseases or conditions but in terms of what they can do (Partridge, Johnston, & Morris, 1996). The importance of this notion is evident in Canada's National Advisory Council on Aging's definition of successful aging, which includes the ability to adapt to change and compensate for limitations (www.naca.ca). We are interested in activity restriction or limitations to daily functioning, also known as functional disability. Not all seniors with diagnosed health problems experience restriction in their daily activities. Overall, 40.5 percent of those age 65 and over experience such restrictions (31.2 percent for those age 65 to 74; 53.3 percent for those age 75 and over) (Statistics Canada, 2002e). Interestingly, functional disability is not necessarily permanent. About one-third of seniors who were dependent in 1994/95 were independent two years later (Hum & Simpson, 2002). Furthermore, while the onset of disability is age-related, age is not a predictor of recovery.

Pain is a problem for a substantial number of seniors: 25.4 percent suffer chronic pain or discomfort, increasing to 28.7 percent among those age 75 years and over. Most are taking some form of medication, either prescription or over-the-counter (84 percent), and over half are taking two or more (Statistics Canada, 1999b, 2001a).

As noted in Chapter 8, illnesses of the mind are viewed as diseases by the medical profession and are typically believed to have physical causes (e.g., serotonin levels that are too low). Dementia is considered to be a disease, even though the physical cause remains undetected. As noted previously, seniors are more likely than younger persons to suffer from dementia; the most prevalent form is Alzheimer's disease. However, the vast majority of seniors are not likely to suffer from dementia. *The Canadian Study on Health and Aging* (1994), Canada's first and only national study to establish the prevalence of dementia, has revealed that between 6 and 8 percent of seniors suffer from this disease. Among those aged over 85, 1 in 13 have dementia. Another 16 percent have less severe symptoms referred to as mild cognitive impairment (National Advisory Council on Aging, 2004). Three-quarters of those who are elderly and suffer from dementia reside in a long-term care facility.

Despite their health problems, the majority of seniors perceive their general health to be good, very good, or excellent (73 percent), with men and women very similar in this regard (73.7 percent for men and 72.7 percent for women). This decreases to 67.8 percent among those age 75 years and over. Box 9.1 gives an illustration of the subjective nature of health self-assessment. Among those in this older age range, women are more likely to rate their health as only fair or poor than are men (Statistics Canada, 2001a). This is consistent with measures of psychological well-being. Data from the 1994 and 1995 *National Population Health Survey* (NPHS) reveal that while 28 percent of Canadians have a high sense of coherence (a view of the world that life is meaningful, events are comprehensible, and challenges are manageable), those over age 75 years are three times more likely than 18- to 19-year-olds to score high on a sense of coherence (Health Canada, 1996).

A review of research in the West found many studies showing that older women report lower life satisfaction, happiness and self-esteem than men (Pinquart & Sorenson, 2001a). These differences, though, are so small that the researchers conclude they are of limited importance. The greatest differences are in terms of loneliness, with older women more likely to feel lonely, probably due to the fact that they are more likely to be widowed or to be socialized to need support than are men.

Box 9.1 *Self-Assessed Health*

Mrs. G. is 84 years old. She has been widowed for five years, an experience for which she was totally unprepared—she expected her husband to outlive her. Since they had lived in different countries of the world, and away from their Canadian-born children, widowhood meant a return to Canada and settling in a new city without friends nearby. She chose a city where one son lives. She was determined to live on her own near a senior centre, to become active and involved, and to make new friends. She did all this. Now at 84 years, she is taking medication for high blood pressure, has persistent and re-occurring skin cancer on her cheek, and has recently experienced a fall that has left her wrist painful and swollen. Probably most disturbing is her very noticeable short-term memory loss— she cannot remember where she put the groceries she just bought, she cannot find her purse, she cannot remember whom she had lunch with earlier in the day, and she cannot remember where she puts things such as her jewellery and passport. However, she is still managing on her own, with family and friends close by, although there is now discussion that she should enter assisted living.

If you ask her how her health is, she will respond immediately and enthusiastically about how good it is. She will comment on the fact that she is still very mobile and living on her own and able to do most things that she wants to do.

Medication will not be mentioned unless you specifically ask her if she is taking any, and then she will note that she is taking just a little for blood pressure. And if you explicitly ask her about her memory, she will tell you how well she is doing. If you further ask if she forgets the odd thing every once in a while and perhaps give her some examples, she will tell you that yes, it is frustrating that some nights she spends hours looking for her wallet or a letter or some other object. She will go on to tell you how, compared with others her age, she is doing much, much better. They are all taking many more medications and many of them can hardly walk at all. She will tell you how lucky she is to have her children who call or drop in and attend to her needs. She will add that she does not know what she would do without them.

She is lucky, too, because she doesn't have to worry about money. She is not rich, she wishes she were a millionaire, but she is very frugal and has everything she needs to get by. Her husband left enough for her to live modestly; the provincial pharmacare program covers the costs of her drugs and, fortunately, she lives in Canada so she can visit physicians without out-of-pocket expenses. Does she worry about money? What if she had unforeseen expenses? She smiles a relaxed smile—"My kids would look after me."

Despite the fact that older women are more likely to be widowed, have lower socio-economic status (SES) and suffer from more health problems, they rate their subjective well-being almost as highly as do men. This suggests that women have self-protective mechanisms despite their disadvantages. Social support, discussed in the next chapter, might be one of those mechanisms.

In other words, even though Canadian seniors are far more likely than younger Canadians to suffer from physical illnesses and conditions, they experience psychological well-being—in fact, they are often happier than younger adults (Federal, Provincial, and Territorial Advisory Committee on Population Health, 1999) : 89.4 percent of seniors are satisfied with their lives, compared to 83.7 percent of 15-to-24-year-olds (Statistics Canada, 2004g). Gender differences are insignificant. Attitude is important; a study that examined health changes for Canadian seniors between 1994/95 and 2002/03 found that seniors with a strong sense of coherence experienced fewer health problems at the end of the eight-year period (Martel, Bélanger, Berthelot, & Carrière, 2005). A positive attitude towards life enhances our chances of healthy aging.

In summary, while women live longer than men, they are more likely to suffer from both chronic conditions and limitations in their activities of daily living. And while older Canadians are more likely to suffer from physical health declines than are younger adults, they appear in many ways to be psychologically more resilient. Furthermore, the majority of elderly Canadians do not suffer from mental decline to the point of dementia. Although chronic conditions, by definition, are not fatal, they can seriously affect the quality of our lives. Because of the prevalence of chronic conditions in old age, there is a major concern in social gerontology with quality of life.

Wellness

We know much more about illness and disease than we do about wellness and quality of life. This is because **health** has typically been defined in terms of absence of disease. However, we want to distinguish not only between health and sickness, but also between disease and illness. The term **sickness** includes both disease and the experience of illness (Segall & Chappell, 2000). People experience illness; physicians diagnose and treat disease. **Disease** is a modern biomedical concept related to changes in specific organs of the body caused by pathogenic agents, such as germs. **Illness** is the subjective phenomenon that individuals experience when they are not feeling well. Illness, as opposed to disease, is based on personal perception, evaluation, and response to symptomatic conditions.

Modern medicine believes that each disease has a particular cause or specific etiology; it attempts to control the causes, for example, through drug therapy, surgery, or both. This has often been described as a **mechanistic model** because disease is viewed as objective, as an altered functioning of the biological organism, that is, the human body. Disease constitutes deviation from normal biological functioning. This biomedical model of disease has seen some important success against acute infectious diseases.

However, its appropriateness has been questioned with older populations, where chronic degenerative diseases, not acute infectious diseases, are most prevalent. Chronic conditions result from multiple etiological factors and have no known cure. Medicine has increasingly come under attack for its inability to deal with chronic conditions and its failure to give credence to the individual's experience of the disease.

Part of the difficulty in talking about the concept of health arises because we tend to take health for granted unless we experience illness. We usually do not notice our health when we are feeling fine. It is typically when we feel ill that the lack of good health becomes apparent. Over half a century ago, the World Health Organization (1948) stated that good health is more than the absence of illness and disease. Within a positive definition, it is a state of complete physical, mental, and social well-being. This includes subjective feelings as well as adequate performance at the physical, psychological, and social levels of functioning.

More recently, the concept of **wellness** has become popular, referring to a broader concept that usually includes, but extends beyond, good health. Litva and Eyles (1994) describe feelings of healthiness as a sense of psychosocial well-being. Emotional well-being is related to such factors as a sense of control and coherence and feelings of purpose, belonging, and satisfaction with one's life. Wellness is often spoken of as including a level of fitness, which may refer to physical and mental fitness, as well as social fitness (being able to perform one's social roles and the demands of everyday living adequately).

Health does not mean the same thing to all people; people who are living with chronic medical conditions may, nevertheless, define themselves as being in good health. For example, arthritis is becoming a normal part of later life. Seniors suffering from arthritis may consider themselves healthy. Indeed, as we saw in the preceding section, when seniors are asked about their perceptions of their health, the majority say that their health is good to excellent. Health and illness, therefore, are relative terms; they are not static but are constantly evolving. For example, not long ago stress was not considered an illness or a predictor of disease. It is now common for workplaces to allow leave for individuals certified by a physician to be suffering from stress.

When asked how their health is, people overwhelmingly define it in physical terms. Among a Dutch sample of people younger than 40 and older than 60, 80 percent referred to physical aspects when asked this question (Simon, De Boer, Joung, Bosma, & Mackenbach, 2005). Virtually no reference was made to mental health. Among those with a history of ill-health (predominantly the elderly respondents) it was less the presence of the problems than their ability to cope with them that determined their health assessment. Litva and Eyles (1994) also report that, when asked to define health, people did so in general and abstract terms, focusing on physical aspects, often the absence of disease and illness.

However, when asked to talk about the personal meaning of being healthy, they spoke about quality of life and psychological well-being, such as feeling happy, enjoying life, and feeling good about oneself. That is, people make a distinction between *health* and *being healthy*. Health is viewed very much in physical terms, as lack of disease, as a physician would view it. Being healthy on the other hand, is viewed much more as the World Health Organization defines health—a more holistic concept that takes into account subjective feelings as well as physical state. Because of the traditional emphasis on biomedical disease, we are much better at measuring sickness than at measuring wellness, and we have more information about diseases than about health in old age. Nevertheless, increasing attention is focused on wellness. It is important to examine all aspects of health, especially given that physical health declines in old age but psychological health does not necessarily decline.

Another important distinction is that between personal or individual health and population health. **Population health** involves a multi-dimensional approach to health and encompasses a societal, rather than an individual, focus. It refers to all members of a group or a society, including those who are healthy and those who are ill, those who are at risk and those who are not. Often, we measure population health by examining individual health in the aggregate (such as men versus women, young versus old). In addition, though, population health also includes societal measures, such as the proportion of gross national product spent on health and the number of physicians available per 100 000 population. When a population health perspective is used, it focuses on the interrelationship of factors that influence the health of populations over the life course, and variations in patterns of occurrence in order to improve the health and well-being of those populations (Hayes & Dunn, 1998).

Gender Differences in Health

There are numerous differences between women and men in both the diagnosis and experience of health and illness, differences that extend into old age. This was evident in the figures provided in earlier chapters and at the beginning of this chapter on life expectancy, chronic conditions, and psychological well-being, as well as causes of death.

The extent to which these differences will dissipate as women take on lifestyles more similar to those of men is unknown. However, female lung cancer rates are increasing as smoking rates increase among young women, whereas male lung cancer rates are remaining stable or decreasing. Breast cancer rates among women are increasing at a faster rate than are prostate cancer rates among men. Data from the *National Population Health Survey of Canadians* in 1994 reveals that women are more likely than men to report multiple health problems associated with chronic conditions, such as arthritis and rheumatism, high blood pressure, back problems, and allergies. Women are more likely to have taken medications for their problems than are men, even when birth control and menopause-related drugs are excluded. Women are also more likely to have consulted a physician about their health problems, although there was no gender difference in contacts with other health professionals, such as dentists and physiotherapists (Millar & Beaudet, 1996).

Contrary to the argument that as women and men adopt more similar lifestyles, they will experience similar health problems, the factors influencing each could be different. Denton and Walters (1999), for example, find that social structural factors such as being in a high income category, working full time, caring for a family, and social support are stronger determinants of health for women, whereas for men, it is personal health practices, such as smoking and alcohol consumption. In addition, the multiple roles of women, such as parenting and being employed, can result in role overload and role conflict and, therefore, strain. Increased stress and excessive demands on time and energy (the *double day* for women) are major factors in psychological distress and poorer health.

Social acceptability due to socialization and to traditional roles may mean it is more acceptable for women than for men to adopt the sick role. They may be more willing to admit to being sick and to accept help in dealing with their health problems. Women discuss their health more freely than do men, they discuss it with many more individuals, they are more accepting of a wider variety of health actions, and they are more likely to seek the help of a professional (Kandrack, Grant, & Segall, 1991). Men traditionally have been socialized to deny experiencing symptoms of illness and disease, are reluctant to adopt the sick role, and discuss their health concerns with far fewer people (Cameron & Bernardes, 1998). The extent to which women's and men's socialization and life experiences differ will influence how these differences extend into later life. For current cohorts, old age will be a gendered experience.

While feminism, as an ideological perspective, developed only recently, it has much relevance to those who are seniors today and has much to offer in our understanding of health and illness. The perspective is critical of the biomedical model of disease, which does not take the whole person into account, excluding social, psychological, and spiritual factors. Furthermore, the biomedical model privileges the expertise of physicians while discounting the feelings and experiential knowledge of those who experience health and illness and of informal caregivers (see Chapter 12). As noted by Hooyman (1990), women play a major role in the health of families and yet have been largely uncompensated and unrecognized for their contributions. Because so much of women's caring work is invisible and unpaid, that is, it takes place in the private sphere, and because the labour of nurturance and health maintenance has been devalued, they have received relatively little attention until very recently.

This perspective is important for those who are seniors today, regardless of whether they are aware of it or accept it. The current cohort of seniors lived most of their lives within a greater traditional and paternalistic division of labour than will be true of the baby boom generation as it enters old age. Women's role as nurturers and as caregivers is more characteristic of those who are elderly today than may be the case in future cohorts.

Frailty

Before leaving our discussion of health, it is important to understand the notion of frailty. In Chapter 2, you learned various definitions of old age together with their inadequacies. Thus far in this chapter, you have learned about the variation in health among Canada's senior population. Because of this variation and the related fact that not all seniors are in poor health, even poor physical health, there is concern that "old" and "old age" do not adequately convey that period of life when only some of us become very debilitated, the negative stereotype of old age. In addition, decline in old age is typically characterized by the coexistence of several conditions not simply one, such as kidney problems or arthritis. The 2003 Canadian Health Survey (Statistics Canada, 2003f) reveals that 56 percent of older adults have two or more chronic conditions and 33 percent have three or more. (Comparable figures for those aged 30 to 64 are 25 percent and 11 percent respectively.) The term **frailty** conveys this notion.

As part of the Canadian Initiative on Frailty and Aging, Hogan, MacKnight, and Bergman (2003; Bergman, 2003) have summarized thinking about what frailty is. They note that it was during the 1970s that the term "frail elderly" was introduced into the United States in recognition of the heterogeneity of the older population and to signify a segment of that population. Various attempts to build models of frailty include reference to those requiring continuing support because of accumulated debilities with increasing age, sometimes to a loss of adaptability leading to age-related mortality and disability, and sometimes to multiple concurrent impairments. Some researchers restrict their focus to physical frailty. Current thinking argues against equating frailty with disability (otherwise we do not need another term). Typically, the term is used to capture something broader than disability alone. Although social factors have been largely neglected in the past, social support, engagement, and the environment may all be important. The role of socio-economic considerations deserves greater attention. If one has the financial means, modifications to the home, hiring personal assistance, and paying for experimental treatments all become possible.

Definitions often focus on dependency but it is not clear how this differs from disability. Many favour a definition in terms of vulnerability due to the interaction of simultaneous deterioration in multiple organ systems leading to adverse outcomes. It will be noticed that disease state itself is not part of the definition. There is, however, no universally accepted definition of frailty at the present time. Nevertheless, Hogan, MacKnight and Bergman (2003) argue there is an emerging consensus that it is primarily a state of vulnerability to experiencing adverse outcomes.

Part of the appeal of the term frailty is that it distinguishes a segment of the older population rather than grouping all old people into a negative stereotype.

It is not synonymous with chronological age. Indeed, one day *old* might come to be equated with frail.

Determinants of Health

As our conceptualization of health is multi-faceted, it should not be surprising that the determinants of health are also multiple. Canada has been a world leader in recognizing this fact. In 1974, Marc Lalonde, then federal minister of health, published *A New Perspective on the Health of Canadians*, acknowledging that major determinants of health include not only formal health-care services but also human biology, lifestyles, and environment. A decade later, then federal minister of health Jake Epp (1986) extended this perspective with *A Framework for Health Promotion*, characterizing health as an essential part of everyday living. Health was portrayed as a resource for living, influenced by our circumstances, beliefs, culture, and socio-economic and physical environments.

There is no disputing the biological determinants of health (Figure 9.1) including individual genetic endowment and the functioning of various body systems, such as our immune and hormonal systems. Hereditary factors may well make us susceptible to a variety of diseases, but this does not exclude the influence of environmental factors in the onset and development of diseases. The environment includes both the physical environment and the social environment. The importance of the physical environment is recognized in legislation which ensures clean drinking water and limits exposure to hazardous waste. This is the traditional area of public health. New dangers are becoming recognized in today's post-industrial society, such as industrial air pollution, second-hand smoke, and acid rain.

Figure 9.1 **DETERMINANTS OF HEALTH**

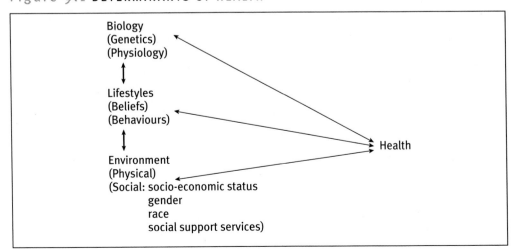

The physical environment also includes the built environment, such as the workplace and housing. Housing is especially important as we age because the physical environment can mean the difference between independence or dependence. For example, if a senior has difficulty going up and down stairs but lives in a place where there are no steps, this lack of mobility does not make him or her dependent. Most people, including older adults, express a preference for staying in their own home, a concept referred to as **aging in place.** This does not mean that they necessarily wish to live in a particular house for their entire lives, but rather that they settle into a place in their later middle years and early old age and are not uprooted. They do not want to be moved from a space that has become familiar and easy to manoeuvre, from a location that they know well and in which they can meet their needs, and be put in an unfamiliar institutional environment or one distant from family and friends. They do not want to leave behind personal belongings that have history and meaning to them.

Assisted living (also known as supportive housing) is currently receiving much attention in Canada and elsewhere. This form of housing typically consists of apartments that provide, at minimum, a general on-site manager who checks on residents and is available for more than physical maintenance of the building, a personal alarm system in case of emergency, and group meals for those who want them. Canada Mortgage and Housing lists five key components: residential character, supportive physical environment, access to necessary support services, progressive management philosophy, and affordability and choice (Davis, 2000). Assisted living is for those whose health has begun to deteriorate; it is a built environment that allows them to age in place.

Health-care services, including services provided in assisted living environments, are a determinant of health, particularly for those who have fallen ill. However, they do little to promote health and wellness. They have a role in risk reduction (for example, providing immunization) but do little to provide people with the knowledge and skills necessary to adopt healthy living practices. The focus in this chapter is on the social-psychological and social determinants of health: health beliefs, health behaviours, and social structure. More is said about health-care services in Chapter 15.

Two types of determinants of health are examined in greater detail here: **personal health determinants,** which take place at the individual level and include beliefs and personal health behaviours, and **structural determinants,** which occur at the societal level and include, for example, the social and economic environment, gender, race, and social support. In examining these determinants, we are interested in the determinants of health and wellness, not simply the determinants of disease or disease avoidance.

Health Beliefs

Health beliefs, also referred to as lay conceptions of good health, are personal determinants of individual and population health. We all have our beliefs about what makes us healthy and what makes us ill. These beliefs give meaning to our experiences when we are healthy and help us interpret the meaning of illness and determine what actions we will take when we fall ill. Interpretive frameworks for explaining health and illness have been classified as professional (scientific, modern, and expert) and popular (non-scientific, traditional, and lay), each offering a set of ideas of shared meaning. The lay public often draws on both belief systems. In our discussion of seniors and aging, we have particular interest in commonsense models of chronic illness. In a study of older adults' meaning and management of chronic illness, Segall and Chappell (1991) report that most believe that medical care is necessary for such conditions as high blood pressure; more than a third also believe that some home remedies are better than prescribed drugs for treating illnesses. That is, consulting a health professional does not preclude self-treatment with, for example, home remedies.

Stoller (1993) reports that among her sample of seniors, the most common symptoms included joint and muscle pain, fatigue, and a runny or stuffy nose. These seniors offered both medical and non-medical interpretations of these symptoms. Medical interpretations included a flare-up of a chronic disease or condition, other medical conditions, or something they caught from someone else. Non-medical (popular) interpretations included normal aging, lifestyle, stress, weather, or season of the year. The most common medical explanation for a symptom was flare-up of a chronic condition, and the most common non-medical explanation was weather or season of the year. Often, seniors cite multiple causes.

Among Chinese seniors in Canada, Chappell and Lai (1998) report that belief in traditional Chinese medicine, which offers a holistic view of individuals and their surroundings, coexists with strong belief in Western medicine and the use of Western health-care services. It should also be pointed out that while we often think of ethnic minorities, such as Chinese seniors or Aboriginal seniors, as having traditional lay beliefs, mainstream Caucasian Canadians also have their beliefs in home remedies. Chicken soup, not sleeping with the window open, and not getting wet to avoid catching a cold are examples.

In contrast to the expert belief system of medicine, which is relatively closed, the lay health belief system is more open and flexible. The two are sometimes related to one another and sometimes reinforce one another. Birthing rooms are now a regular part of hospitals, through the influence of the wishes of women; similarly the treatment of breast cancer among women has been heavily influenced by the desire of women to have their own experiences heard and to be part of therapy. In some jurisdictions, Aboriginal healers are brought into the process as cultural brokers within hospitals (Kaufert & O'Neill, 1990). There is now scientific evidence that one of the substances in licorice root protects the lining of the stomach against erosion by stomach acid, supporting the longstanding use of the licorice plant in folk medicine as a laxative and a digestive aid (Segall & Chappell, 2000).

Importantly, many older adults normalize their symptoms by referring to them as simply part of the aging process. In Stoller's (1993) study, over half attributed at least one of their symptoms to normal aging and even more did so for such symptoms as vision problems, constipation, indigestion, and sleep difficulties. This confirmed earlier research documenting seniors' tendency to attribute many of their symptoms to "normal aging," even symptoms that were not inevitable consequences of the aging process (Kart, 1981). Leventhal and Prohaska (1986) found that common everyday health concerns (general symptomatology) are more likely to be attributed simply to "aging" as one grows older. Older adults are more likely to interpret symptoms such as weakness and aching as simply part of aging, rather than as warning signs of specific illnesses. Interestingly, those who normalize age-related physical decline and functional decline are less bothered by them (Simon, De Boer, Bosma, & Mackenbach, 2005). It is important for those working with older adults to recognize that providing them with information about what is a normal part of aging and what is not can allow them to decide for themselves whether and what action they wish to take.

Chronic illness, as opposed to general symptomatology, however, is not usually attributed to the aging process by older adults. Segall and Chappell (1991) found that half the older adults (age 50 years and over) did not know what caused their chronic illness and could not offer a specific cause. Those who could tended to name heredity, biophysical factors, or lifestyle factors. Only 2 percent attributed chronic illness to old age or the aging process. Middle-aged respondents similarly do not attribute chronic illness to the aging process (Blaxter, 1983).

Another important belief that we hold about illness concerns its **controllability**, that is, whether or not it can be managed by the individuals themselves, other persons in the informal network, or the formal health-care system. The concept of general locus of control and, more specifically, **health locus of control** has been studied in relation to self-rated health, self-initiated preventive care, and behaviour during illness episodes, including use of physician services and compliance with medical regimens. People with an **internal locus of control** believe that they have personal mastery of health and illness. Those with an **external locus of control** put their faith in powerful others, such as health-care providers, or else believe that health outcomes are beyond all control. Research suggests that seniors with a strong internal locus of control have more favourable health outcomes (Waller & Bates, 1992). It may be that those who believe they have some control over their health are more likely to adopt healthy lifestyles (Peterson & Stunkard, 1989).

How does belief in an internal locus of control change with age? A review of the literature (Lachman, 1986) found equal numbers of studies showing increases and decreases in such beliefs with age; still others found no change (Lachman, 1986). Lachman argues the inconsistency is due to methodological problems, including study design, sampling, and measurement, and that both multi-dimensional and domain-specific beliefs must be studied. Lachman's own research found significant differences by age for external locus of control (both control of powerful others and belief in chance outcomes) but not for internal locus. That is, older adults come to believe more in the salience of external factors while maintaining their belief in their own control over their health. The findings support the contention that control beliefs may change with age or remain stable, depending on the domain being examined. A study of elderly Manitobans found that stability in our perception of control was related to better health than fluctuating perceptions (Chipperfield, Campbell, & Perry, 2004).

Furthermore, Shewchuk, Foelker, and Niederehe (1990) adapted measures of locus of control developed for younger adults (for example, not using employment items) and revised the scales so they were more applicable to older adults. They could not confirm the accepted three-factor structure (internal–personal; external–provider; and external–chance). It may well be that one's sense of control over the cause or onset of an illness is different from the sense of personal control over the course of the condition and its management. This distinction has not been studied in relation to the locus of control concept (Segall & Chappell, 2000).

There are, of course, many other beliefs surrounding health and illness, which have generally received less research attention. One such belief is susceptibility. Interestingly, more than 25 years ago Najman (1980) argued for a concept of general illness susceptibility, contrary to the biomedical model in which each illness is believed to have a specific cause. The lay public appears to accept a notion of general susceptibility, such as family susceptibility. Leventhal and Prohaska (1986) reported that older adults have an increased sense of susceptibility to chronic conditions, such as heart disease and high blood pressure.

Some health economists, such as Evans and Stoddart (1990), have argued that the biomedical model errs in its focus on specific causes for particular diseases and that researchers should be examining the individual's host response. This is especially important for research on diseases because currently the vast majority of research dollars are targeted to finding a cure for specific illnesses, such as cancer. If the **host response** or **general susceptibility hypothesis** is valid, then as a cure is discovered for cancer, another illness will emerge to replace it, for example, HIV/AIDS. In other words, those individuals who are susceptible will develop another illness. This is a contentious issue that has not been resolved through research. It does, though, have important implications for whether older adults should address specific health problems individually or from a more holistic perspective.

Another health belief that has received even less attention is belief about seriousness, that is, how serious the disease or condition is. We also know little about beliefs related to stability versus changeability of conditions—their temporary or permanent nature—and the predictability of the symptoms of the illness. Yet all of these beliefs together help an individual make sense of the illness experience. In order to self-manage chronic illness, Kralik, Koch, Price and Howard (2004) argue from qualitative research in Australia, we create a sense of order by recognizing and monitoring the boundaries imposed by the illness; mobilizing resources; managing a shift in identity; and balancing, pacing, planning and prioritizing.

As is obvious from the foregoing, research on health beliefs has focused primarily on beliefs about the nature of illness. It is about making sense of illness, rather than making sense of either good health or preventing disease. An exception is early research conducted by Prohaska, Leventhal, Leventhal, and Keller (1985), who examined age differences in lay beliefs about the preventability of illness. They asked about a variety of health behaviours, such as eating a balanced diet, avoiding too much physical exertion, getting enough sleep, and having regular medical checkups. They reported that while the frequency of health maintenance activities increases with age, there was no age group difference in beliefs about the effectiveness of these health actions. However, older adults believed they were more vulnerable to certain types of illnesses and that they were more serious for them. They were also less likely to consider mild symptoms, such as tiredness, as an indicator of illness. This latter point is important because it means that seniors might be less likely to pursue a remedy or assistance.

In an analysis of the 1990 *Health Promotion Survey*, Penning and Chappell (1993) report that while the vast majority of Canadian adults believe a change in their personal lifestyles would improve their health and well-being, the proportion decreases as one ages. Older adults are less likely than younger adults to expect positive changes from increased exercise, stopping smoking, better dental care, or increased relaxation. Similarly, fewer older adults believe that reducing environmental pollution would benefit their health, and fewer men than women believe in this effect. Similar results are evident when examining social environmental changes, such as improving income or moving to a new neighbourhood. Older adults are less likely to perceive a benefit and, in this instance, women are less likely to perceive a benefit than are men. It would appear that information about the benefits of a variety of lifestyle behaviours is not reaching older Canadians or is not reaching them in a manner that is acceptable to them.

Lay conceptions of health are multi-dimensional and complex. Several studies suggest that for the lay public, an absence of disease is important in their view of health but that it also includes a sense of wholeness as in healthiness. Individuals can perceive themselves as healthy while living with disease. In fact, older adults living with multiple chronic conditions typically report good health. Segall and Chappell (1991) found that fully 74 percent of their respondents described their health as being good or fair for their age, even though, on average, they were living with four different chronic conditions. Most older adults, when comparing their health with others their own age, perceive their health as being good to excellent. They create meaning by drawing on a variety of sources. Being healthy relates to a sense of overall well-being and refers primarily to a psychological, rather than physiological, state.

Our interest in beliefs includes not only understanding the experiential nature of health and illness but also how they are related to health behaviours. We turn next to a discussion of health behaviours. This discussion draws the same distinction between health and illness: behaviours oriented toward maintaining health and those oriented toward dealing with sickness. It will not be surprising that there is more research on illness behaviour than on health maintenance behaviour

Personal Health Behaviours

Illness behaviour refers to activities surrounding the interpretation of symptoms experienced and action taken in response to the condition. **Positive health behaviour** is activity undertaken to prevent disease or detect it early, as well as to promote health. This includes risk-avoiding behaviour, such as wearing seatbelts and not smoking, and preventive medical care, such as having dental checkups and regular physical exams. Positive health behaviour may also include routine daily activities, such as eating nutritious meals, exercising regularly, and getting enough sleep (Mechanic, 1999).

Over two decades ago, Harris and Guten (1979) referred to **health protective behaviours** to describe activities we routinely engage in to protect our health—any behaviour that is intended to protect, promote, or maintain one's health irrespective of the individual's perceived or actual heath status. In their research, they identified three dominant positive health actions: nutrition, relaxation (sleep, rest), and exercise (recreation) activities. In 1985, Green used the term **self-health management** to refer to what we generally do or routinely engage in, including both health-protective behaviours and illness-treatment activities. This includes our own monitoring of our health status by evaluating the meaning of symptoms and bodily conditions and deciding on a course of action. This may include doing nothing, getting more rest, speaking to others about the condition, self-medicating, and so on.

Green argues that self-health management encompasses, but is broader than, self-care behaviour, also including mutual aid and membership in self-help groups. **Self-care** refers to any behaviours that are lay-initiated through a process of self-determination. Self-care necessarily includes lay control over the decision-making process This lay control can be seen as the heart of self-care, incorporating notions of autonomy and responsibility.

Self-Care A recognition of the role that self-care plays in our health is especially important because it changes the nature of the relationships between participants in the health-care system by allowing experiential knowledge of patients into that system. It also acknowledges laypeople as primary providers of health care. Self-care has been recognized for at least a quarter-century as the basic, central, and dominant form of health care practised by individuals (Dean, 1981; Levin & Idler, 1983). Health professionals are just one of many informal and formal resources available to individuals for managing their own health. There is consensus that self-care includes health protective behaviours, symptom evaluation, and self-treatment. It also includes consultation with and use of informal social networks as well as self-referral. Often, the use of preventive medical services is included. Some researchers include the use of health-care services as part of self-care; others do not. We are all health-care providers and health producers, as well as health-care consumers. The predominance of self-care is supported by the finding that 83 percent of an older adult sample used over-the-counter medications and 72 percent engaged in self-care activities (Musil et al., 1998).

Self-care takes on particular significance in later life because of the chronic conditions experienced in that period; because of a pattern of co-morbidity, where typically several chronic health problems coexist at one time; and because traditional acute-care treatment by the health-care system is less likely to be effective. Self-care in the presence of chronic illness becomes more complicated, involving self-monitoring, managing drug therapy at home, deciding whether to take prescribed and non-prescribed medications, and treatment to manage symptoms, especially pain and discomfort. In addition, emotions that accompany chronic illness, including frustration, anger, and depression, must be managed. Often, daily life must be adjusted in order to maintain activities.

Personal Health Practices Individuals engage in any number of **personal health practices**, some of which are believed to be positively related to health and others negatively so. Exercise, rest, and good nutrition are all potentially beneficial; smoking and alcohol consumption are potentially harmful. Similarly, environmental protection and home safety practices (such as having smoke detectors in the home) can have health consequences. Canada's Population Health Survey (1994/95) asked about healthy eating. Over half of Canadians aged 65 and over believe their eating habits are excellent or very good (58 percent) compared with only a third (36 percent) of Canadians ages 20 to 24. Similar figures are apparent when asked whether they are concerned about getting enough starch and fibre in their diet (55 percent of those 65 and over; 36 percent of those aged 20 to 24). More older and younger Canadians are concerned with the amount of fat in their diets (73 percent of seniors; 63 percent of those aged 20 to 24). And most are doing something about it; 92 percent of seniors and 86 percent of those aged 20 to 24 say they are taking action to reduce their fat intake. In other words, older adults tend to engage in practices traditionally believed to enhance health (exercising, eating a good breakfast, and so on), but they are less likely to engage in activities that reflect new thinking about how to improve health, such as environmental practices (e.g., recycling).

In terms of negative health behaviours, specifically smoking and binge drinking, older Canadians have better habits than younger adults. Among all Canadians, 41 percent were smokers in 1978/79, dropping to 28 percent in 1998/99. Among seniors, 22 percent were smokers in 1978/79, dropping to 13 percent in 1998/99. Senior men were more likely to smoke than senior women in 1978/79 (32 percent vs. 15 percent) and the same was true in 1998/99 (15 percent vs. 12 percent) but the difference is now slight. Elderly men have reduced their smoking! Seniors are also less likely to drink heavily. In 1998/99 15 percent of Canadians age 15 and over engaged in binge drinking at least monthly; only 3 percent of seniors did so (Statistics Canada, 1999a).

However, the use of medications (including tranquilizers, diet pills or stimulants, antidepressants, codeine, Demerol or morphine, sleeping pills, and ASA or other pain relievers) increases with age. For example, older adults, especially older women, are much more likely to use sleeping pills. (In the overall population, 7 percent took them within the previous 12 months, but 20 percent of those 70 years and over did so—18 percent of men and 21 percent of women report using sleeping pills). Similarly, only 2 percent of those aged 15 to 29 years report using tranquilizers, but 11 percent of those aged 70 years and over (in this case, there is no significant difference between men and women). These findings are relatively stable between 1990 and 1996–1997 (Statistics Canada, 1999).

Canadians are aware of the importance of personal health behaviours. In Prince Edward Island, researchers asked a number of groups (members of the public, family physicians, service providers, support staff, program managers, senior managers, and board members) about the determinants of health (Eyles et al., 2001). All groups ranked personal health practices first, ahead of employment, formal health care, education, healthy child development, income, social support, and the physical environment. However, when asked to rank where resources should be shifted in order to improve health, the public ranked personal health practices second behind healthy child development, the physical environment, and formal health care, which all tied for first. The public seems to view personal health behaviours as the responsibility of individuals themselves, not of governments. All other groups ranked personal health practices first.

Personal health behaviours are aspects of an individual's broader lifestyle, or general orientation toward life (Wister, 2005). They involve individuals' beliefs, attitudes, values, and behaviours. Our everyday language includes the concepts of healthy (good nutrition, proper exercise, etc.) and unhealthy lifestyles (smoking, excessive drinking, obesity), suggesting a clustering of health behaviours. Early research provided some evidence of such clustering. For example, Harris and Guten (1979) found that some behaviours appear together empirically and, on this basis, postulated five clusters of health protective behaviours:

1. Personal health practices—routine daily positive health actions, such as getting enough sleep and relaxation, eating sensibly, watching one's weight, doing things in moderation, and avoiding overwork.

2. Safety practices—other daily living activities in the home, such as checking the condition of electrical appliances or the car, fixing broken things right away, keeping emergency phone numbers near the phone, having a first aid kit.

3. Preventive health-care practices—the usual preventive medical behaviours, such as seeing a doctor or a dentist for regular checkups.

4. Environmental hazard avoidance, such as avoiding parts of the city with a lot of crime or pollution.

5. Harmful substance avoidance, such as not smoking or drinking.

They reported that preventive health-care practices were unrelated to any of the other clusters.

However, most research has been unable to confirm the existence of such clusterings. A person who exercises may not eat particularly nutritious meals, or may smoke or drink. The one exception seems to be a moderate correlation between smoking and drinking (Krick & Sobal, 1990). Lifestyle behaviours are very complex!

Measurement difficulties may account for the lack of correlation. For example, it might be important to distinguish between routine and spontaneous exercise, and to document actual nutritional intake of a variety of foods. Greater detail on activity patterns would inform us whether some individuals, for example, eat well and exercise during the week, but then eat less healthily and do not exercise on the weekend.

Lifestyle includes behaviours that cluster together and interact with cultural, social, and psychosocial factors. However, to date researchers have been unsuccessful in identifying clusters that constitute lifestyles, perhaps because they are looking for logically consistent behaviour patterns. It could be that many individuals behave in complex and not always logical ways (such as bingeing or drinking a fair amount of alcohol at a party but usually eating well and not drinking alcoholic beverages). Backett, Davison, and Mullen (1994) argue that we trade off positive and negative aspects of health-related behaviour to balance our overall health, rather than choosing certain types of behaviours to the exclusion of others.

Part of the problem is that there is no consensus in theory or practice as to what constitutes "lifestyle." Despite this lack of clarity, the concept of lifestyle appears to be here to stay, for some time at least, perhaps because it is within the control of the individual and because of the belief that, if we could figure it out, it has the potential to have a large effect on our health. This gains in importance with the aging of the population and the increase in chronic degenerative diseases for which medicine has no cure. Healthy behaviours may delay the onset of such conditions and help those who have them manage daily living.

Despite our beliefs that we are eating a healthy diet, there is evidence of a lack of healthy activity in old age. For example, more than 65 percent of Canadian seniors are sedentary (Eakin, 2001), increasing to 70 percent among those age 75 and over. Yet, we know that physical activity can be beneficial even for those with several medical conditions and who are chair-bound. And those benefits accrue even when the activity is initiated late in life (Spirduso, 1995; Hickey & Stilwell, 1992). Lack of activity is related to obesity, which is on the rise. Rates of obesity are lower in old age (25 percent) than in middle age (30 percent), when rates peak (Statistics Canada, 2005d). The known risk factors for diabetes, as for other chronic illnesses, include obesity, poor nutrition, physical inactivity, and low socio-economic status. Lifestyle modifications have been shown to work (Little, 2003; Whitaker, 2000).

This discussion of personal health practices is largely consistent with the premises of activity theory, urging an active lifestyle and focusing on the individual. It assumes individual agency because personal health practices are largely within the control of the individual. However, many of the determinants of our beliefs and actions fall outside of this realm. We turn now to a discussion of some of those factors, notably of social structure (an important influence in all of our lives) as a determinant of health.

Social Structure as a Determinant of Health

Simply put, **social structure** is the pattern of interrelated statuses and roles within society and within subgroups of society that constitute a relatively stable set of social relations. This entails an interrelated set of rights and obligations within a system of interaction. George (1990) describes social structure as the relatively stable pattern of social organization based on a system of social roles, norms, and shared meanings that provide regularity and predictability to social interaction. Examples of social structural variables include age, socio-economic position, and formal roles, such as positions or memberships in an organization or group. Age, for example, defines our occupancy and performance in roles (legal eligibility to attend school, drive a car, drink alcohol, vote, and receive a pension).

Social class refers to our structural position in society and is also referred to as socio-economic status (SES). It is most often measured in terms of income but also often in terms of education and/or occupation. Irrespective of the measure used, it is related to our health. There is no disputing that poverty is related to poor health. Basic necessities are required for life: food, clothing, and shelter. Absolute material deprivation is unhealthy. This is why most countries, including Canada, have basic welfare measures to ensure a minimum level for people to live. Beyond this, however, there is now much research documenting a relationship between SES and health. Those of higher social class have better health than those of lower social class; this has been demonstrated for numerous indicators of health, including mortality, morbidity, functional ability, and perceptions of health. This relationship has persisted over time despite the fact that the primary causes of mortality have shifted away from infectious disease. The relationship between SES and health holds even when controlling for other factors, such as nutritional intake, exercise, and social support. This relationship, furthermore, is strongest in the middle years. Mustard, Derksen, Berthelot, Wolfson, and Roos (1997) identify those aged 30 to 64 years; Torrance, Zhang, Feeny, and Boyle (1992) identify those aged 45 to 64 years; and Wilkins, Adams, & Brancker (1991) identify those aged 25 to 64 years as the age groups with the strongest correlations between SES and health. This is not surprising, given that older individuals are no longer part of the workforce. Although the relationship is not as strong during old age, it is still evident (Hay, 1994).

Wilkinson (1996) describes the relationship between social structure and health as the power of social structure over life and death. Since social structures can be modified, illness is potentially preventable. Indeed, Wilkins and colleagues (1991) have examined how regional disparities in death rates in Canada have changed, showing a decrease from five years in 1941 to 1.5 years in 1986, during a period that saw both major economic growth and national investment in equalizing educational opportunities despite continuing regional differences. That is, social structural change was evident in this time period.

We now know that it is not only the poorest of society who experience more health problems and die sooner, but that those with fewer socio-economic resources than others, irrespective of how high up they are in the societal hierarchy, experience more ill health. Those on the second-highest rung of society are in better health than those on the third-highest rung but in worse health than those on the highest rung. This relationship, referred to as the **social gradient**, holds irrespective of the absolute levels or material standards of living (beyond basic necessities). Inequality per se is bad for health. This gradient is continuous; there is no threshold before or after which it does not apply. Furthermore, it is the distribution of inequality *within* a country that matters, presumably reflecting standards of living within that country. Diseases with the steepest gradients vary from country to country (Wilkinson, 1996). In Canada, men with the lowest 5 percent of earnings before retirement are twice as likely to die between the ages of 65 and 70 years as men with the highest 5 percent of earnings; those in the top earning category, on average, enjoy 12 more years of good health than do low-income earners (CIAR, 1991). This means that the ways in which a society structures opportunities for its citizens and the ultimate availability of a variety of positions become relevant for our health.

It is important, at the same time, to recognize that all individuals have a variety of reference groups in their lives. One can hold a position of value and importance within the local community, within the family, or within a sports club and, provided that the group is salient in one's life, it could have positive health influences. Research on unemployment (another structural factor) and health supports this argument. Although unemployment is generally related to ill health in parts of the country with high overall unemployment rates, in areas where unemployment is the norm, it is not as strongly related to health differentials (D'Arcy, 1988). In other words, we do not all have to be prime minister in order to have good health.

The social gradient has been interpreted in Canada, by economists such as Evans and Stoddart (1990), to mean that it is income and wealth that are related to health and that we should, therefore, turn our efforts to producing wealth. However, as Wilkinson (1994) asks, is the individual's desire for more wealth per se or a desire to improve his or her standing in society? That is, is the equation of social position with material standards in Canada due to the fact that Canada is a capitalist country in which income is a major determinant of social status?

Poland, Coburn, Robertson, and Eakin (1998) argue that it is equity and **redistributive justice** (ensuring that a country's wealth is shared by those less fortunate) that are the key to improving a society's health, not wealth and prosperity per se. Coburn (2004) elaborates, arguing that welfare measures reflect basic social, political, and economic institutions through which a society provides for its citizens or leaves the fate of citizens to the market (neo-liberalism). Said another way, income inequality reflects social conditions that operate through individual and collective, material and psychosocial pathways. Income inequality can be seen as a shorthand for a variety of social conditions. Social welfare measures can buffer the effects of income inequality. This is a complex area of study. As Judge, Mulligan and Benzeval (1998) note, factors potentially affecting the relationship between equity distribution and health must also be taken into account. Such measures would include, for example, measures of prosperity (perhaps average national income) and characteristics of the welfare system. Measures of equity presumably need to take into account taxes, cash benefits, and household composition.

Understanding Why

Knowing that social structure affects health does not tell us why or how this relationship works. Economic advantage is clearly related to health in many ways. It means being able to afford to live in healthy environments and to make healthy choices about such things as nutrition and services. Poor people have few choices about where they live and the food they eat. Fast foods, cigarettes, and alcohol are all relatively accessible in our affluent society, and the poor choose what is accessible, but that means that they must forgo other choices. That is, with money in our capitalist society come the conditions, opportunities and amenities that allow for a healthy life. Whether or not our children will attend university is influenced by where we live, parental expectations, and peer pressure.

However, as shown by the fact that the gradient operates even at high levels, there seems to be some other factor at play. Some authors, such as Syme (1994), argue that it is control or influence over our own actions and a feeling that we are contributing to the larger society that is critical; others suggest that the relationship works through self-esteem, sense of control over our lives, and resiliency (Renaud et al., 1996). While it is not well understood, the clear suggestion is that social-psychological factors, such as coping, self-mastery, and a sense of control are all relevant. Precisely how these connections take place is not known, but it is believed that the social environment affects us psychologically, which in turn affects us physiologically. For example, the immune system is the body's primary defence against bacteria, viruses and cancers. Stress alters the immune system. The nervous and immune systems talk to one another; the social environment can influence biological responses through the nervous system. Hormonal systems also respond to stress (Evans & Stoddart, 1990).

Increasingly, research is investigating the biological pathways through which social factors are related to health. For example, Cohen, Tyrell, and Smith (1991) inoculated volunteers with one of five viruses or a **placebo** (a substance that, unknown to the individual, has no effect). All participants had completed a variety of psychological stress measures. They were quarantined and monitored. Respiratory infections and clinical colds increased in relation to the dose injected, and as the psychological stress of the individual increased, for all five viruses in the study.

Our understanding of how this relationship operates is just starting to be investigated. It is, however, worth noting that non-Western cultures do not embrace the mind–body dichotomy as does Western medicine. The Ayurvedic tradition of South Asian medicine and traditional Chinese medicine view the mind and body as parts of the same whole.

Gender

It is also important to note that women and men experience social class positions differently. Opportunities for men and women are structured differently, as discussed in Chapter 5. Women have been more the nurturers and more likely to have close friends, to be the kin keepers and network builders within the family, and to reach out to others. This is as true in old age as when we are younger (Chappell, 1992; Moore & Rosenberg, 1995). Because of these differences, women have also been excluded from many labour force opportunities, and women who are elderly today lived in a time when gender divisions of labour were more typical than today. However, In addition, similar positions may have different meanings. For example, unemployment might be important for men for different reasons than for women because until recently, men were expected to be employed whereas women were not necessarily expected to be.

As noted earlier, women suffer from more symptomatology than do men, although they have a longer life expectancy. These gender differences may reflect, at least in part, the set of indicators that have dominated health research, such as mortality, morbidity, and functional ability. If other indicators are studied more extensively, such as happiness and stress, we may see different results.

Cultural Minority Status

Health experiences also vary by cultural minority status. Typically, being a member of an ethnic minority is highly correlated with poor health, with the First Nations peoples a dramatic example. Canada's Royal Commission on Aboriginal Peoples (1996) documented the interrelationship between health and race:

- The life expectancy of registered Indians is seven to eight years shorter than that of non–First Nations individuals (statistics were not available for other Aboriginal groups).

- Unemployment rates, incidence of low educational attainment, and welfare dependency are higher in First Nations communities.

- The incidences of violence, physical and sexual abuse, and suicide are higher in First Nations communities.

- First Nations peoples are increasingly affected by such conditions as cancer and heart disease.

- Children in First Nations communities have higher rates of accidental death and injury than other Canadian children.

- Many First Nations communities have higher rates of infectious diseases, such as tuberculosis and AIDS, than non–First Nations.

Since that time the Canadian government confirms that disparities in health status continue. The health of Aboriginal populations remains worse than that of Canadians as a whole; rates of smoking are higher among Indian and Inuit teenagers; the prevalence of diabetes is approximately four times the rate found in the general population; and the rate for tuberculosis is 10 times as high (Health Canada, 2004).

The leading causes of death among First Nations infants (respiratory ailments, infectious and parasitic diseases, accidents) are all indicators of inadequate housing, unsanitary conditions, and poor access to medical facilities. Similarly, rates of death among adults due to infectious and parasitic diseases are consistently above national levels, reflecting differences in lifestyles and living conditions. Reserves often lack central heating, proper ventilation systems, adequate water sources, and sanitation facilities and have fire hazards from wood stoves, improper air circulation, and overcrowding (Young, 1991; Wotherspoon 1994). The Canadian government is working in partnership with First Nations communities to address these many issues (Health Canada, 2004).

In Canada, as in the United States, members of cultural minorities also tend to be economically disadvantaged, so that it is difficult to differentiate the effects of socio-economic status from the effects of cultural minority status. Nevertheless, the National Forum on Health concluded that the consequences of hardships among First Nations peoples are similar to those experienced by others in similar economically disadvantaged circumstances. Supporting the argument that First Nations peoples have worse health because they are more likely to be living in circumstances that are bad for their health, Zong and Li (1994) concluded from a study of 118 countries that economic conditions and nutritional levels, not cultural influence, were responsible for differences between countries in life expectancy and infant mortality rates. This is not to deny the role that racism and discrimination play in the lives and health of cultural minorities.

Box 9.2 looks at some ways that culture and economics may affect health.

Box 9.2 *Cross-Cultural Comparisons*

Historic cultural differences between Asia and North America would suggest a very different aging experience in these different parts of the world. Much is heard of the respect and care provided for seniors in China in contrast to the neglect and alienation of seniors in North America. In Canada, most seniors are not employed and when their spouses die, they tend to live alone. The focus within our capitalist society is on autonomy and independence, together with a youth orientation. Historically, the Chinese have valued and practised filial piety (*xiao*), a reciprocity known as *ci*, referring to kindness in rearing children, and Chinese familism (*Tianlun zhi le*) referring to harmonious family relations and happy family life. Indeed, in 1979, it became a legal obligation of children to care for their elders.

Recent comparative data from seniors living in Shanghai and those living in Victoria, British Columbia, suggest that there are similarities as well as differences. Up to three-quarters of those living in Shanghai have no more than junior high formal education and two-thirds rent, rather than own, their dwellings. Indeed, fully 42 percent have no independent room of their own within their living accommodations. Fully two-thirds live in what are known as old-style lodges, with shared washrooms, often at the end of the hall. There is no universal old-age security payment and a substantial proportion (a quarter) receive financial help from their children and grandchildren, which is their major source of income. In all these ways, they are distinctive from seniors in Canada. Furthermore,

they perceive their health to be worse, and the objective data suggest their perceptions are correct. That is, they seem to suffer from more chronic conditions and from more symptoms (such as chills and flu, being sad or depressed, agitated itchy skin, indigestion). We have already learned that poverty is related to ill health, so this is not surprising. The Shanghaese are less likely to be receiving services, either of a physician or other health-care workers.

However, like seniors in Victoria, and in Canada generally, Shanghaese seniors have others whom they can turn to. In an emergency, or in terms of who their confidants and companions are, the historical value of males emerges. They are much more likely to turn to their sons than is true of Canadian seniors, who more often turn to their spouses or daughters. Most Shanghaese, like most Canadian seniors, have family and friends nearby.

Another similarity emerges when examining happiness among Shanghaese seniors. The major predictors of happiness or life satisfaction are their social support and their health. These are the same factors that emerge consistently in research on happiness among seniors in Canada, in North America generally and, indeed, in Western countries. The form that the social support takes varies (sons are more valued and more popular in Chinese society) but the importance of social support is similar. That is, what brings us happiness in old age seems to span across cultural boundaries.

Source: N.L. Chappell, (2001). *Family care of seniors in Shanghai: Similarities and differences with the West.* Paper presented at the International Symposium on Chinese Elderly, Shanghai, October.

A Health Promotion Perspective

The many determinants of health reviewed in this chapter comprise what is known as a **health promotion perspective.** This perspective recognizes "upstream" factors—that is, psychosocial and environmental factors as influencing our health—and is consistent with the broad World Health Organization definition of health provided earlier in the chapter. Determinants include peace, shelter, education, food, income, a stable ecosystem, sustainable resources, social justice, and equity, in addition to personal health beliefs and behaviours. While recognizing a role for self-care and individual choice, this perspective also recognizes that our structural position within society affects the choices we have. Telling the Inuit to eat fresh fruit and vegetables in the winter is unhelpful when the few available are exorbitantly priced. Similarly, those exposed to harmful chemicals at work have little choice in the effects they may ultimately suffer. Individuals have agency, but there are also limits on that agency.

Early health promotion research focused on individual risk behaviours, such as smoking and poor eating habits. This resulted in a charge of "blaming the victim" (it's your own fault if you are sick because you are not engaging in healthy behaviours). By the 1990s, broader approaches had grown in popularity (Goodman, 2000; Merzel & D'Afflitti, 2003). For example, social ecology embraces a set of principles for examining interdependencies between individual and aggregate manifestations of health problems. It recognizes individual, group, organizational, community, and policy influences on health (Stokols, 1996). The need for collaboration across sectors and levels is emphasized. The Canadian government recognizes the importance of a population health perspective, as is evident from Box 9.3.

Box 9.3 *What Makes Canadians Healthy or Unhealthy*

This deceptively simple story speaks to the complex set of factors or conditions that determine the level of health of every Canadian.

"Why is Jason in the hospital?
Because he has a bad infection in his leg.
But why does he have an infection?
Because he has a cut on his leg and it got infected.
But why does he have a cut on his leg?
Because he was playing in the junkyard next to his apartment building and there was some sharp, jagged steel there that he fell on.
But why was he playing in a junkyard?
Because his neighbourhood is kind of rundown. A lot of kids play there and there is no one to supervise them.
But why does he live in that neighbourhood?
Because his parents can't afford a nicer place to live.
But why can't his parents afford a nicer place to live?
Because his Dad is unemployed and his Mom is sick.

But why is his Dad unemployed?
Because he doesn't have much education and he can't find a job.
But why . . . ?"

Key Determinants

1. Income and social status
2. Social support networks
3. Education and Literacy
4. Employment/Working Conditions
5. Social Environment
6. Physical Environment
7. Personal Health Practices and Coping Skills
8. Healthy Child Development
9. Biology and Genetic Endowment
10. Health Services
11. Gender
12. Culture

Source: From *Toward a healthy future: Second report on the health of Canadians*, Public Health Agency of Canada, (1999). Reproduced with the permission of the Minister of Public Works and Government Services, Canada, 2006.

The Prince Edward Island Study mentioned earlier (Eyles et al., 2001) demonstrates that the Canadian public to a large extent also accepts this perspective, sometimes referred to as a population health perspective. This is evident in the general understanding that our health is influenced by personal health practices but also by early childhood development and the environment.

CHAPTER SUMMARY

This chapter has examined health and illness in old age, emphasizing the importance of incorporating a sense of healthiness as well as a sense of sickness. The domination of medicine together with people's lack of awareness of their health, except primarily when they become ill, has meant that research has concentrated much more on disease and illness than on health and well-being. The determinants of health, including beliefs, behaviours and social structure were then discussed, focusing both on areas of individual agency and on broader forces that affect the individual.

Key ideas to remember from this chapter:

- While women live longer than men, they are more likely to suffer from both chronic conditions and limitations in activities of daily living than are men.
- Despite physical health declines as we age, our psychological well-being seems to improve.
- Gender differences in health are important: women experience more symptomatology in old age than do men; men, however, die younger (that is, the conditions that men experience are more likely to be fatal).
- A major focus in gerontology is an understanding of how we can maintain and enhance quality of life in old age, not simply extend the quantity of life.
- The determinants of health include health beliefs, health behaviours, and social structure. These are all relatively new areas of study in which we have much to learn. However, they are also all factors that we can change in order to improve our health. Although we often think of social structure as being less influenceable than individual factors, governments and community groups can effect change.
- Some health beliefs change as we age (such as the tendency to normalize some symptoms as simply part of aging); others remain stable (such as the actions we should take to help promote and maintain our health). Health beliefs include scientific/expert as well as lay/popular explanations about why we become ill, the course of the illness, and its controllability.
- The general susceptibility hypothesis argues for a host response of the individual to illness. If this is true, those who become ill with one illness would contract another if that illness were conquered.
- Despite the attention paid to sickness and treatment, self-care is the most predominant form of care.
- Personal health behaviours can be positive, neutral, or negative. Positive health behaviours and negative health behaviours may represent two dimensions, rather than opposite ends

of one dimension. To date, researchers have largely failed to demonstrate a clustering of health behaviours that would represent a lifestyle.

- Socio-economic status predicts health. Not only are those living in poverty in worse health, the social gradient suggests that even among those with adequate resources, higher status brings better health.
- A health promotion perspective embraces the social determinants of health.

KEY TERMS

health (p. 224)

sickness (p. 224)

disease (p. 224)

illness (p. 224)

mechanistic model (p. 224)

wellness (p. 225)

population health (p. 226)

frailty (p. 228)

aging in place (p. 230)

assisted living (p. 230)

personal health determinants (p. 230)

structural determinants (p. 230)

health beliefs (p. 230)

controllability (p. 232)

health locus of control (p. 232)

internal locus of control (p. 232)

external locus of control (p. 232)

host response or general susceptibility hypothesis (p. 233)

illness behaviour (p. 235)

positive health behaviour (p. 235)

health protective behaviours (p. 235)

self-health management (p. 235)

self-care (p. 235)

personal health practices (p. 236)

social structure (p. 239)

social class (p. 239)

social gradient (p. 240)

redistributive justice (p. 241)

placebo (p. 242)

health promotion perspective (p. 244)

STUDY QUESTIONS

1. In old age, women and men reveal many differences in their health. Discuss what those differences are and the possible reasons for them.

2. Health has different aspects and different meanings. Discuss what these are and their relevance in old age.

3. How do health beliefs differ in older age from when we are younger, and why is this important for our health?

4. The concept of the host response, if confirmed, will profoundly change how we think about research and treat illnesses. Explain.

5. Do personal health behaviours represent a "lifestyle"? Explain why or why not.

6. What is the social gradient, and what implications does it have for population health?

7. What is the health promotion perspective?

SUGGESTED READINGS

Armstrong, P. (2001). Evidence-based health-care reform: Women's issues. In P. Armstrong & H. Coburn (Eds.), *Unhealthy times: Political economy perspectives on health and care in Canada*, pp. 121–145. Don Mills, ON: Oxford University Press.

Glaser, K., & Grundy, E. (2002). Class, caring and disability: Evidence from the British Retirement Survey. *Ageing and Society*, 22: 325–342.

Litva, A., & Eyles, J. (1994). Health or healthy: Why people are not sick in a Southern Ontarian town. *Social Science and Medicine, 39(8)*, 1083–1091.

Mustard, C.A., Derksen, S., Berthelot, J.M., Wolfson, M., & Roos, L.L. (1997). Age-specific education and income gradients in morbidity and mortality in a Canadian province. *Social Science and Medicine, 45(3)*, 383–397.

Poland, B., Coburn, D., Robertson, A. & Eakin, J. (1998). Wealth, equity and health care: A critique of a "population health" perspective on the determinants of health. *Social Science and Medicine, 46(7)*, 785–798.

Chapter 10

SUCCESSFUL AGING

Learning Objectives

In this chapter, you will learn about

- The history of the successful aging concept.
- The definition of aging as distinct from disease.
- The distinction between normal and abnormal age differences and successful and unsuccessful aging.
- The constraints imposed by research designs on inferences about aging.
- Individual differences that show up on age-dependent variables.
- Age changes on important age-dependent measures that serve as indicators of successful aging.

- Models that include other than age-dependent measures as indicators.
- Individual differences related to health and mental well-being in later life.
- The distinction between successful aging (a process) and successful agers (a group of people).
- Measures used to identify individuals considered mentally and physically successful in later life, and influences on those measures.

Introduction

This chapter begins with an overview of paradigm shifts after World War II that contributed to the development of successful aging and related concepts, and their acceptance not only in the gerontological literature but also by international bodies such as the World Health Organization (WHO). The next section defines aging and discusses the discrimination of aging effects from disease and other sources of variation. Without a clear understanding of distinctions involved, it is impossible to comprehend the scope and limitations of successful aging and its indicators. Conversely, a failure of such comprehension contributes, along with other factors, to a confusing plethora of successful aging models and measures that do not necessarily overlap. The third section examines the influence of individual differences on age-dependent measures and associated models. This section concludes with inferences about the identification of successfully aging people based on age changes in age-dependent measures. The fourth section includes a review and critique of models, measures, and influences that researchers relate to successful aging. Models and measures attempt to identify individuals who have favourable mental and physical profiles in later life. Influences on these measures include lifestyle, life events, and psychological and social resources in addition to a relative absence of disease.

Historical Overview

There are at least two prototypes for the concept of successful aging, each of which originated over half a century ago. The earliest prototype was the definition of health by the WHO as not merely the absence of disease but an optimal state of physical and mental well-being (see Chapter 9). This perspective assumes that health consists of an upper and lower half-range of well-being and pathology, respectively, as discussed in Chapter 8. The WHO definition facilitated the development of perspectives on health care that complement the traditional emphasis on remediation or management of acute and chronic diseases. Health promotion, designed to enable people to increase their control over and improve their health, received a major impetus in countries such as Canada.

A related evolution of ideas occurred in gerontology a few years later. Although generations of gerontologists made explicit the distinction between normal aging and disease, it was not until the 1970s that the "normalcy" of normal aging came under concerted attack. A seminal article by Rowe and Kahn (1987) reviewed evidence showing that personal control over health extended beyond morbidity and mortality to affect the course of aging itself. Out of this realization, the concept of **successful aging** was born.

The second prototype originated in Canada with Murray's (1951) attempt to measure biological aging. Murray was probably the first investigator to measure individual differences on **age-dependent measures** in a quantitative manner, albeit using a methodology that some researchers thought flawed (Costa & McCrae, 1980a; Salthouse, 1990). Age-dependent measures are those expected to show change over time. Later research that attempted to evaluate individual differences with age using qualitative methodology falls under a rubric termed differential aging (Schroots, 1995).

The first acknowledged use of the term *successful aging* was by Havighurst (1961) in the first issue of *The Gerontologist* journal. Synonyms for successful aging since that time include *healthy aging* (McPherson, 1995), *optimal aging* (Baltes & Baltes, 1990), *aging well* (Folts, Ide, Johnson, & Crewe Solomon, 1995), and *vital aging* (Ouaknine, Csank, & Stones, 1997). All of these terms share a common feature: individuals who are thought to be aging successfully are "doing better" in later life than people aging unsuccessfully. What "doing better" means and the ways to achieve that condition are issues discussed in this chapter. The term successful aging gained widespread acceptance in scientific and general discourse following an article by Rowe and Kahn (1987) in the journal *Science*. A series of over 100 published studies on the positive aspects of aging ensued during the following decade, culminating in the publication of a general market book titled *Successful Aging* that attracted a large readership (Rowe & Kahn, 1998).

Successful aging is so accepted as a concept in the modern era that one sometimes forgets how recent its origins are. Examples such as the WHO's agenda on healthy aging in the context of disabilities and the establishment of the Canadian Institute on Healthy Aging (since changed to the Institute on Aging) as a national funding body illustrate how established the concept has become.

Inferences about Aging

Birren and Renner (1977:4) defined aging as "regular changes that occur in mature genetically representative organisms living under representative conditions as they advance in chronological age." This definition distinguishes aging from disease and disability. Aging refers to processes discretely associated with the passage of time. Different diseases may first appear at different ages (e.g., the onset of schizophrenia is generally at a young age; heart disease and cancer appear later; Alzheimer's disease occurs later still), but the causes and symptoms of those diseases are not part of an inevitable progression of chronological aging.

Birren and Renner's (1977) definition is imprecise about the delineation of "genetically representative" organisms and "representative [living] conditions." Although members of the same species share genetically endowed properties (e.g., humans walk on two legs, have large brains, a propensity for language, etc.) and live somewhat similarly (e.g., most people live in fixed dwellings, with family members, as part of larger communities, etc.), the range of individual differences within a species is broad, especially later in life (Nelson & Dannefer, 1992).

Figure 10.1 **HISTOGRAM OF CHANGE SCORES ON THE COGNITIVE PERFORMANCE SCALE IN HOME-CARE CLIENTS**

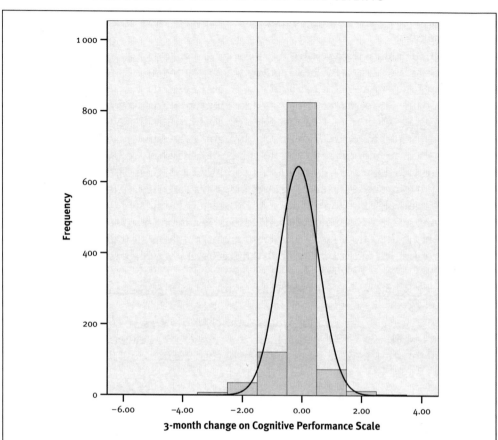

Source: Based on data from the Resident Assessment Instrument Health Infomatics Project (2000–2001).

Distribution of Individual Difference

The distribution of individual differences on any variable frequently approximates a **normal distribution**—a smooth, symmetrical curve with its peak in the middle. Figure 10.1 shows such a distribution for changes over a three-month period on the Cognitive Performance Scale from the Minimum Data Set for Home Care (Morris et al., 1994). The data are from 1077 home-care clients assessed as part of the Resident Assessment Instrument Health Infomatics Project in 2000–2001. Although cognitive performance is an age-dependent measure, we would not normally expect substantial changes within a brief three-month period. However, because home-care clients include individuals recovering from illness or deteriorating because of acute and chronic disease, it is hardly surprising that many people show positive or negative changes.

The concept of a *normal expectation* refers to a population of observations and is meaningful only by reference to a distribution of those observations. Normal scores are representative of the overall distribution and reflect an expected level on the variable measured. The term *abnormal* is the opposite of normal; like a normally expected score, an abnormal score is meaningful only by reference to a distribution of scores. Abnormal scores include those that are unusual and unexpected. With a normal distribution, abnormal scores fall at each extreme. With a differently shaped distribution (e.g., a bimodal distribution with a concentration of scores at each extreme), abnormal scores might lie elsewhere.

Terms that connote an evaluation (e.g., *successful-unsuccessful*; *healthy-unhealthy*), when assigned to differences between people, are also meaningful only in relation to a distribution of observations. These terms do not necessarily coincide with the distinction between normal and abnormal scores. *Abnormal*, in this context, means only that a score deviates from an expected level. The ranges of scores labelled favourable or unfavourable depends on value judgments by the person assigning the labels. If we examine more closely the distribution in Figure 10.1, abnormal scores include those of –2 or less and 2 or more. Fewer than 5 percent of the total sample of scores fall in this range, therefore, these scores are unrepresentative of the population during the period studied. Any score indicating cognitive gain is a favourable score and any score indicative of cognitive loss is an unfavourable score. Collectively, the favourable and unfavourable scores account for nearly 25 percent of the distribution.

Because the scores now classified as favourable and unfavourable represent age changes, it might seem reasonable to ask whether they represent short-term trends of successful and unsuccessful cognitive aging, respectively. The answer, as already indicated, is that any change likely reflects worsening or recovery from disease rather than the normally expected effects of aging. Analysis of other data from the RAIHIP project supports this inference. Generally, clients with unfavourable cognitive change scores had also needed more care over the preceding three months, whereas those with favourable cognitive change scores had needed less care, suggesting that the cognitive changes accompanied changes in overall health.

A somewhat disconcerting implication from these findings is that, even with longitudinal change scores, it is not always feasible to interpret temporal change as unequivocally dependent upon aging effects. Without including other changes in the analyses, researchers could have drawn incorrect causal inferences. Although this example uses a sample to which special conditions apply, causal inference can pose difficulties even in research with healthier samples studied over longer periods. Salthouse, Kausler, and Saults (1986) estimated that with many current measurement procedures, intervals of 30 years might be necessary for longitudinal changes to be statistically significant. If so, psychometric considerations limit the power of all but the longest longitudinal studies to detect age change, and the problem remains of how to disentangle effects directly attributable to aging from those of disease and other life changes.

Individual Differences in Cross-sectional Data

Many recent studies that addressed the topic of successful aging used cross-sectional or short-term prospective designs that sampled only a single older cohort (Almeida, Norman, Hankey, Jamrozik, & Flicker, 2006; Goffaux et al., 2005; Montross et al., 2006; Motta et al., 2005; Phela, Anderson, LaCroix, & Larsen, 2004). However, it is by no means certain that inferences about aging are possible from these designs. The term successful aging (or healthy aging, or optimal aging, etc.) connotes the following:

- The individual difference variable is important;
- The researcher has a means to identify favourable and unfavourable scores;
- The scores are relevant to aging.

Whether the individual difference variable is important and the researcher is able to identify favourable and unfavourable scores relates to values and technical expertise, respectively. Whether the scores are relevant to aging (i.e., as distinct from the aged) is a matter of logic and inference. An inference that the main sources of variability within cross-sectional cohort data relate to aging is usually an unfounded hypothesis (Stones, Kozma, & Hannah, 1990).

Figure 10.2 illustrates this argument with hypothetical data from four individuals at two age levels. If the variable measured were important to success and only data at the old age level were available, the reader would conclude that individuals C and D were aging successfully compared with individuals A and B. If the reader also had access to data at the young age level, the conclusion would be different. Individuals A and C show positive age changes whereas B and D show negative age changes. Consequently, the use of cross-sectional data in this example resulted in incorrect inferences about successful aging because of failure to account for the effects of individual differences present at a younger age.

Stones, Kozma, and Hannah (1990) reasoned that only by making strong assumptions about individual differences at a younger age could researchers justifiably interpret scores in later life as individual differences in age change. The hypothetical data in Figure 10.3 illustrate the assumption, which is that variability in scores at a younger age is negligible compared with the variability in later life. Consequently, the scores at the old age level in Figure 10.3 provide unequivocal estimates of age changes because of an absence of individual differences at a younger age. Inferences about whether the age changes reflect aging effects or other influences (e.g., disease, disability) are uncertain with the data provided. Although Stones and colleagues claimed that unipedal balance (i.e., the length of time a person was able to stand on one foot) satisfied the criterion of minimal variability in young adulthood, most age-dependent measures show substantial variability at all ages and do not satisfy the assumption specified.

Figure 10.2 HYPOTHETICAL DISTRIBUTIONS OF SCORES BY INDIVIDUALS A–D AT DIFFERENT AGES

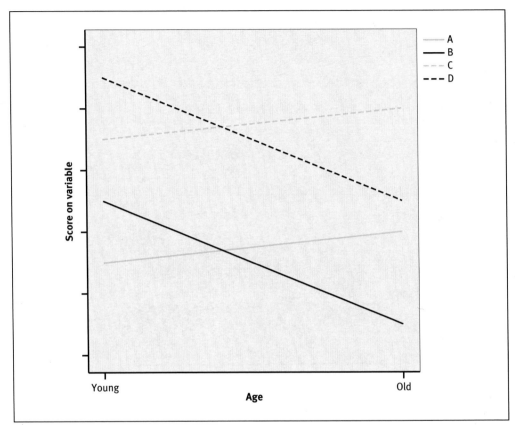

This section illustrated some problems in disentangling the effects of aging from those of disease and other sources of variation in longitudinal data, and in inferring age change with cross-sectional data. The reader should be skeptical about the relevance to aging of studies that claim to measure successful aging with cross-sectional data.

Individual Differences on Age-Dependent Measures

Research on individual differences between humans has a history that dates from the 19th-century beginnings of psychology as the scientific study of behaviour. A longstanding belief in the more recent discipline of gerontology is that older people

Figure 10.3 HYPOTHETICAL SCORES ON A MEASURE BY INDIVIDUALS A–C
AT DIFFERENT AGES

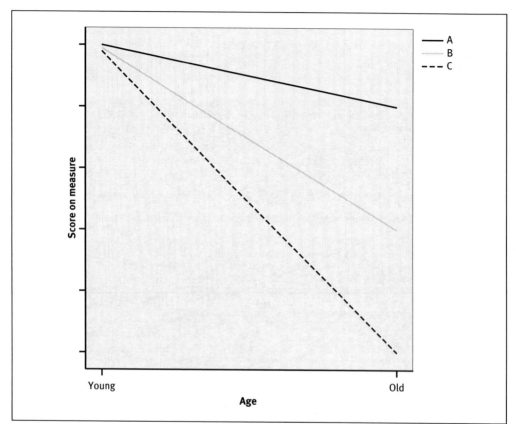

are more heterogeneous than are younger people (Baltes & Willis, 1977; Nelson & Dannefer, 1992). The reasons for this belief include findings of greater diversity among older than younger people on those age-dependent measures that typically decline with age (e.g., many cognitive and physical functions).

Not all measures show this trend of greater heterogeneity in later life. Schaie (1977) proposed three basic models that encapsulate the age trends studied by gerontologists. Possibly the second but certainly the third of these models anticipates a wider range of individual differences in older than younger people:

- The **stability model** assumes an absence of aging effects (e.g., on personality);
- The **irreversible decrement model** assumes ongoing and irreversible aging effects (e.g., on cellular aging);
- The **decrement with compensation model** assumes age deterioration but also the possibility for its remediation (e.g., in cognition, physical fitness).

The models discussed in this section include the irreversible decrement and decrement with compensation models. These are both **process models** that attempt to explain the reasons for individual differences in aging. Before discussion of these models, however, the section begins with a **typological model** that describes individual differences in various life domains. Also discussed in this section are life course and hierarchical models that attempt to provide integrated perspectives on individual differences in aging. The section ends with conclusions about common features of the models and implications about successful and unsuccessful aging.

Typological Models

Individual differences in aging may not be comparable across different domains of life. In fact, most researchers in gerontology conduct their research largely within the confines of a particular life domain. Birren and Renner (1977) described three domains: biological aging, psychological aging, and social aging.

Biological aging encompasses the vital life-limiting organ systems. Individuals with a biological age older than their chronological age are likely have a shorter remaining life expectancy than their chronological age peers. Goffaux and colleagues (2005) confirmed this prediction using a biological age index developed with healthy volunteers aged 70 to 95 years. This index proved to be a stronger predictor than chronological age of three-year mortality and functional outcomes after first coronary artery bypass grafting surgery. However, a problem with measures of biological aging identified by Costa and McCrae (1980a) is that many include items indicative of disease in addition to age-dependent measures. Consequently, the authenticity of findings on the prediction of health outcomes is suspect if the biological age measures include content related to disease (Mitnitski, Graham, Mogilner, & Rockwood, 2002).

Psychological aging refers to the adaptive capabilities of individuals to deal with a changing environment compared with chronological age peers. It includes learning, memory, intelligence, motivations and emotions, and it clearly depends on the conditions of the cardiovascular and central nervous systems. The concept of psychological aging has limitations similar to those of functional age as discussed in Chapter 7 on Cognitive and Physical Performance.

Social aging refers to roles and social habits. Because many social expectations are normative with age, it is reasonable to ask whether a given individual behaves socially in ways that are younger, similar, or older than chronological age peers. Cultural forces can also augment late-life diversity. The life paths of aging people may be more diverse if culture is in transition because of ethnic mixing, changing population structures, and shifting values. Modern Western societies tolerate and encourage individuality, and are relatively open to intercultural and interethnic exchanges. For example, Meintel and Perissini (1993) showed that aged migrant women who lived for many years in Montreal could decide to live alone, in conformity with dominant values of modernity in Canadian urban society, but against norms and values of their own group. In addition, people today live longer and in better health than in earlier times. New social rules that emphasize activity coexist with earlier rules for an orderly disengagement of older people from active living. Consequently, the context of modernity provides a *bouillon de culture* that may accentuate variations between people as they age, giving them both new and old paths to choose from in later life.

Process Models

Irreversible Decrement Irreversible decrement models need not assume a rate of aging that is constant across all members within a species. The effects of caloric restriction provide an example. Researchers in the 1930s restricted young rats' caloric intake by 25–40 percent from weaning on, while maintaining essential nutrients. The rats lived longer, looked younger, and retained abilities longer (McCay & Crowell, 1934). Studies of other species, including non-human primates, found similar effects (Roberts et al., 2001). One interpretation of these findings is that caloric restriction postpones or prevents pathological deterioration in the cardiovascular, renal, and central nervous systems (Lee et al., 2001). Salthouse (1990) likened the distinction between the postponement of pathology and effects on rate of aging to peeling an onion: with all the layers of pathology accounted for, would aging explain any further variability at all?

Decrement with Compensation The decrement with compensation model suggests that although aging effects have adverse implications for functional capability, compensatory mechanisms may postpone or reduce the amount of decrement. Consequently, the extent of variation in individual differences in an older cohort includes differences present at a younger age plus further variation contingent upon the effectiveness of the compensatory mechanisms adopted by different people within the cohort.

Bäckman and Dixon (1992) provide an integrated theory of compensation. They suggest that the origins of compensation arise from a mismatch between demands and skill. Given expectations that are compatible with performance at younger ages, people may change behaviour or expectations.

First, a person can compensate by attempting to raise the level of skill to match the demand. Possible mechanisms include increased practice, the use of latent aspects of skill, or finding an alternative skill. Stones and Kozma (1995) illustrate these three forms of compensation with examples from sport. Martina Navratilova humiliated upcoming tennis star Steffi Graff in the 1987 Wimbledon final with her left-handed sliced serve to the backhand. During the off-season, Graff's coach recruited the help of a hired hand who "lay endless serves against Steffi's backhand until she could whack them back in her sleep (and while wide awake)" (Frayne, 1990:97). This extra practice enabled Graff to drill powerful backhands against Navratilova and win Wimbledon in 1988 and 1989. Prizefighter Sam Longford was well aware that "the legs go first" in aging boxers.

Consequently, he substituted the latent skill of slugging for fancy dodging and leg-work in an attempt to win fights by an early knockout. At the age of 50 in 1929, he compensated for partial blindness and wobbly legs in the simplest way: "Both my eyes were bad then but I could see a bit. So when I got in there, this fella started swingin' that left hand and I blocked it, and he swung again, and I blocked it. An' then I knocked him out." (Frayne, 1990:241). Finally, many athletes who retire from direct competition use their expertise in vocations such as coaching, management, or media activity related to sport. These people compensate by substituting alternative skills related to their former profession.

Second, aging athletes, like everyone else, may lower their expectations to meet declining performance. Even the legendary Muhammad Ali compensated in this way when fighting to regain the world heavyweight boxing championship from Leon Spinks, who was 12 years his junior, in 1978. Whereas the young Ali and his fans demanded that he win with flair and flourish, the old Ali was content simply to win.

Bäckman and Dixon (1992) made three further proposals in their theory. First, compensation occurs only when demand and skill are mismatched. Second, a person faced with such a mismatch does not necessarily engage in compensatory behavior. Third, the behaviour of an older person compensating for declining skill may be different from that of a younger person with intact skill. Salthouse (1984) provided examples of such behavioural differences between younger and older typists even when performing at comparable levels of skill: younger typists had greater manual dexterity than older typists, but the latter used short-term memory more effectively.

Baltes and Baltes (1990) proposed an elaboration of the decrement with compensation model that also included the hypothesis of selective optimization. They suggested that older people restrict their lives to fewer domains of functioning because of age decrements in adaptive capabilities. Within their high-priority domains, they attempt to optimize those capabilities that can enrich and augment the chosen life course. Compensation then occurs if behavioural capabilities fall below a level required for adequate functioning.

Life Course Models   Schroots (1995) proposed a **differential aging** model that provides a metaphor for theory development distinct from gerontological models of the aged, age, or aging, which respectively focus upon late life, age differences, and age change. The differential aging model uses an individual difference metaphor that is consistent with other models that distinguish age-intrinsic processes from the effects of long-term disuse, age-correlated illness, and terminal change (Birren & Cunningham, 1985). These models attribute increasing heterogeneity with age to the multiplicity of processes that can affect functioning in older people.

Schroots's structural model, termed the **branching model**, traces critical transitions in personal life histories. At certain branch points (or choice points) throughout the lifespan, the choice of one alternative over another opens some life paths and closes others, thus affecting subsequent branching. Similarly,

Giddens (1991:243) talks about "fateful moments, . . . at which consequential decisions have to be made or courses of action initiated."

The model anticipates increasing heterogeneity with age because the number of states that a person could occupy increases with age. Limitations to life course models include the use of biographical data in attempts to substantiate the models. Most scientific models attempt to predict contemporaneous or future events. Biographical data use present recollections about the past to explain the present, which raises questions about selective bias in memory and interpretation.

Hierarchical Models **Types of aging models** discriminate between effects of different origin. A change attributable to age alone is an **age-intrinsic effect**; normative effects, and effects with other causes are **age extrinsic** (e.g., disease, disability, lifestyle). Such models assume a hierarchical framework to describe the cumulative effects of age intrinsic and extrinsic factors. They also maintain consistency with an enduring preoccupation in gerontology to separate aging effects from normative influences and life course differences that affect capabilities as people age.

The hierarchical model described by Stones and colleagues (1990) includes the three levels shown in Table 10.1. **Primary aging** includes two levels, termed by Rowe and Kahn (1987) successful and **usual aging**. Successful aging refers to changes owing only to the passage of time (i.e., age-intrinsic changes). Usual aging refers to non-pathological changes commonly observed within a population but brought about by lifestyle or life situation. Examples include the loss in endurance fitness with age, which Smith and Gilligan (1983) estimated to be 50 percent because of age and 50 percent because of disuse of endurance capabilities. The second level, **secondary aging**, refers to changes because of chronic disease. The third level, **tertiary aging**, refers to a dramatic decrease in functional capability as a person approaches death (i.e., called *terminal drop*).

Table 10.1 **THE TYPES OF AGING MODEL**

Classification	Sub-classification	Also known as	Influences
Primary aging	Successful aging	Healthy aging;	Passage of time
	Usual aging	well aging	Life events, lifestyle
Secondary aging			Disease/disability
Tertiary aging		Terminal drop	Impending mortality

Source: Adapted from M.J. Stones, A. Kozma, & T.E. Hannah. (1990). Measurement of individual differences in aging: The distinction between usual and successful aging. In M.L. Howe, M.J. Stones, & C.J. Brainerd (Eds.), *Cognitive and behavioral performance factors in atypical aging.* New York: Springer-Verlag.

This model has heuristic value because it organizes individual differences within a simple hierarchical framework. The hierarchy descends from individuals showing only age-intrinsic decrement (i.e., successfully aging according to the model), through individuals with usual aging decrements because of life course factors (e.g., life conditions, life events, lifestyle), through individuals with chronic illness and disability, to individuals close to death. Limitations to the model include a failure to take account of prior individual differences and a fuzzy separation between category boundaries in empirical paradigms.

An earlier section of this chapter discussed the relevance of individual differences earlier in life to the interpretation of later-life individual differences. The conclusions reached apply to the types of aging model. Consider first an individual difference measure relevant to the model that contains only age-dependent variables (i.e., not items on pathology). It is by no means certain that older individuals lower on the model's hierarchy would have lower scores on the measure than age peers located above them. Individual differences that predate the time of assessment could easily result in someone with chronic illness who is not fully incapacitated scoring at a higher level than someone with only age-intrinsic changes or usual aging effects *if* the person with chronic illness had a higher level of capability in earlier life. Second, even if the measure contains content on chronic pathology, a similar argument could apply to functions unaffected by that pathology (e.g., people with arthritis are likely to have scores on cognitive measures similar to those without the condition). Evidence that gifted individuals continue to perform at high levels despite chronic illness abound in the arts. Whitbourne (2001), who considered creativity in later life to be a yardstick of successful aging, described many such examples:

- Beethoven continued to compose music after becoming deaf;
- Monet continued to paint his vibrant water lilies despite cataracts that affected his visual clarity and colour perception;
- Writer William Carlos Williams produced some of his major works after suffering a stroke and major clinical depression (Whitbourne, 2001).

Clearly, chronic illness does not preclude skillful performance.

The category boundary at the top of the hierarchy—the distinction between successful and usual aging—is not easy to separate empirically. Examples include the effects of physical activity on speed of response, which many researchers consider the index of the speed of processing within the central nervous system. Spirduso (1980) reported that lifelong physical activity contributes to an apparent postponement of the age effect on reaction time. She found that older racquet sport players had reaction times comparable to those of younger racquet sport players and faster than the reaction times of non-athletic age peers. Although such findings might suggest a slowing in cardiovascular and central nervous system aging brought about by physical activity, other authors cited the generalized effects of continued practice in sports that require fast reactions (Stones & Kozma, 1988). The former interpretation suggests an effect of physical activity on age-intrinsic change; the latter may suggest an effect of extended practice (i.e., a form of compensation) that falls under the rubric of age-extrinsic effects.

Lower down the hierarchy, the distinction between usual and secondary aging is often fuzzier than implied by the model. Clinical diagnosis involves a dichotomous decision that classifies an individual either as exhibiting a pathological condition or as normal. However, clinical symptoms precede diagnosis, sometimes by a considerable time. Reisberg, Ferris, deLeon, and Crook (1982) illustrated both a continuum of cognitive decline and a diagnostic dichotomy in their stage model of Alzheimer's disease. The early stages include forgetfulness and confusion that, in the majority of cases, are insufficient in scope and severity to meet the criteria required for a diagnosis of Alzheimer's disease. If given an assessment as part of a research project on successful aging, such an individual ought to score low on cognitive testing but fall within the classification scheme as a usually aging person (i.e., assuming the absence of other chronic disease). Only if cognitive decline is moderate rather than mild are a majority of those afflicted diagnosed with Alzheimer's disease. Consequently, individuals classified within the usual aging category include those without pathology and those with early but undiagnosed pathology. Similar considerations apply to individual differences in the emotive domain, where older individuals with symptoms of depression may not have a depression diagnosis because the symptom profile in later life does not accord closely with current diagnostic criteria (U.S. Department of Health and Social Services, 1999).

Conclusions

The models discussed in this section encompass perspectives on aging ranging from the biological to the anthropological. They all share common features of attempting to account for individual differences in older cohorts while differentiating aging effects from those of disease. The models all have limitations, and applications of the models are also subject to limitations in inference imposed by research design.

Another assumption made by all the models is that individual differences become more heterogeneous as people age. Individuals at both extremes of the distributions lie outside an expected range. However, belonging to these extreme subcategories does not necessarily coincide with an attribution of successful or unsuccessful aging (Salthouse, 1990). The latter connotations depend, among other factors, on the variable under consideration and value judgments by the person assigning the labels.

Perhaps the least controversial inference about successful aging within the contexts of the models described is that

- *People successfully aging include those for whom detrimental age changes on important age-dependent variables are lower than normatively expected.*

This definition makes neither assumptions about the sources of age change (e.g., intrinsic aging, disuse, disease) nor value judgments about those variables considered important. Baltes and Baltes (1990) suggest that older people select and optimize important variables for personal reasons. However, what this inference accomplishes is to locate the concept of successful aging within a framework receptive to distributions of age changes. An implication is that within the scope of Schaie's (1977) three models of stability, irreversible decrement, and decrement with compensation, variables in the first category (i.e., variables not expected to change with age) are not viable indicators of successful aging.

Individual Differences Related to Later-Life Health and Well-Being

This section of the chapter includes discussion of other models and indicators that carry the label of successful aging. Despite its popularity, current usage of the term needs further explanation for three main reasons. First, different researchers use different values and criteria to identify individuals thought to be aging successfully. Values relate to the choice of variables to demarcate the concept, and criteria to the cut-off levels on those variables. Findings reviewed in this section will show considerable disarray in both models and indicators, although there is a greater consensus with regard to influences. Consequently, the term successful aging does not convey a consistent meaning across studies.

A second issue concerns pejorative connotations attached to the latent pole of the concept (i.e., unsuccessful aging). There is a danger that individuals already stigmatized as old might be subject to double stigmatization as old and unsuccessful. Old people are often devalued socially (Dowd, 1980b). A health promotion model that assigns to individuals some responsibility for their own health and well-being (Wallace, 2000) might unfairly stigmatize the "unsuccessful" for deficiencies not of their own making. In contrast, Rowe and Kahn (1998), in the foreword to their book, emphasize the positive aspect of aging. They point out that before their 1987 *Science* article there was a persistent preoccupation in gerontology with disease and disability, and a serious underestimation of the positive implications of lifestyle and psychological resources for the well-being of older people. Their use of the term *successful* to correct these imbalances was intentional and probably appropriate to the time.

Third, the models and associated measures discussed in this section, unlike those described in the preceding section, include variables that are not expected to show regular changes with age but that have relevance to health and well-being.

The use of indicators without age dependency has several implications:

- Such indicators have no direct relevance to aging as a process, with any age changes assumed to arise because of age-extrinsic effects;
- The distributions on the measures are important only with respect to the current levels of the scores (e.g., individual differences that pertain to earlier life have only secondary interpretative significance);
- Longitudinal data are unnecessary (unless the measurement is of change scores);
- The critical criteria for the inclusion of variables include relevance to health and well-being.

These implications suggest that the use of the term *aging* to describe the concept measured by the indicators is probably a misnomer. Aging refers to a temporal process, whereas the indicators measure the state or condition of an individual at a given time. A more appropriate term to describe individuals with favourable scores is that they have successfully *aged*, irrespective of their chronological age at the time of measurement. The following definition is consistent with a distinction between the process (aging) and the person's (i.e., ager's) state with respect to success in later life:

- *Successful agers include individuals with favourable scores on variables considered important to health and well-being.*

This definition makes neither *a priori* assumptions about those variables considered important to health and well-being nor assumptions that individuals with unfavourable scores are poorly adapted. Baltes and Baltes (1990) argue that adaptation in later life includes selecting activity domains for continued engagement or disengagement. These choices are influenced by the individual's values, which may or may not coincide with variables chosen by a researcher (which often depend on the emphasis of the researcher's academic discipline). Models may emphasize mental well-being physical health and autonomy; and mixed models include measures from multiple life domains.

Mental Well-Being Models

Neugarten, Havighurst, and Tobin (1961) advocated the measurement of life satisfaction to index successful aging. Their model included components of zest versus apathy, resolution and fortitude, congruence between desired and achieved goals, self-concept, and mood tone. They developed multiple measures to assess these constructs. Although these measures had reasonable reliability when measured by internal consistency, subsequent research provided very limited support for the model and measures (Kozma, Stones & McNeil, 1991). Several studies failed to replicate the five-component structure of the model. The measures showed only moderate correlations with each other, the internal consistencies were lower than initially reported, test-retest reliability was low, and validity estimates against related indexes were moderate.

Neugarten and colleagues reported that their measure related to marital status and socio-economic status but not to age. The absence of age dependency suggests that their indexes measure successful agers rather than aging.

Ryff's (1989) model includes six components: self-acceptance, positive relationships with others, autonomy, environmental mastery, purpose in life, and personal growth. Although Ryff and Keyes (1995) replicated this structure of the Scales of Psychological Well-Being using a nationally representative sample with ages of 25 years and older, other research failed to provide such replication. Kafka and Kozma (2002) found three components in Ryff's measure, none of which overlapped with the six components that Ryff identified.

Failures to replicate the structure of complex scales are common in psy-chometric research. The reason is that a structure developed with data from a given sample may not apply to samples with other characteristics. The more complex the structure, the more frequent are failures of replication. Only scales with simple structures and based on enduring psychometric models tend to show structural stability regardless of sampling (e.g., the two-component Affect Balance Scale; Bradburn, 1969). Thus, models associated with complex scales may be of uncertain validity.

Other models of mental well-being derived from qualitative research. Fisher (1992) interviewed 19 older individuals with the aim to differentiate between life satisfaction and successful aging. The findings suggest that life satisfaction refers to past expectations and current circumstances, whereas successful aging refers to coping and maintaining a positive attitude in later life. Knight (1999) found that 14 older people nominated by their age peers as examples of suc-cessful agers also considered a positive attitude to be the predominant attribute of successful aging. Some respondents considered a positive attitude to be a yardstick of successful aging regardless of physical health status.

Health and Autonomy Models

Roos and Havens (1991) defined a favourable profile solely in terms of health and functional capability. They measured successful agers by residence in com-munity settings (as opposed to a long-term care home), low home-care usage, self-rated health as better than "fair," adequacy in activities of daily living and instrumental activities of daily living, and absence of cognitive impairment. Findings from the Manitoba longitudinal study indicated that 20 percent of a sample of more than 3500 people aged 65 to 84 satisfied these criteria. Longitudinal risks included poor prior health, widowhood, and compromised cognition.

Other researchers measured health using perceived health measures. Findings with these measures suggest that perceived health is predictive of mor-tality, disease, recovery from disease, and mental well-being (Benyamini, Idler, Leventhal, & Leventhal, 2000). Findings in Chapter 1 show that perceived health and worries about health show no age dependency.

Mixed Models

Mixed models include variables relevant to mental well-being, psychological processes, health and autonomy, and social interaction. The most influential of the mixed models is that of Rowe and Kahn (1987; 1998). This model contains three components: a low risk of disease and disability; high mental and physical func-tions; and active engagement with life. Their 1998 book reviews a multiplicity of findings suggesting practical ways for individuals to become better agers and the benefits of doing so.

Limitations of this model include the absence of an overall measure of the components. This lack led to low consensus about operational definitions and a proliferation of different operational measures (Montross et al., 2006). Nevertheless, a review of recent studies found that a mean of approximately one-third of individuals aged over 60 years satisfied criteria for successful agers, and that the most frequent predictors of unfavourable classifications included age, smoking, disability, arthritis, and diabetes (Depp & Jeste, 2006). Other predictors included physical activity, social contacts, perceived health, depression, and cognitive variability.

There are also concerns about the coherence of the components. In a recent study of more than 600 centenarians, those with the best health status also showed good mental and physical functions; however, even the healthiest were disengaged from life (Motta, Bennati, Ferlito, Malaguarnera, and Motta, 2005). It would appear that for centenarians engagement in life was not necessary to maintain health and functional capabilities.

Ouaknine, Csank, and Stones (1997) described a model and measure of successful agers. The model in Figure 10.4 includes multiple life domains subsequently used in planning by the International Federation of Aging (IFA). The measure that they termed the Well Aging Assessment Battery (WAAB) used published indexes to assess social support, positive and negative aspects of mental health, health attitudes and behavior, nutrition, activities, cognitive and psychomotor functioning, metamemory, autobiographical memory, balance, planning

Figure 10.4 THE INTERNATIONAL FEDERATION OF AGING'S MODEL OF VITAL AGING

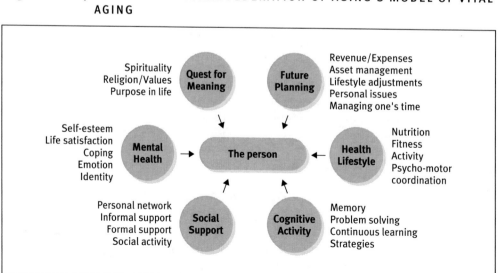

Source: L. Ouaknine, P. Csank, & M.J. Stones. (1997). *The fulfillment of well-aging: A preventative health care intervention program for seniors*. Paper presented to the International Federation on Aging, Durban, South Africa.

for the future, and physical ill-health. The WAAB took considerable time to complete, was available only with interviewer facilitation, and appropriate only for individuals without cognitive impairment. Analyses to reduce the length of the battery eventually resulted in the development of the Successful Aging Quiz (SAQ; <http://successfulaging.ca>).

The SAQ is a 70-item self-administered measure of multiple domains. Knight (2005) carried out an extensive psychometric evaluation of the SAQ that included four separate studies. The findings showed comparability across a paper-and-pencil version, computerized assessment, and interviewer assessment. There were four components in the SAQ: (1) negative orientation; (2) positive orientation; (3) activity; and (4) health. These components were reliable in terms of both internal consistency and stability over time. The measure showed a valid discrimination between hospital and active community residents, with some items sensitive to changes in status over time. An Internet version of the SAQ also provided support for the four-component structure.

Other studies examined the perceptions of older people about their own successful aging compared with those from mixed models. The findings suggest that most people aged over 60 years rate themselves as aging successfully (Montross et al., 2006; Phela, Anderson, LaCroix, & Larsen, 2004).

CHAPTER SUMMARY

Key ideas to remember from this chapter:

- The prototypes for current models of successful aging date from just after World War II. The first known use of the term *successful aging* was in 1961, but after the late 1980s interest grew dramatically.

- Aging refers to "regular changes that occur in mature genetically representative organisms living under representative conditions as they advance in chronological age."

- The terms "successful" and "unsuccessful" connote values attached to individual differences. The distribution of such differences approximates a normal distribution on many variables.

- The terms *successful aging* and *unsuccessful aging* are often used to refer to age change scores either observed directly or inferred (often incorrectly) from cross-sectional data. The extremes on such a distribution do not necessarily coincide with successful and unsuccessful aging.

- Age changes may reflect the effects of an aging process, the effects of disease, and other influences.

- Models of individual differences on age-dependent variables refer to types of variable (biological, psychological, social), underlying process (irreversible decrement, aging with compensation), and the life course. A hierarchical model distinguishes between age-intrinsic changes, the effects of lifestyle and life events, disease, and impending mortality.

- A definition of successful aging is as follows: People successfully aging include those for whom detrimental age changes on important age-dependent variables are lower than normatively expected.
- Other models include measures that do not show regular age changes. These models include selection of measures based on relevance to health and well-being.
- Such models identify successful agers rather than successful aging. Successful agers include individuals with favourable scores on variables considered important to health and well-being.
- Models of successful agers include mental health, health and autonomy, and mixed models. The latter include measures of multiple life domains.
- Canadian mixed models include self-assessment using the Internet.
- Many authors have criticized the concept of successful aging/agers for a lack of consensus in definition. However, there is reasonable agreement about predictors.

Key Terms

successful aging **(p. 250)**
age-dependent measures **(p. 250)**
normal distribution **(p. 252)**
stability model **(p. 256)**
irreversible decrement model **(p. 256)**
decrement with compensation model **(p. 256)**
process models **(p. 257)**
typological models **(p. 257)**
biological aging **(p. 257)**
psychological aging **(p. 257)**
social aging **(p. 257)**

life course model **(p. 259)**
differential aging **(p. 259)**
branching model **(p. 259)**
hierarchical model **(p. 260)**
types of aging model **(p. 260)**
age-intrinsic effects **(p. 260)**
age-extrinsic effects **(p. 260)**
primary aging **(p. 260)**
usual aging **(p. 260)**
secondary aging **(p. 260)**
tertiary aging **(p. 260)**

Study Questions

1. Describe the history of the successful aging concept.
2. Discuss criticisms of the successful aging concept.
3. Does a change score (i.e., the difference in scores from the same person at different times of measurement) unequivocally measure changes because of age? Give evidence.
4. Comment on potential problems with the hierarchical model of successful aging.

5. Can we estimate successful aging from cross-sectional data? Give evidence.

6. Define successful aging and successful agers. Justify your answer.

SUGGESTED READINGS

Bäckman, L., & Dixon, R.A. (1992). Psychological compensation: A theoretical framework. *Psychological Review 112*, 259–283.

Almeida, O.P., Norman, P., Hankey, G., Jamrozik, K., & Flicker, L. (2006). Successful mental health aging: Results from a longitudinal study of older Australian men. *American Journal of Geriatric Psychiatry 14*, 27–35.

Motta, M., Bennati, E., Ferlito, L., Malaguarnera, M., & Motta, L. (2005) Successful aging in centenarians: Myths and realities. *Archives of Gerontology and Geriatrics, 40*, 241–251.

Peel, N.M., McLure R.J., & Barrett, H.P. (2005). Behavioral determinants of healthy aging. *American Journal of Preventive Medicine, 28*, 298–304.

Rowe, J.W., & Kahn, R.L. (1998) *Successful aging.* New York: Dell Publishing.

Chapter 11

FAMILIES AND AGING

Learning Objectives

In this chapter, you will learn about

- Difficulties in defining families.
- Common myths about the family lives of elderly Canadians, past and present.
- How the longevity revolution has affected Canadian families.
- The structure of aging Canadian families, especially regarding marital status and living arrangements.
- Issues concerning mid-life families, including "sandwiching," the departure of grown children from the family residence, and the intergenerational stake.

- The exchange relationships between elderly parents and their children and the issue of private transfers across generations.
- Grandparents and characteristics of the grandparent–grandchild relationship.
- Aspects of the life course transition to widowhood, an especially common transition for older women.
- Characteristics of sibling relationships in later life.
- Conflict and abuse in aging families.

Introduction

The family is a key social institution in all societies, and Canada is no exception. Within gerontology, there has been a substantial amount of research on families—proportionately more than in the standard social science disciplines—in part because of a focus on caregiving (dealt with in detail in the next chapter). It is families who, by and large, do the caregiving. However, this chapter does not focus on caregiving. It has already been pointed out that the majority of older adults in Canada are quite healthy and require little, if any, care. In this chapter, the focus is on the overall characteristics of the family structure and family relationships of Canadian seniors. The possibility and reality of age-related health decline and its effects on family members will not be ignored, but these are not the major concerns of this chapter.

In keeping with the life course perspective introduced in Chapter 3, a distinction is made between mid-life families and older families. Of course, mid-life families will eventually become old families as time goes by, and mid-life families will often interact with the members of old families. Considerable attention will be paid to the life course perspective of linked lives, especially regarding intergenerational relationships.

What Does Family Mean?

Most of us are part of a family; the definition of what a family is seems self-evident. However, it is not easy to capture, for empirical purposes, what a family is or is not. On one level, the standard definition of family as a "group of people related by blood, marriage, or adoption" seems straightforward enough. The difficulty lies in drawing the boundary between families. If you are a 20-year-old woman living with your brother and your parents, is this four-person unit your family? What about your aunts, uncles, and cousins? What about your grandparents? Are you all one big family? What about the siblings of your biological aunt's husband—are they included in your family? Your cousin's common-law husband? Your recently divorced uncle's second wife and her grown-up children?

Statistics Canada has been engaged over many years in efforts to define the term *family* (see Table 11.1). These definitions are important in that many researchers depend on them for their studies and policy-makers and politicians use them in formulating family and related policies. In devising its definitions, Statistics Canada reflects normative understandings of family. In Canadian society, we tend to divide families into nuclear and extended forms. The **nuclear family** is a co-residing unit of parent(s) and dependent children. We further distinguish nuclear families into two types: the family of orientation and the family of procreation. The **family of orientation** is the family into which a person is born (or adopted), and typically consists of co-residing parents (or a lone parent) and dependent children. The **family of procreation** is the family formed when an individual marries (or lives common-law) and has children of his or her own (or adopts them); it typically consists of a co-residing couple (or lone parent) with dependent children.

In Canada, it is assumed that these two families live in different households—that is, when you marry and have children, you no longer live with your parents. This common understanding is reflected in the Statistics Canada definition of **census family**. So, on growing up, an individual moves from one census family in which he or she is a dependent child to another census family in which he or she is part of a couple and likely has dependent children. Since an individual can only be a member of one census family at a given point in time, this normative understanding of family life means that family membership changes over time—as a result of the requirement that nuclear family members must co-reside and must live in the same household.

The **extended family** consists of family members who do not co-reside. Thus, when you grow up and no longer live with your parents, they move from being members of your nuclear family to being members of your extended family. Other non–co-resident kin are also members of your extended family, for example, your married brother and his wife and children. Individuals and families differ in terms of where the line is drawn between kin and non-kin. For example, some will include third cousins as part of their extended family; others will adopt a narrower definition of the extended family.

One's family/household status can become very complicated. Let us follow a hypothetical case of a female, using the family and household definitions in Table 11.1:

1. She grows up with her parents and sister (census family).
2. At 20 years of age, she moves out to live with a platonic friend (non-family household).
3. At 22 years of age, she and her sister live together (economic family, non-family household).
4. At 23 years of age, she lives alone (non-family household).
5. At 24 years of age, she goes back to live with her parents (census family).
6. At 25 years of age, she marries and lives with her husband (census family).
7. At 28 years of age, she divorces and goes back to live with her parents (economic family, family household).
8. At 29 years of age, she lives with her grandmother after her grandfather dies (economic family, non-family household).

This is an extreme example, but it serves to highlight the complexities of categorizing people as members of families/households (or not). Part of the complication stems from our normative practice of making co-residency a defining characteristic of families, that is, of privileging the nuclear family form over the extended family form. This practice has implications for older adults. As long as an older person is married, he or she is considered part of a

Table 11.1 DEFINITIONS OF FAMILY AND HOUSEHOLD

Category	Definition
Census family	A married couple (with or without children of either or both spouses), a couple living common-law (with or without children of either or both partners) or a lone parent of any marital status, with at least one child living in the same dwelling. A couple living common-law may be of opposite or same sex. "Children" in a census family include grandchildren living with their grandparent(s) but with no parents present.
Economic family	Two or more persons who are related to each other by blood, marriage, common-law, or adoption, living in the same household.
Private household	A person or a group of persons (other than foreign residents) who occupy a private dwelling and do not have a usual place of residence elsewhere in Canada.
Family household	A one-family household consists of a single family (e.g., a couple with or without children). A multiple-family household is made up of two or more families occupying the same dwelling.
Non-family household	A non-family household consists either of one person living alone or of two or more persons who share a dwelling, but do not constitute a family (e.g., a couple with or without children).

Source: Statistics Canada, 2001 Census Dictionary. Retrieved from http://www12.statcan.ca/english/census01/Products/Reference/dict/hou014.htm

(census) family—but *not* part of the family of his or her ever-married adult children, unless they live together; in that case, we have a family household. If a woman becomes widowed and she and her granddaughter then co-reside—as in the hypothetical case above—she becomes a family member again, but in a non-family household.

When we consider the family lives of older adults, we need to break down the assumed connection between families and households, between family membership and co-residency. Connidis (2001) emphasizes that nearly all older adults in Canada are family members, regardless of household living arrangements. The majority of elderly Canadians do not live with their children or other family members. However, they are clearly enmeshed in the lives of their children, grandchildren, siblings, and other family members. Separate residence does not mean family estrangement. Rather, separate residence means we have to examine family ties among older Canadian adults with a lens that does not focus only on nuclear families.

Myths about the Family Lives of Older Persons in the Past

It is commonly thought that the family life of older persons was better in the past. We have images of a golden past in which Grandma and Grandpa's house was the hub of a large, happy, and harmonious family of children and grandchildren. The house, although not lavish by today's standards, was big, to accommodate the large and ever-growing family. This image also serves as a standard by which to gauge today's families—which do not measure up, purportedly abandoning their elderly family members in the embrace of materialist consumption.

However, there is something very wrong with our picture of the past. It does not take into account the cruel demographics of life in past generations. Infant and child mortality rates were high, so that the loss of young children was not uncommon. For example, although Canadian women born in 1860 bore, on average, 4.9 children, only 3.2 survived to the age of 20 years (Gee, 1990). Maternal mortality was also high, resulting in the loss of the mother/wife (Guyer, Freedman, Strobino & Sondik, 2000). Life expectancy at birth in the 19th century was well below 60 years, meaning that proportionately few people survived to old age. These mortality conditions meant that the odds of even three generations of a family being alive at the same time were quite low.

The increasing likelihood of a child having at least one parent alive when that child is aged 40, 50, and 60 years is shown in Table 11.2, which provides a vivid portrayal of the longevity revolution. More than half of Canadians born in 1860 were orphans by the time they were aged 40 years; of those born in 1960, 82 percent still had at least one parent alive when they were aged 40 years (in 2000). Among the birth cohort of 1960, nearly one-quarter can expect to have at least one parent alive when they are aged 60 years (in the year 2020); among the cohort of those born 100 years earlier, only 2 percent would have had a parent alive when they were aged 60 years. In addition, women born in the middle of the 19th century were, on average, widowed before their youngest child left home (Gee, 1986).

Table 11.2   **PERCENTAGE OF PERSONS WITH AT LEAST ONE PARENT ALIVE AT AGES 40, 50 AND 60 YEARS: CANADA, PERSONS BORN IN 1860 AND 1960**

AGE	PERSONS BORN IN:	
	1860	1960
40	42%	82%
50	16%	60%
60	2%	23%

Source: Adapted from E.M. Gee. (1990). Demographic change and intergenerational relations in Canadian families. *Canadian Public Policy 16*, 192.

Our image of the past contains the assumption that earlier Canadian families lived in extended (not nuclear) families. Apart from the fact that mortality made this impossible for many families, there is no evidence that earlier generations lived in multi-generational families, even if they could. The Western European family ideal—which came to Canada with the first European settlers—was nuclear family living (Laslett, 1979). Anglophone Canada clearly endorsed this ideal. Even in pre-Confederation Newfoundland (long considered the most traditional society in English-speaking North America), research reveals that extended multi-generational households were few; when they did exist, it was due to dire economic need or situations in which seniors assisted younger family members (McDaniel & Lewis, 1998). In Quebec, on the other hand, there is some evidence of the ideal and the existence of the **stem family**. In the stem family, one son (not necessarily the eldest) remains at the parental home, bringing in a wife and, later, children. Even so, most traditional Quebec families lived as nuclear units.

In traditional First Nations societies, diverse family patterns existed with differing kinship systems—often considerably more complex than those of Western European origin. Overall, these more collectivist-oriented societies preferred multi-generational living arrangements (Dunning, 1959). However, high mortality (particularly in the post-contact period, when infectious diseases brought here by European groups killed many natives, who lacked immunity) meant that most people lived in nuclear or nuclear-type units. Among the traditional Inuit, the few individuals who did live to old age would, when too frail to travel with the group, be left outside to die. In such cases, cultural values emphasized the interests of the group/collectivity over the interests of individuals.

In general, we can conclude that "(t)he great extended families that became part of the folklore of modern industrial society were rarely in existence" (Hareven, 1992:7) and that most of our ancestors "remained poor, died young, and lived out their lives in nuclear families" (McDaniel & Tepperman, 2000).

Another image of the past relates to the treatment and status of the aged in earlier times. The image is one of older persons of the past being venerated, honoured, and well cared for by their children. This is usually contrasted with their treatment today, which is often characterized as one of disrespect and abandonment. The historical evidence, however, suggests that, in the past, Western countries did not revere their elders and that wealth played a large part in the status and treatment of the aged.

Hanawalt's (1986) research on peasants in medieval England reveals much about pre-modern Western families and intergenerational relations. She finds considerable evidence of tension between aged parents, when they survived to older age, and their children, with adult children wanting to gain control of family resources and older parents desirous of retaining control while being assured of care if they needed it. Contracts and wills were established if parents were unsure of receiving care from their families, with the outcomes of such negotiations dependent upon the wealth of the aged. If they had land and goods, they could negotiate with kin (or non-kin) for their care. If they lacked economic resources, they could come to depend on private charity. Similarly in Canada, Snell (1992) finds that maintenance agreements were used in an attempt by older people to ensure economic security in later life.

Most people in pre-industrial and early industrial times lacked property and wealth; "ageing was, for most people, a time of pauperism, degradation and dependency" (Victor, 1994: 73). If seniors could work for pay, the work was low-waged, heavy, and irregular; if they could not work, most families lacked the economic ability to support them. The response in England was to establish poor houses (the Elizabethan Poor Laws), the beginning of state-sponsored support for the old. There is no evidence that state financial assistance for older adults decreased family ties or weakened the family (Quadagno, 1982); indeed, it is more likely that state support for the aged eased intergenerational tensions and reduced feelings of guilt in many who simply could not financially assist their elderly parent(s).

We can conclude that myths of the past over-idealize earlier families. However, a widespread belief in the happy and large multi-generational family of the past, in which elders were treasured and well cared for, persists. Bengtson, Rosenthal, and Burton (1996) identify this disjuncture between everyday belief and scientific evidence as one of the paradoxes about families and aging. There are several reasons for this disjuncture, which parallel the more general "crisis in the family" view that has received considerable media attention. One reason is the rise of the conservative family values movement, with its agenda of a return to a more rigidly gendered society, back to "when girls were girls and men were men" and "we didn't need no welfare state" (lines taken from "Those Were the Days," sung by Archie and Edith Bunker in the TV show *All in the Family*). A less political reason for over-idealizing past families lies in a confusion between the definitions of households and families. If we view family life as occurring only within the confines of the nuclear family residing in a single household, we miss much of what goes on across generations in families.

We now move away from myths of families past to examine contemporary family life for middle-aged and elderly individuals. We begin with structural dimensions, such as marital status and living arrangements, and then move to family ties—that is, the relationships among members of aging families. However, the distinction between structure and ties is somewhat artificial; they are interrelated in the same way that form and content are intertwined. Thus, we will go back and forth between family structure and family interrelationships/ties in the following discussions.

The Structure of Aging Families

Marital Status

We first look at the marital status of the older Canadian population (Table 11.3). Marital status is important; for example, research shows that married seniors are healthier and live longer than their non-married age peers; widows are poorer than elderly married women; separated and divorced elderly persons do not fare as well as the widowed in terms of quality of life, economic status, and social support (Martin-Matthews, 1991; National Advisory Council on Aging, 1994); and unmarried seniors, especially women, are more likely to be institutionalized (Gee, 1995). While there is diversity within each marital status grouping (for example, some widows are rich), marital status remains an important determinant of quality of life in the later years. As can be seen in Table 11.3, it is not possible to talk about marital status without considering gender. Older men are more likely to be married than older women, at all ages—even at 90 years and over. For both groups, advanced age brings less likelihood of marriage and greater likelihood of widowhood.

The difference in the marital status of men and women lies in the differential likelihood of becoming widowed. By age 75, just over 60 percent of women are widowed, making widowhood for women an expectable life event. This gender difference is the combined function of women's greater life expectancy and of the fact that husbands are typically older than their wives. In addition, men are more likely than women to remarry after being either widowed or divorced. This difference in remarriage probability results from a set of factors, chief among them demographic reality: there are not many unmarried older men for widowed women to marry, whereas widowed men have a wide choice of unmarried women. Related to this are sexist social norms that allow older men to marry women who may be quite a bit younger than they are but do not see the converse as appropriate.

There is also some evidence that older widows are less likely to want to remarry than are widowers (Davidson, 2001). In one study, more than half of widows were strongly opposed to the idea of remarrying (Talbott, 1998). Canadian research shows that different factors predict remarriage for widows and widowers; for example, remarriage is positively associated with education among men but not among women, and the presence of children has a negative impact on widow remarriage but not on widower remarriage (Wu, 1995).

As shown in Table 11.3, the marital status categories of never married and divorced are not common within the older Canadian population. Here there is no strong gender difference, although women are somewhat more likely to be in these unmarried statuses. However, it is quite likely that a higher proportion of elderly individuals in the future will be divorced. This is not because a large increase in later-life divorce is expected; rather, more people are entering old age as divorced individuals. Martin-Matthews (2000) estimates—assuming no significant change in marriage, divorce, and remarriage rates—that as many as one-half of all women who turn 65 years in 2025 will not be in a marriage. If this is the case, widowhood will become a less common marital status for older women. The group of older women to watch in the future is the separated and divorced; they enter old age with even less income than widows (Gee, 1995) (also see Chapter 14). If there is a substantial increase in divorced elderly women, the economic situation of older unattached women could worsen.

Table 11.3   MARITAL STATUS OF POPULATION AGED 65 YEARS AND OVER, IN TOTAL, BY GENDER AND AGE, CANADA, 2001

Age 65+

Marital Status[1]	Female(%)	Male (%)
Single (never married)[2]	5.87	5.62
Married[3]	44.38	75.86
Divorced[4]	6.31	5.43
Widowed[5]	43.44	13.10

Total Number of Females (65+): 2 345 537

Total Number of Males (65+): 1 795 482

Age 65–69

Marital Status/Gender	Female(%)	Male (%)
Single (never married)	5.35	5.71
Married	64.24	81.73
Divorced	9.87	7.39
Widowed	20.54	5.18

Total Number of Females (65–69): 607 599

Total Number of Males (65–69): 563 310

Age 70–74

Marital Status/Gender	Female(%)	Male (%)
Single (never married)	5.44	5.66
Married	54.59	79.26
Divorced	7.65	5.97
Widowed	32.32	9.11

Total Number of Females (70–74): 554 550

Total Number of Males (70–74): 487 460

Age 75–79

Marital Status/Gender	Female(%)	Male (%)
Single (never married)	5.65	5.66
Married	41.88	74.98
Divorced	5.35	4.49
Widowed	47.13	14.87

Total Number of Females (75–79): 554 550

Total Number of Males (75–79): 367 267

(continued)

Table 11.3 (CONTINUED)

Age 80–84

Marital Status/Gender	Female(%)	Male (%)
Single (never married)	6.04	5.33
Married	28.63	69.12
Divorced	3.64	3.13
Widowed	61.68	22.42

Total Number of Females (80–84): 376 710

Total Number of Males (80–84): 234 630

Age 85 to 89

Marital Status/Gender	Female(%)	Male (%)
Single (never married)	7.11	5.19
Married	14.98	58.96
Divorced	2.26	2.16
Widowed	75.64	33.69

Total Number of Females (85–89): 204 749

Total Number of Males (85–89): 100 208

Age 90+

Marital Status/Gender	Female(%)	Male (%)
Single (never married)	8.78	6.38
Married	6.43	43.62
Divorced	1.14	1.40
Widowed	83.65	48.60

Total Number of Females (90+): 120 113

Total Number of Males (90+): 42 607

[1]Although marital status definitions correspond to census concepts, only the categories single, married (including common-law), widowed or divorced are considered.

[2]Single persons refers to those who have never been married, or whose marriage has been annulled and who have not remarried, and who are not living common-law.

[3]Married persons (including common-law) refers to those whose husband or wife is living, unless a divorce has been obtained. Persons separated and persons living common-law are also included in this category.

[4]Divorced persons refers to those who have obtained a divorce and who have not remarried, and who do not live common-law.

[5]Widowed persons refers to those who have lost their spouse through death and who have not remarried, and who do not live common-law.

Source: Adapted from Statistics Canada website: http//www12.statcan.ca/english/census01/products/Analytic/companian/fam/livarrang.cfm

Living Arrangements

Who lives (or does not) with whom is an important dimension of family life—even though we must remember that families and households are not necessarily the same thing. Nevertheless, living arrangements are an important issue for elderly people because they are related to social support, family cohesion, economic independence, and age segregation.

Living arrangements are of course related to marital status—for example, it is rare for a married person to live alone, although this can happen in later life if one spouse is institutionalized. But there is not a one-to-one correspondence between marital status and living arrangements; depending on a number of factors, for example, a widow may live alone, with her daughter's family, with her sister, or in a nursing home. As we will see, there is considerable diversity in the living arrangements of seniors, and gender, again, plays a determining role. It is important to remember that the living arrangements of seniors are dynamic and subject to change. Change in marital status (usually widowhood) results in a change in living arrangements; similarly, declines (and improvements) in health can lead to change. Declines in health are associated with moves to institutions or to the households of relatives (Grundy, 1999; Pendry, Barrett & Victor, 1999).

Living with Spouse (Only) Approximately 60 percent of elderly men live with their wives only, in a couple household, and there is little difference between men aged 65 to 74 years and those aged 75 years and over (Table 11.4). In contrast, only 44 percent of women aged 65 to 74 years and fewer than one-quarter of women aged 75 years and over live with a husband. This gender difference is a direct function of differing rates of widowhood between men and women. It means that a majority of older men have a companion in the home and someone who can assist with instrumental activities. While there is no guarantee that these older wives will be healthy and active, much research shows that older wives do a considerable amount of caring for their husbands (see next chapter on caregiving) and that husbands tend to rely more on their wives for social support whereas wives also receive support from their children and friends (Gurung, Taylor, & Seeman 2003; Anderson, Earle & Longino, 1997). This gender difference also means that women are much more likely to experience changes in their living arrangements in later life, a fact that has implications for housing, health, and social support policies.

Living Alone Living alone is a common living arrangement for older adults, especially women—16.0 percent of Canadian men and 34.8 percent of Canadian women 65 or over and living in private households lived alone in 2001, as shown in Table 11.4. While both men and women have experienced an increase in living alone, the trend is far more pronounced for women. This trend is not unique to Canada; all Western industrialized societies have witnessed a substantial increase in living alone, especially among older women, since the end of World War

Table 11.4 **LIVING ARRANGEMENTS OF SENIORS, CANADA 2001**

Sex	Age group	Living alone	Living with spouse or partner (no children)	Living with children	Living in health-care institution	Other living arrangements[1]
Males	Total 65+	16.0	61.4	13.3	4.9	4.4
	65 to 74	14.0	64.4	15.4	2.1	4.0
	75 to 84	18.3	60.7	10.2	6.2	4.6
	85+	22.7	39.5	8.5	22.6	6.7
Females	Total 65+	34.8	35.4	12.1	9.2	8.4
	65 to 74	28.2	48.1	14.1	2.3	7.3
	75 to 84	42.8	27.7	10.8	9.6	9.2
	85+	38.5	7.2	8.4	35.4	10.6

[1]Includes living with other relatives, e.g., a niece or nephew, or with non-relatives, e.g., a lodger.
Source: Adapted from Statistics Canada website: http://www12.statcan.ca/english/census01/Products/Analytic/companion/fam/livarrang.cfm#seniors

II (Wolf, 1990). What factors account for this large increase in living alone? Undoubtedly demographic factors (mortality and fertility) are important. As shown by Wolf (1995), using data from 21 industrialized countries from 1960 to 1992, three demographic variables are important in explaining the rise of living alone among older women. One is the higher increases in female life expectancy, as discussed in Chapter 2, which mean that there is a higher ratio of women to men at older ages now than in the past. Second is declining fertility, so that elderly women have fewer children with whom to live (Gee, 1995). Third is the increased fertility of the second generation (i.e., the parents of the baby boom) so that grandparents have had to compete for space in the homes of the middle generation.

Other factors have been offered to explain the increasing trend of living alone, but there is little consensus and much debate. One long-argued explanation centres on economic feasibility. That is, the improved financial situation of seniors means they can afford to live on their own (Holden, 1988). While this explanation has intuitive appeal, Wolf (1995), in an analysis of 21 countries in North America and

Europe from 1960 to 1992, finds no relationship between living alone and economic variables, such as Gross Domestic Product and expenditures on public pensions. However, McGarry and Schoeni (2000), using U.S. Census data from 1940 to 1990, find that improved pensions and a general increase in economic status are much more important than sociodemographic factors such as decline in number of children in the increase in widows living alone. Similarly, Costa (1999) reports that pension improvements account for a large part of the increase in unmarried elderly women living alone in the United States for the same period.

Another explanation is that more seniors want to live alone because of normative change regarding privacy, independence, and individualism (Angel & Tienda, 1982). Mutchler, Burr, and Rogerson (1997) stress cultural factors but also point out that cultural variables such as ethnicity are related to economic factors (e.g., affordable housing) in determining living arrangement patterns. Other researchers have emphasized health improvements that allow older adults to live independently (Grundy, 1999; Pendry, Barrett & Victor, 1999)

Overall, we can conclude that economic, demographic, and cultural factors are all important in explaining the increase in older women's propensity to live alone, but the jury is still out regarding the relative importance of these determinants.

Multi-generational Living National estimates of multi-generational living are hard to obtain for any of the Western industrialized societies, including Canada. This is because, as we have already seen, the definitions of family and household used by statistical agencies (such as Statistics Canada) focus on nuclear living arrangements. However, the national General Social Survey asked about the grandparents' household composition. In 2001, 2.2 percent of those age 65 to 74 lived in three-generation families including spouse, child, and grandchild. (In the older age groups the sample was too small to compute percentages reliably). It should be noted that these data are conservative estimates of multi-generational living, since they exclude multi-generational living that skips a generation, such as grandchild(ren) and grandparent(s) living together and non-parental arrangements (such as an elderly woman and her niece living together). They also exclude grandparents living with a child and grandchild without a spouse. These living arrangements would fall into the category "other relatives only." Approximately 7 percent of older Canadians live with other relatives only, but we cannot be sure if they are multi-generational (such as in the examples above) or single-generational (such as two elderly sisters living together). It is probably safe to assume that at least 13 percent of Canada's elderly population lives in some kind of multi-generational living arrangement. While this is not a large percentage, it is not inconsequential either.

Ethnicity and immigration status are associated with multi-generational living in Western countries, such as Canada. Families of Asian origins—particularly immigrant families—appear to be the most likely to live in multi-generational arrangements in Canada (Gee, 1997b), the United States (Phua, Kaufman & Park, 2001; Wilmoth, 2001), and Australia (Neupert, 1997). For example, Gee (1997b) finds, on the basis of a random sample of 830 Chinese elders (mostly foreign-born) residing in Vancouver and Victoria in the mid-1990s, that approximately one-half are living in a multi-generational household. This includes both married couples and widows living with children (and often grandchildren). It is not clear whether ethnic minority families are more likely to live multi-generationally due to preference (cultural ideals), economic necessity, or both. Some empirical evidence suggests that minority ethnic group elders have more favourable attitudes towards co-residency and express a higher degree of filial responsibility (Burr & Mutchler, 1999). Neupert (1997) reports that age, gender, and marital status do not explain the higher levels of extended households among ethnic minorities and that the propensity to prefer joint living arrangements is the key factor. However, this propensity contains a mix of cultural, economic, and social factors; we do not know how economic and cultural factors may play intersecting roles.

Attitudes about multi-generational living with aging parents are related to past living arrangements. People who grew up in a multi-generational household or who lived with their parents as adults before they married have more positive attitudes to living with aging parents (Goldscheider & Lawton, 1998). Szinovacz (1997) finds that living in multi-generational households when young predisposes people to view multi-generational living positively *and* to actually bring aging parents into their homes. This research highlights a significant issue in multi-generational living arrangements—that is, who is living in whose house? Multi-generational households living in the parent's home are most likely a nuclear family household continuing into the later years, whereas multi-generational households located in the child's home are most often situations in which a daughter is providing a home for her mother, often due to the mother's care needs. Despite this crucial distinction, gerontological research has tended to assume that multi-generational living is the result of an aging parent or parents moving to a child's home, especially in the face of health declines (Grundy, 1999; Wolf & Soldo, 1988).

Research on Asian Americans shows that they are more likely than other groups both to live in their children's homes and to have adult children living in their homes (Phua, Kaufman & Park, 2001). In the case of elderly Chinese Canadians, Gee (1997b) reports that more seniors in multi-generational family settings are living in their child's home than in their own home—a reversal of the traditional Chinese pattern in which family seniors owned property and exercised economic control over their children. In 1990, Ikels reported that the majority of multi-generation families in mainland China were still living in the parents' home. With the increasing Asian-origin population in Canada, researchers may more closely study the differences between these two patterns.

Structure of Extended Families

The combination of increased longevity and decreased fertility has led to more families that have several generations alive at one time (**vertical extension**), but each generation has fewer members (**horizontal shrinkage**). Families with four and even five generations still alive are sometimes called **beanpole families** (Qualls, 1993). While such families have certainly increased, as Table 11.1 indicates, they are not as common as we sometimes think. About one-third of Americans aged 45 to 64 years are members of four-generation families (Uhlenberg, 1993; Winsborough, Bumpass, & Aquilino, 1991); the research also suggests that four-generational families will never be dominant and that five-generational families will be rare. As Rosenthal (2000:52) states: "While the beanpole family, in the sense of generational depth, is probably more common than in the past, we need to be careful about making sweeping statements about its prevalence." One limiting factor is the increased age of child-bearing. Suppose this trend continues, or even that the age at first birth remains constant. If several generations of women have their first child at, say, 35, how many generations could be alive at the same time—unless there is a huge increase in the human lifespan?

With the increase in divorce has come the formation of **reconstituted families** or **blended families**—that is, families formed by remarriage and involving children from a previous marriage. It is sometimes thought that family reconstitution is having and will have an important effect on aging families. There is some evidence that the adult children of divorce have significantly less contact with their older parents than do adult children raised in a two-parent family (Webster & Herzog, 1995). However, Shapiro (2003) finds that, when divorce occurs after the children are adults, it does not weaken the relationship between the parents and children and it can lead to increased contact especially between the mother and her children. And we must not forget that reconstituted families were not uncommon in the past, and may even have been as common as they are now—the difference being that the cause of remarriage was the death of a spouse, rather than divorce.

Mid-Life Families

Mid-life families are ones in which the household head is aged approximately 45 to 64. They can be of any number of structures, such as a married couple living alone, a married couple or lone parent living with children, a married couple with or without children living in their own home along with one of their parents. Research on mid-life families is not extensive, but we will look at three important issues.

The **sandwich generation** refers to mid-life families, especially women, who are caught in the middle between the care demands of children and the care demands of aging parents. This concept has garnered considerable media attention and is viewed as one of the negative implications of population aging. In Canada, the hugely popular book *Boom, Bust, and Echo* by economist/demographer David Foot (1996) promulgated the notion of the sandwich generation. Important Canadian studies address the issue of the prevalence of such sandwiching. Rosenthal, Martin-Matthews, and Matthews (1996; also see Penning 1995), using data from over 5000 individuals aged 35 to 64 years in 1990, distinguish between those who have the structural *potential* to be sandwiched (i.e., have a living parent, a dependent child, and a paid job) and those who *actually* have an aging parent who needs their assistance and have competing intergenerational responsibilities. They find that 35 percent of women in their late 40s and much smaller proportions of women over the age of 50 years have the structural potential for sandwiching. Among these women, the highest percentage in any group who provide assistance to a parent at least once a month is only 7 percent. Thus, actual sandwiching is not a common phenomenon. Caregiving to elderly parents tends to occur after dependent children have left the home. It is important to remember that the family members who are "caught in the middle"—although not huge in numbers—face a very difficult situation and require a range of choices and supports that currently are often non-existent. In Chapter 12, the more accurate term *serial caregiving* is discussed.

Mid-life families have experienced considerable change with regard to the presence of adult children in the home, leading to discussions of **empty nests, cluttered nests,** and **boomerang kids.** With the increased life expectancy of the 20th century, we came to expect that a married couple would have a period of time on their own after all the children had left home and before the death of one of the spouses ended the marriage. Before the 20th century this empty nest phase of life was not a reality for many couples. It was not uncommon in 18th-century Canada for a marriage to end through death before the last child had left home or shortly thereafter. However, by mid-20th century, the empty nest had become an institutionalized life stage for most mid-life couples. Early research on the empty nest was predicated on the assumption that it represented a difficult life transition, especially for mothers (Myers, 1984). Subsequent research established that the majority of women felt relieved when the children left home: freer, more independent and confident (Guttman, 1994; Helson & Wink, 1992).

In recent years, the empty nest has become increasingly cluttered. Adult children are remaining home until later ages and some adult children are returning (sometimes several times) to the parental home. As a result, rates of adult children co-resident with mid-life parents have increased in the last few decades. The Census of Canada reveals that fully 41 percent of those aged 20 to 29 lived with their parents in 2001. Among those aged 25 to 29, the figure is 19 percent for women and 29 percent for men in this age group. Mitchell, Wister and Gee (2002), using national data, find that the strongest predictor of young Canadian adults aged 25 to 34 years living at home is emotional closeness to the mother when growing up. Gee, Mitchell and Wister (2001), using a Vancouver-based sample of 1800 adult children aged 19 to 35 years, report strong ethnocultural differences; Indo-Canadians display a high propensity for adult children to live with parents, followed, in order, by Chinese Canadians, Canadians of southern European origins, and then Canadians of British origins.

As noted above, one of the factors responsible for the cluttered nest phenomenon is young adult children returning (at least once) to the parental home after they have moved out—the "boomerang kids." In 2001, about 33 percent of men and 28 percent of women aged 20 to 29 returned home at least once after initially leaving home (Statistics Canada, 2004a). Canadian research reveals that boomerang kids are not failures who have been unable to attain full adult status (Mitchell, 2000). A Vancouver-based study of 420 randomly selected families (both child and parent interviewed) reveals that boomerangers are more likely to be never married, be unemployed, and have a step-parent in the parental home (Gee, Mitchell, & Wister, 1995). Approximately one-quarter returned home for reasons of financial difficulty, but another 19 percent returned home to save money (and many indicated that they could afford to live on their own). Economic factors, then, play an important role in returning home. Diminished opportunity structures are also an important factor (Mitchell, 2000). The availability of a welcoming family may be a source of inequality among today's young adults; those who are able to return home have social and economic advantages that others lack (Mitchell & Gee, 1996b).

As with the emergence of the empty-nest phenomenon, initial common-sense speculations are that boomerang kids create stress for parents and cause family disharmony. Media images abound of selfish, lazy, immature boomerangers. However, research by Mitchell and Gee (1996a) finds that the presence of boomerang kids does not negatively affect the marriages of mid-life parents. Mothers, in particular, are quite pleased to have their children back at home. Boomerang kids can have a disruptive family effect if they bounce back and forth several times. This pattern, though, is not common. American research suggests the average length of stay is six months to two years (Stains, 2003).

Intergenerational Stake

It is commonly found that middle-aged parents feel closer to their children than their children feel toward them. The **intergenerational stake hypothesis** (Bengtson & Kuypers, 1971) postulates this is because the two generations have different developmental needs in their relationship. The younger generation has a stake in developing its own autonomous ways of living and values. In contrast, the older generation has a stake in preserving what it has built. Thus, the younger generation tends to maximize intergenerational differences, whereas the older generation tends to minimize them. Overall, studies have found support for this hypothesis (Giarrusso, Stallings, Bengtson, Rossi, & Marshall, 1995). Lynott and

Roberts (1997) find that parents (and grandparents) perceive less of a generation gap than do children, although it is smaller for women and, over time, the perceived gap narrows. Thus, to avoid bias, perceptions of family relationships must be examined for *both* generations.

Family Relationships in Later-Life Families

Several misconceptions exist with regard to the relationships between older adults and their families, particularly their children. One misconception is that children abandon their elderly parents and dump them in nursing homes as soon as they can. Important research by Shanas (1979) over two decades ago put that myth to rest. She found that children provide substantial support to their aging parents and consider institutionalizing a parent only reluctantly and after all other avenues have been exhausted. Unfortunately, stereotypes of abandoned elderly people continue to surface. Shanas's research may have had another consequence, however. Once gerontologists became attuned to the care and assistance that children, especially daughters, were providing to their parents, research on caregiving became very popular. With that research has come the concept of caregiver burden, and images of (mostly) daughters overwhelmed by caregiving duties to their frail parent(s). Inadvertently, such research may have created the impression that seniors are encumbrances to their families, reinforcing stereotypes of the aged as frail, dependent, and useless. However, as we saw in Chapter 9, most seniors are in fairly good health, and little if any caregiving is needed throughout most of the years that adult children and their parents are both alive. This does not dismiss the fact that some families face very heavy caregiving responsibilities that can extend for several years. (See Chapter 12.)

It is important to realize that help and assistance *go both ways* between parents and children. The data in Table 11.5—from both Canadian and American sources—show that parents tend to give more help to children than they receive from them, until very advanced ages. Relatively low percentages of children are involved in giving help to parents, and daughters are more likely to help than sons. These data are quite general; they do not tell us what kinds of help, and how much, is provided or received. The assistance falls into five categories of instrumental help—home maintenance, transportation, household help, personal care, and financial support. This represents a wide range of activities: it is one thing to drive a family member to a doctor's appointment (help with transportation) and quite another to give him or her a bath (help with personal care). Also, giving financial help does not involve much time, whereas cleaning a house can take up a whole day. Nevertheless, it is clear that help does not flow only from children to parents; rather, aging parents and their children are involved in reciprocal relations.

The provision of help among parents and children is related to age and life course stage (Stone, Rosenthal & Connidis, 1998). Parents receive the most help

Table 11.5   HELP GIVEN TO CHILDREN BY PARENTS AND TO PARENTS BY CHILDREN

	Percentage of Children Giving Help to Parents	
Age of Parent:*		
65–69	14%	
70–74	16%	
75+	38%	
Age of Child:**	Daughters	Sons
45–49	15%	8%
50–54	22%	7%
55–59	18%	11%
	Percentage of Parents Giving Help to Children	
Age of Parent:*		
65–69	40%	
70–74	48%	
75+	16%	

Sources: *Data taken from G. Spitze & J. Logan. (1992). Helping as a component of parent–adult child relations. *Research on Aging*, 14, 291–312.
**Data taken from C.J. Rosenthal, A. Martin-Matthews, & S.H. Matthews. (1996). Caught in the middle? Occupancy in multiple roles and help to parents in a national probability sample of Canadian adults. *Journals of Gerontology, 51B*, S274-S283.

when they are at advanced ages; children receive the most help from parents when they are bringing up their own children. This pattern reflects the changing needs of each generation over time. The help that children receive is instrumental, largely in the form of childcare and financial assistance. Kobayashi (1999), in a study of Japanese Canadian families in British Columbia, reports high levels of financial assistance from parents to children. Less assistance with childcare is observed, in part because of the geographic distance between parents and children, a legacy of the internment of Japanese Canadians in several parts of the province during World War II. Soldo and Hill (1995) also report substantial amounts of money transfers from older parents to children (a median value of $1650 in the preceding year). Limited research on aging gays and lesbians suggests they have fewer intergenerational supports, largely due to intrafamilial discrimination (Blando, 2001; Cahill, South, & Spade, 2000).

Until now, we have focused on the *amount* of assistance flowing between the generations, as has most of the research. The amount of assistance is important and speaks directly to the issue of intergenerational equity. The intergenerational equity debate, introduced in Chapter 2, focuses on the fairness of transfers across generations. However, the debate has been framed in terms of public transfers, which appear to favour older people. The data here show us that private transfers are very important and appear to favour the younger generation (and its children). However, as McDaniel (1997) argues, we need to overcome the great divide between public and private intergenerational transfers, both theoretically and in terms of data collection. While the amount of intergenerational transfers is important, other aspects of intergenerational exchange are similarly critical and not yet known.

As Stone and Rosenthal (1998) point out, we need to know whether enough help is available when it is needed. We also need to know more about the meaning of help, the context in which it is given and received in everyday family life. Bengtson (2001) goes further, arguing that intergenerational emotional ties are critical in our lives and we need to know more about the strength and resiliency of intergenerational solidarity over time. Also, he suggests that, with increases in divorce and step-families, multi-generational bonds may become more important than nuclear family ties. In stark contrast, Eggebeen (1992; also see Pezzin & Schone, 1999) suggests that today's older adults lack a tradition of family support and that remarriages (step-families) inhibit intergenerational exchanges. More research is required to know which individuals, and in what circumstances, are most likely to find themselves in which of these scenarios.

Grandparents

More and more people are becoming grandparents, and for longer periods. This is the combined result of increased longevity and a mid-20th century drop in the age at which women bore children. At the current time, there are 5.7 million grandparents in Canada, with an average 4.7 grandchildren each. Nearly two-thirds of women and more than half of men aged 55 to 64 are grandparents; among seniors, 80 percent of women and 74 percent of men are grandparents (Statistics Canada, 2001c). And it is believed that most future seniors will be grandparents. However, recent trends of increased childlessness, lower fertility, and later age at motherhood suggest that they may be grandparents to fewer grandchildren and for shorter periods. The future will also likely see an increase in step-grandparenting as blended families become more common.

Until now, becoming a first-time grandparent has been an event that happens in mid-life—not later life, as is sometimes assumed. The median age at which Canadians become grandparents for the first time is 55 (Schlesinger & Schlesinger, 2004). With life expectancy in the early 80s for women, this means that most women can expect to be grandmothers for almost 30 years. Grandmothers tend to feel that this is the ideal age to take on this role, whereas non-grandmothers are less likely to think there is an ideal age to become a grandmother and, if they do, it is at an older age. Since grandparenthood tends to commence in mid-life, there can be competing demands on grandparents' time. Most will still be employed and some may be dealing with the cluttered nest of late-leaving or returning children. However, with the birth of each successive grandchild, competing demands will likely lessen.

Grandparents provide a considerable amount of assistance—both in kind and financial—to the families of their grandchildren (and great-grandchildren). Bass and Caro (1996) estimated that older Americans who provided help to grandchildren and great-grandchildren in the mid 1990s accounted for $17 to $29 billion per year in economic contributions. The vast majority of grandparents providing such help report that it is a source of pleasure and satisfaction for them. This is another example of private transfers—this time to grandchildren and great-grandchildren—that directly challenges the idea of intergenerational inequity favouring the old. Grandparenting differs by gender. On the demographic level, because women live longer than men and have children at younger ages, they will be grandparents longer than grandfathers. Thus, grandmothers are more likely to have relationships with their grandchildren when they are both children and adults. In addition, men are more likely to be married grandparents, whereas women will be both married and then widowed grandparents.

Both grandsons and granddaughters generally feel emotionally closer to their grandmothers (Roberto & Stroes, 1992). This may be related to findings (Hagestad, 1985) that grandfathers tend to give advice to their grandchildren, whereas grandmothers are engaged in a wider variety of conversation topics as well as activities. However, Hagestad suggests that this gender difference in grandparenting behaviour may be cohort specific. Future grandmothers and grandfathers may be more alike in their interactions with grandchildren.

Grandparent–grandchild relations are also affected by lineage, or line of descent. Given the importance of the mother–daughter relationship in North American families, we would expect maternal grandparents to play a more influential role in grandchildren's lives than paternal grandparents (Rosenthal & Gladstone, 2000). This issue has not been studied much, but there is some evidence that adolescent grandchildren feel closer to their maternal grandparents than their paternal grandparents (Van Ranst, Verschueren & Marcoen, 1995), especially their maternal grandmother.

The relationship between grandparents and grandchildren is mediated by the person who connects them (i.e., the children's parent and the grandparent's child). This makes the grandparent–grandchild tie vulnerable, especially in the event of marital breakdown in the middle generation. The custodial parent may deny grandparents (more often the ex-spouse's parents) access to the grandchildren (Gladstone, 1989). With increasing divorce rates, this is an issue of growing importance to grandparents. In Canada, a number of advocacy groups work on behalf of grandparents who have lost contact with their grandchildren.

In a different vein, grandparents may end up parenting their grandchildren if their own child is unable or unwilling to do so. While this situation is not normative, in 2001, 57 000 grandparents were raising their grandchildren on their own in Canada, a 2 percent increase over the previous decade. Two-thirds were women, and half the children were 14 years of age or younger (Stepan, 2003). Grandparent-headed households often arise because the biological parents are in trouble with the law, due to addictions or other causes; because the parents are dead or ill, sometimes with AIDS; or because of teen pregnancy. All these causes are themselves related to poverty. MacKenzie, Brown, Callahan and Whittington (2005) argue that an increase in grandparents being parents to their grandchildren also arises when governments adopt a strategy of making it more difficult for children to enter the service system and pressuring families to take them in. Grandparents—often at personal sacrifice in terms of free time, working, and financial stress—are coming to the rescue of a growing minority of grandchildren whose parents are not able to raise them. They may do so sporadically rather than continuously as biological parents come back for periods of time.

Widowhood

Most of the research on widowhood focuses on widows; as we have seen, women are much more likely than men to experience the death of their spouse. One of the most striking characteristics of elderly widows is their straitened economic circumstances; approximately one-half of Canadian elderly widows live in poverty (McDonald, 1997b), despite the fact that older widows are more likely than other older women to receive assistance from children (Eggebeen, 1992; Pezzin & Schone, 1999). The poor financial situation of widows highlights the penalties that women face due to their child-rearing and domestic responsibilities, which result in less paid employment over their life course, as discussed in Chapter 2. It is also a function of employer-sponsored pension plans that lack survivor benefits (Schellenberg, 1994). And, overall, it is testimony to the economic dependence of women on men. (Also see the discussion on pensions in Chapter 14).

One important research finding about widowhood is that it is not a cut-and-dried state that necessarily begins on the death of the husband. Neither is the way women experience widowhood simply contingent on what happens after the husband dies (van den Hoonaard, 2001). The distinction between widowhood and non-widowhood may itself be blurry for women. As Martin-Matthews (2000) emphasizes, widowhood is not only an event, it is a process of transition over time. Widowhood is one of the most difficult life transitions to make and the bereavement process is usually long and painful. It is characterized by intense grief, depression, feelings of meaninglessness, and loss of identity. The widow, who was so closely connected to her husband and her role as wife, must deal with who she is now (van den Hoonaard, 2001). This (usually temporary) loss of identity was recognized in the first study of widows in North America (Lopata, 1973) and continues to emerge as an important theme in research on widows.

While most widows feel the loss of their husband and their role as wife very intensely, some experience "an ambiguous loss," as Martin-Matthews (2000) puts it. Mixed feeling are likely when the marriage was not successful and the husband was cruel or nasty. Given that today's elderly women were likely to stay in a bad marriage, some widows are relieved to be no longer married. Presumably, future cohorts of widows will be less likely to face the challenge of having to appear bereaved when they are actually glad, or at least relieved, their husband is dead. Others may experience mixed feelings when a husband with severe dementia dies; the widow may miss her husband tremendously while also feeling relieved that his suffering has ended, as has the heavy burden of providing care.

Whether widowhood is an intensely painful process (as for the majority of women) or a blessing in disguise (for the minority of women in very bad marriages), widows must renegotiate their relations with others. The mother–child(ren) relationship changes with widowhood. A new balance must be achieved. Widows want and need the support of their children, but they also want to maintain their own privacy—at least in mainstream North American society. Children may become overly protective of their mother and even treat her like a child. They need to negotiate a reciprocal relationship to which both the widow and the child feel they are contributing equally (van den Hoonaard, 2001).

Relations with friends also change after a woman is widowed. Maintaining friendships with couples is particularly difficult, given the couple orientation of modern society. An unattached woman may be perceived as a threat by married women friends. Relations with men must also be renegotiated. As van den Hoonaard (2001) points out, most widows do not want to remarry. Nevertheless, they still want to have contacts and friendships with men.

Another category of the widowed that is just beginning to receive research attention is gay widowers. To date, we do not even know how many gay widowers there are. Small-sample research reveals that gay widowers' bereavement process may be made more difficult by an enforced privacy (if others do not know of their homosexuality) but that, overall, gay widowers are able, with time, to transform their lives in positive ways, much like widows (Shernoff, 1997).

Widowhood also creates opportunities for growth and development. Thus, there has been a shift from a doom-and-gloom portrayal of widowhood to one that emphasizes creativity, strength, and positive development. Especially among those elderly today, many women were constrained by traditional spousal roles; during widowhood they can experience a freedom that was absent in their younger years. This new emphasis moves us away from the often hidden ageist assumption that old age is a period of life in which positive developmental change cannot occur. Examples of this new trend in understandings of widowhood are van den Hoonaard's (2001) book on the journey through widowhood and an anthology of

Canadian widows' stories entitled *Beyond Coping: Widows Reinventing Their Lives* (Hurd & Macdonald, 2001).

Sibling Relationships in Later Life

Until recently, most of the research on siblings was conducted in the context of childhood. With population aging and the growth of social gerontology, there has been some refocusing to adult sibling relationships. Norris and Tindale (1994:81) characterize this as a shift in viewpoint "from rivals to allies." Sibling relationships in childhood—which are not voluntary—can be very intense, filled with positive affect and assistance as well as with frictions and rivalries. In young adulthood and early mid-life, sibling relations tend to attenuate somewhat, taking on the characteristics of (voluntary) friendship, as a result of competing demands, especially when children are born. There is more closeness between sisters than between brothers and between brothers and sisters. However, in late mid-life, sibling ties tend to be reactivated by the declining health of the parents. The stresses of elder care may strain sibling relations, especially if siblings perceive an unfair division of labour. This is less likely to happen in families with only two sisters; they tend to share duties the most equitably (Matthews & Rosner, 1988). In families with both brothers and sisters, the sisters are more likely to be engaged in parental caregiving. Sons in brothers-only families do not neglect their parents, but they tend to be reactive, rather than proactive, leaving it to parents to tell them what they need, rather than seeking ways to assist them (Connidis, 2001).

Approximately 80 percent of today's seniors have at least one sibling (Connidis, 2001). The next generation of elders (the baby boomers) are also likely to have at least one surviving sibling, due to the relatively high fertility of their mothers and increased longevity. The following generation (that is, the children of the baby boom) will be somewhat less likely to have a sibling in old age, although the one-child family has never enjoyed much popularity in Canadian society. Future generations of seniors will have more step-siblings and half-siblings, as a result of increased divorce and remarriage. Half-siblings and step-siblings are not new, but now they are more likely the result of divorce, whereas in the past, they were the result of early widowhood. This raises the interesting and yet unanswered question as to how step-siblings and half-siblings define themselves in adulthood, in the past and in the present. Under what circumstances do they come to view each other as real siblings and when does the kin tie disappear over the years?

Many seniors today have a sibling who lives nearby. Close geographical proximity is important to maintaining the sibling tie; in fact, Canadian research shows that geographical closeness is more important for sibling interactions than for older parent–adult child relations (Connidis, 2001; Connidis & Campbell, 1995). Other factors that influence sibling contact in later life include gender, marital status, and parental status. Sisters are far more likely to see each other than are brothers and brother–sister combinations (Connidis, 1989a). Also, sisters are more likely to talk about issues of personal importance to them. Married people are in less frequent contact with their siblings than are the unmarried. Those who never married are most likely to keep sibling ties activated (Connidis, 2001), probably due more to reciprocal feelings of obligation than to greater emotional closeness (Connidis & Campbell, 1995). Childless people are more frequently involved with their siblings than are those with children, and the single and childless are more likely to live near a sibling. Connidis (2001:211) suggests that the "salience of siblings to single, childless persons shapes decisions about where to live." In addition, the existence of a family **kin-keeper** (Rosenthal, 1985) is important; families that have an individual who takes on this role are more likely to keep in contact, and this role is particularly important to the maintenance of sibling relationships.

Sibling relationships are about more than frequency of contact; they are also about emotionality and loyalty. Connidis (1994) reports that among Canadian adults aged 55 years and over, 70 percent say they are somewhat, very, or extremely close to at least one sibling. This sense of closeness comes from a history of shared life (siblings are the longest lasting kin tie); as Connidis (2001) notes, siblings rarely become close in old age if they have not been close in earlier life. Siblings are often confidants in later life; this is especially true for women and for single and childless people. Siblings are more likely to be confidants than companions in later life when geographically proximate, a characteristic more common among friends than siblings (Connidis, 1989b).

But not all family relationships are necessarily harmonious and close. One study (Matthews, Delaney & Adamek, 1989), reported that as many as 35 percent of pairs of brothers were disaffiliated, describing their relationship as not at all close, as characterized by disagreement on important issues, and/or as one in which their brother did not understand them This leads directly to the next section, dealing with family conflict.

Family Conflict

Given the emotionality of family relationships, conflict is to be expected. To assume families are always harmonious is naïve, an expectation grounded in the myths we hold about families past and present. While disagreements and anger are unavoidable in families—at any stage of the life course—and are probably necessary for problem resolution, there are limits on the acceptable expression of conflict. In the last 20 years or so, there has been a growing realization that—in some later-life families—mistreatment of older adults occurs. This mistreatment can take several forms: neglect, physical abuse, psychological abuse, and financial abuse.

While we have much yet to learn about elder maltreatment and abuse, several explanations have been put forward. One of the most popular is that stressful situations, usually referring to the physical and/or mental impairment of the older person, can cause the caregiver to be abusive. Others argue that abuse against older adults stems from learned behaviour; the abusers model violence from witnessing or suffering abuse themselves. It is suggested that children who abuse their frail older parents may have been abused by those parents themselves when they were younger and spouses who abuse their spouse continue the abuse that they began earlier in the relationship (Phillips, 2000). Some claim that physical, emotional and financial dependencies between the victim and the abuser contribute to abuse, as do ageist societal attitudes and beliefs (McDonald & Collins, 2000; Harbison, 1999). Social isolation and psychopathology are two other possible factors (Penhale, 1999). Evidence, however, is limited. Note that not all individuals who are dependent, who have been abused younger in life, or who are under great stress abuse others. This area has been receiving increasing research attention in recent years and no doubt will continue to do so in the years to come.

In Canada, national data from the 1999 General Social Survey (Statistics Canada, 2002f) reveal that 7 percent of seniors said they had experienced some form of emotional or financial abuse by an adult child, caregiver, or spouse in the preceding five years. Emotional abuse is reported most frequently (7 percent) followed by financial abuse (1 percent). Close to 2 percent report experiencing more than one type of elder abuse. Police data on violence against older adults, while capturing only some instances, nevertheless yield important information. Among seniors, as among younger age groups, women are more likely to be victims of police-reported family violence than are males; almost 65 percent of all older adult victims of family violence are women. However, over half of older victims of non-family violence are men (56 percent). Most perpetrators are male; 80 percent of those accused of violently victimizing an older family member were men. Adult children and spouses are the most likely perpetrators, accounting for three-quarters of elder abuse. Older men are most often victimized by their adult children; women may be victimized by spouses or adult children (Statistics Canada, 2002f).

Older women are more at risk of spousal homicide than older men; more than half of older women who were victims of family homicide were killed by their spouses, compared to one-quarter of older men who were victims of family homicide. Older male victims are twice as likely as older female victims to be killed by their adult sons (42 percent versus 24 percent). Furthermore, 43 percent of individuals accused of committing homicide against an older adult family member have a history of family violence with that particular victim. However, family homicide in old age is less common than non-family homicide. Domestic violence in aging families is a difficult issue. It is often hidden; Wiehe (1998) estimates that approximately only one in 14 cases of elder abuse is ever reported.

Research suggests that males, in particular, are more often victims of abuse and maltreatment than official statistics reveal. In England, Pritchard (2002) interviewed 12 male elder abuse victims in depth and others in focus groups. This research suggests that male victims experience the same types of abuse as female victims (financial deprivation, theft, fraud of various kinds, gross physical neglect) and experience similar recurring patterns of abuse throughout their lives. Rather unexpectedly, male victims are very willing to discuss their experiences when encouraged to do so. They are not, however, treated like female victims by social workers or other professionals within the system; their allegations of abuse are often not taken seriously.

Important research supports the findings that older women are more likely to be victimized than older men (Weeks, Richards, Nilsson-Thomy, Kozma, & Bryanton, 2004; Reynolds & Schonfeld, 2004). However, a large population-based survey by Pillemer reported in 1988 found the per capita rate of maltreatment for older men was nearly double that for women, although official statistics often report the reverse (Mouton, Talamantes, Parker, Espino-David, & Miles, 2001). They suggest this is due to several reasons: how senior mistreatment becomes defined and the perception of what constitutes abuse, as well as how men are perceived in present-day Western culture. This is in no way to de-emphasize the significance of abuse of older women, but it is to suggest that we are largely unaware of the maltreatment of older men.

We have the most data on physical abuse. A combination of media images of granny bashing and an understandable clinical focus on the most extreme cases of elder abuse have led to an overemphasis on violence and a lack of knowledge about other forms of elder maltreatment. Also, the estimates of elder abuse by both Podnieks (1992) and Pillemer and Finkelhor (1988) are for community-dwelling elders. Spencer (1994), in a report for Health Canada, points to high levels of abuse among institutionalized seniors. Men are more likely to be perpetrators of violence, whereas women are more likely to be implicated in neglect (Dunlop, Rothman, Condon, Hebert, & Martinez, 2000). Violence against dementia sufferers has received a considerable amount of research attention, in part because it appears that they are at increased risk of abuse, especially if their disease leads them to act in aggressive and violent ways (Buttell, 1999; Penhale & Kingston, 1997).

As Hill and Amuwo (1998) point out, elder maltreatment is more a social than a legal issue. A host of problems, some directly related to aging and health declines, contribute to elder abuse. In most cases, legal notions of guilt and punishment have little relevance. Also, if elders choose not to come forward to the courts, is it ethical for society to take away their right of choice? Would that not be paternalism, reinforcing ageist stereotypes of elderly individuals as incompetent and childlike? Facilitating prevention is likely a more fruitful direction. In some cases, that means prevention of violence much earlier in the family life course. Prevention can also be fostered by providing the right kinds of supports and services to deal with mental illness, caregiving stress, and social isolation.

Chapter Summary

As we have seen, family membership and family ties are important aspects of the lives of elderly Canadians. While most Canadian seniors do not live with anyone other than their spouse, other family members play an important role in their lives. One of the most critical ways in which lives are linked is through families. Nevertheless, there is considerable diversity among older Canadian families—related to age, gender, and ethnicity.

Key ideas to remember from this chapter:

- There are many definitions of family and household. It is difficult to draw a line around where one family ends and another starts. Although we tend to equate households and families, it is important to consider both, and not to privilege the nuclear family over the extended family.

- We need to free ourselves of myths about families and family life in the past; if we compare today's families against an idealized version of the past, contemporary families are guaranteed not to measure up.

- One of these myths is that families in the past were extended, consisting of multi-generational households. Because of high mortality, few families had three generations alive at the same time. Further, at least among Anglo-Canadians, extended families were not preferred.

- Another myth of the past is that seniors were honoured and well cared for by their children. Most people were poor and could not afford to help their parents.

- Gender and marital status are closely related. In later life, women are likely to be widows, whereas men are likely to be married. This gender difference is the combined function of women's greater life expectancy and of the fact that most husbands are older than their wives. Also, men are more likely to remarry if they are widowed or divorced.

- Gender is also related to living arrangements. Men are much more likely to live with a spouse than are women. There has been a substantial increase in living alone among older women in all industrialized countries. Reasons for this trend include demographic, economic, and cultural factors, but there is much debate about the relative importance of these factors.

- Ethnic origin is related to the propensity to live multi-generationally; Asian-origin Canadians—particularly those who are foreign-born—are more likely to live in three-generational households. An important distinction relates to home ownership—is the multi-generational household located in the child's home or the older adult's home?

- Beanpole families—consisting of four or five generations, but with few members per generation—are not as common as sometimes thought. Age at childbearing is an important consideration here; if women have their children at relatively late ages, the age gap between generations is lengthened, making it difficult to achieve beanpole families.

- The image of mid-life families sandwiched between the needs of dependent children and elderly parents is an exaggeration.

- Mid-life families are experiencing a cluttered nest, with children leaving home at older ages and adult children more likely to return.

- Research supports the intergenerational stake hypothesis, which holds that mid-life parents feel closer to their children than their children feel toward them as a result of different developmental stakes. This generation gap, however, decreases over time.

- Private transfers between older parents and their children go both ways. Indeed, research indicates that older parents give more to their children than they receive. This finding has implications for the intergenerational equity debate.

- Most Canadian seniors are grandparents and most experience the transition to grandparenthood in mid-life. Grandparents contribute much to their grandchildren (and great-grandchildren), which is another important finding regarding intergenerational equity. Grandparenting differs by gender: women are more likely to be grandparents for a longer time, and to be emotionally closer to their grandchildren. The grandparent–grandchild tie is mediated by the middle generation. In the event of a divorce in the middle generation, grandparents and grandchildren may be denied contact. In contrast, grandparents can become "parents" if their adult children are unable or unwilling to care for their own children.

- Widowhood is an expectable life event for Canadian women and is associated with financial difficulty. Widowhood is both an event and a process over time; the process is emotionally painful (for most) and necessitates a change in identity. Widows must negotiate new relationships with children and other family members, with friends, and with men.

- The importance of siblings varies over the life course. In later life, sibling ties are important to many people. The importance of sibling ties is influenced by geographical proximity, gender (sisters are closer than other siblings), marital status (siblings are more important to the never-married), and parental status (siblings are more important to the childless).

- Family conflict has not been studied extensively by social gerontologists. We know most about elder abuse, the most extreme form of family conflict but probably not the most common. It is estimated that 4 to 8 percent of elders are victims of abuse and/or neglect in both home and institutional settings. Within the family setting, spouses are more likely to be perpetrators of elder maltreatment than are children. Men are more likely to be physically abusive; women are more likely to be abusive through neglect.

- Violence against aged family members is related to four factors: problems of the abuser, such as mental illness and drug addiction; dependency of the abuser on the victim, particularly financial dependency; social isolation; and external stresses on family members. Part of domestic violence in old age is the perpetuation of wife abuse into later life. Elder abuse is more a social problem than a legal one, and social solutions are needed.

KEY TERMS

nuclear family **(p. 271)**

family of orientation **(p. 271)**

family of procreation **(p. 271)**

census family **(p. 272)**

extended family **(p. 272)**

stem family **(p. 275)**

vertical extension **(p. 284)**

horizontal shrinkage **(p. 284)**

beanpole families **(p. 284)**

reconstituted families **(p. 284)**

blended families **(p. 284)**

sandwich generation **(p. 284)**

empty nests **(p. 285)**

cluttered nests **(p. 285)**

boomerang kids **(p. 285)**

intergenerational stake hypothesis **(p. 286)**

kin-keeper **(p. 294)**

STUDY QUESTIONS

1. In what ways have declines in mortality affected families?

2. Identify at least four myths about aging families and family relationships. Why do you think they exist?

3. List ways that the families of ethnic minority elders differ from those of the mainstream. What are the difficulties in trying to ascertain why these differences exist?

4. Discuss ways in which men's and women's family life courses differ.

5. Discuss how increasing divorce (and remarriage) is affecting older adults in their family lives.

SUGGESTED READINGS

Bengtson, V.L., Rosenthal, C.J., & Burton, L.M. (1996). Paradoxes of family and aging. In R.H. Binstock & L.K. George (Eds.), *Handbook of aging and the social sciences* (4th ed.) (pp. 253–282). New York: Academic Press.

Connidis, I.A. (2001). *Family ties and aging.* Thousand Oaks, CA: Sage.

Gurung-Regan, A.R., Taylor, S.E., & Seeman, T.E. (2003). Accounting for changes in social support among married older adults: Insights from the MacArthur Studies of Successful Aging. *Psychology and Aging, 18*(3), 487–496.

Hareven, T.K. (Ed.). (1996). *Aging and generational relations across the life course.* New York: Walter de Gruyter.

Lowenstein, A. (2005). Global ageing and challenges to families. In Malcolm L. Johnson (Ed.), *The Cambridge handbook of age and ageing.* Cambridge, UK: Cambridge University Press.

Chapter 12

SOCIAL SUPPORT
AND CAREGIVING

Learning Objectives

In this chapter, you will learn about

- What constitutes social support and why it is important.
- The relevance of social support for quality of life in old age.
- Direct and indirect effects of social support.
- Role-specific interpersonal relations in old age, including those with spouses, friends, children, and grandchildren

- Caregiving, a specific type of social support that has critical importance as we age.
- The historical role of the informal network of family and friends in providing the vast majority of care to individuals when they become sick or disabled.
- The largely invisible care system within society.

Introduction

This chapter examines social support—what it is and why it is important in old age. Social support has been and continues to be a popular area of research. Although it still has not captured the attention of clinicians, social support has long been established as important for our well-being and health. More than 25 years ago, Berkman and Syme (1979) demonstrated that a lack of involvement with others was associated with earlier death. Lubben, Weiler, and Chi (1989) are among several researchers who have since confirmed that less involvement with others is also related to more hospitalization. The relationship is as strong as that between smoking and mortality, which led to the government-mandated warning on cigarette packages many years ago.

It can be argued that interacting with others becomes even more important in old age than during the earlier years. In Canada's capitalist society, most older individuals do not work for pay and are, therefore, excluded from society's defining role. Their exclusion from the mainstream, furthermore, has not been replaced by socially sanctioned roles that provide meaningful places for them within society. However, the vast majority of Canadian seniors are nevertheless embedded within social networks and lead active lives.

Social Support: What Is It, and Why Is It Important?

Other people are important throughout our lives; this does not change when we reach age 65. We do not live our lives in social isolation. Even those who live alone do not necessarily feel lonely and isolated. You can be in a crowd and still feel lonely; conversely, you can be alone and not feel lonely. It is subjective measures of emotional connectedness with others (having confidantes and companions) that are related to general well-being (Chappell, 1992). Despite this fact, health-care practitioners tend to measure social isolation in terms of such factors as living alone or having no children, assuming that these are indicators of psychological risk. Such assumptions demonstrate the need for research on social support in old age. We know little about the circumstances when it is beneficial to have other people in our lives and when and for whom they are problematic. Nevertheless, the area is driven by a broad and common-sense understanding that **social interactions** are a necessary part of all our lives and can have critical implications for our happiness.

Social support is a broad term, used variously by researchers, sometimes to refer only to positive interactions with others and at other times to encompass all interactions whether positive, negative, or neutral. The term *informal support* suffers from the same inconsistency; "support" suggests positive interactions and can, therefore, imply that all interaction is necessarily positive, which, of course, is false. The terms *social network* and *informal network* do not have this value-laden implication.

Early research in this area identified the affective and emotional aspects of social support. Lopata (1975) discussed the informal network as the primary support system involving the giving and receiving of objects, services, and social and emotional supports deemed important by the receiver and giver. Cohen and Syme (1985) included the following three components: (1) the emotional function; (2) information that may or may not lead to confirmation or heightening of self-esteem; and (3) tangible support, such as assistance with activities of daily living.

Pearlin (1985) distinguished among *social network, group affiliation,* and *interpersonal interaction.* The social network refers to the entire web of relationships with which the individual is involved either directly or indirectly; it includes all individuals with whom we have contact or exchange. Group affiliation is a narrower concept, including only those social relationships that involve active attachment to the group; these are the social relations that we are likely to turn to for support. Interpersonal interaction is narrower still, including only active affiliations that involve trust and intimacy. For Pearlin, interpersonal interaction refers to individuals, rather than groups, and to qualitative, rather than quantitative, aspects of relationships. Similarly, House and Kahn (1985) categorize social relationships as *social networks, social support,* and *social integration.* Social networks are a set of relationships that can be described in terms of their structure, using such terms as *density* or *homogeneity.* Social support refers only to the functional content of social relationships, such as emotional concern, instrumentality, and information. Social integration and isolation refer to the existence or quantity of relationships.

The lack of consistency in the use of these terms is glaring. Conceptual clarification has not advanced since these earlier works. When reading the literature, you must look for the author's definition of a term because it cannot be assumed. Whichever term is used, it is multi-dimensional, unless a particular researcher specifies otherwise. Table 12.1 lists the use of the various terms by these authors.

Notwithstanding the numerous terms, social support is often used generally to refer to any of these concepts. The majority of research has focused on social networks (primarily their size but also, to a certain extent, their composition) and two of the functional aspects identified by House and Kahn (1985), namely, emotional support and instrumental or tangible support. As will become evident in this chapter, social support varies by gender and socio-economic status. It also changes throughout the life course. The gerontological literature contains much less information on group affiliation, interpersonal interaction, social integration, feelings of belonging, or information.

There has been particular interest in the emotional aspects of social support, including companionship and intimacy (having confidantes). The term **companionship** refers to having other individuals in your life with whom you can spend time and share activities. The term **confidantes** refers to having one or more individuals with whom you feel free to discuss personal matters and share

Table 12.1 SOCIAL SUPPORT TERMS

	LOPATA	COBB	PEARLIN	COHEN & SYME	HOUSE & KAHN
Social network			X		X
Group affliation			X		
Interpersonal interaction			X		
Social integration			·		X
Social support					X
Emotional support	X	X		X	X*
Information		X		X	X*
Feeling of belonging		X			
Tangible support	X			X	X*

* All part of their term "social support."

emotional feelings and events. The same individual could be both confidante and companion, or different individuals could fulfill these roles. Most older people in Canada report having both types of relationships (Chappell & Badger, 1989).

There has also been tremendous interest in **tangible** or **instrumental assistance** during old age. This refers to assistance with activities of daily living (ADL) and can include basic physical and personal care activities necessary for survival, such as walking or being personally mobile, eating, washing, and using the toilet. Few seniors are impaired in all these areas. The loss of functioning in any one, though, can lead to long-term institutional care, especially if there is no informal network to provide assistance. It is not uncommon for seniors to have family and friends who assist with instrumental activities of daily living (IADL): such activities as housework, preparing meals, household maintenance, transportation, shopping, and banking. These activities are important for independence but are not essential for survival. Different types of support may come from the same individual at the same time, and they may not be considered support by any of the parties involved. For example, a daughter may take her elderly mother shopping once a week and in doing so provide companionship, information, and tangible support, but neither may consciously consider any of these functions or even refer to this activity as support. Furthermore, each may view the situation differently; the mother may consider the activity primarily companionship and the daughter may consider it tangible support. And the support we give and receive often changes over time. Read the text in Box 12.1 and identify the different types of support and possible differing interpretations by those involved.

Box 12.1 *Types of Support and Interpretations*

It's 10 o'clock Saturday morning. Helen is 75 years old, widowed, and in relatively good health. She lives on her own, is independent, and is mobile. Her 40-year-old daughter, Nancy, lives in the same city and every Saturday comes round to pick Helen up. They do grocery shopping together. Each does her own and pays for her own groceries. However, the daughter picks up a few special things that she knows her mother likes and slips them into her mother's bags while unloading the car back at her mother's home. Once the groceries are in the house, their routine is to have a cup of tea together and chat.

Nancy is a single mom with two children aged eight and 10 years. Late afternoon, every Tuesday and Thursday, Helen takes the bus over to Nancy's home, prepares dinner for everyone, and looks after the grandchildren, while Nancy goes to her activities. Nancy comes home after work and eats with the family but then goes off immediately afterwards. They have been doing this for a number of years. Helen seems to get along well with her grandchildren, and the grandchildren look forward to her visits.

During the day, Helen takes the bus herself to go to her own activities, to see friends, see the doctor, go shopping, and so on. She has a couple of close friends with whom she shares many activities, and they have known each other for several decades. They do not like to be out after dark, so they typically see each other during the day. They talk on the telephone in the evenings and will call each other to discuss favourite television programs. However, when Helen is sick, it is Nancy who tends to her needs.

Friends call and check on one another, but they themselves are elderly and find it difficult to look after each other if anyone becomes ill. Two years ago, though, when Helen was released from hospital and Nancy had to tend to her full-time job and her two children, her friends would come over for a few hours during the day to stay with her. Even then, with her fierce independence, she was determined not to have home-support workers or other service personnel in her home.

Debunking Myths

As we have seen in earlier chapters, many of society's stereotypes about old people are false. A common stereotype related to social support is that seniors are isolated and alone with their deteriorating health (also see chapters 7 and 9). Because the vast majority of older Canadians are retired, our modern capitalist society tends to devalue them. This is evidenced in ageist attitudes, for example, in media portrayals of seniors, among school-age children, among health-care professionals (Achenbaum, 1995), and among employers faced with older job applicants (McDonald & Wanner, 1984). No socially sanctioned and valued role has developed for seniors in society. Stereotypes of social isolation are fuelled by new concerns about working daughters, who may no longer have sufficient time to care for their parents, and low fertility rates that produce even fewer children to care for us in our old age. Children's mobility can mean that they live great distances from their elderly parents; the technological age has evolved forms of knowledge that simply leave seniors behind.

There is no question that the majority of seniors are not in paid labour (see Chapter 13).

This, however, does not translate into isolation and loneliness or a lack of connectedness with others. On the contrary, seniors confirm the notion of the **modified extended family**. Litwak (1960) noted more than three decades ago that the extended family emphasizes mutual and close intergenerational ties among kin, the strength of intergenerational relations, continuity of responsible filial behaviour, and contact between the generations. This characterization is largely true of Canadian seniors today. Very few are socially isolated; the vast majority report having both companions and confidantes.

Research in the 1970s and early 1980s documented the variety and extent of social interaction during old age. Most elderly individuals have extensive social contacts, with social networks similar in size to those of middle-aged people (Antonucci, 1985): more than 30 people on average (Chappell, 1992). This finding was particularly important in debunking common assumptions at the time that the nuclear family abandoned their seniors to long-term institutional care and that seniors were largely isolated from their families. As noted in earlier chapters, social gerontologists have demonstrated the falsity of these assumptions and debunked the myth of the abandoned elder. There are elderly individuals who experience a decline in the amount and variety of social interaction, but this decrease tends to be characteristic of those who are old-old, in poor health, and have fewer economic resources. It does not characterize seniors as a group. This research, though, assumed that the interaction was supportive, without measuring supportiveness directly (Sauer & Coward, 1985; Walker, McBride, & Vachon, 1977). Indeed, sometimes *social networks* were defined in terms of emotional support, that is, beneficial interaction, although usually benefits were not measured.

Much of the research has focused on marriage, which, during the later years, tends to characterize those who are young-old, rather than old-old. Older married couples tend to have higher incomes than widowed or single seniors, better mental and physical health, assured companionship, and larger social networks (Verbrugge, 1979). For these reasons, it has been argued that marriage is good for people. Indeed, most seniors have positive perceptions of their marriages and greater satisfaction than in the younger married years (Lowenthal & Robinson, 1976), perhaps due to reduced competition from other roles and increased opportunity for companionship. There could also be a selectivity factor at work; those in worse marriages may not have stayed in them. Married men typically name their wives as their confidantes, whereas married women name their husbands plus children or friends; married men name their wives as their best friends, while women name their offspring or female age peers (Strain & Chappell, 1982; 1984). Married men's exclusive emotional reliance on their wives has led to much concern that older men are particularly at risk when they become widowed.

You have already learned that widowhood is a normal life stage for most women, that men are less likely to become widowed, but that those who do are more likely to remarry than are women. The fact that widowhood has become a normal life stage for women means they typically have many peers in the same situation with whom they can form friendships (Martin-Matthews, 1991). The proportion of seniors who have been divorced will increase as the baby boom generation ages, as will the proportion of the never-married. Single people tend to nurture their relationships with their parents, siblings, and friends. Research suggests that life-long singlehood promotes self-reliance (Johnson & Catalano, 1981). As more diverse forms of living together (such as same-sex couples) are evidenced in the baby boom generation than among those who are currently older, and as these individuals age, we can expect to see more research appearing on such relationships.

The sibling relationship is also a special social tie, lasting longer than any other family tie. Siblings share a common cultural background, common genetic pool, and earlier life experiences within the same family. Of those senior today, approximately 80 to 85 percent have at least one living sibling, but less than half of those aged 85 years and over do. Older adults report feeling closer to siblings than to any other relatives, except their own children and perhaps their spouses. They are especially important to the never-married, the childless, the divorced, and the widowed. Siblings tend to keep in contact throughout their lives and have been characterized as standing ready should help be needed (Connidis, 1989a; Cicirelli, 1985).

Among intergenerational relations, the relationship with children has captured the greatest research interest. Contrary to assumptions about the predominance of the isolated nuclear family, the majority of seniors have at least one living child and live with or near one child—no more than half an hour's drive away (Hanson & Sauer, 1985). More than 80 percent of seniors have at least weekly contact with their children (Rosenthal, 1987; Chappell, 1989); and more interaction takes place between older parents and their children than with any other kin. It is dominated by visiting, family get-togethers, and shared leisure activities. As early as 1963, Rosenmayr and Kockeis aptly coined the phrase **intimacy at a distance** to describe seniors' general preference not to live with their children but to maintain close ties.

These relationships are maintained even if there is geographic distance. Letter writing, phone calls, and today e-mail substitute for face-to-face contact. Those with less money tend to have larger kin networks and to live closer to one another. Women usually consider their relationships with their children as more important and more satisfying than do men and there tends to be greater similarity between the views of children and those of their mothers than of their fathers (Connidis, 1989b). Indeed, the mother–daughter tie is one of the closest.

We know much less about seniors' interactions with their grandchildren, although grandparenthood has many symbolic functions. Being there when needed provides stress buffers when there are family crises, such as illness, divorce, or unemployment (Hagestad, 1985). Grandparents provide a key function as symbols of connectedness, having the time to listen and being a link to the past. As noted in Chapter 2, more and more individuals are becoming grandparents and great-grandparents. Three-quarters of Canadians have at least one child, and more than 90 percent of seniors with children are grandparents. Grandmothers tend to be involved in interpersonal dynamics, emphasizing the quality of the relationship, while grandfathers emphasize task-oriented involvements with grandchildren. Same-gender ties tend to be more prevalent among these generations, with the grandmother-granddaughter tie the closest (Hagestad, 1985).

There is also a relative paucity of research on non-kin friendships in old age. Friendships are characterized by voluntary involvement, affective bonds, and consensus, and less by obligation than are kin ties. We choose our friends and are chosen by them. Friends tend to be age peers, to be similar to one another in such characteristics as gender and socio-economic status, to share common experiences and to have lived through similar transitions in society. Chappell (1983) reveals that friendships are especially important for companionship, and Lee (1985) notes their importance for emotional support, affection, and quick integration. They are also more likely to fade away than to end on a bad note, allowing their reactivation if circumstances permit. Seniors have accumulated a large number of social relationships simply by virtue of the amount of time spent meeting people throughout their lives. Antonucci (1985) made the concept of **convoy of social support** famous, arguing that it captures the dynamic aspect of social interaction over time.

We know almost nothing about other relationships, such as cousins, aunts, uncles, and in-laws, or about instrumental relationships with shopkeepers, delivery people, mail carriers, and so on. We do know that most older adults do not belong to voluntary organizations (the major exception being church membership), and most do not belong to seniors' organizations, even if they know about them (Stone & Hubert, 1988).

In summary, early research in the area of social support focused on social interaction more than on social support. It documented the extensiveness of social interaction in old age. We know much more about seniors' interactions with their spouses and with their children than with other kin or non-kin relationships. Research documenting the extent and type of social supports in the lives of seniors continues today. In the 1980s, however, major attention turned to an assessment of the supportiveness of social interaction and to an examination of the relationship between social support and well-being.

Social Support and Well-Being

Much of the research on the relationship between social support and well-being in the 1980s assesses either direct or indirect effects of social support on well-being. Well-being is measured either as the absence of physical or mental illness or more positively as happiness or health. The direct effects view argues that social support is important in meeting needs that require fulfillment on a more or less daily basis, regardless of whether the individual is experiencing stress or not. Simply being a member of a group or receiving support from others is beneficial, but it is mediated through one's perception, that is, through subjective support. While results of empirical research are not entirely consistent, in general, they support the **direct effects view**. Having social support is related to higher well-being and a greater quality of life among seniors (Thomas, Garry, Goodwin, & Goodwin, 1985; Mancini, Quinn, Gavigan, & Franklin, 1980). Exceptions can be found in the literature; for example, Lin, Simeone, Ensel, and Kuo (1979) report a very weak relationship between social support and well-being. Because of the number of studies in this area, several reviews were conducted in the mid-1980s. They concluded that the direct effects view is valid, although the specific aspect of social interaction that is the most crucial for well-being is not always agreed upon. Cohen and Syme (1985) argue that it is the degree to which a person is integrated within the social network; House and Kahn (1985) claim that of all the measures of social support, network size is the most consistently related to health and well-being.

The **indirect effects view** posits that social support is important for quality of life during stressful events or crises. Social support mediates the effect of stressful experiences; it is protective against the harmful effects of stress. Many of the studies examining this view focus on individuals who have experienced stressful life events, such as widowhood, retirement, or illness. Kessler and McLeod (1985) conclude there is evidence for indirect effects in relation to particular stress episodes. They argue that emotional support has a pervasive indirect effect, while membership and affiliative networks do not. Generally, studies find that social support during times of stress enhances quality of life and well-being (House & Kahn, 1985). Antonucci (1990) argues that quality of social support shows a stronger relationship than quantity for both men and women but that the impact is greater for women.

Furthermore, there is more evidence of a link between social support and mental health and between social support and mortality than of a link between social support and physical illness (Cohen & Syme, 1985). And not surprisingly, there is research that does not support the indirect effects view (Andrews, Tennant, Hewson, & Vaillant, 1978). A complication in this research is that many of the life events used to measure stress also measure aspects of social networks. For example, widowhood, retirement, and relocation all entail losses, discontinuation, or disruptions to social ties. There is little research on the indirect effect of social support during ongoing chronic stresses and daily hassles.

Part of the difficulty in this area, alluded to above, is the multi-dimensionality of social support, which is challenging to capture empirically. Researchers often measure different aspects of social support, making comparisons and the drawing of general conclusions difficult. One can measure size of network, perception of emotional support, having confidantes, having companions, living arrangements, feeling of belonging, group affiliation, and so on and then relate any one or more of these measures to any number of outcomes (life satisfaction, happiness, absence of depression, mental health, any number of psychological characteristics, any number of physical health symptoms, etc.). However, many aspects of social support have not been tackled to any extent by research to date. For example, in 1985, Pearlin hypothesized about the specialization of support, wherein different sources of support may be more effective for different problems or for different stages of a particular problem. Problems often have a natural history of their own and may call for different types of support at different times. Little is known about the specialization of support even to this day.

Part of the complexity of social support lies in the fact that social interaction can be simultaneously negative and positive. Rook and Pietromonaco (1987) revealed at least four types of detrimental functions of close relationships: ineffective help, excessive help, unwarranted help, and unpleasant help. As Wortman and Conway (1985) poignantly revealed, healthy people's efforts to cheer up individuals with cancer are unhelpful to the patients, who find such unrelenting optimism disturbing and unauthentic. For example, women who had undergone a mastectomy found it unhelpful when others thought that their major concern was the loss of their breasts; they were more concerned about recurrence, death, and treatment side effects. This example is also a striking reminder that those who provide support and those who receive support may have divergent views of the interaction.

Added to the complexity is the fact that longitudinal research designs are necessary to determine the causal relationship between social support and quality of life, but most research in this area is cross-sectional. We do not know if, for example, those with better well-being or higher quality of life are more likely to engage in social interaction with others or to engage in supportive interactions with others. These options are not either/or; the relationship could occur in both directions. In addition, we do not know if the relationship between social support and quality of life is spurious. The relationship may be due to some other factor, such as social competence, wherein the socially competent may have easier access to social support and may also be more effective in negotiating the health-care system, resulting in optimal care and treatment. Or the explanatory factor may be psychological coping, wherein those with appropriate coping skills are those who receive more social support and also have higher quality of life. Even if the relationship between social support and quality of life is not spurious, we do not know whether there is a threshold effect. Is there an optimal level of social support beyond which the benefits diminish and may even become negative? Is it the absence of social support or minimal social support that is more deleterious, under what circumstances, and for whom? Is there a direct physiological link between our susceptibility to illness (through our neuroendocrinological and immune systems) and our psychological and emotional well-being that is mediated by social support?

Box 12.2 offers two scenarios with similar interactions, but the experience is negative for one person and positive for the other.

Box 12.2 *Two Scenarios*

Scenario 1. Mary is 78 years old, widowed, and with numerous health problems. She lives in an assisted living complex in a large city and is cognitively intact. She has her days fully booked with activities, Monday through Friday. These are organized through the administration of the complex. While she has her own full kitchen, where she makes her breakfast and snacks, she often eats in the main dining room of the building with others. Two of her children live in the same city and one elsewhere in the country. The two children who live in the city call her often and offer to have her come to their places for visits, either for a few hours or a few days, whatever she would like. Similarly, the child who lives at some distance calls often and invites Mary to come for short or extended stays. It is, however, difficult to get in touch with Mary because she refuses to have an answering machine or voice-mail, and her busy schedule means that she is often not at home. When asked, she will tell you proudly about her children and how wonderful they are to her. However, she seldom accepts the invitation to travel to see the child who lives far away, and while she will visit her children in the city on special occasions, such as on

their birthdays or at Christmas time, she finds that she is busy. She is not the grandmotherly type and does not know her grandchildren well but tries hard to remember their birthdays and to send cards. She prefers the company of other seniors and has very close friends within the complex.

Scenario 2. Heather, who also lives in the same complex, is 79 years old, widowed, and with deteriorating physical health. She, too, has children in the city and one who lives some distance away. Heather is also involved in many seniors' activities offered through the complex and busies herself seeing other people. Unlike Mary, Heather has given up just about all the activities that she would do in the evening. She no longer goes out at night, and she no longer bakes, sews, or knits. She thoroughly enjoys and, indeed, longs for the company of others. She signs up for activities, seeking out social interaction. She is, therefore, usually home in the evenings when her children call, and when they do not call any particular evening, she calls them. She eagerly accepts invitations for visits and asks them to visit her more often. She finds the evenings sitting alone in her apartment to be long and wishes the time would pass more quickly.

Research on social support and aging continues today, for example on various social relationships in later life. Recent research demonstrates that social support is more important for the life satisfaction of older women than of older men (Bourque, Pushkar, Bonneville, & Beland, 2005). Barrett and Lynch (1999) confirm earlier research showing that divorced older individuals have smaller social networks than those who are married or widowed; divorced older men have the smallest networks of all. As Denton and Kusch (2006) note, we still know little about the psycho-social effects of divorce in later life, including how its impact may be buffered and how older divorced persons fare over time psycho-socially. Similarly, we know little about who adapts to conjugal bereavement, who does not, and the forces that affect adaptation (Martin-Matthews, 1999). We do know that immigrants who come to Canada after they are age 65 are more likely to be living with a family member (Che-Alford & Stevenson, 1998), probably at least in part due to ethnicity and culture. Many older immigrants also leave Canada, Boyd and Vickers (2000) speculate that they may be returning to their country of origin. However, we know very little about recent immigrants who are seniors, and their social networks.

As well, exciting new lines of inquiry are evident. New research on filial responsibility is examining it as a cultural schema that influences our ideas about appropriate behaviour related to notions such as reciprocity including strong emotions (Holroyd, 2001). The notion of reciprocity, as discussed earlier, is an essential element of a social exchange perspective (Cantor & Brennan, 2000). Whether normative expectations and perceptions are more or less influential than power dynamics is still to be understood, as is the interaction between the two in a given situation (Hong & Liu, 2000). Although a later section of this chapter focuses on caregiving, social support and family life are much broader than caregiving. Notions such as reciprocity and attachment extend beyond caregiving per se (Rosenthal, 2000).

Volunteering

Volunteering is an area of unpaid work from which older adults both give and receive social support. Volunteering, though, has changed throughout the century. At the beginning of the 20th century, there was a critical need, created by industrialization, for social welfare. Charity was largely unorganized; it involved individual, rather than organizational, efforts. By the 1940s, the state had become involved in social welfare with children's services and then transfer payments. The next two decades saw the growth of the welfare state in Canada, with societal institutions evolving in psychiatric care, criminal justice, services for the developmentally handicapped, and geriatric care. The 1960s and 1970s saw growth in the helping professions, including social work, physiotherapy, occupational therapy, speech pathology, psychology, psychometry, child development, and community development. By the latter part of the 20th century, professional human service workers had largely displaced laypeople, including volunteers, who, by implication, could not provide adequate service. Then the end of the 20th century marked a major shift, with government efforts to devolve responsibility back to the community and its not-for-profit sector (Graff, 1991; Gordon & Neal, 1997). A resurgence of interest in volunteering has been evident since that time.

Volunteering today is different in substantial ways from 100 years ago. Societal developments over the last century have included the women's movement, which has spurred the founding of new service-oriented organizations, such as rape crisis centres, shelters for battered women, and women's reproductive health services, which rely heavily on volunteers for direct service work. These organizations tend to be characterized by democratic decision making, involvement of service users, and relatively non-hierarchical structures. New ways of thinking emphasize the importance of understanding how social identities are influenced by social structural variables, such as class, gender, and race. There is increased awareness of the consequences of political and economic culture for lived lives. This has occurred within a climate of changing fiscal policies, in which there is less generous funding to voluntary organizations, when it is available at all. The devolution of service programs previously provided by government to the voluntary sector has enormously increased both the pressure and the opportunities for the voluntary sector. The partial withdrawal of government responsibility has meant that administrative and financial responsibilities for the social safety net for vulnerable persons and groups now fall to the community (Chappell, 1999).

The 1987 Canadian National Survey on Volunteer Activity (NSVA) and the 1997 National Survey on Giving, Volunteering and Participating (NSGVP) have given Canada the richest, most comprehensive national data on volunteering in the world. Two meanings of volunteering are captured within the 1997 NSGVP. Volunteering can be either formal or informal. **Formal volunteer work** is defined in terms of activity with an organization, frequently with paid staff. **Informal volunteer work** is not performed through an organization and includes, for example, helping a friend or a neighbour. The distinguishing characteristic of volunteering is that it is done without pay and of one's own free will.

That survey also includes information on donations and civic participation in local associations and organizations, including attendance at meetings, voting in elections, and being informed about news and public affairs. It finds that individuals who participate in any one form of volunteering, for example, donating, formal volunteering, informal volunteering, or civic participation, are more likely to participate in other forms of volunteering as well. Our interest here is in formal volunteering through organizations. The area of informal volunteering receives much research attention, but it is not referred to as "volunteering" in the literature—rather, it is found within the research on social support, generally and, specifically, on caregiving.

In 1997, just under one-third of Canadians aged 15 years and over engaged in formal volunteering, constituting some 7.5 million persons. This was an increase over the one-quarter of Canadians who engaged in formal volunteering a decade earlier. One-third of volunteers accounted for fully 81 percent of all hours contributed: that is, a small proportion do most of the volunteering. People aged 15 to 24 years, as well as those aged 35 to 54 years, volunteer comparatively more than do other age groups. People aged 15 to 24 years almost doubled their rate of volunteering from 18 percent in 1987 to 33 percent in 1997. These younger individuals, though, contribute fewer hours than do their counterparts in other age groups. Furthermore, the number of hours they contribute decreased over the decade (from 174 hours, on average, to 125 hours per year). Those with more income and more education are more likely to volunteer. In addition, those who volunteer when older tended to volunteer when they were younger (Statistics Canada, 1998b; Hertzog & Kulka 1989).

Almost a quarter of seniors volunteer (22 percent in 1987; 23 percent in 1997). They contribute, on average, more hours per year than any other age group (202 hours, compared with the next largest category of 160 hours for those aged 55 to 64 years, to a low of 125 among those aged 15 to 24 years).

The Benefits of Volunteering

A dominant theme within the literature on formal volunteering is that it is good not only for the recipients of services but for the volunteers themselves. In Canada, Graff (1991) has been a vocal and visible advocate of the benefits of volunteering. She argues that volunteering contributes to the health, self-esteem, and longevity of volunteers. Indeed Aquino, Russell, Cutrona, and Altmaier (1996) find a relationship between volunteer work and life satisfaction, accounted for by social support (confirming earlier research by Hunter and Linn, 1980). Caro and Bass (1997) also report a relationship between health and volunteering, as do Canadians Hirdes and Forbes (1993).

These studies are primarily cross-sectional. Therefore we do not know whether the relationship between volunteering and quality of life is causal or reflects selectivity. Does volunteering maintain and enhance well-being or do those who are in better health and are more satisfied with life volunteer? A review of 37 mostly American independent studies over 25 years (from 1968 to 1994) notes that these studies typically use correlational designs. Even though many of these studies are not longitudinal, many control for the independent effects of health and socio-economic status. They demonstrate that 70 percent of older volunteers enjoy greater quality of life than the average non-volunteer; those involved in direct helping seem to derive greater rewards from volunteering than older adults engaged in more indirect and less formal helping roles (Wheeler, Gorey, & Greenblatt, 1998).

As for those who are served, approximately 85 percent of the people with whom older volunteers work do better than people not receiving the services of volunteers. Greater benefit results from volunteers engaged in enablement or counselling roles than from those engaged in advocacy, mediation, social brokering, or information referral. In addition, the authors conclude that the effectiveness of counselling by older volunteers compares favourably with the effectiveness of paid professional social workers and that probably the most effective form of help combines formal social workers with older volunteers. The benefits for the recipients appear to be related to specific types of social support.

A Special Type of Social Support — Caregiving

Many more people provide informal care than undertake formal volunteering. When the physical and/or mental health of the senior declines, social support typically turns into caregiving, sometimes called simply caring. **Caregiving** refers to support provided to seniors because their health has deteriorated and they can no longer function independently as they once did. Caregiving is a major area of interest in gerontology because physical health declines in old age. Caregiving is becoming a common phase in the family life cycle as our population ages (see Box 12.3). Today's baby boom generation may spend more years caring for a parent than for dependent children (Atchley & Barusch, 2004). The defining characteristic is that the care is required by the individual. This does not mean that the individuals involved necessarily define their interaction as caregiving or as the provision of assistance

Despite media and governmental attention to the formal health-care system, in fact, care and assistance from the informal network of family and friends has been the mainstay of care for seniors throughout history. **Informal care** refers to unpaid assistance from family and friends. Those who are paid, whether by family or by the health-care system, are typically referred to as **formal caregivers**. Summarizing research on caregiving in industrialized countries, Kane, Evans, and MacFayden (1990) conclude that, regardless of whether the country provides universal comprehensive health insurance, the informal network provides 75 to 85 percent of the total personal care received by seniors.

The 1996 national General Social Survey (GSS) reveals that 22 percent of seniors receive assistance because of long-term health problems or physical limitations; 4 percent receive assistance because of a temporary difficulty, such as a short-term illness or minor injury (Keating, Fast, Frederick, Cranswick, & Perrier, 1999). Among older adults receiving assistance for long-term health problems, there are higher proportions of women than men, of the unmarried than the married, of the older rather than younger, and, not surprisingly, of those in poor health. Fully 93 percent of them receive assistance with household tasks. That

Box 12.3 *The Canadian Caregiver Coalition*

The Canadian Caregiver Coalition is the national voice for the needs and interests of family caregivers. We are a bilingual, not-for-profit organization made up of caregivers, caregiver support groups, national stakeholder organizations and researchers.

The Canadian Caregiver Coalition provides leadership in identifying and responding to the needs of caregivers in Canada. We recognize and respect the integral role of family caregivers in society, and we work to make government and the public understand that caregiving is not a substitute for public responsibility in health and social care. The work of the CCC-CCAN involves: policy development, research, education, resource development and communication.

Canadian Caregiver Coalition Mission:

To join with caregivers, service providers, policy makers and other stakeholders to identify and respond to the needs of caregivers in Canada.

Source: Canadian Caregiver Coalition, http://www.ccc-ccan.ca/. Used by permission.

is, most seniors receiving care do so with instrumental activities of daily living and not with the basic activities of daily living that are required for survival. The caregivers to these seniors are more likely to be female than male (61 percent versus 39 percent), with a mean age of 44 for women and 42 for men, somewhat younger than is reported in some other studies. In a province-wide study of caregivers in British Columbia, Chappell and Litkenhaus (1995) find that 73 percent are female; the mean age is 52 years. Of female caregivers, 54 percent in British Columbia are wives and daughters. Nationally, 75 percent of those caring for seniors with dementia are women, usually wives and daughters (Canadian Study on Health and Aging, 1994a).

Women shoulder the major responsibility for the organization and provision of care. Not only are more women than men primary caregivers, but women provide more total weekly hours of caregiving, and more women than men undertake tasks related to homemaking, personal care, and emotional support. Men are more likely to perform instrumental activities, such as home maintenance and repair. Driving and help with finances are just as likely to be undertaken by men as by women.

The distinction between primary and secondary caregivers is an important one. The majority of research on caregiving focuses on the **primary caregiver**. In fact, little is known about others, and even less is known about the differential experiences of these two groups (Chappell & Behie, 2000). Tennstedt, McKinlay, and Sullivan (1989) report that spouse caregivers are the least likely to receive assistance from others but that child caregivers and friends who are primary caregivers usually have secondary caregivers involved with them. When the primary caregiver is a child, she is usually a daughter or daughter-in-law, and the sons and sons-in-law as well as grandchildren living with her often act as **secondary caregivers**. Friends are more typically secondary than primary caregivers. Brody, Hoffman, Klebon, and Schoonover (1989) report that among siblings who are caregivers, one tends to be the primary caregiver, with the others secondary caregivers.

Another study (American Association of Retired Persons and Travellers Company Foundation, 1989) reports that employed caregivers are more likely to have secondary caregivers helping them than primary caregivers who are not working for pay. We do not know whether employed caregivers are more likely to be secondary than primary caregivers themselves. Brody and Schoonover (1986) reported that employed caregiving daughters give just as many hours to caregiving as their unemployed counterparts but that they are involved in different activities. Does employment add stress to the life of the caregiver as another demand? Or does it provide diversion and relief, reducing the stress of the caregiving experience? We do not know. We also know little about whether the involvement of secondary caregivers is helpful or unhelpful to the primary caregiver. Not surprisingly, the little available research reveals contradictory findings; Jutras and Veilleux (1991) report that secondary caregivers help alleviate the burden for primary caregivers but Pruchno (1990) reports that they do not. No doubt each is reality for some caregivers and not for others.

The primacy of the marital relationship continues as we age and as health deteriorates. Spouses, if they are available, are likely to provide care during periods of greater disability and illness and continue doing so even as their own health declines, more than any other caregiver (Hess & Soldo, 1985; Chappell, 1992). Older couples tend to cope by redistributing domestic chores, but there tends to be less relocation when the husband is the one who becomes disabled first. This is because wives' traditional tasks include cooking, cleaning, and attending to their husbands' needs. Because women tend to marry men a few years older than themselves and have a longer life expectancy than men, they tend to be there to provide assistance to their husbands as their health deteriorates in the few years before death. The husband is likely not to be around when the wife's health deteriorates, so it is her child—a daughter if there is one—who steps in to provide the care. Children are the next most frequent caregivers. Among the non-married (including the never-married, divorced, separated, and widowed), half name their children, 29 percent naming daughters and 20 percent naming sons (Chappell, 1990).

Caregiving roles of sons and daughters tend to be different and are often gender based, with daughters providing more hands-on and emotional care and sons providing more supervision and money, if and when needed. If, however, a daughter is unavailable either because there is not one or she is geographically distant, sons provide the needed care (Horowitz, 1981). These early findings on the gendered nature of caregiving have been confirmed more recently (Frederick & Fast, 1999; Wilson, 2000). A son is less likely to be a primary caregiver than a daughter unless he is an only child, lives closer to the care receiver, or has only brothers. Harris and Bichler (1997) propose, as a possible explanation for men's lower participation in caregiving, that children may feel more comfortable providing care to a parent of the same sex. Because women generally have a longer lifespan than men, there are fewer senior men to be cared for, leading to a smaller number of sons as caregivers. Nonetheless, women also predominate as caregivers due to both social structure and ideology. Social structures, such as government, employers and health insurers, place limitations on the availability of formal help (see Chapter 15) and these limitations necessitate informal or unpaid caregiving. Ideological factors are also at work. Paid work is seen as primary for men; caregiving is seen as primary and natural for women (Walker, Osgood, Richardson & Ephross, 1998). A son is less likely than a daughter to offer care to an aging parent but is more likely to provide services when asked, more likely to rely on his spouse or sister as a primary caregiver, and more likely to support the primary caregiver as a peripheral helper or to be involved in particular tasks as a secondary caregiver.

Caregivers to seniors can themselves be seniors. Eight percent of Canadian seniors provide care to other seniors (Stobert & Cranswick, 2004). They are most likely providing care to their spouse (25 percent), close friend (33 percent) or a neighbour (19 percent). The same gendered division of labour noted earlier is evident among seniors caring for seniors.

As we learned in Chapter 11, middle-aged children, primarily daughters, have been identified as the **sandwich generation, hidden victims,** and the **generation in the middle** because they can have multiple demands, including having to care for aging parents, still raising their children, and working in paid labour. However, these terms are misnomers. Despite the popularity of this notion and the media attention given to it, it is not middle-aged adults with young children who are providing extensive help to their parents. It is, rather, children who no longer have their own children living at home (Penning, 1998; Rosenthal, 1986). No more than a quarter of middle-aged caregivers are both caring for their children at home and providing care to a parent (Williams, 2005). The term **serial caregiving** would be more appropriate because most women raise their children, then care for their parents, then care for their husbands, in succession, rather than simultaneously.

Much less is known about caregivers other than spouses and children. Barrett and Lynch (1999) found that fully 88 percent of married respondents reported their primary care provider was their spouse; those who were married or divorced had the smallest caregiving network and it was composed primarily of family members. Seniors who were single or widowed had more diverse caregiving networks, including both family and friends. However, unmarried seniors were also the most likely to receive no assistance at all.

Himes and Reidy (2000) find that friend caregivers tend to be older, provide fewer hours of care, and generally provide short-term care for acute rather than chronic illness. Fischer, Rogne, and Eustis (1990) characterize it as "care without commitment" because the caregivers have neither obligation nor authority. This finding has profound implications for seniors, who, as we have already learned, tend to suffer from long-term chronic illnesses. We do know that elderly persons without families are more likely to live in long-term care institutions.

While still not abundant, research on cultural minorities is beginning to increase. Some other cultures, such as Chinese culture, historically place much emphasis on care for their older adults by children. The notion of filial piety includes respect and care for elderly family members. Sons, notably firstborns, were expected to provide care in old age, often reflected in differential inheritance through a patriarchal system. In this system daughters became members of the husband's family upon marriage and daughters-in-law were expected to help the son in caring for his parents, her parents-in-law. Rapid and tumultuous political and cultural change in the middle of the 20th century, as well as globalization with modern technologies, have brought many changes to the embrace of filial piety. At the present time, it is considered a virtue and praised as a unique aspect of Chinese society, but the focus is on supporting elderly parents as an expression of gratitude rather than economic necessity (Wang, 2004). That is, filial piety is changing as a cultural norm. Nevertheless there is recent evidence that Chinese Canadian families are still distinctive. Parents are more likely to be living with their children even while they are married and living with their spouse than is true of other Canadian families and they are more likely to name a son rather than a spouse as the person they would turn to in an emergency. However, daughters-in-law are less involved in the care of their in-laws than the traditional notion of filial piety would suggest; they are now providing care to their own parents (Chappell, 2003; 2005).

As Chipperfield (1996) correctly points out, we have had much research on the effects of the caregiving experience on the caregiver but comparatively little research on how seniors themselves experience the receipt of informal care. Her own longitudinal study in Manitoba suggests that those who are in poor health and more dependent upon the care provider are more likely to feel they receive inadequate help with IADL. This finding is potentially important; it suggests that those who are dissatisfied with their assistance are actually in need of greater assistance. Newsom and Schulz (1996) report that nearly 40 percent of the care recipients they studied reported some sort of emotional strain associated with receiving help with one or more activities of daily living. This emotional strain was related to depression, even one year later. Keefe and Fancey (2002) find that employed caregivers and their older mothers do not view the caregiving situation in the same light. Daughters tend to emphasize the past contributions that their mothers made to them, whereas the mothers tend to emphasize their current dependent situation, even though they often continue to contribute emotionally and sometimes financially to their daughters. Much more research is needed on seniors' reactions to the care that they receive.

Caregiver Burden

One of the major foci of research on caregivers for seniors has been the stress and burden they experience. Montgomery (1989) identified several terms commonly encountered in the literature, all capturing the essence of the meaning of burden (as a consequence of caregiving), including *stress effects, caregiving consequences,* and *caregiving impact.* George and Gwyther (1986) defined **caregiver burden** as the physical, psychological or emotional, social, and financial problems that can be experienced by family members caring for impaired older adults. Tebb (1995) refers to it as the inability to be resilient. It is commonly understood to have both objective and subjective components, with the subjective particularly important because people's own definitions and assessments of the situation greatly affect their ability to meet their own needs. Objective burden often consists of such things as changes in daily routine, employment, and health, while subjective burden often includes emotional reactions such as low morale, anxiety, and depression.

Much of the caregiving literature has focused on caregivers to sufferers of Alzheimer's disease and other dementias. Those caring for people with dementia are more burdened than those caring for the physically frail (Zarit & Zarit, 1983; George & Gwyther, 1986). It appears to be the behavioural manifestations of dementia that are most problematic for caregivers, rather than the condition per se (Chappell & Penning, 1996) and not all stages of the disease are equally problematic. Particularly distressing behavioural problems include agitation, violence, incontinence, wandering, hallucinations, dangerous and embarrassing behaviours, sleep disturbance, and any behaviour that requires watchfulness and control from the caregiver. Among specific caregiving *tasks*, particularly burdensome are those that must be performed at a particular time and place and those requiring personal bodily contact, such as bathing, dressing, and toileting (Montgomery, Gonyea, & Hooyman, 1985). The relationship between the caregiver and the care receiver makes a difference; close relationships are associated with less burden (Morris, Morris, & Britton, 1988).

The psychological impact of caregiving has been well documented, in terms of depression (Parks & Pilisuk, 1991), guilt, worry/anxiety, loneliness (Barusch, 1988), emotional stress and strain, lowered physical functioning, lower social functioning, or worse general health (Hughes, Giobie-Hurder, Weaver, Kubal, & Henderson, 1999). Indeed, the negative psychological and emotional consequences of caregiving are widely acknowledged. The search for explanatory factors of burden has also received much attention. There is inconsistency in the literature but predictors that emerge include the care receiver's functional ability, gender, hours of caregiving, interruptions of paid employment, the relationship between the caregiver and care receiver, health of the caregiver, and social support (Stull, Kosloski, & Kercher, 1994; Chappell & Penning, 1996). Burden has also been studied as a predictor of other caregiving outcomes, such as well-being or physical health.

One of the most popular theoretical models for studying caregiver burden is the **stress-process model**, proposed specifically for those caring for individuals with Alzheimer's disease (Pearlin, Mullan, Semple, & Skaff, 1990). This model considers caregiver burden a subjective primary stressor that is affected by background characteristics including caregiving history and socio-economic characteristics. Burden then affects outcomes such as depression and physical health directly, as well as indirectly through secondary role strain such as family conflict and economic problems and secondary intra-psychic strain such as self-esteem and competence. This process is mediated by coping and social support. Some support has been evident in research to date (Hughes et al., 1999; Noonan & Tennstedt, 1997). Yates, Tennstedt, and Chang (1999) expanded the popular stress-process model to reflect subjective appraisal by incorporating adaptations derived from Lawton, Moss, Cleban, Glicksman, and Rovine's (1991) appraisal model. Specifically, they modified burden to be a secondary appraisal variable, arguing that it is a subjective assessment. They also modified caregiving assistance, often measured in terms of actual hours of care provided, to be a primary appraisal variable on the argument that the caregiver makes an assessment of how much care is required (also recognizing that it is related to the objective needs of the care recipient). Support for this modification is also evident (Yates, Tennstedt, & Chang, 1999; Chappell & Reid, 2002). (See Figure 12.1.)

Figure 12.1 MODIFIED STRESS PROCESS MODEL

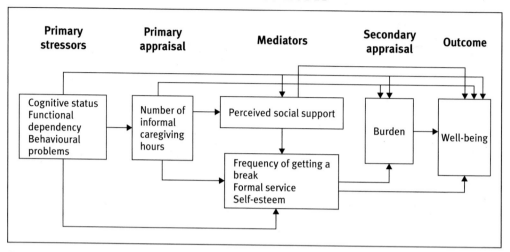

Source: N.L. Chappell & R.C. Reid. (2002). Burden and well-being among caregivers: Examining the distinction. *The Gerontologist*, 42(6): 772–780. Used by permission.

The primary focus in the caregiving literature is on stress and burden during the caregiving experience. Fewer studies examine the caregiver's bereavement, or adjustment to the death of the loved one. An implicit assumption is that once the loved one dies, stress on the caregiver ceases (Montgomery, 1996), which reflects a further assumption that the importance of the role lies in the stresses and burdens, rather than in the satisfaction derived from caring for a loved one. However, the death of a loved one is traumatic, and the bereavement literature generally tells us that wives suffer greater depression than do bereaved husbands. In time the depressive episodes for both tend to decline (Zisook & Shuchter, 1991). Among caregivers in particular, similar results are evident, revealing similar gender and relationship associations (Rudd, Viney, & Preston, 1999; Schulz, Newsom, Fleissner, Decamp, & Nieboer, 1997). The few studies examining the effect of nursing home placement report contradictory findings; some show that the death of a loved one in a nursing home results in greater difficulty for the caregiver than a death at home, while others suggest no difference (Chappell & Behie, 2002).

This focus on the negative aspects of caregiving has resulted in a lack of attention to the positive or more satisfying aspects of the caregiving situation. But, when asked why they provide care, caregivers give a number of reasons, including love, affection, reciprocity, and commitment. In the province-wide B.C. study, Chappell and Litkenhaus (1995) report that the vast majority (93.4 percent) of caregivers can list rewards of caregiving. More than half name something that involves the personal relationship with the care receiver, such as seeing them happy and watching them improve, and the closeness of the relationship;

one-quarter cite being able to help. Fully one-third say that the caregiving relationship is the closest relationship they have ever had with anyone; more than 40
percent say that it is as close as other relationships have been. In the 1996 national
GSS survey, over three-quarters said they were giving back what life had given
to them (87.7 percent) and that strengthened their relationship with their care
receiver (88.7 percent).

Despite the evidence that caregiving is a burden, when one examines prevalence figures, the majority of caregivers do not emerge as overburdened and
unable to cope. In the B.C. study, two-thirds say that they find caregiving stressful; however, two-thirds of those who find it stressful say that the burden is inter-
mittent, and only 9.2 percent say it is extreme. When asked how well they think
they are coping, over 90 percent say that they are coping well. In the national
GSS survey, only 18.2 percent say that they feel burdened in helping others.
Schulz and Williamson (1991) find that most are able to meet their demands
without becoming dysfunctional. Without denying that caregiving can be burdensome and that some require assistance, it is time for gerontology to recognize that not all caregivers are at risk of burn-out and to present a more balanced
picture of caregiving.

We need to turn our attention to identifying the minority of caregivers who
are at risk and require considerable help. We also need to study the positive consequences of caregiving and the beneficial coping skills of caregivers. Some
research links personality characteristics to better coping and less burden among
caregivers. Individuals scoring higher on hardiness, sense of coherence, and personal resiliency are likely to report less burden and better overall well-being, to
use formal services less, and to be in better health (Mockler, Riordan, & Murphy,
1998; Braithwaite, 1998).

Respite

The fact that we know much less about the experience and lives of caregivers
than the abundance of literature on burden would suggest is further evidenced
in recent research on respite for caregivers. Having a break, known as **respite**,
refers conceptually to a pause in or temporary cessation of caregiving tasks and
an interval of rest. However, in practice and in research, it is referred to primarily
as a service or a group of services that provide periods of relief or rest to caregivers
(Feinberg & Kelly, 1995). The services are considered respite care when they
explicitly target the caregiver, rather than the care recipient.

In Canada, they typically refer to three types of services: (1) attendants who
come to the house and look after the senior while the caregiver leaves the home
to do such tasks as shopping or stays in the home but tends to other tasks, such
as cooking or sewing; (2) adult daycare or day hospital programs, where the
care recipient is taken for a few hours; and (3) respite beds in a facility, where
the care receiver stays for a few days or weeks. Respite services aim to strengthen
the efforts of informal caregivers to allow the loved one to remain within the

community by decreasing caregiver burden, providing caregiver education and training, and linking caregivers and care recipients to other community services (Kosloski & Montgomery, 1995).

However, use of respite services is low, with only a small proportion of those eligible using the service when it is offered. Among the many reasons offered for this include unfamiliarity with the service, cost, psychosocial conflict over the appropriateness of using respite care, philosophical values opposed to respite care, feeling a loss of independence, lack of understanding of bureaucratic structures, and negative attitudes toward the receipt of services (Rokowski & Clarke, 1985). Furthermore, research suggests that respite services have a moderate effect at best. Several studies report no effect; other studies report positive outcomes, such as lessened burden for caregivers, higher levels of self-efficacy related to caregiving, lower levels of depression, and improved physical health (Milne, Pitt, & Sabin, 1993; Nolan, Trahar, Clarke, & Blass, 1993; Gottlieb, 1995). Several reviews of the literature in this area arrive at inconsistent conclusions, arguing that respite is either mildly or moderately effective (Kirwin, 1991; Lawton et al., 1991).

One reason that can account for these findings is methodological. Those not receiving formal respite services may be receiving respite (a break) through other means, such as a relative looking after the loved one for a period of time, or the loved one being hospitalized. Therefore, a typical methodological design that compares users of the services with those who are not using them creates a major selectivity problem, since it may be comparing respite services with other types of respite to the caregiver. A different research design is required to more accurately assess the adequacy of the services.

Chappell, Reid, and Dow (2001) argue that researchers and service providers alike have gone astray by conceptualizing respite as a service, rather than as an outcome. Caregivers must first be asked to define for themselves what it means to have a break. Despite the emphasis on a task orientation (assistance with ADL and IADL) by both researchers and service providers, it is the emotional aspects of caregiving that appear to be the most important to both the caregiver and the loved one receiving care (Abel, 1990; Hasselkus, 1988). Informal caregivers realize the importance of their invisible work: decision making and protecting the senior's self-image, sense of identity, and autonomy. They see this as their most important task. Since caregivers view their role differently from researchers and service providers, it should be not be surprising that they view respite differently as well.

Using in-depth qualitative interviews and confirmation in a random sample of 250 caregivers in British Columbia, Chappell, Reid, and Dow (2001) derived a typology of what respite means to caregivers. It is very different from what researchers and service providers had assumed. Six meanings of respite were derived (Table 12.2). *Stolen moments* refers to brief periods away from the actual tasks of caregiving, involving activities or situations that temporarily take the caregiver away from caregiving tasks while maintaining the daily caregiver routine. It includes all manner of activities, such as taking the dog for a walk, taking a bath, cooking, having a haircut, grocery shopping, and so on—generally activities that have to be done anyway.

Other meanings include: *connections* (social involvement, that is, making connections with people in the world "out there," either in a social sense or as part of a support group); *relief* (separation from caregiving, a complete physical and mental break); *mental or physical stimulus* (challenges not associated with caregiving that engage the mind and/or the body in an all-encompassing manner); *angst-free care receiver* (occasions when the care receiver is relatively happy, comfortable); *minimize the importance* (they do not need a break. Often, secondary caregivers and those with fewer caregiving responsibilities fall into this category). These different meanings of respite, based on experiential evidence from caregivers themselves, reveal that fully half the caregivers define having a break differently from how the health-care system and researchers have in the past, with the most prevalent category (*stolen moments* at almost 50 percent) entirely new and unexpected. Interestingly, the meaning of respite for caregivers is unrelated to gender or to social class.

Not one caregiver defined a break or spoke of the experience in relation to service provision. These meanings, nevertheless, have important implications for service delivery, pointing to the fact that policy makers and service providers should redefine respite as an outcome, rather than a service. Assessment protocols should ask caregivers what a break means to them and how they can best receive a meaningful break. New types of interventions based on the reconceptualization of respite as an outcome may see increased use of respite services.

Table 12.2 **THE MEANINGS OF RESPITE ACCORDING TO CAREGIVERS:
DOMINANT THEMES**

Stolen moments	48.1%	
Minimize importance	12.0%	61.3%
Angst-free care receiver	1.2%	
External respite relief	18.3%	
Mental/physical boost	11.2%	38.6%
Connections	9.1%	

N=241 caregivers to seniors in Victoria, B. C.

Note: Numbers do not total 100% due to rounding

Source: N.L. Chappell, R.C. Reid, & E. Dow (2001). Respite reconsidered: A typology of meanings based on the caregiver's point of view. *Journal of Aging Studies, 15*(2), 201–216.

New interventions, such as instruction in self-care, may be appropriate. Another might be teaching strategies to reduce stress levels and to deal with anxiety and guilt.

Caregiving in the Future

While we do not discuss the health-care system until a later chapter, nevertheless there is much interest in future projections of informal caregiving because of its relationship with the formal care system. Keefe, Légaré, and Carrière (2004) used Canada's 1996 National Population Health Survey to project the availability of informal support and its possible impact on chronic home-care services. Between 2001 and 2031, they project a steady increase in the proportion of senior women without any surviving children, likely translating into less informal support. Even if the proportion of seniors requiring assistance remains stable, the growth in the size of the elderly population means that the expected decrease in availability of informal support will result in both an absolute and relative increase in the need for formal support. If we assume the increased educational levels of future cohorts of seniors means increased awareness of and demand for formal services then seniors of the future might expect even more health care than those elderly today. If major health problems seen in younger populations continue, the need for assistance will increase even more. On the other hand, if the compression of morbidity hypothesis discussed much earlier were to become reality one might see less of an increase in demand for formal services.

The relationship between the receipt of informal care and formal services received some attention years ago, (Chappell, 1987; Chappell & Guse, 1989; Penning & Chappell, 1990) but still has not caught the attention of most researchers. Nevertheless, it is critical for understanding policy issues. If family and friend care is perceived as a substitute for formal care, then policies that encourage informal care can be seen as savings to the formal care system (albeit they are at a cost of increased burden and increased financial demands on private individuals and families). If, on the other hand, the formal and informal care systems are seen as complementary then policy makers should consider how the two affect one another. Dosman, Fast, and Keating (2005) recently analyzed the 2002 General Social Survey to understand this issue. Networks consisting of a spouse alone receive the least formal care. When formal care is introduced, family and friend care increases, especially when the care networks are predominantly close kin. This confirms earlier research (Chappell & Blandford, 1991) supporting the complementary nature of the two systems of care. The informal care system is the system of first resort, with the formal system entering either when there is no informal care available or when the needs of the recipient become too great for the informal care system to manage on its own. In this case, formal services are sought to assist the informal care network.

Chapter Summary

Interaction with others is a normal part of virtually everyone's life. As human beings, we are social creatures. The concept of social support receives much recognition in research. However, capturing the essence of social support in precise scientific terms and then being able to translate this into accurate measurement is another matter.

Key ideas to remember from this chapter:

- Social support, particularly in gerontological research, has focused on emotional support and instrumental or task-oriented support, and on the size and composition of social networks.
- Early research in gerontology measured social interaction, assumed it was supportive, and debunked the notion that the vast majority of seniors were lonely and isolated. On the contrary, it documented the social embeddedness and extensiveness of social ties in old age.
- Most seniors prefer intimacy at a distance: not living with their children, but maintaining close ties.
- Most research has focused on the marriage relationship and also the relationship of seniors with their children. We know much less about other relationships, such as those with siblings, grandchildren, and distant relatives.
- Social support is structured by gender and SES.
- Research in the 1980s empirically examined the supportiveness of social interactions and confirmed a relationship between social support and well-being. Social support is directly related to our well-being; those with more social support have increased well-being. Social support is also important for our well-being during times of stress. Those with social support during times of stress have greater well-being than those without social support.
- Despite an abundance of evidence documenting the relationship between social support and well-being, little is longitudinal; logically, one would expect the relationship could be reciprocal.
- Although there is relatively little attention focused upon organizational participation, including volunteering, research suggests that volunteering is good for the volunteers' health. There may well be a selectivity factor operating, but among those who do volunteer, it appears to be beneficial to their health and well-being. Social support derived from this role appears to be one of the reasons.
- Caregiving is especially important as health declines during old age. Informal caregiving from family and friends, not the formal health-care system, is the mainstay of care for seniors.
- Most of the research in this area focuses on the primary caregiver, that is, the individual providing most of the care to the loved one. Women predominate as caregivers, especially wives and daughters.
- Despite the popularity of the terms *sandwich generation, hidden victims,* and *generation in the middle* to describe caregivers, research suggests a more appropriate term would be

serial caregiving. In reality, women raise their children, then provide care to their parents, and then provide care to their husbands. This tends to happen in a serial fashion, rather than simultaneously.

- Typically, there is a gender division of labour when men and women are caregivers, with women providing more hands-on personal care and emotional support; men are more likely to provide advice and monetary assistance.
- There is a major emphasis in the caregiving literature on caregiver burden. This literature reveals the many stresses associated with caregiving, including psychological, physical, emotional, and economic. However, most caregivers can also name satisfactions they derive from this role, and most cope and are not at risk of having to forfeit this role or to receive health-care services themselves.
- The fact that we have much to learn about the caregiving experience is vividly portrayed in the meanings of respite (having a break) for caregivers themselves. Fully half refer to stolen moments, a concept that is foreign to the thinking of researchers and service providers alike when they discuss respite for caregivers.

KEY TERMS

social interactions **(p. 301)**

social support **(p. 301)**

companionship **(p. 302)**

confidantes **(p. 302)**

tangible assistance **(p. 303)**

instrumental assistance **(p. 303)**

modified extended family **(p. 305)**

intimacy at a distance **(p. 306)**

convoy of social support **(p. 307)**

direct effects view **(p. 308)**

indirect effects view **(p. 308)**

formal volunteer work **(p. 312)**

informal volunteer work **(p. 312)**

caregiving **(p. 314)**

informal care **(p. 314)**

formal caregivers **(p. 314)**

primary caregiver **(p. 315)**

secondary caregiver **(p. 315)**

sandwich generation **(p. 317)**

hidden victims **(p. 317)**

generation in the middle **(p. 317)**

serial caregiving **(p. 317)**

caregiver burden **(p. 318)**

stress process model **(p. 319)**

respite **(p. 321)**

STUDY QUESTIONS

1. What is social support, and why is it important as we age?
2. Why is Litwak's concept of the modified extended family appropriate for discussions of seniors in today's society?

3. Discuss the differential importance to seniors of various relationships, such as spouse, daughter, son, sibling, and friend.

4. Discuss the relationship between social support and well-being in old age.

5. Who are the caregivers to seniors, and what do they do?

6. How important is the notion of caregiver burden?

SUGGESTED READINGS

Braithwaite, V. (1998). Institutional respite care: Breaking chores or breaking social bonds? *Gerontologist, 38*(5), 610–617.

Chappell, N.L., & Reid R.C. (2002). Burden and well-being among caregivers: Examining the distinction. *Gerontologist, 42*(6), 772–780.

Chappell, N.L., Reid, R.C., & Dow, E. (2001). Respite reconsidered: A typology of meanings based on the caregiver's point of view. *Journal of Aging Studies, 15*(2), 201–216.

Jackson, J.S., Brown, E., Antonucci, C., & Daatland, S.O. (2005). Ethnic diversity in ageing, multicultural societies. In Malcolm L. Johnson (Ed.with Vern L. Bengtson, Peter G. Coleman, & Thomas B.L. Kirkwood), *The Cambridge handbook of age and ageing.* Cambridge, UK: Cambridge University Press.

Yates, M.E., Tennstedt, S., & Chang, B.H. (1999). Contributors to and mediators of psychological well-being for informal caregivers. *Journal of Gerontology: Psychological Sciences, 54B*(1), 12–22.

Chapter 13

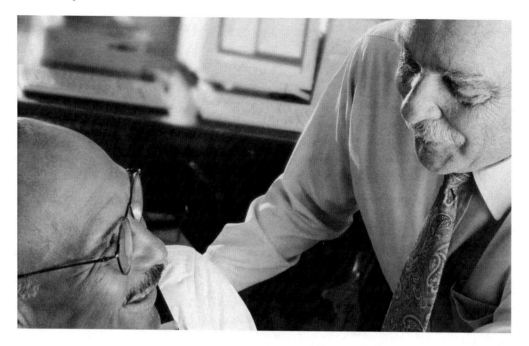

WORK AND RETIREMENT

Learning Objectives

In this chapter, you will learn about

- The history of the institutionalization of retirement.
- A description of the "new" retirement as we know it today.
- The various definitions of retirement and their links to gerontological theories.
- The linkages between work and retirement—the different work experiences of men and women and how they influence the transition into retirement and post-retirement social and economic status.
- Why and when people retire, how they retire, and the consequences of retirement.

Introduction

Most scholars would agree that retirement is a social invention that emerged in modern industrialized societies at the start of the 20th century. As labour force participation rates of older workers began to plummet in most industrialized economies, retirement became a deeply rooted social institution by the end of the 1980s. As a social institution, retirement was designed to move the older worker out of the labour force in a systematic manner without causing unwarranted economic hardship, while solving the societal problem of what to do with an aging labour force. As a consequence, retirement emerged as the last segment of the life course and helped define old age as a distinct life phase, a phase chronologically set apart from the first phase, typically dedicated to education, and the middle phase, devoted to work. Understanding the emergence and development of retirement is, therefore, crucial to an understanding of the last phase of life, since retirement is not only the principal gateway to later life but is the conduit that links the institutional structures of work and non-work to prepare the foundation for well-being in old age.

The History of Retirement in Canada

The Pre-industrial Agrarian Era

Retirement did not exist prior to the industrialization of Canada. People appeared to adjust their work with their diminishing physical capacities as they aged. As historian Andrejs Pakans has aptly observed, people **stepped down** from their work, but the process of withdrawal was informal. It could be long and drawn out (Pakans, 1989:176) or, sometimes, sudden and unexpected as a result of illness or accident (McDonald & Wanner, 1990). In agrarian Canada in the latter half of the 19th century, ownership of the family farm lent itself to stepping down because the farmer had the power to control the process. The farmer could continue to work but could also gradually reduce his more demanding tasks by delegating them to his sons and sons-in-law without losing control of the land. At a time determined by the older farmer, he would pass the farm on to his children, mainly his sons, with provisions made for the care and maintenance of himself and his wife in their old age. The promise of inheriting the farm served to maintain the interest of adult children in the farm and provided the mechanism for maintaining older people in their old age. Maintenance agreements were used to document the nature of the inheritance and the care to be provided to the older couple to make sure that the terms were implemented (Snell, 1992; 1996). Since men legally owned the property, women likely stepped down in tandem with their husbands, perhaps passing some of their more onerous tasks on to daughters or daughters-in-law, although this is not known. If a woman's husband died, her care in old age was passed on to her male relatives, such as sons. Often, the husband left explicit instructions as to how she was to be cared for, including which rooms in the house she could use (Cohen, 1988). If she remarried, the will usually stipulated that she lost her inheritance, so that husbands often exerted control over their wives even from their graves.

Not all workers owned farms, although farming was the mainstay of the economy. Men tended to work in such industries as the fur trade, iron-making industries, timber firms, and water transportation (McDonald & Wanner, 1990), while the majority of women who were employed worked as domestic servants (Cohen, 1971). Most people worked until they could no longer fulfill the responsibilities attached to their jobs, at which time they were moved to less onerous jobs that matched their capacities. The paternalistic nature of labour relations in the 1850s, driven by serious labour shortages, led to a personal concern for workers because employers were anxious to retain them in their firms (Pentland, 1981). There is some evidence that the Hudson's Bay Company offered a type of annuity plan that paid 4 percent on any of a worker's wages left in the care of the company, but only if the worker was considered deserving. Katz (1975), in a study of citizens of Hamilton, found that businessmen, if they fared well financially, would retire and pass their business on to their sons. What became of the women who were domestics, took in boarders, or ran small businesses (such as taverns) is not clear. It is likely that they simply worked until they could cope no more. If they were destitute and bereft of family, they likely ended up in a poorhouse.

The evidence about retirement in pre-industrial Canada suggests that it was an ad hoc event. For the farmer and entrepreneur, stepping down was rooted in the Canadian system of inheritance, while the paid worker was at the mercy of his or her employers. Women, it would seem, were dependent on the family economy and were to be cared for by their male relatives in old age.

The Industrial Era

The industrial revolution in Canada, which spanned the period between the 1840s and the 1930s, caused a momentous transformation of Canada from a rural, agrarian society to an urban, industrialized society. This era is usually considered by historians to be a crucial time in the development of retirement because it was during this period that retirement began to take shape as an institutionalized phase of the life course. The development of retirement is consistent with the **life course institutionalization hypothesis** (O'Rand & Henretta, 1999:181). This hypothesis suggests that, over the long term, individual lives have become increasingly organized by institutions of the state and of the workplace. In this process, individuals have been freed from the bonds of family and the earlier paternalistic relationships of the workforce. The bureaucratic structures of firms tend to be age based; so, for example, permission from an employer to continue to work is replaced by age as the criterion for retirement (Graebner, 1980). In the same vein, the availability of public or private pensions at a specific age encourages exit from the labour force at that age and tends to reduce individual discretion.

Snell (1996) argues that the effects of industrialization were gradual in Canada and that a minority of older workers were pushed out of the labour force into poverty. It was this minority who compelled the social activists in Canada to fight for pensions, which led to the establishment of the *Old Age Pensions Act* of 1927, a type of social assistance, subject to a means test. The ungenerous administration of the Act led to activism on the part of elderly people, which ultimately helped establish the *Old Age Security Act* of 1951, the first universal pension plan in Canada. With the universal pension came a steady income for older workers that made retirement a distinct reality for many Canadian older workers.

Advanced industrialization contributed in several ways to the trend that institutionalized retirement. Most importantly for older workers, firms became bigger and more bureaucratic, with specialized divisions of labour, hierarchical chains of command, and centralized authority—all of which depersonalized the firm, making it almost impossible to meet the individual needs of older workers. At the same time, scientific management (Taylor, 1947) was introduced into organizations, which divided the production process into small, repetitive operations that emphasized physical efficiency and speed—a case of deskilling older workers. In the faster-paced industries where technological change speeded up production levels even further, older workers had trouble keeping up, making them more vulnerable to unemployment (Haber & Gratton, 1994).

Once older workers were deskilled, the traditional discipline attached to the crafts disappeared, and turnover rates of workers were high. To combat this problem, Ford Motor Company created a set of graduations among identical jobs within the factory, establishing a false hierarchy based on seniority rather than skill. Because of seniority, older workers moved to the top of the hierarchy and ended up being paid more than younger workers for the same work. To avoid high costs and to be more efficient, management required a cutoff point. The cutoff was **mandatory retirement**, which was usually set at age 65. At about the same time, the wear-and-tear theory of aging was popular, which suggested that old workers were worn out and should retire. As the great Canadian Dr. William Osler suggested, ". . . men above 60 years of age were useless . . . " (*The Globe*, 1905:7). In short, a number of factors converged during industrialization that set the stage for the institutionalization of retirement. Some workers were forced out of the labour force, expedited by growing ageism and fixed time schedules for retirement.

Pensions and the Institutionalization of Retirement

In 1908, the *Government Annuities Act* was passed as a delayed response to the majority report of the Royal Commission on the Relations of Labour and Capital in 1889, which detailed the more appalling labour force conditions of early industrialism. The *Annuities Act* was not particularly successful in reaching the people who needed it the most, namely, working class labourers, who made up only 4 percent of the population (Bryden, 1974). Nor did it treat women fairly—they received lower returns than men for the same investment (Strong-Boag, 1993).

Retirement, at this time, continued to be an ad hoc affair available to the wealthiest and to those few privileged workers with a pension. The seeds had been sown, however, for the idea of retirement in both government and business.

The poverty of older workers forced out of the labour force caused great concern on the part of social reformers. After much debate in the House of Commons, the *Old Age Pensions Act* of 1927 was passed. There were three serious problems with this Act that made retirement difficult to achieve. First, the state could recover the cost of the pension from the pensioner's estate when he or she died, which violated the spirit of the Canadian system of inheritances. Second, the miserly pensions, paid on the basis of a means test, were too small to make retirement possible. Third, although this legislation was considered the first "gender-inclusive" Act (Struthers, 1992), officials maintained the gendered nature of marriage in its administration, making sure that women received lesser pensions than their husbands because women were still viewed as dependent on male relatives for their retirement income. What other family members, such as sons, could contribute to their mothers was more stringently considered in calculating women's pensions than in the calculation of men's pensions. This problem with the administration of the pension deterred parents interested in retiring because they did not wish to burden their children.

On the heels of the Great Depression and World War II, there was a demand for better pensions because Canadians desperately wanted to avoid the devastation wreaked by the Great Depression in the 1930s. The problems with the Act of 1927 also strengthened the resolve of Canadians to agitate for change. The *Old Age Security Act* of 1951, a universal, flat-rate pension plan financed and administered by the federal government, operated on the principle of social insurance for older workers, as opposed to social assistance. At this time, the *Old Age Assistance Act*, a form of social assistance, was also passed for those aged 65 to 69 years and was based on a means test. Private pension schemes also grew during World War II in response to labour force shortages. Taken together, both public and private developments facilitated the spread of retirement, linking it to a specific age and normalizing the retirement experience for most Canadians. As can be seen in Figure 13.1, the labour force participation rates of men aged 65 years and over dropped substantially from 37.9 percent in 1951 to 26.2 percent in 1966, when the next round of pension changes occurred. Women's rates remained stable during this time, because most women were not in the labour force in 1951. The labour force participation rate of women in 1966 was about 24 percent because the belief at the time was that a woman's place was in the home.

Through the 1960s, the *Old Age Security Act* was restructured to increase pension benefits and the qualifying age of 70 years was reduced by one year every year until it became age 65 in 1970. The Canada/Quebec Pension Plan (C/QPP) was added as a second tier to the pension system in 1965, as a compulsory, contributory plan with benefits linked to contributions based on waged labour. Because Canadians who were already retired would not benefit from the C/QPP, the

Figure 13.1 **PARTICIPATION RATES FOR AGE GROUPS 55-64 AND 65+ BY SEX, CANADA, 1946-2004**

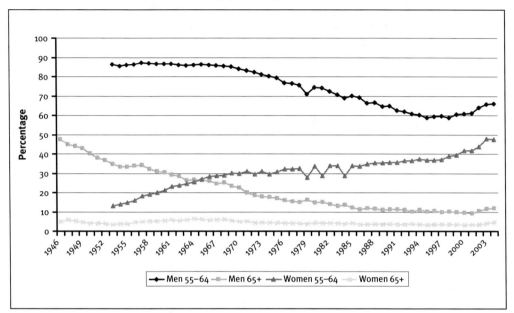

Source: Adapted from Statistics Canada, *Labour force historical review, 2004*, Catalogue No. 71F0004XCB (February 18, 2005).

Guaranteed Income Supplement was introduced in 1966, as an income-tested interim measure to be phased out when the C/QPP fully matured in 1976. The third tier of the pension system included personal savings and assets, private pensions, and the Registered Retirement Savings Plan of 1957, to secure the idea of retirement. With the three tiers of the pension system firmly in place, retirement became economically attractive, was financially guaranteed by the state, and was felt to be a desired event by most Canadians.

The first national retirement study in Canada was conducted in 1975. It found that 75 percent of women were retired at age 63 years, while 60 percent of men were retired at age 65 years (Ciffin & Martin, 1977). By the 1980s, retirement was a widespread institution, which moved Canadians from the labour force into the last segment of the life course in an ordered and systematic manner—a shift based on age and defined by the state through public pensions and by private pensions in the workplace (McDonald & Wanner, 1990; Myles, 1984). According to Figure 13.1, in 1989, only 11.1 percent of men 65 years and over were in the labour force, compared with 3.5 percent of women at the same age.

It is important to note that the labour force experiences of women were quite limited in the formative years of retirement. Most women did not work outside the home and, if they did, their work was considered secondary to the work of their husbands, who were the chief breadwinners. Also, if women worked, their unpaid work at home occurred simultaneously with their paid work in the labour force at a time when housework was hard physical labour. Thus women's circumstances made their link to the labour force more tenuous than men's—differences that ultimately call into question the accepted view of the history of retirement and its application to women (McDonald, 2002).

Retirement in the 21st Century

The Extent of Retirement

Today, in Canada, retirement is the norm for older workers. Canadians want to retire, and preferably early. The General Social Survey of 2002 asked people aged 45 to 59 years at what age they planned to retire. Forty-seven percent of men thought that they would retire before age 65, 22.6 percent at age 65 and 3.3 percent at age 66 or later. About 27 percent of men said they did not know when or if they would retire. Over a decade ago, the percentages were different. In 1991, 51 percent of men said they planned to retire early; 22.5 percent said they would retire at age 65 while 2 percent said they would retire at age 66 or older. About 24 percent did not know their retirement age or did not intend to retire. Today, there are fewer men taking early retirement, more men considering a later retirement age, and more men uncertain about their age of retirement (Schellenberg, 2004). In 2002, 49.7 percent of women intended to retire early, 21.7 at age 65 years, and 2 percent after age 65. About 27 percent of the women did not know when or if they would retire (Schellenberg, 2004). In 1991 more women planned to retire early (51 percent) fewer planned to retire at age 65 (20 percent) and fewer worked past age 66 (1 percent).

The desires of Canadians are reflected in their retirement behaviour. As seen in Figure 13.2, the median age of retirement for men in 2003 was 63.3, down from the median age of 65.1 in 1976. For women, the median age of retirement dropped from 64.8 in 1976 to 60.4 in 2003.

As we saw in Figure 13.1, in 2004, 66 percent of men aged 55 to 64 years remained in the labour force, compared with 86.5 percent in 1953 (McDonald & Wanner, 1990). For men aged 65 years and over, the labour force participation rate was 11.8 percent in 2004, compared with 47.5 percent in 1947, a dramatic drop by any measure. The data in Figure 13.1 flag three retirement trends. Although there has been a decline for all ages, declines for men have been greater for those over age 65; the decline over age 65 appears to have stabilized; and, during the 2000s, labour force participation seems to have fluctuated in an upward direction. The fluctuations may represent such factors as older workers going back to work after retirement or not retiring at all.

Women's labour force participation, as seen in Figure 13.1, is different from men's because the rates represent two developments: the dramatic increase in women's labour force participation starting in the 1960s and the trend toward

Figure 13.2 **RETIREMENT AGE BY SEX, CANADA, 1976–2004**

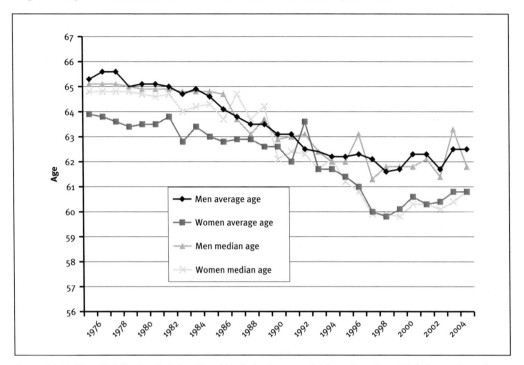

Source: Adapted from Statistics Canada, *Labour force historical review, 2004*, Catalouge No. 71F0004XCB (February 18, 2005).

early retirement. In 1954, only 12.9 percent of women aged 55 to 64 years were in the labour force, compared with almost 50 percent in 2003. At the same time, the labour force participation rates for women aged 65 years and over have never exceeded the rate of 6.3 percent in 1964 and have remained the same since 1946, suggesting that the two trends offset each other According to Figure 13.3, the flat participation rates of women during the 1990s probably represent the full integration of women into the labour force (McDonald, 2006c; Beaudry & Lemieux, 1999) The other possibility is that the participation rates of successive generations have become more similar, leading to slower growth (Sunter, 2001). What is clear in Figure 13.3 is that the decline in the participation rates of men, as we saw above, has served to narrow the gap between men and women and the participation rates of women are beginning to resemble the rates of men (Hicks, 2002; McDonald, 2006c).

The New Retirement

Having argued that the life course has become institutionalized, some researchers now debate whether or not the life course is coming undone (Guillemard & Rein,

Figure 13.3 **PARTICIPATION RATES BY AGE AND SEX, CANADA, 1976 AND 2004**

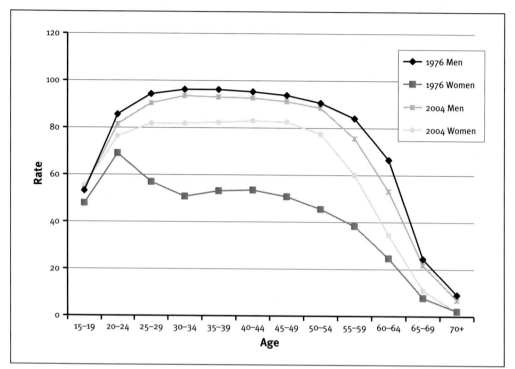

Source: Adapted from Statistics Canada, *Labour force historical review, 2004*, Catalouge No. 71F0004XCB (February 18, 2005).

1993), is simply becoming longer and fuzzier (Kohli & Rein, 1991), is more asynchronous (O'Rand & Henretta, 1999; Han & Moen, 1999; O'Rand, 2003; Settersten, 2006a), or is subject to shifts in the boundaries between the "boxes" of education, work and leisure (Settersten, 2006a:5). Ekerdt's article "Born to Retire" discusses retirement planning for high school students, capturing early life changes that affect retirement (Ekerdt, 2004). A study of the discursive trends in a Canadian newspaper illustrates how the message about the ideal retirement is being re-shaped—and probably won't work since it resists aging (Laliberte Rudman, 2006). In short, retirement does not always represent an abrupt transition from work to non-work: it can be gradual, it can involve multiple exits, and it may never happen. Retirement is a multi-layered process, governed by multiple institutional schedules and by the diverse pacing of individual biographies that intersect with institutional timetables. All of this leads to variability in the age of retirement (Han & Moen, 1999). Guillemard (2000) specifically argues that the retirement pension system no longer regulates early retirement in Europe; rather, disability insurance creates the bridge between work and retirement. Henretta

(2003) argues that the life course is still uniform but becoming more variable in timing. Gardyn (2000) argues that retirement is being reinvented to include not only second careers but also continuing education and volunteerism. Settersten (2006a:5) suggests that there are extensions in education at the front end of the life course, earlier retirement and increased longevity at the back end, and a shorter period of gainful employment in the middle. Whatever the precise nature of the changes, most scholars agree that there have been some adjustments in the temporal order of the stages of the life course and changes in the time spent in the various stages (McDonald, 2006).

Gerontologists are discussing a "new retirement," although they do not agree on what exactly is new (McDonald, 2006). Retirement today is evolving into a process without a clear beginning or end: it is much less likely to be chronologically determined; it is not as tightly regulated by the state through public pensions or by the employing institution through the relationship to the labour force; and there are a multitude of pathways leading to retirement. The evidence for these changes is growing.

While the continuing lowering of the age of retirement could still arguably be tied to public and private pensions, 11 percent of Canadians reported, in 2002, that they did not know at what age they would retire. The average planned retirement age of employed persons was 60.8 years, well below what is considered the normal age of retirement at age 65 years (Schellenberg, 2004). New routes to retirement have come to the forefront in recent years. In the Survey of Persons Not in the Labour Force, 26 percent of men and 12 percent of women indicated that they had retired unexpectedly because they were offered an early retirement package (McDonald, Donahue, & Marshall, 2000). According to the General Social Survey (GSS) 2002, approximately 12 percent of women and 6 percent of men had retired in order to take care of a family member. Disability benefits provide another route into retirement. Disability benefits were originally intended to provide income for those who could not earn a living because they had a severe disability. However, in a number of countries, they were used as a vehicle to remove older workers from the labour force in response to high levels of unemployment. The uptake was so sharp that in 1990, recipients of disability benefits outnumbered those in receipt of unemployment benefits in 12 of 23 OECD countries (McDonald & Donahue, 2000).

Some Canadians have also reversed their retirement decision and returned to the labour force—about 22 percent of retired Canadians; 23 percent of men and 15 percent of women (Schellenberg, Turcotte, & Ram, 2005). Financial needs were the most important reason for returning to work (38 percent), followed by not liking retirement (22 percent), while 19 percent went back because they liked their work (Schellenberg, Turcotte, & Ram, 2005). In a small, non-random study of a telecommunications company in Canada, almost 47 percent of male and 25 percent of female early retirees went back to work (Marshall, Clarke, & Ballantyne, 2001). Most people who went back to work took up part-time work (45 percent), and they tended to have left the labour force before age 60, to have previously

Figure 13.4 **CARTOON**

"If we take a late retirement and an early death, we'll just squeak by."

worked in a professional occupation, and to be in good health (Schellenberg, Turcotte, & Ram, 2005). In the United States, it is now estimated that between 30 and 50 percent of people move into their final retirement via **partial retirement** or use **bridge jobs** from their career jobs into retirement (Mutchler, Burr, Pienta, & Massagli, 1997; Quinn, 1999).

Perhaps even more revealing is the number of Canadians who have no intention of ever retiring. Sixteen percent of Canadians stated they had no intention of retiring (Schellenberg, 2004). Over one-quarter of recent retirees in the GSS 2002 said they would have continued to work if they had been able to reduce their work time without affecting their pensions, either by working fewer days or by working shorter days (Morissette, Schellenberg, & Silver, 2004). Using the longitudinal Health and Retirement Survey in the United States, Ekerdt, Hackney,

Kosloski, and DeViney (2001) showed that the uncertainty about the form and timing of retirement is substantial. In their analyses, 40 percent of workers aged 51 to 61 could not state how they would exit their job, and about 12 percent did not know the date or age of their retirement. Uncertainty was less likely among those who led a more "socially attended life," meaning a more public life influenced by people on the job and at home, and by friends.

Although there is preliminary evidence that the very nature of retirement is changing, only time will define the magnitude and the permanence of these changes. Close to 78 percent of Canadians currently remain retired, so change is slow. Recent evidence supports the idea that the institutionalization of retirement is still strong in North America (Settersten, 2003). One study found that retirement anticipation was normative among older workers (Ekerdt, Kosloski, & DeViney, 2000), and another found that institutionalized retirement criteria have been strongly internalized to anchor people's self-definition as a retiree (Szinovacz & DeViney, 1999).

Explaining Retirement

Definitions

As would be anticipated, contemporary retirement research does not share a common definition of **retirement**. Even though retirement generally refers to late-life separation from waged labour, there are still many variations in definitions. Conceptually, retirement has been defined as an institution, an event, a process, a social role, and a phase (O'Rand & Henretta, 1999; Kohli & Rein, 1991; McDonald & Wanner, 1990). Usually, the conceptual definition chosen by a researcher depends upon what aspects of retirement the researcher wishes to explore.

Those interested in broader societal issues tend to view retirement as a social institution rather than on an individual level. As an institution, retirement functions to remove older workers from the labour force in a timely and orderly fashion, which is seen to be beneficial for the individual and society. Kohli and Rein (1991), for example, focus on institutionally based pathways, such as state policies and work regulations, that define retirement. For example, provincial policies allowing companies to impose mandatory retirement may force people to retire against their will.

Retirement, as an event, usually refers to the formal end of employment, which is usually accompanied by some rite of passage, such as a party or special luncheon and the giving of a commemorative gift. Retirement as a one-time occasion has not been studied extensively by gerontologists, so we know little about the ceremonial aspects of the occasion. Retirement as a social role, a social process, and a phase have received far more attention. Those who study retirement as a social role are interested in knowing the rights and obligations of the retiree in the retirement role and, as a process, how the role is approached, assumed, and relinquished.

How researchers measure retirement also varies. The simplest and most commonly available measure is the one used above—labour force participation rate—a static measure that ignores how people may move in and out of the labour force. In addition, being out of the labour force does not necessarily mean that an older person is retired. For example, he or she may have temporarily left the labour force to care for an older family member. Other measures that are often used are number of hours worked in the past year, a reduction in work responsibilities, age at which the person left his or her career job, receipt of social security benefits, receipt of a private pension, a self-definition of retirement, and any combination of the preceding indicators.

Recent analyses of the many measures of retirement concluded that there was no optimal measure of the term; all definitions have flaws (O'Rand & Henretta, 1999; McDonald, 1996). The standard definitions of retirement are somewhat inadequate in light of the new retirement noted above or in the case of women's retirement, since almost all definitions of retirement imply a relationship to the labour force and not all women have had such a relationship. How retirement is measured is important, however, for three reasons. The measure used determines (1) who will or will not be included in the study; (2) whose perception of retirement matters; and (3) why research findings on the same issue may be contradictory.

Theories

Theories explicitly designed to explain retirement are few and far between and generally reflect the theories found in mainstream gerontology that have emerged over the last 50 years (see Chapter 3). Retirement, however, has usually played only a minor role in the classical social theories developed to explain the broader issue of social aging. Moreover, there has been an apparent reluctance by retirement scholars to undertake theory building, leaving little in the way of new theories. Most theories either focus on the micro-level of individual actors or the macro-level of social structure (Estes, Linkins, & Binney, 2001). Very few theories attempt to link both.

Micro-Theories At the micro-level of theory development, many of the leading theories of social aging have been influenced by the functional paradigm, which explains social phenomena in terms of how they are functional to society. The early theories of disengagement, activity, and continuity shared the underlying assumptions of this approach and, as a result, emphasized the inevitability of physical, social, and psychological aspects of the aging process, the importance of scripted roles, and how people adjusted to these roles. Thus, disengagement theory viewed retirement as part of a normal, mutual, and beneficial withdrawal of the individual and society from each other (Cumming & Henry, 1961). Activity theory, developed in opposition to the assumptions of disengagement theory, considered retirement a break in healthy activity, which had to be replaced following the withdrawal from work. Continuity theory (Costa & McRae, 1980a) treated retirement as a discontinuity to be replaced with other forms of social activity.

All three approaches assumed that retirement was natural, and that the individual was responsible for the quality and quantity of his or her own level of social activity. Retirement could be potentially traumatic, since prescriptions were offered for how to accomplish retirement—no activity or plenty of activity. The difficulties with these theories were that retirement seemed to occur in a vacuum, unaffected by social, political, or economic factors (McDonald & Wanner, 1990).

Modern-day versions of these theories, the successful aging framework (Rowe & Kahn, 1997) and the productive aging framework (Estes, Mahakian, & Weitz, 2001; Holstein, 1992) are based on similar principles. Successful aging identifies the risk factors for unsuccessful aging along with the personal choices to be successful, while productive aging seeks to reverse the "decline and deficit" view of aging and replace it with the view that older people produce valuable goods and services for society. Both frameworks focus on activities and individual responsibility, and pay no heed to structural factors, such as race or social class. The end result is that these perspectives are in danger of "blaming the victim" if retirement does not proceed in a healthy and productive fashion.

Macro-Theories   The macro-theories that touch on retirement—modernization theory and age stratification theory—are cut from the same structural–functional cloth. Life course theory currently exhibits fewer characteristics of functionalism but, in earlier times, was thought to belong to this paradigm. Modernization theory, developed by Cowgill and Holmes (1972), is a theory about how the status of the aged has declined over time with the modernization of society and how retirement facilitated this process. With the growth of an aging population, the intergenerational competition for jobs increased. The accompanying modern technological innovations, which were more suited to the young, meant that there were fewer suitable jobs available for older workers, and as a result of these two developments, retirement was created. Retirement, in turn, inevitably led to lower incomes, and lower incomes produced lower social status for the aged. Retirement in this theory is simply an inevitable outcome of the unidirectional evolution of society toward modernization.

Age stratification theory conceives of life as a series of roles linked together on the basis of age. Behaviour is explained according to the role occupancy of a group of people who were born at about the same time and who share the same experiences as they move through the linked roles (Riley, Johnson, & Foner, 1972). Retirement is a role that applies to a cohort of people, with age criteria for entrance and exit. Indeed, at the time of the development of the theory, if the retirement role was not carried out according to appropriate age norms (e.g., people retiring precisely at age 65 years), they were labelled *age deviants* (Nelsen & Nelsen, 1972). This theory has been criticized as relying on a static concept of social structure (Quadagno & Reid, 1999), which overlooks inequality based on race, gender, and social class. A newer version, the aging and society paradigm, introduces the idea of an age-integrated society, where age stratification disappears (Riley, Foner, & Riley, 1999; Riley & Riley, 1994). In this model, retirement would no longer be explained on the basis of the age criterion—but no other criteria are offered to replace age.

Bridging Theories   Theories of the life course attempt to bridge micro- and macro-levels of analysis by simultaneously considering the individual and society as the unit of analysis. A model proposed by Giele and Elder (1998) suggests that the age structures developed by a given society (as borrowed from age stratification theory) provide road maps for moving through life within a context of historical and cultural change. Retirement would be one of life's age-graded transitions on the road map and is the last stage of the life course. Kohli (1988) and Moen (1996) are rare researchers who have taken account of the life course in explaining retirement. In different ways, both argue that there are significant links between the past and the present in the lives of individuals and that these links create a unique retirement for each individual, even though everyone is influenced by the same institutional characteristics of retirement. For example, two women with the same job, but with different records of work interruptions over their working lives, will have different incomes in retirement. Henretta (2003) argues that three challenges face gerontologists if we view retirement through the lens of the life course. The first is to determine the extent to which social structure is based on age and on how this may change over time. The second is to explain why the three periods of education, work, and retirement occur sequentially and not simultaneously. Finally, the theory must describe exactly how the institutional life course and individual trajectories are linked.

Political Economy Perspective and Critical Theory   To offset the one common flaw of inattention to structural issues in both the micro- and macro-theories, the political economy perspective emerged in the late 1970s and early 1980s with the work of Estes (1979), Guillemard (1980), Walker (1981), and Phillipson (1982). Although more a perspective than a theory, the political economy approach argues that aging is a socially constructed process that is conditioned by one's location in the social structure and the economic, political, and social factors that affect it (Estes, Swan, & Gerard, 1984). When retirement is explained within this perspective, it is seen as a marginal and dependent status occupied by the aged, which is the culmination of the effects of social, economic, and political processes prior to retirement. For example, Myles concludes, "Both the right to retire—and hence to become old—and the rights of retirement today, are the products of national legislation" (Myles, 1984: 175).

The political economy approach has recently undergone a metamorphosis and is considered to be part of critical theory by some theorists, as we saw in Chapter 3. Atchley (1993) was the first to propose a "critical gerontology of retirement," which would expose the hidden power struggles and patterns of domination influencing retirement. As an example, he reinterprets his own institutional view of retirement to show how removing workers from the labour force serves the interests of capitalists and is of questionable value to society. He argues that retirement, as an institution, ensures that society has no obligation to provide a job for an older worker who may wish to be gainfully employed. In addition, the institution reinforces the erroneous view that older workers are less productive. Phillipson (1999; 2003), using a critical approach to the study of retirement, argues that the changes we see today in work and retirement reflect the trends associated with the emergence of postmodern societies. The replacement of mass production with flexible forms of work, the globalization of social life, and the weakening of social security policies that govern the retirement transition generated the new retirement mentioned above. As an illustration, he invokes Beck (1992, 1994) and Giddens (1991, 1994) and their views on reflexive modernity to suggest that the self, as reflexive, can influence the retirement transition, thereby inventing more social constructions of retirement in the process. The pension side of this argument is echoed by Walker in his development of international political economy (Walker, 2005).

The major criticisms of the political economy approach are diametrically opposed, depending on which version is used to explain retirement. The versions emanating from the original Estes school have been criticized for their over-reliance on structural explanations at the expense of neglecting human agency in the aging process and, by association, the retirement transition. The use of critical theory by Phillipson (1999) can be criticized on the same grounds as the reflexive modernity theory of Giddens and Beck, namely, that the role of structural factors are in danger of receiving short shrift. Estes and colleagues have crossed over to the critical side in a new book in which they attempt to integrate micro-, mid-range and macro-perspectives to defuse this argument (Estes, Biggs, & Phillipson, 2003).

The Link between Work and Retirement

The bridge between the work and retirement phases of the life course has been conceptualized in three ways, all of which have to do with inequality in old age. The first hypothesis, related to the life course perspective, emphasizes economic continuity over time and is called the **status maintenance hypothesis**. The competing hypothesis, the **status levelling** or **redistribution hypothesis**, posits that the links among occupation, income, and retirement are tenuous because social security levels income differences or redistributes income when the retiree receives public pensions. A newer hypothesis, also reflective of a life course perspective, is the **cumulative advantage/disadvantage hypothesis,** which postulates that a shift from work to retirement means an increase in the relative importance of differences in income—workers with more resources, such as education, will have accumulated more pension benefits by the time they retire than workers with fewer resources. Retirement is a critical threshold that can increase inequality. There is mixed support for the three hypotheses, due mainly to methodological problems, including the measure of inequality and the use of cross-sectional versus longitudinal data. Frequently, distinctions are not made between men and women, who, in practice, have different trajectories of inequality into retirement.

The Status Maintenance Hypothesis

According to this hypothesis, the effects of various statuses are maintained across the life course. In the case of retirement, a person's educational attainment influences the nature of his or her occupation and industrial placement to produce a certain level of income-related pension benefits and other types of economic resources. The pension benefits and the assets serve as the connection between work and retirement and operate to maintain the individual's relative status in later life (O'Rand & Henretta, 1999). The status maintenance hypothesis implies that post-retirement inequality represents a continued effect of inequalities prior to retirement (Crystal & Shea, 1990). In a longitudinal study using two waves of the Social Security Beneficiary survey in the United States, a decided link was found between women's economic situation earlier in life and their financial status in old age (Gregoire, Kilty, & Richardson, 2002).

The Status Levelling or Redistribution Hypothesis

The status levelling hypothesis posits that old age, and the increased dependence on public transfers that accompanies it, level status differences that developed in the workplace. The underlying rationale is that public transfers are distributed more equally than are wages and salaries and investment income. Workers at the lower echelons of the income ladder receive a greater rate of return to contributions to social security programs than wealthier workers because it is assumed that political institutions can mould the processes that determine income. To examine trends in income inequality over the middle and later stages of the life course, Prus (2000) used a synthetic cohort from the Survey of Consumer Finances (that is, a cohort made up by using age groups cross-sectionally instead of the same cohort over time). Prus's analysis showed that income inequality decreases within a cohort as it grows older, suggesting that the Canadian retirement income system smoothed out the distribution of income in later life. Myles (2000), using the longitudinal aspects of the same survey, showed that small proportional increases from all public government sources, including the earnings-related Canada/Quebec Pension Plan, tended to reduce inequality in old age.

The Cumulative Advantage/Disadvantage Hypothesis

The cumulative disadvantage/advantage perspective proposed by Crystal and Shea (1990) and promoted by Dannefer (2003) as important to gerontology, incorporates the status maintenance conceptualization, but goes further. The inequalities created by work histories prior to retirement are not only perpetuated after retirement but may become amplified by cumulative effects over time. Having the resources to purchase a house when young allows this asset to grow in value over time, whereas renting over the same time drains resources. Their study, using American panel data, found that income inequality within a cohort increased with age and that income inequality was the highest after age 64. In a recent example, O'Rand and Hamil-Luker (2005) found that early disadvantage and childhood illness had severe enduring effects and increased the risk for heart attack in later life. Whatever hypotheses gain ascendancy as the research accumulates, the transition from work to retirement is crucial for most Canadians, since it helps set the parameters for well-being in the later phases of life.

Issues in Retirement: Who Retires, When, and Why?

Undoubtedly, the most enduring theme in the retirement literature has been the timing of retirement, which began with the spread of early retirement. Early retirement was considered to occur any time prior to the normal age of retirement at age 65 years, while late retirement was thought to be any time after age 65 years. Since the end of the 1980s, there has been a growing diversity in the age of retirement, with an increase in retirement for those between the ages of 60 and 64 years, a decline in those retiring right at age 65 years and an increase in people retiring after age 65 years. Knowing who retires when is a critical question, since the answer has significant consequences for individual Canadians and for Canadian society as a whole. As we have already seen, the timing of retirement helps define when a person is considered to be entering old age, it lays the foundation for the economic well-being of individuals, and it has implications for the economic stability of society at large.

The most frequently studied factors believed to affect the timing of retirement are sociodemographic characteristics, health, potential wealth in retirement, the work environment, unemployment, and family contingencies.

Characteristics of Retirees

There is continuing controversy about the function of sociodemographic characteristics in the timing of retirement. The newer life course models have begun to show that early life circumstances, such as family of orientation or number of children, have a direct impact on retirement behaviour and sometimes serve to modify the effects of factors found to be significant in earlier cross-sectional studies. Overall, the life course research tends to support the earlier research. The recent research has shown that unmarried men have a greater probability of retiring before age 65 years. Men with higher personal incomes and previous jobs in the core industrial sector of the economy (where jobs are the most stable and high paying), also tend to retire earlier. Generally women tend to retire earlier than men (Schellenberg, 2003). The level of a woman's household income, as opposed to her personal income, decreases the age of her retirement, highlighting the important place of marriage in women's economic security in later life (Szinovacz, 2006; McDonald, 1996, 1997b; Peracchi & Welch, 1994). Being in fair or poor health prior to retirement is also an important predictor of early retirement. Living in Quebec or Atlantic Canada is associated with earlier retirement, as is having worked in a managerial or professional job (Schellenberg, 2003).

The findings on the presence of dependants in the family are fairly consistent. The presence of children in the family significantly reduces the probability of early retirement for men (Tompa, 1999; Hayward, Friedman, & Chen, 1998). Pienta (1994; 1999) found that the more children a woman had, the greater were her chances of working full time in later life and that the later she had the children, the later she would work before retiring. More recently she found that when children live at home, both men and women in the family are less likely to retire (Pienta, 2003).

While the research is thin on the influence of race and ethnicity on the timing of retirement, several differences have been found between African and Caucasian Americans (Flippen & Tienda, 2000; Hayward et al., 1998). One Canadian study found that after age and gender have been taken into account, the odds of being retired are uniformly lower for all foreign-born groups in Canada than for the Canadian-born. People from Asia, Africa, and Latin America have the least chance of retiring early and tend to retire later than the general Canadian population (Wanner & McDonald, 1989).

Workers who work past the age of 65 are a growing group. About 1 in 12 people 65 and over had a job in 2001 (Duchesne, 2004) compared to 1 in 13 in 1996 (Duchesne, 2002). Those 65 to 69 accounted for over half of older workers, those 70 to 74 over a quarter, and those 75 plus over almost 17 percent (Duchesne, 2004). Canadians who retire after age 65 are more likely to be well educated, with higher occupational status, to be self-employed, or to be immigrants (Schellenberg, 2004). Farming and retail trade were the most popular occupations but many older adults worked in professional occupations such as accounting, medicine, religion, and law. While men were found in such occupations as judge, women were more likely to be found in typically female occupations such as secretary and babysitter. The factor most closely associated with a late retirement age is a higher education. In 2001, 1 in 5 seniors with a university degree was employed compared with only 1 in 20 with less than a Grade 9 education (Duchesne 2004). However, women with the same education as men are much less likely to be working. The rising educational attainment and employment rates likely represent the more extensive schooling of the younger cohorts and will likely increase as the well-educated boomers enter late life (Duchesne, 2004).

The Health versus Wealth Debate

Most Canadians agree today that health and wealth are very important to them. In a poll in 2004, health care and retirement income were the top priorities of Canadians (NUPGE, 2004). Researchers have asked if it is the push of poor health or the pull of a pension that leads to early retirement. Early retirement has been viewed on the one hand as an involuntary response to poor health, and on the other, as a voluntary response to unearned income from pensions and assets. The answers offered by scholars have varied over time, depending on the historical context and the interests of the researchers. In the initial retirement research, ill health was found to be a very important predictor of early retirement (Reno, 1971) but was viewed with some suspicion. At the time, early retirement was not the norm, so researchers thought that retirees might have used poor health as a cover for supposedly less acceptable reasons for retirement, such as pursuing a hobby. This view, now referred to as the **health justification hypothesis,** has received little support in the literature. In Canada those who retired for poor health did indeed report fair to poor health and 3 in 10 reported that their health had declined since the previous year (Pyper, 2006).

With the introduction of early retirement incentive plans in the 1980s, the focus swung to pension income (both public and private) as the more important predictor of early retirement. The lure of early retirement pensions was thought to be so powerful that policy changes to social security were instituted in the United States and Europe to make it less attractive to draw pensions at younger ages (Wise, 1993). Some critics, however, thought that the influence of public pensions was overestimated in explaining early retirement (Rein & Turner, 1999; Epsing-Anderson, 1994). For example, it is difficult to explain why the rate of early retirement is lowest in countries with the most generous early public pension plans, such as Norway and Sweden (Epsing-Anderson, 1994). In contrast, other researchers were more inclined to think that early retirement represented a response to high unemployment rates and early pension options for retirement (Peracchi & Welch,1994; Kolberg & Epsing-Anderson, 1991).

The early 1990s saw a renewed flurry of interest in health as a major factor in the early retirement decision (McDonald & Donahue, 2000). The thinking was that healthy workers could continue to work and would not need to use expensive early pension options. Current research about reduced mortality and morbidity and the compressed morbidity of older workers implies that health should no longer be a main reason for early retirement (Council of Economic Advisors, 1999; Woodbury, 1999). Research surfaced that supported this view. For example, at least two American studies have shown a decline in disability of about 2 percent per year (Crimmins, Reynolds, & Saito 1999; Fries, 2003).

While the research documenting improvements in workers' health is encouraging, some older workers genuinely suffer ill health and are forced to retire early. The most recent literature confirms that poor health is an important consideration in the early retirement decision (Dwyer & Mitchell, 1998; Quinn, 1999; OECD, 1998).

In Canada, the research has shown that poor health is an important reason for retirement. In the General Social Survey, 2002, one-third of recent retirees retired for health reasons (Schellenberg & Silver, 2004). The 2003 Canadian Community Health Survey (CCHS) found that more older women were not working because of their health (Pyper, 2005). In an analysis of unexpected early retirement, retirement because of poor health reduced retirement income by over $7000 a year (McDonald, Donahue, & Marshall, 2000).

The most recent research also offers support for the pension side of the debate, although most research does not assess the relative importance of health and pensions. When changes to the Quebec Pension Plan (QPP) in 1984 and the Canada Pension Plan (CPP) in 1987 made substantial benefits available at age 60, Frenken (1991) reported that Canadians did not hesitate to respond. In 1984, three out of every four people receiving QPP pensions for the first time were between the ages of 60 and 64 years. Two-thirds of new CPP beneficiaries were aged 60 to 64 years. Using a longitudinal administrative data file covering 1982 to 1994 to examine the age at which individuals begin to draw benefits from the CPP, Tompa (1999) found that income amounts from various sources had a significant impact on the take-up of CPP benefits, as did family characteristics and health status. He noted a definite trend to early take-up of CPP benefits, providing further evidence for the effects of pensions on retirement. Similar findings have been confirmed in later studies of different occupations and/or retirees in different provinces (Statistics Canada, 2003g)

When private pension plans and other employee benefits such as health coverage are considered, there is growing evidence that they affect the early retirement decisions of a substantial number of individuals. According to recent retirees in the General Social Survey 2002, 40 percent retired because they were eligible for a pension (Schellenberg, 2003). Generally, more men than women who have a private pension plan have been found to retire earlier (Fronstin, 1999; Tompa, 1999; Monette, 1996). McDonald, Donahue, and Marshall (2000) found that 26 percent of men and 12 percent of women retired early and unexpectedly because they were offered early retirement incentive packages.

It is important to note that this decision is not always truly voluntary. Some workers are coerced into accepting a package by the threat of layoffs and downsizing. In an American study, 49 percent of workers who elected to take an early retirement package indicated that it was not a desirable choice (Gowan, 1998). In a Canadian study of a major telecommunications company, some workers leaving the company with an early retirement incentive program (ERIP) felt ambiguous about their degree of choice in leaving (Robertson, 2000). Marshall (1995) calls this the retirement incentive game, where the company offers the lowest possible retirement incentives to the worker in the hope that the older worker will accept the package in order to help reduce staff levels in the company. The worker, usually within a short time frame, must decide to take the package, hold out for a better package, or risk being displaced.

Work and the Timing of Retirement

The type of employment at the time of retirement has an effect on the timing of retirement. Within the Canadian context, workers who held non-standard jobs, such as part-time work, temporary jobs, or self-employment, retired at later ages, possibly out of economic need. Among men, part-time workers retired, on average, at age 64.2, compared with age 60.8 years for full-time workers. Self-employed women retired at an average age of 60, compared with age 59 for salaried workers (Monette, 1996).

The type of occupation a person had prior to retirement, in combination with the type of employment (full-time, part-time or self-employed,) also affects the retirement age. For example, men who retired at age 60 from sales and services were full-time employees with a job-related pension, while colleagues in the same occupations who were self-employed without a pension retired on average at 64. Similarly, salaried professionals with a pension retired at age 61 years, while self-employed professionals without a pension retired at age 63 years. All the data point to the importance of a pension in the early retirement decision. It is therefore important to note that pension coverage is particularly problematic for contingent workers, who are most likely to be women. For the last 30 years, 69 percent of women have been in non-standard jobs (Townsend, 2006).

Another factor is the centrality of work in people's lives. Some studies have demonstrated that workers who were highly committed to their work or liked their work delayed retirement, while those with opposite views retired earlier (Duchesne, 2004; Vickerstaff, Baldock, Cox, & Keen, 2004; Hansson, DeKoekkoek, Neece, & Patterson, 1997; Reitzes, Mutran, & Fernandez, 1996). One study found that jobs high in intrinsic reward and positive social relationships were related to low planning for retirement (Kosloski, Ekerdt, & DeViney, 2001). Is the work environment or the non-work domain more important in the retirement decision? As would be anticipated, several studies have shown both domains to be important (Beehr, Glazer, Nielson, & Fanner, 2000; Stetz & Beehr, 2000).

Most recent research has focused on the relationship of stress and strain in the workplace to retirement. Part of the reason for the interest is to find ways to retain older workers in the labour force to slow down the trend to early retirement. Job strain is usually defined as a measure of the balance between the psychological demands of a job and the amount of control it affords (Turcotte & Schellenberg, 2005). A Norwegian study found that older workers who took early retirement because of a disability experienced more job strain, and that both disability and non-disability early retirements were related to low autonomy in job tasks (Blekesaune & Solem, 2005). A Canadian study found that older workers with high job strain in managerial, professional, or technical jobs retired earlier than those with low strain in their jobs. Strain was not related to early retirement for older workers in sales, services, clerical or blue-collar occupations (Turcotte & Schellenberg, 2005).

One of the more serious issues in the workplace is the presence of age discrimination (Tougas, Lagacé, & de la Sablonnière, 2004). Several studies have found that age discrimination has led to early retirement (Longino, 2005; Johnson & Neumark, 1997; McDonald, Donahue, & Moore, 1997b). Although McMullin and Marshall (2001) reported little age discrimination in their study of garment industry workers in Montreal, they did report that age-related declines in dexterity and physical ability were rationales used to force workers to leave employment.

One need not look further than the Supreme Court of Canada and its decision on mandatory retirement to find sanctioned discrimination against older workers, even though 65 percent of Canadians do not support it (Lowe, 1991). A landmark ruling by the Supreme Court on December 7, 1990, upheld the principle of mandatory retirement, a decision that was reaffirmed in later rulings in 1992 and 1995 (Klassen & Gillin, 1999). The majority position of the court was that age discrimination was definitely a violation of individual rights but could be upheld under Section 1 of the Charter of Rights and Freedoms as a "minor infringement" of people's rights in favour of the greater benefits that would accrue to Canadian society. While there is no federal statute that forces a worker to retire at age 65, the Supreme Court decision supported the mandatory retirement provisions in provinces that did not have provincial human rights legislation prohibiting mandatory retirement. Currently, Alberta, Manitoba, Quebec, Ontario, Prince Edward Island, Yukon, the Northwest Territories, and Nunavut have human rights legislation banning mandatory retirement as discriminatory, except in certain specific occupations set out by federal law.

The envisioned benefits to society include the creation of opportunities for job openings for younger people, a short-sighted reason favoured by corporations at a time when Canada was in the throes of a recession. There was no evidence to suggest that mandatory retirement created openings for younger workers, because employers tended not to fill vacant positions (McDonald, 2000). Perhaps more disturbing was the message sent to Canadians about older workers. According to Klassen and Gillin (1999), the decision of the Court was based on the stereotyping of older workers as being less competent than younger workers and failed to provide the older worker with any protection against discrimination based on age. In addition, the decision was detrimental to women, who frequently have to work longer to accumulate pension benefits because of interrupted work periods and their shorter time in the labour force (McDonald, 2000). The decisions were also short-sighted when considered within a global context. Many countries are now implementing policies to slow early retirement because they are concerned about the escalating public costs of social security and the possibility of worker shortages (McDonald & Chen, 1993). Indeed, some countries (such as the United States, Italy, and France) have recently raised the statutory age of retirement.

Today more recent judicial opinions seem to re-emphasize the importance of human rights over economic utility. In fact the Court of Appeal in British Columbia upheld a decision against mandatory retirement. Justice Prowse stated " . . . I would urge the Supreme Court of Canada to reconsider this issue [à la McKinney] . . . The extent to which mandatory retirement policies impact on other equality rights, and on the mobility of the workforce, have become prominent social issues" (Gillin & Klassen, 2005:63).

The Spectre of Unemployment

Unemployment rates were high in Canada during two recent recessions: one in the early 1980s and one at the beginning of the 1990s. The accumulated effects of these recessions had a long-term influence on older workers that affected their retirement behaviour. Many researchers have been quick to suggest that a large portion of early retirement was actually unemployment (Rowe & Nguyen, 2003; Hutchens, 1999; Tompa, 1999; Gee & Gutman, 1995). While the unemployment rates for older workers are relatively low in Canada—about 5.4 percent for both men and women aged 55 to 64 years, compared with 12.4 percent for those 15 to 24 years of age (Statistics Canada, 2005e)—the move into retirement probably masks the actual numbers of older unemployed workers. However, part of the problem for older Canadian workers is that, although they are less likely to lose long-term jobs than are younger workers, if they do lose a job they face longer periods of unemployment and instability. For example, the long-term unemployment rate (52 weeks or more) was 17 percent for those 45 years of age and over compared to 3.2 percent for those aged 15 to 24 years of age. The probability of job loss is lower among older workers but once unemployed, they have greater difficulty finding work (Dubé, 2004).

Tompa (1999) showed that individuals receiving employment insurance or who were out of the labour force were more likely to exit to retirement. Another good example of unemployment comes from the Survey of Persons Not in the Labour Force. Of those who retired unexpectedly early, 8 percent of men and 10 percent of the women stated that they had left work for retirement because their company closed, because they were laid off, or because of downsizing (McDonald, Donahue, & Marshall, 2000). The same study found that for every month of joblessness, family income in retirement was decreased by approximately $100 per year. Workers who do not find jobs tend to be discouraged out of the labour force, a finding confirmed in the garment-industry study in Montreal (McMullin & Marshall, 2001).

A Family Approach to Retirement

With the increased labour force participation of women, family contingencies have taken on a whole new meaning for both men and women. In the early retirement literature, researchers considered women to be homemakers and "retired" only if their spouse was retired. Because they spent more years doing unpaid work at home than paid work in the labour force, women were essentially invisible workers and hence invisible retirees. Today, women's paid and unpaid work is publicly acknowledged, with the resulting recognition of the interdependence of life domains and their influence on retirement status. Researchers have now developed models of family retirement linkages grounded in a life course perspective (Szinovacz, 2006; Pienta, 2003). Today the marital context and family contexts are significant areas of retirement study.

A number of dimensions of marriage have been linked to retirement decisions, including age, marital history, work and pension characteristics of both spouses, caregiving, and the quality of the marital relationship. It seems that today dual-career couples will have to make two decisions about retirement instead of one.

Women's increased labour force participation, their larger contributions to household income, their increased pension coverage and increased presence in professional and managerial occupations make them more crucial to the retirement decision. Wives with much older husbands are less likely to retire early, as are married men with younger wives (Szinovacz, 2002). Most couples apparently want to retire at the same time. Tompa (1999) found that both men and women tend to make joint retirement decisions with their spouses. Recent research found that almost half of dual-career couples plan to retire together, but only about one-third manage to do so (Schellenberg, Turcotte, & Ram 2006). This matters because marital quality is more likely to decline for the retired spouse of a working spouse (Moen, Kim, & Hofmeister, 2001). Szinovacz and Davey (2005) found that retired husbands have a difficult time staying home alone when their wives are still working.

The marital history of the couple may also have some bearing on retirement; remarried widowers are less likely to retire, and remarried widows are more likely to retire (Szinovacz & DeViney, 2000). One Canadian study found that married Canadian women retired, on average, at age 56 years, that their retirement was voluntary, and that they were more likely to retire because they wanted to stop working. In contrast, widowed women retired later (age 61 years), and their retirement was less likely to be voluntary (McDonald, Donahue, & Moore, 2000b).

Because of the stronger presence of women in the labour force there is some suggestion that the pensions of both spouses are important in the retirement decision. In a Canadian study of joint retirement, a wife who had her own pension was less likely to retire jointly with her husband, presumably because wives, being younger than their husbands, would not be eligible for a pension at the same time (Schellenberg, Turcotte, & Ram 2006). This constraint did not apply to the husband.

Family care obligations may also impinge on retirement decisions, usually for women, who provide the bulk of family care. As noted above, about 12 percent of women and 6 percent of men retire to provide care. Interestingly, most Canadian women do not anticipate caregiving as a reason for retirement (Zimmerman, Mitchell, Wister, & Gutman, 2000) For example, a Vancouver study found that actual retirement timing was affected by health and stress, a preference for early retirement, caregiving, and spouse's retirement; however, women planning for their future retirement did not anticipate caregiving or health/stress as factors.

Although there is considerable research on the effects of caregiving on employment, it is difficult to ascertain whether caregiving in the years close to retirement leads to early retirement or whether a spell of caregiving makes it difficult to rejoin the labour force when the caregiving is over (McDonald, Donahue, & Sussman, 2003; Pavalko & Artis, 1997). The average age women retire for caregiving is quite low: 48 years in the General Social Survey 1994 (Monette, 1996). What happens to the women when the caregiving is over? Will their family savings see them through retirement or will they have to go back to work, and, if so, will they secure a job?

If they remain in retirement, will they live in poverty? These questions are only beginning to be addressed within the Canadian context.

Finally, there appears to be some evidence that spouses in close relationships, those with joint interests, and those wishing to spend more time together are inclined to retire earlier, whereas couples in conflict-ridden relationships may delay retirement (Henkens, 1999; Szinovacz & Schaffer, 2000). Another study reports that satisfaction with retirement was lower for those retirees whose decision to retire was strongly influenced by their spouse (Smith & Moen, 2004).

Living in Retirement

Making the Transition from Work to Retirement

Most research has found that the vast majority of men and women suffer few, if any, ill effects as a result of the transition from work to retirement. Gerontologists today no longer consider retirement to be a crisis, as they once did, and now focus on the issues of planning for retirement, partial retirement, involuntary retirement, and **reverse retirement** as part of the transitional process. Reverse retirement means returning to work, whether full- or part-time, after having retired.

Retirement Preparations   Approximately 31 percent of Canadians aged 45 to 59 do not feel that they are adequately prepared financially for retirement (Schellenberg, 2004). More than one-third believe that their retirement income will be barely adequate, inadequate, or very inadequate. A slightly larger proportion of women than men believe their financial preparations to be inadequate and the widowed, separated and divorced are most likely to say their preparations are inadequate. Older workers who assess their health to be fair or poor are almost twice as likely to view their preparations as inadequate as those who assess their health as excellent. Similarly, in a study of preparation for later life, it was found that people in better health are more likely than those in poorer health to make plans for retirement (Denton et al., 2000). A qualitative study found that three conditions affected planning for retirement: financial, personal, and familial. As an example, job loss would constrain financial planning for later life (Kemp, Rosenthal, & Denton, 2005).

In contrast, American research found that poor health was related to increased retirement planning (Ekerdt, DeViney, & Kosloski, 1996; Taylor & Shore, 1995). Workers with jobs high in intrinsic enjoyment or positive social relations are less likely to plan for retirement (Kosloski, Ekerdt & DeViney, 2001). More highly educated workers, older workers, and men are more likely to report having plans for retirement and to discuss them with friends and co-workers.

Moen, Sweet, and Swisher (2001) have developed a model predicting retirement planning that takes into account five factors: the nature of the labour force, **biographical pacing**, financial resources, spousal considerations, and organizational location. In their study of dual-income couples, they found some support for their model, especially biographical pacing. Belonging to a different cohort indicated different times for the onset of retirement planning. Younger workers in this study reportedly started planning earlier than the baby boom cohort (Moen, Sweet, & Swisher, 2001). In the case of couples, each partner needs an individualized planning program (van Solinge & Henkens, 2005).

Involuntary Retirement Even though most Canadians experience a positive transition into retirement, the 27 percent of Canadians who retire involuntarily do not always fare well in the transition (Szinovacz & Davey, 2005; Schellenberg, 2003; McDonald, Donahue, & Marshall, 2000). The primary reasons for **involuntary retirement** are poor health (42 percent), unemployment (25 percent), and mandatory retirement (9 percent). Involuntary retirees were more likely to have poor health and to be immigrants and less likely to be married. Involuntary retirement was more common between 1992 and 1996 than between 1997 and 2002, possibly because of the recession at the earlier time. Many involuntary retirees experienced lower incomes in retirement, dissatisfaction in retirement, and a decrease in overall well-being, and rated themselves as having poorer mental and physical health (Szinovacz & Davey, 2005; Schultz, Morton & Weckerle, 1998; Sharpley & Layton, 1998). In a related process, the emergence of the new retirement has also contributed to what some scholars have referred to as instability in the retirement transition, unstable exits involving moving in and out of the labour force. These exits were associated with adverse health effects for both men and women in a study of a telecommunications company in Canada (He, Colantonio, & Marshall, 2006; Marshall, Clarke, & Ballantyne, 2001).

Partial Retirement Contributing to the blurring of the boundaries between work and retirement is partial retirement, which is the most common pattern of post-retirement work for Canadians. According to the GSS 2002, about 22 percent of Canadians went back to work after retiring (Schellenberg, Turcotte, & Ram, 2005), of whom almost half (45 percent) worked part-time. Part-time work was more common among women (58 percent, compared to 37 percent of men) and was most common among older women with a university degree. As age increased so did the return to part-time work. Two types of retirees are most likely to go back to work part time: professionals whose skills allow them to find work fairly easily (Schellenberg, Turcotte, & Ram, 2005) and those forced out of work because of loss of jobs but who can find lesser jobs at the margins of the economy in smaller, less bureaucratized firms (McDonald, 1997a).

There are many barriers to partial retirement, including the public and private pension systems. For example, a serious obstacle is the problem of losing current income and future pension income while in partial retirement. Only 1 percent of an elite group of British Columbia government managers took up a deferred salary leave program when offered on a trial basis, highlighting the difficulties related to protecting present and future incomes (Lussier & Wister, 1995).

This pattern has been evident in most industrialized countries, especially where older workers have been assured large pensions at full retirement (Latulippe & Turner, 2000).

Stages One of the first conceptual frameworks gerontologists used to study post-retirement life was the idea that retirees went through stages as they moved through retirement. The classic stage model of retirement is based on continuity theory and suggests that retirees transit through the honeymoon phase, in which they are satisfied with their new roles, then move to the disenchantment phase, in which retirement may not live up to expectations, on to a readjustment phase, called the reorientation phase, which settles into a stable phase, ultimately ending in death (Atchley, 1976). There has been some empirical support for this model (Reitzes & Mutran 2004; Gall, Evans, & Howard, 2000; Theriault, 1994) but the evidence is slim. More recent models have attended to the gender issue. Monk (1997) found three main adjustment patterns for men (withdrawal, compensation, and accommodation), while Price (2000) uncovered a developmental stage model in interviews with professional women who went through three successive stages (decision to retire; relinquishing professional identity; and re-establishing order). The stage approach to retirement adjustment is extremely complicated and likely depends on a broad array of interrelated factors for both men and women.

Well-Being in Retirement

There has been extensive study of the impact of retirement on individuals, how people adjust to retirement, and the resources required for an individual's satisfaction with retirement. Given differences in research designs, time post-retirement at assessment, and the measures used to rate adjustment and satisfaction, the findings can be confusing and are frequently inconsistent. In some studies retirees have reported greater depression and loneliness than workers, lower life satisfaction and happiness, and negative attitudes to retirement (Rosenkoetter & Garris, 1998; de Grâce, Joshi, Pelletier, & Beaupré, 1994). Other studies show that older workers look forward to retirement and are satisfied in retirement (Nuttman-Shwartz, 2004; Sharpley & Layton, 1998; Gall, Evans, & Howard, 2000). As we have also seen, the issue of retirement is distinctly different for women, and so, by definition, their situation in retirement is different (Smith & Moen, 2004). For example, Quick and Moen (1997) found that later retirement was associated with lower retirement quality for women, whereas the pre-retirement job was more important to the quality of men's retirement.

Satisfaction Some longitudinal studies have shown that recent retirees report the highest levels of satisfaction, whereas long-term retirees express less satisfaction (Warr, Butcher, Robertson, & Callinan, 2004). Other studies report the opposite (Richardson & Kilty, 1991; Beck, 1982) or variations depending on the length of retirement (Kim & Moen, 2002). At least one study has shown that life satisfaction remains constant from pre- to post-retirement (Gall, Evans, & Howard, 2000). In a study of six European countries, all countries except one expressed high satisfaction with retirement (Fouquereau, Fernandez, Fonseca, Paul, & Uotinen, 2005). We know very little about Canadians' satisfaction with life in retirement. We do know that in the GSS 2002 42 percent of Canadians reported that they enjoyed life more after retirement, 14 reported that they enjoyed life less, and 44 percent enjoyed life about the same. There is an embryonic body of research about retirement satisfaction and marriage which shows varying effects on satisfaction in retirement. The thinking behind the research is that retirement may increase marital satisfaction because of more opportunities for interaction; it may decrease marital satisfaction because of an invasion of privacy; or the level of satisfaction may not change. Marital status directly affects retirement satisfaction of women (Price & Joo, 2005) and men (Szinovacz & Davey, 2004b) as does the way the transition is made (Szinovacz & Davey, 2005b) Retired husbands are least satisfied if their wives remain employed and had more say in decisions prior to retirement. The converse applies to women: they are least satisfied if their husbands are still employed and if the husbands had more say prior to retirement (Szinovacz & Davey, 2005). Recent Canadian data indicate that couples fare better in retirement when they are both retired; the higher the woman's contribution to household income, the lower they rate their relationship; the more children at home there are at home, the lower they rate the quality of their relationship; and age difference does not appear to matter—unlike the American data (Chalmers & Milan, 2005).

Health and Wealth The two main resources of the retiree known to affect the quality of retirement include health and wealth. Physical health consistently predicts adjustment to retirement for both men and women (Hyde, Ferries, Higgs, Mein, & Nazroo, 2004; Dorfman, 1995; Hardy & Quadagno, 1995; Hibbard, 1995). The effect of retirement on physical health seems to vary depending whether the retirement was voluntary or not. Involuntary retirees seem to be in poorer health (Hyde et al., 2004; Schellenberg, 2003). An exception to this pattern is a Canadian study of the impact of pre-retirement expectations for income and satisfaction on the quality of men's lives six to seven years after retirement (Gall, Evans, & Howard, 2000). These researchers found that changes in physical health and psychological distress did not change the long-term quality of life in later retirement. The differences in findings may be attributed to the fact that the Canadian study was longitudinal, unlike most of the earlier studies.

Although research on physical health is abundant, there has been less research on mental health and retirement. Longitudinal data from a large British national study found that strong mental health prior to retirement was repeated post-retirement, and that being male and in good health also predicted better mental health in retirement (Hyde et al., 2004). A nation-wide study of mental health in Australia found that retirees—particularly male early retirees—displayed a higher prevalence of mental disorders than those in the labour force (Butterworth et al., 2005). An American study using two different national data sets found support for two opposing views: that retirement was good for mental health and that it was not. In one data file, retirees with higher activity levels had lower anxiety and distress (Drentea, 2002). In both data sets, retirement was associated with a lower sense of control. Another study found that self-esteem did not decline in the transition to retirement (Reitzes et al., 1996), while in a longitudinal study, anxiety levels steadily decreased with time in retirement (Theriault, 1994). In studies of married couples based on the longitudinal aspects of the Health and Retirement Survey in the United States, Szinovacz & Davey (2004a) found that women's, but not men's, well-being was negatively affected if retirement occurred in combination with a spouse's disability. In a different analysis, these researchers found that recently retired husbands reported higher depressive symptoms if their wives continued to work outside of the home (Szinovacz & Davey, 2004b).

Like health, wealth has been found to be a significant resource in contributing to well-being or higher satisfaction in retirement. When asked about their financial situation in retirement, 18 percent of Canadians reported that they were better off, 30 percent reported that their position was worse, and 52 percent said it was about the same as before retirement. Using 25 years of data from a U.S. panel study, researchers found that work history was the most important predictor of transition into poverty after retirement, a condition most likely to affect women (McLaughlin & Jensen, 2000). In the British Whitehall Study II, being male had a very strong positive affect on retirement income (Hyde et al., 2004). In a study of retired widows, low incomes severely constrained older women's activities and made day-to-day living a challenge. As an illustration, one widow reported turning her hearing aid off while at home because she could not afford the batteries (McDonald, Donahue, & Moore, 1997b).

Marriage is a double-edged sword for women. On the one hand, it is a major economic resource that buffers women against poverty in retirement; on the other hand, it prevents women from building their careers and pensions because of their family responsibilities (McDonald et al., 1997a). One national study in Canada found that 49 percent of retired widows, 53 percent of divorced or separated women, and 28 percent of ever-single women lived below the low income cut-offs for Canada, compared with 15 percent of married women (McDonald et al., 1997a). In a later study, McDonald and Robb (2004) found that separated and divorced women were the worst off of all Canadians when they retired. When marital support disappears, women's secondary poverty becomes all too evident in retirement (Logue, 1991). It is no surprise that married and single women are more likely than divorced and separated women to find their income in retirement satisfactory (McDonald & Robb, 2004).

Chapter Summary

This chapter has provided an overview of retirement from its inception until the present day. Key ideas to remember from this chapter:

- Retirement is a social construct that evolved from a process of stepping down within the confines of the family into an age-based, society-wide institution, supported by a national pension system.
- The mould for retirement, as we know it today, is based on a linear, male, 19th-century life course model, where a woman's place was in the home, supported by the husband as sole breadwinner.
- Historically, women have been invisible in the labour force and invisible in retirement, so we know little about their retirement history.
- Most Canadians want to retire, and they want to retire early; only about 8 percent of Canadians who say they will never retire. The main reasons for early retirement are poor health and financial security. For women, an important reason for early retirement is caregiving.
- The new retirement has been characterized as having no clear beginning or end. It is not necessarily dependent upon age. It is not as tightly regulated by public or private pensions, and there are many routes into retirement, if one chooses to retire at all.
- There is a wide variety of definitions, measures, and theories explaining retirement that spans structural and individual circumstances and a few that attempt to show the interplay between the two. The life course perspective shows considerable promise in representing the complexity of retirement.
- Three competing hypotheses on inequality in retirement all have some empirical support: (1) the status maintenance hypothesis, which claims that the older person's situation remains the same after retirement; (2) the status levelling or redistribution hypothesis, which postulates that state pensions redistribute income to make people more equal in old age; and (3) the cumulative advantage/disadvantage hypothesis, which claims that inequalities become magnified in retirement.
- Canadians who retire early tend to be married men and women, men who had stable jobs in the core of the economy, and men with higher incomes. Women with large household incomes are more likely to retire early. Late retirees are highly educated, have high occupational status, are more likely to be self-employed and to be immigrants. People who go back to work after retirement appear to have high levels of education that make them attractive to employers.
- Mandatory retirement is a sanctioned form of age discrimination in Canada.
- About a third of Canadians do not believe that they are adequately prepared for retirement, at least financially; most prefer part-time work if they work post-retirement.
- Overall, most Canadians adjust to and are satisfied with their retirement. Good health and a decent income predict greater satisfaction.

KEY TERMS

step down **(p. 329)**

life course institutionalization
hypothesis **(p. 330)**

mandatory retirement **(p. 331)**

partial retirement **(p. 338)**

bridge jobs **(p. 338)**

retirement **(p. 339)**

status maintenance hypothesis **(p. 343)**

status levelling or redistribution
hypothesis **(p. 343)**

cumulative advantage/disadvantage
hypothesis **(p. 343)**

health justification hypothesis **(p. 347)**

reverse retirement **(p. 353)**

biographical pacing **(p. 353)**

involuntary retirement **(p. 354)**

STUDY QUESTIONS

1. Having reviewed the history of retirement, what do you think retirement will look like 50 years from now? Do you think you will retire, and what would be your reasons for this decision?

2. Compare and contrast the different ways retirement has been conceptualized and their links to different theories.

3. Inequalities related to gender and ethnicity in employment over the life course usually translate into inequalities in retirement. Do you think social policy could be used as a tool to change these outcomes? If your answer is yes, what policies would you propose? If your answer is no, why do you think social policies will not work? Are there other ways to offset life-long inequities?

4. Given the fact that most older Canadians experience good health in retirement and that a sizable proportion go back to work after retiring, do you think we should abolish mandatory retirement? Why or why not?

SUGGESTED READINGS

Adams, G.A., & Beehr, T.A. (Eds.) (2003). *Retirement: Reasons, processes, and results.* New York: Springer.

Gillin, T.A., MacGregor, D., & Klassen, T. R. (Eds.) *Time's up! Mandatory retirement in Canada.* Toronto: Lorimer.

Stone, L. (Editor-in-Chief) (2006). *The new frontiers of research on retirement.* (Catalogue No. 75-511-XPE). Ottawa: Ministry of Industry.

Chapter 14

PENSIONS AND ECONOMIC SECURITY FOR OLDER CANADIANS

Learning Objectives

In this chapter, you will learn about

- How Canada came to be awarded a B grade by NACA in how well older Canadians fare economically.
- How this affects the financial situation of Canadian women and of people who live alone.
- Changes in average income and total assets within the last decade.

- The development of the pension system and what the system looks like today.
- What the future might hold for the retirement income system and why it matters to all Canadians.

Introduction

The National Advisory Council on Aging (NACA) issued a *Report Card on Seniors in Canada* which rated how well older Canadians were doing economically. In 2001 they awarded an overall B grade, which meant good, but with improvements needed (NACA, 2001). In 2005 they issued the same grade (NACA, 2006). See Table 14.1 for the indicators that were used to assign the grade. As we saw in Chapter 9, people's health and overall quality of life depend to a great degree on their economic status. A classic Canadian study discovered that the higher earnings of Canadian men in the decades prior to age 65 were associated with low mortality during the ensuing nine years (Wolfson, Rowe, Gentleman, & Tomiak, 1993). Furthermore, older people who have wealth in the form of assets or income can either own or afford to buy goods and services that will allow them to exercise control over their own lives. In short, wealth at older ages contributes to an independent and healthy life.

The pension system in Canada makes a significant contribution to the incomes of older people. For example, Old Age security transfers reached $28.6 billion by 2004 (2005 constant dollars). According to the 2001 Census, older adults with a low income received two-thirds of their income from Old Age Security and the Guaranteed Income Supplement (Poon, 2005). As one recently retired woman stated about her old age pension, "I am thankful for what I am getting because I never had anything before" (McDonald, Donahue, & Moore, 1997b:53). In contrast, a divorced woman aged 70 stated about her old age pension, " . . . it is just so hard to take sometimes, please don't think I am greedy but I worked hard, I took care of my family and now, . . . well now, I am worse off than ever . . ." (McDonald, Donahue, & McKnight, 2005).

The Retirement Wage: A History of Pensions in Canada

As we outlined in Chapter 13, retirement is a modern social invention that marks the transition to old age. Some scholars further suggest that retirement would never have been possible on such a large scale unless there was a second invention, namely, the pension system, which has often been called the **citizen's wage** or the **retirement wage** (Snell, 1996; Myles, 1995). The public pension system is central to the development of the contemporary welfare state in Canada, as in most other capitalistic democracies—so much so that the welfare state has been hailed as a welfare state for the elderly (Myles & Street, 1995). Large government expenditures on older adults are responsible for this description. For example, in 2003, government transfers accounted for 47.7 percent of the income of people over age 65, compared to about 34 percent from private pensions (Statistics Canada, 2006a).

Traditionally, welfare states have been portrayed as systems that curb the stratification created by market and social forces and, in the process, foster greater equality among citizens. The underlying theme is that workers are oppressed by

Table 14.1 HOW WELL ARE OLDER ADULTS FARING ECONOMICALLY?

THEME	INDICATORS	REFERENCE PERIOD	TREND OF THE SITUATION	GRADE
Income	Mean income of seniors after tax, by gender and family type	1999 to 2003	Improving	B
	Mean income of senior families compared to other Canadian families	1999 to 2003	Worsening	B
	Gap in mean income of men and women	1999 to 2003	Stable	D
	Median income, by gender and family type	1999 to 2003	Improving	B
Source of income	Percentage of income from public and private pension plans, OAS and other sources	1995 to 1999	Improving	B
Income distribution	Distribution of seniors' income	1999 to 2003	Improving	B
Low income	Percentage of low income seniors	1999 to 2003	Improving	B
	Persistence of low income	1993 to 1998 and 1996 to 2001	Worsening	C
Guaranteed Income Supplement (GIS)	Percentage of seniors receiving GIS	1999 to 2004	Improving	B
	Number of seniors eligible for GIS but who do not receive it	1999 to 2001 2002 to 2005	Unknown Worsening	D D
	Number of seniors applying late for GIS			
Assets and debts	Financial and non-financial assets	No new data	—	—
	Indebtedness			
Economic well-being	Financial situation versus expectations prior to retirement	2002	Unknown	—

Source: Seniors in Canada: Report card, Division of aging seniors, Public Health Agency of Canada, 2001. Adapted and reproduced with the permission of the Minister of Public Works and Government Services, 2006.

capitalism, which buys and sells their labour and, in so doing, turns it into a commodity. However, with the advent of social rights based on citizenship, social protection for workers is institutionalized in modern social welfare policies in the form of social insurance and universal benefits, a critical transformation from social relief to social security. Although capitalists have greater resources in the market, workers, because of their numbers, have greater political resources. Workers will use their political resources to temper market processes and to extend their social rights. Theorists who use this approach tend to highlight the distinction between **social assistance**, which aims to provide subsistence to those in need, and **social insurance**, which provides income security and continuity in living standards. It is this analytical framework, a power resources account, that most gerontologists use to explain the development of the retirement wage in capitalist societies, including Canada.

Social Assistance for the Older Worker

Until the introduction of the Old Age Security Act in 1951, destitute older workers relied for help on the good graces of their families or employers or on social relief. At the time, there were isolated examples of private pension plans for older workers, such as at the Hudson's Bay Company. The Company offered some protection for their fur traders who " . . . in case of sickness and old age " were allowed a pension in "any case that was deserving." (Simpson, 1975:33-34). The Hudson's Bay Company also offered a primitive annuity plan that paid 4 percent on any funds the fur trader left in the keeping of the company, but this was rare because workers were paid very little (McDonald & Wanner, 1990). The *Superannuation Act* of 1870, passed by the new federal government, provided an early occupational pension plan for federal employees in order to " . . . get rid of persons who had arrived at a time of life when they could no longer perform their work efficiently" (Morton & McCallum, 1988:6). The Act was as much a political strategy designed to rid the new government of officials inherited from an earlier government as a genuine retirement pension for civil servants.

It was the Grand Trunk Railway (later the Canadian National Railway) that established one of the first compulsory industrial pension plans in Canada in 1874. In order to impose discipline on a large body of employees spread across Canada, the company looked to the military for inspiration. Besides adopting uniforms, hierarchies, and strict regulations, the organization also introduced a contributory pension at age 65 to shore up the workers' commitment to the company. Because workers contributed part of their salary to the plan, they were less likely to leave the company, while the strongly held Canadian value of thrift was reinforced because pensions were a reward for saving. In the ensuing years, these types of benefits were offered by a growing number of businesses such as banks and became known as **corporate welfare**. An Imperial Oil employee observed that the private pension was " . . . a cold blooded business proposition" (quoted in Morton & McCallum, 1988:11). Pensions at this time were a *gift* designed to insure that older workers did not antagonize their employers by actions such as strikes, in return for a secure old age. Indeed, in 1910, in the course of an acrimonious strike, the Grand Trunk Railway wiped out the pension rights of the workers who had struck the company.

Not wanting to take responsibility for the pensions of Canadians, the federal government emulated the railways and banks in their approach to pensions. In order to encourage individual responsibility for pension plans, the federal government took action on two fronts. It passed the *Pension Funds Societies Act* in 1887, which allowed workers in federally chartered organizations to set up pension plans to which their employer could contribute. And in 1908 it introduced the *Government Annuities Act*, a savings plan which offered reasonable interest rates to workers. These actions were followed up by the *Income War Tax Act* in 1917, which allowed employer contributions to employee pension plans to be claimed as tax deductions. The problem, of course, was that few people were covered by such pensions or could set aside money from their paltry wages. Although the government of the day boasted that the *Annuities Act* would eliminate the need for a government program of old age pensions, in the last year of the existence of the Act in 1927, only 9000 contracts were signed (Morton & McCallum, 1988).

In the 1880s, Bismarck instituted the first state pensions for working class men in a rapidly industrializing Germany:

> The State must take the matter into its own hands, not as alms giving but as the right that men have to be taken care of when, from no fault of their own, they have become unfit for work. Why should regular soldiers and officers have old age pensions, and not the soldier of labour? (Quoted in Donahue, Orbach, & Pollack, 1960:351).

Canadian politicians were, however, indifferent to the plight of the soldier of labour, although a number of organized groups, like the Social Service Congress and the Trades and Labour Congress of Canada, demanded old age pensions for the poor. Witnesses to parliamentary committees testified as to the devastation of industrialism and the inability of poor families to provide for their aged members (House of Commons Debates, 1921). Canada's first *Pension Act*, however, was not enacted until 1919, and applied only to soldiers returning from World War I. It was reportedly a draconian piece of legislation with stringent eligibility criteria (Finalyson, 1988). Earlier, in 1911, Newfoundland, still a British colony, introduced the first state-run old age pension program, which, true to the ethos of the day, did not include women because they were assumed to be unpaid family labourers—even though about 13 percent of women actually worked in the paid labour force in 1911.

Canada's first national pension legislation was not enacted until 1927. The *Old Age Pensions Act* (OAP), promoted by social crusaders J.S Woodsworth and A.A. Heaps, both members of the Labour Party, was nothing more than " . . . a classic piece of 'social assistance' legislation . . ." (Myles & Teichroew, 1991: 87). This Act, which established a cost-shared program between the provinces and the federal government, copied the Elizabethan poor laws, targeting benefits only to the poorest: workers who were 70 years of age and over and indigent (making less than $350 per year). The pension, which was administered at the provincial level by pension boards, was worth $240 a year, or a maximum of $20 per month, and was subject to a means test. A worker could earn up to $350 dollars a year including the pension amount—well below the average worker's wage of $2460 per year. Natives, as defined under the *Indian Act,* were not eligible, nor were immigrants to Canada who were not British subjects. Women were eligible but were treated differently in the administration of the Act, as we saw in Chapter 13. By the time the OAP was replaced by the *Old Age Security Act* (OAS) in 1951, less than half of the aged population received benefits (Myles & Teichroew, 1991).

From Social Assistance to Social Security

Following World War II, a universal, flat-rate pension plan was instituted in 1951, on the advice of the Joint Committee of the Senate and House of Commons on Old Age Security, as a first step on the road to social security. The advice followed the recommendations of several strong lobby groups such as the Canadian Congress of Labour and the Canadian Welfare Council and was buttressed by the rise of Keynesian economics, which promoted government responsibility for economic growth and social security, an attractive policy following the Great Depression. The *Old Age Security Act* of 1951 was financed and administered by the federal government and operated on the principle of social insurance for all older Canadians. All Canadians aged 70 and over were paid a flat rate of $40 per month and were not subjected to the unpopular means test of the 1927 Act. Eligibility was based only on age and citizenship, so women were automatically included, independent of their marital status. At the same time, the *Old Age Assistance Act,* a form of social assistance equally shared with the provinces, was also passed for those aged 65 to 69, but was based on a means test. Through the 1960s, the *Old Age Security Act* was restructured to increase pension benefits and the qualifying age of 70 was reduced by one year every year until it became 65 in 1970.

As Myles (1984) has shown, the problem with the flat-benefit structure was that retired workers were equal—equally poor in an otherwise wealthy society. The benefit rates were not meant to replace market income; they were to provide a social safety net. The Minister of National Health and Welfare (Paul Martin Sr.) was careful to make the point:

> I am sure that as this new program comes to be integrated into the existing pattern of retirement provisions provided by individuals, by employers and in other ways, it will be recognized for what it is intended to be—not as a total retirement security scheme in itself, replacing and supplanting all others, but as the core, the keystone of a national savings and retirement plan, around which each individual in the country will be encouraged to build his own retirement security program in a manner and to an extent peculiarly suited to his own needs (quoted in Clark, 1960:239–240).

It was not long before Canada, along with a host of other countries with flat-benefit structures (e.g., Britain, Sweden), recognized that the benefits were not enough to allow workers to withdraw from the labour force without a drastic drop in their income, a problem that became glaring as inflation eroded the value of the benefits even further in the 1950s. Although the rate was raised in 1963, an automatic upward adjustment tied to the consumer price index was instituted in 1972. Tinkering with the rates was not enough to achieve a sufficient level of income security for workers to retire, so a second tier of contributory pensions was added to the flat-benefit program.

The Canada Pension Plan and the Quebec Pension Plan (C/QPP) were introduced in 1965 as compulsory, contributory plans with benefits linked to contributions based on a person's earnings. The CPP was the result of considerable finagling between the federal government and the provinces, while Quebec opted to establish its own plan, the QPP. Equal contributions were required from the employee and the employer and were originally set at 3.6 percent of earnings in 1966, meaning the employee and employer each paid 1.8 percent of the contribution. The C/QPP, at the time, replaced approximately 25 percent of the average industrial wage.

The C/QPP is what Myles (1988) refers to as the citizen's wage because it is a hybrid of market-based and citizenship entitlements (it is open to all Canadian citizens). Even though market-based inequalities were part of the formula (contributions based on earnings), overall, the benefit formula was redistributive, with higher returns on past contributions to people in lower income groups.

In order to aid those already retired, the Guaranteed Income Supplement (GIS), an income-tested program, and thus a form of social assistance, was introduced in conjunction with the C/QPP as an amendment to the *Old Age Security Act* in 1966. The GIS was originally an interim measure until the C/QPP matured in 1976, but is still with us today. For married couples, the GIS was calculated on their combined income and was less than double a single person's GIS because of the view that two could live more cheaply than one. In 1975, an income-tested Spouse's Allowance (SPA), a controversial program that favoured heterosexual marriages, became payable to 60-to-64-year-old spouses of GIS recipients.

These initial pension programs were never meant to completely replace pre-retirement income, since the thinking at the time was that they were a platform upon which Canadians would build their own pension nest eggs. It was anticipated that the first two tiers of the pension system would eventually be complemented by a **third tier** or private income sources. This was to consist of employer pensions (registered pension plans or RPPs) and individual savings in registered retirement savings plans (RRSPs), which were introduced in 1957 as an amendment to the *Income Tax Act*. (Although such plans were seen as private income, they were actually publicly subsidized through tax concessions on contributions and monies that accumulated within the fund.) Looked at another way, the pension system was characterized by government-administered pension programs, employer-sponsored pension plans, and pension plans purchased by individuals.

By the beginning of the 1970s, then, the Canadian pension system was a complex package of public and private programs. The principal components of the three tiers were the Old Age Security system, made up of Old Age Security pension (OAS), the Guaranteed Income Supplement (GIS), and the Spouse's Allowance (SPA); the Canada and Quebec Pension Plans; and private pensions comprised of registered pension plans and registered retirement savings plans.

At the outset, these three tiers of programs firmly established the structural design of the Canadian pension system that has endured over time. The pre-war welfare state in Canada was a social assistance system based on the Poor Law tradition, and was designed to provide subsistence to the poorest older workers and their families. In contrast, the post-war improvements introduced in the 1960s and 1970s aimed to provide a welfare state built on social security that provided a modest, but secure standard of living for older Canadians.

These two major historical developments have culminated in a system that tends to have a dual nature: it still has remnants of social assistance for the poor (GIS) alongside social insurance (OAS, C/QPP), usually taken advantage of by the more fortunate. Understanding this fault line helps to explain some of the continuing debates about pensions that have occupied Canadians for the last 35 years. At some point in most pension debates, the issues ultimately revolve around the degree to which Canadians' collective vision of the pension system favours a social assistance or a social insurance model, or a combination of both. As a simple illustration, when the *Globe and Mail*, one of Canada's national newspapers, calls for the gutting of the OAS and C/QPP to be replaced with a universal super-RRSP for Canadians, the argument is for the further privatization of the pension system and the termination of the social insurance model for pensions (*Globe and Mail*, 1995:D6).

The Great Pension Debate

The **great pension debate** (Townson, 2000; Myles & Street, 1995) erupted between 1976 and 1984 when it became obvious that the third tier of the pension system did not live up to expectations. Anticipated private pension coverage did not materialize and RRSPs attracted few investors. Private pension plans covered about 39 percent of paid workers in 1965, reached 48 percent in 1980 and dropped back down to 45 percent in 1983 (Statistics Canada, 1996). As late as 1974, only one working woman in four had private coverage, mainly because so many women, then as now, worked in the services sector where private pensions were the exception to the rule. Seldom was there coverage for self-employed or part-time male or female workers. As well, the C/QPP, which was originally designed to suit a linear, male economic life course of school, work, and retirement (Chapter 13), did not match the more complicated lives of women. Even though women's participation in the labour force was escalating rapidly, only 53 percent of Canadian women were contributing to the C/QPP in 1976, compared to 94 percent of men (Dulude, 1981).

More telling of the system's failure were the poverty rates. Although there is no official poverty line in Canada, researchers often use as an indicator the **low income cut-offs (LICO)** developed by Statistics Canada, which essentially identify those significantly worse off than the average. About 68.6 percent of

Canadians aged 65 and older had incomes below the low income cut-offs of Statistics Canada—71.6 percent of unattached women and 68.6 percent of unattached men in 1980. Only 10 percent of female taxpayers were able to contribute to RRSPs in 1982 (Statistics Canada, 2000a).

Both women's groups and the Canadian Labour Congress began to agitate for improvements in the system as the shortcomings quickly became obvious. They called for more social insurance, like an expanded C/QPP, and homemaker pensions. However, they faced a powerful business lobby that doggedly resisted any reform because they believed it was not good for business. A major review of the Canadian pension system was set into motion accompanied by a national pension conference in 1981 and a blizzard of reports from numerous groups inundated the public (e.g., reports from the Task Force on Retirement Income Policy, 1979; the Economic Council of Canada, 1983; Special Committee on Retirement Age Policies, 1979; the famous green paper by the federal government, 1982; the Royal Commission on the Status of Pensions in Ontario, 1980; and the Parliamentary Task Force, Canada, 1983). The end result of almost 10 years of debate was the *Pension Benefits Standards Act* in 1985, which set minimum standards for private pension plans. However, with the arrival of the 1982/1983 recession, talk about pensions dwindled, only to be revived in the early 1990s on the heels of another recession.

In the 1990s Canadians were subjected, once again, to a round of debates about their pension system that was driven by what Myles and Street (1995) labelled the **politics of the debt**. With a mounting national deficit, a high debt, and soaring rates of unemployment in the early 1990s, Canada concentrated on how to contain the costs of the public pension system, a rather dramatic turnaround from the 1980s debate. Seen in an international context, the about-face was part of a larger attempt to contain the runaway costs of social insurance programs in many developed countries (OECD, 1998). The greying of Canadians and the anticipated costs of the pension system in the future were seen as the culprit responsible for many of Canada's economic woes, even though this was not borne out by the evidence (Gee, 2000). A number of changes were proposed to ensure the viability of the pension system. Despite fierce opposition from a number of quarters, changes to the administration of the OAS and the C/QPP ultimately reduced the amounts of some benefits under the program that we see today. We now turn to a description of the pension system today.

The Current Canadian Pension System

Government-Administered Programs

The retirement income system is presented in Figure 14.1. Government-administered programs include the Old Age Security pension, the Guaranteed Income Supplement and two programs that replaced the Spouse's Allowance and the Widowed Spouse's Allowance. Together these programs constitute what is

Figure 14.1 CANADA'S RETIREMENT INCOME PROGRAMS

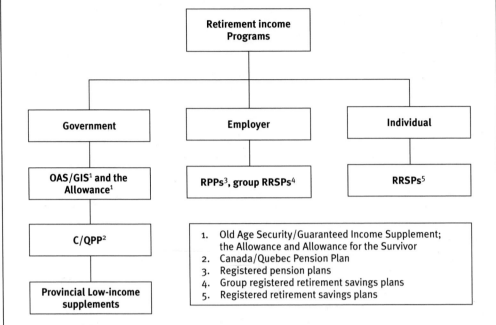

Source: Created from Statistics Canada, *Pension plans in Canada: Statistical highlights and key tables, January 1, 1999,* Catalogue No. 74-401 (January 1, 2000).

generally referred to as the **first tier of the pension system**. The Canada and Quebec Pension Plans are also administered by the federal government, but are considered to be the **second tier of the pension system** because they are based on labour force participation.

Old Age Security (OAS)

The OAS is a flat-rate monthly benefit that is fully taxable. The program is financed from general revenues and is administered by Social Development Canada. To be eligible for the full OAS pension, a person must be 65 years or older and a Canadian citizen or legal resident of Canada, and have resided in Canada for at least 10 years after reaching age 18. Partial pensions may be awarded wherein a person can earn one-fortieth of their pension for each year spent in Canada after age 18. The OAS program also includes reciprocal agreements with other countries that allow time spent in another country to count toward the OAS and the Allowance.

The universal aspect of the OAS pension was terminated in 1989. It is currently means-tested through a **clawback**. A person's pension is clawed back at a rate of

15 cents on every dollar of OAS benefits for every dollar of income over $62 144 in 2006. Since July 1996, the government has imposed the clawback before paying the benefit, so the amount of OAS older people actually receive in any year depends upon the income they declared in their tax return the previous year. A person who is expected to have an income of $100 914 or more in 2006 will not receive an OAS pension.

The OAS rates are adjusted four times a year to reflect any increases in the consumer price index. The average benefit paid in the fourth quarter in 2005 was $454.12 and the maximum benefit that could be paid was $479.83 (Social Development Canada, 2005b). In June 2005, 52.1 percent of OAS beneficiaries were women compared to 47.9 percent who were men (Social Development Canada, 2005a, p. 104, table 41Y). In October 2005, 4.2 million OAS benefits were paid to Canadians, and the cost to the national treasury for that month was over $2 billion dollars.

The loss of the universal aspect of the OAS is a significant step in the development of Canada's welfare system for two reasons. First, the end of universality heralds a renewed receptiveness to a social assistance model for the Canadian welfare state, one that targets dollars to those most in need and moves the federal government out of the pension arena. Second, the income level at which the clawback takes effect is not indexed to inflation below 3 percent, which means the cut-off level will decline each year so that, over the long run, most older Canadians will become subject to the clawback. In a worst case scenario it is predicted that by the year 2036 the pension legislation will generate a sixfold increase in the incidence of low income in Canada (Murphy & Wolfson, 1991). Whether this will occur remains to be seen, but what is clear is that the OAS is fast becoming a social assistance program for the poor and there is a good chance that the trend will continue (Myles & Street, 1995).

The Guaranteed Income Supplement (GIS)

The Guaranteed Income Supplement, a program that was intended to be phased out with the maturation of the C/QPP in 1976, is a vital component of the pension system. The GIS is a means-tested, non-taxable monthly benefit available to OAS recipients with low income. Generally, sponsored immigrants to Canada are not eligible for the GIS during their period of sponsorship, usually 10 years. Eligibility and the amounts of benefits are determined by total family income in the previous year, which must be lower than a specific level. The rates for the fourth quarter of 2005 are presented in Table 14.2. A single person must have an income lower than $13 704, not including OAS, to qualify for the GIS, while a retired married/common-law couple would qualify if their income is under $17 856. The average monthly benefit is $383.55 for a single person and the maximum benefit is $570.27 for a single person. Like the OAS, the GIS is indexed to the consumer price index, which is adjusted four times a year. The GIS benefits are reduced by $1 for every $2 of income for single recipients and by $1 for every $4 of combined income for married couples where both partners receive OAS.

Table 14.2 OLD AGE SECURITY BENEFIT RATES, OCTOBER–DECEMBER 2005

Type of Benefit	Average Monthly Benefit July 2005 $	Maximum Monthly Benefit Oct – Dec $	Maximum Annual Income $	Amount Paid Oct 2005 $ M
Old Age Security	454.12	479.83	60 806*	1,914.9
Guaranteed Income Supplement				430.9
Single person	383.55	570.27	13 704	363.2
Spouse/Common-law partner of a nonpensioner	377.01	570.27	33 168	31.2
Spouse/Common-law partner of a pensioner	234.63	371.46	17 856	107.1
Spouse/Common-law partner of an Allowance recipient	308.36	371.46	33 168	19.7
The Allowance				
Regular Allowance	326.08	851.29	25 536	20.8
Allowance for Survivor	507.47	939.84	18 744	15.7

* Pensioners with an individual net income above $60 806 must repay part or all of the maximum Old Age Security pension amount. The repayment amounts are normally deducted from their monthly payments before they are issued. The full OAS pension is eliminated when a pensioner's net income is $98 850 or above.

Source: Old Age Security (OAS) payment rates 2005. Retrieved December 19, 2005, from http://www.sdc.gc.ca/en/isp/oas/oasrates.shtml. Reproduced with the permission of the Minister of Public Works and Government Services, 2006.

Of the 1.55 million GIS beneficiaries in June 2005, 35.9 percent were men, 64.1 percent were women (Social Development Canada, 2005a, p. 104, table 41Y). About 80 percent of all single recipients of GIS are women, an indication of who is most at risk for poverty in old age. Reliance on the GIS is uneven across Canada and is very high in certain provinces and territories. For example, 67 percent of the seniors of Newfoundland and Labrador and 63 percent of the seniors of the Northwest Territories and Nunavut depended on this source of income in 2000 (NACA, 2006).

In 2005 the federal budget announced a long-awaited increase in the GIS. Maximum benefits rose by $36 for single older adults and $58 for couples beginning in January 1, 2006. This increase is a historic event, given that the last raise occurred as long ago as 1984.The maximum GIS increased by 3 percent from approximately $6780 in 2005 to $7131 in 2006 for singles, and to $7486 in 2007, representing a 4 percent increase. Maximum GIS payments for couples rose by 4 percent from a projected $8832 in 2005 to $9367 in 2006 and $9885 in 2007, for a total increase of 8 percent. Because the rise is so small it is likely to reduce poverty only slightly. As the Caledon Institute says " . . . one cannot expect miracles from so small a rise in the Guaranteed Income Supplement" (Battle, Torjman, Mendelson, & Pomeroy, 2005:42).

The effectiveness of the GIS in reducing poverty depends upon how poverty is defined. As you might expect, there are many definitions, all controversial. Statistics Canada's low income cut-offs (LICO), although not considered an official measure of poverty, are the most widely used indicators in Canada. While **the low income rate** measures the proportion of people below the LICO, the **income gap** is a measure of the depth of low income among those who fall below the cut-off. It is difficult to use the poverty rate because the GIS enhancements have just begun. Using the income gap, a single pensioner with the maximum OAS and GIS benefits would have an estimated income in 2007 of $13 421 (after the enhancement to the GIS), which is well below the after-tax LICO of $17 678 for metropolitan centres over 500 000. In comparison, without the GIS enhancement, the income would be $12 989 in 2007. The enhancement reduces the income gap from $4689 to $4257. For couples, the increase brings income just over the LICO: at the old rates, the maximum OAS and GIS would amount to an estimated $21 059, $512 below the LICO; but with the increase, maximum OAS and GIS benefits reach $21 755 which is $185 above the LICO (Battle et al., 2005).

A more disturbing issue is the fact that only 41 percent of those who needed to apply for GIS in 2001 actually did so; these people tended to be among the oldest old and were likely to receive small benefits (less than $2000). Undoubtedly there are a number of barriers to receiving GIS, like having to apply and renew annually through the tax system or through paper applications, especially for those who have to apply for the first time or after losing eligibility. In 2005, 115 000 people did not reapply for their GIS benefit within the prescribed time period (NACA, 2006). The theoretical annual cost of payments for eligible non-recipients is estimated to be around $300 million (Poon, 2005). Box 14.1 discusses a move to seek compensation for lost income.

The Allowance and the Survivor's Allowance   The Spouse's Allowance (SPA) was available to Canadians aged 60 to 64 who were married to a GIS recipient or to 60-to-64 year old widows and widowers. The SPA program has been replaced with a new program called simply the Allowance, which took effect in July 2000 and extended benefits to same-sex couples. The Allowance may be paid to the spouse or common-law partner of an old-age pensioner, or to a survivor. The same age regulations apply: the person must be between the ages of 60 to 64 and must have lived in Canada for at least 10 years after turning 18. To qualify, the combined yearly income of the couple, or the annual income of the survivor, cannot exceed certain limits which are established quarterly: $25 536 for couples and $18 744 for survivors in 2005. The Allowance is discontinued when

Box 14.1 *GIS Lawsuit*

He thinks Ottawa owes him a total of nearly $6000, but Andre Le Corre says he was also in court yesterday to help hundreds of thousands of Canada's poorer pensioners who, like him, didn't realize that they were eligible for extra pension benefits. Yesterday, a Quebec court judge began hearing Mr. Le Corre's application to launch a class-action suit that, if successful, could cost Ottawa up to $3-billion in arrears, according to one estimate.

A 76-year-old retired medical-lab technician from Longueuil, south of Montreal, Mr. Le Corre says the federal government was negligent in failing to notify Canada's poorer pensioners that they were eligible for the Guaranteed Income Supplement. "It could have made a huge difference. Think of all the awful events that could have been prevented, the rent that could have been paid, the medications that could have been bought," he said in an interview. Mr. Le Corre's lawsuit says Ottawa acted carelessly toward poor elderly people because it could have easily used revenue databanks to spot people who weren't getting their full pension benefits.

Madam Justice Pepita Capriolo of the Quebec Superior Court will hear arguments until Monday, then will consider the matter before ruling whether a class-action suit can proceed. A parliamentary committee looking into the problem has estimated that more than 380,000 pensioners were eligible but did not receive the supplement. This could add up to $3 billion, said one of Mr. Le Corre's lawyers. However, under current rules, Ottawa will pay only for the previous 11 months, should an entitled pensioner apply for missed GIS.

Mr. Lesperance, a federal lawyer, told the court the government has since launched a media blitz and sent 100 000 letters to OAS beneficiaries. Mr. Le Corre said he took it as a sign that federal officials are conceding that they had done something wrong. "It shows they were feeling guilty," he said.

Source: Condensed from Tu Thanh Ha, "Senior seeks to sue Ottawa over unpaid supplement," *The Globe and Mail*, 31 January 2003, p. A7. Reprinted with permission from *The Globe and Mail*.

the person becomes eligible for OAS. The maximum amount paid to a partner of a pensioner is the combined full OAS and the GIS at the married rate. Over the time that the SPA program was offered, Spouse Allowance recipients were concentrated among women. Close to 91 percent of recipients were women in 2005 (Social Development Canada, 2005a).

The former SPA discriminated on the grounds of marital status; individuals who had never married, or who were divorced, separated, or married to a partner not yet 65, were not entitled to benefits under the program. The SPA was unsuccessfully challenged in the Federal Court of Canada and was deemed a reasonable limitation under section 1 of the Canadian Charter of Rights and Freedoms. The problem is likely to continue with the new Allowance and may be challenged again in court. The Allowance increased at the same rate as the GIS starting in 2006.

Canada/Quebec Pension Plan (C/QPP) The Canada/Quebec Pension Plan makes up the smaller second tier of programs administered by government. The C/QPP is not funded by the government. It is a compulsory plan financed by employees, employers, the self-employed, and CPP investments. Contributions are paid on a portion of a worker's earnings that falls between specified minimum and maximum amounts of income. The maximum amount of income, equivalent to the average Canadian industrial wage ($41 100 in 2005), is adjusted annually, and the minimum has been frozen at the 1997 level of $3500. A worker who makes $3500 or less does not pay into the C/QPP, nor does his or her employer, and no contribution is required on earnings above the maximum amount. The contribution rate for 2005 was 9.9 percent—4.95 percent for the worker and 4.95 percent for the employer, or 9.9 percent for the self-employed, who pay both portions. The C/QPP covers all workers between the ages of 18 and 70 whether they work for wages full-time or part-time or are self-employed. The C/QPP allows for a flexible retirement age since workers can retire and claim benefits at any time between the ages of 60 and 70. Those who claim retirement benefits prior to age 65 receive an actuarially reduced benefit, and those who claim after age 65 receive an actuarially improved benefit.

The C/QPP replaces approximately 25 percent of a worker's pre-retirement income, averaged over his or her annual lifetime earnings up to the maximum noted above. A worker's earnings and contributions over the years constitute a worker's **pension credits**. There are provisions in the Plan that allow a worker to drop or exclude periods of low or no income from the contributory period in the calculation of the average earnings on which the pension benefit will be based. Up to 15 percent of the months when the person's income was lowest in the contributory period can be excluded—the **general drop-out provision**. There is also a **child drop-out provision** that accommodates child-rearing responsibilities, a feature very important to women. The period when a worker has a child under the age of seven can be dropped from the calculation of pension benefits.

Besides retirement pensions, both plans also provide disability pensions, benefits to dependent children of deceased C/QPP contributors and to children of disability recipients, surviving spouse/partner benefits, and lump-sum death benefits to help cover the costs of funerals. The rates for the main programs are presented in Table 14.3. The maximum rate for a new beneficiary is $828.75 per month and, as presented in Table 14.4, the C/QPP constitutes about the same proportion of income for men and women (20.2 percent for men compared to 20.5 percent for women). The amounts, however, are quite dissimilar because the Plan, to a certain degree, reproduces the income differentials generated during the working years. Women received, on average, $342.10 for the month of November 2005 from the C/QPP, which is 59 percent of the $584.26 paid to men for the same month (Social Development Canada, 2005c, table 10). Even though women's benefits are lower than men's, the proportion of women receiving CPP benefits is about the same as that of men—50.4 percent of men compared to 49.6 percent of women (Social Development Canada, 2005a, Table 11y, p.41).

It is important to note that pensions can be equally shared by partners so that each receives a pension cheque, even though one partner may not have contributed.

Table 14.3 **THE CANADA PENSION PLAN AND THE QUEBEC PENSION PLAN**

Type of Benefit	New Benefits Maximum Rate (2005)	
	$	$
Individual Pensions	CPP	QPP
Retirement (age 65)	828.75	828.75
Disability	1 010.23	1 010.20
Survivors		
Under 65	462.42	—
Over 65	491.25	497.25
Death (lump sum)	2 500.00	2 500.00
Combined pensions		
Survivors/Retirement	828.75	828.75
Survivors/Disability	1 010.23	1 305.72

Calculation of CPP Maximum Monthly Rates for New Benefits
Retirement: 25% of 1.5 x the average yearly maximum pension earned for last five years
Disability: (retirement x 0.75) + flat rate ($388.67 [2005])
Survivors: 65 and over: (retirement x 0.60)

Source: The CPP & OAS stats book 2005: Statistics related to Canada pension plan and old age security programs, Tables 14A, p. 44; 14B, p. 45; 14C, p. 46; calculations from Appendix D, p. 126; http //www.sdc.gc.ca/asp/gateway.asp?hr=/en/isp/statistics/ statbook.shtml&hs=ozs Reproduced with the permission of the Minister of Public Works and Government Services, 2006.

Where both partners have worked, the pension can be divided equally even though one person may be eligible for a higher pension benefit. C/QPP pension credits can also be equally split on divorce or separation even if one partner did not contribute. For these reasons, along with the child drop-out provision and the survivors benefit, the C/QPP has been described as woman-friendly (Townson, 2000). In fact, the C/QPP has been credited with improving the financial situation of women in old age and has been shown to have reduced their poverty rates, at least through the 1980s (Myles, 2000).

The Canada and Quebec Pension Plans are very similar programs but not identical. They are financed somewhat differently. The Canada Pension Plan can be changed only with the approval of two-thirds of the provinces, including Quebec. Both programs are coordinated so that credits accumulated are fully portable between the provinces, territories and Quebec. The C/QPP program also includes reciprocal agreements with other countries that allow time spent in another country to count toward the benefit or permit the beneficiary to receive benefits from either Canada or the country in which the person previously worked. All C/QPP benefits are taxable and all benefits, except the death benefit, are adjusted at the beginning of each year according to the consumer price index. During the fiscal year 2004/2005, almost 4.5 million Canadians received approximately $23.7 billion in benefits (Social Development Canada, 2005a, table 6A, p. 10; table 8, p. 14).

Originally the CPP was a pay-as-you-go plan, which means that contributions made by employers and employees in the current workforce were used to finance the benefits of those who were retired. In a pure pay-as-you-go system there is generally no fund from which benefits are paid. In 1998, however, the financing of the CPP changed to become a partial pay-as-you-go system in response to concerns about the demands the future baby boom would place on the pension system. The federal government calls the new system **steady-state financing**. Under steady-state financing, the contribution rate increased sharply from 5.6 percent in 1996 to 9.9 percent in 2003 and is expected to remain at this steady rate thereafter. This approach will generate funds that exceed the amount that must be paid out to beneficiaries between 2001 and 2020 when the last of the baby boomers will retire. The excess funds are transferred to a new CPP Investment Board, created in 1998, which invests the money and, over time, creates a large enough reserve to insure the viability of the Plan.

Other significant changes were also made to the CPP in 1998, which have resulted in slightly lower retirement pensions, the freezing of the death benefit at $2500 (down from $3580 in 1997); the freezing of the $3500 level below which contributions are exempt; and restrictions on who receives the combined survivor and disability/retirement benefits. Despite these changes, the C/QPP are sound programs that cover virtually all workers; they follow workers when they change jobs; and they are linked to inflation. Most importantly, they are accommodating to the needs of women.

Having read our view of the strengths of the C/QPP, examine an opposing view by visiting http://www.canada-pension-plan.com/. The author of this website argues that the C/QPP exploits younger taxpayers to benefit wealthier older ones, and that poverty among older adults is a myth. There are definite flaws in his argument, not the least of which is a disregard for the facts. As we saw in Chapter 5, the burden of poverty of women is carried by the separated and the divorced and is not about single women. Perhaps worse, why should older people be expected to sell their homes or take reverse mortgages so they can survive?

Provincial and Territorial Supplements Older people living in Newfoundland, New Brunswick, Ontario, Manitoba, Saskatchewan, Alberta, British Columbia, Yukon, the Northwest Territories, and Nunavut receive income supplements on top of their federal income security benefits (National Council of Welfare, 1999). The amounts, based on need, vary from area to area, and are administered on a variety of schedules by a variety of governmental departments. In 2006, a single older person living in the Northwest Territories would receive $135 per month, compared to $83 per month for a person living in

Ontario. The benefits are not indexed to keep them current with the cost of living and benefits have not been raised on a regular basis, if at all. According to a dated but unrepeated study, there are more than 300 000 seniors receiving supplements, valued at a total of more than $250 million (National Council of Welfare, 1999). The problem with these benefits, according to the National Council of Welfare, is that they ignore the greater financial requirements of single older persons. For information on provincial benefits, go to http://www.phac-aspc. gc.ca/seniors-aines/index_pages/provlinks_e.htm.

Looking at the overall picture for government-administered programs, Table 14.4 displays the degree to which Canadian seniors depend upon government transfers in their annual incomes. Government transfers account for 41.4 percent of older men's income and 55.3 percent of older women's income. In 2003, 31.7 percent of all income of women aged 65 and over came from OAS/GIS, compared with 18 percent for their male counterparts (Statistics Canada, 2006a).

Keeping in mind that no component of the program theoretically raises income over the low income cut-offs for individuals, it begins to make sense that Canada was awarded a B grade by NACA. At best, the system guarantees very modest incomes to Canadians and is beginning to tilt towards more of a social welfare system than a social insurance system with the changes to the Old Age Security Pension.

Table 14.4   **SOURCES OF INCOME FOR CANADIANS AGE 65 AND OVER BY GENDER, 2003**

Source	Men	Women	Total
Employment	8.1	4.3	6.4
Investments	8.8	12.6	10.5
Retirement Pensions	40.5	26.3	34.0
Other Income	1.3	1.5	1.4
Income from Government Transfers			
OAS/GIS	18.3	31.7	24.5
C/QPP	20.2	20.5	20.4
Other Transfers	2.9	3.1	2.8
Total Government Transfers	**41.4**	**55.3**	**47.7**
Total	100%	100 %	100%

Source: Adapted from Statistics Canada. Canada's retirement income programs: 2006 edition (74-507-XBC). *The Daily.* Retrieved March 14, 2006, from http://www.statcan.ca/Daily/English/060207/d060207b.htm

Employer and Individually Administered Programs

Almost all Canadians require other sources of income if they are to avoid a substantial drop in their income when they leave the labour force. As we indicated above, employer pension plans and RRSPs are supposed to make up the rest of people's incomes in old age, usually up to approximately 70 percent of their pre-retirement earnings to maintain their standard of living. This third tier of the pension system does not achieve this goal for most Canadians.

Employer-Sponsored Pension Plans

Employer-sponsored pension plans are also called registered retirement pension plans (RPPs), occupational pension plans, private pension plans, or company pension plans. At bottom, the plans are a form of deferred wages, which postpone the receipt of some of a worker's current wages to provide income when the worker retires. These plans are provided by employers or by unions in both the public and private sectors of the economy, usually on a voluntary basis. The plans are called registered plans because they are registered with Canada Revenue Agency to obtain a tax exemption and, in many cases, with the federal or a provincial regulatory authority. Provincial and federal legislation govern the minimum standards, funding, and investments of the RRPs. A smaller number of plans, covering about 20 percent of members, are not subject to regulatory legislation because they may be covered by their own Acts, as in the case of some federal and provincial public servants or small individual plans (Statistics Canada, 2004d).

At the beginning of 2004, 5.6 million workers were covered by occupational pension plans, a 1 percent increase since 2000 (Statistics Canada, 2006a). More men than women were members of plans, although the number of female members did increase slightly in the last few years (Statistics Canada, 2004d). The increase in women over time can be directly attributed to the growing proportion of women in the workforce and to changes in legislation that allowed part-time employees, mainly women, to be covered. In 1993 men represented 57.7 percent of plan members but in 2003 they represented only 53.7 percent of plan members, reducing the gender gap by 7.2 percentage points (Statistics Canada, 2004d).

Table 14.5 displays the extent of coverage of employer-sponsored pension plans in Canada. Experts use two ways of looking at private pension coverage, the percentage of *paid workers* who are covered by a plan and the percentage of the *labour force* that is covered by a plan. The labour force measure includes the self-employed, the unemployed, and unpaid family workers who do not have an employer-employee relationship (for example, relatives who work in a family-owned store). Including this group of people in the measure will reduce the percentage covered by an occupational pension, so that knowing what indicator is used is important in considering these statistics.

Table 14.5   COVERAGE OF EMPLOYER-SPONSORED PENSION PLANS,
PERCENTAGE OF LABOUR FORCE AND PAID WORKERS

	1992	1994	1996	1998	2000	2002
Women						
Labour force	34.2	33.6	32.8	32.3	33.3	33.3
Paid workers	41.6	41.1	40.3	39.1	39.3	39.2
Men						
Labour force	37.5	35.6	34.3	33.4	34.3	32.8
Paid workers	48.1	45.3	43.4	41.9	41.8	39.9
Total						
Labour force	36.0	34.7	33.6	32.9	33.8	33.0
Paid workers	45.1	43.4	42.0	40.6	40.6	39.6

Source: Statistics Canada, http://www.40.statcan.ca/101/cst01/labor26a.htm.

According to Table 14.5, 39.2 percent of paid workers, or 33.3 percent of the labour force, enjoyed pension coverage in 2002. As Table 14.5 shows quite clearly, the coverage rate for paid workers has steadily declined—from 45.1 percent in 1992 to 39.6 percent in 2002—and the decline has been more pronounced for men than for women. In the case of women, as their labour force participation slowed so did their membership in RRPs (Statistics Canada, 2004d). An analysis of this drop found that a decline in union membership and a move to low-coverage jobs adversely affected many workers. Increased competition, increases in contributions by employers to other pension plans, and the administrative costs of certain types of plans may also have had an effect (Morissette & Drolet, 2001).

Generally, there are two types of plans: non-contributory plans, in which the employer makes all the contributions, and contributory plans, in which both employer and employee pay a share. Employees might pay anywhere from 5 to 10 percent of their earnings into a plan, which is tax-deductible; the employer's contributions, which are also tax deductible, will be calculated according to some contribution formula guaranteed to keep the plan actuarially sound. About 58 percent of plans were contributory in 2003 (Statistics Canada, 2004d).

Within these two types of plans, various methods are used to calculate retirement benefits. The two most common methods are found in defined contribution plans and defined benefit plans. In defined contribution plans, pension benefits vary depending on the contributions accumulated for each individual and the return on the investment of these contributions. In this type of plan, both employers and employees contribute a fixed percentage of a worker's earnings into a fund for investment. In defined benefit plans, benefits are established by a formula specified in the contract with the employer, based on earnings and years of service. Defined benefit plans have the advantage of guaranteeing members a fixed percentage of their preretirement earnings, which does not occur in defined contribution plans. In Canada, defined benefit plans are the most common, with 82 percent of Canadians covered by this type of plan in 2003 (Statistics Canada, 2004d). The majority of defined benefit plan members are in the public sector. Some observers have argued that there is a growing movement towards providing defined contribution plans, which are cheaper for the employer because no minimum payout is guaranteed (Townson, 2000).

Employer-sponsored pension plans and the C/QPP are now similar in a number of features. Ever since the federal and provincial governments agreed, in 1986, to tighten the standards governing private pensions and to make them consistent in all provinces, pension contributions are locked in and vested once a worker has belonged to an employer's plan for two years. *Locking in* benefits means that the benefits cannot be paid until a later date, usually at age 55; and vesting means that workers have a right to future benefits from contributions that they and their employer have made, even if the worker leaves the employer. Benefits are *portable*; that is, the worker can transfer vested pension benefits to the pension plan of the new employer, to an RRSP, or to an annuity. In addition, some part-time workers are now covered, survival benefits are available, and there is credit-splitting upon divorce in some provinces, such as in Manitoba, where a 50-50 split is mandatory.

Employer-sponsored pension plans differ from the C/QPP on two counts—they do not cover everyone and they are not indexed to inflation. As is evident in Table 14.4, occupational pension plans make up only 26.3 percent of older women's income compared to 40.5 percent of older men's incomes. Older women receive more than $7000 less per person on average from private pensions than do older men—a dismal showing in both instances (Statistics Canada, 2006c). Finally, inflation, which can make a pension worth less over time, is covered only in about half of defined benefit plans (and of course, not in any defined contribution plans).

A very serious problem with private pension plans is that they are not a very useful source of retirement income for workers who make lower wages because they replicate the inequality found in the labour market. In 1996 only 10 percent of wage earners making $20 000 or less belonged to plans. It is women who bear the brunt of this problem, since about 47 percent of women have incomes below $20 000. In addition, the average contribution to an employer-sponsored pension plans rises as income rises, so that people with lower incomes (usually women) make lower contributions and, as a result, receive lower pensions. For example, a person making $10 000 would make an average contribution of $253, a small sum that will not add up to much in the long run. In contrast, a person making $50 000 would make a contribution of about $3 121, which could be substantial over time (National Council of Welfare, 1999:39). To add to this disparity, workers with more income get a better tax break on their pension contributions than poorer workers. Again we can see why the National Advisory Council on Aging decided on a B grade for Canada.

Registered Retirement Savings Plans (RRSPs)

Registered retirement savings plans have been increasing, mainly because, unlike RPPs, they are available to all workers. About 5.6 million people, or 38 percent of all eligible tax filers aged 25 to 64, made contributions to RRSPs in 2004, totalling $25.2 billion (Statistics Canada, 2006a). People aged 45 to 64 were the biggest contributors, increasing by 50 percent between 1992 and 2004. By comparison, there was only a 3 percent increase among people aged 25 to 34 years.

RRSPs allow taxpayers to save for their old age through tax breaks. A person is allowed to make an annual contribution of up to 18 percent of earned income to an RRSP, to a maximum limit currently set at $18 000 in 2006 for those who do not have a private pension plan. Members of occupational pension plans have this limit reduced. The worker can then deduct the full amount of the contribution from the year's taxable income. The money in RRSPs is usually invested and the interest earned is not taxed until the RRSP is terminated. People can cash in their RRSPs at any time but at retirement they usually buy an annuity that provides them with a regularly paid benefit. The annuities are taxable income, but after retirement people are usually in a lower tax bracket, so they achieve a net tax saving. A person who does not contribute the maximum allowable amount may carry over unused RRSP room to the following year, a rule that allows people to make up for lean years with larger contributions in more prosperous years. The pattern of contributions for men and women from 1982 to 2002 can be seen in Figure 14.2 as a slow upward trend

In 2004, 54 percent of male tax filers contributed to an RRSP while 46 percent of female tax filers made a contribution. The median contribution of men was $3000, compared to $2200 for women. As would be expected, income affects whether a person participates in an RRSP and the amount of contributions. In 2004, 76 percent of tax filers with incomes of $80 000 or more contributed to RRSPs, compared to 3 percent of tax filers with incomes below $10 000 (Statistics Canada, 2006a).

Although Canadian tax filers contributed over $25 billion to RRSPs in 2004, they also withdrew a considerable amount of money in the same year. About 9 percent of tax filers received on average $4905 per person in RRSP income, down, however, from $6918 in 1994. Surprisingly, these withdrawals were lower among older adults, even though annuities were included in the withdrawals. Almost 9 percent of withdrawers aged 25 to 64 cashed in all or part of their RRSP savings under the Home Buyers Plan to finance the purchase of a home. The Lifelong Learning Plan, introduced in 1999 to finance education or training, was barely used—by fewer than half of 1 percent of tax filers (Statistics Canada, 2006a).

It is useful to remember that taxes not paid represent a reduction in government revenues. For example, the net loss of income to governments in 2003

Figure 14.2 **AVERAGE RRSP CONTRIBUTIONS OF WOMEN AND MEN IN CONSTANT 2002 DOLLARS, 1982 TO 2002**

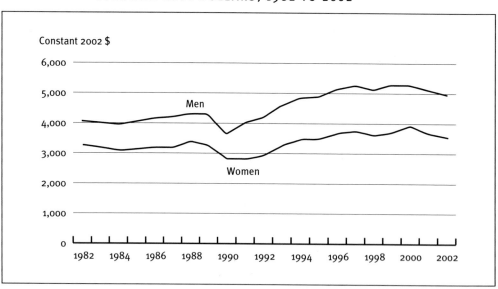

Source: Statistics Canada, *Women in Canada: a gender-based statistical report, 2005*, Catalogue No. 89-503 (March 13, 2006).

as a result of RRSPs was projected to be over $9 billion, while registered pension plans represent a projected net loss of over $5 billion dollars (Department of Finance, 2001). The total cost of pensions, then, includes not only benefits paid by contributors but also forgone taxes. When observers call for cutting the costs of the pension system they often overlook this feature and choose to focus more on cutting the amounts of benefits, which of course hurts lower income people more.

Why a B Grade for Canada?

Improvements in Income

With an overview of the retirement income system it becomes easier to see how well the pension system protects older Canadians. In terms of income levels and measures of income distribution, the relative economic position of older persons in Canada, as in many industrialized nations, has noticeably improved over the last several decades. The improvement has been so dramatic that the National Council of Welfare has called it " . . . one of Canada's biggest success stories in social policy during the latter part of the 20th century" (National Council of Welfare, 2000:79). However, as recently as 1980, close to 61 percent of unattached older men and 72 percent of unattached older women lived below Canada's LICO, as reported above. Comparative studies in the 1980s of six countries placed Canada near the bottom of the list in terms of the number of older adults with low incomes. The gap between men's and women's incomes was considered to be particularly unacceptable at this time.

In 2003, depending on the measure of poverty used, 17.7 percent of **unattached persons** 65 years of age and over lived below the after-tax LICO. Close to 19 percent of unattached women, the lowest number ever, and 14.7 percent of unattached men, lived in poverty as of 2003 (Figure 14.3). Using a slightly different measure, which considers income before taxes, the equivalent poverty figures are 38.3 percent for all older unattached persons: 31.6 percent for unattached males and 40.9 percent for unattached females (Figure 14.4). These figures are more in line with how the poverty rates were originally used in the 1980s and are a better gauge of the gains in income.

The protection afforded by family against poverty is extraordinary. As Figures 14.3 and 14.4 illustrate, the proportion of older people in families below the LICO is only 2.2 percent after taxes and 5.3 percent before taxes and reflects the presence of a male income. Although we do not wish to enter into the debate about the choice of indicators, the point remains that poverty has been reduced amongst the elderly but, by any measure, too many older unattached people are still poor. Moreover, Figure 14.5 shows that the incomes of older families have been declining while the incomes of the unattached have remained fairly constant since 1989.

Figure 14.3 **PEOPLE AGED 65+ WITH LOW INCOME AFTER TAXES**

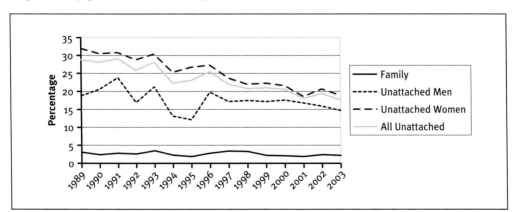

Source: Statistics Canada, CANSIM, table 202-0802 and Catalogue No. 75-202-X. http://www40.statcan.ca/101/cst01/famil19a.htm; http://www40.statcan.ca/101/cst01/famil19c.htm; http://www40.statcan.ca/101/cst01/famil19e.htm

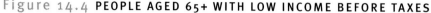

Figure 14.4 PEOPLE AGED 65+ WITH LOW INCOME BEFORE TAXES

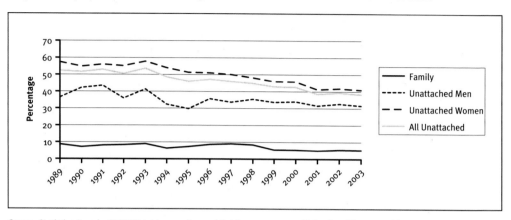

Source: Statistics Canada, CANSIM, table 202-0802 and Catalogue no. 75-202-X. Retrieved from http://www40.statcan.ca/101/csto1/famil41a.htm; http://www40.statcan.ca/101/csto1/famil41c.htm; http://www40.statcan.ca/101/csto1/famil41e.htm

One of the major reasons for the turnaround in the circumstances of Canada's elderly is that the C/QPP has become fully operational, becoming an increasing source of older people's incomes. The C/QPP was designed to come to maturity very quickly so that full benefits were in place 10 years after its introduction in 1966. As a result, recent cohorts who are more likely to be covered by the C/QPP have displaced older cohorts and, due to the increased labour force participation of women, more women are receiving their own C/QPP benefits. According to one study, the percentage of unattached women receiving a C/QPP rose from 44 to 78 percent between 1980 and 1996, while married people in families receiving one C/QPP benefit rose from 74 to 93 percent over the same period (Myles, 2000).

Figure 14.5 AVERAGE TOTAL INCOME (BEFORE TAX) BY FAMILY TYPE FOR PERSONS AGED 65+ YEARS (IN CONSTANT 2003 DOLLARS)

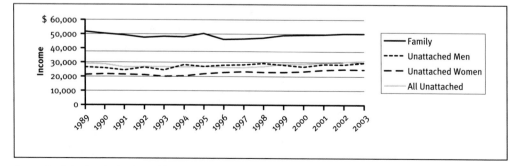

Source: Statistics Canada, CANSIM, table 202-0403 and Catalogue no. 75-202-XIE. Retrieved from http://www40.statcan.ca/101/csto1/familo5a.htm; http://www40.statcan.ca/101/csto1familo5b.htm

Unfortunately, the changes that have occurred are part of the planned maturation of the C/QPP and are not likely to continue in the foreseeable future. Changes that will occur are likely to be related to RRSPs and RRPs, which, as we have seen, favour the wealthy over the poor and men over women. So, while improvements have been made, the poverty of the elderly in Canada has not been eradicated, contrary to what many people believe. Changes still have to made to accommodate the poor elderly who are, in the main, women. The B grade assigned by NACA acknowledges this progress and the need for further improvement.

The Mismatch between the Lives of Canadians and the Pension System

Our review of the three tiers of the Canadian pension system shows where the flaws are and who is most vulnerable to their effects. Older women, especially those who are unattached, depend on the public pension system for most of their income, and are unable to use the private pension system to their advantage. Unattached older men, the next most vulnerable group, are in a similar situation, especially if they are in the secondary labour market. Men at both ends of the age spectrum have been affected by high levels of unemployment in the last decade, moving in and out of the labour force into a series of often non-standard jobs. Their wages have been stagnant and, as we saw earlier, they are now less likely to be covered by private pensions. In effect, one could argue that some men's career trajectories are beginning to look more like women's, rather than women's careers emulating those of men (McDonald, 2006c). The fundamental problem with the pension system is that it was developed to meet the needs of the 19th-century male worker, who was a lone breadwinner supporting a family. The pension system today, with its emphasis on job tenure in a life-long career job, excludes many Canadians who do not match this profile. In other words, pension policy does not match the life course of a substantial number of Canadians.

In particular, pension policy does not match women's lives. The financial situation of women in their later years is a function of their family and labour force histories. Many of today's older women are poor because they belonged to a cohort where the primary occupation of women was that of housewife and mother. As one widowed woman observed, " . . . I was born in the days when the men didn't want women to work . . . so women didn't work . . . , I mean there was no jobs for them anyway . . . ." Another widow was told, "Mrs. X, I hope you realize that the policy is that when you are in a family way, you must give notice . . . ." In the 1930s and 1940s most women had to depend upon their spouses for support in old age; if they worked, it was "just a job" to bring home extra money (McDonald, Donahue, & Moore, 1997b:38, 40). Most women did not have surviving spouse benefits if their husband died and had to rely on the public pension system which, as we saw above, does not provide enough income to raise a person above the LICO. Indeed, in this particular study, 49 percent of the widows who previously worked lived below the LICO in 1991.

Today, many economic analysts argue that the next generation of women, namely the baby boomers, will have been in paid employment for most of their lives and will have their own private pensions, RRSPs, and C/QPP benefits. While this may be true, least two overriding factors suggest that their pension incomes will still not be equal to men's: first, private and semiprivate (C/QPP) components of the pension system replicate the inequality in the labour market; second, women's interrupted work histories due to family responsibilities will affect their ability to save and accumulate pension benefits.

Women are concentrated in non-standard and part-time work; they are under-represented in unions and over-represented in the services sector; and they continue to work largely in traditional female and lower-paid occupations. In fact, the number of women working in non-standard work is slowly increasing, including temporary workers, part-time workers, self-employed workers, and multiple job holders. In 2004, 14 percent of female employees compared to 12 percent of male employees had a temporary job arrangement. In 2004, 6 percent of women were multiple job holders, compared to 4 percent in 1987. Women accounted for 34 percent of all self-employed workers in 2004. Part-time employment continues to be the most common form of non-standard work for women. Since the middle of the 1970s, women have accounted for approximately 70 percent of all part-time employees even though, in 2004, 26 percent of these women reported that they would prefer full-time work (Statistics Canada, 2006c:109-110).

People in part-time jobs not only work fewer hours but also have lower hourly earnings. In 2001, for example, part-time workers worked less than 800 hours compared to 1961 hours for standard workers and earned $11.58 per hour compared to $18.89 per hour for standard workers (Kapsalis & Tourigny, 2005:31). Only 32 percent of women are covered by unions, and this is an improvement from 16 percent in 1966. In comparison, men have been losing ground at a rapid rate. Men's union membership declined in the same period from 40 percent to 32 percent in 2004 (Statistics Canada, 2006c). In terms of the distribution of women's occupations, two-thirds of all employed women in 2004 worked in teaching, nursing and related health occupations, clerical or other administrative jobs, and sales and services occupations (Statistics Canada, 2006c:113), down from 78 percent in 1982 (Statistics Canada, 2000c). It is well known that female occupations traditionally attract lower wages. The female-to-male earnings ratio for full-time full-year workers was 70.5 in 2003, and shows little sign of dropping since the ratio was 70.6 in 2000 (Statistics Canada, 2006c, table 6.9, p.152). When all is said and done, it comes as no surprise that in 2003, the average annual pre-tax income of women aged 16 and over from all sources was $24 400, compared to $39 300 for men (Statistics Canada, 2006c:133). The income of women working on a full-time, full-year basis in 2003 was $36 500 compared to $51 700 for men (Statistics Canada, 2006c, table 6.9, p.152).

Tomorrow's older women may have their own pensions but their position will be only marginally improved because RPPs, the C/QPP, RRSPs and savings all depend on earnings and length of time in the labour market. Unless these conditions are modified, any change in the size of women's benefits will be small. To add to women's financial problems, they outlive men, so their private pensions are more likely to be subject to inflation in the long run. Family responsibilities are linked to women's work histories and have a significant effect on their work patterns and, therefore, their incomes in old age. Almost two-thirds of women who have ever worked have had a work interruption in paid work of six months or more. Most women on maternity leave (86 percent) return to work within one year after giving birth; however, one study has shown that, after a work interruption, women are not as likely as men to return to the same job or to a full-time job if they had a one prior to their interruption (Fast & Da Pont, 1997). In 2004, women employed full-time missed an average of 10 days due to personal and family commitments, up from four days per year in 1980s. In comparison full-time paid men lost only about a day and a half from work for family responsibilities, a figure barely changed from the 1970s (Statistics Canada, 2006c).

Another study found that, if a labour force adjustment must be made to accommodate family responsibilities, it is usually the woman who makes the adjustment (Townson, 2000). Of the men and women with family responsibilities who made adjustments in 1995, two-thirds of women adjusted their work schedules compared to about one-third of men. The adjustments included part-time work, irregular schedules, voluntary job absences, and voluntary joblessness. In the face of a growing demand for the care of aging parents and relatives, women are also more likely to provide care: 15 percent of women, compared to 9 percent of men, cared for both children and an aging relative in 1996. The data from one study suggest that employed women provide elder care by carrying out some of their paid work at home and by working in off hours (Marshall, 1998). While more research needs to be done to establish the exact effect of family responsibilities on women's work, and ultimately their financial security in old age, there is enough evidence now to suggest that their futures might not be as rosy as predicted.

Pension policy barely recognizes the burden of institutionalized lower earnings for women or the costs of their unpaid work and ignores the multiple job changes that both men and women have experienced in the last 10 years. At its best, the pension system offers social welfare to the poor in the guise of OAS and GIS, which, in the final analysis, does little to relieve their poverty. While the C/QPP has great potential to accommodate people's lives, the benefits are small and have become even smaller with the adjustments made in 1998. To successfully prevent poverty, improvements to public or private pensions would have to start with a new vision of the life course that reflected the actual lives of Canadians.

Looking to the Future

Currently, most of the pension changes on the immediate horizon focus on tinkering with the pension system to save money by looking to the markets for solutions. Three main strategies have been considered in Canada: raising the age of retirement (as has been done in the United States, Germany, and Italy); introducing partial retirement through the use of flex time, job-sharing, and part-time work (as in Germany); and shifting pension costs from the government sector to the private sector (as in Great Britain). The last solution has been the solution of choice for Canada. The pension debate in the 1990s resulted in several changes to the Canadian pension system, such as adjustments to increase contribution rates to the C/QPP, reductions in the size of C/QPP retirement and disability benefits, the move to a market solution to bolster the CPP, and the improvements to RRSP regulations. These were all, at the core, cost-cutting measures and nothing more. It is instructive that nothing was done to curtail tax expenditures, the silent side of pension costs. Rather than expand benefits to the poor or find ways to improve private pension coverage, the system committed to contraction, a stand that does not bode well for Canada's poor older adults and that threatens any progress we have already made.

Today's pension policy leans precariously closer to a social assistance model of income security but has not gone all the way down the road to social welfare. For example, in 1998 the federal government abandoned the proposed Seniors Benefit, which was intended to target only the poor and to save $8.2 billion in 2030. It remains to be seen whether the emphasis continues to be on reducing the role of the state in providing pensions and on downloading costs to the private sector. Pension policy is a complicated matter influenced by changing economic conditions like a skittish stock market, trends in people's behaviour (such as investing in RRSPs), lobbying by interest groups such as corporations, and the political will of the Canadian people.

CHAPTER SUMMARY

This chapter has provided an overview of the history of the development of the pension system and how the system has changed and operates today.

Key ideas to remember from this chapter:

- The pre-war welfare state in Canada was a social assistance system based on the Poor Law tradition and was designed to provide subsistence to the older worker and his or her family. In contrast, the post-war improvements introduced in the 1960s and 1970s aimed to provide a different welfare state built on social security that provided a modest but secure standard of living for older Canadians.
- The first private pension plans in Canada, which appeared before state pensions, were a result of a new set of management tools designed to encourage the loyalty of the workers to the company. When they were first offered they were considered a gift that

could be revoked by the company at any time for any untoward behaviour on the part of the worker.

- Canada's first national pension legislation, the *Old Age Pension Act* (OAP), which established a cost-shared program between the provinces and the federal government, copied the Elizabethan Poor Laws, targeting benefits only to workers who were 70 years of age and over and indigent.

- The *Old Age Security Act* of 1951 operated on the principle of social insurance for all older Canadians and was financed and administered by the federal government. All Canadians aged 70 and over were paid a flat rate of $40 per month.

- The Canada Pension Plan and the Quebec Pension Plan (C/QPP) were introduced in 1965 as compulsory, contributory plans with benefits linked to contributions based on a person's earnings. The pension has often been called the *citizen's wage* or a *retirement wage* because it is a hybrid of market-based and citizenship entitlements.

- In order to aid those already retired, the Guaranteed Income Supplement (GIS), an income-tested program and therefore a form of social assistance, was introduced in conjunction with the C/QPP. The GIS was supposed to have been phased out when the system matured but is still needed today.

- The principal tiers of the of the pension system today include the first tier, comprising the Old Age Security pension (OAS), the Guaranteed Income Supplement (GIS) and the Allowance; the second tier, made up of the Canada and Quebec Pension Plans; and the third tier of private pensions comprising registered pension plans and registered retirement savings plans.

- The universal aspect of the OAS pension was terminated in 1989 and the OAS pension is currently means-tested through a clawback. A person's pension is clawed back at a rate of 15 percent for every dollar of income over $62 144 (for 2006).

- The great pension debate of the early 1980s was about how the system could be expanded to provide a more adequate income for Canadians. The economic security of older women was one of the prime issues of concern. The non-debate about the pension system in the 1990s was about how to reduce the costs of the very same system in order to reduce the national debt and deficits.

- The Seniors Benefit, an income-tested plan, was proposed in 1995. The Benefit would have replaced the OAS and GIS and two tax credits directed to older people. The Benefit was dropped in 1998 in response to strong opposition. Changes were made to the CPP instead that essentially reduced benefits and increased contribution rates.

- The problems with private pension plans are that they are not indexed to inflation and they do not cover enough workers, while RRSPs are more useful for the wealthy than for the poor.

- Even though the economic security of older Canadians has improved since the 1980 because of the maturation of the C/QPP, there still are too many Canadians who depend on the system for most of their income and who live in poverty.

- About 17.7 percent of people 65 years of age and over live below the low income cut-offs after taxes have been removed. Older persons who do not live in a family are at the highest risk for poverty. About 19 percent of unattached women, and 14.7 percent of unattached men, lived in poverty as of 1998.

KEY TERMS

citizen's wage (p. 361)

retirement wage (p. 361)

social assistance (p. 363)

social insurance (p. 363)

corporate welfare (p. 363)

third tier (p. 366)

great pension debate (p. 367)

low income cut-off (p. 367)

politics of the debt (p. 368)

first tier of the pension system (p. 369)

second tier of the pension system (p. 369)

clawback (p. 369)

low income rate (p. 372)

income gap (p. 372)

pension credits (p. 374)

general drop-out provision (p. 374)

child drop-out provision (p. 374)

steady-state financing (p. 376)

unattached persons (p. 383)

STUDY QUESTIONS

1. Do you agree with the National Advisory Council on Aging that the economic security of older Canadians is good but could use some improvement? If improvements are to be made to the public pension system, what changes would benefit you when you retire?

2. What are the differences between social insurance and social assistance, and how are they reflected in our national pension system? When you retire do you think the system will lean more toward social insurance or social assistance?

3. What plans are you making now that will eventually influence your economic security in old age? Do you think the public pension system will be there to support you in your old age? Why or why not? Will RRPs and RRSPs take on more importance in the future?

4. How do gender and marital status affect the size of private and public pensions? Do these factors have any influence on who lives above or below the LICO?

Suggested Readings

McDonald L., & Robb, L. (2004). The economic legacy of divorce and separation for older women. *Canadian Journal on Aging, 23*(Suppl.2), S1, S83–S97.

Ginn, J., Street, D., & Arber, S. (Eds.) (2001). *Women, work and pensions: International issues and prospects*. Philadelphia: Open University Press.

Denton, F.T., Fretz, D., & Spencer, B. (Eds.) (2000). *Independence and economic security in old age*. Vancouver: University of British Columbia Press.

Myles, J. (2000). *The maturation of Canada's retirement income system: Income levels, income inequality and low-income among the elderly*. Ottawa: Statistics Canada and Florida State University. Catalogue No. 11F0019MPE No. 147. Accessed September 28, 2006 at http://www.statcan.ca/bsolc/english/bsolc?catno=11F0019M2000147.

Chapter 15

HEALTH-CARE SYSTEM AND POLICY

Learning Objectives

In this chapter, you will learn about

- Jurisdictional issues, established with the formation of the country, that have affected the evolution of Canada's health-care system, the historic development of medicare, and the health-care system as it exists today.
- Health-care reform of the 1990s; what led to such questioning of the established health-care system; the implications for medicare; and the vision of a new, more appropriate

and effective health-care system.
- Health-care reform since the mid-1990s.
- An assessment of health-care reform as it exists at the beginning of the millennium, including a discussion of vested interests in the established system and of broader societal forces (such as capitalism).
- What the future holds if we continue with health-care reform as it appears at the present time.

Introduction

The health-care system is of particular concern when studying an aging population because, as has become evident in earlier chapters, our physical health tends to decline as we age. To recap, these declines occur gradually over time, beginning long before retirement. They tend to include chronic conditions, rather than acute conditions or infectious disease. Mental health, however, does not necessarily deteriorate as we age, although the prevalence of certain mental illnesses, such as dementia, increases with aging. When our health fails, the informal network consisting primarily of family is the first and predominant source of care. This continues in old age. Formal health-care services tend to be utilized either when no informal care is available or the when the needs of the older adult exceed the care family members are able to provide. In examining the Canadian health-care system, we are interested in knowing whether the services it provides are the most appropriate for the illnesses and disabilities suffered as we age and whether the treatments provided are effective. We can also ask: Is the major focus of the health-care system on *health*, that is, on promoting the nation's health and preventing illness and disability? Is the system effective in these efforts? When illness and disability occur, does the system provide appropriate and effective services for dealing with them?

Historical Roots of Canadian Health-Care Policy

The health-care system in Canada has been shaped from Confederation in 1867. The *British North America Act* (BNA) made no mention of welfare measures. The government's contribution to this arena was restricted to poor relief administered at the local level. Needy individuals relied primarily on religious organizations or private charities. Neither the federal government nor the provincial governments were concerned with income security or social-service programs. The working assumption of the day was that individuals were responsible for providing for the contingencies of life for themselves and their families; these included health care. Such family-based welfare is known as **residual welfare**.

The BNA assigned to the federal government responsibility for quarantine centres and marine hospitals, and for special groups, such as the armed forces and veterans. The provinces were responsible for other hospitals, asylums, charities, and charitable institutions. Importantly, any jurisdiction not assigned to the federal government was to fall within the provincial domain if it arose later. Because health and welfare were not specifically mentioned, they were provincial jurisdictions when they arose later (Bryden, 1974). This is why Canada, to this day, has a split federal–provincial responsibility for health care. Although health care falls within provincial jurisdiction, the federal government, as will become clear below, plays a significant role through funding.

Community care, or care in the community, also known as home care or home support, was present long before the health-care system was created. It existed largely on a volunteer basis. For example, the Grey Nuns, formed in 1838, visited the sick in their homes. The Victorian Order of Nurses was established in 1898 to provide nursing services in the home. Most provinces adopted workers' compensation laws between 1851 and 1928. Throughout this time, local government was involved in providing health-care services, including, for example, medical services, hospital outpatient departments for the indigent (extremely poor) and near indigent, and public clinics for treating tuberculosis and sexually transmitted infections. There were health insurance plans as well, but they were few and were operated by many industries. **Public health** was also being implemented: vital statistics collection; sanitary inspection; supervision of water, milk, and food; and the disposal of sewage and garbage (Government of Canada, 1970). What used to be referred to as public health is now often referred to as preventive medicine.

It was also during the latter part of the 1800s and the early 1900s that the public acceptance of the efficacy of medicine evolved. From 1900 to 1920, medical licensing laws were passed, medical schools were standardized, restrictions on entry into the medical field were enforced, and the income and status of the medical profession increased. It was a period, however, when private enterprise dominated the health-care field; that is, doctors, dentists, and nurses sold their services privately. Similarly, drugs and medications were sold on the open market: a prescription from a physician was not required (Brown, 1979; Chappell, 1983). It was after the Depression, which exposed the inadequacy of many private schemes for health care, that the federal government entered into health care in a serious way. It accepted the argument that the risks of illness were relatively easy to establish, relatively constant, and not subject to cyclical fluctuations or sudden emergencies, and that the universal risks of sickness and invalidity in old age should be underwritten by the community as a whole. Thus, the principle was established in Canadian health care of equity for all Canadians: no one should be disadvantaged in the receipt of health care because they could not afford it. This principle provides a just system to the extent that those who have more money are not more likely to receive better or more service and to the extent that most communities have services available and accessible to them (which has not always been the case in the remote and rural areas of Canada).

In the 1950s, during the economic upturn after the Depression, hospitals emerged throughout the country as locations where complex medical procedures were performed. Hospitals were transformed: they were no longer places where the poor went to die but the arenas of skilled medical specialists who used complex technologies (Coburn, Torrance, & Kaufert, 1983). With the establishment of hospitals, the development of hospital insurance was inevitable, given the high costs of this care. This became reality in 1957. As the number of hospitals throughout the country grew and physicians became more hospital minded, increasingly specialized, and accustomed to expensive therapies and a cadre of paramedical workers to assist in their work, dollars flowed readily from the public purse. Doctors were transformed from independent entrepreneurs to participants in a major and complex medical and industrial institution. In 1966, the *Medical Care Act* was passed, implemented in 1968, providing national insurance for physician services. Thus arose Canada's medicare system of universal physician and acute hospital care.

By 1972, all provinces and territories had become partners in the federal government's cost-shared medical insurance program. The federal government paid one-half the cost; the provinces paid the other half and delivered the programs. The provinces had to meet criteria set out by the federal government: universal coverage, reasonable access to services, portability of benefits, comprehensive services, and non-profit administration by a public agency. These criteria are still in effect today, although the funding arrangements have changed. The federal government still transfers dollars to the provinces but it is no longer on a 1:1 basis. In 1977, through the Extended Health Care Services Program, the federal government for the first time provided dollars for long-term care. This resulted in the development of provincial long-term care facilities (nursing homes) and home-care/support programs.

Funds were also separated from specific health expenditures, which limited the rate of growth of federal costs. It also gave greater control over health expenditures to the provinces, since the federal government removed the dictate that the money had to be used for physicians and acute-care hospital services. Removing these strictures, however, did little to assist the provinces because of the large medical/hospital complex already in place. Rather, the result for the provinces was increased demand on provincial coffers. Some provinces allowed **extra billing** by physicians (additional charges to patients, over and above the payment schedule) and hospital user fees to raise more monies to cover costs. Concerns arose that reasonable access, as required under the terms of the agreement, was threatened. In 1984, the *Canada Health Act* (CHA) allowed for a reduction in the financial contributions from the federal to the provincial governments equal to the amount of extra billing and user charges implemented in the province. The CHA effectively ended these practices.

However, the economic recession continued into the 1980s and the federal government sought means to halt the continual rise in health expenditures. In 1986, the block funding legislation was amended to further reduce the rate of growth of federal contributions, with more reductions announced in subsequent years. The plan was to steadily decrease federal contributions to the provinces until they became nil—with timelines varying from province to province. In return, the provinces' taxing powers were to be increased. This action removed any clout the federal government had to enforce the five criteria of medicare noted above. Simultaneously, the federal government also lost its ability to ensure comparable services from province to province and left open a greater possibility for differing quality health care in economically depressed areas (Segall & Chappell, 2000).

As the provinces struggled with their ever-increasing health-care costs, media stories were rampant about declining quality in health care. There were pressures to move to the private sector, on the argument that public health care does not work. However, national polls demonstrated that Canadians overwhelmingly supported universal medicare and even saw it as a defining characteristic of the

Canadian identity. In February 1999, the federal government re-entered funding with budget transfers to the provinces for health care once again. This move came at a time of economic surplus when the federal debt had been paid off; funding has continued in subsequent budgets. In 2001, the federal government gave large transfers to the provinces, with few strings attached other than that the money had to be spent on health care.

In summary, Canada's health-care system evolved only in the mid-1900s after a severe economic depression and in times of economic prosperity. It was a reflection of societal beliefs in the credibility and hope represented by medicine for the health of the nation. The government embraced hospital care unquestioningly as the most appropriate care to ensure healthy individuals. Canada also embraced an equitable system, in which all citizens would receive health care on the basis of need, irrespective of ability to pay. While establishing a publicly funded and equitable insurance system, Canada did not choose to establish socialist medicine. Physicians are, by and large, paid on a fee-for-service basis for each service delivered. That is, physicians operate as private entrepreneurs with their incomes guaranteed. Citizens also have the right to choose the physician of their liking.

With no limits on the amount of billings and no limits on the utilization of hospitals, in retrospect, the unprecedented growth of physician services and hospital treatment is not surprising. There was no process to assess whether this system was leading to appropriate and effective care for the recipients of service, the patients. Health economist R.G. Evans (1976) clearly demonstrated the dominance of physicians in this health-care system a decade after universal physician insurance was implemented. He estimated physicians controlled approximately 80 percent of health-care costs, even though only 19 percent of total health-care expenditures were going directly to physicians. They largely controlled hospital use (accounting for about half of all health-care costs), prescribing of drugs, ordering of laboratory tests, and, after the initial visit to the system, recommending return visits. Physicians are the gatekeepers to medicare; they have expert knowledge not shared by patients and make decisions on patients' behalf. The system is, to a large extent, provider driven, not user or patient driven.

The 1990s and Discontent

By the late 1980s, Canada's health-care system had grown and matured. Canada, like virtually all other industrialized countries (the United States being the main exception), had universal medicare for physician and hospital services. Each province had its own unique configuration of other services, including a variety of home-care services (home nursing, home personal care, home physiotherapy, and so on) and other services (adult daycare, mental health teams, nursing homes, and so on), but there was no consistency among provinces in services offered, referral mechanisms, or user fees charged.

Research demonstrated that in Canada, use of medicare services was determined largely by the individual's need (ill health), rather than by non-medical factors, such as financial status. Lower-income groups, seniors, and women receive more services because they have worse health than higher-income groups, younger adults, and men (McDonald, McDonald, Steinmentz, Enterline, & Salter, 1973; Manga, 1978; Broyles, Manga, Binder, Angus, & Charette, 1983). Prior to the introduction of universal medicare, economic ability often determined whether or not people received these services. Similar findings had been demonstrated in the United Kingdom (Rein, 1969; Stewart & Enterline, 1961).

The Andersen and Newman model (1973) was popular for examining utilization of physician and hospital services. These authors argued that the utilization of health services could be understood in terms of social determinants, such as technology and social norms; the health services system, including resources and organizations; and individual determinants. Most research has focused on the individual determinants of the model, assessing the influence of three types of factors: (1) the predisposition of the individual to use the services, (2) the ability to secure services, and (3) the need for services. **Predisposing factors** (which exist prior to the onset of specific illness and increase people's likelihood of using more services) include demographic, social structural, and attitudinal–belief variables, such as age, gender, education, occupation, and a strong belief in the effectiveness of medical treatment. **Enabling conditions** (which allow the individual to use the service) include such factors as income or region of the country where one lives. **Need** refers to ill health, including chronic health conditions, physical disability, perceived ill health, and diseases (Figure 15.1).

Figure 15.1 **DETERMINANTS OF SERVICE USE**

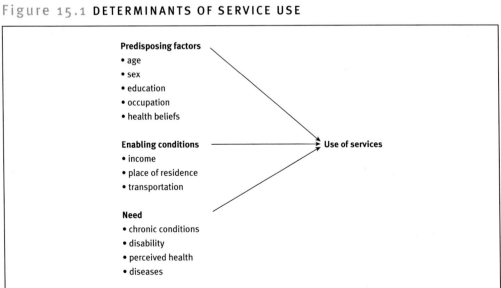

The Andersen-Newman model has been criticized because it fails to tap the underlying decision-making processes that lead an individual to the doctor's office (finding and interpreting symptoms, seeking the advice of others, coming to a decision to use or not use services) and because it fails to take into account the broader structural context within which physician services operate. Nevertheless, the extensive research using this model supports the notion that, where universal medicare exists, need is the driving factor behind its use. Those in need are the ones who use the services.

The Discontent   During the 1980s and 1990s, medicare was increasingly coming under attack. Governments were struggling with spiralling costs and research was questioning the long-held belief that the decline in mortality since the turn of the century was due to medical treatment. Medical intervention is, even to this day, usually cited as the major reason for this decline. However, McKeown, Record, and Turner (1975) showed that the rise in medical care expenditures and, therefore, widespread medical intervention, began after almost all (92 percent) of the modern decline in mortality had already occurred, except for the eradication of smallpox, which accounted for about 5 percent of the reduction. Rather, it would appear that public health measures and rising standards of living (reflected in improved diet, improved hygiene, and increased natural immunity to some microorganisms) were the reasons for the decline in mortality. McKeown and colleagues (1975) suggested nutrition was the major influence. (Also see McKinlay & McKinlay, 1977.) In addition, Badgely (1991) reviewed Canadian research since the introduction of medicare and concluded that there was little significant improvement, if any, in the disparities in longevity and the prevalence of illness between the rich and the poor.

Research was also revealing that medicine was not as scientific as the public often believes. Roos and Roos (1994) concluded that

- Patterns of medical practice differ substantially from one physician to another.
- A significant amount of care is inappropriate.
- There is a lack of evidence of clear benefit from certain procedures (such as Caesarean section).
- Clinical uncertainty explains some practice variation; that is, decisions or choices are not always grounded in evidence.
- Informed patients tend to prefer conservative treatment when there are risks involved.
- Both expert panels and cost-effectiveness studies tend to overestimate the benefits of treatment.
- Applying practice guidelines does not guarantee low surgical rates.

Box 15.1 gives further findings on the use of medical technology.

Shapiro (1991) recorded variations in surgical rates among different areas of Manitoba, citing differences of opinion among physicians in selecting patients for elective surgery, underestimation of risk, and possible overestimation of benefits

Box 15.1 *An Assessment of Medical Technology in Canada*

Guyatt and his colleagues, in 1986, published criticisms of medical practice in Canada. They found that

- Technologies are too often accepted for use without evaluation.
- When evaluations are done, technologies are often put into use before they are complete.
- Technologies that have been evaluated and accepted for use are often used for conditions that were not covered by the evaluations.

- Technologies that have been evaluated, accepted, and used for their intended purposes are often utilized too much.
- Even for technologies that avoid all of these problems, value may be dubious, because there is an equally effective and less costly technology that is not being used.

Source: G.H. Guyatt, P.X. Tugwell, D.H. Feeny, R.B. Haynes, & M. Drummond. (1986). A framework for clinical evaluation of diagnostic technologies. *Canadian Medical Association Journal, 134*(6): 587–594.

associated with some procedures. Differences in hospital admission rates among geographical areas were due, in large measure, to the adoption of new procedures before the risks and benefits were fairly studied, physician practice style, and the way physicians deal with medical uncertainty. International research suggested that between 15 percent and 30 percent of medical procedures were inappropriate (Lomas, 1990). Fee-for-service payment of physicians was exposed as less than optimal. Evidence of inappropriate hospital utilization, especially under fee-for-service remuneration, was documented (Lloyd, Lupton, & Donaldson, 1991).

At the same time, there was increasing recognition that the benefits derived from a medical approach may be reaching their limits; spending more dollars on health care will not necessarily enhance the health of the population. The American government noted that only 10 percent of premature deaths were attributable to inadequate health services, while 50 percent were due to unhealthy lifestyles, 20 percent to environmental factors, and 20 percent to human biological factors (General Accounting Office, 1991). Research was appearing throughout the industrialized world that national health insurance, while treating the ill, did nothing to prevent illness, disability, or disease and that poverty (as seen in Chapter 9) was a major correlate of ill health (Evans, 1994). The acute-care focus of medicine was seriously questioned for an aging population in which chronic illness dominates, not acute conditions. Medicine has no cures for chronic conditions. Furthermore, the conditions of old age are frequently non-specific, so there is always something more that a physician can try or check, raising the possibility of over-servicing of seniors (Barer, Evans, & Hertzman, 1995).

Even worse than over-servicing, there are sometimes harmful consequences from medicine itself. Illich (1976) introduced the concept of iatrogenic illness more than 30 years ago to convey this idea. **Iatrogenic illness** includes, in a narrow sense, those diseases that would not have occurred if sound and professionally recommended treatments had not been applied. In a broader sense, clinical iatrogenic illness refers to all clinical conditions for which remedies, physicians, and hospitals are the pathogens or the "sickening" agents. Such errors as when individuals are given the wrong drug, an old drug, or a contaminated drug, and harmful interactions of drugs would be included here, as would cases where people become addicted to prescription drugs or where antibiotics alter the normal bacterial flora of the body and induce a super-infection. Illich goes on to argue that depersonalization of diagnosis and therapy has turned malpractice from an ethical problem into a technical problem, where, within the complex technological medical environment of the hospital, negligence becomes "random human error" or "system breakdown"; callousness becomes "scientific detachment"; and incompetence becomes "a lack of specialized equipment."

Concomitant with the declining reverence for medicine is a growing acceptance of alternative approaches to health, including herbal medicines, non-Western approaches to holistic living, homeopathy, and naturopathic approaches. As Sinnott (2000) notes, where health is concerned, people choose whatever works. Interest in complementary systems of healing is booming; these are now a multi-billion dollar business in the United States. It is difficult to pick up a popular magazine or newspaper without reading about nutrition, exercise, home remedies, and other aspects of life that promise to maintain and/or improve our health (see Box 15.2).

In addition to medical intervention per se, the organization of the delivery of health care has also come under attack. Until the 1990s, countries had been focusing their attention on equity, extending equal financial protection and access to health-care services to most or all of the population. They did not question the adequacy of the care being provided. No overall mechanism to evaluate interventions, to assess delivery efficiency or effectiveness, or to ensure cost accountability was established. For the first time since medicine achieved prominence in health care in the industrialized world (about 100 years ago), the 1990s saw the consumers of care, both public and private, questioning the quality of that care. They started asking questions such as: How much of current medical intervention is warranted? Would some of the dollars currently spent on medical care have a greater effect on health if they were spent on such things as home

Box 15.2 Health in the Headlines

Maclean's, April 9, 2006

- When zero fat is not zero fat
- Peanut allergy? Give peas a chance
- When it's not on your plate it doesn't count
- Raise a glass of red wine to aging well

Reader's Digest, April 9, 2006

- Taking control of your diabetes
- Vitamins & minerals Q & A

- Well-being questionnaire
- Curing everyday ailments the natural way
- Eat well, stay well

Flare, April 9, 2006

- Body forecast
- Dieting
- Pay attention to your health—now

care, better housing, or air quality? How do we ensure that medical intervention is beneficial, rather than simply causing no harm? What is the effectiveness
of many medical interventions? Are we organizing and delivering health care
in the most appropriate and effective way?

A New Vision

By the late 1980s and early 1990s, there was a major questioning of medicare for
the first time since it had been established. Criticisms of medicare were not new.
What was new in the 1990s was an official acceptance of the criticisms and an
apparent willingness to act on them. Despite the criticisms of medicare, there
remained widespread acceptance of the principles of universal access and public funding upon which that system is based.

In the early part of the 1990s, Mhatre and Deber (1992) reviewed available
reports from various working groups, task forces, and committees and found
remarkable consistency in the vision of a new health-care system for Canada.
The shared characteristics of these various reports included

- broadening the definition of health beyond to the biomedical aspects, to include
  the social and psychological aspects;
- seeking the collaboration of multiple sectors;
- shifting the emphasis from curing illnesses to promoting health and preventing
  disease;
- switching the focus from institution-based to community-based care;
- providing more opportunities for individuals to participate with service providers
  in decisions on health choices and policies;
- decentralizing of the provincial systems to some form of regional authority;
- improving human resources planning, with particular emphasis on alternative
  methods of remuneration for physicians other than fee-for-service;
- enhancing efficiency in the management of services, through the establishment
  of councils, coordinating bodies, and secretariats;
- increasing funds for health services research, especially in the areas of utilization,
  technology assessment, program or system evaluation, and information systems.

Subsequent committees throughout the 1990s reached virtually the same conclusions. There was widespread acceptance that both emphasis and dollars
should be redistributed from medical and institutional care to a broader base of
community health-care services.

The new vision was embraced as promising a more appropriate system of
care that would cost less, or at least no more, than the current medicare system.
The new vision reformulates the role of government from a provider to a partner
in care and places greater emphasis on a reliance on family and community social
care. The envisioned health-care system embraces a broader paradigm of health,
as noted in the report of the National Forum on Health (1997): being healthy

requires a clean, safe environment; adequate income; meaningful roles in society; and good housing, nutrition, education, and social support. The National Forum concluded that Canadians strongly support the basic principles of medicare and that they value equity, compassion, collective responsibility, individual responsibility, respect for others, efficiency, and effectiveness. It also argued that the social and economic determinants of health merit particular attention, including the factors that lie outside the traditional health-care system, such as unemployment, labour market conditions, and cultural status. It recommended that Canada's health-care system be expanded to publicly fund all medically necessary services, explicitly naming home care and prescription drugs, and that primary care funding, organization, and delivery be reformed.

Reforming Canada's Health-Care System

By the mid-1990s, both levels of government were ready to take action. They wanted to reduce costs. Hospitals became the first target because they represented the largest single expense in the public health-care system. In Canada, hospitals are private, non-profit organizations provided with global budgets (excluding funds for medical technologies), which had offered few incentives for devising adequate information systems to allow them to assess cost per patient or per case. As Rachlis and Kushner (1989) had noted, hospitals are about the only business that has no idea what its product (healthy patients) costs to produce. Global budgeting makes it difficult for provincial ministries of health to influence actual hospital expenditures. Typically, there was closure of long-term or chronic care beds within hospitals (for example in Nova Scotia and Newfoundland), closure of entire hospitals (in Saskatchewan), and a moratorium on building long-term institutional beds (in British Columbia). During this period, there were no increases or only minor increases to acute-care hospital budgets, with small increases to community and home-care budgets in many provinces (Chappell, 1993a; 1993b).

Medical schools agreed to reduce new admissions and post-graduate training by 10 percent, to implement tighter restrictions on foreign-trained physicians' practice, and to have differential fees to encourage physicians to settle in under-serviced areas. However, by 2005, some provinces (such as British Columbia) were expanding medical school enrolment, and then prime minister Paul Martin was urging the greater use of foreign-trained doctors. Incentives for physicians to work in under-serviced areas have thus far been largely unsuccessful. Some provinces also introduced aggregate caps on physician billings through negotiation with provincial medical associations, but physician work stoppages and work-to-rule campaigns have been largely successful in obtaining monetary increases. User fees are being charged in some areas where they did not exist before, such as for equipment in Manitoba; income testing is being imposed for higher room and board fees in long-term care facilities, such as in British Columbia; and private for-pay services are growing, especially in Alberta and British Columbia.

Attempts to redistribute health-care dollars from expensive acute-care hospitals to less expensive home care have resulted in a major shift in the nature of community services. A rationale for funding post-hospital care is that much of the care that could be given only in the hospital when medicare was established can now be provided effectively in the home, offering a less expensive form of care in a location often preferred by individuals. This is indeed true; however, providing acute care in the community is often intensive and expensive care compared with long-term chronic care for seniors. It thus uses up a larger portion of the comparatively small home-care budgets. As more and more of the home-care budget is used to service post-acute care, less remains for long-term chronic home care, the service most needed by older adults.

In the Capital Health Region of British Columbia, there are fewer people receiving services; those who are receiving services need higher levels of care and are receiving more hours of service (Penning, Allan & Brackley, 2001). In other words, these data suggest there has been a reduction, not an expansion, of community home-based service. Services are being redirected away from the less ill clients who may have the greatest potential for prevention to more intensive, medically focused, post-acute care. Home care is providing more medical support and less social care.

This shift is even more pronounced following the report of the Commission on the Future of Health Care in Canada, *Building on Values* (Romanow, 2002). The Romanow report recommended that funding over the next two years be allocated to transfer money to the provinces for short-term home care, including medically necessary home mental-health-care management and intervention services; care for post-acute patients, including medication management and rehabilitation services; and palliative care services. While the report uses the aging of the population as one of the justifications for supporting short-term home care, there is no mention made of long-term support. The Romanow report appears not to have grasped that the greatest need of older adults is for long-term chronic home care.

For mental health problems, the absence of long-term support suggests a lack of understanding of the chronic nature of many of these problems. Short-term care tends to be crisis intervention; without long-term support it will do little to ensure sustainable solutions. Furthermore, while the federal government has made short-term transfers to the provinces, home care has not been added to the *Canada Health Act*—not even short-term home care. As will become evident later in this chapter, this leaves such services vulnerable to erosion.

Research from British Columbia demonstrates that recent shifts are not cost effective. Hollander (2001) compared four health units that differentially implemented cuts to home support services. Units that cut homemaking-only services paid for more services for these individuals three years later through their greater use of hospital beds, increased use of home-care services in the second and third years after the cuts, and increased rates of admission to nursing homes. Importantly, the greater overall costs did not emerge immediately. This suggests that social services such as homemaking are cost effective, and that a preventive and maintenance function of home care should be taken seriously.

Other B.C. research compared the costs of similar levels of care for clients receiving home care and clients in nursing homes. Hollander and Chappell (2001) analyzed data from 1987 to 1997. The costs for home care clients were 40 to 75 percent of the costs of facility care; the differential is greater for lower levels of care than for higher levels of care. Furthermore, the greatest cost of home care is in the transitions; that is, those who change their type or level of care cost considerably more than clients who remain within their level of care, even though individuals in transition still cost less than facility-care clients. The only home-care clients who cost more than nursing-home clients are those who die while on home care, and the increased costs are due to hospitalization. That is, hospitalization and not home care is the cost driver. In a separate project conducted in Winnipeg and Victoria, Chappell, Havens, Hollander, Miller, and McWilliam (2004) compared the costs of nursing home care with the costs of providing the same level of care at home. They took into account costs of informal care (that is, costs incurred by family and friends in caring for the senior), counting their time at minimum wage. The conclusion was the same: even counting the cost of informal care, home care costs less than does nursing-home care.

Most provinces (Ontario being the major exception) have now regionalized, on the argument that it allows for integration and decision making at the local level. However, in almost all instances, only hospital care and community care are integrated, excluding both physician payments and drug payments. It is, therefore, at best only partial integration, excluding major decision makers (physicians) and cost escalators (drugs). It has the disadvantage of marrying a well-established and powerful vested interest within the system (acute-care hospitals) with a historically weak distant cousin (home care). There is the very real danger of the home-care sector losing visibility and having even less influence than it had prior to regionalization.

To examine the effect of regionalization in British Columbia, Penning, Allan, and Brackley (2001) compared three regions. They found that the utilization of acute-care hospital services, physician services, and community-based home-support services prior to and for two years after regionalization did not differ among the regions, even though their socio-demographic makeup varied. Allan and Penning (2001) similarly examined health regions in British Columbia from 1990/1991 to one year after regionalization. They report no differences before and after regionalization in terms of visits to specialists, inpatients leaving hospital, or home-support use. Differences in visits to general practitioners, outpatient hospital separations, and home-nursing-care clients all decreased. That is, there seems to be more standardization between regions in their health care, rather than less, as one would expect as care moves "closer to home." Both studies report that the observed trends began long before regionalization and continued afterwards. A decrease in the supply of acute-care and extended-care beds began prior to 1997, with both admissions and lengths of stay decreasing.

This decline continued after regionalization. However, extended-care and day-surgery rates increased prior to regionalization and decreased afterward. Utilization of physician services—especially specialist services—increased, and the increase was even greater after regionalization. Furthermore, outpatient hospital utilization rates increased prior to regionalization but have declined recently.

There is little evidence that consumers have increased participation through the establishment of regional boards. As Sullivan and Scattolon (1995) suggest, regional boards with no budget- or policy-setting authority will be unsuccessful in ensuring consumer participation. For this strategy to work, administrative and budget authority over service provision must be provided. It is too early to tell whether regional populations in Canada contain too few people to effect economies of scale or the coordination of services. In British Columbia, the provincial government decreased the number of regions through amalgamation to increase their size.

The Romanow report also recommended a move towards a primary care model. At the time of writing, provinces were starting to move beyond the discussion phase. Primary care is often touted as integrated health care. Although defined in a variety of ways, it is generally considered the first level of contact with the health-care system and delivered as close to home as possible. It includes health promotion, illness prevention, and curative, supportive, and rehabilitation services. It should lead to improved accessibility, quality, and coordination of services as well as responsiveness to individual needs (Marriott & Mable, 1998). It is, in other words, more consistent in its image with the vision of health reform than many of the changes that have been taking place. Key elements include

- general practitioners working in a group environment that could also include a network of solo practices;
- multidisciplinary teams, including general practitioners as well as others, such as nurse practitioners, counsellors, and nutritionists;
- patient registration or rostering, whereby the organization is responsible for specific individuals, rather than a geographic area;
- funding on a population or a capitation basis, that is, a set number of dollars per person;
- core services, including health promotion, sickness prevention, diagnosis and treatment of illness, urgent care, 24-hour accessibility, and management of chronic illness;
- high-quality, specific records that allow for greater certainty for costing and better analysis of the benefits.

It is to be noted that both the broader health reform vision and proposals for primary care include health promotion and sickness prevention, but reforms to date still place the main emphasis on physician-dominated medical care. There is no necessary inclusion of home care and they do not extend to the larger structural elements of the community, such as the workplace or educational institutions. Where health promotion and illness prevention are included, there is little evidence that it means more than providing information on healthy lifestyles, such as proper nutrition, or on the harmful effects of smoking.

It is clear that Canada's health-care system is under reform. Whether that change will lead to a health-care system consistent with the vision of health reform that emerged in the 1990s is questionable. There has been widespread recognition that the system is fragmented, operating in silos, each sector with different rules. For example, physician services are paid through a fee-for-service mechanism, hospitals receive global budgets, and assistive devices receive a percentage subsidy. There has been no provision for the transfer of monies from one administrative unit to another, and historically there is little interaction between them. This is a major reason given for integration. However, the changes that have taken place over the last decade suggest that structural change within the system is leading in some instances to greater fragmentation, not less.

This can be seen in relation to home care, the service most appropriate for an aging population. In the past, long-term home care had been slowly building but now there is little care left in the community. The short-term home care that remains is heavily medically focused. This shift splinters the system and solidifies the divide between medical services, which are publicly funded, and social services, which are increasingly becoming the responsibility of the individual. The question is, whose responsibility is it to pay for social services that are medically necessary (Hollander, Chappell, Prince, & Shapiro, 2005)?

The rhetoric of health reform is being replaced with that of a market model. Physicians and other fee-for-service providers, such as walk-in clinics and physiotherapists, continue, by and large, to be based on a market allocation model, wherein practitioners are paid for their services to clients who choose to see them. Hospitals are still largely funded on a global budget basis. Reimbursement is a function of the volume and mix of services delivered. There has been little activity to shift the emphasis from curing illness to promoting health and preventing disease, providing more opportunities for individuals to participate with service providers in making decisions on health choices and policies, or enhancing efficiency in the management of services through councils, coordinating bodies and secretariats.

Women

There has been little attention paid to the saliency of women as recipients of care, as the majority of formal care providers, and as those most affected by health reform. The top managerial positions (such as hospital CEOs) are typically filled by men. Despite the increased number of women entering medicine, there is evidence from several countries that they hit a **glass ceiling**, beyond which they tend not to be promoted. They are largely concentrated in traditional specialties, such as pediatrics, or as general practitioners (Lorber, 1993; Riska & Wegar, 1993). Other than physicians, the majority of health-care workers are women. This is especially true among nurses and home-care workers. With health-care restructuring, there is a clear shortage of nursing jobs, yet, when nurses are retained, they have little or no say in decision making; nurses are finding themselves in contracted-out positions, often with no career trajectory and little in the way of benefits. With home care being transformed into an intensive acute-care support system and the dismantling of long-term home care, the jobs being lost tend to be the housekeeping and homemaking positions that also belong to women.

Women have little say in when and how health-care reform happens (Armstrong & Armstrong, 1999). With the reforms taking place, it can be argued that there is medical retrenchment—a return to a more physician-directed model. This leaves even less room for women's perspectives that have argued for a more holistic approach to health care, including care during childbirth and treatment of diseases such as breast cancer. Responsibility for caring work is typically not acknowledged by policy makers. As health care becomes more commodified (see next section), women's traditional care work is neither recognized nor valued. Indeed, the current trend toward a market approach risks commodifying care relationships, and in the process, eroding ties built on affection and obligation (Medjuck, Keefe, & Fancey, 1998; McDaniel, 2002).

A major issue for health reform is how to work with an existing system and effect changes in that system while creating a new system. The existing structure of the system is, therefore, relevant for any new system that evolves, as are vested interests within that system. Included within the area of vested interests is the private sector. We turn to that discussion now.

Vested Interests

Canada's medicare system is universal and publicly financed but includes only a limited number of services. Canadians have rejected a private health-care system as is found in the United States. These basic facts are particularly important in health reform. Privatization risks diminished control of health by citizens (through government) and increased control by multinational business interests. As health economist R.G. Evans (1984) noted decades ago, health care is not a market commodity like automobiles or appliances. Health is not something that applies only to the rich, nor is it a commodity about which the consumer can be expected to have perfect or even adequate knowledge to choose between alternatives. In supporting medicare, Canadians have rejected the notion that health should be only for those who can afford it and that health care should be available as market forces dictate. Thus, current debates and many current reforms focused on privatization of health care are emotional issues for Canadians.

Profitization

Privatization has various meanings, including (1) increasing control by private groups—private in the sense of anything that is not public—thereby reducing the size and scope of government involvement; (2) empowering individuals and communities through increased reliance on families, churches, and other non-profit institutions, rather than governments; and (3) laissez-faire capitalism, with free markets and the profit motive working to produce innovation, efficiency, good management, and responsiveness to individual choice. But public and private arrangements are not dichotomies. *Private* bodies includes for-profit as well as not-for-profit organizations. Charitable and non-profit sectors frequently work closely with government and may not charge for services. However, the discussion within health services generally refers to private as for-profit and has business and corporate connotations (Deber et al., 1998). Critics' concern is not so much with privatization per se; doctors and hospitals have always been private providers under medicare. The concern has more to do with **profitization** of health care, that is, the provision of health services as a profit-making business (Williams, Deber, Baranek, & Gildiner, 2001).

As a capitalist society, we can expect there will be pressures toward privatization and profitization. And with health reform, we are headed in that direction. The proportion of private funding in health care increased from 23.6 percent in 1975 to 30.2 percent in 2000 (Mendelson & Divinsky, 2000). Compare this with the United States, where the private-sector figure is 53.6 percent, and with the United Kingdom, where it is 15.4 percent.

Increased profitization is consistent with the internationalization of capital so often referred to as **globalization** (Coburn, 2001; 2004). In this era of the free trade agreement, business influence within Canada increased greatly to counter the perceived threat of capital mobility (the flight of capital from Canada). The Canadian government, threatened with a reduced credit rating, higher interest rates, and/or withholding business investment in the 1980s, slashed government expenditure, reduced deficits, and paid down the debt. Canada became more market oriented, and the power of the state was reduced. Trade with the United States increased dramatically, now far outstripping intra-Canada activity in virtually every region of the country (Mendelson & Divinsky, 2000). The increased favour of a for-profit ideology brought with it a business–state coalition to rationalize health care. Part of the impetus came from American businesses, which had more or less saturated the American health-care market (Armstrong, 2001; McKee, 2001). By the mid-1990s, for-profit health maintenance organizations dominated the market in the United States, and for-profit hospitals also became good business. Hospitals, for example, saw their aggregate profits rise by 25 percent in 1996. By the end of the 1990s, they were looking to Canada to expand their investment and demanded greater freedom to deliver health-care business in Canada under the North American Free Trade Agreement (NAFTA).

Hospitals became central to the new business approach to health care. They represented the single largest expense within Canada's publicly funded system and they were most amenable to new strategies taken from the private sector. As hospitals were restructured, their appropriate business (acute care) became more narrowly defined; surgeries were shifted to outpatient status, and nursing positions were lost and downsized. Patient stays grew shorter, and services were contracted out. Some rehabilitation services and the provision of prescription drugs, nursing care, and custodial care were either no longer offered or were offered as home care. These services are thus outside of medicare and, therefore, no longer universally insured and publicly provided.

Home care has been shifting to a mixed mode of managed competition in which the local health authority purchases services from a mix of not-for-profit and for-profit service providers on behalf of consumers (the Ontario Continuing Care Access Centres are but one example). In Ontario, as in British Columbia, citizens are means-tested when they are assessed for services but are not necessarily provided with needed services. This mixed mode of delivery is supposed to ensure competition and, thereby, keep the price down. However, evidence suggests that for-profit firms are more likely to skimp on quality or to select only consumers who are in the least need in order to keep profits up (Bendick, 1989; Williams, Deber, Baranek, & Gildiner, 2001); that those cared for at private for-profit hospitals have higher risk-adjusted mortality rates than those cared for at private not-for-profit hospitals; and that private for-profit hospitals result in higher payments for care than private not-for-profit hospitals (Devereaux et al., 2004). In addition, managed care plans in the United States can drop coverage or reduce benefits if they are losing money.

When for-profit multinationals buy home-care agencies in Canada, profits, more often than not, leave this country. The problems do not stop there. Under NAFTA, the Canadian government can allow for-profit entry into the health-care field, but once it does, it cannot then return that area to public provision without providing compensation to for-profit firms for their foregone future profits. Moreover, the terms and conditions of compensation are set not by Canadian bodies but by an international tribunal. It therefore becomes increasingly difficult and expensive, if at all possible, to reverse the for-profit trend (Evans, 2001; Shrybman, 2001).

What of the argument that for-profit care cuts costs? For-profit health care is less expensive for governments, but more expensive for consumers. A large part of this increased expense comes not only through profits but also through administrative overhead. In large American health maintenance organizations and in private plans in Canada not covered under medicare, overhead costs run around 26 percent. Costs were similar for private prepayment and commercial health insurance carriers prior to medicare in Canada. In contrast, the cost of overhead within universal medicare is only 1 percent. Canada's system costs less in total than the American system: $2250 per person in 1998 compared to $4270 per person in the United States (Marmor & Sullivan, 2000). Moreover, in the United States, only 84 percent of the population are insured, while in Canada 100 percent are.

Our vision of **health-care reform** argues for expanding the mandate under Canada's medicare system, acknowledging the social determinants of health, and defining health as something broader than medicine. Yet we see a paradigm shift within society that has increased the dominance of American-style capitalism and allowed it to become increasingly pervasive within health care. Within this transformation, medicare becomes more narrowly defined, and therefore, the territory expands for for-profit firms. With health reform has come an increased role for private clinics, which used to be restricted mainly to specialized or elective services. We now see the purview of these private clinics extending beyond abortions, in vitro fertilization, and laser eye surgery and moving into the arena of private hospitals.

For an aging population, the **hollowing out** of medicare means that many of the home-care and community-support services required by seniors are no longer available or are becoming privatized. Concerns that the aging of the baby boom generation will bankrupt the universal health-care system are simply unfounded but nevertheless fuel the arguments for more profitization (recall the discussion of apocalyptic demography in Chapter 2). It is the old-old, those aged 75 years and over, who use health-care services disproportionately, and this population will grow from 5.8 percent of the population in 2001 to 6.7 percent in 2016. Even if it is assumed that this population currently accounts for fully 50 percent of health-care expenditures, the growth in this segment of the population will add only about 1.1 percentage points to health-care expenditures as a percentage of GDP. While this represents growth, it hardly warrants the alarmist writings one often sees in the media (Mendelson & Divinsky, 2000).

Pharmaceuticals

A particularly powerful for-profit interest group that has relevance in any discussion of health care is the pharmaceutical manufacturing industry. The pharmaceutical industry is tied uniquely to physicians, since physicians are the only individuals who can prescribe drugs. (Prescription drugs are not part of medicare, unless they are provided within an acute-care hospital.) Payment schedules vary from province to province. Pharmaceuticals, an essential element of our modern culture of health care, have seen an explosion of knowledge, whereby physicians and other health-care workers, citizens, and governments are deluged with masses of often conflicting information (Segall & Chappell, 2000). In 1993, Lexchin estimated that there were 3500 prescription products available to Canadian physicians. New information on side effects and drug interactions continually emerge, as do computer programs to warn doctors and pharmacists. Most physicians stay current by relying on information from *detail men*—drug company representatives (Rachlis & Kushner, 1989). This relationship, interestingly, is not viewed as a conflict of interest, but rather as experts (who happen to be employed by drug manufacturers) providing information to physicians.

Yet, as noted by the Saskatchewan Commission on medicare, there is solid evidence from Ontario and Quebec that physicians often prescribe drugs poorly. To cite from the commission's report, "Antibiotics are often prescribed for viruses where they are totally ineffective. An estimated 20 percent of elderly admissions to hospital are associated with an adverse drug reaction. Evidence from Ontario and British Columbia suggests that expensive drugs are routinely prescribed when cheaper drugs will do . . . " (Fyke, 2001: 72). In their review of prescription drug use among seniors, Tamblyn and Perreault (2000) conclude that the potential benefits of drug treatment are compromised by the underuse and overuse of prescribed medications for certain conditions, errors in the drug dose and duration of therapy prescribed, and suboptimal compliance. They note that drug-related illness is now cited as the sixth leading cause of mortality in the United States.

There has also been an unprecedented increase in the cost of prescription drugs. In Ontario, from 1987 to 1993, the average price per prescription (excluding the dispensing fee) went from $12.48 to $24.09, a rise of 93 percent; during that period the consumer price index rose 23.1 percent. More than half the rise in these costs was due to the introduction of new patented medications. The year 1987 saw the introduction of Bill C-91, which extended the monopoly for new drugs coming on the market, abolished compulsory licensing, and gave multinational manufacturing companies 20 years of patent protection for their products (Lexchin, 2001). Compulsory licensing had allowed generic competitors to come on the market within five to seven years after the appearance of the original product, typically priced 25 percent lower than the brand name product; and when there were three or four generics, the price differential would be 50 percent (Lexchin, 1993). However, both NAFTA and the General Agreement on Tariffs and Trade (GATT) were used to eliminate this system. At around the same time, the pharmaceutical industry invested heavily in Quebec; indeed a key feature of the province's industrial strategy was the development of the pharmaceutical industry. The Quebec government is an affiliate member of the Pharmaceutical Manufacturers Association of Canada (PMAC). A perceived threat to the economic viability of the pharmaceutical industry, therefore, is also a perceived threat to the Quebec government, which could be used by separatists should the federal government take a position against PMAC (Lexchin, 2001).

In an effort to deal with increasing drug prices, provinces often increase the deductible for eligible pharmacare programs or restrict the population groups (such as seniors) who are eligible. In an effort to contain escalating costs, British Columbia introduced reference-based pricing (RBP), whereby the cheapest of the most effective drugs with the least side effects is reimbursed through the provincial drug plan. Decisions on which drugs to reimburse are made by an expert panel. The PMAC launched a public relations campaign to convince the public that RBP was not acceptable. They argued that individuals under this scheme would receive the oldest and cheapest drugs only, that provincial economic needs were being placed before patient needs, that there would be multiple adverse effects on the quality of care and consequently on health, that bureaucrats and not physicians were making medical decisions, and that there was lack of consultation when developing the policy (Brunt, Chappell, Maclure, & Cassels,

1998). The provincial government countered this public media campaign with messages that the profit motive of drug companies was driving the opposition to the policy, that the program reflects good stewardship of threatened resources, and that the policy offers flexibility and safety. A province-wide survey of seniors showed strong support for RBP; seniors viewed the media campaign by the pharmaceutical manufacturers as driven by self-interest (Chappell, Maclure, Brunt, Hopkinson, & Mullett, 1997). PMAC sued the provincial government for lost revenues but lost in the courts. It appealed and lost; the Supreme Court of Canada denied PMAC permission for further appeal.

Canada currently spends 16.9 percent of its total public health spending on drug expenditures (2003 figures; OECD, 2005), close to the 17.8 percent average for all countries in the Organisation of Economic Co-operation and Development (OECD). However, of 25 OECD countries, only eight spend less than Canada on drug expenditures when computed on a per capita basis. When compared using purchasing power parities (PPPs) to permit cross-country comparisons, OECD countries spend an average of 366 PPPs while Canada spends only 200.

The provinces have been increasing deductibles and patient co-payments in their public drug plans. The cost of prescription drugs is still increasing and, at the time of writing, there seems to be no appetite among provincial or federal governments to add pharmacare to the Canada Health Act and, therefore, to medicare. However, among Romanow's (2002) 47 recommendations was funding for two years to establish a Catastrophic Drug Transfer to fund a portion of the increasing costs of drug plans and to reduce disparities in coverage among jurisdictions. He also recommended a new National Drug Agency to evaluate and approve new prescription drugs, provide ongoing evaluation of existing drugs, negotiate and contain drug prices, and provide objective information. A national prescription dug formulary was also recommended. Discussions are taking place on these issues.

The Future?

Health-care reforms of the 1990s opened the door for a greater role for private interests within Canada's health-care system. The discussion of the provision of health care has been reformulated. During the 1990s, the role of government switched from the provider of care, as in the past, to a partner that enables and empowers individuals to exert control over their lives. Partnerships have become a key concept and are expected—at least so the rhetoric maintains—to improve the efficiency, effectiveness, and responsiveness of public organizations. This has represented a fundamental shift in the approach to health care in Canada and has facilitated a greater role for private interests. This is within a climate in which the United Nations Declaration of Human Rights (Article 25) recognizes the right to health care as a human right, not a privilege. The need for health care for serious illnesses is understood as a vital need, that is, one for which there is a right to obtain fulfillment. This provides a moral argument for legislation to establish equal access for all to basic health care, and, since it emanates from the United Nations, it is applicable to all countries (Tranoy, 1996). Furthermore, Canadians strongly believe that their government's role in social policy should not be minimized but, rather, that social policy is at the forefront of defining Canadian identity (Peters, 1995). Canadians consider health a right for all; they do not want a two-tier system where those who cannot afford to pay are disadvantaged.

Canadians' strong support of the medicare program is one of the reasons why we are witnessing the current strategy unfold. Public outcries that it is being eroded mean that it is very difficult for governments to explicitly dismantle this program. They must, therefore, be seen to be maintaining medicare. Current restructuring and redefinitions of acute care, which specify that only the most severely ill can receive immediate treatment, can be presented as improved efficiency in the delivery of medicare. The consequence, though, is to make medicare even more medical and narrow, contrary to the broadened vision for reform. It results in the hollowing out of medicare (Williams, Deber, Baranek, & Gildiner, 2001). More and more individuals, many of whom are women (who experience more symptomatology than men) and are elderly (the greatest users of health-care services), are defined as being outside the protection of medicare.

The Saskatchewan Commission on medicare (Fyke, 2001) notes that the two biggest challenges of modern health care are accountability and sustainability. Unfortunately, many of the reforms being witnessed today will lead neither to public accountability nor to sustainability. Particularly for an aging population, public health, home care, chronic disease management, and mental health are of paramount importance and yet are receiving short shrift within reform. While health care requires a cultural transformation, the major paradigm shift taking place in Canada at this time is not going to lead to a more appropriate and more effective health-care system for seniors. This is despite the fact that the vision of health care reform outlined a new health-care system for Canadians that would have provided more cost effective, intervention effective, and appropriate services for an aging society.

Although the actions of reform bear little resemblance to the vision of health reform, that vision has allowed the dismantling of the health-care system as we knew it. The call for a broader perspective on health, less medicalized health care, and less institutionalized health care have provided the opportunity for provincial governments to downsize acute-care hospitals, shorten lengths of stay, and so on. But governments have not, to date, demonstrated a willingness to expand community care outside of hospitals, to expand a definition of health beyond biomedicine, or to embrace other types of health-care workers in addition to physicians. The vision of health-care reform, in other words, has allowed a shifting of the burden of care in old age from the public purse onto individuals and families, even though this was not part of the rhetoric or vision of health-care reform. While we do not know what the health of seniors will be in the future, we do know that with the aging of the baby boom generation, there are going to be significantly more seniors and they are going to expect a just and civil society to provide them with appropriate care.

Not only are those services most required by an aging population the very ones that are not included in medicare, evidence now available suggests that the neo-liberal agenda in favour of American-style global capitalism is not producing the economic prosperity its has promised. Navarro (2002a, 2002b) demonstrates that, where profit shares and rates have increased, this seems due to declines in wages rather than increases in investment. The capitalist economic agenda is resulting in increased unemployment in all OECD countries, increased salary differentials (meaning the gap between rich and poor is widening) in most, decreased social expenditures, and transfers of income from labour to capital. Working-class rights are being undermined, and part-time, home-based work, self-employment, contracting out and temporary work are all increasing (Coburn, 2004). Importantly, countries such as Canada with more developed welfare states and therefore more re-distributive public policies show fewer wage and income inequalities than other countries (notably the United States and Great Britain). Even Canada is showing the same trends, although they are thus far less pronounced than, for example, in the United States.

CHAPTER SUMMARY

In this chapter, we have examined Canada's health-care system, its historical roots, its evolution throughout the 20th century, and present-day health-care reform.

Key ideas to remember from this chapter:

- Canada's universal health-care system, medicare, emphasizes medical aspects of illness care, covering only physician care and acute hospital care.
- Other aspects of care, particularly those that could be considered from a social perspective, are not covered in medicare. These include, for example, home care, long-term institutional care, and care by alternative practitioners, such as chiropractors, massage therapists, and naturopaths.
- Canada's health-care system emphasizes the most expensive forms of care for illness treatment, rather than health promotion or disease prevention.
- Despite provincial jurisdiction to deliver health care, the federal government has played a critical role in health care through funding.
- Provincial discontent with what they perceived as federal interference in their jurisdiction, cumulative research suggesting there were more efficient and effective forms of delivery, and widespread acceptance of alternative definitions of health, health promotion, and health care led to a new vision for health care in the early 1990s.

- The vision of health-care reform embraced a more appropriate health-care system for seniors that included a broadened definition of health. Biomedicine and institutional care were to be de-emphasized; community care strengthened; and evidence-based decision making was to be recognized. The movement called for the management of health care to be reorganized and citizens to participate more in their own care.
- The 1990s differed dramatically from the preceding decades in the political willingness to take action to change the health-care system. By the mid-1990s, there was clear evidence of attempts at reform, including capping hospital budgets, and closing hospital beds and, in some cases, entire hospitals.
- Recent evidence suggests that regionalization and downsizing of acute care hospitals are producing results that are inconsistent with the vision of health-care reform. Indeed, evidence suggests that the Canadian health-care system is becoming more medicalized, rather than less medicalized, although there is some de-institutionalization taking place.
- The vision of health reform embraced in virtually all quarters of the country permitted a major change to our system. It has allowed dismantling of some parts of the system without follow-through to build those aspects of the system that were deemed necessary within health-care reform.
- The voice of women and a women's perspective are difficult to find within health-care reform.
- Health-care reform has opened the door to privatization of the health-care system.
- The pharmaceutical industry is a powerful, established vested interest group within the health-care system.
- The federal Romanow Commission, perhaps inadvertently, has enabled the further retrenchment of medical care by fragmenting long-term home care from the system.
- American-style capitalism is eroding Canada's publicly funded health-care system.
- The future of health-care reform does not inspire optimism when judged against the vision of health-care reform.

Key Terms

residual welfare **(p. 393)**

public health **(p. 394)**

extra billing **(p. 395)**

predisposing factors **(p. 397)**

enabling conditions **(p. 397)**

need **(p. 397)**

iatrogenic illness **(p. 399)**

glass ceiling **(p. 406)**

privatization **(p. 407)**

profitization **(p. 408)**

globalization **(p. 408)**

health-care reform **(p. 409)**

hollowing out **(p. 410)**

Study Questions

1. How did Canada end up with a primarily medical health-care system?

2. What are the reasons for wanting to reform medicare?

3. Why is the system within the vision of health-care reform more appropriate for seniors than the current system?

4. How are reforms "hollowing out" medicare?

5. Why are current trends in health-care reform not optimal for seniors?

Suggested Readings

Armstrong, P., Armstrong, H., & Coburn, D. (2001). Unhealthy times. *Political economy perspectives on health and care in Canada.* Toronto, Ontario: Oxford University Press.

Barer, M.L., Evans, R.G., & Hertzman, C. (1995). Avalanche or glacier? Health care and the demographic rhetoric. *Canadian Journal on Aging, 14*(3), 193–224.

Coburn, D. (2004). Beyond the income inequality hypothesis: Class, neo-liberalism, and health inequalities. *Social Science and Medicine, 58,* 41–56.

McDaniel, S.A., & Chappell, N.L. (1999). Health care regression: Contraindications, tensions and implications for Canadian seniors. *Canadian Public Policy, 15*(1), 123–132.

Navarro, V. (2002). Neoliberalism, "globalization," unemployment, inequalities and the welfare state. In V. Navarro (Ed.), *The political economy of social inequalities,* 33–106. Amityville, NY: Baywood.

Chapter 16

END-OF-LIFE ISSUES

Learning Objectives

In this chapter you will learn about

- Place of death: Where do people die?
- Defining death: How do we know when people are dead?
- The process of dying, which is different from death.
- Understanding that those who are dying are still living and the important implications for care of the dying.
- Non-life-sustaining measures, euthanasia, and assisted suicide.
- How people with cognitive impairments make their wishes known for end-of-life decisions.
- Competence and advance directives.
- Family and friends who must cope with the process of dying and ultimately with the death of a loved one.
- The funeral—rituals and business.
- Increased recognition of end-of-life issues.

Introduction

A message throughout this book is that old age is not equal to dying. Although the older we become the closer to death we are, old age is a time of continued living. Nonetheless, we all die; it is, as they say, a fact of life. However, death at the beginning of the 21st century differs from death earlier in history. Now that most individuals can expect to live to old age, we know that most will die in old age. At the present time, this means that most will die after suffering from chronic illnesses and organ system failures. There is, in other words, a long trajectory of dying before one is dead. The juncture at which one is no longer simply living with chronic illness but is dying is not necessarily clear for the individuals themselves, for their family members, or for the clinicians caring for them. As we shall learn in this chapter, death is not simply biological. There are social, psychological, and spiritual aspects to this process.

Death and Dying in the 21st Century

Death in modern society occurs overwhelmingly in hospitals, although this proportion is decreasing. In 1997, 73 percent of deaths occurred in hospitals (Heyland, Tranmer, Feldman, & Stewart, 2000); in 2002 the figure was 68.7 percent (Statistics Canada, 2002g). However, in 1950, only 45 percent of deaths occurred in hospitals. Most deaths in hospitals occur among patients who are over 65 years of age and were living in the community; i.e., not living in nursing homes. If you are in a long-term care facility when the end comes, you are likely to die there. If you are living in the community when the end comes, you are likely to be taken to a hospital and die there. In part, this reflects the difficulty of knowing when the end is here; the move to the hospital often represents an effort to cure or care for an ailment experienced by the living. In part, it also represents families', physicians', and the health-care system's difficulty in accepting death. Indeed, hospitalization at the end of life can result in a prolongation of dying, rather than a good death.

Death due to suicide increases near the end of life but the reasons for this are not well understood. It may reflect a rational alternative to a demeaning and punishing decline, but this may not always be the case (Prado, 1998). We understand little about the role of anxiety, fears, or threats of losing aspects of our identity as reasons for suicide in late life. Suicide in old age tends to happen among those who have severe health problems; most have not attempted suicide before; and, unlike suicide among younger people, it is equally likely for the married and the single. Older men are more likely to commit suicide than are older women (Statistics Canada, 2002g).

While death comes to all of us and is final, even its definition has become problematic in present-day society. Traditionally, when someone's heartbeat and breathing stopped permanently, they were considered dead. During the 20th century, the question arose as to whether an individual could be dead even though his or her heart was pumping blood and the lungs were working. The concept of whole-brain death, or just **brain death**, arose, allowing the declaration of death if an individual's entire brain ceases functioning.

Dying

While death is defined in biological terms, dying is also social, emotional, and spiritual. Over 30 years ago, Kübler-Ross (1969), who counselled terminally ill patients, developed her theory of five stages inherent within the process of dying: denial, then anger, then bargaining, then depression, and, finally, acceptance. These stages are not necessarily linear or sequential and vary from person to person. It is important to recognize that dying involves more than biological changes; there is meaning in life even when death is impending.

As we saw in earlier chapters, most individuals today can expect to live to old age. During old age, we are likely to suffer from chronic conditions before we die. Older people, by virtue of their proximity to death, are assumed to accept death; it is assumed that they do not find it frightening and need not even discuss death. Clarke and Hanson (2000), however, find that older individuals in the United Kingdom do want to talk about death, although they are not obsessed by or overly preoccupied with it. They appreciate the opportunity to discuss their impending death. It is a myth that just because one is aged, one is necessarily completely prepared for death. Some may be and others may not.

Preparing for death can include a desire to bring meaning to one's life. Because of the prolongation of the dying process due to chronic illness in old age, there has been increased interest in **spirituality** and the meaning of life toward the end. As Bevans and Cole (2001) argue, as long as our focus is on technology, treatments, procedures, and documents, that is, on problems toward the end of life, the mystery of the end of life is ignored. When we talk about the meaning of life, we are talking about spirituality. Dying individuals can have **crises of meaning**, also referred to as **soul pain** (Kearney, 1996), where they experience a lack of meaning, coherence, or comfort with their life. Meaning refers to existential well-being and is more than physical or psychological well-being. Where an individual finds spirituality will vary from person to person because it refers to bringing integrity and coherence to one's life. For some, there may be a particular emphasis on religion; for others it may be on friendships.

Quality-adjusted life years (QALYs) refer to the duration of life in various compromised health conditions. The concept has been around for nearly 30 years. QALYs all score one full year of healthy life at 1.0. Less than optimal health receives a score of less than 1.0. There are different ways of computing QALYs. The standard "gamble technique" asks a respondent to make a hypothetical choice between continued life in their present state or a gamble that would result in either perfect health or death. A different method refers to time trade-off, in which individuals are asked how much time they would be willing to give up in order to be in a better state of health. Another approach uses a simple rating scale in which individuals rate health conditions on a scale ranging from 0 to 10 or 0 to 100.

Valuing Life

Lawton prefers to approach the topic through death, anxiety, and the wish to live (Lawton et al., 1999). While health-related quality of life considers the extent to which distress from illness or side effects associated with treatment reduce the person's wish to live, much less is known about the desire to live. Lawton argues that years of desired life is not determined entirely by quality of life but is mediated by an intervening cognitive affective schema referred to as **valuation of life** (VOL). VOL is defined as the extent to which the person is attached to his or her present life due to enjoyment and the absence of distress, as well as hope, futurity, purpose, meaningfulness, persistence, and self-efficacy. VOL is an existential concept, capturing the concept of total reason for living. Lawton and his associates find that people choose fewer years of life if life is marred by functional and cognitive impairment or pain. Cognitive loss is much less desirable than either functional impairment or pain. Pain is the least threatening of the three. They find that VOL predicts years desired to live independent of other measures of psychological well-being and, therefore, contend that it is not simply another measure of positive mental health. They argue VOL is an attitude that motivates people for continuing to live longer and that its incorporation of purpose may be critical as a sustaining force in the desire to live.

In addition to valuation of life, one can have **fear of death**, referring either to fear of the unknown or to fear of the process of dying. Fear of dying is associated with being younger, of lower socio-economic status, female, white rather than black, having a more external locus of control, and being less religious. Greater fear of the unknown is associated with having a more external locus of control, less perceived social support, less religiousness, and indirectly with being older, of lower socio-economic status, male, and white rather than black (the research was conducted in the United States) (Cicirelli, 1999).

Individuals have been asked directly what the quality of the end of life means to them. Canadians identified five domains of quality end-of-life care: (1) receiving adequate pain and symptom management, (2) avoiding inappropriate prolongation of dying, (3) achieving a sense of control, (4) relieving burden, and (5) strengthening relationships with loved ones (Singer, Martin, & Kelner, 1999).

The role of religiousness seems to depend on the specific beliefs held by the individual. For example, a belief that suffering is a punishment from God affects a person differently from a belief in a forgiving God. And people can be afraid of dying without being afraid of death. There could be a sense of no further time to make restitution or receive forgiveness from another individual, there may be guilt, and there may be despair. On the other hand, an individual could find great comfort in the belief that he or she will soon be with loved ones in an after-life. Some believe that religious coping is especially prevalent in old age because, with impending death, there can be an existential or health crisis. Religious coping resources can allow for the integration of the self, retention of feelings of control over the environment, continuation of intimate relations with others, and coming to terms with mortality. The general notion that our religious beliefs become much stronger near death does not receive empirical support. Attendance at religious services declines somewhat, probably due to physical decline. Feelings of religiousness and strength or comfort received from religion are either stable or increase slightly (Idler, Stanislav, & Hayes 2001).

Our discussion has emphasized life near death and concern beyond the physiological aspects of dying. This is in contrast to a medical focus on pain and suffering associated with death. Rather, quality of life at the end focuses on life, rather than death, even in terminally ill patients. Bradley, Fried, Stanislav, and Idler (2001) discuss the notion of quality-of-life trajectories because it suggests that dying is a social process that changes over time. **Trajectory** refers to a particular path and can include a change in the pattern of health status. In end-of-life trajectories, you can think of one trajectory as sudden death from an unexpected cause, such as an accident or heart attack. A second trajectory could refer to a steady decline in health status from a progressive and fairly predictable disease, such as cancer. A third trajectory could refer to a long period of chronic illness with gradual decline and periodic crises, any of which may result in sudden death. Congestive heart failure would be an example. Note that all of these trajectories define living near death in terms of health status. This is not surprising, given that death is defined in terms of physiological factors.

Quality-of-life trajectories, in contrast, include all dimensions of living that characterize **a good death**. Reviewing the different domains, Bradley and associates (2001) report that between 20 and 70 percent of dying patients are inadequately treated for pain. Other common physical symptoms experienced by the dying include fatigue, drowsiness, nausea, difficulty breathing, and insomnia. A decrease in physical function and an increase in physical symptoms are related to nearness to death. Psychologically, it appears that depression increases with nearness to death and that suicide rates are higher among terminally ill adults than among healthy adults. Some individuals lack social supports to meet both instrumental and emotional needs at this time of their lives. And, as already noted, religious beliefs do not seem to change much with impending death. Those who are not religious are more likely to be depressed. Communication is also important, both so that the individual has sufficient information about the situation to maintain control and make decisions, and so that the individual can convey his or her wishes. When multiple dimensions of life are taken into account in examining quality of life near the end, it becomes clear that you can have poor physical health but high overall quality of life, even in the face of death. For some, social and spiritual health may have greater importance than physical health. Quality-of-life trajectories (rather than health-status trajectories) include, for example, good psychological health, a strong sense of self and of control of your dying process, loved ones close by, and good communication with health-care professionals and with loved ones, whether in prolonged physical decline or in swift decline.

Discussions about dying, rather than death, about living during the end of life, and about quality of life near the end place the emphasis on continued life, even near death. This emphasis ensures the inclusion of psychological, social, and spiritual issues, in addition to physiological concerns. It leads to a particular type of care for those who are at the end of their lives. We turn now to a discussion of care at the end of life.

Care of the Dying

At the end of life, seniors want candid but sensitive communication; they also want respect and recognition and a multidisciplinary approach that focuses on medical needs as well as on psychosocial, spiritual, and emotional needs. High value is placed on **comfort**, a term that puts the focus on the person receiving the care rather than on the provider. Comfort is subjective; only the individual knows whether or not she or he is comfortable. Overall comfort includes physical comfort, but it also includes a state of contented well-being, both psychological and spiritual. *Comfort* has been examined in terms of three different aspects: a state of ease and contentment; relief from discomfort; and transcendence, or being strengthened and invigorated. *Transcendence* refers to being free to take control of your own decisions and your own destiny, in the dying process as well as in living (Hurley, Volicer, & Mahoney, 2001).

Comfort leads to the broader issue of quality of care for the dying, in a time in which chronic illness has extended the trajectory of dying and blurred the boundaries between living with chronic illness and dying. Advanced technologies are not necessarily compatible with dying with dignity. Leading causes of death are now from chronic progressive organ system failure—heart disease, cancer, stroke. After interviewing people with life-threatening illness, surviving family members or significant others, and informal and professional caregivers, Teno, McNiff, and Lynn (2001) summarized the areas that they believe are relevant for quality of care: spirituality and personal growth while dying; a natural death in familiar surroundings with loved ones; symptom management; sensitive communication to allow decision making and planning; family and patient treated as a unit; absence of financial, emotional, and physical burden for family members; autonomy or right of self-determination for the patient.

Despite the fact that seniors themselves seem to know what they want for end-of-life care, research on health-care providers, most notably physicians, suggests that seniors do not have a say in this decision; health-care professionals do not provide care consistent with the wishes of the patient. Physicians, in particular, often make decisions about care for dying patients without much input from others (Baggs & Schmitt, 2000). In Israel, for example, physicians are likely to use life-sustaining treatment more often than older adults want (Carmel, 1999). Similarly, a significant number of nurse practitioners are ill-informed about legal guidelines and few incorporate advance care planning into their clinical practice (Schlegel & Shannon, 2000).

Now that death occurs primarily in old age from chronic illnesses, the dividing line between when one is ill and when one is dying is not clear cut. Chronic illnesses evolve in a gradual fashion. Determining when one is dying is, therefore, a clinical judgment. Medical care tends to focus on survival, even survival at all costs. Interestingly, Kaplan and Schneider (2001) note that this tendency to prolong life at all costs is contrary to the Hippocratic corpus, wherein physicians are urged that when a disease is too strong for available remedies, the physician should not expect it to be overcome by medicine and should not attempt what does not belong to nature.

The role of the physician at the end of life is important. Most adults want realistic estimates of how long they can expect to live. Physicians' communication with patients is therefore of particular importance near the end of life. Yet, more often than not, there has been a lack of communication, both because of the difficulty of definitive diagnoses and prognoses and because of a desire to maintain the hopes of the patient. In addition, there is often professional discomfort in discussing death. This is not an easy area; the physician must maintain a balance between honesty and compassion (Bradley, Fried, Stanislav, & Idler, 2001). Yet accurate communication can be especially important so individuals have an opportunity to prepare themselves and their families for death. They need to make important decisions about the type of treatment they wish to receive, set their financial affairs in order, and speak with and see certain people.

What is considered appropriate information varies by cultural group. For example, First Nations culture has values prohibiting direct communication involving terminal prognosis or palliative care options. Kaufert (1999) found that younger patients favoured more explicit communication about these matters than did older patients. Such cultural attitudes make direct communication difficult. In addition, cultural attitudes can change over time. Researchers in the Netherlands (Wouters, 1990) note that the period from 1930 to 1955 was characterized by silence regarding impending death, described as "the sacred lie." By the 1955 to 1965 period, it had become more acceptable to talk about one's own and others' emotions in order to gain an acceptance of the impending death. Post-1970 is referred to as a period of secularization, in which emotional expression and coping strategies for dealing with death had become acceptable and considered desirable. In the United States, Korean and Mexican seniors are less likely than African and European seniors (35, 48, 63, 69 percent, respectively) to believe that a patient should be told of a terminal prognosis and less likely to believe that the patient should make decisions about the use of life-supporting technologies. Korean and Mexican seniors are more likely to hold a family-centred model of medical decision making rather than one that favours patient autonomy (Blackhall, Murphy, Frank, & Michel, 1995).

Palliative Care

Because of the perception that acute care in hospitals and medical care in general are not adequately meeting the needs of dying persons in the 21st century, many advocate an expansion of **palliative care**, also known as **hospice care**. The first such program was established in Canada in 1974 in Montreal at the Royal Victoria Hospital under Dr. Balfour Mount. A few months later, Dr. Paul Hentleff established a similar program at St. Boniface Hospital in Winnipeg. In Quebec, the term *palliative care* was used, rather than *hospice*, and is a unique Canadian use of the term. (American usage differentiates between the terms *hospice* and *palliative care*, with *hospice* representing a formal set of practices and closely linked to federal requirements for Medicare funding and *palliative care* a more general descriptive term. Canadian usage does not distinguish in this way.)

In the early 1980s the Palliative Care Foundation of Canada was established, closing in 1991. Later that year, the Canadian Palliative Care Association was established, now known as the Canadian Hospice Palliative Care Association. Provincial associations began first in Ontario (1982) and British Columbia (1983) and are now evident in all provinces.

In 2001, the B.C. government announced the establishment of the Palliative Care Benefits Program to remove financial barriers for terminally ill persons who wish to receive care at home. This program ensures the same pharmaceutical benefits, medical supplies, and equipment people would receive if they remained in hospital. The vast majority of those enrolled are cancer patients because, to be eligible, individuals must be in the terminal stages of a life-threatening disease or illness with a life expectancy of up to six months. The terminal stage of cancer is relatively easy to diagnose, whereas the terminal stage for many illnesses (such as Alzheimer's disease) is not. Hospice care is therefore not available to many people. In 2003, the federal government announced the Compassionate Care Benefit, allowing Canadians to receive employment insurance if they temporarily leave their jobs to care for a dying family member.

Hospice care has arisen as an alternative to institutional care. It provides care as near to home and in as home-like a setting as possible, if not in the home itself. In some instances, palliative care units or wards are established within acute-care hospitals; sometimes they are free standing. Canada now has a federal minister with special responsibility for palliative care and, in 2001, a secretariat on palliative care became the focal point for end-of-life issues within Health Canada. A senate subcommittee released their report on palliative care, entitled *Quality End-of-Life Care: The Right of Every Canadian* that same year.

The palliative care information sheet for seniors, made available by the Division of Aging and Seniors of the federal Ministry of Health, states that the goal of palliative care is to provide the best quality of life for the critically or terminally ill by ensuring their comfort and dignity. It meets not only the physical needs but also the psychological, social, cultural, emotional, and spiritual needs of the ill person and his or her family. Palliative care is an idea whose time has come in Canada. The hospice movement is an effort to move away from the medicalization of death. Many of the hospices, though, are used primarily by cancer or AIDS patients, denying many older individuals this specialized care offered. Many are thereby denied a good death by being denied control of their own dying process. Palliative care represents person-centred care, in which the dying individual develops a trusting relationship with care providers and is treated within a biographical approach, wherein her or his lived life and present anxieties and needs are voiced.

The holistic view of hospice care is consistent with incorporating comfort into care. The focus in palliative care is on maximum comfort and not simply maximum survival. It refers to a comprehensive, interdisciplinary, and systematic patient–family approach to coordinated end-of-life care and services. Comfort care is often consistent with limitations on aggressive medical interventions. Aggressive medical care would include, for example, aggressive diagnostic tests and treatment of co-existing medical conditions. It can include transfer to acute-care hospitals or units of hospitals and tube feeding if normal eating is not possible. Limitations to treatment that are consistent with a comfort approach include, for example, no cardiopulmonary resuscitation, no transfer to acute care for technological interventions, no aggressive treatment of intercurrent infections, and no artificial feeding. It would include medical interventions that increase comfort level. Hospice care includes care of family members immediately following death. Effective grieving requires the treatment and prevention of coping problems related to death; coaching patient and family through grieving; assessing and responding to incidents of anticipatory grief; preventing premature death; and identifying need for grief work—such as effecting reconciliation, assessing the potential for complicated grief, and assisting the family in integrating the memory of their loved one into their lives.

There are criticisms of hospice care. Hospice care is not necessarily appropriate for everyone. Some individuals may not wish to forgo curative and life-sustaining treatment interventions. They may wish that everything possible, including aggressive medical treatment, be used to prolong their lives. There are difficulties with pain management, depending on the disease one is suffering. It has been estimated that between 10 and 50 percent of patients receiving palliative care report significant pain (Cicirelli, 2001). For others, increased dosages of pain medication can lead to decreased cognitive functioning, unconsciousness, and terminal sedation—which all interfere with maintaining a quality of life while dying. Part of the difficulty arises from the fact that there tends to be an increase in symptoms near the end of life and increased severity of many symptoms as death nears (Miller, Mor, Gage, & Coppola, 2001). Adding to the difficulties, as many as 50 percent of patients in the two weeks prior to death and 80 percent of patients in the one week prior to death are reportedly unable to convey their symptom status.

Non-Life-Sustaining Measures, Euthanasia, Assisted Suicide

There is now general consensus that heroic life-sustaining efforts that simply prolong the dying process are unnecessary and unacceptable. There is less consensus on active euthanasia and assisted suicide. Aggressive medical care seems to improve neither life expectancy nor quality of life among those who are dying.

In a survey of more than 2000 Canadian adults, 85 percent of Canadians agreed with forgoing life-sustaining treatment in a competent individual if that individual is unlikely to recover and 35 percent if the person is likely to recover (Singer, Choudhry, Armstrong, Meslin, & Lowry). For the individual unlikely to recover, 58 percent also approved of assisted suicide and 66 percent approved of euthanasia. Some people prefer a greater say in their own decision making at the end of life, whereas others prefer to delegate the decision making to physicians, to God, or to fate. In the United States, Cicirelli (1995) found that more than half the seniors he studied favoured going on living, regardless of the situation; one-third favoured deferring or delegating an end-of-life decision to someone close or to a physician; and about one-tenth favoured ending life through suicide, assisted suicide, or voluntary active euthanasia. African Americans, those with less education, those with a fundamentalist church background and high religiousness, as well as those with higher self-esteem, less depression, and less fear of the dying process were more likely to favour going on living, regardless of the situation. Caucasian Americans seem to be more likely than African Americans to limit care and withhold treatment before death. African Americans seem more likely to want all possible care in order to prolong life.

In an Israeli study, Carmel and Mutran (1999) found that over a two-year period, these preferences are largely stable among older persons. There was remarkable stability in preference for life-sustaining treatments among severely ill older adults. Most stable of all are those who, at baseline, do not want to prolong their lives. Among a Canadian sample of seniors in a chronic care hospital, most preferred to retain some control in decision making at the end of their lives. Most wanted to make their exit quickly and painlessly with as much privacy and dignity as possible and linked euthanasia and assisted suicide with severity of illness. The more severe the illness, the more likely they were to consider euthanasia and assisted suicide acceptable (Kelner, Meslin, & Wahl, 1994).

The topic of euthanasia and assisted suicide is, perhaps, the most difficult. This area can include **passive euthanasia**, referring to the withholding or withdrawing of artificial life support or other medical treatment and allowing the patient to die; **physician-assisted suicide** or **active voluntary euthanasia**, wherein the physician administers a lethal dose of medication to a competent person who requests it; **involuntary euthanasia** and **non-voluntary euthanasia**, referring to ending the life of a mentally incompetent person who is unaware of what is happening and is not able to request it. Euthanasia, furthermore, can include rapid mercy killing or slow procedures—clinical practices of treating a terminal patient that lead to a comfortable but not particularly quick death.

The extent to which seniors support euthanasia and/or assisted suicide is unclear, although a significant proportion clearly do. A survey in the United States reports that only 41 percent of seniors approve of legalizing physician-assisted suicide (Seidlitz, Duberstein, Cox, & Conwell, 1995). A multiracial study, including Chinese Americans, Filipino Americans, Hawaiians, Japanese Americans, and Caucasian Americans holidaying in Hawaii, found that except for Filipino

Americans, 75 percent or more of each ethnic group believed that those in pain and with a terminal illness should have access to assistance with dying. Over half the respondents said this would also be acceptable for persons with current physical disability for which they needed help with "every little thing" (Koch, Braun, & Pietsch, 1999).

In 1994, Oregon became the first American state to legalize physician-assisted suicide. Mangus, Dipiero, and Hawkins (1999) found that 60 percent of medical students, both in Oregon and outside the state, favoured the legalization of physician-assisted suicide. However, Oregon students were less willing to write a lethal prescription themselves (52 percent of Oregon students versus 60 percent of students outside Oregon). This hesitancy on the part of physicians is also reported in a study by Carver and colleagues (1999) that included neurologists, neuro-oncologists, and specialists in amyotrophic lateral sclerosis (ALS). Just over a third think it is illegal to administer analgesics in doses that risk respiratory depression to the point of death; 40 percent believe they should obtain legal counsel when considering stopping life-sustaining treatment; and 50 percent believe physician-assisted suicide should be made legal by statute for terminally ill patients.

Other research by Doukas and colleagues (1999) demonstrates how physicians' personal values are reflected in their attitudes toward physician-assisted death. Those holding personal values promoting continued life-sustaining treatment in their own terminal care and with strong values against their own withdrawal of treatment were more likely to be opposed to physician-assisted death. This is often a dilemma for practitioners. If they practise in an area where physician-assisted suicide is legal, they may be asked to practise against their own personally held beliefs. Even removing life-sustaining supports is contentious. In the United States, for example, all 50 states now have laws permitting the refusal of life-support, but there seems to be a gap between physician practice and patient and family wishes. Physicians are not good at perceiving patient preferences (Bevans & Cole, 2001). Indeed, physician, nurse, and surrogate understanding of patient preferences is only moderately better than chance (Covinsky et al., 2000).

Advance Directives

Given that some individuals suffer from cognitive impairment, including dementia, towards the end of life, not everyone is able to make their own end-of-life decisions. The ability to make decisions is referred to as **competence** or *decision-making capacity*. Only a court can rule that an individual is incompetent to make his or her own decisions. Courts focus on various aspects of a person's decision-making capacity, including whether the individual is able to understand information, to deliberate, and to communicate. It is not, however, clear cut—many individuals have fluctuating competence. That is, they may be competent at some times and not at others, or in some areas and not in others. **Advance directives** are instructions people can leave in case they become unable to make their own decisions.

Both living wills and durable powers of attorney for health care are considered advance directives. A **living will** is a document in which the individual expresses his or her treatment preferences in specific situations. A **durable power of attorney for health care** is a document in which an individual appoints a proxy decision maker who will make treatment decisions for the individual if he or she is unable to do so. When a person is considered incompetent and there is no advance directive, a decision can be made using the *substituted judgment standard*, in which another individual, a surrogate, is called upon to make the decision the surrogate believes the individual would make if he or she were still capable. Alternatively, the surrogate may use a *best interests standard*, deciding on the basis of the individual's well-being. Often, it is a family member who is closest to the individual who is asked to be the surrogate. Unfortunately, even when family members are appointed to make decisions for seniors, there is little congruence between what the family member believes the elderly person would choose and what the elderly person says they would choose (Zweibel & Cassel, 1989).

The Royal Dutch Medical Association believes that, in exceptional circumstances, voluntary euthanasia or physician-assisted suicide can be justified. The association names early-stage dementia, in which the patient has a clear diagnosis and a persistent and well-considered wish to die, as an exceptional circumstance. Another such circumstance is severe dementia when the individual has left an advance directive specifying life termination should there be mental incompetence or where the individual's prior wishes can be ascertained with certainty. In the United States, approximately two-thirds of all physicians support the use of advance directives but older African American physicians are less likely to do so than younger African American or Caucasian American physicians (Mebane, Orman, Kroonen, & Goldstein, 1999). Caucasian American physicians are much more likely to agree that tube feeding terminally ill patients is heroic than is true for African American physicians. Caucasian American physicians are also much more likely to support physician-assisted suicide, for themselves personally as well as for their patients. The majority of American Veterans Affairs physicians believe that physicians should be responsible for initiating discussions about advance directives and most report having done so with their older patients (Markson et al., 1997).

Unfortunately, it appears that even when there are advance directives, there is little likelihood that they will be followed. Evidence suggests that the presence of an advance directive does not affect costs of end-of-life care (Lawton, 2001; Kaplan & Schneider, 2001). Thus, there is little evidence to suggest that advance directives affect the treatment provided. This is where an effective advocate can be important, to point out the advance directive and monitor to ensure it is followed.

Even within nursing-home populations, it appears that discussions concerning advance directives are not frequent. Indeed, Bradley, Peiris, and Wetle (1998) report that 71.5 percent of nursing-home residents in their study had no discussion of future treatment preferences in their medical records. Similarly, in a study of seriously ill hospitalized patients, only a quarter of patients had written advance directives (Heyland, Tranmer, Feldman, & Stewart, 2000). However, 80 percent wanted an active role, either shared or informed, in decisions about end-of-life care. Some have reported the same black–white divide noted earlier. Hopp and Duffy (2000) report that African Americans are less likely to have advance directives or durable power of attorney for health care and less likely to request restriction of treatment than are Caucasian Americans. However, Dupree (1998) found that African Americans did not want unconditional aggressive end-of-life treatment. Cultural differences surrounding these issues are especially important in a multicultural society such as Canada. The health-care system, to date, has not given much attention to cultural variations in death and dying. In Japan, for example, interest in advance directives seems to be considerably less than in North America, because Japanese culture tends to entrust all decisions to the family (Voltz, Akabayashi, Reese, Ohi, & Sass, 1998). We do not know whether Japanese Canadians feel this way.

Advance directives can include preferences related to withholding life-sustaining treatments as well as requests for euthanasia and assisted suicide under some circumstances. Aid in dying is particularly controversial and can include both assisted suicide—as when an individual provides the means for another to end their own life, such as a physician prescribing a drug in a lethal dose that can be taken by the individual—and euthanasia—when the actions of an individual cause the death of another in order to relieve their suffering, such as when a physician administers a lethal dose of a drug to a patient. Physicians are often critical to this process because, as noted earlier, individuals tend to die in hospitals and physicians are the only ones who can legally prescribe drugs. Assisted suicide and euthanasia, therefore, are medical as well as legal issues. It is often believed that individuals request aid in dying in order to relieve pain and discomfort, and some argue that an expansion of hospice services would take away the need for euthanasia (see, for example, Byock, 1993). Hospice care focuses on life and the alleviation of suffering so that individuals can be confident they will not be abandoned in their dying; in these conditions it is thought that the desire for euthanasia will dissipate. However, a U.S. study of over 1000 older people near death found that dissatisfaction with comfort care was not associated with requests for aid in dying and that those with hospice care were *more* interested in assisted suicide or euthanasia. Some suggest that one of the reasons for wishing aid in dying is not physical pain but a lack of hope and purpose (Bevans & Cole, 2001; Jacobson, 1995).

Certainly, not all or even most people at the end of the life want to hasten their death, but a significant minority do. In a Swedish study of palliative-care physicians, physicians from the Swedish Association for the Study of Pain and physicians in specialties of care of dying adult patients, more than half the physicians said that some of their patients had expressed a wish to die. One-third of the physicians had given analgesics or other drugs in sufficient doses to hasten a patient's death. A third had been asked for active euthanasia, and 10 percent had been asked to assist suicide. More than 20 percent of all social workers in a B.C. study, and nearly 40 percent of those who worked with medical employers, said they had been consulted by a patient about assisted suicide or voluntary euthanasia (Ogden & Young, 1998). Data from the Netherlands reveal that among physicians attending deaths, only 2.4 percent claim that the death resulted from euthanasia and only 0.2 percent from assisted suicide in 1995, virtually no change from a similar survey in 1990. In 0.7 percent of the cases, life was ended without the patient's explicit consent (VanderMaas et al., 1996). And an English hospital study (Seale & Addington-Hall, 1994) reports that 24 percent wished to die sooner than they did; 4 percent requested euthanasia.

The issue is not easy. Given that end-of-life suffering is now largely due to chronic illnesses and that many medical and technological advances have resulted in prolongation of dying, the question is often when to stop prolonging the dying process. Ethicists debate whether killing to relieve suffering is moral or immoral. When is the individual's right to control his or her own destiny morally correct? Cicirelli (2001) summarizes euthanasia at the present time:

- Attitudes toward physician-assisted suicide and euthanasia are becoming more accepting over time.
- A small but significant proportion of older adults would choose this course if their quality of life were low enough.
- There seems to be a preference for one of these options over suicide.
- Physicians would prefer assisted suicide to euthanasia.
- Fewer physicians favour aid in dying than is true of older adults.

Family and Friends at the End of Life

When examining end-of-life issues, the focus tends to be on the dying individual. However, many do not die alone, and most leave behind family and friends. Palliative care, as noted earlier, embraces both the older individual and the family as clients. Indeed, sometimes families support palliative care because they have watched a loved one suffer in the hospital, with the dying process prolonged by technological means. Among the family members of people who died in hospital in the United States, 16 percent were dissatisfied with patient comfort and 30 percent were dissatisfied with communication and decision making (Baker et al., 2000). Hanson and associates (1997) report, after interviewing family members, that less than 10 percent wanted more or different treatment than their loved one received. For loved ones who had received hospice care, families were very satisfied (91 percent), while of those whose loved ones had died in a nursing home, only half gave very positive scores for the care received.

Although generally, families are trusted to make the right and best decisions, conflicts can and do arise between the dying individual and family members. There is not always consensus and congeniality. Family members must face the death of a loved one and the accompanying bereavement and grieving. The grieving process involves not only the depth of numerous emotions, including powerlessness, anxiety, depression, and immobilization, but also the challenges and opportunities of relearning one's social worlds and the relationship to self and to the deceased. Part of the grieving process is now believed to entail not necessarily letting go of the one who has died but finding ways to maintain connections to loved ones. Memories, rituals, dreams, and thoughts can all be part of this process (Attig, 1995; Stajduhar & Davies, 1999).

One area in which wishes of the dying person and of family members can conflict is a death at home. The senior may view staying at home as critical to maintaining independence and self-identity. In spite of the growing popularity of this option, it can cause great demands on family members. Stajduhar and Davies (1998) note that death at home has become a gold standard among palliative-care practitioners. However, while it is widely believed that dying at home can increase a sense of normalcy, security, and familiarity, the situation can turn the home environment into a medicalized and institutionalized setting, disrupting the daily routine of family members.

Often, supports within community services are not available to assist families. Indeed, Stajduhar (2001) notes that because of the idealization of dying at home, caregivers may feel pressured into providing care at home when they do not particularly want to and when the necessary supports are not in place to permit a good death in this environment. Her findings also suggest that the wishes of the dying person are often privileged over those of family caregivers. The fact that caregivers overlook their own needs and focus their energy and attention on the needs of the elderly person is not new (Chappell, 1998). The trend to medicalize palliative care may be counter to some of the basic tenets of that movement. (Note the parallels with the discussion in Chapter 15 of how trends in health-care reform run counter to the vision of health-care reform.) This can increase the burden on family members.

The role of non-kin, that is of friends of the dying individual, is not well prescribed within society. Often, professionals and family members exclude (not necessarily intentionally) friends, disenfranchising them in the dying process. Indeed, friends may be seen as an intrusion into the family at this time. Family ties at the end of life are considered so strong that often individuals do not know what to do with friends, and friends do not know how to approach the family to see someone of value to them. We do not know the extent to which dying people have a preference for non-kin to be with them. Institutions often have a policy barring non-kin from visiting those who are very ill and/or dying. Similarly, airlines tend to restrict compassionate fares to immediate family members.

For a growing number of people, the end comes in a nursing home. Especially in Canada, nursing homes are a place of last abode. Few leave before they die. Nevertheless, nursing homes tend to emphasize that they are places for living, not for dying, death, and bereavement. Moss (2001) notes that the **living-dying interval**, the interval between knowledge of impending death and death itself, characterizes the nursing home environment and its exclusion from mainstream society. And while deaths occur frequently in nursing homes, the term dying is reserved for the very last days of life, and the ritual surrounding death tends to be invisible to nursing home residents (Marshall, 1976). Stated differently, a conspiracy of silence has been reported around death and dying in nursing homes, perhaps reflecting the staff's own discomfort and fear of their own mortality. Nursing home staff try to maintain a routine of normalcy in an environment in which death occurs regularly. The dying are sequestered even within the nursing home (Froggatt, 2001).

At the present time, nursing homes tend not to provide hospice care, although this could change. This may be due partly to the fact that hospice care has developed around cancer patients and cancer is not a major cause of death in nursing homes. One could think of hospice wards in nursing homes for individuals, where physicians certify that they are expected to die within six months. In the nursing home, as in other parts of society, friends made within the residence tend not to be incorporated into the grieving process when someone dies. This tends to be reserved for family members.

Death Rituals

We all die and we need a means both to dispose of the physical remains and to cope with this important transition. **Death rituals** are rites of passage that provide formal recognition of the transition from life to death. They assist those left behind, psychologically and emotionally, to accept the death of a loved one and to continue on with life without that person. As noted in the National Advisory Committee's Guide to End-of-Life Care for Seniors (2000; also see Auger, 2000), funerals serve to

- increase the reality of death
- provide a legitimate public occasion for expressing and validating grief
- provide evidence of the worth of the person who has died
- provide social support for the survivors
- help occupy the bereaved person's time in a difficult situation
- provide predictability and organization in the midst of an uncontrollable situation
- present an opportunity to reflect on one's own mortality
- reaffirm ethnic or religious identity for some
- emphasize the cohesiveness of the family or larger group beyond the loss of one of its members
- remind survivors that structure, organization, and life go on
- reaffirm social order
- help children to learn about death and about the comfort, love, and support that humans can provide each other in times of crisis
- mirror the values and expectations of a society
- provide an opportunity to examine the nature of life within a cultural group.

Most people in Canada are buried in the earth after they die. Entombment—the placing of the casket in a mausoleum above ground, arranged in rows stacked one above the other—occurs much less often. Cremation, however, is increasing in popularity. Cremation increased by fully 55 percent in the decade between 1977 and 1987 (Tipper, 1989). While cremation had been practised in Europe since 1400 BC, Canada's first crematorium was built in Montreal in 1901. The reasons for this increase in popularity are believed to include the growing scarcity of urban space as well as cost. Cremation expenses have been estimated to be as much as 30 percent lower than traditional burial services.

The funeral business has received some attention from researchers because of its role within a youth-oriented, capitalistic society. The dramaturgical aspects of the funeral industry (preparing the dead to be presentable for viewing in such a way that the horrors of mortality are tolerable) have often been highlighted. These include the demeanour of funeral directors when dealing with the public. Fulton and Metress (1995) have demonstrated this through the language usage of funeral directors. For example, they favour the term *cremains* over *ashes*; *interment* over *burial*; *final resting place* over *graveyard* or *cemetery*; *casket* over *coffin*; *remains, the deceased, loved one* or (the individual's name) over *corpse* or *dead body*; *passing on* or *lying in repose* over *dead* or *death*; *funeral director* over *embalmer, mortician,* or *undertaker*; *preservation* or *restoration* over *embalming*; *funeral home* over *mortuary*; and *monument* over *tombstone*.

In Wernick's (1995) terms, funeral homes are in the business of imaging death. They have also commodified death, turning it into a lucrative business endeavour. This author points out that the North American practice of embalming and the popularity of park-like cemeteries are all attempts at making death acceptable by removing the signs of death from the ritual. This contradiction feeds on a denial of death.

There is an increase in arranging one's own funeral, that is, bypassing the funeral director. A doctor or hospital can often provide the necessary forms and permissions. There are now, in various parts of the country, consumer-run memorial societies and funeral cooperatives, which provide simple, no-frills, inexpensive funerals.

Funeral traditions differ both within and among groups. Subcultural groups often differ from the host society. First Nations peoples are more likely to live in rural and isolated areas and to adhere to the circle of life, wherein death is perceived as a reunion with other family members. People will relate a dream in which a mother or father or other departed family member is beckoning the elder to join them. Here, death is seen as another stage in the circle of life. On reserves, men and boys often share in the digging of graves by hand while stories are shared about the deceased and women provide sustenance to the workers and mourners. Among some tribes, totem poles are built to honour the dead. They draw on their visions, dreams, and spirits to help them deal with death. It is important, though, to recognize that beliefs may differ from tribe to tribe and that not all First Nations persons adhere to traditional tribal beliefs.

Recognizing the Importance of the End of Life

Despite the universality of death and dying, and notwithstanding funeral practices, this aspect of life has not received particular attention. It is significant therefore that in the 21st century, the federal government is recognizing the importance of this area. In early 2001, the subcommittee of the standing Senate Committee on Social Affairs, Science, and Technology issued recommendations for quality end-of-life care. This subcommittee urged the development of a national strategy for end-of-life care and made the following recommendations:

- The federal government must assess the need for home care and pharmacare for the dying, working with the provinces to develop funding for the programs. Income security and job protection for family members who care for the terminally ill should also be implemented.

- Professionals involved in end-of-life care require multidisciplinary training and education. The federal government should explore such programs with provincial governments and educational agencies.

- The federal government should have an interdepartmental approach to end-of-life care and consider the establishment of a federal, provincial, and territorial strategy for this issue with appropriate funding.

- End-of-life research is needed and should be coordinated by the federal minister of health.

- The Canadian Institutes of Health Research should focus on end-of-life issues and the Canadian Institute for Health Information should develop indicators for quality end-of-life.

Similarly, the Canadian Palliative Care Association has identified as priority issues the availability of and access to end-of-life care, professional education, research and data collection, support to families and caregivers, and public education and awareness.

Such recognition of end-of-life issues arises from the fact that virtually all of us can now expect to live to old age and can expect to have a prolonged period of dying before death occurs. In the years ahead, we can expect much greater attention to this area.

Chapter Summary

This chapter has focused on end-of-life issues, including living while dying and death itself. More than ever before, dying is a topic of old age because so many of us now die in old age. Key ideas to remember from this chapter:

- Death occurs for most of us in hospital, although this is less true of those who are living in long-term care institutions prior to death.

- Given the association of prolonged chronic illness with old age, it is difficult to diagnose when one has entered the dying process as opposed to simply being ill.
- Death is no longer defined only as the stopping of the heartbeat or the cessation of breathing. One can be brain dead.
- Dying is social, emotional, and spiritual, as well as biological. Preparation for death and the dying process can include bringing meaning to one's life. Valuation of life is a concept distinct from fear of death. One can examine trajectories of life at the end of life as well as trajectories of dying.
- A holistic model of care of the dying places focus on meaning of life and on comfort in addition to attending to the physiological needs of the individual.
- A palliative care movement has arisen because of the inappropriateness of much intensive high-tech medical care in hospitals. Hospice or palliative care is an alternative to institutional care, providing care as near to home and in as home-like a setting as possible.
- The prolongation of the dying process and appropriate care of the dying lead to issues involving euthanasia and assisted suicide. Evidence to date suggests that most health-care workers, including physicians, do not take dying individuals' wishes into account in terms of these issues.
- Similarly, even when advance directives are issued by individuals, current research suggests that physicians do not abide by them.
- There is little literature on the experiences and needs of family and friends of the dying individual. There is some evidence that friends tend to be shut out of this experience because of cultural beliefs that family members are the only ones who should be involved at the very end, despite wishes to the contrary by friends.

KEY TERMS

brain death **(p. 419)**

spirituality **(p. 419)**

crises of meaning **(p. 419)**

soul pain **(p. 419)**

quality-adjusted life years (QALYs) **(p. 419)**

valuation of life (VOL) **(p. 420)**

fear of death **(p. 420)**

trajectory **(p. 421)**

a good death **(p. 421)**

comfort **(p. 422)**

palliative care **(p. 423)**

hospice care **(p. 423)**

passive euthanasia **(p. 426)**

physician-assisted suicide **(p. 426)**

active voluntary euthanasia **(p. 426)**

involuntary euthanasia **(p. 426)**

non-voluntary euthanasia **(p. 426)**

competence **(p. 427)**

advance directives **(p. 427)**

living will **(p. 428)**

durable power of attorney for health care **(p. 428)**

living–dying interval **(p. 431)**

death rituals **(p. 432)**

Study Questions

1. What do we mean by a good death?

2. Why has palliative care developed and what does it strive to offer?

3. How does support for non-life-sustaining measures, euthanasia, and assisted suicide differ between seniors and health-care providers?

4. Discuss the pros and cons of advance directives.

5. What do we know about the differential experience of friends and family of dying people at the end of life?

6. Why is the need for quality care at the end of life now being recognized and what issues need to be addressed?

Suggested Readings

Carmel, S. (1999). Life-sustaining treatments: What doctors do, what they want for themselves, and what elderly persons want. *Social Science and Medicine, 49*(10), 1401–1408.

Cicirelli, V.G. (1999). Personality and demographic factors in older adults' fear of death. *Gerontologist, 39*(5), 569–579.

Froggatt, K. (2001). Life and death in English nursing homes: Sequestration or transition? *Ageing and Society, 21*(3), 319–332.

Lawton, M.P., Moss, M., Hoffman, C., Grant, R., Have, T.T., & Kleban, M.H. (1999). Health, valuation of life, and the wish to live. *Gerontologist, 39*(4), 406–416.

Stajduhar, K., & Davies, B. (1998). Death at home: Challenges for families and directions for the future. *Journal of Palliative Care, 14*(3), 8–14.

REFERENCES

Abel, E.K. (1990). Daughters caring for elderly parents. In J.F. Gubrium & A. Sankar (Eds.), *The home care experience: Ethnography and policy* (pp. 189–286). Newbury Park, CA: Sage Publications.

Abramson, T.A., Trejo, L., & Lai, D. (2002). Culture and mental health: Providing appropriate services for a diverse older population. *Generations, 26*(1), 21–27.

Achenbaum, W.A. (1995). *Old age in a new land.* Baltimore, MD: Johns Hopkins University Press.

Achenbaum, W.A. (1997). Critical gerontology. In A. Jamieson, S. Harper, & C. Victor (Eds.), *Critical approaches to ageing and later life* (pp. 16–26). Buckingham, UK: Open University Press.

Achenbaum, W.A. & Bengtson, V.L. (1994). Re-engaging the disengagement theory of aging: On the history and assessment of theory development in gerontology. *Gerontologist, 18,* 756–763.

Ackerman, P.L., Beier, M.E., & Boyle, M.E. (2005) Working memory and intelligence: The same or different constructs. *Psychological Bulletin, 131,* 30–60.

Administration on Aging. (1998). The National Elder Abuse Incidence Study: Final Report, September 1998. Administration of Aging and National Centre on Elder Abuse at the American Public Human Services Association.

Ajzen, I., & Fishbein, M. (1977). Attitude-behavior relations: A theoretical analysis and review of empirical research. *Psychological Bulletin, 84,* 888–918.

Allan, D.E., & Penning, M. (2001, July). *An early look at regionalization in British Columbia: Regional equity or equality?* Paper presented at the International Association of Gerontology, Vancouver, B.C.

Allen, J.S., Bruss, J., & Damasio, H. (2005). The aging brain: The cognitive reserve hypothesis and hominid evolution. *American Journal of Human Biology, 17*(6), 673–689.

Allport, G.W. (1935). Attitudes. In C. Murchison, (Ed.), *Handbook of social psychology* (pp. 798–844). Worcester, MA: Clark University Press.

Almeida, O. & Fenner, S. (2002). Bipolar disorder: Similarities and differences between patients with onset before and after age 65. *International Psychogeriatrics, 14*(3), 311–322.

Almeida, O.P., Norman, P., Hankey, G., Jamrozik, K., & Flicker, L. (2006). Successful mental health aging: Results from a longitudinal study of older Australian men. *American Journal of Geriatric Psychiatry, 14*(1), 27–35.

Alwin, D.F., & Campbell, R.T. (2001). Quantitative approaches: Longitudinal methods in the study of human development and aging. In H. Binstock & L.K. George, (Eds.), *Handbook of aging and the social sicences* (pp. 22–43). San Diego, CA: Academic Press.

American Association of Retired Persons (AARP). (2001). Public attitudes toward aging, beauty, and cosmetic surgery. Retrieved April 3, 2006, from http://research.aarp.org./consume/ cosmetic_1.html

American Association of Retired Persons and Travelers Company Foundation. (1989). *National survey of caregivers: Working caregivers report.* Washington. DC: AARP; Hartford, CT: Travelers Company Foundation.

American Psychiatric Association. (1994). *Diagnostic and statistical manual of mental disorders* (4th ed.) (DSM-IV). Washington, DC: APA.

Andersen, K.L., Masironi, R., Rutenfranz, J., & Seliger, V. (1978). *Habitual physical activity and aging.* Copenhagen: World Health Organization.

Andersen, R., & Newman, J.F. (1973). Societal and individual health determinants of medical care utilization in the United States. *The Milbank Memorial Fund Quarterly, 51*(1), 95–124.

Anderson, J.K. (1991). Racial discourse in Canada, 1875–1980: Race, place and the power of definition. In K.J. Anderson (Ed.), *Vancouver's China Town.* (pp. 8–33). Montreal/Kingston: McGill–Queen's University Press.

Anderson, T.B., Earle, J.R., & Longino, C.F. (1997). Therapeutic role in later life: Husbands, wives and couples. *International Journal of Aging and Human Development, 45*(1): 49–65.

Andrews, F.M. (1991). Stability and change in levels and structure of subjective well-being: USA 1972 and 1988. *Social Indicators Research, 25,* 1–30.

Andrews, G., Tennant, G., Hewson, D., & Vaillant, G. (1978). Life event stress, social support, coping style, and risk of psychological impairment. *Journal of Nervous and Mental Disease, 166,* 307–316.

Angel, R., & Tienda, M. (1982). Determinants of extended household structure: Cultural pattern or economic need? *American Journal of Sociology, 87,* 1360–1385.

Antonucci, T.C. (1990). Social supports and social relationships. In R.H. Binstock & L.K. George, (Eds.), *Handbook of aging and the social sciences* (3rd ed.). New York: Academic Press.

Antunes, H.K., Stella, S.G., Santos, R.F., Bueno, O.F., & de Mello, M.T. (2005). Depression, anxiety and quality of life scores in seniors after an endurance exercise program. *Revista brasileira de psiquiatria, 27*(4), 266–271.

Aquino, J.A., Russell, D.W., Cutrona, C.E., & Altmaier, E.M. (1996). Employment status, social support, and life satisfaction among the elderly. *Journal of Counseling Psychology, 43*(4), 480–489.

Arbuckle, T.Y., Maag, U., Pushkar, D., & Chaikelson, J.S. (1998). Individual differences in trajectory of intellectual development over 45 years of adulthood. *Psychology and Aging, 13,* 663–675.

Armstrong, P. (2001). Science, enterprise and profit: Ideology in the knowledge-driven economy. *Economy and Society 30*(4), 524–552.

Armstrong, P., & Armstrong, H. (1999). Women, privatization and health care reform: The Ontario scan. Working Paper #10 for the Health Reform Reference Group, Centres of Excellence for Women's Health Program, Women's Health Bureau. Toronto: The National Network of Environments and Women's Health, York University

Armstrong, P., & Armstrong, H. (2001). *The double ghetto: Canadian women and their segregated work* (3rd ed.). Toronto: McClelland & Stewart.

Aronson, J., Denton, M., & Zeytinoglu, I. (2004). Market-modeled home care in Ontario: Deteriorating working conditions and dwindling community capacity. *Canadian Public Policy, 30*(1), 111–125.

Atchley, R. (1971). Disengagement among professors. *Journals of Gerontology, 26*, 183–190.

Atchley, R. (1976). *The sociology of retirement.* New York: Wiley and Sons.

Atchley, R. (1989). A continuity theory of normal aging. *Journals of Gerontology: Social Sciences, 52*, 183–190.

Atchley, R.C. (1993). Critical perspectives on retirement. In T.R. Cole, W.A. Achenbaum, P.L. Jakobi, & R. Kastenbaum (Eds.), *Voices and visions of aging: Toward a critical gerontology (pp. 3–19).* New York: Springer.

Atchley, R.C., & Barusch, A.S. (Eds.), (2004). *Social forces and Aging: An Introduction to Social Gerontology* (10th ed.). Toronto: Thomson Wadsworth.

Atkinson, R.C., & Shriffrin, R.M. (1968). Human memory: A proposed system and its control processes. In K.W. Spence, & J.T. Spence, (Eds.), *The psychology of learning and motivation: Advances in research and theory* (Vol. 2). New York: Academic Press.

Atkinson, T. (1982). The stability and validity of quality of life measures. *Social Indicators Research, 10*, 113–132.

Attig, T. (1995). Can we talk? On the elusiveness of dialogue. *Death Studies, 19*(1), 1–19.

Auger, J.A. (2000). *Social perspectives on death and dying.* Halifax, NS: Fernwood Publishing.

Backett, K., Davison, C., & Mullen, K. (1994). Lay evaluation of health and healthy lifestyles: Evidence from three studies. *British Journal of General Practice, 44*, 277–280.

Bäckman, L. (2001). Learning and memory. In J.E. Birren & K.W. Schaie, (Eds.), *Handbook of the psychology of aging* (5th ed) San Diego, CA: Academic Press.

Bäckman L., & Dixon, R.A. (1992). Psychological compensation: A theoretical framework. *Psychological Bulletin, 112*(2), 259–283.

Badgely, R.F. (1991). Social and economic disparities under Canadian health-care. *International Journal of Health Services, 21*(4), 659–671.

Baggs, J.G., & Schmitt, M.H. (2000). End-of-life decisions in adult intensive care: Current research base and directions for the future. *Nursing Outlook, 48*(4), 158–164.

Bahrick, H.P., Bahrick, P.O., & Wittlinger, R.P. (1975). Fifty years of memory for names and faces: A cross-sectional approach. *Journal of Experimental Psychology: General, 104*, 54–75.

Baker, A.B., Tang, Y.Q., &Turner, M.J. (2003). Percentage decline in masters superathlete track and field performance with aging. *Experimental Aging Research, 29*(1), 47–65.

Baker, M. & Lero, D. (1996). Division of labour: Paid work and family structure. In M. Baker, (Ed.), *Families: Changing trends in Canada* (3rd ed.). Toronto: McGraw Hill Ryerson

Baker, R., Wu, A.W., Teno, J.M., Kreling, B., Damiano, A.M., Rubin, H.R., et al. (2000). Family satisfaction with end-of-life care in seriously ill hospitalized adults. *Journal of the American Geriatrics Society, 48*(suppl. 5), 61–69.

Balakrishnan, T.R., Lapierre-Adamcyk, E., & Krotki, K.J. (1993). *Family and childbearing in Canada: A demographic analysis.* Toronto: University of Toronto Press.

Baltes, P.B. (1993). The aging mind: Potential and limits. *Gerontologist, 33*, 580–594.

Baltes, P.B., & Baltes, M. (1990). Psychological perspectives on successful aging: The model of selective optimization with compensation. In P.B. Baltes & M. Baltes, (Eds.), *Longitudinal research and the study of successful (optimal) aging* (pp.1–49). Cambridge, UK: Cambridge University Press.

Baltes, P.B., & Staudinger, U. (1993). The search for a psychology of wisdom. *Current Directions in Psychological Science, 2*, 75–80.

Baltes, P.B., & Willis, S.W. (1977). Toward psychological theories of aging and development. In J.E. Birren & K.W. Schaie (Eds.), *Handbook of the psychology of aging* (pp. 128–154). New York: Van Nostrand Reinhold.

Barak, Y., Aizenberg, D., Szor, H., Swartz, M., Maor, R., & Knobler, H.Y. (2005). Increased risk of attempted suicide among aging Holocaust survivors. *American Journal of Geriatric Psychiatry, 13*, 701–704.

Barer, M.L., Evans, R.G., & Hertzman C. (1995). Avalanche or glacier? Health care and the demographic rhetoric. *Canadian Journal on Aging, 14*, 193–224.

Barer, M.L., McGrail, K.M., Cardiff, K., Wood, L., & Green, C.J. (2000). *Tales from the other drug wars.* Vancouver: University of British Columbia Centre for Health Services and Policy Research.

Barrett, A.E. (1999). Social support and life satisfaction among the never married. *Research on aging. 21*(1): 46–72.

Barrett, A.E., & Lynch, S.M. (1999). Caregiving networks of elderly persons: Variation by marital status. *The Gerontologist, 39*(6), 695–704.

Barrett, R., Kazawa, C.W., McDade, T., & Armelagos, G.J. (1998). Emerging and re-emerging infectious diseases: The third epidemiologic transition. *Annual Review of Anthropology, 27*, 247–271.

Bar-Tur, L., Savaya, R., and Prager, E. (2001). Sources of meaning in life for young and old Israeli Jews and Arabs. *Journal of Aging Studies, 15*, 253–269.

Barusch, A.S. (1988). Problems and coping strategies of elderly spouse caregivers. *Gerontologist, 28*, 677–685.

Basavarajappa, K.G. (1998). *Living Arrangements and Residential Overcrowding: The Situation of Older Immigrants in Canada, 1991*. Family and Community Support Systems, Statistics Canada. Catalogue 11F0019MPE No. 115.

Basavarajappa, K.G., & Jones, F. (1999). Visible minority income differences. In S.S. Halli & L. Driedger (Eds.), *Immigrant Canada: Demographic, economic, and social challenges* (pp. 230–257). Toronto: University of Toronto Press.

Bass, S.A., & Caro, F.G. (1996). Economic value of grandparent assistance. *Generations, 20*, 29–33.

Battle, K., Torjman, S., Mendelson, M., & Pomeroy, S. (2005, March). *The vote or veto budget: An analysis of the 2005 federal budget*. Ottawa: Caledon Institute of Social Policy.

Beaudry, P., and Lemieux, T. (1999). Evolution of the female labour force participation rate in Canada, 1976–1994. *Canadian Business Economics 7*(2), 57–70.

Beaujot, R. (1995). Family patterns at mid-life (marriage, parenting, working). In R. Beaujot, E.M. Gee, F. Rajulton, & Z.R. Ravanera, *Family over the life course* (pp. 37–75). (Catalogue No. 91-643E). Ottawa: Statistics Canada.

Beaujot, R. (2000). *Earning and caring in Canadian families*. Peterborough, ON: Broadview.

Beaujot, R., & Bélanger, A. (2001). Perspectives on below replacement fertility in Canada: Trends, desires, and accommodations. *Discussion paper 01–6*. London, ON: University of Western Ontario, Population Studies Centre.

Beaulieu, M., & Bélanger, L. (1997). Intervention in long-term care institutions with respect to elder mistreatment. In M.J. MacLean (Ed.), *Abuse and neglect of older Canadians: Strategies for change* (pp.27–37). Toronto: Thompson.

Beck, S.H. (1982). Adjustment to and satisfaction with retirement. *Journals of Gerontology, 37*(5), 616–624.

Beck, U. (1992). *Risk society: Towards a new modernity*. London: Sage Publications.

Beck, U. (1994). The reinvention of politics: Toward a theory of reflexive modernization. In U. Beck, A. Giddens, & S. Lash (Eds.), *Reflexive Modernization* (pp. 1–55). Stanford, CA: Stanford University Press.

Bédard, M., Stones, M.J., Guyatt, G.H., & Hirdes, J.P. (2001). Traffic-related fatalities among older drivers and passengers: Past and future trends. *Gerontologist, 41*(6): 751–756.

Beehr, T.A., Glazer, S., Nielson, N.L., & Fanner, S.J. (2000). Work and nonwork predictors of employees' retirement ages. *Journal of Vocational Behavior, 57*(2), 206–225.

Bélanger, A., Carrière, Y., & Gilbert S. (Eds.), 2000. *Report on the demographic situation in Canada, 2000*. (Catalogue No. 91-209-XPE). Ottawa: Statistics Canada.

Bélanger, A., & Malenfant, É.C. (2005, March). *Population projections of visible minority groups, Canada, provinces and regions* (Catalogue No. 91-541-XIE). Ottawa: Demography Division, Statistics Canada.

Bendick, M., Jr. (1989). Privatizing the delivery of social welfare services: An ideal to be taken seriously. In S.B. Kamerman & A.J. Kahn, (Eds.), *Privatization and the welfare state* (pp. 97–120). Princeton, NJ: Princeton University Press.

Bengtson, V.L. (2001). Beyond the nuclear family: The increasing importance of multigenerational bonds. *Journal of Marriage and the Family, 63*, 1–16.

Bengtson, V.L., Burgess, E.O., & Parrott, T.M. (1997). Theory, explanation, and a third generation of theoretical development in social gerontology. *The Journals of Gerontology: Social Sciences, 52*, S72–S88.

Bengtson, V.L., & Kuypers, J.A. (1971). Generational differences and the developmental stake. *Aging and Human Development, 2*, 246–260.

Bengtson, V.L., Rice, C.J., & Johnson, M.L. (1999). Are theories of aging important? Models and explanations in gerontology at the turn of the century. In V.L. Bengtson, V.L. Schaie, & K.W. Schaie, (Eds.), *Handbook of theories of aging* (pp. 3–20). New York: Springer.

Bengtson, V.L., Rosenthal, C.J., & Burton, L.M. (1996). Paradoxes of family and aging. In R.B. Binstock & L.K. George, (Eds.), *Handbook of aging and the social sciences* (4th ed., pp. 253–282). New York: Academic Press.

Benyamini, Y., Idler, E.L., Leventhal, H., & Leventhal, E.A. (2000). Positive affect and function as influences on self-assessments of health: expanding our view beyond illness and disability. *The journals of gerontology. Series B, Psychological sciences and social sciences, 55*(2), 107–116.

Bergman, H. (2003). The Canadian initiative on frailty and aging. *Aging Clinical and Experimental Research, 15*(suppl. 3): 1–2.

Bergman, M., Blumenfeld, V.G., Casardo, D., Dash, B., Levitt, H., & Margulies, M.K. (1976). Age-related decrement in hearing for speech: Sampling and longitudinal studies. *Journals of Gerontology, 31*, 533–538.

Berkman, L.F., & Syme, S.L. (1979). Social networks, host resistance, and mortality: A nine-year follow-up study of Alameda County residents. *American Journal of Epidemiology, 109*(2), 186–204.

Berman, L., & Sobkowska-Ashcroft, I. (1987). Images and impressions of old age in the great works of Western literature (700 B.C.–1900 A.D.). Lewiston, NY: The Edwin Mellen Press.

Berry, J., & Kalin, R. (1990). *Some psychological and cultural implications of multiculturalism: A social cost benefit analysis from the perspectives of a larger society*. Ottawa: Economic Council of Canada.

Beullens, J., Marcoen, A., Jaspaert, H., & Pelmans, W. (1997). Medical students' knowledge about and attitudes towards aging and the impact of geriatric training: A review study. *Netherlands Journals of Gerontology and Geriatrics, 28*(4), 178–184.

Bevans, M., & Cole, T. (2001). Ethics and spirituality: Strangers at the end of life? In M.P. Lawton (Ed.),

Annual Review of Gerontology and Geriatrics: Vol. 20. Focus on the end of life: Scientific and social issues (pp.16–38). New York: Springer.

Biggs, S., Lowenstein, A., & Hendricks, J. (2003). *Need for theory: Critical approaches to social gerontology.* Amityville, NY: Baywood.

Biggs, S. & Powell, J.L. (2001). A Foucauldian analysis of old age and the power of social welfare. *Journal of Aging & Social Policy, 12*(2), 93–112.

Binet, A., & Simon, T. (1905). Méthodes nouvelles pour le diagnostic du niveau intellectuel des anormaux. *L'Année Psychologique, 11,* 191.

Binstock, R.H. (1997). The 1996 election: Older voters and implications for policies on aging. *Gerontologist, 37,* 15–19.

Biribili, M. (2000). Translating from one language to another. *Social Research Update, 31,* 1–6.

Birren, J.E., & Bengtson, V.L. (Eds.), (1988). *Emergent theories of aging.* New York: Springer.

Birren, J.E., & Cunningham, W. (1985). Research on the psychology of aging: Principles, concepts and theory. In J.E. Birren & K.W. Schaie (Eds.), *Handbook of the psychology of aging* (2nd ed., pp. 3–34). New York: Van Nostrand Reinhold.

Birren, J.E., & Renner, V.J. (1977). In J.E. Birren & K.W. Schaie (Eds.), *Handbook of the Psychology of Aging.* New York: Van Nostrand Reinhold.

Bittman, M. (1999). Parenthood without penalty: Time use and public policy in Australia and Finland. *Feminist Economics, 5,* 27–42.

Black, C. (1995). Using existing data sets to study aging and the elderly: An introduction. *Canadian Journal on Aging, 14*(suppl.), 135–150.

Black, S.A., Kyriakos, S.M., & Miller, T.Q. (1998). Correlates of depressive symptomatology among older community dwelling Mexican-Americans: The Hispanic EPSE. *Journals of Gerontology, Series B 53,* S198–S208.

Blackhall, L.J., Murphy, S.T., Frank, G., & Michel, V. (1995). Ethnicity and attitudes toward patient autonomy. *Journal of the American Medical Association, 274*(10), 820–825.

Blakemore, K., & Boneham, M. (1994). *Age, Race and Ethnicity: A comparative approach.* Buckingham: Open University Press.

Blando, J.A. (2001). Twice hidden: Older gay and lesbian couples, friends, and intimacy. *Generations, 25,* 87–89.

Blaxter, M. (1983). The causes of diseases: Women talking. *Social Science and Medicine, 17,* 59–69.

Blekesaune, M., & Solem, P. (2005). Working conditions and early retirement. *Research on Aging, 27*(1), 3–30.

Blumenthal, J., Babyak, M., Moore, K.A., Craighead, W.E., Herman, S., Khatri, et al. (1999). Effects of exercise training on older patients with major depression. *Archives of Internal Medicine, 159,* 2349–2356.

Bohlmèijer, E., Smit, F., & Cuijpers, P (2003). Effects of reminiscence and life review on late-life depression: A meta-analysis. *International Journal of Geriatric Psychiatry, 18*(12), 1088–1094.

Borkan, G.A., & Norris, A.H. (1980). Assessment of biological age using a profile of physical parameters. *Journals of Gerontology, 35,* 177–184.

Botwinick, J., West, R., & Storandt, M. (1978). Predicting death from behavioral test performance. *Journals of Gerontology, 33,* 755–762.

Bouchard, T.J. & McGue, M. (1990). Genetic and rearing environmental influences on adult personality: An analysis of adopted twins reared apart. *Journal of Personality, 58,* 263–292.

Bourque, P., Pushkar, D., Bonneville, L., & Beland, F. (2005) Contextual effects on life satisfaction of older men and women. *Canadian Journal on Aging, 24,* 31–44.

Boyd, M. (1991). Immigration and Living Arrangements: Elderly Women in Canada. *International Migration Review, 25,* 4–7.

Boyd, M., & Vickers, M. (2000). 100 years of immigration in Canada. *Canadian Social Trends,* Autumn, 2–12, Catalogue No. 11-008.

Boyd, N. (2000). *The beast within: Why men are violent.* Vancouver, BC: Greystone Books.

Bradburn, N.M. (1969). *The structure of psychological well-being.* Chicago: Aldine.

Bradley, E.H., Fried, T.R., Stanislav, V.K., & Idler, E. (2001). Quality-of-life trajectories of elders in the end of life. In M.P. Lawton (Ed.), *Annual review of gerontology and geriatrics: Vol. 20. Focus on the end of life: Scientific and social issues* (pp.64–96). New York: Springer.

Bradley, E.H., Peiris, V., & Wetle, T. (1998). Discussions about end-of-life care in nursing homes. *Journal of the American Geriatrics Society, 46*(10), 1235–1241.

Braithwaite, V. (1998). Institutional respite care: Breaking chores or breaking social bonds? *Gerontologist, 38*(5), 610–617.

Breckler, S.J. (1984). Empirical validation of affect, behavior, and cognition as distinct components of attitude. *Journal of Personality and Social Psychology, 47,* 1191–1205.

Brink, P., Stewart, S., & Stones, M. J. (2004). Institutional reactions to verbally abusive behaviour by residents of long-term care facilities. Proceedings of Ontario Network for the Prevention of Elder Abuse Conference. Retrieved May 5, 2006, from http://onpea.org/Strategy/Communication/Conference04Eng.htm

British Columbia Inter-Ministry Committee on Elder Abuse and Continuing Care Division, Ministry of Health and Ministry Responsible for Seniors. (1992, February). *Principles, procedures, and protocol.*

Brody, E.M., Hoffman, C., Kleban, M.H., & Schoonover, C.B. (1989). Caregiving daughters and their local siblings: Perceptions, strains, and interactions. *The Gerontologist, 29,* 529–538.

Brody, E.M., & Schoonover, C.B. (1986). Patterns of parent-care when adult daughters work and when they do not. *The Gerontologist, 26,* 372–381.

Brotman, S. Ryan, B. & Cormier, R. (2003). The health and social service needs of gay and lesbian elders and their families in Canada. *The Gerontologist, 43,* 192–202.

Brown, D, (2004) A literature review exploring how healthcare professionals contribute to the assessment and control of postoperative pain in older people. *Journal Of Clinical Nursing, 13,* 74–90

Brown, E.R. (1979). *Rockefeller medicine men: Medicine and capitalism in America.* Berkeley, CA: University of California Press.

Browne, C.V. (1998). *Women, feminism and aging.* New York: Springer.

Broyles, R.W., Manga, P., Binder, D.A., Angus, D.E., & Charette, A. (1983). The use of physician services under a national health insurance scheme. *Medical Care, 21,* 1037–1054.

Brunt, J.H., Chappell, N.L., Maclure, N., & Cassels, A. (1998). Assessing the effectiveness of government and industry media campaigns on seniors' perceptions of reference-based pricing policy. *The Journal of Applied Gerontology, 17*(3), 276–295.

Bryden, K. (1974). Old age pensions and policy making in Canada. Montreal: McGill-Queen's University Press.

Bryman, A. (2001). *Social research methods.* New York: Oxford.

Burr, J.A. & Mutchler, J.E. (1993). Nativity, acculturation, and economic status: Explanations of Asian American living arrangements in later life. *Journals of Gerontology: Social Sciences, 48,* S55–S63.

Burr, J.A., & Mutchler, J.E. (1999). Race and ethnicity variation in norms of filial responsibility among older persons. *Journal of Marriage and the Family, 61,* 674–687.

Burton, L.M. & Bengtson, V.L. (1985). Black grandmothers: Issues of timing and continuity of roles. In V.L. Bengston & J.F. Robertson, (Eds.), *Grandparenthood* (pp. 61–77). Beverly Hills, CA: Sage.

Butler, R.N. (1963). The life review: An interpretation of reminiscence in the aged. *Psychiatry, 26,* 65–76.

Butler, R.N. (1975) *Why survive? Being old in America.* New York: Harper & Rowe.

Butler, R.N., & Gleason, H.P. (1985). *Productive aging: Enhancing vitality in later life.* New York: Springer.

Butler, R.N., & Lewis, M.I. (2002). *The new love and sex after 60.* (4th ed.) New York: Ballantine.

Butler, R.N., Lewis, M.I., and Sutherland, T. (1998). *Aging and mental health: Positive psychosocial and biomedical approaches.* Needham Heights, MA: Allyn and Bacon.

Butler, R., & Schechter, M. (2001). Productive aging. In G. Maddox, (Ed.), *The Encyclopedia of Aging,* Vol. II (3rd ed., pp. 824–825). New York: Springer.

Buttell, F.P. (1999). Relationship between spouse abuse and the maltreatment of dementia sufferers by their caregivers. *American Journal of Alzheimer's Disease, 14,* 230–232.

Butterworth, P., Gill, S., Rodgers, B., Anstey, K., Villamil, E. & Melzer, D. (2005). Retirement and mental health: Analysis of the Australian national survey of mental health and well-being. *Social Science and Medicine, 62,* 1179–1191.

Byock, I.R. (1993). Consciously walking the fine line: Thoughts on a hospice response to assisted suicide and euthanasia. *Journal of Palliative Care, 9*(3), 25–28.

Cahill, S., South, K., & Spade, J. (2000). *Outing age: Public policy issues affecting gay, lesbian, bisexual and transgender elders.* Washington, DC: Policy Institute of the National Gay and Lesbian Task Force.

Calasanti, T.M. (1996) Incorporating diversity: Meaning, levels of research, and implications for theory. *The Gerontologist, 36*(2), p.147–156.

Calasanti, T.M, & Slevin, K.F. (2001). *Gender, social inequalities, and aging.* New York: AltaMira Press.

Calasanti, T. (2004). Feminist gerontology and old men. *Journals of Gerontology, 59B*(6), S305–S314.

Cameron, E., & Bernardes, J. (1998). Gender and disadvantage in health: Men's health for a change. *Sociology of Health and Illness, 20,* 673–693.

Campbell, D.T. (1963). Social attitudes and other acquired behavioral dispositions. In S. Koch, (Ed.). *Psychology: A study of a science* (pp.94–172). New York: McGraw-Hill.

Campbell, D.T., & Fiske, D.W. (1959). Convergent and discriminant validation by the multitrait-multimethod matrix. *Psychological Bulletin, 56,* 81–105.

Canada. (1970). *Vital Statistics* (84–202). Dominion Bureau of Statistics.

Canada Pension Plan Home Page. (2005, Copyright James Lovee). CPP: Bad Social Policy—Squeezing the young to benefit the wealthier old. Retrieved April 14, 2006, from http://www.canada-pension-plan.com/

Canadian Institute for Advanced Research. (1991). *The determinants of health* (CIAR Publication, No. 5).Toronto: CIAR.

Canadian Institute for Health Information. (1998). *Provincial mini-status report: The quality of caring: Chronic care in Ontario.* Ottawa: CIHI.

Canadian Institute for Health Information (2005). Comparable health and health system performance indicators for Canada, the Provinces, and Territories, November 2004.

Canadian Study of Health & Aging Working Group. (1994a). The Canadian study of health and aging: Study methods and prevalence of dementia. *Canadian Medical Association Journal, 150,* 899–913.

Canadian Study of Health & Aging Working Group (1994b). The Canadian study of health and aging: Risk factors for Alzheimer's disease in Canada. *Neurology, 44,* 2073–2080.

Cantor, M.H. & Brennan, M. (2000) *Social care of the elderly: The effects of ethnicity, class and culture.* New York: Springer.

Carmel, S. (1999). Life-sustaining treatments: What doctors do, what they want for themselves and what elderly persons want. *Social Science and Medicine, 49*(10), 1401–1408.

Carmel, S., & Mutran, E.J. (1999). Stability of elderly persons' expressed preferences regarding the use of life-sustaining treatments. *Social Science and Medicine, 49*(3), 303–311.

Caro, F.G., & Bass, S.A. (1997). Receptivity to volunteering in the immediate postretirement period. *Journal of Applied Gerontology, 16*(4), 427–441.

Carver, A.C., Vickrey, B.G., Brnat, J.L., Keran, C., Ringel, & S.P., Foley, K.M. (1999). End-of-life care: A survey of US neurologists' attitudes, behavior, and knowledge. *Neurology, 53*(2), 284–293.

Chalmers, L. & Milan, A. (2005). Marital satisfaction during the retirement years. *Canadian Social Trends.* (Catalogue No. 11-008). Pp. 14–17.

Chamberlain, K. & Zika, S. (1992). Stability and change in subjective well-being over short periods of time. *Social Indicators Research, 26,* 101–117.

Chan, K.B. (1983). Coping with aging and managing self-identity: The social world of the elderly Chinese women. *Canadian Ethnic Studies.* 15, 36–50.

Chappell, N.L. (1983). Informal support networks among the elderly. *Research on Aging, 5*(1), 77–99.

Chappell, N.L. (1987). The interface between three systems of care: Self, informal and formal. In R. Ward & S. Tobin (Eds.), *Health in aging: Sociological issues and policy directions* (pp. 159–179). New York: Springer.

Chappell, N.L. (1989). Health and helping among the elderly, gender differences. *Journal of Aging and Health, 1*(1), 102–120.

Chappell, N.L. (1990). In-group differences among elders living with friends and family other than spouse. *Journal of Aging Studies, 5*(1), 61, 76.

Chappell, N.L. (1992). *Social support and aging.* Toronto: Butterworths.

Chappell, N.L. (1993a). The future of health care in Canada. *Journal of Social Policy, 22*(4), 487–505.

Chappell, N.L. (1993b). Implications of shifting health care policy for caregiving in Canada. *Journal of Aging and Social Policy, 5*(142), 39–55.

Chappell, N. (1995). Gerontological research in the '90s: Strengths, weaknesses and contributions to policy. *Canadian Journal on Aging, 14*(suppl.), 23–36.

Chappell, N.L. (1998). Maintaining and enhancing independence and well-being in old age. In *Determinants of health, adults and seniors* (Vol. 2) (pp.89–137). Canada Health Action: Building on the Legacy, Papers Commissioned by the National Forum on Health.

Chappell, N.L. (1999). *Volunteering and healthy aging—What we know.* Victoria, BC: Volunteer Canada, Manulife Financial and Health Canada.

Chappell, N.L. (2001). *Family care of seniors in Shanghai; Similarities and differences with the West.* Paper presented at the International Symposium on Chinese Elderly, Shanghai, October.

Chappell, N.L. (2003). Correcting cross-cultural stereotypes: Aging in Shanghai and Canada. *Journal of Cross-Cultural Gerontology, 18*(2), 127–147.

Chappell, N.L. (2005). Perceived change in quality of life among Chinese Canadian seniors: The role of involvement in Chinese culture. *Journal of Happiness Studies.* 6(1), 69–91

Chappell, N.L. & Badger, M. (1989). Social isolation and well-being. *Journals of Gerontology: Social Sciences, 44*(5), S169–S176.

Chappell, N.L. & Behie, G.E. (2000). Is there life after caregiving? A comparison of caregivers before and after the death of a loved one. Gerontological Society of America annual meetings, Washington, November.

Chappell, N.L., & Blandford, A.A. (1991). Informal and formal care: Exploring the complementarity. *Aging and Society, 11*(3), 299–317.

Chappell, N.L., & Guse, L.W. (1989). Linkages between informal and formal support. In K.S. Markides & C.L. Cooper (Eds.), *Aging, Stress and Health* (pp. 219–237). New York: John Wiley & Sons, pp. 219–237.

Chappell, N.L., Havens, B., Hollander, M.J., Miller, J., & McWilliam, C. (2004). Comparative costs of home care and residential care. *The Gerontologist, 44*(3), 389–400.

Chappell, N., & Lai, D. (1998). Health care service use by Chinese seniors in British Columbia, Canada. *Journal of Cross-Cultural Gerontology, 13,* 21–37.

Chappell, N. & Lai, D. C. (2001). Social support of the elderly Chinese: Comparisons between China and Canada. In I. Chi, N. Chappell, & J. Lubben (Eds.) *Elderly Chinese in Pacific Rim Countries: Social Support and Integration.* Hong Kong: Hong Kong University Press.

Chappell, N. Lai, D. & Gee, E. (1997). A study of the Chinese elderly in British Columbia. Ottawa: National Health and Research and Development Program (NHRDP).

Chappell, N., Lai, D., & Gee, E. (2004). Ethnic group membership and old age: The Chinese elderly in British Columbia. Centre on Aging, University of Victoria. Retrieved April 19, 2006, from www.coag.uvic.ca

Chappell, N.L. & Litkenhaus, R. (1995). *Informal caregivers to adults in British Columbia.* Joint Report of the Centre on Aging, University of Victoria and The Caregivers Association of British Columbia.

Chappell, N.L., Maclure, M., Brunt, H., Hopkinson, J., & Mullett, J. (1997). Seniors' views of medication disbursement policies: Bridging research and policy at the point of policy impact. *Special Joint Issue of the Canadian Journal of Public Policy and the Canadian Journal on Aging* (spring suppl.), 114–131.

Chappell, N.L., & Penning, M.J. (1984). *Informal Supports: Examining Ethnic Variations.* Paper presented at the Annual meeting of the Gerontological Society of America, San Antonio, Texas.

Chappell, N.L. & Penning, M. (1996). Behavioural problems and distress among caregivers of people with dementia. *Aging and Society, 16,* 57–73.

Chappell, N.L. & Penning, M.J. (2001). Sociology of aging in Canada: Issues for the millennium. *Canadian Journal on Aging, 20,* (suppl.), 82–110.

Chappell, N.L. & Reid R.C. (2002). Burden and well-being among caregivers: Examining the distinction. *The Gerontologist 42*(6), 772–780.

Chappell, N.L., Reid, R.C., & Dow, E. (2001). Respite reconsidered: A typology of meanings based on the caregiver's point of view. *Journal of Aging Studies, 15*(2), 201–216.

Charmaz, K. (2000). Grounded theory: Objectivist and constructivist methods. In N. Denzin & Y. Lincoln, (Eds.), *Handbook of qualitative research* (2nd ed., pp. 509–535). Thousand Oaks, CA: Sage Publications.

Charness, N., Holly, P., Feddon, J., & Jastrezembski, T. (2004). Light pen use and practice minimize age and hand performance differences in pointing tasks. *Human Factors, 46*(3), 373–384.

Che-Alford, J., & Stevenson, K. (1998). Older Canadians on the move. (Catalogue No. 11-008-XPE). *Canadian Social Trends, Spring,* 15–18. Ottawa: Statistics Canada.

Chen, J., Ng, E., & Wilkins, R. (1996). The Health of Canada's immigrants in 1994–95. *Health Reports, 7*(4), 33–45.

Chen, P., Ganguli, M., Mulsant, B., & DeKosky, S. (1999). The temporal relationship between depressive symptoms and dementia. *Archives of General Psychiatry, 56,* 261–266.

Childs, H.W., Hayslip, B., Radika, L.M., & Reinberg, J.A. (2000). Young and middle-aged perceptions of elder abuse. *Gerontologist, 40,* 75–85.

Chipperfield, J. (1996). Perceived adequacy of instrumental assistance: Implications for well-being in later life. *Journal of Aging and Health, 8*(10), 72–95.

Chipperfield, J.G., Campbell, D.W., & Perry, R.P. (2004). Stability in perceived control: Implications for well-being among older individuals. *Journal of Aging and Health, 16,* 116–147.

Chipperfield, J.G., Havens, B., & Doig, W. (1997). Method and description of the Aging in Manitoba project: A 20-year longitudinal study. *Canadian Journal on Aging, 16*(4), 606–625.

Chipperfield, J.G., & Segall, A. (1996). Seniors' attributions for task performance difficulties. *Journal of Aging and Health, 8*(4), 489–511.

Chodzko-Zajko, W.J. (1994). Assessing physical performance in older adult populations. *Journal of Aging and Physical Activity, 2,* 103–104.

Chou, K.-L., Chow, N.W.S., & Chi, I. (2004). Leisure participation among Hong Kong Chinese older adults. *Ageing & Society, 24,* 617–629.

Chung, U. (1994). *The case for culturally sensitive health care: A comparative study of health beliefs related to culture in six north-east Calgary communities.* Executive Summary. Edmonton: Alberta Community Development, Citizen and Heritage Secretariat.

Cicirelli, V.G. (1985). The role of siblings as family caregivers. In W.J. Sauer & R.T. Coward, (Eds.), *Social support networks and the care of the elderly.* New York: Springer.

Cicirelli, V.G. (1995). *Personality factors related to elders' end-of-life decisions: Final report* (Study I). Lafayette, IN: Purdue University, Department of Psychological Sciences.

Cicirelli, V.G. (1999). Personality and demographic factors in older adults' fear of death. *Gerontologist, 39*(5), 569–579.

Cicirelli, V.G. (2001). Healthy elders' early decisions for end-of-life living and dying. In M.P. Lawton (Ed.), *Annual Review of Gerontology and Geriatric: Vol. 20. Focus on the end of life: Scientific and social issues* (pp.163–192). New York: Springer.

Ciffin, S. & Martin, J. (1977). *Retirement in Canada: When and why people retire.* Staff Working Paper SWP–7804. Ottawa: Health and Welfare Canada.

Citizenship and Immigration Canada. (1999). *Facts and figures, 1998.* (Catalogue No. MP43-333/1999E). Ottawa: Minister of Public Works and Government Services Canada.

Citizenship and Immigration Canada. (2005). *Facts and figures: Immigration overview, permanent and temporary residents* (Catalogue No. CI1-8/2004E). Ottawa: Research and Evaluation Branch.

Clark, P.G. (1999). Moral economy and the social construction of the crisis of aging and health care: Differing Canadian and U.S. perspectives. In M. Minkler & C.L. Estes, (Eds.), *Critical gerontology: Perspectives from political and moral economy* (pp. 147–167). Amityville, NY: Baywood.

Clark, R.M. (1960). *Economic security for the aged in the United States and Canada. A report prepared by the Government of Canada, Vol. III.* Ottawa: The Queen's Printer and Controller of Stationery.

Clarke, A., & Hanson, E. (2000). Death and dying: Changing the culture of care. In A.M. Warnes, L. Warren, & M. Nolan (Eds.), *Care services for later life—transformations and critiques* (pp.204–218). London, UK: Jessica Kingsley Publishers.

Clausen, A. (1998). Life reviews and life stories. In J.Z. Giele & G.H. Elder Jr. (Eds.), *Methods of life course research: Qualitative and quantitative approaches* (pp.89–212). Thousand Oaks, CA: Sage Publications.

Clausen, J.A. (1993). *American lives: Looking back at the children of the depression.* New York: Free Press.

Clément, R., Singh, S.S., & Gaudet, S. (2006). Identity and adaptation among minority Indo-Guyanese: Influence of generational status, gender, reference group and situation. *Group Processes & Intergroup Relations, 9*(2), 289–304.

Clyburn, D.L., Stones, M.J., Hadjistavropoulos, T., & Tuokko, H. (2000). Disturbing behavior in Alzheimer's disease and its relationship to caregiver distress. *Journals of Gerontology, 55B,* S2–S13.

Coale, A.J. (1956). The effects of changes in mortality and fertility on age composition. *Milbank Memorial Fund Quarterly, 34,* 79–114.

Coburn D. (2001). Health, health care, and neo-liberalism. In P. Armstrong, H. Armstrong, & D. Coburn,

(Eds.), *Unhealthy times. Political economy perspectives on health and care in Canada.* (pp. 45–65). Toronto: Oxford University Press.

Coburn, D. (2004). Beyond the income inequality hypothesis: Class, neo-liberalism, and health inequalities. *Social Science & Medicine, 58*(1), 41–56.

Coburn, D., Torrance, G.M., & Kaufert, J.M. (1983). Medical dominance in Canada: The rise and fall of medicine. *International Journal of Health Services, 13,* 407–432.

Cohen, M. 1988. *Women's work, markets and economic development in nineteenth-century Ontario.* Toronto: University of Toronto Press.

Cohen, S., & Syme, S.L. (1985). Issues in the study and application of social support. In S. Cohen (Ed.), *Social Support and Health* (pp. 3–22). Orlando, FL: Academic Press.

Cohen, S., Tyrrell, D.A., & Smith, A.P. (1991). Psychological stress in humans and susceptibility to the common cold. *New England Journal of Medicine, 325,* 606–612.

Cohen, W. (1971). *Social security: The first thirty-five years: Papers from the 23rd Annual Conference on Aging, August 12-14,1970.* Ann Arbor, MI: Institute of Gerontology, University of Michigan–Wayne State University.

Collings, P. (2001) "If you got everything, it's good enough": Perspectives on successful aging in a Canadian Inuit community. *Journal of Cross-Cultural Gerontology,16,* 127–155.

Connidis, I.A. (1989a). Contact between siblings in later life. *Canadian Journal of Sociology, 14,* 429–442.

Connidis, I.A. (1989b). *Family ties and aging.* Toronto: Butterworths.

Connidis, I.A. (1994). Growing up and old together: Some observations on families in later life. In V. Marshall & B. McPherson (Eds.), *Aging: Canadian perspectives* (pp. 195–205). Peterborough, ON: Broadview.

Connidis, I.A. (2001). *Family ties and aging.* Thousand Oaks, CA: Sage.

Connidis, I.A., & Campbell, L.D. (1995). Closeness, confiding, and contact among siblings in middle and late adulthood. *Journal of Family Issues, 16,* 722–745.

Cook, P. (1994). Chronic illness beliefs and the role of social networks among Chinese, Indian, and Angloceltic Canadians. *Journal of Cross-Cultural Psychology, 25*(4), 452–465.

Cool, L.E. (1981). Ethnic identity: A source of community esteem for the elderly. *Anthropological Quarterly. 54,* 179–181.

Costa, D.L. (1999). Home of her own: Old age assistance and the living arrangements of older unmarried women. *Journal of Public Economics, 72,* 39–59.

Costa, P.T., & McCrae, R.R. (1980a). Functional age: A conceptual and empirical critique. In S.G. Haynes & M. Feinleib (Eds.), *Proceedings of the Second Conference on the Epidemiology of Aging.* Bethesda, MD: National Institute on Aging.

Costa, P.T., & McCrae, R.R. (1980b). Still stable after all these years. In P.B. Baltes & O.G. Brim (Eds.), *Life Span Development and Behaviour.* Vol. 3, (pp. 65–102). New York: Academic Press.

Costa, P.T., McCrae, R.R., & Zonderman, A. (1987). Environmental and dispositional influences on well-being: Longitudinal follow-up of an American national sample. *British Journal of Psychology, 78,* 299–306.

Council of Economic Advisors. (1999). Work and retirement among the elderly. *Population and Development Review, 25*(1), 189–196.

Couper, D.P. (1994, Sept./Oct.). What's wrong with this picture? Aging and education in America. *Aging Today, 3.*

Covinsky, K.E., Fuller, J.D., Yaffe, K., Johnston, C.B., Hamel, M., Lynn, J., et al. (2000). Communication and decision-making in seriously ill patients: Findings of the SUPPORT project. *Journal of the American Geriatrics Society, 48*(suppl. 5), 187–193.

Cowgill, D.O., & Holmes, L.D. (1972). *Aging and Modernization.* New York: Appleton Century-Crofts.

Craik, F.I.M., & Jennings, J.M. (1992). Human memory. In F.I.M. Craik & T.A. Salthouse (Eds.), *Handbook of aging and cognition* (pp. 51–110). Hillsdale, NJ: Lawrence Erlbaum.

Creswell, J. (1998). *Qualitative enquiry and research design: Choosing among five traditions.* Thousand Oaks, CA: Sage Publications.

Crimmins, E.M. (1990). Are Americans healthier as well as longer-lived? *Journal of Insurance Medicine, 22,* 89–92.

Crimmins, E.M., Reynolds, S.L., & Saito, Y. (1999). Trends in health and ability to work among the older working-age population. *Journals of Gerontology: Series B: Psychological Sciences and Social Sciences, 54B*(I): S31–S40.

Crystal, S., & Shea, D. (1990). Cumulative advantage, cumulative disadvantage, and inequality among elderly people. *The Gerontologist, 30*(4), 437–443.

Csank, P., Gauron, K., Knight, C., Obadia, F., Ouaknine, L., & Stones, M.J. (1997). Happy and healthy seniors: The measurement and meaning of well-aging, Durban, SA: International Federation on Aging.

Cumming, E. (1963). Further thoughts on the theory of disengagement. *International Social Science Journal, 15,* 377–393.

Cumming, E. & Henry, W. (1961). *Growing old: The process of disengagement.* New York: Basic Books.

Dannefer, D. (1988). *Differential gerontology and the stratified life course: Conceptual and methodological issues.* New York: Springer.

Dannefer, D. (2003). Cumulative advantage/disadvantage and the life course: Cross-fertilizing age and social science theory. *The Journals of Gerontology. 58B*(6), S327–S337.

D'Arcy, C. (1988). *Reducing inequalities in health.* Health Services and Promotion Branch Working Paper 88–16. Ottawa: Health and Welfare Canada.

Davidson, K. (2001). Late life widowhood, selfishness and new partnership choices: A gendered perspective. *Ageing and Society, 21,* 297–317.

Davies, L. (2003). Singlehood: Transitions within a gendered world. *Canadian Journal on Aging, 22*(4), 343–352.

Davis, C.K. (2000). *Supportive housing for seniors.* Prepared for CMHC by Social Data Research Ltd. Ottawa: Canada Mortgage and Housing.

Dean, K. (1981). Self-care responses to illness: A selected review. *Social Science and Medicine, 151,* 673–687.

Deber, R., Narine, L., Baranek, P., Sharpe, N., Masnyk Duvalko, K., Zlotnik-Shaul, R., et al. (1998). The public-private mix in health care. *Canada Health Action: Building on the Legacy,* pp. 423–546, National Forum on Health.

de Grâce, G.R, Joshi, P., Pelletier, R., & Beaupré, C. (1994). Conséquences psychologiques de la retraite en fonction du sexe et du niveau occupationel antérieur. *Canadian Journal on Aging, 13,* 149–168.

Dennis, W. (1996). Creative productivity between the ages of 20–80 years. *Journals of Gerontology, 21,* 1–8.

Denton, F.T., Feaver, C.H., & Spencer, B.G. (1998). The future population of Canada, its age distribution and dependency relations. *Canadian Journal on Aging, 17,* 83–109.

Denton, F.T., & Spencer, B.G. (1999). *Population aging and its economic costs: A survey of the issues and evidence.* SEDAP Research Paper No. 1. Hamilton, ON: McMaster University. Retrieved April 15, 2006, from http://socserv2.mcmaster.ca/~sedap/

Denton, F.T., & Spencer, B.G. (2002). Some demographic consequences of revising the definition of "Old Age" to reflect future changes in life table probabilities. *Canadian Journal on Aging, 21*(3): 349-356.

Denton, M., & Kusch, K. (2006) *Well-being throughout the senior years. Issue paper on key events in transition in later life.* Prepared for the Expert Roundtable on Seniors. Ottawa: Social Development Ministry.

Denton, M., Raina, P., Lian, J., Gafni, A., Joshi, A., French, S., et al. (2000). Health, age and financial preparations for later life. In F.T. Denton, D. Fretz, & B. Spencer (Eds.), *Independence and economic security in old age* (pp. 136–155). Vancouver: University of British Columbia Press.

Denton, M., & Walters, V. (1999). Gender differences in structural and behavioural determinants of health: An analysis of the social production of health. *Social Science and Medicine, 48,* 1221–1235.

Denzin, N.K., & Lincoln, Y.S. (Eds.) (2005). *The Sage handbook of qualitative research* (3rd ed.). Thousand Oaks, CA: Sage.

Department of Finance. (2001). Tax expenditures and evaluations. (Catalogue No. F1-27/2001E). Ottawa: Her Majesty the Queen in Right of Canada.

Depp C.A., & Jeste, D.V. (2006). Definitions and predictors of successful aging: A comprehensive review of larger quantitative studies. *American Journal Of Geriatric Psychiatry, 14,* 6–20.

Devereaux P.J., Heels-Ansdell, D., Lacchetti, C., Haines, T., Burns, K.E.A., Cook, D.J., et al. (2004). Payments for care at private for-profit and private not-for-profit hospitals: A systematic review and meta-analysis. *Canadian Medical Association Journal, 170*(12), 1817–1824.

De Vries J. (1995). Ethnic language maintenance and shift. In S.S. Halli, F. Tovato, & L. Dreidger (Eds). *Ethnic demography* (pp. 163–177). Ottawa: Carleton University Press.

Diener, E., Sandvik, E., Parvot, W., & Gallagher, D. (1991). Response artifacts in the measurement of subjective well-being. *Social Indicators Research, 24,* 35–56.

Diener, E., Sandvik, E., Seidlitz, L., & Diener, M. (1993). The relationship between income and subjective well-being: Relative or absolute. *Social Indicators Research, 28,* 225–244.

Diener, E., Suh, E.M., Lucas, R.E., & Smith, H.L. (1999). Subjective well-being: Three decades of progress. *Psychological Bulletin, 125,* 276–302.

Dietz, T.L., John, R., & Roy, C.L. (1998). Exploring intra-ethnic diversity among four groups of Hispanic elderly: Patterns and levels of service utilization. *International Journal of Aging and Human Development, 46*(3), 247–266.

Dionigi, R.A. (2002). Empowerment and resistance through leisure: The meaning of competitive sport participation to older adults. *Society and Leisure, 25*(2), 303–328.

Donahue, P., & McDonald, L. (2005). Gay and lesbian aging: Current perspectives and future directions for social work practice and research. *Families and Society, 88*(3), 359–367.

Donahue, W., Orbach, H.L., & Pollack, O. (1960). Retirement: The emerging social pattern. In C. Tibbitts, (Ed.), *Handbook of social gerontology: Social aspects of aging.* Chicago: University of Chicago Press.

Donlon, M.M., Ashman, O., & Levy, B.R. (2005). Revision of older television characters: A stereotype-awareness intervention. *Journal of Social Issues, 61*(2), 307.

Dorfman, L.T. (1995). Health conditions and perceived quality of life in retirement. *Health and Social Work, 20*(3), 192–199.

Dosa, PA. (1999). (Re) imaging aging lives: Ethnographic narratives of Muslim women in diaspora. *Journal of Cross-Sectional Gerontology, 14,* 245–272.

Dosman, D., Fast, J., & Keating, N. (2005). *Care Networks of Frail Seniors and the Formal-Informal Interface.* (Hidden Costs/Invisible Contributions Research Program). Edmonton, AB: University of Alberta, Department of Human Ecology.

Doukas, D.J., Gorenflo, D.W., & Supanich, B. (1999). Primary care physician attitudes and values toward end-of-life care and physician-assisted death. *Ethics and Behavior, 9*(3), 219–230.

Dowd, J.J. (1975). Aging as exchange: A preface to theory. *Journals of Gerontology, 30,* 584–594.

Dowd, J.J. (1980a). Exchange rates and old people. *Journals of Gerontology, 35*, 596–602.

Dowd, J.J. (1980b). *Stratification among the aged.* Monterey, CA: Brooks/Cole.

Dowd, J.J., & Bengston, V.L. (1978). Aging in minority populations: An examination of the double jeopardy hypothesis. *Journals of Gerontology, 33*, 427–436.

Dowd, R.L., Sisson, R.P., & Kern, D.M. (1981). Socialization to violence among the aged. *Journals of Gerontology, 36*, 350–361.

Drentea, P. (2002). Retirement and mental health. *Journal of Aging and Health. 14*(2), 167–194.

Driedger, L. (2003). *Race and ethnicity: Finding identities and equalities* (2nd ed.). Don Mills, ON: Oxford University Press.

Driedger, L., & Chappell, N. (1987). *Aging and ethnicity: Toward an interface.* Toronto: Butterworths.

Driedger, L., & Halli, S. (2000). Racial integration: Theoretical options. 55–76. In L. Driedger & S. Halli (Eds.), *Race and racism.* Montreal and Kingston: McGill-Queens University Press.

Drolet, M. (1999). *The persistent gap: New evidence on the Canadian gender wage gap* (Catalogue No. 75F0002MIE-99008). Ottawa: Income Statistics Division, Statistics Canada.

Dubé, V. (2004). Sidelined in the labour market. *Perspective on labour and income, 16*(2), 25–31.

Duchesne, D. (2002). Seniors at work. *Perspective on labour and income, 14*(2), 33–43.

Duchesne, D. (2004). More seniors at work. *Perspective on labour and income, 16*(1), 55–67.

Dulude, L. (1981). *Pension reform with women in mind.* Ottawa: Canadian Advisory Council on the Status of Women.

Dumas, J., & Péron, Y. (1992). *Marriage and conjugal life in Canada.* (Catalogue No. 91-534E) Ottawa: Statistics Canada (p. 107).

Duncan, C., & Loretto, W. (2004) Never the right age? Gender and age-based discrimination in employment. *Gender Work and Organization, 11*(1), 95.

Dunlop, B.D., Rothman, M.B., Condon, K.M., Hebert, K.S., & Martinez, I.L. (2000). Elder abuse: Risk factors and use of case data to improve policy and practice. *Journal of Elder Abuse and Neglect, 12*, 95–122.

Dunn, J.R., & Dyck, I. (2000). Social determinants of health in Canada's immigrant population: Results from the national population health survey. *Social Science & Medicine, 51*, 1573–1593.

Dunning, R.W. (1959). *Social and economic change among the northern Ojibwa.* Toronto: University of Toronto Press.

Dupree, C.Y. (1998). The attitudes of black Americans toward advance directives. *Dissertation Abstracts International, 59*(04), 1347A.

Durin, J.V., & Passmore, R. (1967). *Energy, work and leisure.* London, UK: Heinemann.

Duxbury, L., & Higgins, C. (1994). Families in the economy. In M. Baker, (Ed.). *Canada's changing families: Challenges to public policy.* Ottawa: Vanier Institute of the Family.

Dwyer, D.S., & Mitchell, O.S. Health problems as determinants of retirement: Are self rated measures endogenous? *Journal of Health Economics, 18*(2), 173–193.

Eagly, A.H., & Chaiken, S. (1993). *The psychology of attitudes.* New York: Harcourt Brace Jovanovich.

Eakin, E. (2001). Promoting physical activity among middle-aged and older adults in health care settings. *Journal of Aging and Physical Activity, 9*(suppl.), S29–S37.

Eaves, L.J., Eysenck, H.J., & Martin, N.G. (1989). *Genes, culture, and personality: An empirical approach.* London, UK: Academic Press.

Eggebeen, D.J. (1992). Family structure and intergenerational exchanges. *Research on Aging, 14*, 427–447.

Ekerdt, D. (2004). Born to retire: The foreshortened life course. *The Gerontologist, 44*(1), 3–9.

Ekerdt, D.J., DeViney, S., & Kosloski, K. (1996). Profiling plans for retirement. *Journals of Gerontology: Series B: Psychological sciences and social sciences, 51*(Bn3): S140.

Ekerdt, D.J., Hackney, J., Kosloski, K., DeViney, S. (2001). Eddies in the stream: The prevalence of uncertain plans for retirement. *Journals of Gerontology, 56B*(3), S162–S170.

Ekerdt, D.J., Kosloski, K., & DeViney, S. (2000). The normative anticipation of retirement by older workers. *Research on Aging, 22*(1), 3–22.

Elder, G.H. Jr. (1974). *Children of the great depression: Social change in life experience.* Chicago: University of Chicago Press.

Elder, G.H. Jr. (1975). Age differentiation and the life course. *Annual Review of Sociology, 1*, 165–190.

Elder, G.H. Jr. (1978). Approaches to social change and the family. *American Journal of Sociology, 84*, S1–S38.

Elder, G.H. Jr. (Ed.). (1985). *Life course dynamics: Trajectories and transitions, 1968–1980.* Ithaca, NY: Cornell University Press.

Elder, G.H. Jr. (1987). War mobilization and the life course: A cohort of World War II veterans. *Sociological Forum, 2*, 449–472.

Elder, G.H. Jr. (1992). Models of the life course. *Contemporary Sociology, 21*, 632–635.

Elder, G.H. Jr. (1994). Time, human agency, and social change. *Social Psychology Quarterly, 57*, 4–15.

Elder, G.H. Jr. (2000). The life course. In E.F. Borgatta & R.J.V. Montgomery, (Eds.), *The encyclopedia of sociology, Vol. 3* (2nd ed., pp. 939–991). New York: Wiley.

Elder, G.H. Jr., & Caspi, A. (1990). Studying lives in a changing society: Sociological and personological explorations. In A.I. Rubin, R.A. Zucker, & S. Frank, (Eds.), *Studying persons and lives* (pp. 210–247). New York: Springer.

Ellerby, J.H., McKenzie, J., McKay, S., Gariépy, G.J., & Kaufert, J.M. (2000). Bioethics for clinicians: 18. Aboriginal cultures. *Canadian Medical Association Journal, 163*(7), 845–850.

Employment Equity Act, 1995, c. 44, s. 3.

Epp, J. (1986). *Achieving health for all: A framework for health promotion.* Ottawa: Health and Welfare Canada.

Epsing-Anderson, G. (1994). Welfare states and the economy. In N.J. Smelser & R. Swedberg (Eds.), *The handbook of economic sociology* (pp. 711–732). Princeton, NJ: Princeton University Press.

Erlandson, D.A., Harris, E.L., Skipper, B.L., & S.D. Allen. (1993). Doing naturalistic enquiry: A guide to new methods. Newbury Park, CA: Sage.

Estes, C.L. (1979). *The Aging Enterprise.* San Francisco: Jossey-Bass.

Estes, C.L. (1991). The new political economy of aging: Introduction and critique. In *Critical perspectives on aging: The political and moral economy of growing old* (pp. 19–36). New York: Baywood.

Estes, C.L. (1999). Critical gerontology and the new political economy of aging. In M. Minkler & C.L. Estes (Eds.), *Critical gerontology: Perspectives from political and moral economy* (pp. 17–35). Amityville, NY: Baywood.

Estes, C., Biggs, S., & Phillipson, C. (2003). *Social theory, social policy and ageing: A critical introduction.* Maidenhead, UK: Open University Press.

Estes, C.L., Gerard, L.E., Zones, J.S., & Swan, J.H. (1984). *Political economy, health and aging.* Boston: Little, Brown and Company.

Estes, C., Linkins, C.W., & Binney, E.A. (2001). Critical perspectives on aging. In C. Estes et al. (Eds.), *Social policy and aging: A critical perspective* (pp. 23–44). Thousand Oaks, CA: Sage.

Estes, C.L., Linkins, K.W., & Binney, E.A. (1996). The political economy of aging. In R.H. Binstock & L.K. George (Eds.), *Handbook of aging and the social sciences* (4th ed, pp. 346–361). San Diego, CA: Academic Press.

Estes, C.L. Mahakian, J.L., & Weitz, T.A. (2001). A political economy critique of "productive aging." In C.L. Estes and Associates, *Social policy and aging: A critical perspective.* Thousand Oaks, CA: Sage Publications.

Estes, C.L., Swan, J.H., & Gerard, L.E. (1984). Dominant and competing paradigms in gerontology: Towards a political economy of aging. In M. Minkler & C.L. Estes (Eds.), *Readings in the political economy of aging.* Farmingdale, NY: Baywood.

Evans, R.G. (1976). Does Canada have too many doctors? Why nobody loves an immigrant physician. *Canadian Public Policy, 2,* 47–160.

Evans, R.G. (1984). Strained mercy: The economics of Canadian health care. Toronto: Butterworths.

Evans, R.G. (1994). Health care as a threat to health: Defense, opulence, and the social environment. *Daedalus, 123*(4), 21–42.

Evans, R.G. (2001). Ideology, religion, and the WTO. In A. Ostry & K. Cardiff (Eds.), *Trading away health? Globalization and health policy* (pp. 6–10). Report from the 14th Annual Health Policy Conference of the Centre for Health Services and Policy Research. HPRU 2002:10D. Vancouver, B.C., November 9, page 6–10.

Evans, R.G., McGrail, K.M., Morgan, S.G., Barer, M.L., & Hertzman, C (2001). Apocalypse no: Population aging and the future of health care systems. *Canadian Journal on Aging, 20* (suppl. 1), 160–191.

Evans, R., & Stoddart, G. (1990). Producing health, consuming health care. *Social Science and Medicine, 31,* 1347–1363.

Eyles, J., Brimacombe, M., Chaulk, P., Stoddart, G., Pranger, T. & Moase, O. (2001). What determines health? To where should we shift resources? Attitudes towards the determinants of health among multiple stakeholder groups in Prince Edward Island, Canada. *Social Science and Medicine,* 53, 1611–1619.

Falcón, M., & Tucker, K.L. (2000). Prevalence and correlates of depressive symptoms among Hispanic elders in Massachusetts. *Journals of Gerontology: Social Sciences, 55B*(2), S108–S116.

Fast, J., & Da Pont, M. (1997). Changes in women's work continuity. *Canadian Social Trends, 46*(Autumn), 2–7.

Federal, Provincial, and Territorial Advisory Committee on Population Health. (1999). Statistics Canada, Ottawa, ON.

Feinberg, L.F., & Kelly, K.A. (1995). A well-deserved break: Respite programs offered by California's statewide system of caregiver resource centers. *The Gerontologist, 35*(5), 701–706.

Fellegi, I.P. (1988, Oct.). Can we afford an aging society? *Canadian Economic Observer,* 4.1–4.33.

Ferraro, K.F. (1997), (Ed.). *Gerontology: Perspectives and issues* (2nd ed.). New York York Springer.

Fiksenbaum, L.M., Greenglass, E.R., & Eaton, J. (2006). Perceived social support, hassles, and coping among the elderly. *Journal of Applied Gerontology, 25*(1), 17–30.

Fine, M. (1992). *Disruptive voices: The possibilities of feminist research.* Ann Arbor, MI: University of Michigan Press.

Finlayson, A. (1988). *Whose money is it anyway? The showdown on pensions.* Markham, ON: Viking.

Fischer, D.H. (1977). *Growing old in America.* New York: Oxford University Press.

Fischer. L.R., Rogne, L., Eustis, N.N. (1990). Support systems for the familyless elderly: Care without commitment. In J.F. Gubrium & A. Sankar, (Eds.), *The home care experience: Ethnography and policy.* Newbury Park, CA: Sage Publications.

Fisher, B.J. (1992). Successful aging and life satisfaction: A pilot study for conceptual clarification. *Journal of Aging Studies, 6,* 191–202.

Fitzgerald, J.M. (1988). Vivid memories and the reminiscence phenomenon: The role of a self-narrative. *Human Development, 31,* 260–270.

Fleras, A., & Elliot, J.L. (1992). *Multiculturalism in Canada: The challenge of diversity.* Scarborough, ON: Nelson Canada.

Flippen C., & Tienda, M. (2000). Pathways to retirement: Patterns of labour force participation and retirement: Some evidence on the role of pensions and social security in the 1970s and 1980s. *Journal of Labour Economics, 17*(4), 757–783.

Fluehr-Lobban, C. (2005). *Race and racism: An Introduction.* Lanham, MD: AltaMira Press.

Folts, W.E, Ide, B.A., Johnson, T.F., Crewe Solomon, J.C. (1995). *Aging well: A selected, annotated bibliography.* Westport, CT: Greenwood Press, 156.

Foot, D.K, with Stoffman, D. (1996). *Boom, bust and echo: How to profit from the coming demographic shift.* Toronto: Macfarlane Walter and Ross.

Forbes, W.F., Jackson, J.A., & Kraus, A.S. (1987) *Institutionalization of the elderly in Canada.* Toronto: Butterworths.

Ford, A.B., Haug, M.R., Roy, A.W., Jones, P.K., & Folmar, S.J. (1992). New cohorts of urban elders: Are they in trouble? *Journals of Gerontology, 47,* S297–S303.

Ford, D. & Nault, F. (1996). Changing fertility patterns, 1974 to 1994. *Health Reports, 8*(3), 39–46. (Catalogue No. 82-003). Ottawa: Statistics Canada.

Fortin, P. (1996). The Canadian fiscal problem: The macroeconomic connection. In L. Osberg & P. Fortin, (Eds.), *Unnecessary debts* (pp. 26–38). Toronto: James Lorimer.

Foster, C. (1996). *A Place called Heaven: The meaning of being Black in Canada.* Toronto: Harper Collins.

Foucault, M. (1972). *The archaeology of knowledge.* London, UK: Tavistock.

Fouquereau, E., Fernandez, A. Fonseca, A., Paul, M. & Uotinen, V. (2005). Perceptions of satisfaction with retirement: A comparison of six European Union countries. *Psychology and Aging, 20*(3), 524–528.

Fowler, F.J., Jr. (2001). *Survey research methods* (3rd ed.). Beverly Hills, CA: Sage.

Fox, R. (1991). Presentation to the Canadian Medical Association Conference on Challenges and Changes in the Care of the Elderly.

Fozard, J.L. (1990). Vision and hearing in aging. In J.E. Birren, & K.W. Schaie (Eds.), *Handbook of the psychology of aging* (3rd ed., pp. 150–171). San Diego, CA: Academic Press.

Fozard, J.L., & Gordon-Salant, S. (2001). Sensory and perceptual changes with aging. In J.E. Virren & K.W. Schaie (Eds.), *Handbook of the psychology of aging* (5th ed.). San Diego, CA: Academic Press.

Frayne, T. (1990). *The tales of an athletic supporter.* Toronto: McClelland & Stewart.

Frederick, J. & Fast, J. (1999, Autumn). Eldercare in Canada: Who does how much? *Canadian Social Trends.*

Frenken, H. (1991). Women and RRSPs. Perspectives on labour and income. Ottawa: Statistics Canada.

Frideres, J.S. (1994). The future of our past: Native elderly in Canadian society. In *Writings in gerontology 15.* Ottawa: National Advisory Council on Aging.

Fries, J.F. (1983). Compression of morbidity. *Milbank Memorial Fund Quarterly, 61,* 397–419.

Fries, J.F. (2003). Measuring and monitoring success in compressing morbidity. *Annals of Internal Medicine, 139,* 455–459.

Froggatt, K. (2001). Life and death in English nursing homes: Sequestration or transition? *Ageing and Society, 21*(3), 319–332.

Fronstin, P. (1999). Retirement patterns and employees' benefits: Do benefits matter? *The Gerontologist, 39*(1): 37–47.

Fry, C.L. (2003). The life course as a cultural construct. In R.A. Settersten (Ed.), *Invitation to the life course: Toward new understandings of later life* (pp. 269–295). Amityville, NY: Baywood.

Fuller-Thomson, E. (2005). Canadian First Nations grandparents raising grandchildren: A portrait in resilience. *International Journal of Aging and Human Development, 60*(4), 331–342.

Fulton, G., & Metress, E. (1995). *Perspectives on death and dying.* Boston: Jones and Bartlett.

Fyke, K. (2001). Caring for medicare. Sustaining a quality system. Commission on Medicare. Government of Saskatchewan.

Galarneau, D. & Sturrock, J. (1997). Family income after separation. *Perspectives on Labour and Income, 9*(2), 18–28. (Catalogue No. 75-001-XPE). Ottawa: Statistics Canada.

Gall, T.L, Evans, D.R., & Howard, J. (2000). Preretirement expectations and the quality of life of male retirees in later retirement. *Canadian Journal of Behavioural Science, 32*(3), 187–197.

Gallo, J., Rabins, P., & Hopkins, J. (1999). Depression without sadness: Alternative presentations of depression in late life. *American Family Physician, 60,* 820–826.

Galton, F. (1883). *Inquiries into human faculty and its development.* New York: Macmillan.

Gardyn, R. (2000). Retirement redefined. *American Demographics, 22*(11), 52–57.

Garner, J.D. (1999). *Fundamentals of feminist gerontology.* New York: Haworth Press.

Gee, E.M. (1980). Population. In R.B. Hagedorn, (Ed.). *Sociology* (pp. 191–235). Toronto: Holt, Rinehart and Winston of Canada.

Gee, E.M. (1986). The life course of Canadian women: An historical and demographic analysis. *Social Indicators Research, 18,* 263–283.

Gee, E.M. (1990). Demographic change and intergenerational relations in Canadian families: Findings and social policy implications. *Canadian Public Policy, XVI,* 191–199.

Gee, E.M. (1995). Contemporary diversities. In N. Mandell & A. Duffy, (Eds.), *Canadian families: Diversity, conflict and change* (pp. 79–109). Toronto: Harcourt Brace.

Gee, E.M. (1996, October). *Aging and immigration in Canada: The elderly foreign-born population.* Paper presented at the meeting of the National Symposium on Immigration and Integration. Winnipeg: University of Manitoba.

Gee, E. (1997a). Editorial: Policy and research on aging: Connections and conundrums. *Canadian Public Policy, 23,* i-viii.

Gee, E.M. (1997b). The living arrangements of Chinese Canadian elders: The effect of demographic, economic, and cultural variables. Paper presented at the annual meeting of the American Sociological Association, Toronto, ON, August.

Gee, E. M. (1999). Ethnic identity among foreign-born Chinese Canadian elders. *Canadian Journal on Aging. 18*(4) 415–429.

Gee, E.M. (2000). Population and politics: Voodoo demography, population aging, and Canadian social policy. In E.M. Gee & G.M. Gutman, (Eds.), *The overselling of population aging: Apocalyptic demography, intergenerational challenges, and social policy* (pp. 5–25). Toronto: Oxford University Press.

Gee, E., & Gutman, G. (1995). (Eds). *Rethinking retirement.* Vancouver, BC: Gerontology Research Centre, Simon Fraser University.

Gee, E.M., & Gutman, G.M. (2000). *The overselling of population aging. Apocalyptic demography, intergenerational challenges and social policy.* Don Mills, ON: Oxford University Press.

Gee, E.M. & Kimball, M.M. (1987). *Women and aging.* Toronto: Butterworths.

Gee, E.M., Kobayashi, K.M., & Prus, S.G. (2004). Examining the healthy immigrant effect in mid- to later life: Findings from the Canadian Community Health Survey. *Canadian Journal on Aging* (suppl.), S55–S63.

Gee, E.M., Mitchell, B.A., & Wister, A.V. (1995). Returning to the "parental nest": Exploring a changing Canadian life course. *Canadian Studies in Population, 22,* 121–144.

Gee, E., M., Mitchell, B.A., & Wister, A.V. (2001). Homeleaving trajectories in Canada: Exploring cultural and gendered dimensions. Paper presented at a joint session at the annual meetings of the Canadian Sociology and Anthropology Association and the Canadian Population Society, Laval University, QB, May.

Gelfand, D. (1994). *Aging and ethnicity: Knowledge and services.* New York: Springer.

Gelfand, D. (2003). *Aging and ethnicity: Knowledge and services.* (2nd ed.). New York: Springer.

General Accounting Office. (1991). *Canadian health insurance: Lessons for the United States.* Gaithersburg, MD: U.S. General Accounting Office.

George, L.K. (1990). Social structure, social processes, and social-psychological states. In R.H. Binstock & L.K. George, (Eds.), *Aging and the social sciences* (3rd ed., pp. 186–204). San Diego, CA: Academic Press, Inc.

George, L.K., & Gwyther, L.P. (1986). Caregiver well-being: A multidimensional examination of family caregivers of demented adults. *The Gerontologist, 26,* 253–259.

Gescheider, G.A. (1997). *Psychophysics: The fundamentals.* Mahwah, NJ: Erlbaum.

Gfellner, B.M. (1982). *Case study analysis: A field placement program in the study of aging.* Paper presented at the Canadian Association on Gerontology 11th Annual Scientific and Educational Meeting, Winnipeg, MB.

Giarrusso, R., Stallings, M., Bengtson, V.L., Rossi, A.S., & Marshall, V.W. (1995). "Intergenerational stake" hypothesis revisited: Parent-child differences in perceptions of relationships 20 years later. In V.L. Bengtson, K.W. Schaie, & L. Burton, (Eds.), *Adult intergenerational relations: Effects of societal change* (pp. 227–296). New York: Springer.

Giddens, A. (1991). *Modernity and Self-Identity.* Cambridge: Polity.

Giddens, A. (1994). Living in a post-traditional society. In U. Beck, A. Giddens, & S. Lash (Eds.), *Reflexive Modernization* (pp. 56–109). Stanford, CA: Stanford University Press.

Giele J.Z., & Elder Jr., G.H. (Eds.). (1998). *Methods of life course research: Qualitative and quantitative approaches.* Thousand Oaks, CA: Sage Publications.

Gilbert, S., & Bélanger, A. (2001). Impact of causes of death on life expectancy at higher ages from 1951 to 1996. In A. Bélanger, Y. Carriere, & S. Gilbert (Eds.), *Report on the Demographic Situation in Canada, 2000.* Ottawa: Statistics Canada: 137–151.

Gillin, T. & Klassen, T. (2005). The shifting judicial foundation of legalized age discrimination. In T. Gillin, D. MacGregor, & T. Klassen (Eds.), *Time's up! Mandatory retirement in Canada.* Toronto: James Lorimer & Co. Ltd.

Ginn, J., Street, D., & Arber, S. (Eds.), (2001). *Women, work and pensions: International issues and prospects.* Buckingham, UK: Open University Press.

Gladstone, J.W. (1989). Grandmother–grandchild contact: The mediating influence of the middle generation following marriage breakdown and remarriage. *Canadian Journal on Aging, 8,* 355–365.

Glaser, B., & Strauss, A. (1967). *The discovery of grounded theory.* Chicago: Aldine.

Glazer, N., & Moynihan, D.P. (1963). *Beyond the Melting Pot.* Cambridge, MA: M.I.T. Press.

The Globe (1905, March 2). Link took chloroform. p. 7.

Globe and Mail. (1995, March 11). *Toward a renewed pension system.* p. D6.

Godin, G., Jobin, J., & Bouillon, J. (1986). Assessment of leisure time exercise behavior by self-report: A concurrent validity study. *Canadian Journal of Public Health, 77,* 359–362.

Goffaux, J., Friesinge, G.C., Lambert, W., Shroyer, L.W., Moritz, T.E., McCarthy, et al. E. (2005). Biological age—a concept whose time has come: A preliminary study. *Southern Medical Journal, 98*(10), 985–993.

Goffman, E. (1961). Asylums: Essays on the social situation of mental patients and other inmates. Garden City, NY: Anchor.

Goldscheider, F.K., & Lawton, L. (1998). Family experiences and the erosion of support for intergenerational co-residence. *Journal of Marriage and the Family, 60,* 623–632.

Gordon, J., & Neal, R. (1997). Voluntary non-profit organizations: A new research agenda. *Society/Société* (Newsletter of the Canadian Sociology and Anthropology Association), *21*(1), 15–19.

Gottlieb, B.H. (1995, February). *Impact of day programs on family caregivers of persons with dementia*. Report by the Gerontology Research Centre & Psychology Department, University of Guelph, Guelph, ON.

Government of Canada. (1970). *Income security and social services: Government of Canada working paper on the Constitution*. Ottawa: Queen's Printer.

Government of Canada. 1996a. *Profiles: Hong Kong*. C&I-110-06-96 (Hong Kong).

Government of Canada. 1996b. *Profiles: People's Republic of China*. C&I-110-06-96 (China).

Government of Canada. (2005). *Canada's performance: The government of Canada's contribution (annex 3)* (No. BT1-10/2005). Ottawa: Treasury Board of Canada Secretariat.

Gowan, M.A. (1998). Preliminary investigation of factors affecting appraisals of the decision to take early retirement. *Journal of Employment Counseling, 35*, 124–140.

Graebner, W. (1980). *A history of retirement*. New Haven: Yale University Press.

Graff, L. (1991). *Volunteer for the health of it*. Etobicoke, ON: Volunteer Ontario.

Green, K. (1985). Identification of the facets of self-health management. *Evaluation and the Health Professions, 8*, 323–338.

Gregoire, T., Kilty, K., & Richardson, V. (2002). Gender and racial inequalities in retirement resources. *Journal of Women and Aging. 14*(3/4), 25–39.

Grindstaff, C.F. (1996). The costs of having a first child for women aged 33–38, Canada 1991. *Sex Roles, 35*, 137–151.

Grindstaff, C.F., & Trovato, F. (1990). Junior partners: Women's contribution to family income in Canada. *Social Indicators Research, 22*, 229–253.

Grundy, E. (1999). *Living arrangements and the health of older persons in developed countries*. New York: United Nations Secretariat, Department of Social and Economic Affairs, Population Division.

Guba, E.G., & Lincoln, Y.S. (2005). Paradigmatic controversies, contradictions, and emerging confluences. In N. Denzin & Y. Lincoln (Eds.), *Handbook of qualitative research* (3rd ed., pp. 191–215). Thousand Oaks, CA: Sage Publications.

Guberman, N., & Mahue, P. (2003/2004). Beyond cultural sensitivity: Universal issues in caregiving. *Generations, 27*(4), 39–43.

Gubrium, J.F., & Holstein, J.A. (Eds.) (2000). *Aging and everyday life*. Oxford, UK: Blackwell.

Gubrium, J.F., & Holstein, J.A. (Eds). (2003). *Ways of aging*. Oxford, UK: Blackwell.

Guillemard, A.M. (1980). *La vieillesse et l'état*. Paris, France: Presses Universitaires de France.

Guillemard, A.M. (2000). *Aging and the welfare state crisis*. Newark, NJ: University of Delaware Press.

Guillemard, A.M., & Rein, M. (1993). Comparative patterns of retirement: Recent trends in developed societies. *Annual Review of Sociology, 19*, 469–503.

Gum, A. (2004) Older adults with cognitive impairment and informed consent for research: Review of ethical issues and empirical findings. *Journal of Mental Health and Aging. 10*(4), 257–268.

Gunderson, M. (1998). *Flexible retirement as an alternative to 65 and out*. C.D. Howe Institute, Canada.

Guruge, S., McGilton, K., Yetman, L., Campbell, H., Librado, R., Bloch, L., et al. (2005). Unit manager's role with family members of clients in complex continuing care settings: An untold story. *Canadian Journal on Aging, 24*(2), 127–138.

Gurung, R., Taylor, S., & Seeman, S. (2003). Accounting for changes in social support among married older adults: Insights from the MacArthur Studies of Successful Aging. *Psychology and Aging, 18(3)*, 487–496.

Guttman, D. (1994). *Reclaimed powers: Men and women in later life* (2nd ed.). Evanston, IL: Northwestern University Press.

Guttman, L. (1941). The qualification of a class of attributes: A theory and method of scale construction. In P. Horst, (Ed.)., The prediction of personal adjustment. Bulletin No. 48 (pp. 319–348). New York: Social Science Research Council.

Guyatt, G.H., Tugwell, P.X., Feeny, D.H., Haynes, R.B., & Drummond, M. (1986). A framework for clinical evaluation of diagnostic technologies. *Canadian Medical Association Journal, 134*(6), 587–594.

Guyer, B., Freedman, M.A., Strobino, D.M., & Sondik, E.J. (2000). Annual summary of vital statistics: Trends in the health of Americans during the 20th century. *Pediatrics, 106*, 1307–1317.

Haber, C., & Gratton, B. (1994). *Old age and the search for security: An American social history*. Bloomington, IN and Indianapolis, IN: Indiana University Press.

Habermas, J. (1972). *Knowledge and human interests*. London, UK: Heinemann.

Hadjistavropoulos, T. (Ed.) (2001). Pain and aging (Special Issue). *Pain Research and Management, 6*(3), 113–168.

Hagestad, G.O. (1985). Continuity and connectedness. In V.L. Bengtson & J.F. Robertson (Eds.), *Grandparenthood* (pp. 31–48). Beverly Hills, CA: Sage.

Hagestad, G.O. (1990). Social perspectives on the life course. In R.H. Binstock & L.K. George (Eds.), *Handbook of aging and the social sciences* (3rd ed., pp. 151–168). San Diego, CA: Academic Press.

Hagestad, G.O. & Dannefer, D. (2001). Concepts and theories of aging: Beyond microfication in social science approaches. In R.H. Binstock & L.K. George (Eds.), *Handbook of aging and the social sciences* (5th ed., pp. 3–21). San Diego, CA: Academic Press.

Hagestad, G. & Uhlenberg, P. (2005). The social separation of old and young: A root of ageism. *Journal of Social Issues, 61*, 343–360.

Haldemann, V., & Lévy, R. (1995). Oecuménisme méthodologique et dialogue entre paradigms. *Canadian Journal on Aging, 14*(suppl.), 37–51.

Hall, D.R. (1996). Marriage as a pure relationship: Exploring the link between premarital cohabitation and divorce in Canada. *Journal of Comparative Family Studies, 27*, 1–12.

Hall, D.R., & Zhao, J.Z. (1995). Cohabitation and divorce in Canada: Testing the selectivity hypothesis. *Journal of Marriage and the Family, 57*, 421–427.

Hamil-Luker, J. (2001). The prospects of age war: Inequality between (and within) age groups. *Social Science Research, 30*, 386–400.

Hammersley, M. (1992). *What's wrong with ethnography? Methodological explorations.* London, UK: Routledge.

Han, S.-K., & Moen, S. (1999). Clocking out: Temporal patterning of retirement. *American Journal of Sociology,* 105:191–236.

Hanawalt, B.A. (1986). *The ties that bound: Peasant families in medieval England.* New York: Oxford University Press.

Hanson, E.J., Danis, M., & Garrett, J. (1997). What is wrong with end-of-life care? Opinions of bereaved family members. *Journal of the American Geriatrics Society, 45*(11), 1339–1344.

Hanson, S.M., & Sauer, W.J. (1985). Children and their elderly parents. In W.J. Sauer & R.T. Coward, (Eds.), *Social support networks and the care of the elderly.* New York: Springer.

Hansson, R.O., DeKoekkoek, P.D., Neece, W.M., & Patterson, D.W. (1997). Successful aging at work: Annual review, 1992–1996: The older worker and transitions to retirement. *Journal of Vocational Behaviour, 51*, 202–233.

Harada, M. (1994). Early and later life sport participation patterns among the active elderly in Japan. *Journal of Aging and Physical Activity, 2*, 105–114.

Harbison, J. (1999). Models of intervention of elder abuse and neglect: A Canadian perspective on ageism, participation and empowerment. *Journal of Elder Abuse and Neglect, 10* (3/4), 1–17.

Harding, S.G. (2004). *The feminist standpoint theory reader: Intellectual and political controversies.* New York: Routledge.

Hardy, M.A., & Quadagno, J. (1995). Satisfaction with early retirement: Making choices in the auto industry. *Journals of Gerontology: Social Sciences, 5OB,* S217–S228.

Hareven, T.K. (1992). Family and generation relations in the later years: A historical perspective. *Generations, 16*, 7–12.

Harkins, S.W., Price, D.D., & Martelli, M. (1986). Effects of age on pain perception. *Journals of Gerontology, 41*, 58–63.

Harris, D., & Guten, S. (1979). Health protective behavior: An exploratory study. *Journal of Health and Social Behavior, 20*, 17–29.

Harris, P.B., & Bichler, J. (1997). *Men giving care: Reflections of husbands and sons.* New York: Garland Publishing.

Hasher, L. Goldstein, D., & May, C. (2005). It's about time: Circadian rhythms, memory and aging. In C. Izawa & N. Ohta (Eds.), *Human learning and memory: Advances in theory and application.* Kansas: Lawrence Erlbaum Associates.

Hasher, L., & Zacks, R.T. (1979). Automatic and effortful processes in memory. *Journal of Experimental Psychology: General, 108*, 356–388.

Hasselkus, B.R. (1988). Meaning in family caregiving: Perspectives on caregiver/professional relationships. *The Gerontologist, 28*(5), 686–691.

Havens, B. (1995). Overview of longitudinal research on aging. *Canadian Journal on Aging, 14*(suppl.), 119–134.

Havens, B. (1997). *Annotated bibliography of papers, articles & other documents resulting from the Aging in Manitoba 1971, 1976, 1983, 1990, 1996 Cross-Sectional & Panel Studies.* Compiled by M.K. Hall.

Havens, B. (2001, November). *Healthy aging: From cell to society.* Planning workshop for the Canadian Longitudinal Study on Aging. Canadian Institute for Healthy Aging, Ottawa, ON.

Havens, B. & Chappell, N. (1983). Triple jeopardy: Age, sex and ethnicity. *Canadian Ethnic Studies, 15*(3): 119–132.

Havighurst, R.J. (1961) Successful aging. *The Gerontologist, 1*, 8–13.

Havighurst, R., & Albrecht, R. (1953). *Older people*: New York: Longmans, Green.

Hawley, K.S., Garrity A.W., & Cherry, K.E. (2005). Knowledge of normal versus pathological memory aging among police officers. *Educational Gerontology, 31*(1), 1–18.

Hay, D.I. (1994). Social status and health status: Does money buy health? In B.S. Bolaria & R. Bolaria, (Eds.), *Racial minorities, medicine and health* (pp. 9–51). Nova Scotia & Saskatchewan: Fernwood Publishers and University of Saskatchewan.

Hayes, M.V., & Dunn, J.R. (1998). *Population health in Canada: A systematic review.* Ottawa: Canadian Policy Research Networks, CPRN study H01.

Hayward, M.D., Crimmins, E.M., & Saito, Y. (1998). Cause of death and active life expectancy in the older population of the United States. *Journal of Aging and Health, 10*, 192–213.

Hayward, M.D., Freidman, S., & Chen, H. (1998). Career trajectories and older men's retirement. *The Journals of Gerontology: Series B: Psychological Sciences and Social Sciences, 53B*(2), S91–Sl03.

He, Y., Colantonio, A., & Marshall, V. (2006). The relationship between career instability and health condition in older workers: A longitudinal analysis. In Stone, L. (Editor). *The New Frontiers of Research on Retirement.* (pp. 321–342). (Catalogue No. 75-511-XPE). Ottawa: Minister of Industry.

Heady, B. & Wearing, A. (1988). The sense of relative superiority—central to well-being. *Social Indicators Research, 20,* 497–517.

Health Canada. (1996.) *Report on the 1994–1995 National Population Health Survey (NPHS): Nutrition Component.* Unpublished report by the Nutrition Programs Unit, 1996. Ottawa, ON.

Health Canada. (1998a). *Reaching out: A guide to communicating with Aboriginal Seniors.* Ottawa: Minister of Public Works and Government Services, Canada. Catalogue No. H88-3/20-1998E.

Health Canada. (1998b). *Canada's seniors at a glance.* Ottawa: Canadian Council on Social Development for the Division of Aging and Seniors, Health Canada. Retrieved May 27, 2002 from http://www.hc-sc.gc.ca/seniors-aines/pubs/poster/seniors/page5e.htm.

Health Canada. (1999). *Canadian research on immigration health: An overview.* Ottawa: Minister of Public Works and Government Services. Catalogue No. H21-149/1999E.

Health Canada. (2000). Retrieved May 28, 2002 from http://www.hc-sc.gc.ca/seniors-aines/pubs/factoids/en/no41.htm.

Health Canada (2002). *Diabetes in Canada.* (2nd ed.). Retrieved May 4, 2006 from http://www.phac-aspc.gc.ca/publicat/dic-dac2/english/10intro_e.html.

Health Canada. (2004). Aboriginal health. *Healthy Canadians: Report on comparable health indicators, 2004.* Ottawa, ON.

Health & Welfare Canada. (1987). *Aging: Shifting the emphasis.* Working paper, Health Services and Promotion Branch, Ottawa, ON.

Health & Welfare Canada, Seniors Independence Program. (1990). *Today's projects enhancing the future, 1988–1989, 1989–1990* (Catalogue No. H7430/1990E). Ottawa: Supply and Services Canada.

Helson, R., & Wink, P. (1992). Personality change in women from the early 40s to the early 50s. *Psychology and Aging, 7,* 46–55.

Hendricks, J. (1996). The search for new solutions. *The Gerontologist, 36,* 141–144.

Henkens, K. (1999). Retirement intentions and spousal support: A multifactor approach. *Journals of Gerontology: Social Sciences, 54B,* 863–874.

Henretta, J. (2003). The life-course perspective on work and retirement. In R. Stettersten, Jr. (Ed.), *Invitation to the life course: Toward new understandings of later life* (pp. 85–106). Amityville, NY: Baywood Publishing.

Hepworth, M. (2005). Culture and decline: Age awareness and life review. *Ageing and Society, 25(5),* 785–793.

Herdt, G., & de Vries, B. (2004). *Gay and lesbian aging.* New York: Springer.

Heron, A., & Chown, S. (1967). *Age and function.* Boston, MA: Little Brown.

Hertzog, C., Dixon, R.A., & Hultsch, D.F. (1990). Metamemory in adulthood: Differentiating knowledge, belief, and behavior. In T. M. Hess, (Ed.), *Aging and cognition: Knowledge organization and utilization.* Amsterdam: Elsevier.

Herzog, A. R., & Kulka, R. A. (1989). Telephone and mail surveys with older populations: A methodological overview. Sampling rare population. In M. Powell Lawton & A.R. Herzog, (Eds.), *Special research methods for gerontology* (pp. 63–90). Amityville, NY: Baywood.

Hess, B.B., & Soldo, B.J. (1985). Husband and wife networks. In W.J. Sauer & R.T. Coward, (Eds.), *Social support networks and the care of the elderly.* New York: Springer.

Heyland, D.K, Tranmer, J., Feldman, & Stewart, D. (2000). End-of-life decision making in the seriously ill hospitalized patient: An organizing framework and results of a preliminary study. *Journal of Palliative Care, 16*(suppl.), 31–39.

Hibbard, J.H. (1995) Women's employment history and their post-retirement health and resources. *Journal of Women and Aging, 7*(3), 43–54.

Hickey, T., & Stilwell, D.L. (1992). Chronic illness and aging: A personal contextual model of age-related changes in health status. *Educational Gerontology, 18,* 1–15.

Hicks, P. (2002). *New policy research on the population aging and life-course flexibility.* Ottawa: Policy Research Initiative. Retrieved July 31, 2006 from http://policyresearch.gc.ca/page.asp?pagenm=v6n2_art_02.

Hill, J.B., & Amuwo, S.A. (1998). Understanding elder abuse and neglect. In N.A. Jackson & & G.C. Oates (Eds.), *Violence in intimate relationships: Examining sociological and psychological issues* (pp. 195–216). Boston, MA: Butterworth-Heinemann.

Himes, C.L., & Reidy, E.B. (2000). The role of friends in caregiving. *Research on Aging, 22*(4), 315–336.

Hirdes, J.P., & Brown, K.S. (1994). The statistical analysis of event histories in longitudinal studies of aging. *Canadian Journal on Aging, 13*(3), 332–352.

Hirdes, J.P., & Forbes, W.F. (1993). Factors associated with the maintenance of good self-rated health. *Journal of Aging and Health, 5*(1) 101–122.

Hirdes, J.P., Fries, B.E., Morris, J.N., Steel, R.K., LaBine, S., Beaulne, P., et al. (2000). Integrated health information systems based on the RAI/MDS series of instruments. *Hospital Management Forum, 12,* 30–40.

Hirdes, J.P., Zimmerman, D.R., Hallman K.G., & Soucie, P. (1998). Use of the MDS quality indicators to assess quality of care in institutional settings. *Canadian Journal of Quality Health Care, 14,* 5–11.

Ho, B., Friedland, J., Rappolt, S., & Noh, S. (2003). Caregiving for relatives with Alzheimer's disease:

Feelings of Chinese-Canadian women. *Journal of Aging Studies, 17,* 301–321.

Hochschild, A. (1975). Disengagement theory: A critique and proposal. *American Sociological Review, 40,* 553–569.

Hofer, S.M., Sliwinski M.J., & Flaherty, B.P. (2002). Understanding ageing: Further commentary on the limitations of cross-sectional designs for ageing research. *Gerontology, 48,* 22–29.

Hogan, D.B., MacKnight, C., & Bergman, H. (2003). Models, definitions, and criteria of frailty. *Aging Clinical and Experimental Research, 15* (suppl. 3): 3–29.

Holden, K.C. (1988). Poverty and living arrangements among older women: Are changes in economic well-being underestimated? *Journals of Gerontology, 43,* S22–S27.

Hollander, M.J. (2001). *Final report on the comparative cost analysis of home care and residential care services.* A report prepared for the Health Transition Fund, Health Canada.

Hollander, M., & Chappell, N.L. (2002). *Final report of the National Evaluation of the Cost Effectiveness of Home Care.* Prepared for the Health Transition Fund, Health Canada.

Hollander, M.J., Chappell, N.L., Prince, M.J., & Shapiro, E. (2005). *Key policy issues for the frail elderly.* Unpublished paper for the Canadian Initiative on Frailty and Aging.

Holroyd, E. (2001). Hong Kong Chinese daughters' intergenerational caregiving obligations: A cultural model approach. *Social Science and Medicine, 53,* 1125–1134.

Holstein, M. (1992). Productive aging: Troubling implications. In M. Minkler & C.L. Estes (Eds.), *Critical gerontology: Perspectives from political and moral economy* (pp. 359–373). Amityville, NY: Baywood.

Homans, G.F. (1961). *Social behavior: Its elementary forms.* New York: Harcourt Brace Jovanovich.

Honeyman, M. (1991). Challenges and changes in the care of the elderly. Ottawa: Canadian Medical Association.

Hong, Y., & Liu, W.T. (2000). The social psychological perspective of elderly care. In William T. Liu & Hal Kendig (Eds.), *Who should care for the elderly: An East-West value divide* (pp. 165–182). Singapore: Singapore University Press, National University of Singapore, and World Scientific Publishing.

Hooyman, N. (1990). Women as caregivers of the elderly: Social implications for social welfare policy and practice. In D.E. Biegel & A. Blum, (Eds.), *Aging and caregiving—Theory, research and policy* (pp. 221–241). Newbury Park, CA: Sage Publications Inc.

Hooyman, N. & Kiyak, H. (2005). *Social gerontology: A multidisciplinary perspective* (7th ed.).Boston: Allyn & Bacon.

Hopp, F.P., & Duffy, S.A. (2000). Racial variations in end-of-life care. *Journal of the American Geriatrics Society, 48*(6), 658–663.

Horn, J.L. (1982). The theory of fluid and crystallized intelligence in relation to concepts of cognitive psychology and aging in adulthood. In F.I.M. Craik & S. Trehub (Eds.), *Aging and cognitive processes* (Vol. 8). New York: Plenum.

Horowitz, A. (1981). *Sons and daughters as caregivers to older parents: Differences in role performance and consequences.* Paper presented at the annual meeting of the Gerontological Society of America, Toronto, ON.

Hou, F., & Omwanda, L. (1997). A multilevel analysis of the connection between female labour force participation and divorce in Canada, 1931-1991. *International Journal of Comparative Sociology, 38,* 271–288.

House, J.S., & Kahn, R.L. (1985). Measures and concepts of social support. In S. Cohen & S.L. Syme, (Eds.), *Social support and health.* Orlando, FL: Academic Press.

House of Commons Debate (1921, Feb 14). *House of Commons Debates of the Dominion of Canada. Fifth Session—Thirteenth Parliament.* Ottawa: King's Printer.

Hovland, C.I. (1959). Reconciling conflicting results derived from experimental and survey studies of attitude change. *American Psychologist, 14,* 8–17.

Hsu, H.-C., Lew-Ting, C.-Y., & Wu, S.-C. (2001). Age, period and cohort effects on the attitude toward supporting parents in Taiwan. *The Gerontologist, 41*(6), 742–750.

Hudson, M.F. (1991). Elder mistreatment: A taxonomy with definitions by Delphi. *Journal of Elder Abuse and Neglect, 3,* 1–20.

Hudson, M.F., Armachain, W.D., Beasley, C.M., & Carlson, J.R. (1998). Elder abuse: Two Native American views. *Gerontologist, 38*(5), 538–548.

Hudson, M.F., & Carlson, J.R. (1998). Elder abuse: Expert and public perspectives on its meaning. *Journal of Elder Abuse and Neglect, 9,* 77–97.

Hughes, S.L., Giobbie-Hurder, A., Weaver, F.M., Kubal, J.D., & Henderson, W. (1999) Relationship between caregiver burden and health-related quality of life. *The Gerontologist, 39*(5), 534–545.

Hultsch, D.F. (1971). Adult age differences in free classification and free recall. *Developmental Psychology, 4,* 338–342.

Hultsch, D.F., Hammer, M., & Small, B.J. (1993). Age differences in cognitive performance in later life: Relationships to self-reported health and activity life style. *Journals of Gerontology: Psychological Sciences, 48,* P1–P11.

Hum, D., & Simpson, W. (2002). Disability onset among aging Canadians: Evidence from panel data. *Canadian Journal on Aging, 21*(1), 117–136.

Hunter, K.I., & Linn, M.W. (1980). Psychosocial differences between elderly volunteers and non-volunteers. *International Journal of Aging and Human Development, 12*(3), 205–213.

Hurd, M. & Macdonald, M. (2001*). Beyond coping: Widows reinventing their lives.* Halifax, NS: Pear Press.

Hurley, A.C., Volicer, L., & Mahoney, E.K. (2001). Comfort in older adults at the end of life. In M.P. Lawton (Ed.), *Annual review of gerontology and geriatrics: Vol. 20. Focus on the end of life: Scientific and social issues* (pp.120–143). New York: Springer.

Hutchens, R. (1999). Social Security benefits and employer behaviour: Evaluating Social Security early retirement benefits as a form of unemployment insurance. *International Economic Review, 40*(3): 659–678.

Hyde, M., Ferries, J., Higgs, P., Mein, G. & Nazroo, J. (2004). The effects of pre-retirement factors and retirement route on circumstances in retirement: Findings from the Whitehall II Study. *Ageing and Society, 24,* 279–296.

Idler, E.L., Stanislav, V.K., & Hayes, J.C. (2001). Patterns of religious practice and belief in the last year of life. *Journals of Gerontology: Social Sciences, 56B*(6), S326–S334.

Ikels, C. (1990). Resolution of intergenerational conflict: Perspectives of elders and their family members. *Modern China, 16*(4), 379–406.

Illich, I. (1976). *Limits to medicine. Medical nemesis: The expropriation of health.* London, UK: Marion Boyars Publishers.

Isajiw, W.W. (1999). *Understanding diversity: Ethnicity and race in the Canadian context.* Toronto: Thompson.

Jacob, A.G. (1994). Social integration of Salvadoran refugees. *Social Work. Journal of the National Association of Social Workers, 39*(3), 307–312.

Jacobson, S. (1995). Overselling depression to the old folks. *Atlantic Monthly, 275*(4), 46–49.

Jacoby, S. (1999). Great sex: What's age got to do with it? Special report: The 1999 AARP/Modern Maturity survey on sexual attitudes and behavior. *Modern Maturity,* special report.

James, C.E. (2003). *Seeing ourselves* (3rd ed.). Toronto: Thompson.

James, W. (1890). *Principles of psychology.* New York: Henry Holt.

Janevic, M.R., & Connell, C.M. (2001). Racial, ethnic, and cultural differences in the dementia caregiving experience: Recent findings. *The Gerontologist, 41*(3), 334–347.

Jayachandran, J. (2000). Contributions of socioeconomic, sociopsychological and biological factors to fertility differentials in Canada. *Canadian Studies in Population, 27,* 329–354.

Jerant, A.F., Franks, P., Jackson, J.E., & Doescher, M.P. (2004). Age-related disparities in cancer screening: Analysis of 2001 Behavioral Risk Factor Surveillance System data. *Annals of Family Medicine, 2*(5), 481–487.

Jett, K.F. (2006). Mind-loss in the African American community: Dementia as a normal part of aging. *Journal of Aging Studies, 20*(1), 1–10.

Jimenez, M. (1987). *Changing faces of madness: Early American attitudes and treatment of the insane.* Hanover and London: University Press of New England.

Johnson, C.L., & Catalano, D.H. (1981). Childless elderly and their family supports. *The Gerontologist, 21,* 610–618.

Johnson, R. W., & Neumark, D. (1997). Age discrimination, job separations, and employment status of older workers: Evidence from self-reports. *Journal of Human Resources, 32*(4), 779–811.

Johnson, W. (2006). *The challenge of diversity.* Montreal: Black Rose Books.

Joiner, T.E. Jr. (1996). A confirmatory factor-analytic investigation of the tripartite model of depression and anxiety in college students. *Cognitive Therapy and Research, 20*(5), 521–539.

Judge, K., Mulligan, J. A., & Benzeval, M. (1998). Income inequality and population health. *Social Science and Medicine, 46*(4–5), 567–579.

Jutras, S. & Veilleux, F. (1991). Informal caregiving: Correlates of perceived burden. *Canadian Journal on Aging, 10*(1), 40–55.

Kafka, G.J., & Kozma, A. (2002) The construct validity of Ryff's Scales of Psychological Well-Being (SPWB) and their relationship to measures of subjective well-being. *Social Indicators Research, 57,* 171–190.

Kamo, Y., & Zhou, M. (1994). Living arrangements of elderly Chinese and Japanese in the United States. *Journal of Marriage and the Family, 56,* 544–558.

Kandrack, M.-A., Grant, K., & Segall, A. (1991). Gender differences in health related behaviour: Some unanswered questions. *Social Science and Medicine, 32,* 579–590.

Kane, M.N. (2004). Ageism and intervention: Do social work students believe a person should be treated differently because of age? *Educational Gerontology: An International Journal of Research and Practice, 30*(9), 767–784.

Kane, R.L., Evans, J.G., & MacFayden, D. (1990). *Improving the health of older people: A world view.* World Health Organization Report. Geneva: WHO.

Kaplan, R.M., & Schneider, D.L. (2001). Medical decision making toward the end of life: Ethical, economic, and health policy implications. In M.P. Lawton (Ed.), *Annual review of gerontology and geriatrics: Vol. 20. Focus on the end of life: Scientific and social issues* (pp. 39–63). New York: Springer.

Kapsalis, C. & Tourigny, P. (2005). Duration of nonstandard employment. *Perspectives on Labour and Income, 17*(1), 31–39. Catalogue No. 75–001–XPE.

Karademas, E.C. (2006). Self-efficacy, social support and well-being: The mediating role of optimism. *Personality and Individual Differences, 40,* 1281–1290.

Karavidas, M., Lim, N.K., & Katsikas, S.L. (2005). The effects of computers on older adult users. *Computers in Human Behaviour, 21*(5) 697–711.

Kart, C. (1981). Experiencing symptoms: Attribution and misattribution of illness among the aged. In M. Haug (Ed.), *Elderly patients and their doctors* (pp. 70–78). New York: Springer.

Kart, C.S., & Kinney, J.M. (2001). *The realities of aging* (6th ed.). Boston, MA: Allyn and Bacon.

Kart, C.S., & Longino, C.F. (1987). The support systems of older people: A test of the exchange paradigm. *Journal of Aging Studies, 1,* 239–251.

Kasl, S.V. (1995). Strategies in research on health and aging: Looking beyond secondary data analysis. *Journals of Gerontology: Social Sciences, 50*(4), S191–S193.

Katz, M.B. (1975). *The people of Hamilton, Canada West.* Cambridge, MA: Harvard University Press.

Katz, S. (1996). *Disciplining old age: The foundations of gerontological knowledge.* Charlottesville, VA: University Press of Virginia.

Katz, S. (2005). *Cultural aging: Life course, lifestyle and senior worlds.* Peterborough, ON: Broadview Press.

Kaufert, J.M. (1999). Aboriginal patients in Canada. *Anthropology and Medicine, 6*(3), 405–421.

Kaufert, J. & O'Neill, J. (1990). Biomedical rituals and informed consent: Native Canadians and the negotiations of clinical trust. In G. Weisz (Ed.), *Social Science Perspectives on Medical Ethics* (pp. 41–63). Philadelphia: University of Pennsylvania Press.

Kearney, M. (1996). *Mortally wounded: Stories of soul pain, death & healing.* New York: Torch Stone/Simon & Schuster.

Keating, N., Fast, J., Frederick, J., Cranswick, K., & Perrier, C. (1999). *Eldercare in Canada: Context, content and consequences.* (Catalogue No. 89-570-XPE). Ottawa: Statistics Canada, Housing, Family and Social Statistics Division.

Keefe, J.M. & Fancey, P.J. (2002). Work and eldercare: Reciprocity between older mothers and their employed daughters. *Canadian Journal on Aging 21*(2), 229–241.

Keefe, J., Légaré, J., & Carrière, Y. (2004). *Projecting the future availability of informal support and assessing its impact on home care services.* Executive Summary. Ottawa, ON: Health Canada.

Keefe, J. Rosenthal, C., & Béland, F. (2000). Impact of ethnicity on helping older relatives. *Canadian Journal of Aging, 19,* 317–342.

Kelly, G.A. (1991). *The psychology of personal constructs.* London: Routledge. (Original work publishing 1955 by Norton, New York.)

Kelner, M.J., Meslin, E, & Wahl, J. (1994). *Patient decision-making in critical illness: A Canadian study.* International Sociological Association, Centre for Studies on Aging, University of Toronto, Ontario.

Kemp, C., Rosenthal, C. & Denton, M. (2005). Financial planning for later life: Subjective understandings of catalysts and constraints. *Journal of Aging Studies, 19,* 273–290.

Kemp, K. L. (2005). Dimensions of grandparent–adult grandchild relationships: From family ties to intergenerational friendships. *Canadian Journal on Aging,* 24(2) 161–178.

Kempen, G.I.J.M., & Suurmeijer, T.P.B.M. (1990). The development of a hierarchical polychotomous ADL-IADL scale for noninstitutionalized elders. *The Gerontologist, 30,* 497–502.

Kendall, R.E. (2001). The distinction between mental and physical illness. *British Journal of Psychiatry, 178,* 490–493.

Kessler, R.C., & McLeod, J.D. (1985). Social support and mental health in community samples. In S. Cohen & S.L. Syme, (Eds.), *Social support and health.* Orlando, FL: Academic Press.

Kim, H.-K., Hisata, M., Kai, I., & Lee, S. (2000). Social support exchange and quality of life among Korean elderly. *Journal of Cross-Cultural Gerontology, 15*(4), 331–347.

Kim, J. & Moen, P. (2002). Retirement transitions, gender, and psychological well-being: A life-course, ecological model. *Journals of Gerontology, 57B*(3), P212–P222.

Kim, U. (1987). Illness behaviour patterns of Korean immigrants to Toronto: What are the hidden costs? In K.V. Ujimoto & J. Naidoo (Eds.), *Asian Canadians: Contemporary issues* (pp. 194–219). Guelph: University of Guelph.

Kincheloe, J., & McLaren, P. (2005). Rethinking critical theory and qualitative research. In N. Denzin & Y. Lincoln (Eds.), *Handbook of qualitative research* (3rd ed., pp. 303–342). Thousand Oaks: Sage Publications.

King, L.A., Hicks, J.A., Krull, J.L., & Del Gaiso, A.K. (2006). Positive affect and the experience of meaning in life. *Journal of Personality and Social Psychology, 90*(1), 179–196.

Kipper. 2001. Unpublished M.A. thesis, Lakehead University.

Kirwin, P.M. (1991). *Adult day care: The relationship of formal and informal systems of care.* New York: Garland Press.

Klassen, T.R., & Gillin, C.T. (1999). The heavy hand of the law: The Canadian supreme court and mandatory retirement. *Canadian Journal on Aging, 18*(2), 259–275.

Kline, D.W., & Schaie, K.W. (Eds.). (1996). *Handbook of the psychology of aging* (4th ed.). San Diego, CA: Academic Press.

Knight, C. (1999). Unpublished MA thesis, University of Waterloo.

Knox, V.J., & Gekoski, W.L. (1989). The effect of judgement context on assessments of age groups. *Canadian Journal on Aging, 8,* 244–254.

Knox, V., Gekoski W.L., & Kelly, L.E. (1995). The age group evaluation and description (AGED) inventory: A new instrument assessing stereotypes of and attitudes towards age groups. *International Journal of Aging and Human Development, 40*(1), 39–55.

Knox, V.J., Gekoski, W.L., & Johnson, E.A. (1984). The relationship between contact with and perceptions of the elderly. Paper presented at the Canadian Association on Gerontology 13th Annual Scientific and Educational Meeting, Vancouver, B.C.

Kobayashi, K.M. (1999). *Bunko no tanjyo (Emergent culture): Continuity and change in older nisei (second generation) parent–adult sansei (third generation) relationships in Japanese Canadian families*. Unpublished doctoral dissertation, Simon Fraser University.

Kobayashi, K.M. (2000). The nature of support from adult *sansei* (third generation) children to older *nisei* (second generation) parents in Japanese Canadian families. *Journal of Cross-Cultural Gerontology, 15,* 185–2000.

Koch, T., Braun, K.L., & Pietsch, J.H. (1999). Social necessity, individual rights, and the needs of the fragile: Euthanasia in the context of end-of-life decision making. *Journal of Ethics, Law and Aging, 5*(1), 17–28.

Kohli, M. (1988). *New patterns of transition to retirement in West Germany*. Tampa, FL: International Exchange Centre on Gerontology, University of South Florida.

Kohli, M. & Rein, M. (1991). The changing balance of work and retirement. In M. Kohli, M. Rein, A.M. Guillemard, et al., *Time for Retirement: Comparative Studies of Early Exit From the Labour Force* (pp. 1–35). Cambridge: Cambridge University Press.

Kojima, H. (1996). Determinants of attitudes toward population aging in Japan. The *Journal of Population Problems, 52*(2), 15.

Kolberg, J.E., & Epsing-Andersen, G. (1991). Welfare states and employment regime. In Kolberg, J.E. (Ed.), *The welfare state as employer* (pp. 3–35). Armonk, NY: M.E. Sharpe.

Kopec, J.A., Williams, J.I., To, T., & Austin, P.C. (2001). Cross-cultural comparisons of health status in Canada using the health utilities index. *Ethnicity & Health, 6*(1), 41–50.

Kosloski, K., Ekerdt, D., & DeViney, S. (2001). The role of job-related rewards in retirement planning. *The Journals of Gerontology. 56B* (3).

Kosloski, K., & Montgomery, R.J.V. (1995). The impact of respite use on nursing home placement. *The Gerontologist, 35(1),* 67–74.

Kotlikoff, L.J. (1993). *Generational accounting: Knowing who pays, and when, and what we spend*. New York: Free Press.

Kotynia-English, R., McGowan, H., & Almeida, O.P. (2005). A randomized trial of early psychiatric intervention in residential care: Impact on health outcomes. *International Psychogeriatrics 17*(3): 475–485.

Kovar, M.G., & LaCroix, A.Z. (1987). Aging in the eighties: Ability to perform work-related activities. *National Centre for Health Statistics Advance Data, 136,* 1–12.

Kozma, A., Stone, S., & Stones, M.J. (2000). Stability in components and predictors of subjective well-being (SWB): Implications for subjective well-being structure. In E. Diener (Ed.), *Advances in quality of life theory and research*. Dordrecht, The Netherlands: Kluwer.

Kozma, A., Stone, S., Stones, M.J., Hannah, T.E., & McNeil, K. (1990). Long-and short-term affective states in happiness. *Social Indicators Research 22,* 119–138.

Kozma, A., & Stones, M.J. (1980). The measurement of happiness: Development of the Memorial University of Newfoundland Happiness Scale (MUNSH). *Journals of Gerontology, 35,* 906–912.

Kozma, A., & Stones, M.J. (1983). Predictors of happiness. *Journals of Gerontology, 38,* 626–628.

Kozma, A., & Stones, M.J. (1987). Social desirability in measures of subjective well-being: A systematic evaluation. *Journals of Gerontology, 42,* 56–59.

Kozma, A., & Stones, M.J. (1988). Social desirability in measures of subjective well-being: Age comparisons. *Social Indicators Research, 20,* 1–14.

Kozma, A., & Stones, M.J. (1990). Decrements in habitual and maximal performance with age. In Perlmutter, M., (Ed.). *Late life potential* (pp. 1–23). Washington D.C.: The Gerontological Society of America.

Kozma, A., Stones, M.J., & Hannah, T.E. (1991). Age, activity, and physical performance: An evaluation of performance models. *Psychology and Aging, 6,* 43–49.

Kozma, A., Stones, M.J., & Kazarian, S. (1985). The usefulness of the MUNSH as an index of well-being and psychopathology. *Social Indicators Research, 17,* 49–55.

Kozma, A., Stones, M.J., & McNeil, K. (1991). Subjective well-being in later life. Toronto: Butterworths.

Kralik, D., Koch, T., Price, K., & Howard, N. (2004) Chronic illness self-management: Taking action to create order. *Journal of Clinical Nursing, 13*(2), 259–267.

Krick, J., & Sobal, J. (1990). Relationships between health protective behaviors. *Journal of Community Health, 15,* 19–34.

Kritz, M., Gurak, D., & Chen, L. (2000). Elderly immigrants: Their composition and living arrangements. *Journal of Sociology and Social Welfare, 27*(1), 85–114.

Kronebusch, K. & Schlesinger, M. (1994). Intergenerational transfers. In V.L. Bengtson & R.A. Harooytan, (Eds.), *Intergenerational linkages: Hidden connections in American society*. New York: Springer.

Krueger, J. & Heckhausen, J. (1993). Subjective conceptions versus cross-sectional contrasts. *Journals of Gerontology, 48B*(3), P100–P108.

Kübler-Ross, E. (1969). *On death and dying*. New York: Macmillan.

Kuhn, T. (1962). *The structure of scientific revolutions*. New York: Norton.

Kuhn, T. (1970). *The structure of scientific revolutions* (2nd ed.). Chicago, IL: University of Chicago Press.

Lachman, M. (1986). Locus of control in aging research: A case for multidimensional and domain-specific assessment. *Journal of Psychology and Aging, 1,* 34–40.

Laczko, L.S. (1997). Language, region, race, gender, and income: Perceptions of inequalities in Quebec and English Canada. In A. Frizzell & J. H. Pammett (Eds.), *Social Inequality in Canada* (pp. 107–126). Ottawa: Carlton University Press.

Ladson-Billings, G. & Donnor, J. (2005). The moral activist role of critical race theory scholarship. In N. Denzin & Y. Lincoln (Eds.) *Handbook of qualitative research* (3rd ed., pp. 279–301). Thousand Oaks: Sage Publications.

Lai, D.W (2000a). Depression among the elderly Chinese in Canada. *Canadian Journal on Aging, 19*(3), 409–429.

Lai, D.W (2000b). Prevalence of depression among the elderly Chinese in Canada. *Canadian Journal of Public Health, 9*(1), 64–66.

Lai, D.W. (2003). Health and predictors of health among older Chinese-Canadians in British Columbia. *BC Medical Journal, 45*(8) 382–390.

Lai, D.W.L. (2004a). Health status of older Chinese in Canada: Findings from the SF-36 health survey. *Canadian Journal of Public Health, 95*(3), 193–197.

Lai, D.W.L. (2004b). Impact of culture on depressive symptoms of elderly Chinese immigrants. *Canadian Journal of Psychiatry, 49*(12), 820–827.

Lai, D. W. L. (2004c). Use of homecare services by elderly Chinese immigrants. *Home Health Care Services Quarterly, 23*(3), 41–56.

Lai, D.W.L., & Kalyniak, S. (2005). Use of annual physical examinations by aging Chinese Canadians. *Journal of Aging and Health, 17*(5), 573–591.

Laing, R.D. (1960). *The divided self: A study of sanity and madness.* London, UK: Tavistock.

Laliberte Rudman, D. (2006). Shaping the active autonomous and responsible modern retiree: An analysis of discursive technologies and their links with neo-liberal political rationality. *Ageing and Society, 2,* 181–201.

Langer, E.J., & Rodin, J. (1976). The effects of choice and enhanced personal responsibility for the aged. *Personality and Social Psychology, 34,* 191–198.

Larsen, R., & Diener, E. (1987). Affect intensity as an individual difference characteristic: A review. *Journal of Research in Personality, 21,* 1–39.

Larson, E.B., Wang, L., Bowen, J.D., McCormick, W.C., Teri, L., Crane, P., et al. (2006). Exercise is associated with reduced risk for incident dementia among persons 65 years of age and older. *Annals of Internal Medicine, 144*(2), 73–81.

Laslett, P. (1979). *The world we have lost* (2nd ed.). London, UK: Methuen.

Latulippe, D., & Turner, J. (2000). Partial retirement and pension policy in industrialized countries. *International Labour Review, 139*(2): 179–195.

Laub, J. H., & Sampson, J. (1998). Integrating qualitative and quantitative data. In J.Z. Giele & G.H. Elder Jr. (Eds.), *Methods of life course research: Qualitative and quantitative approaches* (pp. 231–230). Thousand Oaks, CA: Sage Publications.

Lawton, M.P. (2001). *Annual Review of Gerontology and Geriatrics: Vol. 20. Focus on the end of life: Scientific and social issues.* New York: Springer.

Lawton, M.P., Moss, M., Hoffman, C., Grant, R., Have, T.T., & Kleban, M.H. (1999). Health, valuation of life, and the wish to live. *The Gerontologist, 39*(4), 406–416.

Lawton, M.P., Moss, M., Kleban, M.H., Glicksman, A., & Rovine, M. (1991). A two factor model of caregiving appraisal and psychological well-being. *Journals of Gerontology: Psychological Sciences, 46,* 181–189.

Leacy, F.H. (Ed.). (1983). *Historical statistics of Canada* (2nd ed.). Ottawa: Statistics Canada (STC 11–516). Retrieved April 18, 2006, from http://www.statcan.ca/english/freepub/11-516-XIE/sectiona/toc.htm

LeBourdais, C. & Marcil-Gratton, N. (1996). Family transformations across the Canadian/American border: When the laggard becomes the leader. *Journal of Comparative Family Studies, 27,* 415–436.

Lee, G.R. (1985). Theoretical perspectives on social networks. In W.J. Sauer & R.T. Coward, (Eds.), *Social support networks and the care of the elderly.* New York: Springer.

Lee, I.M., Blair, S.N., Allison, D.B., Folsom, A.R., Harris, T.B., Manson, J.E., et al. (2001). Epidemiologic data on the relationships of caloric intake, energy balance, and weight gain over the life span with longevity and morbidity. *The Journals of Gerontology. Series A, Biological Sciences and Medical Sciences, 56A* (special issue I), 7–19.

Lehman, H.C. (1953). *Age and achievement.* Princeton, NJ: Princeton University Press.

Lemon, B., Bengston, V., & Peterson, J. (1972). Activity types and life satisfaction in a retirement community. *Journals of Gerontology, 27,* 511–523.

Leung H.H. & McDonald, L. (2002). *Chinese immigrant women who care for aging parents.* Toronto: Joint Centre for Excellence for Research on Immigration and Settlement.

Leventhal, L.A., & Prohaska, T.R. (1986). Age, symptom interpretation and health behavior. *Journal of the American Geriatrics Society, 34,* 185–191.

Levin, L.S., & Idler, E.L. (1983). Self-care in health. *Annual Review of Public Health, 4,* 181.

Lewis-Beck, M., Bryman, A.E., & Liao, T.F. (2004). *The Sage encyclopedia of social science research methods.* Thousand Oaks, CA: Sage.

Lexchin, J. (1993). The effect of generic competition on the price of prescription drugs in the Province of Ontario. *Canadian Medical Association Journal, 148,* 35–38.

Lexchin, J. (2001). Pharmaceuticals: Politics and policy. In P. Armstrong, H. Armstrong, & D. Coburn, (Eds.), *Unhealthy times. Political economy perspectives on health and care in Canada.* (pp.31–44). Toronto: Oxford University Press.

Li, P.S. (1990). Race and Ethnicity. 3–17. In P. S. Li (Ed.). *Race and ethnic relations in Canada.* Don Mills, ON: Oxford University Press.

Li P.S. (1998). *The Chinese in Canada* (2nd ed.). Toronto: Oxford University Press.

Li, P.S. (1999). Race and ethnicity. In P.S. Li (Ed.), *Race and ethnic relations in Canada* (2nd ed., pp. 3–20). Don Mills, ON: Oxford University Press.

Li, P.S. (2000). Earning disparities between immigrants and native-born Canadians. *Canadian Review of Sociology and Anthropology, 37*(3), 289–311.

Liang, J., Krause, N.M., & Bennett, J.M. (2001). Social exchange and well-being: Is giving better than receiving? *Psychology and Aging, 16,* 511–523.

Liang, J. & Lawrence, R. (1989). Secondary analysis of sample surveys in gerontological research. In

M. Lowell Lawton & A.R. Herzog (Eds.), *Special research methods for gerontology* (pp. 31–61). Amityville, NY: Baywood Publishing, Inc.

Lichtenberg, P.A. (1997). Clinical perspectives on sexual issues in nursing homes. *Topics in Geriatric Rehabilitation, 12*(4), 1–10.

Likert, R. (1932). A technique for the measurement of attitudes. *Archives of Psychology, 140*, 5–53.

Lin, N., Simeone, R.S., Ensel, W.M., & Kuo, W. (1979). Social support, stressful life events, and illness: A model and empirical test. *Journal of Health and Social Behaviour, 20*, 108–119.

Linville, P.W. (1982). The complexity-extremity effect and age based stereotyping. *Journal of Personality and Social Psychology, 42*, 193–211.

Lithwick, M., Reis, M., Stones, M.J., Macnaughton-Osler, K., Gendron, M.J., Groves, D., et al. (1997). Exploring definitions and developing community-based projects on the awareness and prevention of elder abuse in different cultural communities. Montreal: CLSC Rene-Cassin and Foundation for Vital Aging.

Lithwick, M., Stones, M.J., & Reis, M. (1998). *Exploring definitions and developing community based projects on the awareness and prevention of senior mistreatment in ethnocultural communities.* Halifax, NS: Canadian Association on Gerontology.

Little, D. (2003). Non-pharmacological management of diabetes: The role of diet and exercise. *Geriatrics & Aging, 6*(1), 27–29.

Litva, A., & Eyles, J. (1994). Health or healthy: Why people are not sick in a Southern Ontario town. *Social Science and Medicine, 39*, 1083–1091.

Litwak. E. (1960). Geographic mobility and extended family cohesion. *American Sociological Review, 25*, 385–394.

Litwak, E. & Longino, C.F. (1987). Migration patterns among the elderly: A developmental perspective. *The Gerontologist, 27*, 266–272.

Ljunggren, G., Phillips, C.D., & Sgadari, A. (1987). Comparison of restraint use in nursing homes in eight countries. *Age and Ageing, 26*(suppl. 2), 43–48.

Lloyd, P., Lupton, D., & Donaldson, C. (1991). Consumerism in the health care setting: An exploratory study of factors underlying the selection and evaluation of primary medical services. *Australian Journal of Public Health, 15*(3): 194–201.

Logue, B.J. (1991) Women at risk: Predictors of financial stress for retired women workers. *The Gerontologist, 31*(5): 657–665.

Lomas, J. (1990). Finding audiences, changing beliefs: The structure of research use in Canadian health policy. *Journal of Health Politics, Policy and Law, 15*, 525–542.

Longino, C. (2005). The future of ageism: Baby boomers at the doorstep. *Generations, 29*(3), 79–83.

Longino, C.F., & Kart, C.S. (1982). Explicating activity theory: A formal replication. *Journals of Gerontology, 37*, 713–722.

Lopata, H.Z. (1973). *Widowhood in an American city.* Cambridge, MA: Schenkman.

Lopata, H.Z. (1975). Support systems of elderly urbanites: Chicago of the 1970s. *The Gerontologist, 15*, 35–41.

Lopata, H.Z. (1995). Feminist approaches in social gerontology. In R. Bleizner & V. Hilkevitch Bedford, (Eds.), *Handbook of aging and the family* (pp. 114–151). Westport, CT: Greenwood Press.

Lorber, J. (1993). Why women physicians will never be true equals in the American medical profession. In E. Riska & K. Wegar, (Eds.), *Gender, work and medicine. Women and the medical division of labour* (pp. 62–76). International Sociological Association; SAGE Publications, Ltd.

Lowe, G.S. (1991, autumn). Retirement attitudes, plans and behavior. *Perspectives, Statistics Canada*, 8–17.

Lowenthal, M.F., & Robinson, B. (1976). Social networks and isolation. In R.H. Binstock & E. Shanas, (Eds.), *Handbook of aging and the social sciences.* New York: Van Nostrand Reinhold.

Lubben, J., & Becerra, R.M. (1987). Social support among Black, Mexican, and Chinese elderly. In D.E. Gelfand & C.M. Berresi (Eds.), *Ethnic dimensions of aging* (pp. 130–144). New York: Springer.

Lubben, J.E., Weiler, P.G., & Chi, I. (1989). Health practices of the elderly poor. *American Journal of Public Health, 79*, 731–734.

Lubomudrov, S. (1987). Congressional perceptions of the elderly: The use of stereotypes in the legislative process. *Gerontologist, 27*(1), 77–81.

Lussier, G. & Wister, A.V. (1995). Study of workforce aging of the British Columbia public service, 1983–1991. *Canadian Journal of Aging, 14*(3): 480–497.

Lykken, D., & Tellegen, A. (1996). Happiness is a stochastic phenomenon. *Psychological Science, 7*, 186–189.

Lynott, P.P. & Roberts, R.E.L. (1997). Developmental stake hypothesis and changing perceptions of intergenerational relations, 1971–1985. *The Gerontologist, 37*, 394–405.

Lyubomirsky, S. (2001). Why are some people happier than others? The role of cognitive and motivational processes in well-being. *The American Psychologist, 56*(3), 239–249.

MacCorquodale, K., & Meehl, P.E. (1948). On a distinction between hypothetical constructs and intervening variables. *Psychological Review, 55*, 95–107.

MacKenzie, P., Brown, L., Callahan, M., & Whittington, B. (2005). *Grandparents raising their grandchildren.* Paper presented at the Canadian Association on Gerontology, Halifax, NS.

Malenfant, É.C. (2004). Suicide in Canada's immigrant population. *Health Reports, 15*(2), 9–17.

Mallard, A.G.C., Lance, C.E., & Michalos, A.C. (1997). Culture as a moderator of overall life satisfaction–life facet satisfaction relationships. *Social Indicators Research, 40*, 259–284.

Mancini, J.A., Quinn, W., Gavigan, M.A., & Franklin, H. (1980). Social network interaction among older adults:

Implications for life satisfaction. *Human Relations, 33*, 543–554.

Manga, P. (1978). *The income distribution effect of medical insurance in Ontario*. Occasional Paper No. 6. Toronto: Ontario Economic Council.

Mangus, R.S., Dipiero, A., & Hawkins, C.E. (1999). Medical students' attitudes toward physician-assisted suicide. *Journal of the American Medical Association, 282*(21), 2080–2081.

Mann, P. (1991). The influence of peers and parents on youth life satisfaction in Hong Kong. *Social Indicators Research, 24*, 347–366.

Manuel, D.G., & Schulz, S.E. (2001). *Adding years to life and life to years: Life and health expectancy in Ontario. Research atlas*. Toronto: Institute for Clinical Evaluative Sciences.

Manulife Financial. (1999). *Manulife healthstyles study*. Toronto: Market Facts of Canada Ltd.

Marcil-Gratton, N. (1998). *Growing up with mom and dad? The intricate family life courses of Canadian children*. (Catalogue No. 89-566-XIE). Ottawa: Statistics Canada.

Markides, K.S. (1983). Minority aging. In M.W. Riley, B.B. Hess, & K. Bond (Eds.), *Aging in society: Reviews of recent literature*. Hillsdale, NJ: Lawrence Erlbaum.

Markides, K.S., & Black, S. (1996). Race, ethnicity and aging. In R.H. Binstock & L.K. George (Eds.), *Handbook of aging and the social sciences* (4th ed.) San Diego, CA: Academic Press.

Markides, K.S. Liang, J., & Jackson, J.S. (1990). Race, ethnicity and aging: Conceptual and methodological issues. In R.H. Binstock & L.K. George (Eds.), *Handbook of aging and the social sciences* (3rd ed., pp. 112–129). New York: Academic Press.

Markson, L., Clark, J., Glantz, L., Lamberton, V., Kern, D., & Stolleran, G. (1997). The doctor's role in discussing advance preferences for end-of-life care: Perceptions of physicians practicing in the VA. *Journal of the American Geriatrics Society, 45*(4), 399–406.

Marmor, T.R., & Sullivan, K. (2000, July/August). Canada's burning! Media myths about universal health coverage. *Washington Monthly*.

Marriott, A., Donaldson, C., Tarrier, N., & Burns, A. (2000). Effectiveness of a cognitive-behavioural family intervention in reducing the burden of care in carers of patients with Alzheimer's disease. *British Journal of Psychiatry, 176*, 557–562.

Marriott, J., & Mable, A.L. (1998). Integrated models. International trends and implications for Canada. In *Canada health action: Building on the legacy* (pp. 547–676). National Forum on Health.

Marshall, K. (1998). Couples working shift. *Perspectives on Labour and Income, 10*(3), 9–14.

Marshall, V.W. (1976). Organizational features of terminal status passage in residential facilities for the aged. In L.H. Lofland (Ed.), *Toward a sociology of death and dying* (pp. 115–134). Beverly Hills, CA: Sage.

Marshall, V.W. (1995). Rethinking retirement: Issues for the twenty-first century. In E. Gee & G. Gutman (Eds.), *Rethinking retirement* (pp. 31–50). Vancouver: Gerontology Research Centre, Simon Fraser University.

Marshall, V.W. (1996). The state of theory in aging and the social sciences. In R.H. Binstock & L.K. George, (Eds.), *Handbook of aging and the social sciences* (4th ed., pp. 12–30). San Diego, CA: Academic Press.

Marshall, V.W., Clarke, P.J., & Ballantyne, P.J. (2001). Instability in the retirement transition: Effects on health and well-being in a Canadian study. *Research on Aging, 23*(4).

Martel, L., & Bélanger, A. (2000). Dependence-free life expectancy in Canada. *Health Reports, 58*, 26–29. (Catalogue No. 11-008). Ottawa: Statistics Canada.

Martel, L., Belanger, A., Berthelot, J.-M., & Carriere, Y. (2005). *Healthy today, healthy tomorrow? Findings from the National Population Health Survey*. Ottawa: Statistics Canada, Demography Division.

Martens, A., Goldenberg, J.L., & Greenberg, J. (2005). A terror management perspective on ageism. *Journal of Social Issues, 61*, 223–239

Martens, A., Greenberg, J., Schimel, J., & Landau, M. J. (2004). Ageism and death: Effects of mortality salience and similarity to elders on distancing from and derogation of elderly people. *Personality and Social Psychology Bulletin, 30*, 1524–1536.

Martin, H.W., Hoppe, S.K., Marshall, V.W., & Daciuk, J.F. (1992). Sociodemographic and health characteristics of anglophone Canadian and U.S. snowbirds. *Journal of Aging and Health, 4*, 500–513.

Martin, N.J., Stones, M.J., Young, J., & Bédard, M. (2000). Development of delirium: A cohort prospective study in a community hospital. *International Psychogeriatrics, 12*, 117–126.

Martin-Matthews, A. (1987). Widowhood as an expectable life event. In V. Marshall (Ed.), *Aging in Canada: Social perspectives* (2nd ed, pp. 343–366). Markham, ON: Fitzhenry & Whiteside.

Martin-Matthews, A. (1991). *Widowhood in later life*. Toronto: Butterworths.

Martin-Matthews, A. (1999) Widowhood: Dominant renditions, changing demography, and variable meaning. In S. Neysmith (Ed.), *Critical issues for future social work practice with aging persons* (pp. 27–46). New York: Columbia University Press.

Martin-Matthews, A. (2000). Change and diversity in aging families and intergenerational relations. In N. Mandell & A. Duffy (Eds.), *Canadian Families: Diversity, conflict and change* (2nd. ed., pp. 323–360). Toronto: Harcourt Canada.

Martin-Matthews, A., & Béland, F. (Eds). (2001). Northern lights: Reflections on Canadian gerontological research on the occasion of the 17th World Congress of the International Association of Gerontology, Vancouver, Canada, July 2001. *Canadian Journal on Aging, 20*, 1–211.

Martin-Matthews, A. & Joseph, A.E. (1994.) Growing old in aging communities. In. V. Marshall & B. McPherson (Eds.), *Aging: Canadian perspectives* (pp. 20–35). Peterborough, ON: Broadview Press.

Mata, F., & Valentine, J. (1999). *Selected ethnic profiles of Canada's senior age cohorts.* Strategic research and Analysis, Multiculturalism Department of Canadian Heritage.

Matthews, A.M., Tindale J.A., & Norris J.E. (1985). The facts on aging quiz: A Canadian validation and cross-cultural comparison. *Canadian Journal on Aging, 3,* 165–174.

Matthews, B.J. (1999). The gender system and fertility: An exploration of the hidden links. *Canadian Studies in Population, 26,* 21–38.

Matthews, S. (1979). *The social world of older women: Management of identity.* Beverly Hills, CA: Sage.

Matthews, S.H., Delaney, P.J., & Adamek, M.E. (1989). Male kinship ties: Bonds between adult brothers. *American Behavioral Scientist, 33,* 58–69.

Matthews, S.H. & Rosner, T.T. (1988). Shared filial responsibility: The family as the primary caregiver. *Journal of Marriage and the Family, 50,* 185–195.

Matthias, R.E., Lubben, J.E., Atchison, K.A., & Schweitzer, S.O. (1997). Sexual activity and satisfaction among very old adults: Results from a community-dwelling Medicare population survey. *Gerontologist, 37*(1), 6–14.

Maurier, W.L., & Northcott, H.C. (2000). *Aging in Ontario.* Calgary: Detselig Enterprises Ltd.

McAdams, D.P., & de St. Aubin, E. (1992) A theory of generativity and its assessment through self-report, behavioral acts, and narrative themes in autobiography. *Journal of Personality and Social Psychology, 62,* 1003–1015.

McCay, C.M., & Crowell, M.F. (1934). Prolonging the life span. *Science Monthly, 39,* 405–414.

McConatha J.T., Hayta V., Rieser-Danner L., McConatha, D., & Polat T.S. (2004). Turkish and U.S. attitudes toward aging. *Educational Gerontology, 30*(3), 169–183.

McConatha J.T., Schnell F., Volkwein K., Riley L., & Leach E. (2003). Attitudes towards aging: A comparative analysis of young adults from the United States and Germany. *International Journal of Aging and Human Development, 57(3),* 203–215.

McCracken, C.F.M., Boneham, M.A., Copeland, J.R.M., Williams, K.E., Wilson, K., Scott, A., et al. (1997). Prevalence of dementia and depression among elderly people in black and ethnic minorities. *British Journal of Psychiatry, 171,* 269–273.

McCrae, R.R. (1986). Well-being scales do not measure social desirability. *Journals of Gerontology, 41,* 390–392.

McCrae, R.R., Arenberg, D., & Costa, P.T., Jr. (1987). Declines in divergent thinking with age: Cross-sectional, longitudinal, and cross-sequential analyses. *Psychology and Aging, 2,* 130–137.

McDaniel, S.A. (1997). Intergenerational transfers, social solidarity and social policy: Unanswered questions and policy challenges. *Canadian Journal on Aging/Canadian Public Policy* (suppl.), 1–21.

McDaniel, S.A. (2002). Women's changing relations to the state and citizenship: Caring and intergenerational relations in globalizing western democracies. *Canadian Review of Sociology and Anthropology, 39*(2), 125–150.

McDaniel, S.(2004). Generationing gender: Justice and the division of welfare. *Journal of Aging Studies, 18*(1), 27–44.

McDaniel, S.A., & Chappell, N.L. (1999). Health care in regression: Contraindications, tensions and implications for Canadian seniors. *Canadian Public Policy,* 15(1), 123–132.

McDaniel, S.A., & Lewis, R. (1998). Did they or didn't they? Inter-generational supports in Canada's past and a case study of Brigus, Newfoundland, 1920–1949. In L. Chambers & E-A. Montigny (Eds.), *Family matters: Papers in post-confederation Canadian history* (pp. 475–497). Toronto: Canadian Scholars Press.

McDaniel, S.A., & Tepperman, L. (2000*). Close relations.* Scarborough, ON: Prentice Hall Allyn and Bacon Canada.

McDonald, A.D., McDonald, J.C., Steinmetz, N., Enterline, P.E., & Salter, V. (1973). Physician services in Montreal before universal health insurance. *Medical Care, 11,* 269–286.

McDonald, L. (1996). *Transitions into retirement: A time for retirement.* Toronto: Centre For Applied Social Research, Faculty of Social Work, University of Toronto.

McDonald, L. (1997a). The link between social research and social policy options: Reverse retirement as a case in point. *Canadian Public Policy/ Canadian Journal of Aging* (special joint issue, suppl.), 90–113.

McDonald, L. (1997b). Invisible poor: Canada's retired widows. *Canadian Journal on Aging, 16,* 553–583.

McDonald, L. (2002). *The invisible retirement of women.* Social and Economic Dimensions of Aging Paper (SEDAP) 69. Retrieved July 1, 2006 from http://socserv/mcmaster.ca/sedap/papers02.htm.

McDonald, L. (2006a) Elder abuse. In E. Birren, *The Encyclopedia of Gerontology* (2nd ed.). Academic Press. (In press).

McDonald, L. (2006b). *The economic security of minorities in Canada.* Toronto: Canadian Sociology and Anthropology Association.

McDonald, L. (2006c). Gendered retirement: The welfare of women and the "new" retirement. In Leroy O. Stone (Ed.), *New Frontiers of Research on Retirement.* Catalogue No. 75-511-XPE. Ottawa: Statistics Canada. (in press).

McDonald, L. & Chen, M.Y.T. (1993). The youth freeze and the retirement bulge: Older workers and the impending labour shortage. *Journal of Canadian Studies, 28*(1), 75–101.

McDonald, L., & A. Collins. (2000). *Abuse and neglect of older adults: A discussion paper.* Ottawa: Family Violence Prevention Unit, Health Canada.

McDonald, L., Dergal, J, & Cleghorn, L. (2006). Living on the margins: Homelessness among older adults in Toronto. *Journal of Gerontological Social Work.* (In press).

McDonald, L., & Donahue, P. (2000). Poor health and retirement income: The Canadian case. *Ageing and Society, 20,* 493–522.

McDonald, L., Donahue, P., & Marshall, V. (2000). The economic consequences of early unexpected retirement. In F.T. Denton, D. Fretz, & B. Spencer (Eds.), *Independence and Economic Security in Old Age* (pp. 267–292.) Vancouver: University of British Columbia Press.

McDonald, L., Donahue, P., McKnight, K. (2005). *Older women separated and divorced in retirement.* Paper presented at the Annual Conference of the Canadian Association on Gerontology, October 21, 2005, Halifax, Nova Scotia.

McDonald, L., Donahue, P., & Moore, B. (1997a) The Economic Casualties of Retiring to Caregiving. Toronto: Centre for Applied Social Research, Faculty of Social Work, University of Toronto.

McDonald, L., Donahue, P., & Moore, B. (1997b). *Widowhood and retirement: Women on the margin.* Toronto: Centre for Applied Social Research.

McDonald, L., Donahue, P., & Moore, B. (2000a). Widowhood in retirement. In F.T. Denton, D. Fretz, & B. Spencer, (Eds.), *Independence and economic security in old age* (pp. 329–345). Vancouver: University of British Columbia Press.

McDonald, L., Donahue, P., & Moore, B. (2000b). The poverty of retired widows. In F. T. Denton, D. Fretz, & B. Spencer (Eds.), *Independence and economic security in old age* (pp. 328–345). Vancouver: University of British Columbia Press.

McDonald, L., Donahue, P., & Sussman, T. (2003). *The costs of retiring to caregive: Hearing the voices of former caregivers.* Paper presented at 1st National Gerontological Social Work Conference, CSWE, Atlanta Georgia.

McDonald, L., George, U, Daciuk, J., Yan, M., & Rowan, H. (2001). *A study on the settlement related needs of newly arrived immigrant seniors in Ontario.* Toronto: Centre for Applied Social Research, University of Toronto.

McDonald, L. & Robb, L.A. (2004). The economic legacy of divorce and separation for women in old age. *Canadian Journal on Aging* (suppl.), S83–S97.

McDonald, L. & Wanner, R.A. (1984). Socioeconomic determinants of early retirement in Canada. *Canadian Journal on Aging, 3*(3), 105–116.

McDonald, L., & Wanner, R.A. (1990) Retirement in Canada. Toronto: Butterworths.

McGarry, K., & Schoeni, R.F. (2000). Social security, economic growth, and the rise in elderly widows' independence in the twentieth century. *Demography, 37,* 221–236.

McKee, M. (2001). Europe and North America: A clash of cultures? In A. Ostry & K. Cardiff (Eds.), *Trading away health? Globalization and health policy* (pp. 25–28). Report from the 14th Annual Health Policy Conference of the Centre for Health Services and Policy Research, Vancouver, B.C.

McKeown, T. (1976). *The modern rise of population.* London, UK: Edward Arnold.

McKeown, T. (1988). *The origins of human disease.* Oxford, UK: Basil Blackwell.

McKeown, T., Record, R.G., & Turner, R.D. (1975). An interpretation of the decline of mortality in England and Wales during the twentieth century. *Population Studies, 29,* 391–422.

McKinlay, J.B., & McKinlay, S.M. (1977). The questionable contribution of medical measures to the decline of mortality in the United States in the twentieth century. *Health and Society,* 405–428.

McLaughlin, D.K., & Jensen, L. (2000). Work history and U.S. elders' transitions into poverty. *Gerontologist, 40*(4), 469–479.

McMullin, J.A. (2000). Diversity and the state of sociological aging theory. *The Gerontologist, 40*(5) S517–530.

McMullin, J.A. & Marshall, V.W. (2001). Ageism, age relations, and garment industry work in Montreal. *The Gerontologist, 41*(1): 111–122.

McNeil, J.K., LeBlanc, A.M., & Joyner, M. (1991).The effect of exercise on depressive symptoms in the moderately depressed elderly. *Psychology and Aging, 6,* 487–488.

McNeil, J.K., Stones, M.J., Kozma, A., & Andres, D. (1994). Age differences in mood: Structure, mean level, and diurnal variation. *Canadian Journal on Aging, 31,* 201–220.

McNeill, W.H. (1973). *Plagues and People.* New York: Doubleday.

McPherson, B.D. (1995). Aging from the historical and comparative perspective: Cultural and subcultural diversity. In R. Neugebauer-Visano (Ed.), *Aging and inequality: Cultural constructions of differences* (pp. 31–67). Toronto: Canadian Scholars' Press Inc.

McQuillan, K., & Belle, M. (2001). Lone-father families in Canada, 1971–1996. *Canadian Studies in Population, 28,* 67–88.

McVittie, C., McKinlay, A., & Widdicombe, S. (2003). Committed to (un)equal opportunities? 'New ageism' and the older worker. *British Journal of Social Psychology, 42*(4), 595–612.

Mebane, E.W., Orman, R.F., Kroonen, L.T., & Goldstein, M.K. (1999). Influence of physician race, age, and gender on physician attitudes toward advance care directives and preferences for end-of-life decision making. *Journal of the American Geriatrics Society, 47*(5), 579–591.

Mechanic, D. (1999). Correlates of physician utilization: Why do major multivariate studies of physician utilization find trivial psychosocial and organizational effects? *Journal of Health and Social Behavior, 20,* 387–396.

Medjuck, S., Keefe, J.M., & Fancey, P.J. (1998). Available but not accessible, an examination of the use of workplace policies for caregivers of elderly kin. *Journal of Family Issues, 19*(3), 274–299.

Meier, R. (2000). *Ethnoracial issues: Barriers to mental health care.* Canadian Mental Health Association.

Meintel, D., & Perissini, M. (1993). Seule et âgée en milieu urbain. *Revue internationale d'action communautaire, 69,* 37–48.

Mendelson, M., & Divinsky, P. (2000). *Canada 2015: Globalization and the future of Canada's health and health care.* Draft report prepared for the Future of Global and Regional Integration Project, Institute of Intergovernmental Relations. Kingston: Queen's University.

Menec, V.H., & Chipperfield, J.G. (2001). Prospective analysis of the relation between self-rated health and health care use among elderly Canadians. *Canadian Journal on Aging, 20*(3), 293–306.

Menec, V., Lix, L., MacWilliam, L. & Soodeen, R. (2003). *Trends in the health status of older Manitobans, 1985 to 1999.* Paper presented at the Canadian Association on Gerontology, Toronto.

Merton, R.K. (1968). *Social theory and social structure.* New York: Free Press.

Merzel, C. & D'Afflitti, J. (2003). Reconsidering community-based health promotion: Promise, performance, and potential. *American Journal of Public Health, 93*(4), 557–574.

Mhatre, S.L., & Deber, R.B. (1992). From equal access to health care to equitable access to health: A review of Canadian provincial health commissions and reports. *International Journal of Health Services, 22*(4), 56–68.

Michalos, A.C. (1985). Multiple discrepancies theory (MDT). *Social Indicators Research, 16*(4), 347–413.

Michalos, A.C. (1991). Global report on student well-being. New York: Springer-Verlag.

Millar, W., & Beaudet, M. (1996). Health facts from the 1994 National Population Health Survey. *Canadian Social Trends, 40,* 24–27.

Miller, B., Campbell, R.T., Davis, L., Furner, S., Giachello, A., Prohaska, T., et al. (1996). Minority use of community long-term care services: A comparative analysis. *Journals of Gerontology: Social Sciences, 51B,* S70–S81.

Miller, S.C., Mor, V., Gage, B., & Coppola, K. (2001). Hospice and its role in improving end-of-life care. In M.P. Lawton (Ed.), *Annual Review of Gerontology and Geriatrics: Vol. 20. Focus on the end of life: Scientific and social issues* (pp.193–223). New York: Springer.

Mills, C.W. (1959). *The sociological imagination.* New York: Oxford University Press.

Milne, D., Pitt, I., & Sabin, N. (1993). Evaluation of a career support scheme for elderly people: The importance of "coping." *British Journal of Social Work, 23*(2), 157–168.

Miner, S. & Montoro-Rodriguez, J. (1999). Intersections of society, family, and self among Hispanics in middle and later life. In C.D. Ryff & V.W. Marshall (Eds.), *The self and society in aging processes* (pp. 423–552). New York: Springer.

Minkler, M. (1999). Introduction. In M. Minkler & C. Estes (Eds.), *Critical gerontology: Perspectives from political economy and moral economy* (pp. 1–13). Amityville, NY: Baywood.

Minkler, M., & Estes, C.L. (Eds.), (1984). *Readings in the political economy of aging.* Farmingdale, NY: Baywood.

Mitchell, B.A. (2000). The refilled "nest": Debunking the myth of families in crisis. In E.M. Gutman & G.M Gutman, (Eds.), *The overselling of population aging: Apocalyptic demography, intergenerational challenges, and social policy* (pp. 80–99). Toronto: Oxford University Press

Mitchell, B.A. & Gee, E.M. (1996a). Boomerang kids and mid-life parental marital satisfaction. *Family Relations, 45,* 442–448.

Mitchell, B.A. & Gee, E.M. (1996b). Young adults returning home: Implications for social policy. In B. Galaway & J. Hudson, (Eds.), *Youth in transition to adulthood: Research and policy implications* (pp. 61–71). Toronto: Thompson.

Mitchell, B.A., Wister, A.V., & Gee, E.M. (2002). "There's no place like home": An analysis of young adults' mature coresidency in Canada. *International Journal of Aging and Human Development, 54,* 57–84.

Mitnitski, A.B., Graham, J.E., Mogilner, A.J., & Rockwood, K. (2002). Frailty, fitness and late-life mortality in relation to chronological and biological age, *BMC Geriatrics, 2:*1.

Mockler, D., Riordan, J., & Murphy, M. (1998). Psychosocial factors associated with the use/non-use of mental health services by primary carers of individuals with dementia. *International Journal of Geriatric Psychiatry, 13*(5), 310–314.

Moen, P. (1996). Gender, age, and the life course. In R.H. Binstock & L.K. George (Eds.), *Handbook of aging and the social sciences* (4th ed., pp. 171–187). San Diego, CA: Academic Press.

Moen. P., Kim, J. & Hofmeister, H. (2001). Couples' work/retirement transitions, gender, and marital quality. *Social Psychology Quarterly, 64,* 55–71.

Moen, P., Sweet, S., & Swisher, R. (2001). *Customizing the career clock: Retirement planning and expectations.* Bronfenbrenner Life Course Centre Working Paper #01-08. Ithaca, NY: Cornell Employment and Family Careers Institute, Cornell University.

Moller, V. (1992). Spare time use and perceived well-being among black South African youth. *Social Indicators Research, 26,* 309–352.

Monette, M. (1996). *Canada's changing retirement patterns: Findings from the general social survey.* Ottawa: Statistics Canada.

Monk, A. (1997). *Transition to retirement.* New York: Springer.

Montepare, J.M., & Lachman, M.E. (1989). "You're only as old as you feel": Self-perceptions of age, fears of aging, and life satisfaction from adolescence to old age. *Psychology of Aging, 4*(1), 73–78.

Montgomery, D. (2000). Attitudes of college students toward the elderly. Unpublished manuscript.

Montgomery, R.J.V. (1989). Investigating caregiver burden. In K.S. Markides & C.L. Cooper (Eds.), *Aging, Stress and Health* (pp. 201–218). New York: John Wiley & Sons Ltd.

Montgomery, R.J.V. (1996). Advancing caregiver research: Weight efficacy and feasibility of interventions. *Journals of Gerontology, 51B*(3), S109–S110.

Montgomery, R.J.V., Gonyea, J.G., & Hooyman, N.R. (1985). Caregiving and the experience of subjective and objective burden. *Family Relations, 34,* 19–25.

Montross, L.P., Depp, C., Daly, J., Reichstadt, J., Golshan, S., Moore, D., et al. (2006). Correlates of self-rated successful aging among community-dwelling older adults. *The American Journal of Geriatric Psychiatry, 14*(1), 43–51.

Moon, A., & Williams, O. (1993). Perceptions of elder abuse and help-seeking patterns among African-American, Caucasian American, and Korean-American elderly women. *Gerontologist, 33*(3), 386–395.

Moore, E.G., & Rosenberg, M.W. (1994). Residential mobility and migration among Canada's elderly. In V. Marshall & B. McPherson, (Eds.), *Aging: Canadian perspectives* (pp. 51–69). Peterborough, ON: Broadview Press.

Moore, E.G., & Rosenberg, M.W. (1995). *Population health among Canada's elderly. Sociodemographic and geographic perspectives.* NHRDP.

Moore, E.G., & Rosenberg, M.W., with McGuinness, D. (1997). *Growing old in Canada: Demographic and geographic perspectives.* Toronto: Statistics Canada and ITP Nelson.

Morioka-Douglas, N., Sacks, T., & Yeo, G. (2004). Issues in caring for Afghan American elders: Insights from literature and focus groups. *Journal of Cross-Cultural Gerontology. 19*(1) 27–40.

Morris, J.N., Chave, S.P., Adam, C., Sirey, C.F., & Epstein, L. (1956). Vigorous exercise in leisure time and the incidence of coronary heart disease. *Lancet, ii,* 569–570.

Morris, J.N., Fries, B.E., Mehr, D.R., Hawes, C., Phillips, C., Phillips, C., Mor, V. et al. (1994). MDS Cognitive Performance Scale. *Journals of Gerontology, 49*(4), M174–M182.

Morris, J.N., Fries, B.E., & Morris, S.A. (1999). Scaling ADLs within the MDS. *The Journals of Gerontology. Series A, Biological sciences and medical sciences, 54*(11), M546–M553.

Morris, J.N., Murphy, K., & Nonemaker, S. (1995). *Long-term care facility resident assessment instrument user's manual.* Brigg Health Care Products.

Morris, R.G., Morris, L.W., & Britton, P.G. (1988). Factors affecting the emotional wellbeing of the caregivers of dementia sufferers. *British Journal of Psychiatry, 153,* 147–156.

Morissette, R., & Drolet, M. (2000). *Pension coverage and retirement savings of young and prime-aged workers in Canada: 1986–1997.* Ottawa: Statistics Canada, Minister of Industry.

Morrisette, R., Schellenberg, G, & Silver, C. (2004). Retaining older workers. *Perspective on labour and income, 16*(4), 33–38.

Morton, D., & McCallum, M.E. (1988). Superannuation to indexation: Employment pension plans. *Research Studies, 2.* Toronto: Queen's Printer for Ontario.

Moss, M.S. (2001). End of life in nursing homes. In M.P. Lawton (Ed.), *Annual review of gerontology and geriatrics: Vol. 20. Focus on the end of life: Scientific and social issues* (pp.224–258). New York: Springer.

Motta, M., Bennati, E., Ferlito, L., Malaguarnera, M., & Motta, L. (2005). Italian Multicenter Study on Centenarians (IMUSCE) Successful aging in centenarians: Myths and reality. *Archives of Gerontology and Geriatrics, 40*(3), 241–251.

Moustakas, C. (1994). *Phenomenological research methods.* Thousand Oaks, CA: Sage.

Mouton, C.P., Talamantes, M., Parker, R.W., Espino–David, V. & Miles, T. (2001). Abuse and neglect in older men. *Clinical Gerontologist, 24*(3–4), 15–26.

Mullan, P. (2000). *The imaginary time bomb: Why an ageing population is not a social problem.* London, UK: IB Tauris.

Mullins, L.C., & Tucker, R.D. (Eds.). (1988). *Snowbirds in the sunbelt: Old Canadians in Florida.* Tampa, FL: University of South Florida, International Exchange Center on Gerontology.

Murphy, B., & Wolfson, M. (1991*). When the baby boom grows old: Impacts on Canada's public sector.* Ottawa: Statistics Canada.

Murray, C.J.L., & Lopez, A.D. (1996). *The global burden of disease: A comprehensive assessment of mortality and disability from diseases, injuries, and risk factors in 1990 and projected to 2020.* Boston, MA: Harvard School of Public Health on behalf of the World Health Organization and the World Bank

Murray, I.M. (1951). Assessment of physiologic age by combination of several criteria—vision, learning, blood pressure and muscle force. *Journals of Gerontology, 6,* 120–126.

Murzello, F. (1991). Quality of life of elderly East Indian immigrants. MSW Thesis. Calgary: University of Calgary.

Musil, C.M., Ahn, S., Haug, M., Warner, C., Morris, D., & Duffy, E. (1998). Health problems and health actions among community-dwelling older adults: Results of a health diary study. *Applied Nursing Research, 11*(3), 138–147.

Mussen, P., Honzik, M.P., & Eichorn, D.H. (1982). Early adult antecedents of life satisfaction at age 70. *Journals of Gerontology, 37,* 316–322.

Mustard, C.A., Derksen, S., Berthelot, J.M., Wolfson, M., & Roos, L.L. (1997). Age-specific education and income gradients in morbidity and mortality in a Canadian province. *Social Science and Medicine, 45*(3), 383–397.

Mutchler. J.E., Burr, J.A., Pienta, A.M., & Massagli. M.P. (1997). Pathway to labour force exit: Work transitions and work instability. *Journals of Gerontology: Social Sciences, 52B,* S4–S12.

Mutchler, J.E., Burr, J.A., & Rogerson, P.R. (1997). *Minority aging in a diverse society: Community, family, and individual determinants of living arrangements.* Buffalo, NY: Research Foundation of the State University of New York.

Myers, D.G. (2000). The funds, friends, and faith of happy people. *American Psychologist, 55*(1), 56–67.

Myers, D.G., & Diener, E. (1995). Who is happy? *Psychological Science, 6,* 10–19.

Myers, W.A. (1984). *Dynamic therapy of the older patient.* New York: J. Aronson.

Myles, J. (1984). *Old age and the welfare state.* Boston, MA: Little, Brown and Company.

Myles, J. (1988). Decline or impasse? The current state of the welfare state. *Studies in political economy, 26,* 73–107.

Myles, J. (1995). *The market's revenge: Old age security and social rights.* Ottawa: Caledon Institute of Social Policy.

Myles, J. (2000). *The maturation of Canada's retirement income system: Income levels, income inequality and low-income among the elderly.* Ottawa: Statistics Canada; Florida State University.

Myles, J. & Quadagno, J. (Eds.), (1991). *States, labour markets, and the future of old age policy* Philadelphia. PA: Temple University Press.

Myles, J., & Street, D. (1995). Should the economic life course be redesigned? Old age security in a time of transition. *Canadian Journal on Aging, 14*(2), 335–359.

Myles, J., & Teichroew, L. (1991). The politics of dualism: Pension policy in Canada. In J. Miles & J. Quadagno (Eds.), *States, labour markets, and the future of old-age policy* (pp. 84–104). Philadelphia, PA: Temple University Press.

Nagel, J. (1994). Constructing ethnicity: Creating and recreating ethnic identity and culture. *Social Problems, 41,* 152–176.

Najman, J. (1980). Theories of disease causation and the concept of general susceptibility. *Social Science and Medicine, 14A,* 231–237.

Namiash, D. (2000). Do our society's values, systems and policies contribute to the abuse and neglect of older adults? *Vital Aging Bulletin, 6*(3)

National Academy on an Aging Society. (1999). *Demography is not destiny.* Washington, DC: National Academy on an Aging Society.

National Advisory Committee (2000). A guide to end-of-life care for seniors. Ottawa ON: Tri-Co Printing Inc.

National Advisory Council on Aging (NACA). (1994*). Marital disruption in later life.* Ottawa: National Advisory Council on Aging.

National Advisory Council on Aging (NACA). (2001). *Seniors in Canada: A report card.* Ottawa: Minister of Public Works and Government Services Canada.

National Advisory Council on Aging (NACA). (2004). *The NACA position on Alzheimer disease and related dementias.* Ottawa: Minister of Public Works and Government Services Canada.

National Advisory Council on Aging (NACA). (2005). *Seniors from ethnocultural minorities.* (Catalogue No. H88-5/1-2005E). Ottawa: Minister of Public Works and Government Services Canada.

National Advisory Council on Aging (NACA). (2006). *Seniors in Canada: A Report Card.*

National Council of Welfare. (1999). *A pension primer.* Ottawa: NCW.

National Council of Welfare. (2000). *Poverty profile 1998.* Ottawa: NCW.

National Forum on Health. (1997). *Canada Health Action: Building on the legacy.* Volume I: The Final Report of the National Forum on Health and Volume II: Synthesis Reports and Issue Papers. Ottawa: NFH.

National Institute on Aging. (1996). *In search of the secrets of aging.* Bethesda, MD: National Institutes of Health.

National Population Health Survey (1994, 1995). *N.P.H.S. public use microdata documentation.* Ottawa: Statistics Canada.

National Union of Public and General Employees (NUPGE) (2004). NUPGE Poll. http://www.nupge.ca/news_2004/n04oc04a.htm.

Navarro, V. (2002a). Neoliberalism, "globalization," unemployment, inequalities and the welfare state. In V. Navarro (Ed.), *The political economy of social inequalities: Consequences for health and quality of life* (pp. 33–107). Amityville, NY: Baywood.

Navarro, V. (2002b). The political economy of the welfare state in developed capitalist countries. In V. Navarro (Ed.), *The political economy of social inequalities: Consequences for health and quality of life* (pp. 121–169). Amityville, NY: Baywood.

Near, J. & Rechner, P.L. (1993). Cross-cultural variations in predictors of life satisfaction: An historical view of differences among West European countries. *Social Indicators Research, 29,* 109–121.

Nelson, E.A., & Dannefer, D. (1992). Aged heterogeneity: Fact or fiction? The fate of diversity in gerontological research. *Gerontologist, 32*(1), 17–23.

Nelsen, N.E., & E.E. Nelsen. (1972). *Passing in the age stratification system.* Paper presented at the Annual Meeting of the American Sociological Association, New Orleans.

Neugarten, B.L. (1974). Age groups in American society and the rise of the young old. In F.R. Eisele, (Ed.). *Political consequences of aging* (pp. 187–198). The Annals of the American Academy of Political and Social Science.

Neugarten, B.L., Havighurst, R.S., & Tobin, S.S. (1961). The measurement of life satisfaction. *Journals of Gerontology, 16*, 134–143

Neundorfer, M.M., Harris, P.B., Britton, P.J., & Lynch, D.A. (2005). HIV-risk factors for midlife and older women. *The Gerontologist, 45*(5), 617–626.

Neupert, R.F. (1997). Demographic decomposition of household arrangements among the ethnic aged. *Australian Journal on Ageing, 16*, 213–217.

Newbold, K.B. (2005). Health status and health care of immigrants in Canada: A longitudinal analysis. *Journal of Health Services Research & Policy, 10*(2), 77–83.

Newbold, K. B., & Danforth, J. (2003). Health status and Canada's immigrant population. *Social Science & Medicine, 57*, 1981–1995.

Newsome, J. & Schultz, R. (1996). Social support as a mediator in the relation between functional status and quality of life in older adults. *Psychology and Aging, 11*(1), 34–44.

Ng, E., Wilkins, R., Gendron, F., & Berthelot, J.-M. (2005). *Dynamics of immigrant's health in Canada: Evidence from the national population health survey* (Catalogue No. 82-618-MWE2005002). Ottawa: Statistics Canada.

Noh, S., & Avison, W.R.(1996). Asian immigrants and the stress process: A study of Koreans in Canada. *Journal of Health and Social Behaviour, 37*(2), 192–208.

Nolan, K.A., Trahar, M.F., Clarke, C., & Blass, J.P. (1993). Respite retreat for dementia caregivers: A demonstration. *American Journal of Alzheimer's Care and Related Disorders and Research, 8*(1), 34–38.

Noonan, A.E., & Tennstedt, S.L. (1997). Meaning in caregiving and its contribution to caregiver well-being. *The Gerontologist, 39*,177–185.

Norris, J.E. & Tindale, J.A. (1994). *Among generations: The cycle of adult relationships.* New York: Freeman.

Northcott, H.C. (1994). Public perceptions of the population aging "crisis." *Canadian Public Policy, 20*, 66–77.

Nussbaum, J.F., Pitts, M.J., Huber, F.N., Raup Krieger, J.L., & Ohs, J.E. (2005). Ageism and ageist language across the life span: Intimate relationships and non-intimate interactions. *Journal of Social Issues, 61*(2), 287.

Nuttman-Schwartz, O. (2004). Like a high wave: Adjustment to retirement. *The Gerontologist, 44*(2), 229–236.

Ogden, R., & Young, M.G. (1998). Euthanasia and assisted suicide: A survey of registered social workers in British Columbia. *British Journal of Social Work, 28*(2), 161–175.

O'Hanley, S., Ward, A., Zwirren, L., McCarron, R.F., Ross, J., & Rippe, J.M. (1987). Validation of a one-mile walk test in 70–79 year olds. *Medicine and Science in Sports and Exercise, 19*, 356–362.

Olesen, V.L. (2005). Early millennial feminist qualitative research: Challenges and contours. In N. Denzin & Y. Lincoln (Eds.), Handbook of qualitative research (3rd ed., pp. 235–278). Thousand Oaks: Sage Publications.

Olsen, J.M., Vernon, P.A., Harris, J.A., & Jang, K.L. (2001). The heritability of attitudes: A study of twins. *The American Psychological Association, 80*(6), 845–860.

Olshansky, S.J., & Ault, A.B. (1986). The fourth stage of the epidemiologic transition: The age of delayed degenerative diseases. *Milbank Memorial Fund Quarterly, 64*, 355–391.

Olshansky, S.J., Carnes, B.A., Rodgers, R.G., & Smith, L. (1997). Infectious diseases—New and ancient threats to world health. *Population Bulletin, 52*(2), 1–52. Washington, DC: Population Reference Bureau, Inc.

Olson, L. (Ed.) (2001). *Age through ethnic lenses: Caring for the elderly in a multicultural society.* Lanham, MD: Rowan & Littlefield.

Omran, A.R. (1971). The theory of epidemiological transition. *Milbank Memorial Fund Quarterly, 49*, 509–538.

O'Rand, A. (2003). The future of the life course: Late modernity and life course risks. In J. Mortimer & S. Shanahan (Eds.), *Handbook of the life course* (pp.693–702). New York: Kluwer Academic/Plenum Publishers.

O'Rand, A., & Hamil-Luker, J. (2005). Process of cumulative adversity: Childhood disadvantage and increased risk of heart attack across the life course. *Journals of Gerontology, 60B* (special issue II), 117–124.

O'Rand, A.M., & Henretta, J.C. (1999). *Age and inequality: Diverse pathways through later life.* Boulder, CO: Westview Press.

O'Reilly, P., & Caro, F.G. (1994). Productive aging: An overview of the literature. *Journal of Aging & Social Policy, 6*(3), 39–71.

Organisation for Economic Cooperation and Development (OECD). (1998). *The retirement decision in OECD countries.* OECD Working Papers, 6(38). Paris: OECD.

Organisation for Economic Cooperation and Development (OECD). (2005). *OECD Health Data 2005. How does Canada compare.* Briefing note for OECD Health Data 2005: Canada. Retrieved Apr 20, 2006 from http://www.oecd.org/dataoecd/16/9/349696633.pdf

Osberg, L. & Fortin, P. (1996). Credibility mountain. In L. Osberg & P. Fortin, (Eds.) *Unnecessary debts* (pp. 157–172). Toronto: James Lorimer.

Ouaknine, L., Csank, P., & Stones, M.J. (1997). *The fulfillment of well-aging: A preventative health care intervention program for seniors.* Durban, South Africa: International Federation on Aging.

Pacey, M. (2002). *Living alone and living with children: The living arrangements of Canadian and Chinese-Canadian seniors.* SEDAP Research Paper Series No.74. Hamilton: McMaster University.

Pakans, A. (1989). Stepping down in former times: A comparative assessment of retirement in traditional Europe. In D.I. Kertzer & K. Warner Schaie (Eds.),

Age structuring in comparative perspective (pp. 175–195). Hillsdale, NJ: Lawrence Erlbaum Associates.

Palmore, E.B. (1971). Attitudes toward aging as shown in humor. *The Gerontologist, 11*, 181–186.

Palmore, E.B. (1988). *The facts on aging quiz: A handbook of uses and results.* New York: Springer.

Palmore, E.B. (1990). Aging: Positive and negative. New York: Springer.

Pang, K.Y. (1998). Causes of dysphoric experiences among elderly Korean Immigrants. *Clinical Gerontologist, 19*(4), 17–33.

Parkin, A.J., & Walter, B.M. (1992). Recollective experience, normal aging, and frontal dysfunction. *Psychology and Aging, 7*, 290–298.

Parks, S.H. & Pilisuk, M. (1991). Caregiver burden: Gender and the psychological costs of caregiving. *American Journal of Orthopsychiatry, 61*(4): 501–509.

Partridge, C., Johnston, M., & Morris, L. (1996). Disability and health: Perceptions of a sample of elderly people. *Physiotherapy Research International 1*(1), 17–29. Centre for Health Services Studies, University, Canterbury, UK.

Pavalko, E.K., & Artis, J.E. (1997). Women's caregiving and paid work: Causal relationships in late life. *Journals of Gerontology Series B Psychological Sciences and Social Sciences, 52B*(4), S170–S179.

Pavalko, E.K., & Elder, G.H. Jr. (1990). World War II and divorce: A life course perspective. *American Journal of Sociology, 95*, 1213–1234.

Payne, B.J., & Strain, L. A. (1990). Family social support in later life: Ethnic group variations. *Canadian Ethnic Studies, 22*(2), 99–100.

Payne, B.K., & Berg, B.L. (1999). Perceptions of nursing home workers, police chiefs, and college students regarding crime against the elderly: An exploratory study. *American Journal of Criminal Justice, 24*, 139–149.

Pearlin, L.I. (1985). Social structure and processes of social support. In S. Cohen & S.L. Syme (Eds.), *Social support and health.* Orland, FL: Academic Press.

Pearlin, L.I., Mullan, J.T., Semple, S.J., & Skaff, M.M. (1990). Caregiving and the stress process: An overview of concepts and their comments. *The Gerontologist, 30*, 583–594.

Peel, N.M., McLure R.J., & Barrett, H.P. (2005). Behavioral determinants of healthy aging. *American Journal of Preventive Medicine 28*, 298–304.

Pendakur, K., & Pendakur, R. (1998). The colour of money: Earnings differentials among ethnic groups in Canada. *Canadian Journal of Economics, 31*(3), 518–548.

Pendakur, R., & Hennebry, J. (1998). *Multicultural Canada: A demographic overview 1996.* Canadian Heritage Multiculturalism.

Pendry, E., Barrett, G., & Victor, C. (1999). Changes in household composition among the over sixties: A longitudinal analysis of the Health and Life Surveys. *Health and Social Care in the Community, 7*, 109–119.

Peng, I., & Lettner, M. (2004). *Socio-economic inclusion: Demographic aging among immigrant populations and implications for health policy in Ontario.* Prepared for Health Canada, Ontario/Nunavut Region.

Penhale, B. (1999). Bruises on the soul: Older women, domestic violence, and elder abuse. *Journal of Elder Abuse and Neglect, 11*, 1–22.

Penhale, B. & Kingston, B. (1997). Elder abuse, mental health and later life: Steps towards an understanding. *Aging and Mental Health, 1*, 296–304.

Penning, M. (1983). Multiple jeopardy: Age, sex and ethnic variations. *Canadian Ethnic Studies, 15* (3), 81–105.

Penning, M.J. (1995). Cognitive impairment, caregiver burden and the utilization of health services. *Journal of Aging and Health, 7*(2), 233–253.

Penning, M.J. (1998). In the middle: Parental caregiving in the context of other roles. *Journals of Gerontology: Social Sciences, 53B*, S188-S197.

Penning, M.J., Allan, D.E., & Brackley, M.E. (2001, July). *Home care and health reform: Changes in home care utilization in one Canadian province, 1990–1998.* Paper presented at the International Association of Gerontology, Vancouver, B.C.

Penning, M.J., & Chappell, N.L. (1990). Self care in relation to informal and formal care. *Ageing and Society, 10*(1), 41–59.

Penning, M.J., & Chappell, N.L. (1993). Age-related differences. In T. Stephens & D.F. Graham (Eds.), *Canada's Health Promotion Survey 1990: Technical report.* (Catalogue No. H39-263/2-1990E). Ottawa: Minister of Supply and Services Canada.

Pentland, H.C. (1981). *Labour and capital in Canada, 1650–1860.* Toronto: James Lorimer.

Peracchi, F., & Welch, F. (1994). Trends in labour force transitions of older men and women. *Journal of Labour Economics, 12*(2): 210–242.

Peressini, T., & McDonald, L. (1998). An evaluation of a training program on alcoholism and older adults for health care and social service practitioners. *Journals of Gerontology and Geriatrics Education, 4*(18).

Peters, S. (1995). *Exploring Canadian values: Foundations for well-being.* Ottawa: Renouf Publishing.

Peterson, C. (2000). The future of Optimism. *American Psychologists, 55*, 44–55.

Peterson, C., & Stunkard, A. (1989). Personal control and health promotion. *Social Science and Medicine, 28*, 819–828.

Pezzin, L.E., & Schone, B.S. (1999). Parental marital disruption and intergenerational transfers: An analysis of lone elderly parents. *Demography, 36*, 287–297.

Phillips, L.R. (2000). Domestic violence and aging women. *Geriatric Nursing, 21*,188–195.

Phillipson, C. (1982). *Capitalism and the construction of old age.* London, UK: Macmillan.

Phillipson, C. (1999). The social construction of retirement: Perspectives from critical theory and political economy. In M. Minkler & C.L. Estes, (Eds.), *Critical*

Gerontology. Perspectives from Political and Moral Economy (pp. 315–327). Amityville, NY: Baywood Publishing.

Phillipson, C. (2003). Globalization and the reconstruction of old age: New challenges for critical gerontology. In S. Biggs, A. Lowenstein, & J. Hendricks (Eds.), *The need for theory: Critical approaches to social gerontology* (pp. 163–179). Amityville, NY: Baywood.

Phipps, S., Burton, P., & Lethbridge, L. (2001). In and out of the labour market: Long-term economic consequences of child-related interruptions to women's paid work. *Canadian Journal of Economics, 34,* 411–429.

Phua, V.C., Kaufman, G., & Park, K.S. (2001). Strategic adjustments of elderly Asian Americans: Living arrangements and headship. *Journal of Comparative Family Studies, 32,* 263–281.

Pienta, A. (1999). Early childbearing patterns and women's labour force behaviour in later life. *Journal of Women in Aging* 11(1): 69–84.

Pienta, A. (2003). Partners in marriage: An analysis of husbands' and wives' retirement behaviour. *Journal of Applied Gerontology, 22*(3), 340–358.

Pienta, A.M., Burr, J.A., & Mutchler, J.E. (1994). Women's labour force participation in later life: The effects of early work and family experiences. *Journals of Gerontology: Social Sciences, 49,* S231–S239.

Pillemer, K., & Finkelhor, D. (1988). Prevalence of elder abuse: A random sample survey. *The Gerontologist, 28,* 51–57.

Pinquart, M. & Sorenson, S. (2001a). Gender differences in self-concept and psychological well-being in old age: A meta-analysis. *The Journals of Gerontology: Psychological Sciences, Vol 56B*(4), P195–P213.

Pinquart, M., & Sorensen, S. (2001b). How effective are psychotherapeutic and other psychosocial interventions with older adults? A meta-analysis. *Journal of Mental Health and Aging, 7*(2), 207–243.

Podnieks, E. (1992). National Survey on Abuse of the Elderly in Canada. *Journal of Elder Abuse and Neglect* 4: 5–58.

Podnieks, E. & Baille, E. (1995). Education as the key to the prevention of elder abuse and neglect. In Maclean, M., (Ed.). *Abuse and neglect of older Canadians— Strategies for change.* (pp. 81–94). Toronto: Thompson Educational Publishing.

Poland, B., Coburn, D., Robertson, A., & Eakin, J. (1998). Wealth, equity and health care: A critique of a "population health" perspective on the determinants of health. *Social Science and Medicine, 46*(7), 785–798.

Poon, R. (2005). Who's missing out on the GIS? *Perspectives on Labour and Income, 17*(4), 18.

Population Reference Bureau. (2001). *2001 World population data sheet.* Washington, DC: Population Reference Bureau, Inc.

Population Reference Bureau. (2005). *2005 World population data sheet.* Washington, DC: Population Reference Bureau, Inc.

Porter, E.J., Ganong, L.H., Drew, N., Lanes, T.I. (2004). A new typology of home-care helpers. *The Gerontologist. 44*(6) 750–759.

Powell, J. (2006). *Social theory and aging.* Lanham, MD: Rowan & Littlefield.

Prado, C.G. (1998). Last choice: Preemptive suicide in advanced age (2nd ed.). Westport, CT: Greenwood Press.

Preston, S.H. (1984). Children and the elderly: Divergent paths for America's elderly. *Demography, 21,* 435–457.

Price, C.A. (2000). Women and retirement: Relinquishing professional identity. *Journal of Aging Studies, 14*(1), 81–101.

Price, C. & Joo, E. (2005). Exploring the relationship between marital status and women's retirement satisfaction. *Journal of Aging and Human Development, 61*(1) 37–35.

Pritchard, J. (2002). *Male victims of elder abuse: Their experiences and needs.* York, UK: Joseph-Rowntree Foundation.

Proctor, W.R. & Hirdes, J.P. (2001). Pain and cognitive status among nursing home residents in Canada. *Official Journal of the Canadian Pain Society, 6*(3), 119–125.

Prohaska, T.R., Leventhal, E.A., Leventhal, H., & Keller, M.L. (1985). Health practices and illness cognition in young, middle-aged, and elderly adults. *Journals of Gerontology, 40,* 569–578.

Pruchno, R.A. (1990). Effects of help patterns on the mental health of spouse caregivers. *Research on Aging, 12*(1), 57–71.

Prus, S. (2000). Income inequality as a Canadian cohort ages. *Research on Aging, 22*(3), 211–238.

Prus S. (2004). A life course perspective on the relationship between socio-economic status and health: Testing the divergence hypothesis. *Canadian Journal on Aging* (suppl.), S145–S153.

Public Health Agency of Canada. (2005). Inventory of falls prevention initiatives in Canada.

Pyper, W. (2006). Aging, health and work. *Perspective on labour and income, 18*(1) 48–58.

Quadagno, J. (1982). *Aging in early industrial society.* New York: Academic Press.

Quadagno, J., & Reid, J. (1999). The political economy perspective in aging. In V.L. Bengston & K.W. Schaie (Eds.), *Handbook of theories of aging* (pp. 344–358). New York: Springer.

Qualls, S.H. (1993). Family therapy with older adults. *Generations, 17,* 73–74.

Quick, H.E., & Moen, P.B. (1997). Gender, employment, and retirement quality: A life course approach to the differential experiences of men and women. Ithaca, NY: Bronfenbrenner Life Course Centre, Cornell University.

Quinn, J.F. (1999) Retirement patterns and bridge jobs in the 1990s. *EBRI Issue Brief,* No. 206, 1–22.

Rachlis, M., & Kushner, C. (1989). *Second opinion: What's wrong with Canada's health care system and how to fix it.* Toronto: Collins.

Raina, P., McIntyre, C., Zhu, B., McDowell, I., Santaguido, L., Kristjansson, B., et al. (2004). Understanding the influence of the complex relationships among informal and formal supports on the well-being of caregivers of persons with dementia. *Canadian Journal on Aging, 23,* S49–S59.

Rajulton, F. & Ravanera, Z.R. (1995). The family life course in twentieth century Canada: Changes, trends and interrelationships. In R. Beaujot, E.M. Gee, F. Rajulton, & Z.R. Ravanera (Eds.), *Family over the life course* (pp. 115–150). (Catalogue No. 91-643E). Ottawa: Statistics Canada.

Rakowski, W., & Clark, N.M. (1985). Future outlook, caregiving and care-receiving in the family context. *The Gerontologist, 25,* 618–623.

Raphael, D., Brown, I., & Wheeler, J. (Eds.). (2000). *A city for all ages: Fact or fiction? Effects of government policy decisions on Toronto seniors' quality of life.* Toronto: Centre for Health Promotion, University of Toronto. Retrieved April 23, 2006, from http://www.utoronto.ca/seniors.

Rasulo, D., Christensen, K., & Tomassini, C. (2005). The influence of social relations on mortality. *The Gerontologist, 45*(5), 601–608.

Rattenbury, C., & Stones, M.J. (1989). A controlled evaluation of reminiscence and current-topics discussion groups in a nursing home context. *The Gerontologist, 29,* 768–771.

Rein, M. (1969). Social class and the utilization of medical care services: A study of British experience under the National Health Service. *Hospitals, 43,* 43.

Rein, M., & Turner, J. (1999). Work, family, state and market: Income packaging for older households. *International Social Security Review, 52*(3), 93–106.

Reinhardt, U.E. (2001). Commentary: On the apocalypse of the retiring baby boom. *Canadian Journal on Aging, 20* (suppl. 1), 192–204.

Reisberg, B., Ferris, S.H., deLeon, M.J. & Crook, (1982). Relationships in late midlife. *The Journals of Gerontology: Series B: Psychological Sciences and Social Sciences, 52B*(4), SI70–S179.

Reitzes, D., & Mutran, E. (2004). The transition to retirement: Stages and factors that influence retirement adjustment. *International Journal of Human Development, 59*(1), 63–84.

Reitzes, D.C., Mutran, E.J., & Fernandez, M.E. (1996). Preretirement influences on postretirement self-esteem. *Journals of Gerontology: Series B: Psychological Sciences and Social sciences, 51B*(5), S242–S249.

Renaud, M., Good, D., Nadeau, L., Ritchie, J., Way-Clark, R., & Connolly, C. (1996). *Determinants of health working group synthesis report, Canada health action: Building on the legacy: Synthesis reports and issues papers, Vol. II.* Ottawa: National Forum on Health.

Reno, V. (1971). *Why men stop working at or before age 65.* U.S. Department of Health, Education and Welfare, Social Security Administration, Office of Research and Statistics.

Retherford, R.D. (1975). *The changing sex differential in mortality.* Westport, CT: Greenwood Press.

Reynolds, S.L., & Schonfeld, L. (2004). Using Florida's adult protective services data in research: Opportunities and challenges. *Journal of Elder Abuse and Neglect, 16*(1), 1–22.

Richardson, C.J. (1992). The implications of separation and divorce for family structure. Report prepared for the *Review of Demography and its Social and Economic Implications,* Health and Welfare Canada.

Richardson, V., & Kilty, K.M. (1992). Retirement intentions among Black professionals: Implications for practice with older Black adults. *The Gerontologist, 32*(1), 7–16.

Riley, M.W. (1971). Social gerontology and the age stratification of society. *Gerontologist, 11,* 79–87.

Riley, M.W. (1987). On the significance of age in sociology. *American Sociological Review, 52,* 1–14.

Riley, M.W. (1997). *Age integration: Challenge to a new institute.* Raleigh, NC: University of North Carolina, Institute on Aging.

Riley, M.W. (1998). A life course approach: Autobiographical notes. In J.Z. Giele & G.H. Elder Jr. (Eds.), *Methods of life course research: Qualitative and quantitative approaches* (pp. 28–51). Thousand Oaks, CA: Sage Publications.

Riley, M.W., Foner, A. & Riley, J.W., Jr. (1999). The aging and society paradigm. In V.L. Bengtson & K.W. Schaie (Eds.), *Handbook of theories of aging* (pp. 327–343). New York: Springer.

Riley, M.W., Johnson, M., & Foner, A. (1972). *Aging and society, Vol.3: Sociology of age stratification.* New York: Russell Sage Foundation.

Riley, M.W., & Riley, J.W. Jr. (1994). Age integration and the lives of older people. *The Gerontologist, 34*(1), 110–115.

Riska, E., & Wegar, K. (1993). *Gender, work and medicine. Women and the medical division of labour.* Newbury Park, CA: Sage.

Roberto, K., & Stroes, J. (1992). Grandchildren and grandparents: Roles, influences and relationships. *International Journal of Aging and Human Development, 34,* 227–239.

Roberts, S.B., Pi-Sunyer, X., Kuller, L., Lane, M.A., Ellison, P., Prior, J.C., et al. (2001). Physiologic effects of lowering caloric intake in nonhuman primates and nonobese humans. *The Journals of Gerontology. Series A, Biological Sciences and Medical Sciences, 56*(1), 66–75.

Robertson, A. (2000). "I saw the handwriting on the wall": Shades of meaning in reasons for early retirement. *Journal of Aging Studies, 14*(1), 63–79.

Rogers, R.G., Hummer, R.A., & Nam, C. (2000). *Living and dying in the USA.* San Diego, CA: Academic Press.

Romanow, R.J., Commissioner. (2002). *Building on values. The future of health care in Canada.* Commission on the future of health care in Canada. Final Report. National Library of Canada.

Romanucci-Ross, L., De Vos, G. & Tsuda, T. (2006). *Ethnic identity: Problems and prospects for the 21st century.* Lanham MD: AltaMira Press.

Rook, K.S., & Pietromonaco, P. (1987). Close relationships: Ties that heal or ties that bind? In W.H. Jones & D. Perlman, (Eds.), *Advances in personal relationships.* Greenwich, CT: JAI Press.

Roos, N.P. & Havens, B. (1991). Predictors of successful aging: A twelve year study of Manitoba elderly. *American Journal of Public Health, 81,* 63–68

Roos, N.P., Havens, B., & Black, C. (1993). Living longer but doing worse: Assessing health status in elderly persons at two points in time in Manitoba, Canada, 1971 and 1983. *Social Science and Medicine, 36,* 273–282.

Roos N.P., & Roos L.L. (1994). Small area variations, practice style and quality of care. In R.G. Evans, M.L. Barer, T.R. Marmor (Eds): *Why are some people healthy and others not? The determinants of health of populations.* Hawthorne, NY: Aldine de Gruyte Press.

Rorty, R. (1991). *Objectivity, relativism, and truth.* Cambridge, UK: Cambridge University Press.

Rosenau, P.M. (1992). *Post-modernism and the social sciences: Insights, inroads and intrusions.* Princeton, NJ: Princeton University Press

Rosenbluth, G. (1996). The debt and Canada's social programs. In L. Osberg & P. Fortin (Eds.), *Unnecessary debts* (pp. 90–111). Toronto: James Lorimer.

Rosenkoetter, M.M., & Garris, J.M. (1998). Psychosocial changes following retirement. *Journal of Advanced Nursing, 27,* 966–976.

Rosenmayr, L., & Kockeis, E. (1963). Propositions for a sociological theory of aging and the family. *International Social Science Journal, 15,* 410–426.

Rosenthal, C.J. (1983). Aging, ethnicity and the family: Beyond the modernization thesis. *Canadian Ethnic Studies, 15*(3), 1–16.

Rosenthal, C.J. (1985). Kinkeeping in the familial division of labor. *Journal of Marriage and the Family, 47,* 965–974.

Rosenthal, C.J. (1986). Differentiation of multigenerational households. *Canadian Journal on Aging, 5,* 27–42.

Rosenthal, C.J. (1987). Aging and intergenerational relations in Canada. In V.W. Marshall (Ed.), *Aging in Canada: Social Perspectives* (2nd ed, pp. 311–342). Markham: Fitzhenry and Whiteside.

Rosenthal, C.J. (2000). Aging families: Have current changes and challenges been "oversold"? In E.M. Gee & G.M. Gutman (Eds.), *The overselling of population aging: Apocalyptic demography, intergenerational challenges, and social policy* (pp. 45–63). Toronto: Oxford University Press.

Rosenthal, C.J., & Gladstone, J. (2000). *Grandparenthood in Canada.* Ottawa: The Vanier Institute of the Family.

Rosenthal, C.J., Martin-Matthews, A., & Matthews, S.H. (1996). Caught in the middle? Occupancy in multiple roles and help to parents in a national probability sample of Canadian adults. *Journals of Gerontology, 51B,* S274–S283.

Rothman, D.J. (1971). *The discovery of the asylum: Social order and disorder in the new republic.* Boston, MA: Little, Brown.

Rowe, G., & Nguyen, H. (2003). Older workers and the labour market. *Perspective on labour and income, 15*(1), 55–58.

Rowe, J.W., & Kahn, R.L. (1987). Human aging: Usual and successful. *Science, 237,* 143–149.

Rowe, J.W., & Kahn, R.L. (1997). Successful aging. *The Gerontologist, 37*(4), 433–440.

Rowe, J.W., & Kahn, R.L. (1998). *Successful aging.* New York: Pantheon Books/Random House.

Royal Commission on Aboriginal Peoples. (1996). *Looking Forward, Looking Back—Report of the Royal Commission on Aboriginal Peoples. Vol.1.* Ottawa: Ministry of Supply and Services Canada.

Rubin, A., & Babbie, E. (2005). *Research methods for social work* (5th ed.). Pacific Grove, CA: Brooks/Cole.

Rubin, D.C. (1999). Autobiographical memory and aging: Distributions of memories across the life-span and their implications for survey research. In N. Schwarz, & D.C. Park (Eds.), *Cognition, aging, and self-reports* (pp. 163-183). Hove, UK: Psychology Press/Erlbaum.

Rudd, M.G., Viney, L.L, & Preston, C.A. (1999). Grief experienced by spousal caregivers of dementia patients: The role of place of care of patient and gender of the caregiver. *International Journal of Aging and Human Development, 48*(3), 217–240.

Rupp, D.E., Vodanovich, S.J., & Crede, M. (2005). The multidimensional nature of ageism: Construct validity and group differences. *Journal of Social Psychology, 145,* 335–362.

Ruth, J.E., & Birren, J.E. (1985). Creativity in adulthood and old age: Relations to intelligence, sex, and mode of testing. *International Journal of Behavioral Development, 8,* 99–109.

Ryff, C.D. (1989) Beyond Ponce de Leon and life satisfaction: New directions in the quest for successful aging. *International Journal of Aging and Human Development, 12,* 35–55.

Ryff, C.D., & Keyes, C.L.M. (1995). The structure of psychological well-being revisited. *Journal of Personality and Social Psychology, 69,* 719–727.

Safford, F. (1995). Aging stressors for holocaust survivors and their families. *Journal of Gerontological Social Work 24*(1–2), 131–153.

Salthouse, T.A. (1984). Effects of age and skill in typing. *Journal of Experimental Psychology: General, 113,* 345–371.

Salthouse, T.A. (1990). Influence of experince on differences in cognitive functioning. *Human Factors, 32*(5), 551–569.

Salthouse, T.A., & Babcock, R.L. (1991). Decomposing adult age differences in working memory. *Developmental Psychology, 27*(5), 763–776.

Salthouse, T.A., Kausler, D.H., & Saults, J.S. (1986). Groups versus individuals as the comparison unit in cognitive aging research. *Developmental Neuropsychology, 2,* 363–372.

Sankar, A., & Gubrium, J.F. (1994). *Qualitative methods in aging research.* Thousand Oaks, CA: Sage.

Sato, S., Shimonaka, Y., Nakazato, K., & Kawaai, C. (1997). A life-span developmental study of age identity: Cohort and gender differences. *The Japanese Journal of Developmental Psychology, 8*(2), 88–97.

Sauer, W.J., & Coward, R.T. (1985). The role of social support networks in the care of the elderly. In W.J. Sauer & R.T. Coward (Eds.), *Social support networks and the care of the elderly: Theory, research, and practice.* New York: Springer.

Schaie, K.W. (1977). Quasi-experimental designs in the psychology of aging. In J.E. Birren & K.W. Schaie (Eds.), *Handbook of the psychology of aging* (pp. 39–58). New York: Van Nostrand Reinhold.

Schaie, K.W. (1996). Intellectual development in adulthood. The Seattle longitudinal study. New York: Cambridge University Press.

Schaie, K.W., & Hofer, S.M. (2001). Longitudinal studies in aging research. In J. E. Birren & K.W. Schaie (Eds.), *Handbook of Aging* (pp. 53–57). New York: Academic Press.

Schaie, K.W., & Willis, S.L., (1993). Age difference patterns of psychometric intelligence in adulthood: Generalizability within and across ability domains. *Psychology and Aging, 8*(1), 44–55.

Schellenberg, G. (1994). *The road to retirement: Demographic and economic changes in the 90s.* Ottawa: Canadian Council on Social Development.

Schellenberg, G. (2003). Retirement transitions in Canada: Evidence from the 2002 General Social Service. The 2003 Symposium on New Issues in Retirement, Ottawa, September 5–6, 2003.

Schellenberg, G. (2004). *The retirement plans and expectations of non-retired Canadians 45 to 59.* (Catalogue No. 11F0019MIE). Ottawa: Statistics Canada.

Schellenberg, G., & Silver, C. (2004) You can't always get what you want: Retirement preferences and experiences. *Canadian Social Trends* (Catalogue No. 11-008). Ottawa: Statistics Canada, 2–7.

Schellenberg, G., Turcotte, M., Ram, B. (2005). Post-retirement employment. *Perspective on labour and income, 17*(4) 14–17.

Schellenberg, G., Turcotte, M., & Ram, B. (2006). The changing characteristics of older couples and joint retirement in Canada. In L. Stone. (Ed.), *The new frontiers of research on retirement* (pp.199–218). (Catalogue No. 75-511-XPE). Ottawa: Minister of Industry.

Schlegel, K.L., & Shannon, S.E. (2000). Legal guidelines related to end-of-life decisions: Are nurse practitioners knowledgeable? *Journal of Gerontological Nursing, 26*(9), 14–23.

Schlesinger, R.A., & Schlesinger, B. (2004). Grandparents and adult grandchildren: Roles and influences, *Transition, 34*(3).

Schonfield, A.E.D., & Robertson, B.A. (1966). Memory storage and aging. *Canadian Journal of Psychology, 20,* 228–236.

Schonfield, D. (1982). Who is stereotyping whom and why? *The Gerontologist, 22,* 267–272.

Schonknecht, P., Pantel, J., Kruse, A., & Schroder, J. (2005). Prevalence and natural course of aging-associated cognitive decline in a population-based sample of young-old subjects. *American Journal of Psychiatry, 162*(11), 2071–2077.

Schroots, J.J.F. (1995). Psychological models of aging. *Canadian Journal on Aging, 14,* 44–67.

Schultz, K.S., Morton, K.R., & Weckerle, J.R. (1998). Influence of push and pull factors on voluntary and involuntary early retirees' retirement: Decision and adjustment. *Journal of Vocational Behaviour, 53,* 45–57.

Schulz, R., Beach, S., Ives, D.G., Martire, L.M., Aariyo, A.A., & Kop, W.J. (2000). Association between depression and mortality in older adults. *Archives of Internal Medicine, 160,* 1761–1768.

Schulz, R., Newsom, J.T., Fleissner, K., Decamp, A.R., & Nieboer, A.P. (1997). The effects of bereavement after family caregiving. *Aging and Mental Health, 1*(3), 269–282.

Schulz, R., & Williamson, G.M. (1991). Two year longitudinal study of depression among Alzheimer's caregivers. *Psychology and Aging, 6*(4), 569–578.

Schupf, N., Tang, M.X., Albert, S.M., Costa, R., Andrews, H., Lee, J.H., et al. (2005). Decline in cognitive and functional skills increases mortality risk in nondemented elderly. *Neurology, 65*(8), 1218–1226.

Schwandt, T.A (2001). *Qualitative inquiry: A dictionary of terms* (2nd ed.). Thousand Oaks, CA: Sage.

Schwartz, W.B. (1998). *Life without disease: The pursuit of medical utopia.* Berkeley, CA: University of California Press.

Schwartzman, A.E., Gold, D., Andres, D., Arbuckle, T.Y., & Chaikelson, J. (1987). Stability of intelligence: A forty-year follow-up. *Canadian Journal of Psychology, 41,* 244–256.

Seale, C., & Addington-Hall, J. (1994). Euthanasia: Why people want to die earlier. *Social Science and Medicine, 39,* 647–654.

Seccombe, K., & Ishii-Kuntz, M. (1994). Gender and social relationships among the never-married. *Sex Roles, 30,* 585–603.

Segall, A., & Chappell, N. (1991). Making sense out of sickness: Lay explanations of chronic illness among older adults. *Advances in Medical Sociology, 2,* 115–133.

Segall, A., & Chappell, N.L. (2000). *Health and health care in Canada.* Toronto: Prentice Hall.

Seidlitz, L., Duberstein, P.R., Cox, C., & Conwell, Y. (1995). Attitudes of older people toward suicide and assisted suicide: An analysis of Gallup Poll findings. *Journal of the American Geriatrics Society, 43*(9), 993–998.

Settersten, R.A. Jr. (1999). *Lives in time and place: The problems and promises of developmental science.* Amityville, NY: Baywood.

Settersten, R.A. (2003). *Invitation to the life course: Toward new understandings in later life.* Amityville, NY: Baywood.

Settersten, R.A. (2006a). Aging and the life course. In R. Binstock & L. George (Eds.), *Handbook of aging and the social sciences* (pp 3–19). Burlington MA: Elsevier Academic Press.

Settersten, R.A. (2006b). When nations call: How wartime military service matters for the life course and aging. *Research on Aging. 28*(1), 12–36.

Settersten, R.A, & Hagestad, G.O. (1996). What's the latest? Cultural age deadlines for family transitions. *Gerontologist, 36,* 178–188.

Settersten, R.A. & Hagestad, G.O. (2001). What's the latest? II. Cultural age deadlines for educational and work transitions. *The Gerontologist, 36*(5) 602–613.

Shanahan, M.J., Elder, G.H. Jr., & Miech, R.A. (1997). History and agency in men's lives: Pathways to achievement in cohort perspective. *Sociology of Education, 70,* 54–67.

Shanas, E. (1979). Social myth as hypothesis: The case of the family relations of old people. *The Gerontologist, 19,* 3–9.

Shannon, M., & Kidd, M.P. (2001). Projecting the trend in the Canadian gender wage gap 2001–2031: Will an increase in female education acquisition and commitment be enough? *Canadian Public Policy, XXVII,* 447–467.

Shapiro, A. (2003). Later-life divorce and parent–adult child contact and proximity: A longitudinal study. *Journal of Family Issues, 24*(2), 264–285.

Shapiro, E. (1991). *Manitoba health care studies and their policy implications.* Winnipeg, MB: Manitoba Centre for Health Policy and Evaluation, Department of Community Health Sciences, University of Manitoba.

Shapiro, E. & Tate, R. (1988). Who is really at risk of institutionalisation? *The Gerontologist, 28,* 237–245.

Sharpley, C.F., & Layton, R. (1998). Effects of age of retirement, reason for retirement, and pre-retirement training on psychological and physical health during retirement. *Australian Psychologist, 33*(2), 119–124.

Shephard, R.J. (1969). Endurance fitness. Toronto: University of Toronto Press.

Shephard, R.J. (1978). Physical activity and aging. Chicago, IL: Yearbook Medical Publishers.

Shernoff, M. (1997). *Gay widowers: Life after death of a partner.* New York: Haworth Press.

Shewchuk, R., Foelker, G., & Niederehe, G. (1990). Measuring locus of control in elderly persons. *International Journal of Aging and Human Development, 30,* 213–224.

Shmotkin, D (1991). The role of time orientation in life satisfaction across the life span. *Journals of Gerontology: Psychological Sciences, 46,* 243–250.

Shrybman, S. (2001). International trade agreements. In A. Ostry & K. Cardiff (Eds.), *Trading away health? Globalization and health policy.* Report from the 14th Annual Health Policy Conference of the Centre for Health Services and Policy Research, Vancouver, B.C., November 9, 2001 (pp. 11–15).

Simich, L., Beiser, M., & Mawani, F.N. (2003). Social support and the significance of shared experience in refugee migration and resettlement. *Western Journal of Nursing Research, 25*(7), 872–891.

Simich, L., Beiser, M., Stewart, M., & Mwakarimba, E. (2005). Providing social support for immigrants and refugees in Canada: Challenges and directions. *Journal of Immigrant Health, 7*(4), 259–268.

Simon, J.G., De Boer, J.B., Joung, I.M.A., Bosma, H., & Mackenbach, J.P. (2005). Perceived health: How is your health in general? A qualitative study on self-assessed health. *European Journal of Public Health, 15*(2), 200–208.

Simoneau, G.G., & Leibowitz, H.W. (1996). Posture, gait, and falls. In J.E. Birren & K.W. Schaie (Eds.), *Handbook of the psychology of aging* (4th ed.). San Diego, CA: Academic Press.

Simonton, D.K. (1990). Creativity and wisdom in aging. In. J.E. Birren & K.W. Schaie (Eds.), *Handbook of the psychology of aging* (3rd ed., pp. 320–329). San Diego, CA: Academic Press.

Simpson, I.H. (1975). Review symposium on work in America. *Sociology of Work and Occupations, 2,* 182–187.

Singer, P.A., Choudhry, S., Armstrong, J., Meslin, E.M., & Lowy, F.H. (1995). Public opinion regarding end-of-life decisions: Influence of prognosis, practice and process. *Social Science and Medicine, 41*(11), 1517–1521.

Singer, P.A., Martin, D.K., & Kelner, M. (1999). Quality end of life care: Patients' perspectives. *Journal of the American Medical Association, 28*(2), 163–168.

Singleton, R.A. Jr., and Straits, B.C. (2005). *Approaches to social research* (4th ed.). New York: Oxford University Press.

Sinnott, J.D. (2000). *Growing and healing while aging: The role of spirituality in typical and complementary healing systems.* Paper presented at the Gerontological Society of America Conference, Washington, DC, November.

Slife, B.D. & Williams, R.N. (1995). *What's behind the research? Discovering hidden assumptions in the behavioral sciences.* Thousands Oaks, CA: Sage.

Smith, D. & Moen, P. (2004). Retirement satisfaction for retirees and their spouses: Do gender and the retirement decision-making process matter? *Journal of Family Issues, 25*(2), 262–285.

Smith, E.L., & Gilligan, G. (1983). Physical activity prescription for the older adult. *The Physician and Sportsmedicine, 11,* 91–101.

Smith, P. (1998). A comparative analysis of female lone parent families in Canada and the United States. In *Contributions to family demography: Essays in honour of Dr. Wayne W. McVey*, (pp. 184–204). Edmonton, AB: University of Alberta, Department of Sociology.

Snell, J.G. (1992). Maintenance agreements for the elderly: Canada, 1900–1951. *Journal of the Canadian Historical Association, 3*, 197–216.

Snell, J.G. (1996). *The citizen's wage: The state and the elderly in Canada, 1900–1951*. Toronto: University of Toronto Press.

Social Development Canada. (2005a). *The CPP & OAS stats book 2005: Statistics related to Canada pension plan and old age security programs*. Ottawa: Forecasting, Information & Analysis, Social Development Sectors, Social Development Canada.

Social Development Canada. (2005b, September 30). *Old Age Security (OAS) payment rates*. Retrieved December 19, 2005, from http://www.sdc.gc.ca/en/isp/oas/oasrates.shtml

Social Development Canada. (2005c, November). *Statistical Bulletin: Canada Pension Plan, Old Age Security*. Ottawa: Social Development Canada.

Soldo, B.J. & Hill, M.S. (1995). Family structure and transfer measures in the Health and Retirement Study. *Journal of Human Resources, 30* (suppl.), S108–S137.

Speare, A., & Avery, R. (1993). Who helps whom in older parent-child families? *Journals of Gerontology, 48*, S64–S73.

Spearman, C. (1927). *The abilities of man*. New York: Macmillan.

Spencer, C. (1994). Abuse and neglect of older adults in institutional settings. Ottawa: Health Canada, Health Services Directorate, Mental Health Division.

Spirduso, W.W. (1980). Physical fitness, aging, and psychomotor speed. *Journals of Gerontology, 35*, 850–865.

Spirduso W.W. (1995). *Physical dimensions of aging*. Champaign, IL: Human Kinetics.

Spitze, G., & Logan, J. (1992). Helping as a component of parent–adult child relations. *Research on Aging, 14*, 291–312.

Stacey, C., Kozma, A., & Stones, M.J. (1985). Simple cognitive and performance changes resulting from improved physical fitness in persons over 50 years of age. *Canadian Journal on Aging, 4*, 67–73.

Stains, L.R. (2003). Look who's back. *American Association of Retired Persons Newsletter, 1* (1A), 36–38.

Stajduhar, K. (2001). *The idealization of dying at home: The social context of home-based palliative caregiving*. Unpublished doctoral dissertation, University of British Columbia, Vancouver, B. C.

Stajduhar, K., & Davies, B. (1998). Death at home: Challenges for families and directions for the future. *Journal of Palliative Care 14*(3), 8–14.

Stajduhar, K., & Davies, B. (1999). Death, loss, and grief. In B.W. DuGas, L. Esson, & S.E. Ronaldson (Eds.), *Nursing foundations: A Canadian perspective* (2nd ed). Scarborough, ON: Prentice Hall.

Standardized Test of Fitness. (1981). Ottawa: Government of Canada (Fitness and Amateur Sport).

Stanfield, J.H., II. (1994). Ethnic modeling in qualitative research. In K. Denzin & Y. Lincoln, (Eds.), *The handbook of qualitative research* (pp. 175–188). Thousand Oaks, CA: Sage.

Starr, B.D. (1985) Sexuality and aging. *Annual Review of Gerontology and Geriatrics, 5*, 97–126.

Statistics Canada. (1996). *Canada's retirement income programs: A statistical overview*. (Catalogue No. 74-507-XPB). Ottawa: Minister of Industry.

Statistics Canada. (1998a). *The earnings of men and women*. (Catalogue No. 13-217-XBP). Ottawa: Statistics Canada.

Statistics Canada. (1998b). National Survey of Giving, Volunteering and Participating (NSGVP), (Catalogue No. 11-001E). *The Daily*, 3–7, 1997.

Statistics Canada. (1999a). Personal health practices: Smoking, drinking, physical activity and weight. *Health Reports, 11*(3).

Statistics Canada. (1999b). *A portrait of seniors in Canada*. (Catalogue No. 89-519-XPE). Ottawa: Statistics Canada, Minister of Industry. October.

Statistics Canada. (2000a). *Pension plans in Canada: Statistical highlights and key tables (January 1, 1999)*. (Catalogue No. 74-401-SIB). Ottawa: Minister of Industry. Reprinted with permission from Statistics Canada.

Statistics Canada (2000b). Criminal victimization in Canada. *Juristat, 20*(10).

Statistics Canada. (2000c).*Women in Canada, 2000: A gender-based statistical report*. (Catalogue No. 89-503-XPE). Ottawa, ON: Statistics Canada

Statistics Canada. (2001a). *Health Indicators*. Ottawa: Statistics Canada, Minister of Industry.

Statistics Canada. (2001b). Living arrangements of seniors aged 65 and over by sex and age group, Canada, 2001. Retrieved July 31, 2006 from http://www12.statcan.ca/english/census01/Products/Analytic/companion/fam/livarrang.cfm

Statistics Canada (2001c). General Social Survey.

Statistics Canada. (2002a, October 22). *Census of Canada, 2001: Age groups (12B), family structure (7A) and sex (3) for children, 1981–2001*. Ottawa: Statistics Canada. Retrieved April 20, 2006, from http://prod.library.utoronto.ca:8090/datalib/datar/cc01/cot/005/97F0005XCB01002.IVT

Statistics Canada. (2002b, October 22). *Census of Canada, 2001: Census family status (6), age groups (17A) and sex (3) for population in private households* [computer file]. Ottawa, ON: Statistics Canada [producer and distributor], Canadian overview tables; 97F0005XCB01003, http://p8090-prod.library.utoronto.ca.myaccess.library.utoronto.ca/datalib/datar/cc01/cot/005/97F0005XCB01003.IVT

Statistics Canada. (2002c, October 22). *Census of Canada, 2001: Household living arrangements (10), age groups (17A)*

and sex (3). Ottawa: Statistics Canada. Retrieved April 20, 2006, from http://prod.library.utoronto.ca:8090/datalib/datar/cc01/cot/005/97F0005XCB01004.IVT.

Statistics Canada. (2002d, October 22). *Census of Canada, 2001: Legal marital status (6), age groups (19), and sex (3)*. Ottawa: Statistics Canada. Retrieved April 18, 2006, from http://p8090-prod.library.utoronto.ca.myaccess.library.utoronto.ca/datalib/datar/cc01/cot/004/97F0004XCB01001.IVT.

Statistics Canada. (2002e). *A profile of disability in Canada, 2001*. Ottawa: Statistics Canada.

Statistics Canada (2002f). *Family violence in Canada: A statistical profile, 2002*. Catalogue No. 85-224-XIE. Ottawa: Statistics Canada.

Statistics Canada. (2002g). Suicide deaths and suicide attempts. *Health Reports, 13*(2). Catalogue No. 82-003.

Statistics Canada (2002h). *Profile of languages in Canada: English, French and many others*. (Catalogue No. 96F 0030XIE2001005). Ottawa: Minister of Industry.

Statistics Canada. (2003a, February 11). *Census of Canada, 2001: Occupation—2001 National Occupational Classification for Statistics (143), class of worker (6) and sex (3) for labour force 15 years and over*. Ottawa: Statistics Canada. Retrieved April 14, 2006, from http://p8090-prod.library.utoronto.ca.myaccess.library.utoronto.ca/datalib/datar/cc01/cot/012/97f0012xcb01020.ivt.

Statistics Canada. (2003b, May 13). *Census of Canada, 2001: Income status (4) and census family structure for census families, sex, age groups and household living arrangements for non-family persons 15 years and over and sex and age groups for persons in private households (87*. Ottawa: Statistics Canada. Retrieved April 16, 2006, from http://p8090-prod.library.utoronto.ca.myaccess.library.utoronto.ca/datalib/datar/cc01/cot/020/97f0020xcb01006.ivt.

Statistics Canada (2003c). *Canada's ethnocultural portrait: The changing mosaic*. (Catalogue No. 96F0030XIE2001008). Ottawa: Statistics Canada.

Statistics Canada (2003d). *Ethnic diversity survey: Portrait of a multicultural society*. (Catalogue No. 98-593-XIE). Ottawa: Minister of Industry.

Statistics Canada (2003e). *Aboriginal peoples of Canada: A demographic profile*. (Catalogue No. 96F0030XIE2001007). Ottawa: Minister of Industry.

Statistics Canada (2003f). *Canadian community health survey*. Retrieved April 20, 2006 from http://www.biomedcentral.com/1472-6874/4/S1S17.

Statistics Canada (2003g). Retirement. *Perspective on labour and income*. 15(4) 67–68.

Statistics Canada. (2003h, March 25). *Census of Canada, 2001. Labour force activity (8), age groups (17b), sex (3), immigrant status and period of immigration (10b) and marital status (7) for population 15 years and over*. Ottawa: Statistics Canada. Retrieved April 24, 2006, from http://p8090-prod.library.utoronto.ca.myaccess.library.utoronto.ca/datalib/datar/cc01/cot/012/97f0012xcb01001.ivt.

Statistics Canada. (2003i, January 21). *Census of Canada, 2001. Ethnic origin (232), sex (3) and single and multiple responses (3) for population, for Canada, provinces, territories, census metropolitan areas 1 and census agglomerations, 2001 census—20% sample data*. (Catalogue No. 97F0010XCB2001001). Ottawa: Statistics Canada.

Statistics Canada. (2004a, January 19). *Census of Canada, 2001. Legal marital status (6), common-law status (5), age groups (12a), sex (3) and household living arrangements (11) for population 15 years and over*. Retrieved April 11, 2006, from http://prod.library.utoronto.ca:8090/datalib/datar/cc01/cot/004/97f0004xcb01040v2.ivt.

Statistics Canada. (2004b, November). *General Social Survey*. Cycle 15, 2001. Retrieved April 18, 2006, from http://r1.chass.utoronto.ca/cgi-bin/sda/hsda?harcsda+gss15m.

Statistics Canada. (2004c, December 21). CANSIM: table 101-1002—mean age and median age of grooms and brides (opposite-sex), by marital status, Canada, provinces and territories, annual. Ottawa: Statistics Canada. Retrieved April 11, 2006, from http://www.statcan.ca/english/freepub/84F0212XIE/84F0212XIE2002000.htm.

Statistics Canada (2004d). *Pension plans in Canada. Pension and wealth research paper Series*. (Catalogue No. 13F0026MIE-No.001). Ottawa: Minister of Industry.

Statistics Canada. (2004e, June 1). Pilot survey of hate crime. *The Daily*. Retrieved April 11, 2006, from http://www.statcan.ca/Daily/English/040601/d040601a.htm.

Statistics Canada (2004f, August 19). *The Daily*. Retrieved April 19, 2006, from http://www.statcan.ca/Daily/English/040819/d040818e.htm.

Statistics Canada. (2004g). *Canadian Community Health Survey, Mental Health and Well-being, 2002* (updated in September 2004). Table 21.

Statistics Canada. (2005a, February 18). *Labour force historical review, 2004*. Labour force estimates by detailed age groups, sex, Canada, province, annual average. Ottawa: Statistics Canada. Retrieved May 4, 2006, from http://prod.library.utoronto.ca:8090/datalib/datar/cstdsp/71f0004xcb/2004/cd1t01an.ivt.

Statistics Canada (2005b). *Population projections of visible minority groups, Canada, provinces and regions*. (Catalogue No. 91-541-XIE). Ottawa: Minister of Industry.

Statistics Canada (2005c). *Projections of the Aboriginal populations, Canada, provinces and territories*. (Catalogue No. 91-547-XIE). Ottawa: Minister of Industry.

Statistics Canada. (2005d). *Nutrition: Findings from the Canadian Community Health Survey Issue No. 1*. Ottawa: Minister of Industry.

Statistics Canada (2005e). *Labour force characteristics by age and sex.(rates)*. Retrieved May 3, 2006, from http://www40.statcan.ca/101/cst01/labor20b.htm.

Statistics Canada (2006a, February 7). Canada's retirement income programs: 2006 edition (74-507-XBC).

The Daily. Retrieved March 14, 2006, from http://www.statcan.ca/Daily/English/060207/d060207b.htm.

Statistics Canada. (2006b, March). *Women in Canada: A gender-based statistical report* (5th ed., Catalogue No. 89-503-XIE). Ottawa: Minister of Industry.

Statistics Canada. (2006c, June). *Health Indicators.* (Catalogue No. 82-221-XIE.) Ottawa: Minister of Industry.

Steffens, D.C., Skoog, I., Norton, M.C., Hart, A.D., Tschanz, J.T., Plassman, B.L., et al. (2000). Prevalence of depression and its treatment in an elderly population. *Archives of General Psychiatry, 57,* 601–607.

Stepan, C. (2003, December 11). Seniors are becoming moms and dads again. *Hamilton Spectator.*

Stephens, T., Craig, C. & Ferris, B. (1986). Adult physical activity in Canada: Findings from the Canada Fitness Survey. *Canadian Journal of Public Health, 77,* 285–290.

Sternberg, R. J. (1984). Toward a triarchic theory of human intelligence. *Behavioral and Brain Sciences, 7,* 269–315.

Stetz, T.A., & Beehr, T.A. (2000). Organizations' environment and retirement: The relationship between women's retirement, environmental munificence, dynamism and local unemployment rate. *Journals of Gerontology: Series B Psychological Science and Social Sciences, 55B*(4), S213–S221.

Stevens, J.C., Cruz, A., Marks, L.E., & Lakatos, S. (1998). A multimodal assessment of sensory thresholds in aging. *Journals of Gerontology: Psychological Sciences, 53B,* 263–272.

Stewart, W.H., & Enterline, P.E. (1961). Effects of the NHS on physician utilization and health in England and Wales. *New England Journal of Medicine, 265,* 1187.

Stobert, S. & Cranswick, K. (2004, Autumn). Looking after seniors: Who does what for whom? *Canadian Social Trends,* 2–6.

Stokols, D. (1996). Translating social ecological theory into guidelines for community health promotion. *American Journal of Health Promotion, 10,* 282–298.

Stoller, E. (1993). Interpretations of symptoms by older people. *Journal of Aging Health, 5,* 58–81.

Stone, L.O. & Hubert, F. (1988). *Canada's seniors: A dynamic force.* Ottawa: Statistics Canada.

Stone, L.O. & Rosenthal, C.J. (1998). *How much help is exchanged in families? Towards an understanding of discrepant research findings.* Social and Economic Dimensions of an Aging Population (SEDAP) research paper No. 2. Hamilton, ON: McMaster University.

Stone, L.O., Rosenthal, C.J., & Connidis, I.A. (1998). *Parent-child exchanges of supports and intergenerational equity.* (Catalogue No. 89-557-XPE). Ottawa: Statistics Canada

Stones, L., & Stones, M.J. (1996). Sex may be wasted on the young. Toronto: Captus Press.

Stones, L. & Stones, M.J. (2005). *Sex may be wasted on the young* (2nd ed.). Toronto: Captus Press.

Stones, M.J. (1995). Scope and definition of elder abuse and neglect in Canada. In Maclean, M. (Ed.), *Abuse and neglect of older Canadians—Strategies for change* (pp. 111–116). Toronto: Thompson Educational Publishing.

Stones, M.J. (2001a). Are satisfaction surveys satisfactory for evaluating quality of care? Case Mix 2001 Conference: New frontiers in health information. Niagara Falls, ON.

Stones, M.J. (2001b). Deconstructing depression. *Gerontology, 47*(suppl. 1), 573.

Stones, M.J. (2005a). Ontario's provincial strategy to combat elder abuse. *Stride* (2nd quarter), 23–24.

Stones M.J. (2005b). Outlooks on agitation in old people. *Stride,* (4th quarter), 14.

Stones, M.J. & Bédard, M. (2002). Higher thresholds for elder abuse with age and rural residence. *Canadian Journal on Aging.*

Stones, M.J., Clyburn, L.D., Gibson, M.C., & Woodbury, M.G. (in press.) Predicting diagnosed depression and antidepressant treatment in the institutionalized elderly by symptom profiles: A closer look at anhedonia and dysphoria. *Canadian Journal on Aging.*

Stones, M.J., Hadjistavropoulos, T., Tuokko, H., & Kozma, A. (1995). Happiness has traitlike and statelike properties: A reply to Veenhoven. *Social Indicators Research, 36,* 129–144.

Stones, M.J., & Kirkpatrick, W. (2002).Deconstructing depression: Dormancy & dysphoria. *Stride,* 14–19.

Stones, M.J., & Kozma, A. (1980). Issues relating to the usage and conceptualization of mental health constructs employed by gerontologists. *International Journal of Aging and Human Development, 11,* 269–281.

Stones, M.J., & Kozma, A. (1986). Age trends in maximal physical performance: Comparison and evaluation of models. *Experimental Aging Research, 12,* 207–215.

Stones, M.J., & Kozma, A. (1988). Physical activity, age, and cognitive/motor performance. In M.L. Howe & C.J. Brainerd (Eds.), *Cognitive development in adulthood: Progress in cognitive development research* (pp. 273–321). New York: Springer Verlag.

Stones, M.J., & Kozma, A. (1995). Compensation in athletic sport. In R. Dixon & C. Bäckman (Eds.), *Psychological compensation: Managing losses and promoting gains.* Hillsdale, NJ: Lawrence Erlbaum.

Stones, M.J., & Kozma A. (1996). Activity, exercise and behavior. In: J. Birren & K.W. Schaie (Eds.), *Handbook of the psychology of aging* (5th ed.). Orlando, FL: Academic Press.

Stones, M.J., Kozma, A., & Hannah, T.E. (1990). Measurement of individual differences in aging: The distinction between usual and successful aging. In M.L. Howe, M.J. Stones, & C.J. Brainerd (Eds.), *Cognitive and behavioral performance factors in atypical aging.* New York: Springer-Verlag.

Stones, M.J., Kozma, A., Hirdes, J., Gold, D., Arbuckle, T., & Kolopack, P. (1995). Short happiness and affect research protocol. *Social Indicators Research, 37,* 75–91.

Stones, M.J., Linkewich, E., Porter Brysch, E., Taylor, J., Brink P. (2004). *Final report to Health Canada and Veterans Affairs on activities. Thunder Bay Falls Prevention Coalition: 2002–2004.* Retrieved May 4, 2006 from http://www.phac-aspc.gc.ca/seniors-aines/pubs/fall_prevention_initiatives/index.htm.

Stones, M.J., & Pittman, D. (1995). Individual differences in attitudes about elder abuse: The Elder Abuse Attitude Test. *Canadian Journal on Aging, 14,* 61–71.

Stones, M.J., & Stones L. (2006). Sexuality, sensuality, and intimacy. In J. Birren (Ed.), *Encyclopaedia of Gerontology* (2nd ed.). Amsterdam: Elsevier.

Strain, L.A. & Chappell, N. (1982). Confidantes: Do they make a difference in quality of life? *Research on Aging,* 4(4), 479–502.

Strain, L.A., & Chappell, N. (1984). *Social support among elderly Canadian Natives: A comparison with elderly Non-Natives.* Paper presented at the annual meeting of the Canadian Association on Gerontology Vancouver, B.C.

Strong-Boag, V.J. (1993). *The new day recalled: Lives of girls and women in English Canada 1919–1939.* Mississauga, ON: Copp Clark Pitman.

Struthers, J. (1992). Regulating the elderly: Old age pensions and the formation of a pension bureaucracy in Ontario, 1929–1945. *Journal of the Canadian Historical Association,* 235–255.

Stull, D.E., Kosloski, K., & Kercher, K. (1994). Caregiver burden and generic well-being: Opposite sides of the same coin? *The Gerontologist, 34(1),* 88–94.

Sugiman, P, & Nishio, H.K. (1983). Socialization and cultural duality among Japanese Canadians. *Canadian Ethnic Studies, 15*(3), 17–35.

Sullivan, M.J., & Scattolon, Y. (1995). Health policy planning: A look at consumer involvement in Nova Scotia. *Canadian Journal of Public Health, 86*(5), 317–320.

Sunter, D. (2001, spring). Demography and the labour market. (Catalogue No. 75-001-XPE). *Perspectives on Labour and Income,* 28–39.

Suwal, J., & Trovato, F. (1998). Canadian aboriginal fertility. *Canadian Studies in Population, 25,* 69–86.

Syme, S.L. (1994). The social environment and health. *DAEDALUS, Journal of the American Academy of Arts and Sciences, 123*(4), 79–86.

Szasz, T. (1961). *The myth of mental illness: Foundations of a theory of personal conduct.* New York: Hoeber-Harper.

Szinovacz, M. (1997). Adult children taking parents into their homes: Effects of childhood living arrangements. *Journal of Marriage and the Family, 59,* 700–717.

Szinovacz, M. (2002). Couple retirement patterns and retirement age. *International Journal of Sociology, 32*(2), 30–54.

Szinovacz, M. (2006). Families and retirement. In L. Stone (Ed.), *The new frontiers of research on retirement* (pp. 165–198). (Catalogue No. 75-511-XPE). Ottawa: Minister of Industry.

Szinovacz, M., & Davey, A. (2004a). Retirement transitions and spouse disability: Effects on depressive symptoms. *The Journals of Gerontology,* 59B(6), S333–S342.

Szinovacz, M., & Davey, A. (2004b). Honeymoons and joint lunches: Effects of retirement and spouse's employment on depressive symptoms. *The Journals of Gerontology,* 59B(5), P233–P245.

Szinovacz, M. & Davey, A. (2005). Retirement and marital decision-making: Effects on retirement satisfaction. *Journal of Marriage and the Family, 67,* 387–398.

Szinovacz, M. & DeViney, S. (1999). The retiree identity: Gender and race differences. *Journals of Gerontology: Social Sciences, 54B,* S207–S218.

Szinovacz, M.E., & DeViney, S. (2000). Marital characteristics and retirement decisions. *Research on Aging, 22*(5), 470–498.

Szinovacz, M., & Schaffer, A.M. (2000). Effects of retirement on marital conflict management. *Journal of Family Issues, 21,* 367–389.

Talbott, M.M. (1998). Older widows' attitudes towards men and remarriage. *Journal of Aging Studies, 12,* 429–449.

Tamblyn, R, & Perreault, R. (2000). Prescription drug use and seniors. *Canadian Journal on Aging, 19*(suppl.1), 143–175.

Taylor, B. & Bengston, V. (2001). Sociological perspectives on productive aging. In N. Morrow-Howell, J. Hinterlog, & M. Sherradon (Eds.), *Productive aging: Concepts and challenges* (pp. 120–144). Baltimore: The John Hopkins Press.

Taylor, F. (1947). *Scientific Management.* New York: Harper.

Taylor, M.A., & Shore, L.M. (1995). Predictors of planned retirement age: An application of Beehr's model. *Psychology and Aging, 10*(1), 76–83.

Tebb, S.S. (1995). Aid to empowerment: A caregiver well-being scale. *Health and Social Work, 20*(2), 87–92.

Tedlock, B. (2000). Ethnography and ethnographic representation. In N. Denzin & Y. Lincoln, (Eds.), *Handbook of qualitative research* (2nd ed., pp. 455–486). Thousand Oaks, CA: Sage Publications.

Tennstedt, S., & Chang, B.H. (1998). The relative contribution of ethnicity versus socioeconomic status in explaining differences in disability and receipt of informal care. *Journals of Gerontology, 53B*(2), S61–S70.

Tennstedt, S.L., McKinlay, J.B., & Sullivan, L.M. (1989). Informal care for frail elders: The role of secondary caregivers. *The Gerontologist, 29,* 677–683.

Teno, J.M., McNiff, K., & Lynn, J. (2001). Measuring quality of medical care for dying persons and their families: Preliminary suggestions for accountability. In M.P. Lawton (Ed.), *Annual review of gerontology and geriatrics: Vol. 20. Focus on the end of life: Scientific and social issues* (pp.97–119). New York: Springer.

Theriault, J. (1994). Retirement as a psychosocial transition: Process of adaptation to change. *International Journal of Aging and Human Development, 38,* 153–170.

Thomas, D. (2005, spring). "I am Canadian." *Canadian Social Trends, 76,* 2–7.

Thomas, K., & Wister, A. (1984). Living arrangements of older women: The ethnic dimensions. *Journal of Marriage and the Family, 46,* 301–311.

Thomas, P.D., Garry, P.J., Goodwin, J.M., & Goodwin, J.S. (1985). Social bonds in a healthy elderly sample: Characteristics and associated variables. *Social Science and Medicine, 20,* 365–369.

Thurstone, L.L. (1928). Attitudes can be measured. *American Journal of Sociology, 33,* 529–554.

Thurstone, L.L. (1938). *Primary mental abilities.* Chicago, IL: University of Chicago Press.

Tierney, W.G. (2000). Undaunted courage: Life history and postmodern challenge. In N. Denzin & Y. Lincoln, (Eds.), *Handbook of qualitative research* (2nd ed., pp. 537–553). Thousand Oaks, CA: Sage Publications

Tinetti, M.E., (1986). Performance-oriented assessment of mobility problems in elderly patients. *Journal of the American Geriatrics Society, 34,* 119–126.

Tipper, S. (1989, August). Cremation is an opportunity for funeral directors. *Canadian Funeral News,* 10–11.

Tjam E.Y., & Hirdes, J.P. (2002). Health, psycho-social and cultural determinants of medication use in the Chinese-Canadian elderly. *Canadian Journal on Aging 21*(1).

Tompa, E. (1999). *Transition to retirement: Determinants of age of social security take up.* Paper No. 6, Social and Economic Dimensions of an Aging Population. Hamilton, ON: McMaster University.

Torczyner, J.L. (1997). *Diversity, mobility and change: The dynamics of Black communities in Canada.* McGill Consortium for Ethnicity and Strategic Planning. Ottawa: Multiculturalism Branch, Department of Canadian Heritage.

Torrance, G.W., Zhang, Y., Feeny, D., & Boyle, M.H. (1992). Multi-attribute preference functions for a comprehensive health status classification system. [Unpublished]. Hamilton, ON: Centre for Health Economics and Policy Analysis, McMaster University.

Tougas, F., Lagacé, M., & de la Sablonnière, R. (2004). A new approach to the link between identity and relative deprivation in the perspective of ageism and retirement. *International Journal of Human Development, 59*(1), 1–23.

Townsend, P. (1962). *The last refuge. A survey of residential institutions and homes for the aged in England and Wales.* London: Routledge and Kegan Paul.

Townsend, P. (1981). The structured dependency of the elderly: A creation of social policy in the twentieth century. *Ageing and Society, 1*(1), 5–28.

Townsley, C.A., Selby, R., & Siu, L.L. (2005). Systematic review of barriers to the recruitment of older patients with cancer onto clinical trials. *Journal of Clinical Oncology, 23*(13), 3112–3124.

Townson, M. (2000). *Reducing poverty among older women: The potential of retirement incomes policies.* Ottawa: Status of Women Canada.

Trammer, R., Croxford, R., & Coyte, P.C (2003). Dementia in Ontario: Prevalence and health service utilization. *Canadian Journal on Aging, 22*(4), 369–379.

Tranoy, K.E. (1996). Vital needs, human rights, health care law. *Medical Law, 15*(2), 183–188.

Tulving, E., Hayman, C.A.G., & MacDonald, C.A. (1991). Long-lasting priming in amnesia: A case experiment. *Journal of Experimental Psychology: Learning, Memory, and Cognition, 17,* 595–617.

Turcotte, M., & Schellenberg, G. (2005). Job strain and retirement. *Perspective on labour and income, 17*(3), 35–39.

Turner, F. (1995). Shame, beauty, and the tragic view of history. *American Behavioral Scientist, 38*(8), 1060–1075.

Uhlenberg, P. (1993). Demographic change and kin relationships in later life. In G. Maddox & M.P. Lawton (Eds.), *Annual review of gerontology and geriatrics, Vol. 13* (pp. 219–238). New York: Springer.

Uhlenberg, P. & Miner, S. (1996). Life course and aging: A cohort perspective. In R.H. Binstock & L.K. George, (Eds.), *Handbook of aging and the social sciences* (4th ed., pp. 208–228). San Diego, CA: Academic Press

Ujimoto, K. (1995). Ethnic dimension of aging in Canada. In R. Neugebauer-Visano (Ed.), *Aging and inequality: Cultural constructions of differences* (pp. 3–29). Toronto: Canadian Scholars' Press.

Ujimoto, K.V., Nishio, H.K., Wong, P.T.P., & Lam. L. (1995). Cultural factors affecting self assessment of health satisfaction of Asian Canadian elderly. In R. Neugebauer-Visano (Ed.), *Aging and inequality: Cultural constructions of differences* (pp. 131–141). Toronto: Canadian Scholars' Press.

United Nations. (2001). *World population prospects: The 1998 revision. Volume III: Analytical report.* New York: United Nations.

United Nations Secretariat. (1988). Sex differentials in life expectancy and mortality in developed countries: An analysis by age groups and causes of death from recent and historical Data. *Population Bulletin of the United Nations, 25,* 65–106.

U.S. Department of Health and Social Services. (1999). Mental health: A report of the Surgeon General.

Vallee, R. (1998). *Caregiving across cultures.* Washington, D.C.: Taylor and Francis.

van den Hoonaard, D.K. (2001). *The widowed self: The older woman's journey through widowhood.* Waterloo, ON: Wilfrid Laurier University Press.

VanderMaas, P.J., vanderWal, G., Haverkate, I., deGraaff, C.L.M., Kester, J.G.C., Onwuteaka-Philipson, B.D., et al. (1996). Euthanasia, physician-assisted suicide, and other medical practices involving the end of life in the Netherlands. *New England Journal of Medicine, 335*(22), 1699–1705.

van der Suiijs, H.A. (1972). A standardized analysis of daily energy expenditure and patterns of physical activity. In J.M. Dirken, (Ed.), *Functional age of industrial workers.* Groningen, The Netherlands: Walters-Noordhof.

Van Maanen, H. (1991). Canadian Medical Association. Challenges and changes in the care of the elderly. Ottawa: CMA.

Van Ranst, N., Verschueren K., & Marcoen, A. (1995). The meaning of grandparents as viewed by adolescent grandchildren: An empirical study in Belgium. *International Journal of Aging and Human Development, 41,* 311–324.

van Solinge, H. & Henkens, K. (2005). Couples' adjustment to retirement: A multi-actor panel study. *Journals of Gerontology: Social Sciences, 60B*(1), S11–S20.

Veenhoven, R (1994). Is happiness a trait? Tests of the theory that a better society does not make people any happier. *Social Indicators Research, 33,* 101–160.

Veevers, J.E. (1984). Age-discrepant marriages: Cross-national comparisons of Canadian-American trends. *Social Biology, 31,* 18–27.

Veevers, J.E., Gee, E.M., & Wister, A.V. (1996). Homeleaving age norms—Conflict or consensus? *International Journal of Aging and Human Development, 43,* 1–19.

Ventegodt, S., Flensborg-Madsen, T., Abdersen, N.J., & Merric, J. (2005). Factors during pregnancy, delivery and birth affecting global quality of life of the adult child at long-term follow-up. Results from the prospective Copenhagen Perinatal Birth Cohort 1959–61. *Scientific World Journal, 5,* 933–941.

Verbrugge, L.M. (1979). Marital status and health. *Journal of Marriage and the Family, 41,* 267–285.

Verbrugge, L.M. (1984). A longer life but worsening health? Trends in health and mortality of middle-aged and older persons. *Milbank Memorial Fund Quarterly, 62,* 475–519.

Vernon-Scott, S.A. (2003). *Rethinking elder abuse: Words and actions* M.A. thesis, Lakehead University.

Vickerstaff, S., Baldock, J., Cox, J., & Keen, L. (2004). *Happy retirement? The impact of Employers' policies and practice on the process of retirement.* Bristol Avon: Policy Press.

Victor, C.R. (1994). *Old age in modern society.* London, UK: Chapman & Hall.

Victorino, C.C., & Gauthier, A.H. (2005). Are Canadian seniors becoming more active? Empirical evidence based on time-use data. *Canadian Journal on Aging, 24*(1) 45–56.

Voltz, R., Akabayashi, A., Reese, C., Ohi, G., & Sass, H.M. (1998). End of life decisions and advance directives in palliative care: A cross-cultural survey of patients and health-care professionals. *Journal of Pain and Symptom Management, 16*(3), 153–162.

Waldron, I. (1985). What do we know about causes of sex differences in mortality? A review of the literature. *Population Bulletin of the United Nations, 18,* 59–76.

Waldron, I. (1998). Sex differences in infant and early childhood mortality: Major causes of death and possible biological causes. In *Too young to die: Genes or gender?* New York: United Nations.

Walford, R.L. (1983). *Maximum life span.* New York: Norton.

Walker, A. (1981). Towards a political economy of old age. *Ageing and Society, 1*(1), 73–94.

Walker, A. (Ed.) (1996). *The new generational contract: Intergenerational relations, old age, and welfare.* London, UK: UCL Press.

Walker, A. (2005). Towards an international political economy. *Ageing and Society, 25,* 815–899.

Walker, B.L., Osgood, N.J., Richardson, J.P., & Ephross, P.H. (1998). Staff and elderly knowledge and attitudes toward elderly sexuality. *Educational Gerontology, 24*(5), 471–489.

Walker, K.N., McBride, A., & Vachon, M.L.S. (1977). Social support networks and the crisis of bereavement. *Social Science and Medicine, 11,* 35–41.

Wallace, J.B. (1994). Life stories. In J.F. Gubrium & J.A. Sankar (Eds.), *Qualitative methods in research* (pp. 137–154). Thousand Oaks, CA: Sage.

Wallace, S.P. (2000). American health promotion: Where individualism rules. *The Gerontologist, 40,* 273–276.

Waller, N.G., Kojetin, B.A., Bouchard, T.J. Jr., Lykken, D.T., & Tellegen, A. (1990). Genetic and environmental influences on religious interests, attitudes, and values: A study of twins reared apart and together. *Psychological Science, 1,* 138–142.

Wang, D. (2004). Ritualistic coresidence and the weakening of filial practice in rural China. In C. Ikels (Ed.), *Filial piety, practice and discourse in contemporary East Asia* (pp.16–33). Stanford, CT: Stanford University Press.

Wanner, R.A. and McDonald, L. (1989). Ethnic diversity and patterns of retirement. In J. Frideres (Ed.), *Multiculturalism and Intergroup Relations.* New York: Greenwood Press.

Warr, P., Butcher, V., Robertson, I., & Callinan, M. (2004). Older people's well-being as a function of employment, retirement, environmental characteristics and role preference. *British Journal of Psychology, 95*(3), 297–324.

Watson, D., Clark, L.A., Weber, K., & Assenheimer, J.S. (1995). Testing a tripartite model: II. Exploring the symptom structure of anxiety and depression in student, adult and patient samples. *Journal of Abnormal Psychology, 104*(1), 15–25.

Webster, P.S., & Herzog, R.A. (1995). Effects of parental divorce and memories of family problems on relationships between adult children and their parents. *Journals of Gerontology, 50B,* S24–34.

Wechsler, D. (1958). *The measurement and appraisal of adult intelligence.* Baltimore, MD: Williams & Wilkins.

Wechsler, D. (1972). "Hold" and "Don't Hold" tests. In S.M. Chown (Ed.), *Human aging.* New York: Penguin.

Weeks, L.E., Richards, J.L., Nilsson-Thomy, Kozma, A., & Bryanton, O. (2004). Gendered analysis of the abuse of older adults: Evidence from professionals. *Journal of Elder Abuse and Neglect, 16*(2), 1–15.

Weigel, R.H., & Newman, L.S. (1976). Increasing attitude-behavior correspondence by broadening the scope of the behavioral measure. *Journal of Personality and Social Psychology, 33*, 793–802.

Weissman, M.M., Bland, R.C., Canino, G.J., Faravelli, C., Greenwald, S., Hwu, H.G., et al. (1996). Cross-national epidemiology of major depression and bipolar disorder. *Journal of the American Medical Association, 276*, 24–31.

Wells, D. (1997). A critical ethnography of the process of discharge decision-making for elderly patients. *Canadian Journal on Aging, 16*(4), 682–699.

Wernick, A. (1995). Selling funerals, imaging death. In M. Featherstone & A. Wernick (Eds.), *Images of aging* (pp. 280–293). London: Routledge.

Wheeler, J.A., Gorey, K.M., & Greenblatt, B. (1998). Beneficial effects of volunteering for older volunteers and the people they serve: A meta-analysis. *International Journal of Aging and Human Development, 47*(1), 69–79.

Whitaker, J. (2000). *Reversing hypertension.* New York: Warner Brooks.

Whitbourne, S.K. (2001) *Adult development and aging: Biopsychological perspectives.* New York: John Wiley & Sons.

Whitfield, K., & Baker-Thomas, T. (1999). Individual differences in aging minorities. *International Journal of Aging and Human Development, 48*(1), 73–79.

Wicker, A.W. (1969). Attitude versus actions: The relationship of verbal and overt behavioral responses to attitude objects. *Journal of Social Issues, 25*(4), 41–78.

Wiehe, V.R. (1998). Elder abuse. In V.R. Wiehe, (Ed.), *Understanding family violence: Treating and preventing partner, child, sibling, and elder abuse* (pp. 127–165). Thousand Oaks, CA: Sage.

Wilkins, R., Adams, O., & Brancker, A. (1991). Changes in mortality by income in urban Canada from 1971 to 1986. *Health Reports, 1*, 137–174.

Wilkinson, R.G. (1994). The epidemiological transition: From material scarcity to social disadvantage? *DAEDALUS, Journal of the American Academy of Arts and Sciences, 123*(4), 61–77.

Wilkinson, R.G. (1996). *Unhealthy societies: The afflictions of inequality.* New York: Routledge.

Williams, A.P., Deber, R., Baranek, P., & Gildiner, A. (2001). From medicare to home care: Globalization, state retrenchment, and the profitization of Canada's health-care system. In P. Armstrong, H. Armstrong, & D. Coburn (Eds.), *Unhealthy times. Political economy perspectives on health and care in Canada* (pp.7–30). Toronto: Oxford University Press.

Williams, C., (2005, summer). The sandwich generation. *Canadian Social Trends,* 16–24.

Williams, D.R., & Wilson, C.M. (2001). Race, ethnicity and aging. In R.H. Binstock & L.K. George (Eds.), *Handbook of Aging and the Social Sciences* (5th ed., pp. 160–178). New York: Academic Press.

Williamson, J.B., & Watts-Roy, D.M. (1999). Framing the generational equity debate. In J.B. Williamson, D.M. Watts-Roy, & E.R. Kingson, (Eds.), *The generational equity debate,* (pp. 3–37). New York: Columbia University Press.

Wilmoth, M. (2001). Living arrangements among older immigrants in the United States. *The Gerontologist, 41*(2), 228–238.

Wilson, Gail. (2000). *Understanding old age.* London, UK: Sage Publications.

Wingfield, A., Tun, P.A., & McCoy, S.L. (2005). Hearing loss in adulthood: What it is and how it interacts with cognitive performance. *Current Directions in Psychological Science, 14,* 144–148.

Winsborough, H., Bumpass, L., & Aquilino, W. (1991). The death of parents and the transitions to old age. NSFH Working Paper No. 39, National Survey of Families and Households. Madison, WI: University of Wisconsin.

Wise, D. (1993). *Firms, pension policy and early retirement. Age, work, and social security.* New York: St. Martin's Press.

Wister, A.V. (2005). *Baby boomer health dynamics: How are we aging.* Toronto: University of Toronto Press.

Wister, A., & Moore, C. (1998). First Nations elders in Canada: Issues, problems, successes in health care policy. In A.V. Wister & G.M. Gutman, *Health systems and aging in selected Pacific Rim countries: Cultural diversity and change* (pp. 103–124).Vancouver, BC: Gerontology Research Centre, Simon Fraser University.

Wolf, D.A. (1990). Household patterns of older women. *Research on Aging, 12,* 463–486.

Wolf, D.A. (1995). Changes in the living arrangements of older women: An international comparison. *The Gerontologist, 35,* 724–731.

Wolf, D.A., & Soldo, B.J. (1988). Household composition choices of older unmarried women. *Demography, 25,* 387–403.

Wolf, R.S. (1997a). Resident abuse in nursing homes. Available from CANE, document N4726–3.

Wolf, R. (1997b). Factors affecting the rate of elder abuse reporting to a state protective services program. Available from CANE, document J4115–23.

Wolf, R. (1997c). Elder abuse and neglect: Causes and consequences. *Journal of Geriatric Psychiatry, 30*(1), 153–174.

Wolfson, M., Rowe, G., Gentleman, J.F., & Tomiak, M. (1993). Career earnings and death: A longitudinal analysis of older Canadian men. *Journals of Gerontology, 48*(4), 167–179.

Wong, P.T., & Reker, G.T. (1985). Stress, coping and well-being in Anglo and Chinese elderly. *Canadian Journal on Aging, 4,* 29–37.

Woodbury, R.G. (1999). Early retirement in the United States. *Statistical Bulletin, 80*(3), 2–7.

World Health Organization (WHO). (1948). *The first ten years of the World Health Organization.* Geneva: World Health Organization.

World Health Organization (WHO) (2004). *2004 Report on the global AIDS epidemic*. (WHO Catalogue No. 92 9173 355 5). Geneva: World Health Organization.

Wortman, C.B. & Conway, T.L. (1985). The role of social support in adaptation and recovery from physical illness. In S. Cohen & S.L. Syme, (Eds.), *Social support and health*. Orlando, FL: Academic Press.

Wotherspoon, T. (1994). Colonization, self-determination and the health of Canada's First Nations peoples. In B.S. Bolaria & R. Bolaria (Eds.), *Racial minorities, medicine and health* (pp. 247–268). Halifax, NS: Fernwood Press.

Wouters, C. (1990). Changing regimes of power and emotions at the end of life: The Netherlands 1930–1990. *The Netherlands Journal of Social Sciences, 26*(2), 151–167.

Wright, R.O. (1997). *Life and death in the United States*. Jefferson, NC: McFarland & Company.

Wu, Z. (1995). Remarriage after widowhood: A marital history study of older Canadians. *Canadian Journal on Aging, 14*, 719–736.

Wu, Z. (2000). *Cohabitation: An alternative form of family living*. Toronto: Oxford University Press.

Wu. Z. & Wang, H. (1998). Third birth intentions and uncertainty in Canada. *Social Biology, 45*, 96–112.

Yaffe, K., Blackwell, T., Gore, R., Sands, L., Reus, V., & Browner, W. (1999). Depressive symptoms and cognitive decline in nondemented elderly women. *Archives of General Psychiatry, 56*, 425–431.

Yates, M.E., Tennstedt, S., & Chang, B.-H. (1999). Contributors to and mediators of psychological well-being for informal caregivers. *Journals of Gerontology: Psychological Sciences, 54B*(1), P12–P22.

Young, C.M. (1991). Changes in the demographic behaviour of migrants in Australia and the transition between generations. *Population Studies, 45*, 67–89.

Zanna, M.P., & Rempel, J.K. (1988). Attitudes: A new look at an old concept. In D. Bar-Tal & A.W. Kruglanski, (Eds.), *The Social Psychology of Knowledge* (pp.315–334). Cambridge, UK: Cambridge University Press.

Zarit, S.H., & Zarit, J.M. (1983). *The burden interview*. Los Angeles, CA: Ethel Percy Andrus Gerontology Centre.

Zimmerman, L., Mitchell, B., Wister, A., & Gutman, G. (2000). Unanticipated consequences: A comparison of expected and actual retirement timing among older women. *Journal of Women and Aging, 12*(1–2), 109–128.

Zisook, S., & Shuchter, S.R. (1991). Depression through the first year after the death of a spouse. *American Journal of Psychology, 148*, 1346–1352.

Zong, L., & Li, P.S. (1994). Different cultures or unequal life chances: A comparative analysis of race and health. In B.S. Bolaria & R. Bolaria (Eds.), *Racial minorities, medicine and health* (pp. 113–126). Halifax, NS: Fernwood Press.

Zweibel, N.R., & Cassel, C.K. (1989). Treatment choices at the end of life: A comparison of decisions by older patients and their physician-selected proxies. *Gerontologist 29*(5), 615–621.

INDEX

Page numbers ending in *f* refer to figures; in *t* to tables.

A

abnormal expectation, 253
Aboriginal peoples, 139, 140, 142, 144, 145, 146–148
  caregiving and values of, 147
  diabetes rates for, 159
  economic resources of senior, 156–157
  health systems and, 160–161
active voluntary euthanasia, 426
activities of daily living (ADL) measures, 184, 184*t*
activity theory, 63–64, 340
ADL hierarchy scale, 184, 184*t*
ADL. *See* activities of daily living (ADL) measures
adult children,
  as caregivers, 317
  gender differences in caregiving roles, 316
  generation-in-the middle, 317
  hidden victims, 317
  sandwich generation, 284–285, 317
  serial caregiving, 317
advance directives, 427–430
affectivity (affective style), 195
age blaming, 48
age deviants, 341
age discrimination, 349
Age Group Evaluation and Description (AGED) Inventory, 4, 7–8, 9
age levelling hypothesis, 153, 154–155
Age of Degenerative and Human-Made Diseases, 38
Age of Delayed Degenerative Diseases, 39
Age of Pestilence and Famine, 38

Age of Receding Pandemics, 38
age strata, 68–69
age stratification theory, 68–69, 68*f*, 69–70, 341
age structure (age composition), 26
age-dependent measures, 250–251
age-extrinsic effect, 260
age-intrinsic effect, 260
age-related capacities, 69
age-related expectations, 69
age-related macular degeneration (AMD), 170
aged dependency ratio, 28
ageism, 3, 7
  education, 4
  elder abuse and, 11–12
  employment, 5–6
  health care and, 4–5
  legislature, 5–6
  measures, 9
  research, 3–4
  roots, 3
  sexuality and, 6
  variations in expression of, 3
aging effect, 104
Aging in Manitoba Study (AIM), 107, 107*f*, 109
aging in place, 230
aging models, types of, 260
aging well, 251
aging,
  creativity and, 177–178
  cross-cultural differences in, 244
  dynamic process of, 87
  ethnicity and, 152–153
  family and, 271
  gender differential in, 40–44
  health during, 221, 222–224
  hearing and, 169–170
  intelligence and, 175–176
  Inuit and, 137
  memory and, 171, 172,

173, 174, 175
  modernization theory of, 70–71
  physical competence and, 180, 183
  sensory system and, 169–171
  social assistance and, 363–365
  social context study of, 87–88
  social policy intertwining, 48
  social problem of, 48, 49
  social support and, 310–311
  studying challenges, 104
  successful, 64, 250–251
  vision and, 169–170
  wisdom and, 178–180
agoraphobia, 212
agreeableness, 204
Agricultural Revolution, 38
AIDS/HIV, 39, 86, 424
Alberta,
  Aboriginal peoples in, 147
  age structure in, 45
Ali, Muhammad, 259
All in the Family (television), 276
allocation, 69
Allowance, 372–373
Alzheimer's disease, 97, 184, 200, 424
  caregiving burden of, 319
  impaired cognitive performance and, 214, 215
  stage model of, 262
amenity-oriented migration, 46
American Association for Health, Physical Education, Recreation, and Dance (AAHPERD), 185
American Association of Retired Persons (AARP), 18, 21

American Association of
    Retired Persons
    (*Continued*)
    survey (1999), 22
    survey (2001), 22
American Psychiatric
    Association, 210, 214
amyotrophic lateral sclerosis
    (ALS), 427
angst-free care receiver, 323
anhedonia (pleasure
    loss), 212, 213, 214
anti-imperialist movement
    in intellectual
    discourse, 61
Apartheid, 205
apocalyptic (voodoo)
    demography hypothe-
    sis, 5, 47–48, 73
    criticisms of, 48–51
appetite disturbance, 213
Aquinas, Thomas, 208,
    211
arthritis, 184, 215, 221
assimilation, 153
    theories, 153–154
assisted living (supportive
    housing), 230
assisted suicide, 426–427
asthma, 221
attitudes, 2
    behaviour and, 10
    beliefs and, 7, 8
    definition of, 6
    elder abuse, 14–16
    group membership, 12
    influences on, 10–11
    long term care toward
        sexuality, 19–20
    measurement of, 6–7
    older people's toward
        sexuality, 18, 19*f*
    professional, 20–21
    public, 21
    response consistency
        and, 8–9
    self and, 21–22
    sexual ageism and,
        16–18
attrition, 109
Ayurvedic medicine, 242

B
baby boom, 32, 107, 221
    in Canada, 119, 120
back translating, 109
Bank of Canada, 50
beanpole families, 284
Beethoven, Ludwig
    van, 261
behaviour, 2
    attitudes and, 10
beliefs,
    attitudes and, 7, 8
bereavement, 320
best interests standard, 428
*Beyond Coping: Widows
    Reinventing their
    Lives*, 293
biographical pacing,
    353–354
biography, 100
biological age, 186
biological aging, 257
biomedical model domi-
    nant, 36
bipolar effective disor-
    der, 210
birthing rooms, 231
Black Death (the
    Plague), 38
boomerang kids, 285, 286
bottom-up models of men-
    tal well-being, 199, 199*f*,
    200–202
brain death, 419
branching model of age
    trends, 259–260
bridge jobs, 338
bridging retirement theo-
    ries, 342
British Columbia Inter-
    Ministry Committee on
    Elder Abuse (1992), 11
British Columbia,
    Aboriginal peoples
        in, 147
    Chinese elders in, 160
    elderly in, 45
    health care costs in, 49
    immigration to, 143
*British North America Act
    (BNA)*, 393

bronchitis, 221
Buddhism, 16
buffer hypothesis, 153, 155
*Building on Values (Romanow
    report)*, 403, 405
Burns, George, 179
Butler, Robert, 80

C
Caledon Institute, 372
Calgary, 46
    East Indian immigrants
        in, 141
Camrose, Alberta, 46
Canada Customs and
    Revenue Agency, 378
Canada Fitness Survey, 183
*Canada Health Act (CHA,
    1984)*, 395
Canada Pension Plan
    (CPP), 50, 348, 375, 376,
    388
Canada,
    age pyramids, 33*f*
    age structures within, 45
    ageism in, 3
    aging population
        in, 29–30, 30*f*
    Alzheimer's disease
        in, 214–215
    baby boom in, 119
    comparative of aging
        population in, 31, 31*t*
    definitions of elder abuse
        in, 11
    dementia in, 214–215,
        222
    dependency ratios
        in, 28–29
    epidemiological transi-
        tion theory in, 38–39
    ethnic origin of popula-
        tion in, 142–145, 144*t*,
        145
    ethnicity in, 137
    health-care system re-
        form, 402–406
    health-care system,
        393–396, 397, 398, 399,
        400–401
    immigration to, 142–143,

143*f*, 146*f*, 148–150, 149*t*
Korean immigrants to, 142
marital status in, 276–277
median age in, 27–28
pension system flaws in, 385–387
pensions, 361–363, 365, 367, 368
poverty rates, 367
retirement in, 329–331, 330–331, 333, 334–335, 335*f*, 336*f*
unemployment in, 350–351
volunteering in, 312
welfare state in, 51
Canada/Quebec Pension Plan (C/QPP), 106, 332–366, 367, 368, 370, 373–374, 375–376, 375*t*, 380, 384–385, 386, 387, 388
Canadian 1999 Manulife Financial survey, 22, 182, 182*f*, 195–196, 197
Canadian Association on Gerontology (CAG), 88
Canadian Caregiving Coalition, 314
Canadian Community Health Survey (CCHS, 2003), 347
Canadian Congress of Labour, 365
Canadian Initiative on Frailty and Aging, 228
Canadian Institute for Health Information, 434
Canadian Institute of Health Research, 434
Canadian Institute on Aging (Canadian Institute on Healthy Aging), 251
Canadian Institute on Health Information (CIHI), 211
Canadian Institutes for Health Research, 106
Canadian Journal on Aging, 88

Canadian Labour Congress, 368
Canadian Longitudinal Survey of Aging, 106
Canadian Medical Association, 5, 20
Canadian Pacific Railway (CPR), 143
Canadian Palliative Care Association, 424, 434
Canadian Population Health surveys, 228, 236, 324
Canadian Study of Health and Aging (1994), 106, 214, 222
Canadian Welfare Council, 365
cancer, 38, 43, 184, 221, 424
cardiovascular disease, 38, 39, 184, 221
caregiving, 271, 313–314, 318
Alzheimer's disease sufferers, 318–319
burden, 318
dementia sufferers, 315, 318–319
future of, 324
respite from, 321–323*t*
retirement and, 352–353
stress of, 318–319, 320–321
Catastrophic Drug Transfer, 412
causes of death, 37–38
cancer, 38
cardiovascular diseases, 38
circulatory diseases, 38
epidemiological transition theory, 38–39, 40
First Nations peoples, 433
infectious diseases, 38, 39
major, among elderly Canadians, 40, 40*t*
malnutrition, 38
census family, 4
Census of Canada, 285

cerebrovascular disease (stroke), 40
Charles, Marjorie, 17, 18
Charter of Canadian Rights and Freedoms, 350, 373
Chicago School of sociology, 153
child drop-out provision, 374
childlessness, 120
Chinese-born Canadians, 46
cholera, 38
chronic bronchitis, 40
chronic illness, 418, 422–423
Churchill, Sir Winston, 179
cigarette smoking, 43, 44, 184, 236, 238
circadian rhythm, 110
circulatory diseases, 40, 43
citizen's wage, 361
clawback, 369–370
cluttered nests, 285, 286
co-residency, 162, 272–273
Coale, Ashley, 32
Cobourg, Ontario, 46
cognition, 2, 168
cognitive impairment, 193, 212
Cognitive Performance Scale, 252
cognitive performance, 168–169
cognitive schemata, 9
cognitive-behavioural intervention, 210
cohabitation, 117, 118
children in, 121
divorce and, 122
cohort centrism, 106
cohort designs, 107, 108*f*
cohort effect, 75, 104–105
cohort flow, 69
Cold War, 39
comfort, 422
Commission on the Future of Health Care in Canada (2002), 403
Commonwealth, 142
Community Care Access Centres (CCAC), 185

community care, 393–394
community psychiatric model, 210
Community Senior Mistreatment Committees (Quebec), 14
companionship, 302
Compassionate Care Benefit, 424
compensation, 180
competence, 180, 427
complexity-extremity hypothesis, 12
compression of morbidity hypothesis, 36
concentration difficulties, 213
Confederation (1867), 393
confidantes, 302–303
Confucianism, 16
conscientiousness, 204
construct validity, 94
constructivist perspectives, 155–156
content validity, 94
continuity theory, 66
contributory pension plans, 379–380
control as scientific guideline, 90–91
controllability, 232
convergent thinking, 177
convergent validity, 9
convoy of social support, 307
corporate welfare, 363
Cowgill, Donald, 70, 71
CPP Investment Board, 376
creativity, 177, 178
credibility, 100
Cree peoples, 146
cremation, 433
crises of meaning, 419
criterion validity, 94
critical paradigm, 102–104
critical theory, 79–80
cross-sectional research, 200
cross-sectional surveys, 95
crossover effect, 141
crystallized intelligence, 176

Cultural/Educational Centres Program, 146
culture, 138, 139
mental health and, 159
cumulative advantage/disadvantage hypothesis, 343, 344
cumulative method (Guttman), 7

D

data collection, 110
de Cervantes, Miguel, 179
de Gaulle, Charles, 179
death, 418–419
causes of, 37
preparing for, 419
rituals, 432–433
debunking stereotypes, 304–307
decision-making capacity, 427
decrement with compensation model of age trends, 256, 258–259
deductive approach to theory, 57, 92
delirium, 193, 214, 215–216
dementia, 19, 193, 221, 318, 427, 428
as disease, 222
impaired cognitive performance and, 214, 215
Demography is Not Destiny (1999), 51
dependency ratios (of age), 28–29
depression, 193, 210, 212, 214, 319
diagnosis of, 213
major, 213
psychological model, 213
self-stated, 197, 198f
symptoms, 212–213
treatment of, 214
Descartes, René, 2
descriptive school of phenomenology, 100
diabetes, 221

Diagnostic and Statistical Manual (DSM), 210
Diagnostic and Statistical Manual of Mental Disorders (DSM-IV, 1994), 211, 214, 215
differential aging, 259
Digits Forward test, 173
direct effects view, 308
discriminant validity, 10
disease, 224
disengagement theory, 58, 64–65, 340
distribution of mental well-being scores, 193, 195–196, 197
demographic influences on, 197
divergent thinking, 177–178
divorce, 121–277, 284
Don Quixote de la Mancha, 179
Doukhbours, 143
Dowd, James, 67
durable power of attorney for health care, 428
Dutch school of phenomenology, 100
dying, 419
at home, 431
care of, 422–423
family and, 430–432
recognition of importance of, 434
religiousness and, 420–421
role of physician in, 423
dysphoria (depressed mood), 212, 213

E

early retirement incentive plan (ERIP), 348
early retirement, 347
Economic Council of Canada, 368
economic modernization, 70, 71
economic resources of older minorities, 156–158

economic-class immigrants, 148
education, 71
ego involvement, 89
Elder Abuse Attitude Test (EAAT), 14
elder abuse, 11
    ageism and, 11–12
    attitude change and, 14–16
    attitudes, 12–13, 14
    institutional, 13, 13*f*
    research, 14–89
Elder, Glen, 63, 73, 75
electroconvulsive shock, 207
Elliot Lake, Ontario, 46
emphysema, 40, 221
empirical generalizations, 58
empiricism, 90
employer-sponsored pension plans. *See* registered retirement pension plans (RPPs)
Employment Equity Act (1995), 150
employment, ageism and, 5
empty nests, 285
enabling conditions, 397
end-of-life decisions, 427
energy loss, 213
entombment, 433
Epidemiological Catchment Area Survey (ECA), 212
epidemiological transition theory, 38–39, 40
epidemiology, 211
episodic memory, 173
epistemology, 92
equal intervals method (Thurstone), 7
essentialist approach, 153
Estes, Carroll, 71, 72, 73
ethics in conducting research, 110–111
Ethnic Diversity Study (2002, Statistics Canada), 142, 150
ethnic group, 138

ethnic origin, 143–144
ethnic stratification, 154–156
ethnicity, 137
    constructivist perspective on, 155–156
    definition of, 137–138, 140
    economic resources and, 156–157
    family support and, 161–163
    health and, 158–159
    influence of, 141–142
    theories, 153–154
ethnocultural variations, as mortality differential, 44–45
ethnogerontology, 137
ethnography, 102
etiology, 224
euthanasia, 426–430
Evans, Robert, 49
event history design, 108
ex post facto hypothesizing, 89
exercise, physical, 181–182, 185, 186, 187, 214
    see also physical competence, fit people
experimental designs, 97–98
extended family, 271, 272
    structure of, 284
Extended Health Care Services Program, 395
extra billing, 395
extremity set, 171
extroversion, 204

F
facts, 56, 58
familial old-age dependency ratio, 29
family of orientation, 271
family of procreation, 271
family structures, extended, 271, 272, 275
    horizontal shrinkage, 284
    living alone, 273, 280–282, 297

multigenerational living, 282–284
    vertical extension, 284
family, 271–273, 273*t*
    conflict, 294–296
    gender roles, 117–118
    mid-life, 284–286
    myths about older family members, 274, 275–276
    relationships in later life, 287–289
    retirement and, 351–353
    work and, 131–132, 133
family-class immigrants, 148
Fatal Accident Reporting System (FARS) (US), 7, 8*f*
Faust, 179
fear of death, 420
Fellegi, Ivan, 37
feminist theory, 77–79
fertility, 32–33, 118–121, 281
Fine, Michele, 78
First Nations Peoples Survey (1991), 159
First Nations peoples, 146–150, 152
    death and, 433
    disability rates for, 159
    dying and, 423
    family patterns in, 275
    health and, 242–243
    health systems and, 160–161
    poverty and, 164
first tier of the pension system, 369
First World Masters Track and Field Championship (Toronto, 1975), 187
Fischer, David Hackett, 71
Fitness with Fun and Fellowship (3F), 187
fitness, 180
five-factor personality theory, 204
fluid intelligence, 176
Foot, David, 285
Ford Motor Company, 331

formal caregivers, 314
formal volunteer
    work, 312
Foucault, Jean, 80
Fox, Roy, 206
frailty, 228
*Framework for Health
    Promotion, A*, 229
Franklin, Benjamin, 179
frontal lobotomy, 207
functional age, 186
funerals, 433

G
gay widowers, 292
gender wage gap, 128
gender, 115–116
    as mortality
        differential, 40–44
    changing life course
        and, 116–117
    family income and, 129,
    health and, 221, 224,
        226–227
    in labour force, 131–132,
        133
    labour force segregation
        and, 130–131, 130*t*
    living arrangements
        and, 280
    part-time work
        and, 128–129
    role socialization, 115
    social class and, 242
    social structure and, 115
    work life course
        and, 126–128
gendered segregation
    of work, 130–131, 130*t*
General Agreement on
    Tariffs and Trade
    (GATT), 411
general drop-out
    provision, 374
General Social Survey
    (GSS), 95, 118, 120,
    282, 295, 314, 324,
    334, 337, 347, 348, 354,
    356
general susceptibility hy-
    pothesis, 233

generation in the mid-
    dle, 317
George III, 208
geriatrics, 4, 206
Gerontological Society of
    America, 64
Gerontologist, The, 251
gerontology, 26
    research, 87–88,
        89, 250
glass ceiling, 406
glaucoma, 168
globalization, 408
Globe and Mail, The, 367
Glory Days (song), 174
Goethe, Johann, 179
good death, 421
Government Annuities Act
    (1908), 331–332, 364
Graff, Steffi, 258
grand theories, 58
Grand Trunk Railway, 363
grandchildren, 290–291
grandparents, 289–291, 307
Gray Panthers group, 179
Gray, Asa, 179
Great Depression, 332, 365,
    394
great pension debate,
    367–368
grounded theory, 101
group affiliation, 302
Guaranteed Income
    Supplement (GIS,
    1966), 333, 361, 367, 368,
    370, 371–372, 373, 387

H
happiness, 193, 195
Health and Welfare
    Canada, 11, 424
health care policy,
    community care, 393–394
    equity in health care, 394
    extra billing, 395
    historical roots of
        Canadian, 393–396,
        397, 398
    hospitals, 394
    jurisdictional issues, 394
    Medicare system, 396

physicians, 394–395
    preventive medicine, 394
    public health, 395–396
    residual welfare, 393
health care reform in
    Canada, 402–406
health care system, 393
    ageism and, 4–5
    privatization of, 407–408
    profitization of, 408
    reform of, 402–406
    women in, 406–407
health justification hypothe-
    sis, 347
health locus of control, 232
health promotion perspec-
    tive, 244–246
Health Promotion Survey
    (1990), 234
health protective behav-
    iours, 235
health, 224–226
    beliefs, 230–234
    cultural minority status
        and, 242–243
    determinants, 229, 229*f*,
        230
    gender differences in, 37,
        226–227
    personal practices, 235,
        236–239
    retirement and, 347–356
    social structure
        and, 239–241, 242
    technology, 70
    unemployment and, 240
healthy aging, 251
healthy immigration
    status, 158–159
Heaps, A. A., 364
Henry VIII, 209
Hentleff, Dr. Paul, 424
heredity, 205, 206
heritability research,
    204–205
hidden victims, 317
hierarchical models of age
    trends, 260, 261–262
high blood pressure, 221
hip fractures, 221
Hippocrates, 211

Hirdes, John, 211
Holocaust, 87, 140
Homans, George, 66
Home Buyers Plan, 381
home care, 406
homogenization of older
    people, 48
Honeyman, Madeline, 20
hospice care, 424–429, 432
host response hypothe-
    sis, 233
housing, 230
Hudson's Bay
    Company, 330, 363
hypertension, 184, 221
hypothesis, 57
hypothetical constructs, 8

I
iatrogenic illness,
    399–400
illness behaviour, 235
Imaginary Time Bomb, The:
    Why an Ageing Population
    is Not a Social Problem
    (2000), 51
immigrants to Canada,
    chronic diseases
        amongst, 158–159
    classes of, 148–149, 155
    demographics
        of, 151–152
    diversity of, 148–149
    healthy immigrant
        thesis, 158
    landed, 148
    mental health of, 159
    reasons for becom-
        ing, 142–143, 148
impression manage-
    ment, 194, 195
Improving the Quality of
    Life of Canadian Seniors
    project, 103
income supplements
    (provincial and
    territorial), 377
Income War Tax Act
    (1917), 364
indirect effects view, 308
individual aging, 69

individual differences in
    aging, 252, 253
    age dependent measures
        of, 255–257
    cross-sectional data
        in, 254, 255
inductive approach to
    theory, 57–58, 92
Industrial Revolution, 38,
    330–331
influenza, 38, 40
informal care, 314
informal voluntary
    work, 312
information acquisition, 174
informed consent, 110
insane asylums, 208, 209
insanity, 208, 211
Institute for Aging, 106
institutional care, 207–208
    current models of,
        209–210
    early models of, 208–209
instrument activities of
    daily living (IADL), 184,
    184t
intelligence quotient
    (IQ), 175
intelligence, 175
    age trends in, 176–177
intergenerational equity de-
    bate, 50–308
intergenerational
    injustice, 48
intergenerational stake hy-
    pothesis, 286
internal locus of control,
    232–233
interpersonal interac-
    tion, 302
interpretive school of phe-
    nomenology, 100
interpretive/constructivism
    approach to knowledge
    generation, 98–100
intervention fidelity, 98
intimacy at a distance, 306
Inuit peoples, 146
    aging and, 137
    health promotion
        and, 245

health systems
    and, 160–161
Inuktitut peoples, 146
involuntary euthanasia, 426
involuntary retirement, 354
irreversible decrement model
    of age trends, 256, 258
Islam, 16

J
Jackson, Andrew, 209
Japan,
    ageism in, 3
Joint Committee of the
    Senate and House of
    Commons on Old Age
    Security, 365

K
Katz, Stephen, 80
kin-keeper, 294
kinesthesis, 171
Kipness, Pamela, 187
knowledge systems, 92–93
Kuhn, Maggie, 179
Kuhn, Thomas, 59

L
Labrador City,
    Newfoundland and
    Labrador, 46
landed immigrant, 148
language, 154
    as barrier to health
        service, 164
Larkin, Erik, 187
latent variables, 8
Legionnaire's Disease,
    39
legislature,
    ageism and, 5–6
life course, 74, 75
    fallacy, 105
    institutionalization
        hypothesis, 330
    model of age
        trends, 259–260
    theoretical perspec-
        tive, 73–77
life cycle, 73–74

life expectancy, 33, 35, 221, 274
  dependency-free, 35, 37
life history, 74
life review, 109
life satisfaction, 22, 194, 195
life-domain satisfactions, 195, 206
Lifelong Learning Plan, 381
lifespan, 33, 35, 74
living alone, 280–282
living arrangements, 280, 281*t*
living wills, 428
living with spouse (only), 280
living-dying interval, 431–432
lone parenting, 123
loneliness, 223
long-term care, 201
  attitudes toward sexuality, 19–20
  homes, 201, 202, 206, 207*f*
long-term memory, 173, 174, 175
longevity, 115
Longford, Sam, 258
longitudinal stability, 199
Longitudinal Study of Aging Danish Twins, 108
longitudinal surveys, 95, 105–106, 115, 198
low income cut-offs (LICOs), 123, 124*f*, 367–368
  Canadian pension system and, 383, 385
  definitions, 372
  ethnic stratification hypothesis and, 156
low income rate measures, 372
low self-esteem, 213
Lyme Disease, 39

M

macro-level of analysis, 61
macro-level retirement theory, 341–342
macro-level theories, 61

major depression, 213
malaria, 39
malignant neoplasms (cancers), 40, 43
  see also cancer
Malleus Maleficarum ("Hammer of Witches," 1486), 16
malnutrition, 38
mandatory retirement, 116–117, 331, 350
Manitoba,
  Aboriginal peoples in, 147
  age structure in, 45
  immigration to, 143
  migration in, 45
Mao Tse-Tung, 179
marital status, 276–278*t*
marriage, 117
  retirement and, 357
Marshall's classification scheme, 62
Martin, Paul, 402
Marx, Karl, 102
Marxist critique, 72
materialist explanations, 131
mating gradient, 118, 126
Matthews, Sarah, 67
McDonald, Lynn, 71
measurement equivalence, 109
mechanistic model of health, 224
median age of population, 27–28
medicare, 396–397, 398, 401, 407, 409–411
  hollowing out of, 410
medication, 237
Memorial University of Newfoundland Scale of Happiness (MUNSH), 194, 195, 200–201
memory, 168
  long-term, 173, 174, 175
  metamemory, 175
  organization, 174
  primary, 172
  retrieval, 174–175

sensory, 172
  short-term, 172–173
  working, 172
mental disorders, 193, 206–207
  diagnosis of, 211
mental health tool (MDS-MH), 211
mental health, 193
  culture and, 159
  retirement and, 356–357
  social support and, 308
mental well being, 192–193
  measurement of, 194–195
  models of, 199, 436
  temporal stability of, 198–199
Merton, Robert, 56
metamemory, 175
Métis peoples, 145–146
Michelangelo, 179
micro-level of analysis, 61
micro-level of retirement theory, 340–341
micro-level theories, 61
microfication, 62
middle-range theories, 58
migration, 37
  amenity-oriented, 46
  as mortality differential, 46–47
Mills, C. Wright, 73
Minimum Data Sets (MDS 2.0), 211, 252
  in home care (MDS-HC), 210
  in psychiatric institutions (MDS-MH), 210–211
Minkler, Meredith, 71
mnemonic techniques, 174
models, 58
modernization theory, 58, 153, 341
  aging and, 70–71
modified extended family, 305
Monet, Claude, 261
mood disorders, 193
mood stabilizers, 210
morale, 194, 195
mortality decline, 33

mortality,
  accident, 44
  infant, 43
  maternal, 44
Mount, Dr. Balfour, 424
multi-generational living, 282–283
multiple jeopardy hypothesis, 153, 154–155
multiple knowledges, 79
multiples of basal metabolic rate (METs), 181
mutual withdrawal, 65
Myles, John, 71
myocardial infarctions (heart attacks), 221
myths,
  abandonment, 305
  aging, 199
  bankruptcy of universal health care system, 410
  caregiver burden, 318
  convoy of social support, 307
  debunking, 304–307
  isolation, 305
  marriage, 305–306
  nuclear family, 306
  sandwich generation, 317
  see also stereotypes

N

National Advisory Council on Aging (NACA), 222, 361, 381, 385
National Council of Welfare, 377, 382–383
National Forum on Health (1997), 243, 401–402
National Institute of Mental Health (US), 211
National Population Health surveys (NPHS), 106, 158, 223, 226
National Survey on Giving, Volunteering and Participating (NSGVP, 1997), 312
National Survey on Volunteer Activity (NSVA, 1987), 312

Navratilova, Martina, 258
need, 397
negatively skewed distributions, 196, 197
neurosis, 210
neuroticism, 145
New Perspective on the Health of Canadians, A, 229
Newfoundland and Labrador Human Rights Code, 5–6
Newfoundland and Labrador, GIS reliance in, 371
Newfoundland Pensioners and Senior Citizens Federation, 17
non-contributory pension plans, 379–380
non-kin friendships, 307
non-voluntary euthanasia, 426
normal distribution, 252
normal expectation, 253
normative timing, 75
North America,
  ageism as an educational topic, 4
North American Free Trade Agreement (NAFTA), 408, 411
Northwest Territories,
  Aboriginal peoples in, 147
  age structure in, 45
  cohabitation in, 117
  ethnic mix in, 144
  GIS reliance in, 371
nuclear family, 271
Nunavut,
  Aboriginal peoples in, 147
  age structure in, 45
  cohabitation in, 117
  GIS reliance in, 371
nursing homes, 210

O

obesity, 184
objectivity, 90
Ojibway peoples, 146
Old Age Assistance Act (1951), 332, 365

Old Age Pensions Act (OAP, 1927), 331, 332, 364, 365
Old Age Security Act (1951), 331, 332, 363, 365
Old Age Security pension (OAS), 361, 367, 368, 369–370, 377, 387
Old Crow, Yukon, 147
One Flew Over the Cuckoo's Nest, 207
Ontario Continuing Care Access Centres, 409
Ontario Longitudinal Survey of Aging (1959–1978), 95, 106
Ontario,
  Aboriginal peoples in, 147
  cohabitation in, 117
  elderly in, 45
ontology, 93
openness to experience, 146
optimal aging, 251
optimum continuity, 66
Organization of Economic Co-operation and Development (OECD), 412, 414
Oshawa, Ontario, 46
Osler, Dr. William, 331
Overselling of Population Aging, The: Apocalyptic Demography, Intergenerational Challenges, and Social Policy (2000), 51

P

pacification policy, 4
pain, 222
Pakans, Andrejs, 329
Palliative Care Benefits Program, 424
Palliative Care Foundation of Canada, 424
palliative care, 424–425
panel study, 106
paradigms, 56, 59, 92–93
Parksville, British Columbia, 46
Parliamentary Task Force, Canada (1983), 368
partial retirement, 338, 354

ParticipAction campaign, 181

passive euthanasia, 426

patriarchy, 123

peer debriefing, 100

Pension Act (1919), 364

Pension Benefits Standards Act (1985), 368

pension credits, 374

Pension Funds Societies Act (1887), 364

pension system flaws, 385–387

pension system,
  B grade for
    Canada's, 382–383, 384–385
  Canada's current, 369–370, 371–372, 373–374, 375–376
  debate about, 367–368
  employer, 378, 379–380
  future of, 388
  history of Canada's, 361–363, 365, 367
  mismatch between Canadians and, 385–387

pensions, 331–333
  older women and, 385–386, 387
  part-time workers and, 386

Pentagon, Washington, D.C., 37

Penticton, British Columbia, 46

perception, 168

period effect, 75, 105

personal construct systems, 2

personal control, 201

personal health
  behaviours, 236–239
  health protective, 235
  illness, 235
  importance of, 237
  life style and, 237, 238
  medication use, 237
  negative, 236
  positive, 235

self-help management, 235, 236

personal health determinants, 230

personal health practices, 236–239

personality research, 202, 206

personality theories, 204

pharmaceutical industry, 49

Pharmaceutical Manufacturers Association of Canada (PMAC), 411

pharmaceuticals, 410–412

phenomenology, 100–101

Phillipson, Chris, 71

phobias, 212

physical competence,
  dependent people, 184
  elite people, 187
  fit people, 186–187
  frail people, 184
  independent people, 185–186

physical environment, 229, 230

physical performance, 180
  age trends in, 181–182
  measures, 181

physician-assisted suicide, 426, 427, 428, 429–430

Pickett, Mike, 17

Pinel, Philippe, 208

place of residence,
  as mortality differential, 45–46

pluralism, 153

pneumonia, 38, 40

political economy of aging theory, 71–73

political economy retirement theory, 342–343

politics of debt, 368

poorhouses, 209, 210

population aging measures, 26, 27–29

Population Association of America, 50

population health, 226

population pyramids, 32–33

positive health behaviour, 235

positivism, 93

post-World War II, 39

postmodern intellectual discourse, 60

postmodern turn, 60

postmodernism, 80

postpositivism, 93, 94, 95

predisposing factors, 397

premature closing, 88

presbycusis, 170

Preston, Samuel, 50

primary aging, 260

primary caregiver, 315

primary memory, 172

primary mental abilities, 176

Prince Edward Island, cohabitation in, 117

procedural memory, 173

process models of age trends, 257, 258, 259, 260, 261–262

productive aging framework, 341

productive aging, 80–81

Productive Aging: Enhancing Vitality in Later Life (1985), 81

prolonged engagement, 100

prospective memory, 173

Provincial Strategy to Combat Elder Abuse (Ontario), 11

proxy respondents, 195

psychiatric hospitals, 209

psychiatry, 206–207, 209–210

psychoanalytic schools, 211

psychogeriatrics, 206

psychological aging, 257

psychomotor retardation, 213

psychosis, 210

psychotherapy, 211

psychotropic medicine, 4–5

public pension system,
  allowance, 372–373
  Canada/Quebec pension

plans, 373–374, 375–376, 375t

clawback, 369–370

guaranteed income supplement, 370, 371–372

old age security, 369–370

provincial and territorial supplements, 376–377

purchasing power parities (PPPs), 412

Q

Quality End-of-Life Care: The Right of Every Canadian, 424

quality-adjusted life years (QALYs), 419

quality-of-life trajectories, 421

quasi-experimental designs, 98

Quebec Pension Plan (QPP), 348, 366, 375

Quebec,
 cohabitation in, 117–118
 elderly in, 45
 ethnic mix in, 144
 ethnicity in, 139

R

race, 137
 definition of, 140–141
 influence of, 141–142

recognition, 174

reconstituted (blended) families, 284

redistributive justice, 241

reference-based pricing (RBP) of drugs, 411–412

reflexivity, 79

refugees, 148

regionalization of healthcare, 404

registered retirement pension plans (RPPs), 378, 379–382, 379t, 382f, 387

registered retirement savings plans (RRSPs), 333, 367, 380, 387, 388

reliability, 90

remarriage, 122–123

reminiscence therapy, 201

Report Card on Seniors in Canada, 361

Research Ethics Boards (REBs), 111

research,
 age levelling hypothesis, 153, 154–155
 aging effect, 104
 buffering hypothesis, 153, 155
 challenges, 87–88
 cohort effects, 75, 104–105
 cohort, 107
 control, 90, 91
 controversy, 92
 data collection challenges, 110
 deductive approach, 57, 92
 description of, 87–88
 empiricism, 90
 essentialist approach, 153
 ethics, 110–111
 explanatory, 87–88
 feminist methods of, 104
 goals of science, 89–90
 inductive approach to, 57–58, 92
 multiple jeopardy hypothesis, 153, 154–155
 objectivity, 90
 period effects of, 75, 105
 purposes of, 89
 reliability of, 90
 scientific guidelines, 90–92
 statistically rare populations, 95
 systems of knowledge, 92–93
 validity of, 90

Resident Assessment Instrument Health Informatics Project (RAIHP), 185, 252

Resident Assessment Instruments (RAIs), 184, 210–211

residual welfare, 393

respiratory diseases, 40, 43–44

respite for caregivers, 321–323t

response consistency attitudes, 8–9

response set, 194

retirement, 329
 caregiving and, 352
 definitions of, 339–340
 ethnicity and, 346
 extent of, 334, 335
 family and, 351–353
 health and, 346–356
 institutionalized, 331
 marriage and, 357
 mental health and, 356–357
 new, 335–339
 planning for, 353
 reverse, 353
 stages of, 355
 theories on, 340–341, 342, 343
 timing of, 345, 346, 348–350
 wage, 361
 well-being in, 355–356

rheumatism, 221

right to privacy, 110

Romanow report. See Building on Values (Romanow report)

Royal Commission on Aboriginal Peoples (1996), 242

Royal Commission on the Relations of Labour and Capital (1889), 331

Royal Commission on the Status of Pensions in Ontario (1980), 368

Royal Dutch Medical Association, 428

Royal Victoria Hospital, Montreal, 424

S

same-sex unions, 123–124

sandwich generation, 284–285, 317

SARS (Severe Acute Respiratory Syndrome), 39
Saskatchewan Commission on Medicare, 410, 413
Saskatchewan,
Aboriginal peoples in, 147
age structure in, 45
immigration to, 143
migration in, 45
schizophrenia, 251
scientific guidelines for social research, 90–92
second tier of the pension system, 369
secondary aging, 260
secondary caregivers, 315
secondary data analysis, 95, 96–97
selective optimization, 180
self, 2
attitudes and, 21–22
self-assessed health, 222–223
self-care, 235, 236
self-health management, 235
semantic memory, 173
Senate Committee on Social Affairs, Science, and Technology, 434
Senior Behaviour Inventory (SBI), 15, 15 , 16
Seniors Benefit, 388
seniors' family life course, 126
sensation, 168
sensory memory, 172
sensory system,
age changes in, 169–171
hearing, 170
kinesthesis, 171
pain, 171
smell, 171
taste, 171
temperature, 171
touch, 171
vision, 169–170
September 11, 2001
attacks, 37, 87
serial caregiving, 317

serotonin reuptake inhibitors, 210
sexuality,
ageism and, 6, 16–18
long term care attitudes toward, 19–20
older people's attitudes toward, 18, 19f
short-term memory, 172–173
sibling relationships (in later life), 293–294, 306
sickness, 224
singlehood identity, 125
situation appraisal, 200
sleep disturbance, 213
smallpox, 38, 39
snowbirds, 47
social acceptability, 227
social aging, 257
social assistance, 332, 363, 365
social class, 239
social desirability scale, 195
Social Development Canada, 369
social exchange model, 12
social exchange theory, 66–68
social gerontology, 56
barriers to theory development in, 59–61
organizing theories, 61–63
research, 87–88
social gradient, 240
social insurance, 363
social integration, 302
social interactions, 302
research, 305
social isolation, 301, 302, 304
social network, 302
social norms (rules), 62
social roles, 69
Social Service Congress, 364
social stereotypes, 304–307
social structure,
class and, 239
defined, 239
economic advantage, 239
equity, 241

ethnicity and, 242–243
gender and, 242
health and, 239–240, 241–242
redistributive justice, 241
social gradient, 240
social support, 301, 302–303, 302t
mental health and, 308
multi-dimensionality of, 308–309
types, 304
well-being and, 307–309, 310–311
social survey, 94–96
socialization, 69–70
socio-economic status (SES), 224
somatic arousal, 213
somatization, 212
soul pain, 419
Special Committee on Retirement Age Policies (1979), 368
Spinks, Leon, 259
Spousal Allowance, 366–367
spousal homicide, 295
Spouse's Allowance (SPA), 368–369, 372–373
Springsteen, Bruce, 174
St. Augustine, 16
St. Boniface Hospital, Winnipeg, 424
stability model of age trends, 256
Standardized Test of Fitness, 185–186
statistically rare populations, 95
Statistics Canada, 12, 26, 123, 124, 152, 221, 271, 367–368, 372
status levelling (redistribution) hypothesis, 343, 344
status maintenance hypothesis, 343, 344
steady-state financing, 376
stem family, 275
stepped down, 329
stereotypes, 2, 3, 16

stolen moments, 322, 323
Stones, Lee, 17, 18
stress effects of
    caregiving, 318, 319
stress process model, 319,
    320*f*
strokes, 221
structural determinants, 230
structural functionalism, 63
structural lag, 115
subjective age, 22
substituted judgement stan-
    dard, 428
Successful Aging (1998), 64,
    251
successful aging, 222
    framework, 341
suicide, 44, 213, 418
    assisted, 426–427
    gender and, 40
    immigration and, 159
summative method
    (Likert), 7, 9, 9*t*
Superannuation Act
    (1870), 363
Supreme Court of
    Canada, 350
Surgeon General's report on
    mental health
    (1999), 213
*Survey of Labour and Income
    Dynamics (SLID)*, 106,
    108
*Survey of Persons Not in the
    Labour Force*, 337, 351
susceptibility, 233
Swedish Association for the
    Study of Pain, 429
symbolic interactionism, 63
symptomatology, 242

T

tangible (instrumental)
    assistance, 303
Taoism, 16
Task Force on Retirement
    Income Policy (19179),
    368
temporally specific mood
    states, 195
termination of research
    project, 110

tertiary aging, 260
theoretical perspectives, 57
theory, 56
    activity theory, 63–64,
        340
    age stratification
        theory, 68, 68*f*, 69–70,
        341
    aging and modernization
        theory, 70–71
    assimilation theories,
        153–154
    bridging retirement theo-
        ries, 342
    continuity theory, 66
    critical theory, 79–80
    deductive approach, 57,
        92
    definition of, 57
    disengagement theory,
        58, 64–65, 340
    epidemiological transi-
        tion theory, 38–39, 40
    ethnicity theories,
        153–154
    feminist theories, 77–79
    five-factor personality
        theory, 204
    grand theories,
        290–291
    grounded theory, 101
    importance of, 61
    inductive approach
        to, 57–58, 92
    macro-level retirement
        theory, 341–342
    micro-level of retirement
        theory, 340–341
    micro-level theories, 58
    middle-range theories, 58
    modernization theory,
        58, 153, 341
    personality theories, 204
    political economy of
        aging theory, 71–73
    political economy retire-
        ment theory, 342–343
    prospective theory, 173
    retirement theories,
        340–342, 343
    social exchange theory,
        66–68

social gerontology organ-
    izing theories, 61–63
    types of, 57–58
therapeutic interventions,
    201, 206
top-down models of mental
    well-being, 199, 199*f*, 202,
    205
total dependency ratio, 28
Trades and Labour
    Congress of Canada, 364
traditional Chinese medicine
    (TCM), 159–160, 231, 242
trait effect, 194, 195, 204
trajectory of life, 421
tranquilizers, 210
transcendence, 422
triangulation, 100
tripartite model of
    depression, 213
Tuke, William, 208
twin research paradigm, 10
typological models of age
    trends, 257
typological perspective,
    184, 185

U

U.S. National Center for
    Health Statistics, 170
unattached older
    adults, 125
unattached persons, 383
unemployment, 241,
    350–351
United Nations Convention
    on Refugees, 148
United Nations Declaration
    of Human Rights, 412
University of British
    Columbia, 49
University of Waterloo, 211
up-down models of mental
    well-being, 199, 199*f*,
    205–206
urbanization, 70

V

validity, 90
valuation of life (VOL), 420
vascular dementia, 214, 215
Viagra (potency drug), 6

vibrotactile sensitivity, 171
Victoria, British Columbia,
  age structure in, 46
Victorian Order of
  Nurses, 394
violence, attitudes
  toward, 12–13
visible minority, 150–152,
  151*t*
vision, 169–170
vital aging, 251
voluntary euthanasia, 428
volunteering, 311–313
  benefits of, 313
von Bismarck, Prince
  Otto, 364
voodoo demography
  hypothesis. *See* apocalyptic (voodoo) demography
  hypothesis

Vuntut Gwitchin peo-
  ples, 147

W
Walker, Alan, 71
Weber, Max, 102
Wechsler Adult Intelligence
  Scale (WAIS), 172, 175
welfare states, 361–363
wellness, 224–226
Western Enlightenment, 60
Whitehorse Star, 147
Widowed Spouse's
  Allowance, 368
widowhood, 124–125, 277,
  280, 291–293, 306
Williams, William
  Carlos, 261
Willis, Francis, 208
Windt, Wilhelm, 179

wisdom, 178–179
Woodsworth, J. S., 364
working memory, 172
workplace
  accommodations, 131–133
World Health Organization
  (WHO), 226, 244, 250
World Trade Center, New
  York, 37
World War I, 364
World War II, 32, 76, 87,
  210, 250, 280, 332, 365

Y
York retreat, England, 208
youth dependency ratio, 28
Yukon,
  Aboriginal peoples
    in, 147
  age structure in, 45